中国残疾人事业统计年鉴

China Statistical Yearbook on the Work for Persons with Disabilities

2013

（总第12期 No. 12）

中国残疾人联合会 编
China Disabled Persons' Federation

中国统计出版社
China Statistics Press

图书在版编目（CIP）数据

中国残疾人事业统计年鉴. 2013 / 中国残疾人联合会编. -- 北京 : 中国统计出版社, 2013.7
ISBN 978-7-5037-6822-4

Ⅰ. ①中… Ⅱ. ①中… Ⅲ. ①残疾人－社会福利事业－统计资料－中国－2013－年鉴 Ⅳ. ①D669.69-66

中国版本图书馆 CIP 数据核字(2013)第 116176 号

中国残疾人事业统计年鉴—2013

作　　者/中国残疾人联合会
责任编辑/王振宇
封面设计/王　鹏
出版发行/中国统计出版社
通信地址/北京市丰台区西三环南路甲 6 号　邮政编码/100073
电　　话/邮购（010）63376909　书店（010）68783171
网　　址/http://csp.stats.gov.cn
印　　刷/河北天普润印刷厂
经　　销/新华书店
开　　本/880×1230mm　1/16
印　　张/20.5　8 彩页
字　　数/680 千字
版　　别/2013 年 8 月第 1 版
版　　次/2013 年 8 月第 1 次印刷
定　　价/180.00 元

如有印装差错，由本社发行部调换。

《中国残疾人事业统计年鉴—2012》
编委会和编辑工作人员

编者说明

《中国残疾人事业统计年鉴—2013》系统收录了全国和各省、自治区、直辖市2012年残疾人工作各方面的统计数据，是一部全面反映中国残疾人事业发展的资料性年刊。

本书内容由六部分组成：第一部分为主要指标数据图；第二部分为统计公报与专文，包括2012年中国残疾人事业发展统计公报和部分业务专题文章；第三部分为综合统计资料，是历年统计情况的综合反映；第四部分为2012年度分省统计资料，记录2012年各省任务指标执行情况和全国汇总情况；第五部分为分省统计报告，包括全国31个省（自治区、直辖市）、新疆生产建设兵团和黑龙江农垦总局的残疾人事业统计公报；第六部分为附录，介绍中国残疾人事业统计有关的政策法规文件。

本年鉴涉及的全国性统计数据均不包括香港、澳门特别行政区和台湾省数据。

本年鉴是根据各地残联报送的统计年报和部分专项业务项目统计结果编制而成。表格中“空格”表示该项统计指标数据不足本表最小单位数、数据不详或无该项数据。

2013年7月

目　录

Contents

第一部分　主要数据图

Part Ⅰ　Charts

第二部分　统计公报与专文

Part Ⅱ　Communiqué and Reports

第三部分　综合统计资料
Part Ⅲ　Comprehensive Statistical Data

第四部分　分省统计资料
Part Ⅳ　Statistical Data of Provinces

康　复
Rehabilitation

第六部分　附　　录
Part Ⅵ　Appendix

1

主要数据图

Charts

图-1 2008-2012年视力残疾康复主要任务完成情况

Chart 1 Rehabilitation for Persons with Visual Disability during 2008-2012

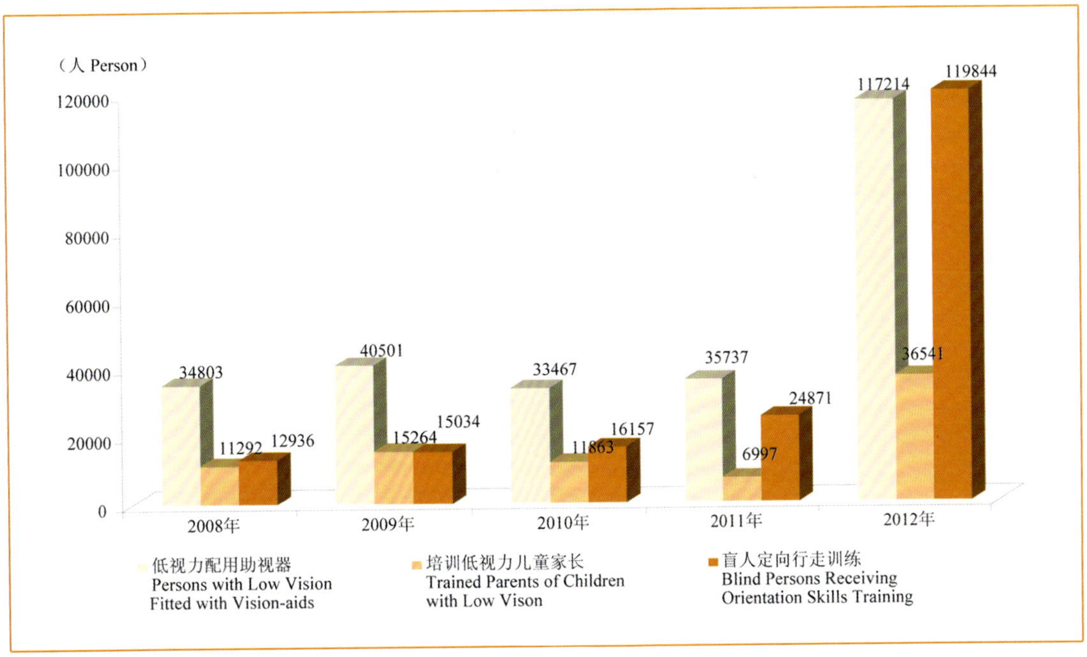

图-2 2008-2012年残疾儿童康复训练情况

Chart 2 Rehabilitation for Children with Disabilities during 2008-2012

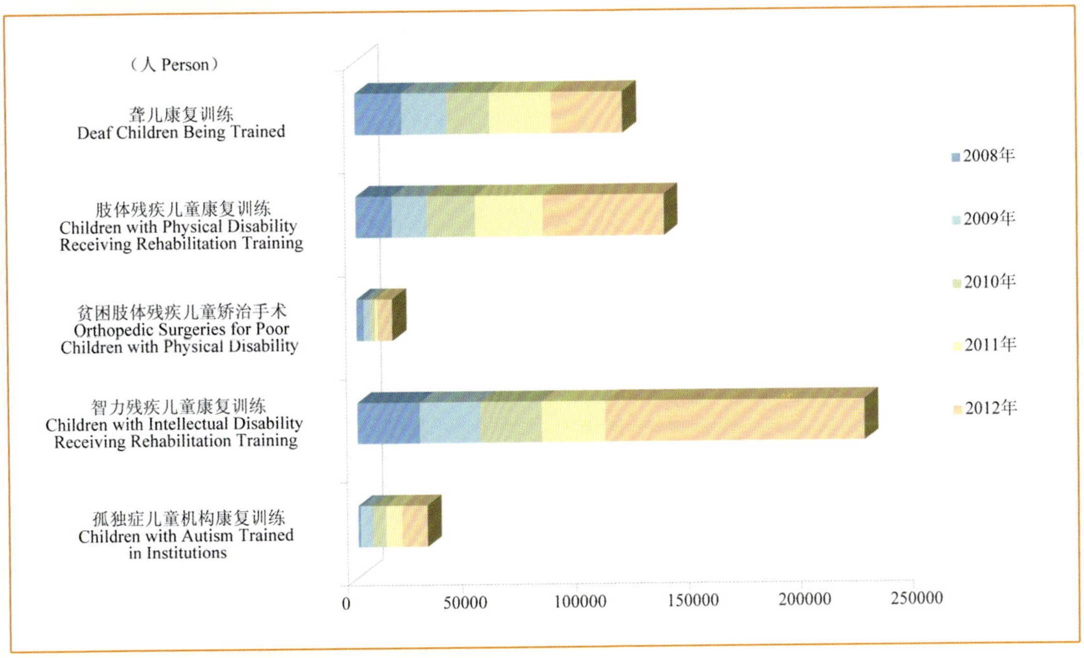

图-3　2008-2012年精神病人监护和救助情况

Chart 3 Custody and Medical Assistance for Persons with Mental Illness during 2008-2012

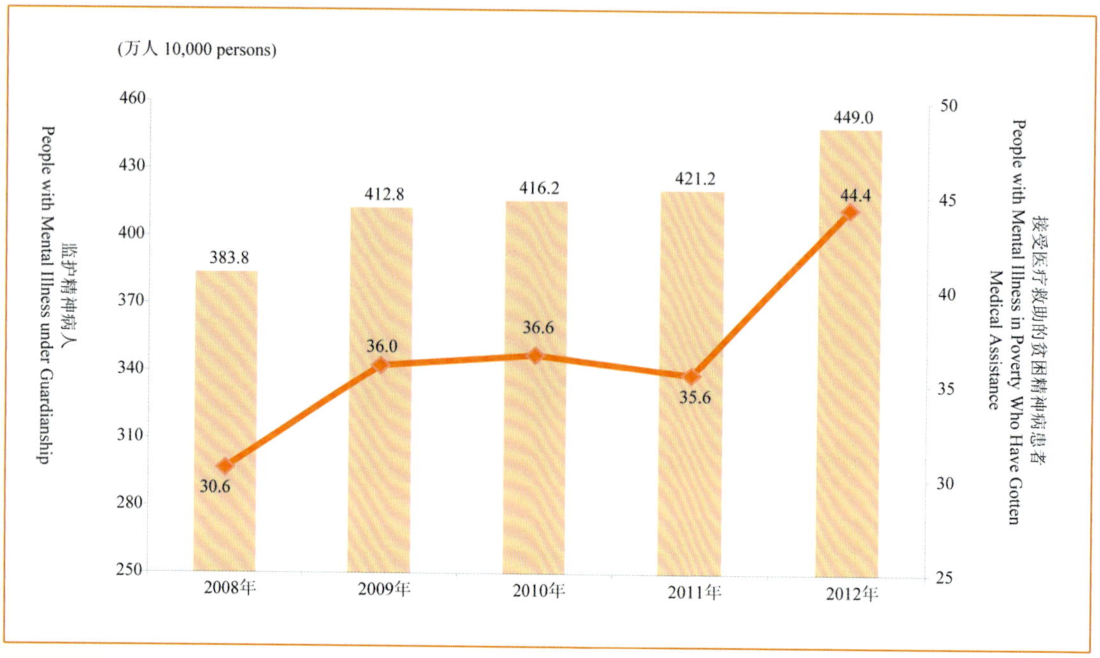

图-4　2008-2012年假肢和矫形器装配情况

Chart 4 Artificial Limbs and Orthotic Devices Fitted during 2008-2012

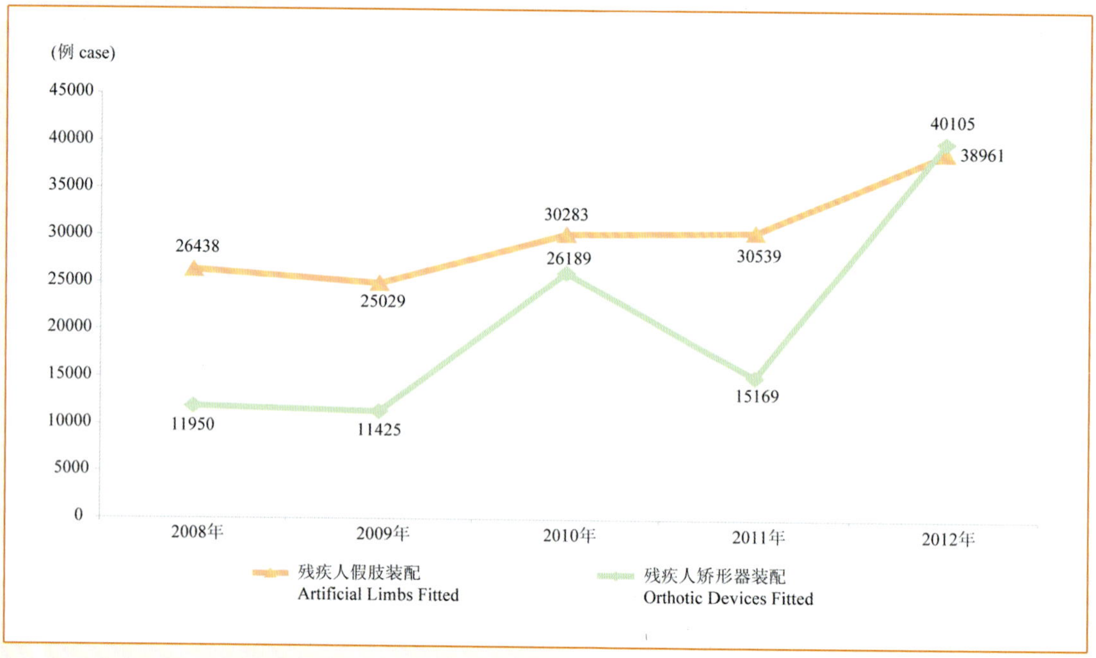

图-5 2008-2012年高等院校录取残疾考生情况

Chart 5 Admission of Disabled Students by Higher Educational Institution during 2008-2012

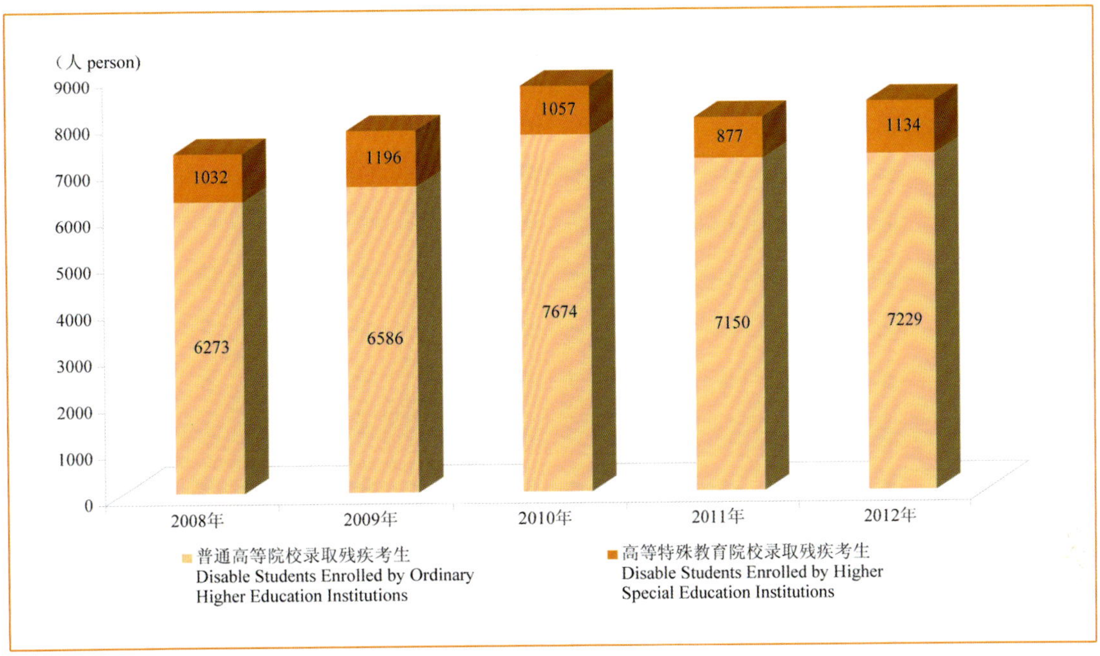

图-6 2008-2012年城镇残疾人新安排就业情况

Chart 6 Newly-added Employment of Disabled Persons in Urban Areas during 2008-2012

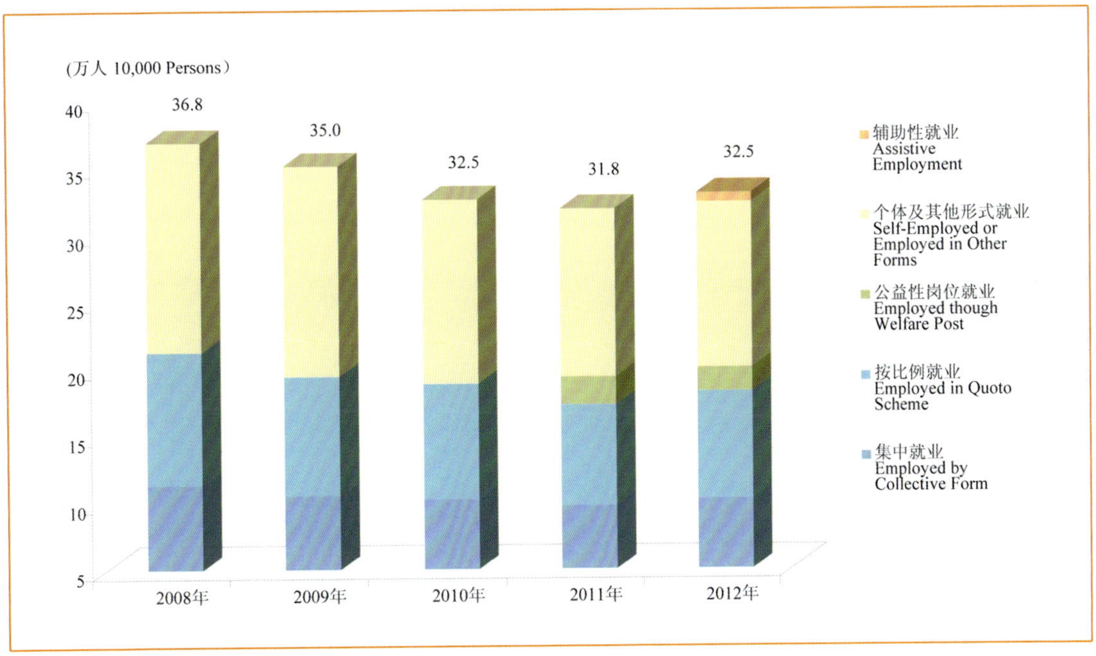

图-7　2008-2012年城乡残疾人社会保障与救助情况

Chart 7 Social Security and Relief for Urban and Rural Disabled Persons during 2008-2012

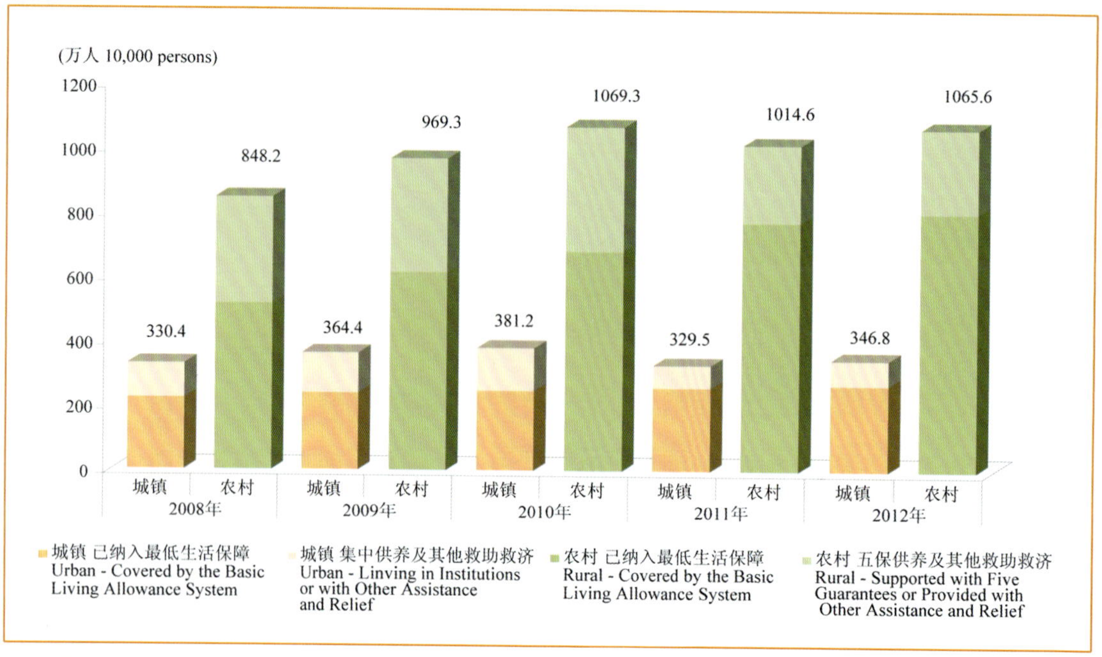

图-8　2008-2012年农村贫困残疾人危房改造情况

Chart 8 House Renovation for Poor PWDs in Rural Areas during 2008-2012

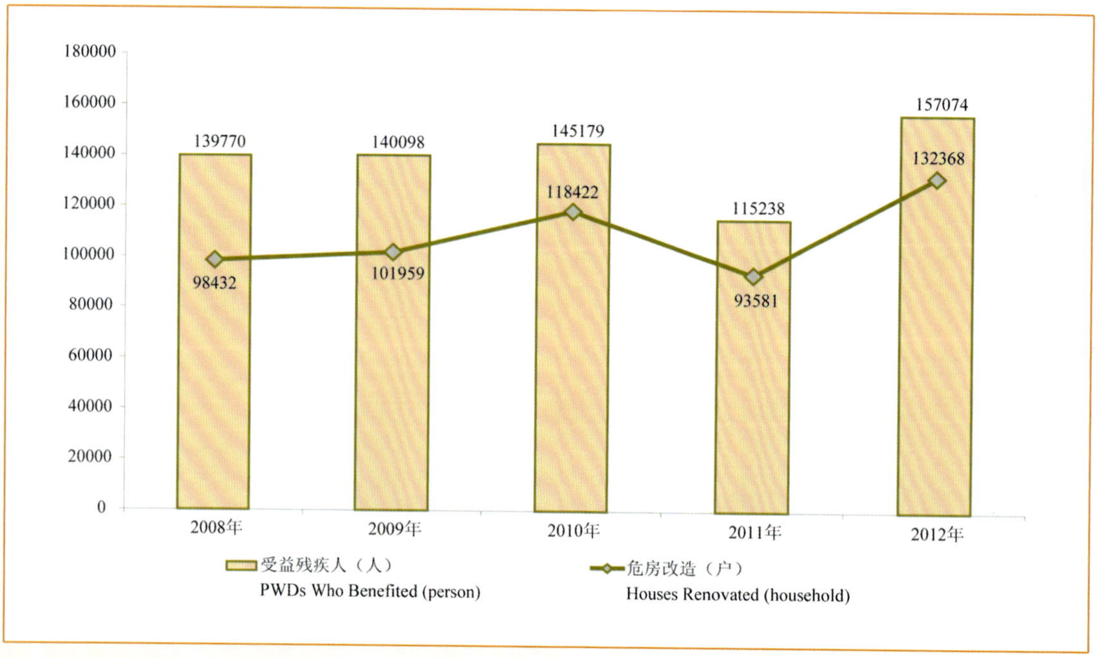

图-9 2008-2012年省、市两级残疾人宣传栏目开展情况

Chart 9 Propaganda Column for PWDs at Provincial and City Level during 2008-2012

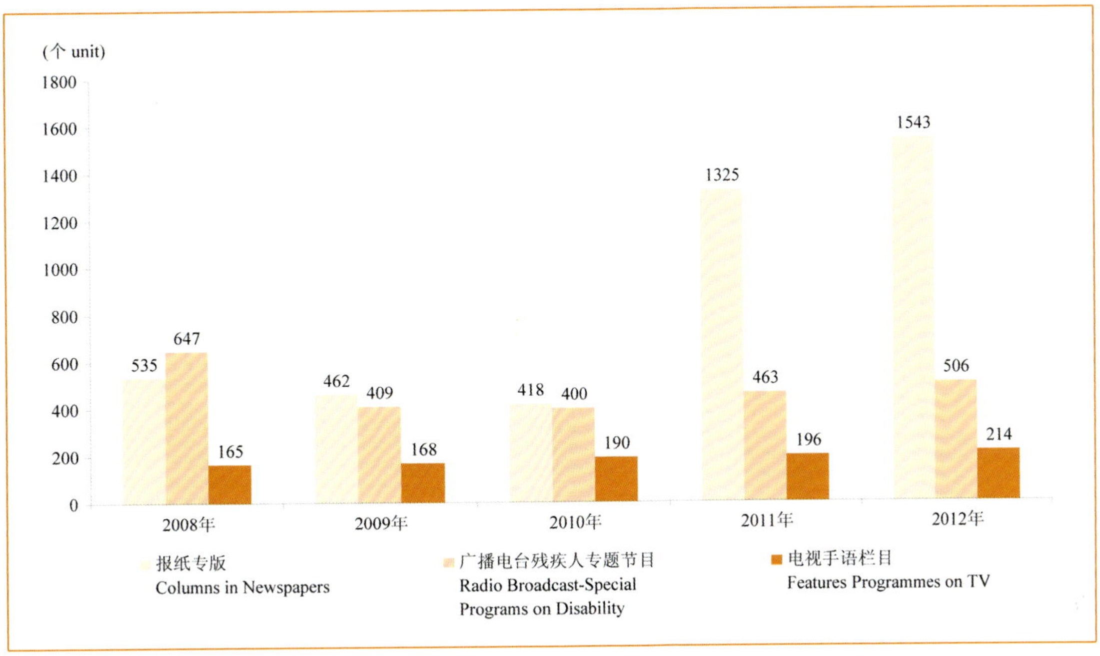

图-10 历届残奥会我国获得奖牌情况

Chart 10 Chinese Medal Tally for Each Paralympic Games

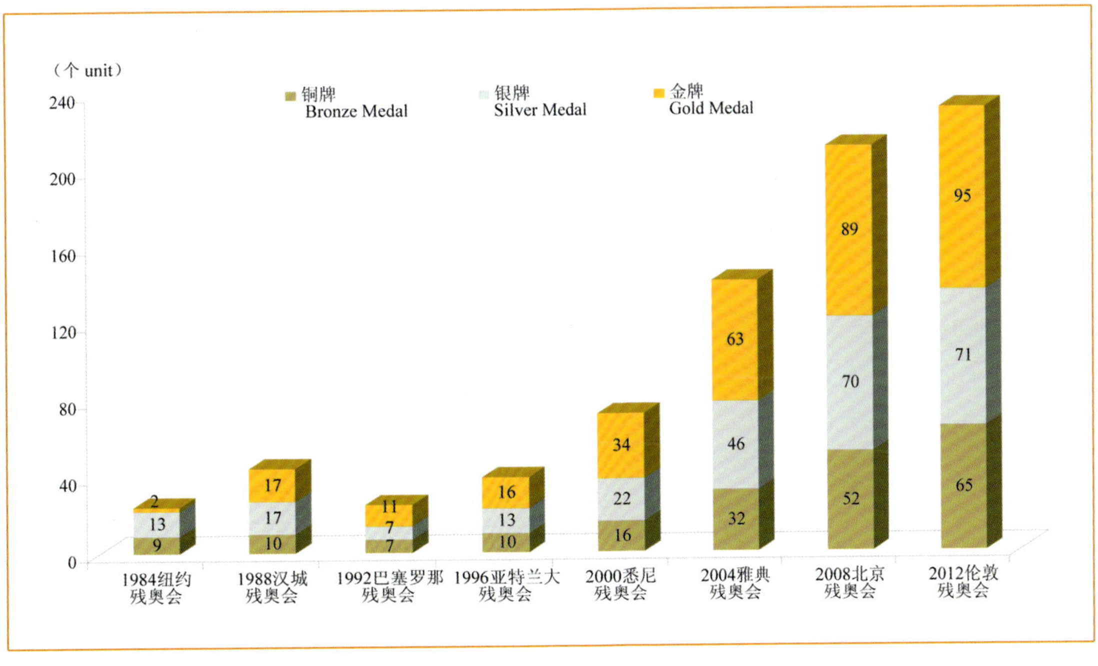

图-11　2008-2012年残疾人法律救助机构及服务情况

Chart 11 Legal Aid Centers(Stations) for PWDS and Their Service during 2008-2012

图-12　2008-2012年残疾人专职委员选聘情况

Chart 12 Full-time Workers on Disability at Grass-roots during 2008-2012

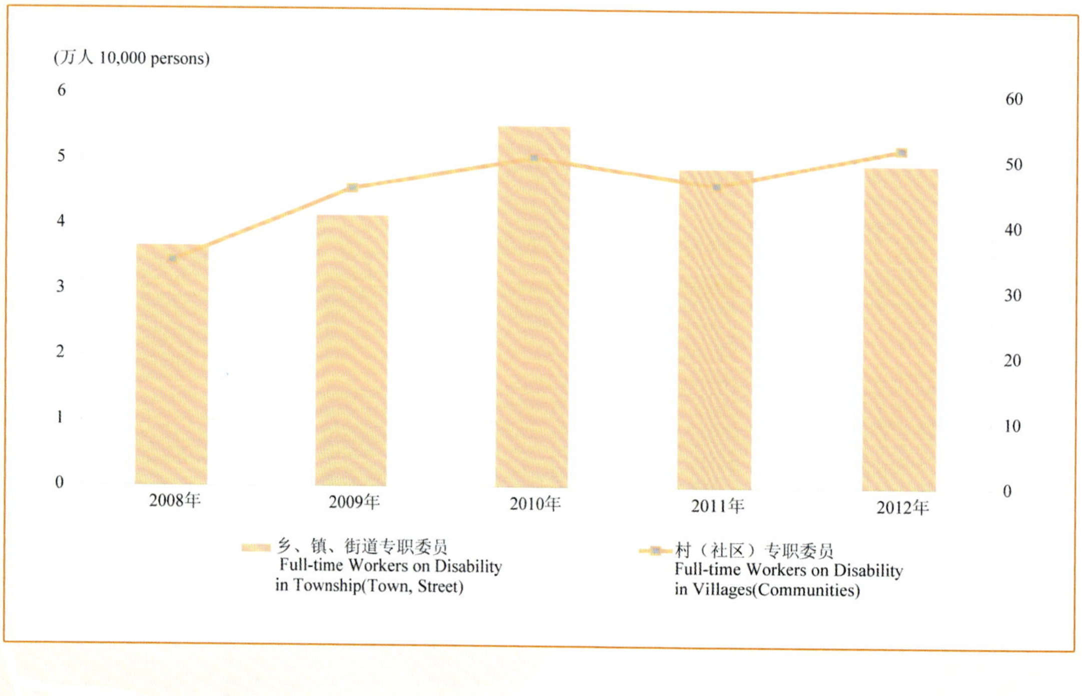

2

统计公报与专文

Communiqué and Reports

2012年中国残疾人事业发展统计公报

2012年是我国发展历史上具有重要意义的一年，党的十八大开启了全面建成小康社会新的伟大征程，揭开了共创中国人民和中华民族更加幸福美好未来的新篇章。残疾人事业保持良好的发展势头，各方面工作取得新成效，广大残疾人得到新实惠。

一、康复

2012年，通过实施一批重点康复工程，使760.2万残疾人得到不同程度的康复。开展全国残疾人社区康复示范区、县培育活动，积极推进残疾人社区康复工作；指导加强残疾人康复服务机构建设力度；实施《全国残联系统康复人才培养规划》，加强人才队伍建设；积极推动残疾人医疗康复保障政策的出台和落实；大力宣传和普及康复知识。

在889个市辖区和1905个县（市）开展了社区康复工作，累计已建社区康复站的社区总数20.5万个，配备35.3万名社区康复协调员。

开展视力残疾康复机构总数达到724个，完成白内障复明手术79.6万例；为33.4万名贫困白内障患者免费施行复明手术；为11.7万名低视力患者配用助视器，培训低视力儿童家长3.7万名，有效开展家庭康复训练。对12.0万名盲人进行定向行走训练。

推进听力语言康复机构规范化管理，完善基层服务网络。已建设省级听力语言康复机构32个，基层听力语言康复机构1011个。年度新收训聋儿2.0万名，在训聋儿3.2万名；规范聋儿家长学校，开展家庭训练，共培训聋儿家长3.9万名；开展各级各类听力语言康复专业技术人员培训，共培训专业人员7731人；实施贫困聋儿人工耳蜗、助听器抢救性康复项目，资助4000名聋儿免费植入人工耳蜗，资助4500名聋儿免费配戴助听器；开展彩票公益金成年听力残疾人（助听器）康复项目，为2万名（含2011年度）贫困成年听力残疾人免费验配助听器，各级康复机构共为3.5万名成年听力残疾人提供技术服务。

大力推广“社会化、综合性、开放式”精神病防治康复工作。在2586个市县开展精神病防治康复工作，对593.6万重性精神病患者进行综合防治康复，监护率达到75.6%，显好率达到67.2%，社会参与率达到52.6%，肇事率0.19%；解除关锁5056人；对44.4万贫困精神病患者进行医疗救助。

建立了30个省级孤独症儿童康复训练机构；1.1万名孤独症儿童在各级机构进行了康复训练。

开展肢体残疾康复训练服务机构达1592个，其中，省级康复机构31个，地市级、县级康复机构1561个；培训各级各类肢体残疾康复人员3.9万人次；全国共对35.7万肢体残疾者实施康复训练；实施救助项目资助3.0万名脑瘫儿童进行机构康复训练，资助6221名贫困肢体残疾儿童实施矫治手术。

为麻风畸残者实施矫治手术458例，开展宣传普及教育，为麻风患者回归社会营造良好社会氛围。

开展智力残疾康复训练服务的机构1206个，其中，省级康复机构29个，地市级、县级康复机构1177个；培训各级各类智力残疾康复人员1.7万人次；全国共对14.0万名智力残疾人进行康复训练；实施救助项目资助2.0万名智力残疾儿童进行机构康复训练，同时培训儿童家长。

加强残疾人辅助器具服务体系建设，深入开展辅助器具供应服务，为残疾人减免费用供应辅助器具114.5万件，其中装配假肢3.9万例、矫形器4.0万例，验配助视器10.5万件。

二、教育

2012年，残疾人受教育权得到了更好保障，进一步提高了残疾人素质和平等参与社会的能力。

残疾人事业专项彩票公益金助学项目，为全国家庭经济困难的残疾儿童享受普惠性学前教育提供资助1.0万人次。各地也积极多渠道争取资金支持，对4429名残疾儿童给予学前教育资助。

已开办特殊教育普通高中班（部）186 个，在校生 7043 人；其中聋高中 121 个，在校生 5555 人；盲高中 22 个，在校生 1488 人。残疾人中等职业学校（班）152 个，在校生 10442 人，毕业生 7354 人，其中 5816 人获得职业资格证书。全国有 7229 名残疾人被普通高等院校录取，1134 名残疾人进入特殊教育学院学习。

截止到 2012 年底，全国有未入学适龄残疾儿童少年 9.1 万人，其中视力残疾儿童 0.6 万人，听力残疾儿童 0.6 万人，言语残疾儿童 0.6 万人，智力残疾儿童 2.8 万人，肢体残疾儿童 2.8 万人，精神残疾儿童 0.3 万人，多重残疾儿童 1.3 万人。

三、就业

2012 年，残疾人就业工作在保持就业局势稳定的基础上取得新进展。城镇新增 32.9 万残疾人就业，其中，集中就业残疾人 10.2 万，按比例安排残疾人就业 8 万，公益性岗位就业 1.8 万，个体就业及其它形式灵活就业 12.3 万，辅助性就业 0.7 万。全国城镇实际在业人数 444.8 万；1770.3 万农村残疾人实现稳定就业，其中 1389.9 万人从事农业生产劳动。

全国残疾人职业培训基地达到 5271 个，其中残联兴办 1927 个，依托社会机构兴办 3344 个，29.9 万人次城镇残疾人接受了职业培训。

盲人按摩事业稳定发展，按摩机构迅速增长。2012 年度培训盲人保健按摩人员 16514 名、盲人医疗按摩人员 4925 名；保健按摩机构达到 12887 个，医疗按摩机构达到 848 个；在专业技术职务资格评审中，分别有 551 人和 1655 人通过医疗按摩人员中级和初级职称评审。

四、社会保障

2012 年残疾人社会保障状况保持平稳。残疾人参加新型农村和城镇居民社会养老保险工作实现了全覆盖，已有 325.3 万城镇残疾人参加了城镇居民社会养老保险，参保率 58.4%。在 60 岁以下的参保残疾人中有 62.8 万重度残疾人，其中 59.2 万得到了政府的参保扶助，有 47.7 万非重度残疾人也享受了全额或部分代缴的优惠政策。领取养老金待遇的人数达到 133.7 万人。

新型农村社会养老保险方面，共有 1333.8 万残疾人参加了新型农村社会养老保险，参保率 63.8%。在 60 周岁以下的参保残疾人中有重度残疾人 236.6 万，其中 224.6 万得到了政府的参保扶助（全部代缴 188.2 万人，部分代缴 36.4 万人），有 150.0 万非重度残疾人也享受了全额或部分代缴的优惠政策。享受养老金待遇的人数达到 507.4 万人。

城镇残疾职工参加社会保险人数达到 280.9 万，城镇残疾居民参加基本医疗保险达到 498.6 万人，城乡 1070.5 万残疾人纳入最低生活保障范围；城镇集中供养残疾人和农村五保供养残疾人分别达到 12.2 万和 68.5 万；261.3 万城乡残疾人获得其他救助救济，239.1 万和 36.3 万符合条件的城乡残疾人分别享受了稳定的生活补贴和护理补贴。

残疾人托养服务工作稳步推进，残疾人寄宿制托养服务机构达到 3903 个，其中事业单位 1107 个，民办非企业 1366 个，其他性质的 1430 个，托养残疾人 11.3 万人。残疾人日间照料机构达到 3372 个，为 7.4 万名残疾人提供托养服务。接受居家托养服务的残疾人达到 56.0 万人。

五、扶贫开发

2012 年，残疾人扶贫开发成效显著，贫困残疾人生产生活状况得到进一步改善。229.9 万贫困残疾人得到扶持，其中 137.3 万人通过扶贫开发实际脱贫；接受实用技术培训的残疾人达到 86.1 万人次。

康复扶贫贴息贷款扶持 5.5 万农村残疾人，6.4 万个单位和 41.3 万个人对贫困残疾人开展结对帮扶。残疾人扶持基地达到 5226 个，安置 10.2 万残疾人就业，扶持带动 25.8 万残疾人户。

完成 13.2 万户农村贫困残疾人危房改造，各地投入危房资金 11.9 亿元，15.7 万残疾人受益。

基层党组织助残扶贫项目帮扶 9.4 万名农村贫困残疾人。万村千乡市场工程助残扶贫项目安置 5968 名贫困残疾人就业，帮扶贫困残疾人创办 2059 个村级农村店。

六、宣传文化

2012 年，残疾人事业宣传工作在全社会大力弘扬人道主义思想，全面反映残疾人事业“两个体系”

建设为残疾人生活带来的明显变化，残疾人事业的社会影响力和关注度得到快速提升，营造了有利于残疾人事业发展的舆论环境。圆满组织以“加强残疾人文化服务 保障残疾人文化权益”为主题的第二十二次全国助残日活动，完成伦敦残奥会、《无障碍环境建设条例》颁布实施、《农村残疾人扶贫开发纲要》颁布、《残疾人权利公约》履约等重大事件和重点工作的宣传报道，把残疾人事业宣传纳入党的“十八大”国家宣传报道计划；举办2010—2011年度残疾人事业好新闻评选和第十届各地人民广播电台残疾人专题节目展播活动，217件新闻作品和48件广播专题节目获等级奖；完善全国残疾人事业宣传报道网络，建立两级宣传调控机制，形成残疾人事业宣传合力。截至2012年底，中央电视台《新闻联播》播出残疾人题材报道68条，全国共开辟省级报刊专版168个，残疾人专题广播节目38个，电视手语新闻栏目30个，28个省建立了省级残疾人事业新闻宣传促进会；共开辟地市级报刊专版1375个，残疾人专题广播节目468个，电视手语新闻栏目184个，建立地市级新促会115个。

残疾人文化生活更加丰富活跃，残疾人受到社会广泛关注并更加全面地参与到社会生活当中。与中宣部等十一部委联合制定并下发了《关于加强残疾人文化建设的意见》；启动全国残疾人文化体育建设示范市（区）工作；残疾人文化周活动深入开展，全国上百万残疾人参与其中；继续推进“残疾人文化进社区”项目，由中国残联扶持的示范社区已达1500个；残疾人题材电影《完美人生》被列入“迎接党的十八大国产重点影片”之一；电影《吴运铎》、图书《雷锋》荣获第十二届精神文明建设“五个一工程”优秀作品奖；举办了“全国残疾人美术大赛”、“兰亭杯全国残疾人书法大赛”、“V歌赛”等残疾人喜闻乐见的文化活动，出版了残疾人散文集《道德的力量》，有效促进了残疾人文化活动的繁荣发展。

七、体育

2012年是残疾人体育发展历程中具有里程碑意义的一年。我国派团参赛伦敦残奥会再创新辉煌，全面实施“残疾人自强健身工程”取得新突破。

2012年8月29日至9月9日，我国派出417人的代表团参加了第14届伦敦残奥会，取得了95枚金牌、71枚银牌、65枚铜牌、231枚奖牌的优异成绩，实现了我国在残奥会上金牌榜和奖牌榜的“三连冠”，创造了新辉煌。

成功举办第二届残疾人健身周活动，全国共有28个省（区、市）结合本地特色，举办了丰富多彩的残疾人健身周活动。积极举办残疾人群众体育赛事活动。2012年，举办了全国盲人跳绳、盲人乒乓球比赛和全国首期轮椅广播操训练营。全国共有30个省（区、市）的338名特教学生及残疾人工作者参加。

推进残疾人群众体育活动示范点建设。2012年出台《自强健身示范点命名资助办法》，已建设了76个国家级残疾人自强健身示范点。

大力推进聋人体育运动和特奥运动。为备赛世界听障奥运会，举办了5项全国聋人锦标赛，共有28个省市、438名聋人运动员参赛。完成了2013年世界冬季特奥会组团工作。举办了特奥融合篮球邀请赛、大学生特奥教练员培训班等9项特奥活动。特奥运动员总数已达到112万。

积极运用社会化工作方式，拓展残疾人体育发展资源。目前，我国开设残疾人体育课题研究及相关活动的院校已达到18所，开展特奥大学计划的院校达到了150所。2012年考核审批了153名国家级裁判员，有3000多名社会体育技术官员参与了残疾人体育活动，全国已设立29所国家级训练基地。

各地深入开展残疾人体育工作。组织省级残疾人群众体育健身活动218次，4.9万多人次参加；建设省级残疾人群众体育活动示范点351个，培训省级残疾人体育健身指导员2836人，组织残疾人体育比赛80多次，参赛运动员达1.3万多人次；省级残疾人体育训练基地已达200个。组织地市级残疾人体育活动3953次，52.5万人次参加；设立地市级残疾人群众体育活动示范点1040个，培训地市级残疾人体育健身指导员6616人。

八、维权

各级残联贯彻落实中国残疾人事业“十二五”发展纲要及实施方案，维权组织建设得到加强，残疾人事业法律法规体系进一步完善，残疾人维权工作全面开展。

2012年，修订《残疾人保障法》地方实施办法12件；制定或修改了关于残疾人的专门法规、规章省级5件、地市级25件；制定或修改保障残疾人权益的规范性文件省级61件、地市级109件。全国县级以上人大进行《残疾人保障法》执法检查923次；政协进行视察和专题调研810次。全国开展普法宣传教育活动8925次，92.8万人参加；举办法律工作者培训班1576个，8.8万人参加。

截至2012年底，全国成立残疾人法律救助工作协调机构1188个，建立残疾人法律救助工作站811个，办理案件6453件。建立残疾人法律援助中心（工作站）2979个，办理案件2.5万件，有力地促进了法律救助和法律援助工作。

残疾人参政议政工作得到加强，各级残联协助人大代表、政协委员提出议案、建议、提案1771件，办理议案、建议、提案1435件。

无障碍建设法规、标准进一步完善。全国共出台了438个省、地市、县级无障碍建设与管理法规、规章；1084个市、县、区系统开展无障碍建设；全国开展无障碍建设检查3354次，无障碍培训3.4万人次；为14.1万个贫困残疾人家庭实施了无障碍改造；为55.4万残疾人发放了残疾人机动轮椅车燃油补贴。

全国各级残联共处理残疾人群众来信5.5万余件，接待残疾人群众来访34.4万人次，其中集体访1096批次、1.5万人次。

九、组织建设

2012年，31个省级残联领导班子中基本上配备了残疾人理事长或副理事长；232个地市级残联在领导班子中配备了残疾人理事长或副理事长；1624个县级残联机关配备了残疾人干部；已建乡镇（街道）残联3.9万个，已建率达到97.5%，选聘残疾人专职委员4.9万名；已建社区（村）残协60.7万个，已建率达到95.6%，选聘残疾人专职委员51.8万名。

全国省市县乡残联实有人员已达12万人。各级残联共举办培训班3万期，培训机关干部、协会干部及残疾人专职委员79万人次。

全国共建立省级以下各类残疾人专门协会15321个，市级专门协会已建比例为98.2%，市辖区专门协会已建比例94.9%；县（含县级市）级专门协会已建比例为89.2%。

十、服务设施建设

残疾人服务设施建设得到全面发展。截至2012年底，全国已竣工并投入使用的各级残疾人综合服务设施1971个，总占地面积444.0万平方米，总建设规模355.8万平方米，总投资96.2亿元；已竣工并投入使用的各级残疾人康复设施231个，总占地面积82.4万平方米，总建设规模67.0万平方米，总投资19.2亿元；已竣工并投入使用的各级残疾人托养服务设施155个，总占地面积71.6万平方米，总建设规模43.1万平方米，总投资12.6亿元。

十一、信息化建设

2012年，中国残联网站加大对残疾人各项政策、地方残疾人工作的宣传，年度访问量达到3450万次，完成1.5万条信息更新。全国33个省级残联、272个地市级残联和1235个县级残联开通网站，为广大残疾人和社会公众提供信息服务，其中7个省级残联及2个计划单列市残联网站开展了无障碍建设。中国残疾人服务网开展面向聋人的央视蛇年春晚（文字+视频）网上直播服务，独立用户访问量14万；发布了近2000个残疾人高端就业岗位。

截至2012年底，全国残疾人人口基础信息数据库累计采集、收录持证残疾人实名信息近2600万条。结合全国农村贫困残疾人扶贫调查，采集农村贫困残疾人扶贫需求信息1350.6万条。作为国家权威的残疾人基础信息资源，残疾人人口基础数据库为残疾人社会保障体系和服务体系建设提供进一步支持和保障。

Statistical Communiqué on the Development of the Work for Persons with Disabilities in 2012

The year of 2012, as one important year in Chinese development history, witnesses the great decision in building a comprehensive Well-off society in the all round way in the 18th CPC and leading the Chinese nation and Chinese into the new stage of bright and happy future. The work on disabilities in China achieves important progress. The work on disabilities makes new strides and achieves new development. The people with disabilities get new benefits from the new policies.

I. Rehabilitation

In 2012, through implementation of some key projects, 7.602 million disabled persons received rehabilitation services of different degrees. The Campaign of Building Model Community or County was staged to vigorously promote community-based rehabilitation (CBR). Guidance was given to the capacity building of rehabilitation institutions. The National Rehabilitation Personnel Training Program was implemented to further the work of personnel training. Measures were taken to enable PWDs in rural areas to be covered by new type of cooperative medical care. Basic knowledge of rehabilitation was publicized and popularized.

Community-based rehabilitation was carried out in 889 districts under the jurisdiction of cities and 1,905 counties with 205,000 CBR stations set up and 353,000 CBR coordinators designated.

724 institutions provided rehabilitation services for patients with visual impairment. In the year, 796,000 cases of cataract sight-restoring surgeries were conducted, including 334,000 free ones for poor cataract patients. 117,000 low-vision patients received vision aids. 37,000 parents of children with low vision got training for more effective family-based rehabilitation. 120,000 blind persons received orientation mobility trainings.

The hearing and speech training institutions were regularized and the grassroots service network was built up. There were 32 provincial-level rehabilitation centers for deaf children and 1,011 grassroots hearing and speech training institutions nationwide. In 2012, 32,000 deaf children across the country got hearing and speech training. In addition, 20,000 new deaf children across the country enrolled in our institution. Parent schools were further regulated and trained 39,000 parents of deaf children. 7,731 various kinds of professionals were trained. A rescuing rehabilitation project was implemented to provide 4000 poor deaf children with free cochlear and 4,500 ones with free hearing aids. The rehabilitation project for the adult with hearing disabilities (hearing aids) was also carry out supported by the public welfare lottery fund. 20,000 poor adult with hearing disability (including the data from 2011) get free hearing aids and 35,000 poor adult with hearing disability get technical services by various levels of rehabilitation institutions.

A "socialized, comprehensive and open" model was promoted for the prevention and rehabilitation of psychiatric diseases. In 2012, the work of prevention and rehabilitation was carried out in 2,586 cities and counties, covering 5.936 million persons with severe mental illness. 75.6 % of the patients lived under guardianship, 67.2% of them showed signs of recovery, 52.6% participated in the society, and 0.19% caused incidents. 5,056 persons with mental illness were released from seclusion and 444,000 poor patients got medical assistance.

30 provincial-level autism rehabilitation institutions were set up and. 11,000 children with autism were provided with rehabilitation training.

The number of institutions able to provide rehabilitation and training services to persons with physical disability reached 1,592, including 31 provincial level rehabilitation institutions and 1,561 city level ones, which altogether conducted corrective surgeries for 6,221 poor children with physical disability, trained 30,000 children with cerebral Palsy and carried out rehabilitation training for 357,000 persons with physical disability nationwide. 39,000 professionals on physical rehabilitation also take their trainings in the institutions.

458 cases of corrective surgeries were conducted on persons with leprosy-induced disabilities. Education campaigns were carried out to build a favorable social atmosphere for these patients to return to society.

The number of institutions providing rehabilitation and training services to persons with intellectual disability reached 1,206, including 29 provincial level rehabilitation institutions and 1,177 city level ones, which trained 140,000 persons with intellectual disability nationwide and 20,000 children with intellectual disability as well as their parents. 17,000 professionals on intellectual rehabilitation also take their trainings in the institutions.

The supply system of assistive devices was built up to improve supply of assistive technology. By the end of 2012, an accumulation of 1.145 million assistive devices, including 39,000 items of cost-effective artificial limbs, 40,000 pieces of prosthetics were provided to poor disabled person at preferential rate or for free,.

II. Education

In 2012, disabled persons' right to education was better guaranteed. The quality of disabled persons and their ability to equally participate in social life were improved.

The education project funded by dedicated lottery fund provided 10,000 person/times of financial support to disabled children from poor families in their preschool education. Fund was also raised through various channels to support 4,429 disabled children in their preschool education.

There were 186 special education classes at senior high schools nationwide, with an enrollment of 7,043 students. Among the schools, 121 were for the deaf with 5,555 enrolled students, 22 were for the blind with 1,488 enrolled students. There were 152 medium-level vocational education institutions (classes) with 10,442 enrolled students, 7,354 graduates, of whom 5,816 were with vocational certification. In 2012, 7,229 students with disabilities were accepted by mainstream higher education institutions, and 1,134 disabled students entered special higher education institutions.

By the end of 2012, there were 91,000 disabled children and youth at school age who did not have access to education, including 6,000 with visual impairment, 6,000 with hearing impairment, 6,000 with speech impairment, 28,000 with intellectual disability, 28,000 with physical disability, 3,000 with psychiatric diseases and 13,000 with multiple disabilities.

III. Employment

In 2012, the work to promote employment of PWDs made new progress. 329,000 disabled persons in urban areas were newly employed, including 102,000 through concentrative placement, 80,000 through quota scheme, 7,000 through supporting employment. 18,000 through welfare post and 123,000 through individual business and other forms of employment. 4.448 million disabled persons were in employment in the urban areas. 17.703 million rural PWDs had employment and 13.899 million of them took part in agricultural productive labor.

There were 5,271 special vocational training institutions nationwide, including 1,927 established by DPFs and 3,344 by social organizations. A total of 299,000 disabled persons in the urban areas received vocational training.

Massage business by the blind grew steadily with big increase of the number of massage institutions. In 2012, 16,514 health blind masseurs and 4,925 medical blind masseurs were trained. The number of healthcare massage institutions reached 12,887 and that of medical massage institutions amounted to 848. 551 and 1,655 medical blind masseurs passed secondary and elementary level qualification exams respectively.

IV Social Security

Social security for disabled persons was further improved in 2012. The disabled persons can make fully participation in the new type of rural cooperative or urban social endowment insurance. 3.253 million or 58.4% of disabled persons in rural areas took part in new type of rural social endowment insurance, including 628,000 persons with severe disabilities under 60 years old, 592,000 of whom received governments' financial assistance. 477,000 persons whose disabilities were not severe enjoyed the preferential treatment of all or part of the premium paid by governments. 1.337 million disabled persons received old-age pension.

In the aspect of new type of rural social endowment insurance, 13.338 million or 63.8% of disabled persons were covered by urban social endowment insurance, including 2.366 million persons with severe disabilities under the age of 60. 2.246 million of whom received governments' financial assistance.1.882 million persons with disabilities received the fully financial assistance from the government. 364,000 persons with disabilities receive partial financial support. 1.5 million Persons whose disabilities were not severe enjoyed the preferential treatment of all or part of the premium paid by governments. 5.074 million Disabled persons received old-age pension.

2.809 million Urban workers with disabilities were covered by social insurance. 4.986 million Urban residents with disabilities were covered by basic medical insurance. 10.705 million Were covered by basic living insurance protection. The number of urban disabled residents with basic medical insurance reached 10.314 million. The number of unban centralized persons with disabilities and the rural five-guarantee disable persons reached 122,000 and 685,000 respectively. 2.613 million Persons with disabilities in the urban and rural areas got social relief. 2.391 million Disabled persons in the urban areas and 363,000 in the rural areas got regular living allowance and care subsidy.

The fostering service for disabled persons made steady progress. The number of boarding fostering service organizations for disabled persons amounted to 3,903, including 1,107 social institutions, 1,366 private non-enterprise units and 1,430 other organizations, which altogether provided services to 113,000 persons with disabilities. The number of day-care organizations for disabled persons increased to 3,372, which provided services to 74,000 persons with disabilities. 560,000 persons with disabilities received services while staying at home.

V. Poverty Alleviation

The work of poverty alleviation made remarkable progress with the living and production conditions of poor disabled persons further improved. In 2012, 2.299 million poor disabled persons were covered by poverty alleviation projects, including 1.373 million who got rid of poverty through the projects. 861,000 persons/times of training of practical technology were provided.

55,000 rural persons with disabilities were granted interest-subsidized loans under poverty alleviation through rehabilitation projects. 64,000 units and 413,000 individuals paired up with poor disabled persons to get them out of poverty. The number of poverty-alleviation bases increased to 5,226, employing 102,000 disabled persons, supporting and leading 258,000 disabled persons.

132,000 poor rural households with disabled persons had their houses renovated. 1.19 billion RMB Yuan were invested, benefiting nearly 157,000 disabled persons. There were 940,000 poor disabled persons in the rural areas get benefit from the poverty alleviation project held by the local organizations.5968 disabled persons get employment through marketing engineering alleviation project and 2059 village-level shops were set up by the disabled persons with the help of the project.

VI. Publicity and Cultural Activities

In 2012, centered on the major tasks of the work on disabilities, humanitarianism was advocated, the social impact of and attention to the work on disabilities were remarkably upgraded, and a conducive public atmosphere was created for the sustainable development of the work on disabilities. Activities were organized on the theme of "strengthening the culture services for the Persons with Disabilities, Safeguarding their culture rights" on the occasion of the 22nd National Day of Assisting Persons with Disabilities. Activities such as the promulgation of the regulations on the accessibility environment construction and the national program for the rural poverty alleviation of the disabled. The big events, such as the London Paralympic Games and the implementation of the UNCRPD were also well publicized. The publicity for the enterprises of people with disabilities was integrated into the broadcasting plan for the spirit of the 18th national congress of the communist Party of China. The broadcasting network for the enterprises of people with disabilities was well organized. By the end of 2012, 68 news on issue of people with disabilities were showed in CCTV. At the provincial level there were 168 special columns and special editions in newspapers and magazines, 38 radio programs on disability, 30 TV news programs with sigh language and 28 disability publicity promotion societies. At the district/city level, there were also 1,375 special columns and special editions in newspapers and magazines, 468 radio programs on disability, 184 TV news programs with sigh language, 115 disability publicity promotion societies.

The cultural life of disabled persons became more active and colorful. PWDs received wide social attention and extensively participated in social life. The guideline on further promotion on the culture civilization for PWDs was jointly formulated and issued by Publicity department of central committee of CPC and CDPF. Together with other 11 ministries and departments. The work of pilot model city (district) for the national culture and sports building for PWDs was also launched this year. The activity of "Culture Week of Disabled Persons" was continuously carried out with millions of participants with disabilities. Inspection and evaluation were done to 1,500 pilot communities under the project of "Culture of Disabled Persons in Communities". The movie named perfect life which reflected the issue for PWDs was listed as one the key movies in celebrating the 18th national congress of the communist Party of China. The movie named Wu Yunduo and the book entitled Lei Feng got the good masterpieces award for the 12th spiritual civilization "five ones" project. Various kinds of activated favored by the PWDs were also be held. Such as the National Art Show for PWDs, Lanting Cup national handwriting competition for PWDs and V singing contest. The essay entitled "the power of morality" was also being published. All of which further promoted the culture activities for PWDs.

VII. Sports

2012 is a milestone in Sport development history for the people with disabilities. Chinese delegation won great success in the 14th London Paralympic Games. The project of promotion of disabled persons' fitness with great efforts was also be fully implemented.

China sent a sports delegation with 417 members to participate in the 14th London Paralympic Games which was held from Aug.29 to Sept. 9, 2012. The delegation brought back a good result of 95 gold medals, 71 silver medals and 65 bronze medals. 231 medals altogether. China topped both in the medal and the gold medal tallies for the third time. .

28 provinces (districts and cities) organized various kinds of activities according to their local situation. Activities like the second "Fitness Week of Disabled Persons", National Rope Jumping Contest of Blind as well as Table tennis Competition of Blind Persons were held. The first national wheelchair radio gymnastics training camp was organized and attended by 338 students and working staff from specials schools of 30 provinces.

The focus was also given to the establishment of the sports activity demonstration sites of disabled persons. The name and support methods on the sports activity demonstration sites of disabled persons was formulated in 2012 and 76 national sports activity demonstration sites of disabled persons have been set up.

Activities were organized to promote the development of spots for the deaf persons and the Special Olympics in China, including organizing 5 national tournaments for the deaf persons in preparation for the world Deaflympics. 438 athletes of deaf sportsman from 28 provinces participated in the tournaments. The excellent persons were included into the sports delegation for world winter Special Olympics 2013. Nine activities for the Special Olympics were held during this year, including Special Olympic Competition of basketball, training courses of coaches for Special Olympics in the university. The number of the athletes for Special Olympics has reaches 1.12 million.

The socialized working methods were actively used in enlarging the resources for sport development for people with disabilities. Up to now, 18 Universities and colleges have researches on sport science of disabled persons and related activities. 150 universities and colleges have programmes for Special Olympics. 153 coaches have passed the national qualification examination by the year 2012. 3000 social sport technical officials participated in the sport activities for the people with disabilities. 29 national training bases have been set up in China.

The sports activity of disabled persons was

extensively carried out in localities. 218 times of fitness activities were organized for disabled persons at provinces, with a participation of 49,000 person/times. 351 sports activity demonstration sites of disabled persons were established, training 2836 coaches for fitness activity of disabled persons. Over 80 sports competitions of disabled persons were organized and participated by 13,000 persons. The number of provincial sports training base of disabled persons amounted to 200. At the city level, 3,953 times of sports activities of disabled persons were organized and participated by 525,000 person/times. 1040 sports activity demonstration sites of disabled persons were established, training 6,616 coaches for fitness activity of disabled persons.

VIII. Rights Protection

In line with the Work Program on Disability during the 12th Five-Year Plan Period and relevant action plans, disabled persons' federations at all levels further strengthened their work in rights protection for disabled persons. They built up their capacities of right protection, improved the legal systems related with disabled persons. The work of rights protection was carried out in an all round way.

In 2012, 12 local implementation method of the Law of P.R.C. on the Protection of Persons with Disabilities were revised. 5 regulations especially for disabled persons at the province level and 25 ones at the city level were formulated or revised. 61 regulations directly related with disabled persons at the province level and 109 ones at the city level were formulated or revised. People's congress at and above the county levels carried out inspections on enforcement of the Law of P.R.C. on the Protection of Persons with Disabilities for 923 times. The Political Consultative Conferences at all levels carried out inspections and studies for 810 times. 8,925times of law publicity and education activities and 1,576 education courses for legal professionals were organized for 928,000 and 88,000 participants respectively.

By the end of 2012, 1,188 coordination organizations of legal assistance for disabled persons and 811 legal aid stations were set up, handling 6,453 cases of rights violation against disabled persons. 2,979 legal aid stations were set up, handling 2,500 cases of rights violation against disabled persons. The work of legal aids and services for disabled persons were greatly promoted.

Disabled persons took a more active part in political consulting process. In 2012, 1,771 pieces of bills and proposals were raised by congress deputies and members of political consultative conferences from disabled persons' federation systems. 1,435 pieces of bills and proposals were dealt with.

Legislation and standards of accessibility were further improved. 438 regulations and administrative decrees on accessibility were issued in the provinces, cities and counties. Systematic accessibility construction was carried out in 1084 cities and counties. 3,354 times of special inspections on accessibility were carried out. 34,000 persons/times received trainings on accessibility. Accessibility renovation was made for 141,000 poor families with disabled persons. 554,000 persons with disabilities received subsidy for petrol used by their motorized wheelchairs.

The disabled persons' organizations at all levels received and handled over 55,000 compliant letters and 344,000 visitor/times in the year. Among the complaint visits, there are 1,096 group visits and 15,000 by individuals.

IX. Disabled Persons' Organizations

In 2012, 31 provincial federations had disabled persons as president or vice presidents. 232 city-level federations had disabled president or vice presidents in their offices. 1,624 county-level federations had disabled staffs in their offices. 39,000 towns (streets) had disabled persons' federations, accounting for 97.5% of the total and recruiting 49,000 disability commissioners. 607,000 communities (villages) had disabled persons' associations, accounting for 95.6% of the total and recruiting 518,000 disability commissioners.

Workers of city, county and township level disabled persons federations amounted to 120,000 persons. Personnel training made new progress. 30,000 training courses were organized for 790,000 person/times. The trainings played an important role in raising the quality of DPF's staff.

Nationwide, there are 15,321 special associations of disabled persons under the provincial level. 98.2 %

of cities and 94.9% of districts under the jurisdiction of cities as well as 89.2% of the counties had special associations.

X. Service facilities

The construction of services facilities for disabled persons was developed in an all round way. By the end of 2012, 1971 complicated services facilities at all levels were completed and put into use, coving an area of 4.44 million square meters, with the construction area of 3.558 million square meters. The total investment is 9.62 billion RMB. 231 complicated rehabilitation services facilities at all levels were completed and put into use, coving an area of 842,000 square meters, with the construction area of 670,000 square meters. The total investment is 1.92 billion RMB. 155 complicated foster services facilities were completed and put into use, coving an area of 716,000 square meters, with the construction area of 431,000 square meters. The total investment is 1.26 billion RMB.

XI. Informationization

In 2012, the official website of China Disabled Persons' Federation put emphasis on disclosure of policies and information and provision of highlight services, the website recorded 34.5 million visits in 2012. 150,000 new information have been updated. 33 disabled persons' federations at the provincial level, 272 at the city level and 1,235 at the county level had constructed their websites. The websites of DPFs had developed as a platform of administrative information and services for the society and disabled persons in particular. Seven provincial DPF and two municipality DPFs developed their accessible websites. CDPF gave an accessible live broadcast on the Spring Festival Gala of CCTV through text and video on the eve of the Spring Festival. The program received over 140,000 visits and 2000 posts for the employment of PWDs has been announced on line.

By the end of 2012, the national basic database of persons with disabilities collected the basic data of 26 million disabled persons. The national survey on the poverty alleviation of disabled persons in the rural areas of China collected data on the poverty alleviation needs of 13.506 million disabled persons. As an authoritative basic information resource, the database played an important role in providing support and guarantee for improvement of social security system and social security level for disabled persons.

全国残疾人人口基础数据库主要数据简报

中国残联 2008 年启动建设全国残疾人人口基础数据库，结合第二代残疾人证核发工作进行持证残疾人的人口基础信息的收集与管理，并通过与公安部“全国公民身份信息服务系统”进行身份认证。全国残疾人人口基础数据库（简称“人口库”）是目前唯一权威的国家级残疾人基础信息数据库。

截至 2013 年 6 月 3 日，人口库中已收录 3795.2 万条基础数据，其中已完成残疾人证审核和办理的数据达到 2651.5 万。按照全国 8502 万残疾人计算，残疾人证办理比例为 27.4 %。

持证残疾人的主要特征为：劳动年龄人口为主（16-59 岁占 61.7%），男性、中轻度、肢体残疾人各占到六成（分别为 60.3%、62.4%和 59.0%），农业户口近四分之三（74.9%），受教育程度以小学和初中为主体（70.5%）。

一、持证残疾人人口学主要特征

1. 性别年龄结构

人口库中 2651.5[1]万持证残疾人的性别构成为：男性 1598.4 万人，占 60.3%；女性 1053.1 万人，占 39.7%。

人口库中 2651.5 万持证残疾人的年龄构成为：0-14 岁 75.6 万人，占 2.8%；15-64 岁 1916.9 万人，占 72.3%；65 岁及以上 659.1 万人，占 24.9%。相对于残疾人总体（2006 年第二次全国残疾人抽样调查数据）以老年人口为主，人口库持证残疾人以 16-59 岁劳动年龄人口为主，达到 61.7%。

2. 民族

人口库中汉族残疾人 2398.9 万人，占 90.5%；少数民族 252.7 万人，占 9.5%。

3. 户口性质

人口库中农业户口的持证残疾人 1984.8 万人，占 74.9%；非农业户口 666.7 万人，占 25.1%。

4. 受教育程度

人口库中 2639.4 万的 6 岁及以上持证残疾人中，受教育程度构成为：文盲 504.6 万人，占 19.1%；小学 1071.1 万人，占 40.6%；初中 790.9 万人，占 30.0%；高中 181.5 万人，占 6.9%；中专 35.3 万人，占 1.3%；大学专科及以上 37.2 万人，占 1.4%；其他 18.7 万人，占 0.7%。

5. 婚姻状况

人口库中 2576.0 万 15 岁及以上持证残疾人的婚姻状况为：未婚 538.2 万人，占 20.9%；已婚 1888.2 万人，占 73.3%；丧偶 32.0 万人，占 1.2%；离异 117.6 万人，占 4.6%。

二、持证残疾人主要残疾特征

1. 残疾类别

人口库中 2651.5 万持证残疾人的类别构成为：视力残疾人 316.4 万人，占 11.9%；听力残疾人 204.4 万人，占 7.7%；言语残疾人 50.7 万人，占 1.9%；肢体残疾人 1564.0 人，占 59.0%；智力残疾人 220.2 万人，占 8.3%；精神残疾人 182.0 万人，占 6.9%；多重残疾人 113.8 万人，占 4.3%。

2、残疾等级

人口库中 2651.5 万持证残疾人的残疾等级构成为：残疾一级 362.9 万人，占 13.7%；残疾二级 633.6 万人，占 23.9%；残疾三级 743.2 万人，占 28.0%；残疾四级 911.8 万人，占 34.4%。

如表 1 所示，除肢体残疾人外，其余各类持证残疾人中一二级重度残疾人所占比例均超过 50%或在 50%左右，比例最高的为多重残疾人，达到 84.8%，其次为言语残疾人，69.6%。但由于肢体残疾人在持证残疾人中占了较大比重（59.0%），而持证肢体残疾人中以三四级中轻度残疾人为主（75.1%），从而影响到全部持证残疾人的残疾等级构成表现为以中轻度残疾人为主（62.4%）。

注：数据简报根据分析时点上收集到的数据进行，即截止到 2013 年 6 月 3 日已完成残疾人证办理的 2651.5 万残疾人数据。

表 1　人口库残疾人分类别残疾等级构成（%）

类　别	残疾一级	残疾二级	残疾三级	残疾四级
合　　计	13.7	23.9	28.0	34.4
视力残疾人	28.1	19.2	16.7	35.9
听力残疾人	24.4	23.9	23.8	28.0
言语残疾人	46.3	23.3	15.1	15.3
肢体残疾人	5.3	19.6	32.2	42.9
智力残疾人	13.0	38.6	30.0	18.4
精神残疾人	12.3	49.6	28.7	9.4
多重残疾人	58.8	26.0	10.9	4.3

三、主要致残原因

1. 视力残疾

人口库 329.7 万视力残疾（含多重）的主要致残原因中，“其他”和“原因不明”占到较大比例，共计 23.6%。在已明确的具体致残原因中，“白内障”排在第一位，占 13.2%，其次“视网膜、色素膜病变”为 11.6%，“遗传、先天异常或发育障碍”10.8%和“外伤”8.9%，“视神经病变”、“角膜病”和“青光眼”分别为 8.1%、7.3%和 6.2%，比例最小的是“中毒”，仅为 0.3%。

2. 听力残疾

在人口库 282.5 万听力残疾（含多重）的主要致残原因中，“原因不明”和“其他”所占比例最高，分别为 24.5%和 19.2%。在已明确的具体致残原因中，“老年性耳聋”排在首位占 15.6%，其次为“遗传”11.1%，此外，“中耳炎”、“药物中毒”所占的比例也较高，分别是 7.1%和 6.9%，比例最低的是“高胆红素血症”，仅占 0.1%。

3. 言语残疾

在人口库 125.7 万言语残疾（含多重）的主要致残原因中，“听力障碍”为最主要因素，占 37.4%，“其他”和“原因不明”所占的比例也较高，分别占 18.3%和 17.3%，其余各种原因所占的比例较低，均在 5%以下。

4. 肢体残疾

在人口库 1597.5 万肢体残疾（含多重）的主要致残原因中，“其他外伤”排在首位，占 22.3%，其次为“其他”，占 15.5%，“骨关节病”、“脑血管疾病”、“原因不明”分别占 11.4%、10.9%和 8.2%，“脊髓灰质炎”占 6.7%，“其他先天性或发育障碍”占 5.0%，“交通事故”占 4.0%，其余各类原因所占比例均很小。

5. 智力残疾

在人口库 240.0 万智力残疾（含多重）的主要致残原因中，“原因不明”和“其他”同样占较大比例，分别为 19.7%和 16.5%。在已明确的具体致残原因中，“脑疾病”所占比例最高，占 31.4%，其次为“遗传”12.0%，“发育畸形”占 4.8%，其余各类原因所占的比例均很小。

6. 精神残疾

在人口库 187.5 万精神残疾（含多重）的主要致残原因中，“精神分裂症”是最主要的原因，占 60.1%，其次为“其他”、“癫痫”和“原因不明”，分别为 8.3%、6.8%和 5.8%，其余各种原因所占的比例较小，均在 4%以下。

3

综合统计资料

Comprehensive Statistical Data

中国残疾人事业“十二五”发展纲要执行简要情况
(2011－2012)

指 标 名 称		Item	
康 复		Rehabilitation	
得到不同程度康复残疾人	(万人)	PWDs Received Rehabilitation Services of	(10,000 persons)
1. 社区康复		Community-based Rehabilitation (CBR)	
开展社区康复服务的县、区	(个)	Counties and Districts Where CBR Has B	(unit)
接受社区康复服务的残疾人	(万人)	Disabled Persons Who Began to Get CBR	(10,000 persons)
社区康复协调员	(万人)	CBR Coordinators at Communties	(10,000 persons)
2. 视力残疾康复		Rehabilitation of Persons with Visual Disability	
白内障复明手术	(万例)	Sight-restoring Surgeries for Cataract Pati	(10,000 cases)
其中：贫困患者免费手术	(万例)	Free Surgeries for Poor Catarat Patients	(10,000 cases)
低视力配用助视器	(万人)	Persons with Low Vision Fitted with Visic	(10,000 persons)
培训低视力儿童家长	(万人)	Trained Parents of Children with Low Vis	(10,000 persons)
盲人定向行走训练	(万人)	Blind Persons Receiving Orientation Skill	(10,000 persons)
3. 听力语言残疾康复		Rehabilitation of Persons with Hearing/Speech Disabilities	
聋儿康复训练	(万人)	Deaf Children Trained	(10,000 persons)
聋儿家长培训	(万人)	Parents Trained	(10,000 persons)
4. 肢体残疾康复		Rehabilitation of Persons with Physical Disability	
肢体残疾(脑瘫)儿童机构康复训练	(万人)	Children with Physical Disability Receivir Training in Institutions	(10000 persons)
肢体残疾人社区、家庭康复训练	(万人)	Persons with Physical Disability Receivin Training in Communities and Families	(10000 persons)
贫困肢体残疾儿童矫治手术	(例)	Orthopedic Surgeries Conducted for Poor Physical Disability	(case)
麻风畸残矫治手术	(例)	Orthopedic Surgeries Conducted for Perso Leprosy- induced Disability	(case)
5. 智力残疾康复		Rehabilitation of Persons with Intellectual Disability	
智力残疾儿童康复训练	(万人)	Children with Intellectual Disability Recei Rehabilitation Training	(10000 persons)
成年智力残疾人社区、家庭康复训练	(万人)	Adults with Physical Disability Receiving Training in Communities and Families	(10000 persons)
6. 精神病防治康复		Prevention and Rehabilitation of Mental Illness (PRMI)	
监护精神病人	(万人)	People with Mental Illness under Guardiar	(10000 persons)
接受医疗救助的贫困精神病患者	(万人)	People with Mental Illness in Poverty Whc Medical Assistance	(10000 persons)
孤独症儿童康复训练机构	(个)	Rehabilitation Institutions for Children wi	(unit)
孤独症儿童康复训练	(人)	Children with Autism Trained in Institutio	(person)

Brief Summary on Development of the Work for Persons with Disabilities during the 12th Five-year Plan Period (2011－2012)

"十一五"完成/达到 the 11th Five-year Accomplishment	"十二五"任务 the 12th Five-year Plan	"十二五"完成情况 the 11th Five-year Accomplishment (2011－2012)		
		累计完成/达到 Total	2011	2012
1037.9	**1300**	**867.9**	**631.8**	**760.2**
2507	2860	2794	2697	2794
1036	—	632.3	303.5	328.8
32.9	30	35.3	31.4	35.3
423.6	328	155.3	75.8	79.6
127.6	—	64.4	31.0	33.4
17.3	50	15.3	3.6	11.7
6.5	20	4.4	0.7	3.7
6.3	50	14.5	2.5	12.0
9.8	10	3.7	1.8	2.0
12.2	10	6.8	2.9	3.9
7.8	3	3.0	1.8	3.0
41.6	85	47.6	14.9	32.8
10535	12000	7532	1311	6221
8254	1000	617	159	458
13.2	41.0	14.3	2.8	11.5
—	—	2.5	—	2.5
416.2	780	449.0	421.2	449.0
36.6	20	79.9	35.6	44.4
426	—	929	839	929
13743	50000	18029	6910	11119

续表 1

指 标 名 称		Item	
7. **残疾人辅助器具供应服务**		**Provision of Assistive Devices**	
辅助器具供应	(万件)	Assistive Devices Provided	(10,000 pieces)
其中：贫困残疾人免费发放	(万件)	Assistive Devices Provided to Disabled Persons Free of Charge	(10,000 pieces)
残疾人普及型假肢装配	(万例)	Low-cost Artificial Limbs Fitted	(10,000 case)
残疾人矫形器装配	(万例)	Orthotic Devices Fitted	(10,000 case)
教　育		**Education**	
1. **学前教育**		**Pre-school Rehabilitation and Education**	
残疾人事业专项彩票公益金助学项目资助	(人)	Support of Educational Project Funded by Dedicated Welfare Lottery Fund	(person)
其他残疾儿童学前教育助学项目资助	(人)	Support of Other Pre-School Educational Project for Disabled Children	(person)
2. **残疾人高级中等教育**		**Senior Secondary Education for PWDs**	
特教普通高中	(个)	Special Education Senior High Schools	(unit)
特教普通高中在校学生	(人)	Students at Special Education Senior High Schools	(person)
中等职业教育机构	(个)	Secondary Vocational Schools	(unit)
中等职业教育在校学生	(人)	Students at Secondary Vocational Schools	(person)
3. **残疾人高等教育**		**Higher Education for PWDs**	
高等特殊教育院校	(个)	Ordinary Higher Education Institutions	(unit)
普通高等院校录取残疾考生	(人)	Disable Students Enrolled by Ordinary Higher Education Institutions	(person)
高等特殊教育院校录取残疾考生	(人)	Disable Students Enrolled by Higher Special Education Institutions	(person)
就　业		**Employment**	
1. **城镇残疾人就业状况**		**Employment of PWDs in Urban Areas**	
在业	(万人)	Employed Disabled Persons	(10,000 persons)
新增安排就业	(万人)	Newly Employed	(10,000 persons)
其中：集中就业	(万人)	Employed by Collective Form	(10,000 persons)
按比例就业	(万人)	Employed in Quoto Scheme	(10,000 persons)
公益性岗位就业	(万人)	Employed though Welfare Post	(10,000 persons)
个体及其他形式就业	(万人)	Self-Employed or Employed in Other Forms	(10,000 persons)
辅助性就业	(万人)	Assistive Employment	(10,000 persons)
2. **农村残疾人就业状况**		**Employment of PWDs in Rural Areas**	
已就业	(万人)	Employed Disabled Persons	(10,000 persons)
3. **残疾人职业培训**		**Vocational Education and Training for PWDs**	
残疾人职业培训基地	(个)	Vocational Training Bases for PWDs	(unit)
城镇残疾人职业培训	(万人次)	Vocational Training for Urban PWDs	(10,000 person-time)
4. **盲人按摩**		**Blind Massage**	
按摩人员培训		**Massage Training**	
保健按摩人员	(人)	Training for Health-care Masseurs	(person)
医疗按摩人员	(人)	Training for Blind Therapeutical Masseurs	(person)
按摩机构		**Institutions of Blind Massage**	
医疗按摩机构	(个)	Therapeutical Blind Massage Clinics	(unit)
保健按摩机构	(个)	Health-care Blind Massage Houses	(unit)

Continued 1

"十一五"完成/达到 the 11th Five-year Accomplishment	"十二五"任务 the 12th Five-year Plan	"十二五"完成情况 the 11th Five-year Accomplishment (2011 - 2012) 累计完成/达到 Total	2011	2012
514.7	500	188.8	74.3	114.5
242.3	50	75.0	41.2	33.8
12.1	7	7.0	3.1	3.9
7.7	5	5.5	1.5	4.0
—	51400	20560	10280	10280
—		11056	6627	4429
99	—	186	179	186
6067	—	7043	7207	7043
147	—	152	131	152
11506	—	10442	11572	10442
—	—	20	18	20
29915	—	14379	7150	7229
5357	—	2011	877	1134
	—			
	—			
441.2	—	444.8	440.5	444.8
179.7	100	64.7	31.8	32.9
53.4	—	19.9	9.7	10.2
49.6	—	15.5	7.5	8.0
—	—	3.8	2.1	1.8
76.8	—	24.8	12.5	12.3
—	—	0.7	—	0.7
1749.7	1800	1770.3	1748.8	1770.3
—	**—**	**5271**	**5254**	**5271**
137.9	**180**	**59.7**	**29.9**	**29.9**
61147	30000	30581	14067	16514
28357	20000	8661	3736	4925
1152	—	848	1031	848
11616	—	12887	12170	12887

续表 2

指标名称		Item	
社会保障		**Social Security**	
1. 城镇残疾人社会保障状况		**Social Security in Urban Area**	
(1)参加社会保险		Disabled Persons Covered by Social Insurance	
残疾职工参加社会保险	(万人)	Urban Workers with Disabilities Covered Social Insurance	(10,000 persons)
参加养老保险	(万人)	Covered by Pension Insurance	(10,000 persons)
参加医疗保险	(万人)	Covered by Medical Care Insurance	(10,000 persons)
残疾居民参加城镇居民医疗保险	(万人)	Urban Residents with Disabilities Covere Medical Care Insurance	(10,000 persons)
(2)接受社会救助		Disabled Persons Covered by Social Relief	
已纳入最低生活保障	(万人)	Covered by the Basic Living Allowance S	(10,000 persons)
集中供养及其他救助救济	(万人次)	Linving in Institutions or with Other Assi	(10,000 person-time)
2. 农村残疾人社会保障状况		**Social Security in Rural Areas**	
参加新型农村社会养老保险	(万人)	Covered by New Types of Rural Pension Ins	(10,000 persons)
接受社会救助		Disabled Persons Covered by Social Relief	
已纳入最低生活保障	(万人)	Covered by the Basic Living Allowance S	(10,000 persons)
五保供养及其他救助救济	(万人次)	Supported with Five Guarantees or Provic Other Assistance and Relief	(10,000 person-time)
3. 托养服务		**Fostering Service**	
寄宿制托养服务机构	(个)	Boarding Fostering Institutions	(unit)
日间照料托养服务机构	(个)	Day-Care Fostering Service	(unit)
寄宿制和日间照料机构内托养	(万人)	PWDs in Boarding and Day-Care Fostering	(10,000 persons)
享受居家托养服务	(万人)	PWDs Recieving Fostering Service an Hom	(10,000 persons)
扶贫		**Poverty Alleviation**	
1. 农村贫困残疾人状况		**Impoverished PWDs in Rural Areas**	
农村贫困残疾人	(万人)	Impoverished PWDs in Rural Areas	(10,000 persons)
当地低收入残疾人	(万人)	PWDs with Low Income	(10,000 persons)
2. 扶贫效果		**Outcome of Poverty Alleviation**	
扶持贫困残疾人	(万人次)	Impoverished PWDs Assisted	(10,000 person-time)
实际脱贫	(万人次)	Out of Poverty	(10,000 person-time)
实用技术培训	(万人次)	Training on Applied Technologies for PWD	(10,000 person-time)
3. 残疾人扶贫资金落实情况		**Poverty Alleviation Fund for PWDs**	
中央安排康复扶贫贴息贷款	(亿元)	Interest-subsidized Loans for Rehabilitation from the Central Fiscal Budget	(100 million yuan)
项目贷款实际落实	(亿元)	Actually Allocated Loans for Project	(100 million yuan)
项目贷款扶持贫困残疾人	(人)	Poor Disabled Persons Supported by Loar	(person)
到户贷款实际落实	(亿元)	Loans Actually Allocated to Households	(100 million yuan)
到户贷款扶持贫困残疾人	(人)	Poor Disabled Persons Supported by Loar	(person)

Continued 2

“十一五”完成/达到 the 11th Five-year Accomplishment	“十二五”任务 the 12th Five-year Plan	“十二五”完成情况 the 11th Five-year Accomplishment (2011－2012)		
		累计完成/达到 Total	2011	2012
283.2	—	280.9	299.3	280.9
198.5	—	173.4	156.8	173.4
155.5	—	164.9	142.2	164.9
355.9	—	495.6	433.1	498.6
246.3	—	—	257.8	266.5
557.2	—	152.1	71.8	80.3
487.1	—	1333.8	1232.5	1333.8
680.8	—	—	773.6	804.0
1704.7	—	502.6	240.9	261.6
	—			
	—			
—	—	3903	3921	3903
—	—	3372	2368	3372
33.3	—	35.2	16.5	18.7
43.5	—	100.2	44.2	56.0
	—			
	—			
1089.1	—	—	1097.0	1393.7
715.4	—	—	758.0	825.6
932.2	1000	441.7	211.8	229.9
618.4	—	229.6	92.3	137.3
414.3	100	178.4	92.3	86.1
40.0	—	21.3	11.0	10.3
15.0	—	12.1	6.4	5.7
12.0	—	6.6	4.2	2.4
8.1	—	9.2	4.6	4.5
7.3	—	6.0	2.9	3.1

续表 3

指标名称		Item	
4. 残疾人扶贫基地建设		**Poverty Alleviation Bases for PWDs in Rural Areas**	
残疾人扶贫基地	(个)	Poverty Alleviation Bases for PWDs	(unit)
安置残疾人就业	(万人)	Providing Employment for PWDs	(10,000 persons)
扶持带动贫困残疾人	(万户)	Supporting and Leading Households with PWDs	(10,000 households)
5. 农村贫困残疾人危房改造		**House Renovation for Poor PWDs in Rural Areas**	
危房改造	(万户)	Houses Renovated for PWDs	(10,000 households)
受益残疾人	(万人)	PWDs Who Benefited	(10,000 persons)
宣传文化		**Publicity and Culture**	
1. 宣传		**Publicity at Provincial and Prefectural/City Level**	
省、市级报纸专版	(个)	Features in Newspapers	(unit)
省、市级广播电台残疾人专题节目	(个)	Radio Broadcast-Special Programs on Disability	(unit)
省、市级电视手语栏目	(个)	Programmes with Sign Language on TV	(unit)
2. 文化		**Culture at Provincial and Prefectural/City Level**	
省、市级盲文及盲人有声读物阅览室	(个)	Reading Rooms with Braille and Audio Reading Materials	(unit)
残疾人文化周	(个)	Culture Week for PWDs	(unit)
残疾人文化艺术类比赛及展览	(个)	Culture or Art Competitions and Exhibitions for PWDs	(unit)
体　育		**Sports**	
1. 残疾人群众体育健身		**Massive Sports and Fitness for PWDs at Provincial and Prefectural/City Level**	
省、市级残疾人群众体育健身活动	(次)	Massive Sports and Fitness Activities for PWDs	(time)
省、市级残疾人群众体育健身活动参加人	(万人次)	Participations in Massive Sports and Fitness Activities for PWDs	(10,000 person-time)
省、市级残疾人群众体育活动示范点	(个)	Sports Activity Demonstration Sites for PWDs	(unit)
省、市级残疾人体育健身指导员	(人)	Coaches for Fitness Activity for PWDs	(person)
2. 残疾人体育比赛		**Sports Events for PWDs at Provincial Level**	
省级残疾人体育比赛	(次)	Sports Events for PWDs	(time)
参加省级残疾人体育比赛运动员	(人次)	Disabled Athletes Who Participated in Sports Events for PWDs	(person-time)
省级残疾人体育训练基地	(个)	Sports Trainong Bases for PWDs	(unit)
维　权		**Safeguarding the Rights of PWDs**	
1. 法规体系和政策文件		**Legal System**	
制定或修改关于残疾人的专门法规、规章	(个)	Regulations Enacted or Reviewed for Assisting PWDs	(unit)
制定或修改保障残疾人权益的规范性文件	(个)	Policies Enacted for Protecting the Rights of PWDs	(unit)
2. 执法检查		**Inspections on Law Enformance**	
人大执法检查	(次)	Inspections by Officials of People's Congresses	(time)
政协视察或专题调研	(次)	Inspections and Investigations by Officials of People's Political Consultative Conferences	(time)

Continued 3

"十一五"完成/达到 the 11th Five-year Accomplishment	"十二五"任务 the 12th Five-year Plan	"十二五"完成情况 the 11th Five-year Accomplishment (2011–2012)		
		累计完成/达到 Total	2011	2012
—	—	5226	3985	5226
—	—	18.8	8.7	10.2
—	—	41.4	15.6	25.8
49.4		22.6	9.4	13.2
68.1	—	27.2	11.5	15.7
418	—	1543	1325	1543
400	—	506	463	506
523	—	214	196	214
441	—	479	438	479
—	—	3208	1426	1782
3164	—	2210	1085	1125
—	—	8264	4093	4171
—	—	109.5	52.0	57.5
—	1200	1391	799	1391
—	30000	9452	4150	9452
519	—	180	100	80
74962	—	24729	12155	12574
221	—	200	220	200
36	—	30	40	30
849	—	1577	871	706
5375	—	1747	824	923
5243	—	1655	845	810

续表 4

指标名称		Item	
3. **法律救助**		**Legal Aid**	
残疾人法律救助工作站	(个)	Legal Assistance Stations for PWDs	(unit)
残疾人法律救助工作站办理的案件	(件)	Cases Handled by Legal Assistance Stations for PWDs	(case)
残疾人法律援助中心(工作站)	(个)	Legal Aid Centers (Stations) for PWDs	(unit)
残疾人法律援助中心(工作站)办理的案件	(件)	Cases Handled by Legal Aid Centers (Stations) for PWDs	(case)
4. **参政议政**		**PWDs Participating in the Administration and Discussion of State Affairs**	
协助人大、政协代表提出议案、建议、提案	(件)	Proposals Put forward at People's Congresses with Assistance of PWDs	(case)
办理人大政协交办的议案、建议、提案	(件)	Handling Proposals of Peoples'Congresses and Motions of People's Political Consultative Conferences	(case)
5. **无障碍设施建设**		**Accessible Environment Building**	
无障碍设施建设法规、政府令	(个)	Regulations and Decrees on Accessible Environment Building and Management	(unit)
贫困残疾人家庭无障碍改造	(万户)	Accessibility Renovation for Homes of Poor PWDs	(10,000 households)
6. **残疾人机动轮椅车燃油补贴**	(万人)	**Subsidy for Petrol Used by Motorized Wheelchairs of PWDs**	**(10,000 persons)**
7. **残疾人信访**		**Complaint Letter and Visit**	
来信	(万件)	Complaint Letter	(10,000 cases)
来访	(万人次)	Complaint Visit	(10,000 person-time)
组织建设		**Organizational Structure**	
1. **省市县乡残联实有人员**	(万人)	**Staff of Disabled Persons'Federations at Provincial, City, County and Township Level**	**(10,000 persons)**
2. **市(地)级残联**		**Disabled Persons'Federations at Cities and Prefectures Level**	
配备残疾人领导干部的残联	(个)	Disabled Persons' Federations Whose Leadership Include PWDs	(unit)
残疾人干部	(人)	Staff with Disability	(person)
3. **县(市、区)级残联**		**Disabled Persons' Federations at County Level**	
配备残疾人干部的残联	(个)	Disabled Persons' Federations Whose Leadership Include PWDs	(unit)
残疾人干部	(人)	Staff with Disability	(person)
4. **乡、镇、街道残联与村(社区)残疾人协会**		**Disabled Persons' Federations in Township(Town, Street) and Villages(Communities)**	
已建乡、镇、街道残联	(万个)	Disabled Persons' Federation Established	(10,000 units)
其中：已配专兼职理事长	(万人)	Full-time(part-time) Presidents	(10,000 persons)
已建村(社区)残疾人协会	(万个)	Associations of Disabled Persons Established in Villages(Communities)	(10,000 units)
已选聘残疾人专职委员	(万人)	Full-time Workers on Disability	(10,000 persons)

Continued 4

"十一五"完成/达到 the 11th Five-year Accomplishment	"十二五"任务 the 12th Five-year Plan	"十二五"完成情况 the 11th Five-year Accomplishment (2011－2012)		
		累计完成/达到 Total	2011	2012
—	500	811	545	811
—	—	10606	4153	6453
2934	—	2979	2933	2979
19607	—	45856	21306	24550
10580	—	3644	1873	1771
7548	—	2805	1370	1435
385	—	438	426	438
—	8	24.3	10.2	14.1
—	—	97.4	41.9	55.4
30.2	—	11.6	6.0	5.5
204.2	—	69.3	34.9	34.4
9.9089	—	12	10.9	12
227	—	232	222	232
328	—	376	375	376
1744	—	1624	1599	1624
2133	—	2207	2114	2207
4.0	—	3.9	3.7	3.9
3.7	—	3.3	2.3	3.3
60.4	—	60.7	61.1	60.7
55.9	70	56.7	51.1	56.7

续表 5

指 标 名 称		Item	
5. 省级以下各类专门协会		**Special Associations below Provincial Level**	
盲人协会	(个)	Associations of Persons with Visual Disability	(unit)
聋人协会	(个)	Associatinss of Persons with Hearing Disability	(unit)
肢残人协会	(个)	Associations of Persons with Physical Disability	(unit)
智力残疾人及亲友协会	(个)	Associations of Persons with Intellectual Disability and Their Relatives and Friends	(unit)
精神残疾人及亲友协会	(个)	Associations of Persons with Psychiatric Disability and Their Relatives and Friends	(unit)
智力残疾人及亲友协会和精神残疾人及亲友协会合一的协会	(个)	Joint Associations of people with Mental or Psychiatric Disability and Their Relatives and Friends	(unit)
残疾人服务设施建设		**Service Facilities for PWDs**	
1. 残疾人综合服务设施		**Comprehensive Service Facilities for PWDs**	
建设完成已投入使用项目	(个)	Accumulated Projects in Operation	(unit)
总建设规模	(万平米)	Construction Area	(10,000 sq.m)
2. 残疾人康复设施		**Rehabilitation Service Facilities for PWDs**	
建设完成已投入使用项目	(个)	Accumulated Projects in Operation	(unit)
总建设规模	(万平米)	Construction Area	(10,000 sq.m)
3. 残疾人托养设施		**Fostering Service Facilities for PWDs**	
建设完成已投入使用项目	(个)	Accumulated Projects in Operation	(unit)
总建设规模	(万平米)	Construction Area	(10,000 sq.m)
信息化建设		**Informatization**	
1. 残疾人人口库综合数据	**(万人)**	**Data of the National Basic Database of Persons with Disabilities**	**(10,000 persons)**
2. 信息化专业人才	**(人)**	**IT Professionals**	**(person)**
3. 省、市、县各级残联网站	**(个)**	**Websites at Provincial, City, County Level**	**(unit)**

Continued 5

"十一五"完成/达到 the 11th Five-year Accomplishment	"十二五"任务 the 12th Five-year Plan	"十二五"完成情况 the 11th Five-year Accomplishment (2011－2012)		
		累计完成/达到 Total	2011	2012
3132	—	3089	3095	3089
3113	—	3073	3077	3073
3168	—	3113	3127	3113
3011	—	2983	2973	2983
3013	—	2985	2973	2985
63	—	78	90	78
	—			
2544	—	1971	1935	1971
487.7	—	355.8	334.0	355.8
—	—	231	224	231
—	—	67.0	60.7	67.0
—	—	155	130	155
—	—	43.1	34.2	43.1
1793.7	3000	2527.2	2195.1	2527.2
869	—	4948	4770	4948
1241	—	1540	1411	1540

全国残疾人人口基础数据库主要数据
Brief Data of the National Basic Information Database of Persons with Disabilities

单位：人　　(截止时间：2013年6月3日)　　(person)

地 区	入库残疾人 PWDs in the Database	已办理证件 PWDs with Disabled Persons Certificate	0-14岁 Age 0-14	15-64岁 Age 15-64	65岁及以上 Age 65 and over
全 国	**37951669**	**26515102**	**755555**	**19168865**	**6590671**
北 京	471500	436611	4926	320085	111600
天 津	253625	232029	3862	189041	39126
河 北	2208397	1417293	39088	1045306	332899
山 西	1015597	748649	20041	576295	152313
内蒙古	1054116	644933	12385	515752	116796
辽 宁	1134277	802316	13563	675046	113702
吉 林	752262	616232	12426	515595	88211
黑龙江	855035	764050	14968	653500	95580
上 海	535128	365488	1037	275693	88758
江 苏	2844233	1345043	25535	974024	345484
浙 江	1010132	1008619	19971	717989	270659
安 徽	1998308	1308217	34646	893066	380504
福 建	1036936	986763	22456	532000	432307
江 西	1008536	841011	31220	621528	188263
山 东	2220962	1826849	47438	1271910	507501
河 南	3431494	1526067	59501	1164813	301753
湖 北	1461728	977689	22326	767958	187405
湖 南	2028004	1064197	32131	815194	216872
广 东	1487528	1051031	47496	744381	259154
广 西	1889222	1297544	37616	658398	601530
海 南	142005	126356	5584	91562	29210
重 庆	828354	739813	22232	544500	173080
四 川	2443375	1817923	56836	1325954	435133
贵 州	1410608	738365	36176	544946	157243
云 南	1237784	1038031	41948	755133	240950
西 藏	65951	64941	6133	47848	10960
陕 西	1375800	1301242	19980	844717	436545
甘 肃	735066	566277	21118	428417	116742
青 海	143077	131395	7516	102701	21178
宁 夏	259899	208884	8498	144204	56182
新 疆	512250	427200	24946	332619	69633
新疆兵团	36399	31265	495	27206	3564
黑龙江农垦	64081	62779	1461	51484	9834

续表 1 Continued 1

单位：人 (person)

地 区	已办理证件残疾人 PWDs with Disabled Persons Certificate					
	性 别 Gender		残疾等级 Disability Grading			
	男 性 Male	女 性 Female	残疾一级 Grade-1	残疾二级 Grade-2	残疾三级 Grade-3	残疾四级 Grade-4
全 国	**15984351**	**10530747**	**3629476**	**6336349**	**7431500**	**9117777**
北 京	249222	187389	54145	104410	118427	159629
天 津	137694	94335	30335	63632	80417	57645
河 北	856352	560941	177005	278521	344675	617092
山 西	475709	272940	86672	174240	196466	291271
内蒙古	395595	249338	73725	146747	198460	226001
辽 宁	506115	296201	102200	184303	254872	260941
吉 林	384114	232118	83768	144481	197253	190730
黑龙江	482917	281133	93880	184040	242235	243895
上 海	202189	163299	49144	65030	99851	151463
江 苏	756133	588910	214523	396148	424522	309850
浙 江	615746	392873	153698	188525	312766	353630
安 徽	758972	549245	209983	583094	282812	232328
福 建	550041	436721	107091	253698	232556	393418
江 西	518015	322995	100354	195506	234015	311136
山 东	1130616	696233	272611	447116	517233	589889
河 南	940748	585319	236155	399593	412141	478178
湖 北	601795	375894	163185	251277	258333	304894
湖 南	686253	377944	162231	244514	281021	376431
广 东	642142	408889	189737	264032	308876	288386
广 西	727962	569582	114774	209882	329009	643879
海 南	75016	51340	44131	22093	31403	28729
重 庆	453495	286318	92975	185351	201145	260342
四 川	1113405	704517	248678	393854	535004	640387
贵 州	473725	264640	79242	118921	197989	342213
云 南	629675	408355	131493	188404	254232	463902
西 藏	34281	30660	10006	12660	15752	26523
陕 西	735600	565642	142886	245026	456495	456835
甘 肃	340005	226272	87297	143132	163432	172416
青 海	77329	54066	23602	46661	31808	29324
宁 夏	116560	92324	27470	65177	56625	59612
新 疆	259312	167888	56107	111975	133218	125900
新疆兵团	19693	11572	3881	5947	9658	11779
黑龙江农垦	37925	24854	6492	18359	18799	19129

续表 2 Continued 2

单位：人 (person)

地区	已办理证件残疾人 PWDs with Disabled Persons Certificate				
	残疾类别 Disability Category				
	视力残疾人 Persons with Visual Disability	听力残疾人 Persons with Hearing Disability	言语残疾人 Persons with Speech Disability	肢体残疾人 Persons with Physical Disability	智力残疾人 Persons with Mental Retardation
全国	**3163824**	**2044071**	**507746**	**15639618**	**2201847**
北京	46533	28886	2707	247427	49275
天津	21444	14942	3480	140458	26888
河北	129604	97960	38097	935742	108869
山西	78612	57975	17193	471395	66948
内蒙古	67864	57988	15410	395482	52316
辽宁	86095	59850	8395	447788	98386
吉林	69645	49089	11578	364286	56351
黑龙江	80794	59758	10788	479428	62691
上海	67721	33804	4113	159120	56008
江苏	166031	82009	9080	754782	171735
浙江	111386	118353	16240	539335	101270
安徽	150521	84010	28081	704680	122893
福建	160639	154337	12076	475269	76177
江西	93741	65257	13012	491903	66771
山东	154252	118507	24280	1165472	161343
河南	142495	113514	45370	994941	128176
湖北	127550	59786	27714	542023	81265
湖南	134896	52344	22484	639221	79185
广东	105951	71889	19940	564047	105114
广西	181522	123827	21346	788538	60367
海南	14178	4260	2576	73248	10380
重庆	120686	41573	12350	416491	58880
四川	267835	113334	34005	1111487	125331
贵州	92847	37445	16508	490878	34815
云南	140974	73567	26787	637161	56930
西藏	10853	6848	3419	31866	2012
陕西	162120	144529	29695	763938	67054
甘肃	61873	41184	10610	334138	45056
青海	16468	15524	3085	72603	10383
宁夏	26047	20239	4076	119689	17065
新疆	61179	35214	11871	235772	32470
新疆兵团	3467	2145	566	17168	3242
黑龙江农垦	8001	4124	814	33842	6201

续表 3　Continued 3

单位：人　(person)

地　区	已办理证件残疾人 PWDs with Disabled Persons Certificate			
	残疾类别 Disability Category		户口性质 Household Register Type	
	精神残疾人 Persons with Mental Disability	多重残疾人 Persons with Multiple Disabilities	农业 Rural	非农业 Non-Rural
全　国	**1819521**	**1138475**	**19848024**	**6667073**
北　京	45189	16594	188792	247819
天　津	22043	2774	98426	133603
河　北	57275	49746	1209644	207649
山　西	32439	24087	608398	140251
内蒙古	32163	23710	429451	215482
辽　宁	74407	27395	430680	371636
吉　林	45253	20030	347417	268815
黑龙江	46190	24401	369683	394367
上　海	44142	580	78802	286686
江　苏	120744	40662	229323	1115720
浙　江	93228	28807	826024	182595
安　徽	133592	84440	1044401	263816
福　建	64218	44047	811667	175096
江　西	67196	43131	671065	169946
山　东	123052	79943	1605140	221708
河　南	58552	43019	1327301	198766
湖　北	89338	50013	763603	214086
湖　南	73571	62496	889171	175026
广　东	125756	58334	783161	267870
广　西	55527	66417	1157821	139723
海　南	15331	6383	93745	32611
重　庆	62695	27138	585761	154050
四　川	110277	55654	1532909	285013
贵　州	22434	43438	646551	91814
云　南	56531	46081	916232	121798
西　藏	3854	6089	59946	4995
陕　西	61774	72132	1112524	188718
甘　肃	27416	46000	477919	88358
青　海	3361	9971	103470	27925
宁　夏	12378	9390	154242	54642
新　疆	27897	22797	292923	134277
新疆兵团	3856	821	556	30709
黑龙江农垦	7842	1955	1276	61503

续表 4 Continued 4

单位：人 (person)

地区	已办理证件残疾人 PWDs with Disabled Persons Certificate					
	15及以上受教育程度 Education of Age 15 and over					
	文盲 Illiterate	小学 Primary School	初中 Junior High School	高中及中专 Senior High School	大学专科及以上 Junior College and above	其他 Other
总计	**4770545**	**10447985**	**7901606**	**2167472**	**371813**	**100112**
北京	62505	82280	160528	81532	31415	13425
天津	29956	57672	88383	40625	9999	1532
河北	162974	592061	492937	111689	16055	2489
山西	93210	258728	297222	65744	11227	2477
内蒙古	109732	215300	225467	69078	11680	1291
辽宁	85060	245041	358370	84524	14291	1462
吉林	59844	195813	247582	90289	8957	1321
黑龙江	59018	242318	328384	101517	14822	3021
上海	31021	80931	156464	71546	19404	5085
江苏	445624	417270	346126	90758	18616	1114
浙江	213004	444462	261951	48401	12337	8493
安徽	331238	559023	310388	61330	10678	913
福建	199493	487015	203122	57234	9626	7817
江西	112488	357830	267670	62324	7400	2079
山东	325908	686005	585658	159451	19858	2530
河南	331045	464590	501725	138801	18974	11431
湖北	190823	309791	328395	110760	14390	1204
湖南	147979	437120	325774	109799	10717	677
广东	159436	425332	299077	85583	14275	19832
广西	173195	699597	309503	65433	8419	3781
海南	24072	39247	43628	12164	1512	149
重庆	83123	386662	199177	41256	5790	1571
四川	272687	941412	443609	89129	13452	797
贵州	196634	302407	165324	29603	7540	681
云南	267922	475365	193334	46274	12186	1002
西藏	32203	23085	2456	689	283	92
陕西	256590	492809	403417	109447	17079	1920
甘肃	175905	195022	123332	43634	6829	437
青海	27449	63819	21142	8707	2455	307
宁夏	56605	75440	49479	14666	3907	289
新疆	47030	171113	122295	47545	13479	790
新疆兵团	1786	6650	14940	6520	820	54
黑龙江农垦	4986	16775	24747	11420	3341	49

4

分省统计资料

Statistical Data of Provinces

1-1　社区康复

Community-Based Rehabilitation(CBR)

地　区	Region	开展社区康复服务的市辖区 Districts Where CBR Has Been Conducted	本年度新开展 Counties and Cities where CBR was Introduced in 2012	开展社区康复服务的县(市) Counties and Cities Where CBR Has Been Conducted	本年度新开展 Counties and Cities Where CBR Was Introduced in 2012
		个 unit	个 unit	个 unit	个 unit
全　国	**Total**	**889**	**21**	**1905**	**114**
北　京	Beijing	14		2	
天　津	Tianjin	13		3	
河　北	Hebei	37		138	11
山　西	Shanxi	23		87	4
内蒙古	Inner Mongolia	22	1	81	11
辽　宁	Liaoning	62		44	
吉　林	Jilin	30	7	40	
黑龙江	Heilongjiang	57	1	62	
上　海	Shanghai	16		1	
江　苏	Jiangsu	59	3	49	1
浙　江	Zhejiang	32		54	
安　徽	Anhui	43		56	3
福　建	Fujian	25		58	
江　西	Jiangxi	23		77	
山　东	Shandong	55		90	
河　南	Henan	57		103	
湖　北	Hubei	39		59	
湖　南	Hunan	36	1	88	3
广　东	Guangdong	58		67	
广　西	Guangxi	36		75	
海　南	Hainan	3		8	1
重　庆	Chongqing	21	2	19	
四　川	Sichuan	28		100	1
贵　州	Guizhou	10		62	24
云　南	Yunnan	11		93	4
西　藏	Tibet	1		9	8
陕　西	Shaanxi	26	4	83	33
甘　肃	Gansu	18		69	
青　海	Qinghai	4		42	
宁　夏	Ningxia	9		13	
新　疆	Xinjiang	10		79	2
新疆兵团	Xinjiang Corps	11	2	73	8
黑龙江农垦	Heilongjiang Land Reclamation			21	

1-1 续表 1 Continued 1

地区	Region	开展社区康复服务的社区(村) Communities (villages) Where CBR Has Been Conducted	社区康复协调员累计 Accumulative CBR Coordinators at Communties	本年度新增社区康复协调员 CBR Coordinators Who Were Engaged in 2012
		个 unit	人 person	人 person
全国	**Total**	**298580**	**353326**	**55796**
北京	Beijing	5517	4472	270
天津	Tianjin	4541	4055	588
河北	Hebei	28018	37044	2753
山西	Shanxi	9757	16586	2408
内蒙古	Inner Mongolia	4662	9831	1974
辽宁	Liaoning	11752	12921	754
吉林	Jilin	6245	8161	531
黑龙江	Heilongjiang	3003	4319	309
上海	Shanghai	648	3847	94
江苏	Jiangsu	16666	19446	2270
浙江	Zhejiang	15472	10753	2899
安徽	Anhui	5605	6602	908
福建	Fujian	9429	10034	1251
江西	Jiangxi	8325	13106	1920
山东	Shandong	48483	49730	2054
河南	Henan	32209	30322	5833
湖北	Hubei	8823	7284	1779
湖南	Hunan	12607	12695	3170
广东	Guangdong	14233	18409	2500
广西	Guangxi	6209	9571	1827
海南	Hainan	562	1342	359
重庆	Chongqing	5926	8045	1630
四川	Sichuan	13789	16148	5242
贵州	Guizhou	2996	5947	2543
云南	Yunnan	6861	10412	746
西藏	Tibet		23	6
陕西	Shaanxi	5293	7317	2793
甘肃	Gansu	4397	7813	4723
青海	Qinghai	2027	1899	408
宁夏	Ningxia	736	1371	777
新疆	Xinjiang	3598	3388	383
新疆兵团	Xinjiang Corps	154	272	27
黑龙江农垦	Heilongjiang Land Reclamation	37	161	67

1-1　续表 2　Continued 2

地　区	Region	接受过培训的社区康复协调员 Trained CBR Coordinators	已建社区康复站的社区累计 Accumulative Communities Where CBR Stations Have Been Established	本年度新建社区康复站的社区 Communities Where CBR Stations Were Established in 2012	已建社区康复服务档案的残疾人 PWDs who have been Established Files of CBR Service	本年度新增接受社区康复服务残疾人 PWDs Who Began to Get CBR Service in 2012
		人 person	个 unit	个 unit	万人 10,000 persons	万人 10,000 persons
全　国	**Total**	**336596**	**205180**	**21534**	**1917.6**	**328.8**
北　京	Beijing	4225	3601	308	35.1	22.5
天　津	Tianjin	2714	1611	47	23.6	14.5
河　北	Hebei	33344	16002	1278	156.5	8.3
山　西	Shanxi	15587	4971	197	43.0	3.2
内蒙古	Inner Mongolia	9701	2017	141	28.4	4.2
辽　宁	Liaoning	12854	10097	377	113.3	13.9
吉　林	Jilin	7979	2744	78	102.3	12.3
黑龙江	Heilongjiang	4258	1258	109	28.2	2.8
上　海	Shanghai	3845	219		33.3	28.2
江　苏	Jiangsu	19368	14501	2395	177.4	25.0
浙　江	Zhejiang	10563	9930	607	65.7	15.9
安　徽	Anhui	6213	3812	605	49.9	8.2
福　建	Fujian	9772	3760	109	65.8	16.5
江　西	Jiangxi	12557	3622	319	56.9	10.2
山　东	Shandong	47741	40568	1529	157.4	27.6
河　南	Henan	29054	47992	10748	165.0	23.0
湖　北	Hubei	7137	4567	433	80.6	5.2
湖　南	Hunan	12418	5245	167	75.2	4.9
广　东	Guangdong	17688	7817	413	115.8	12.6
广　西	Guangxi	9016	2353	151	32.3	2.2
海　南	Hainan	1000	615	7	2.9	0.4
重　庆	Chongqing	8018	3039	593	58.5	18.7
四　川	Sichuan	15769	6772	425	86.2	15.3
贵　州	Guizhou	5430	891	20	18.7	1.6
云　南	Yunnan	8904	2348	64	39.6	5.1
西　藏	Tibet	22	3			
陕　西	Shaanxi	7046	1198	131	32.3	5.8
甘　肃	Gansu	7697	1199	47	39.8	15.1
青　海	Qinghai	1680	461	32	4.2	0.8
宁　夏	Ningxia	1369	477	54	4.6	1.2
新　疆	Xinjiang	3201	1374	141	19.4	3.1
新疆兵团	Xinjiang Corps	272	99	9	1.8	0.3
黑龙江农垦	Heilongjiang Land Reclamation	154	17		3.7	0.1

1-1 续表 3 Continued 3

地 区	Region	开展家长学校工作的残疾人康复机构 Rehabilitation Institutions for Parents Training of PWDs	省级 at Provincial Level	地市级 at Prefectural/ City Level	县级 at County Level	参加培训的家长 Parents Trained	省级 at Provincial Level	地市级 at Prefectural/ City Level	县级 at County Level
		个 unit	个 unit	个 unit	个 unit	人次 person-time	人次 person-time	人次 person-time	人次 person-time
全 国	**Total**	**798**	**11**	**66**	**721**	**55012**	**1696**	**7194**	**46122**
北 京	Beijing	79			79	7665		536	7129
天 津	Tianjin	2			2	143			143
河 北	Hebei	35		4	31	1128		205	923
山 西	Shanxi	40	3	13	24	2193	850	611	732
内蒙古	Inner Mongolia	5	1		4	258	70		188
辽 宁	Liaoning	2			2	339		80	259
吉 林	Jilin	28		18	10	320		151	169
黑龙江	Heilongjiang	2			2	10			10
上 海	Shanghai	310	2		308	20533	350		20183
江 苏	Jiangsu	53		4	49	5070		715	4355
浙 江	Zhejiang	24		5	19	2024	2	1380	642
安 徽	Anhui	30		1	29	3637	12	331	3294
福 建	Fujian	6	1		5	243	30		213
江 西	Jiangxi	6			6	276		20	256
山 东	Shandong	60			60	2824			2824
河 南	Henan	14			14	571	10	20	541
湖 北	Hubei	4			4	358		23	335
湖 南	Hunan	11		1	10	861		206	655
广 东	Guangdong	22		10	12	2569		1992	577
广 西	Guangxi	6			6	133			133
海 南	Hainan					10		10	
重 庆	Chongqing	14	1		13	627	100		527
四 川	Sichuan	17		6	11	1475		657	818
贵 州	Guizhou	2			2	110			110
云 南	Yunnan	3			3	281	65	70	146
西 藏	Tibet								
陕 西	Shaanxi								
甘 肃	Gansu								
青 海	Qinghai	7			7	87	7	7	73
宁 夏	Ningxia	13	3	4	6	801	200	180	421
新 疆	Xinjiang	3			3	466			466
新疆兵团	Xinjiang Corps								
黑龙江农垦	Heilongjiang Land Reclamation								

1-2 视力残疾康复

Rehabilitation of Persons with Visual Disability

地 区	Region	白内障复明 Sight-restoring of Persons with Cataract-induced Blindness		低视力康复 Rehabilitation of Persons with Low Vision		盲人定向行走训练 Skills Training for Blind Persons	
		白内障复明手术 Sight-restoring Surgeries for Cataract Victims	贫困白内障患者免费手术 Free Surgeries for Poor Catarat Victims	低视力者配用助视器 Persons Fitted with Vision-aids	培训低视力儿童家长 Trained Parents of Children with Low Vison	盲人定向行走训练 Blind Persons Who Have Gotten Orientation Skills Training	盲人定向行走训练指导师 Orientation Skills Trainers for Blind Persons
		例 case	例 case	人 person	人 person	人 person	人 person
全 国	**Total**	**795932**	**334162**	**117214**	**36541**	**119844**	**5123**
北 京	Beijing	10356	667	362	25	920	183
天 津	Tianjin	5744	1168	1868	138	1256	78
河 北	Hebei	32661	5676	13375	2322	6272	146
山 西	Shanxi	29124	7046	56	3829	6364	458
内蒙古	Inner Mongolia	10928	5749	1228	162	2038	34
辽 宁	Liaoning	20719	7418	5926	1610	6525	201
吉 林	Jilin	15085	2947	7254	2604	4493	165
黑龙江	Heilongjiang	12217	4300	1141	824	4676	17
上 海	Shanghai	50907	3004	4178	1062	1939	511
江 苏	Jiangsu	60046	17192	6501	1203	8081	153
浙 江	Zhejiang	34640	19001	2002	966	5790	668
安 徽	Anhui	26676	11584	3788	619	3853	220
福 建	Fujian	17677	12641	749	946	4255	50
江 西	Jiangxi	18088	4559	1697	460	4754	29
山 东	Shandong	58238	26806	2795	513	6432	350
河 南	Henan	24671	12165	14402	4843	8695	346
湖 北	Hubei	30000	7456	7297	7304	6668	406
湖 南	Hunan	29938	15606	4928	1115	5121	163
广 东	Guangdong	89302	23238	1442	122	4664	50
广 西	Guangxi	25975	12144	4358	1211	2571	81
海 南	Hainan	4779	3587	159	21	810	39
重 庆	Chongqing	16821	8188	2789	382	1140	127
四 川	Sichuan	45000	22870	2106	909	7353	69
贵 州	Guizhou	15258	8451	2891	402	2788	63
云 南	Yunnan	63415	61038	4191	1003	2593	198
西 藏	Tibet	1056	1056	66		106	
陕 西	Shaanxi	15618	10349	9661	145	3659	57
甘 肃	Gansu	11126	7295	4988	985	2601	39
青 海	Qinghai	2501	2368	246	97	1152	15
宁 夏	Ningxia	2629	1884	2071	437	1127	96
新 疆	Xinjiang	12622	6197	1415	145	656	111
新疆兵团	Xinjiang Corps	1671	452	1004	17	212	
黑龙江农垦	Heilongjiang Land Reclamation	444	60	280	120	280	

1-3 视力残疾康复服务机构
Rehabilitation Institutions for Persons with Visual Disability

地 区	Region	开展视力残疾康复训练服务机构 Rehabilitation Institutions for Persons with Visual Disability	省级 at Provincial Level	地市级 at Prefectural/ City Level	县级 at County Level	本年度新建机构 Established in 2012	本年度注销机构 Cancelled Registration in 2012
		个 unit	个 unit	个 unit	个 unit	个 unit	个 unit
全 国	**Total**	**724**	**21**	**147**	**556**	**192**	**34**
北 京	Beijing	6			6	2	
天 津	Tianjin	5	1		4	1	
河 北	Hebei	18		6	12		4
山 西	Shanxi	41	1	15	25	10	7
内蒙古	Inner Mongolia	10		6	4	3	
辽 宁	Liaoning	26	1	7	18	1	
吉 林	Jilin	49	3	15	31	10	9
黑龙江	Heilongjiang	22	1	7	14	4	2
上 海	Shanghai	30	1		29	3	-2
江 苏	Jiangsu	49	1	4	44	10	1
浙 江	Zhejiang	15	1	3	11	7	
安 徽	Anhui	10	1	4	5	2	
福 建	Fujian	52		5	47	13	1
江 西	Jiangxi	8		3	5	5	
山 东	Shandong	78		14	64	29	6
河 南	Henan	15	1	3	11		
湖 北	Hubei	14		2	12	7	
湖 南	Hunan	24		4	20	8	
广 东	Guangdong	69	1	25	43	12	3
广 西	Guangxi	6	1	1	4		
海 南	Hainan						
重 庆	Chongqing	31			31	6	
四 川	Sichuan	21	1	3	17	4	
贵 州	Guizhou	17		3	14	5	
云 南	Yunnan	27	1	7	19	15	
西 藏	Tibet	1	1				
陕 西	Shaanxi	39	2	3	34	28	
甘 肃	Gansu	15	1	4	10	2	1
青 海	Qinghai	1			1		
宁 夏	Ningxia	4	1	1	2		
新 疆	Xinjiang	21		2	19	5	2
新疆兵团	Xinjiang Corps						
黑龙江农垦	Heilongjiang Land Reclamation						

1-3 续表 Continued

地区	Region	视力残疾康复机构在岗人员 Staff of Rehabilitation Institutions for Persons with Visual Disability			
		在岗人员总数 Total Staff	专业技术人员 Technicians and Professionals	管理人员 Managerial Personnels	其他 Other Staff Members
		人 person	人 person	人 person	人 person
全 国	**Total**	**11060**	**6957**	**1997**	**2106**
北 京	Beijing	126	89	13	24
天 津	Tianjin	24	13	8	3
河 北	Hebei	119	73	29	17
山 西	Shanxi	815	530	146	139
内蒙古	Inner Mongolia	64	24	31	9
辽 宁	Liaoning	198	104	46	48
吉 林	Jilin	641	409	160	72
黑龙江	Heilongjiang	239	172	35	32
上 海	Shanghai	335	160	37	138
江 苏	Jiangsu	854	597	130	127
浙 江	Zhejiang	824	481	224	119
安 徽	Anhui	88	54	15	19
福 建	Fujian	298	170	66	62
江 西	Jiangxi	119	43	36	40
山 东	Shandong	2104	1422	291	391
河 南	Henan	97	49	25	23
湖 北	Hubei	107	52	21	34
湖 南	Hunan	522	341	113	68
广 东	Guangdong	997	640	138	219
广 西	Guangxi	23	8	6	9
海 南	Hainan				
重 庆	Chongqing	526	346	87	93
四 川	Sichuan	217	145	49	23
贵 州	Guizhou	547	362	87	98
云 南	Yunnan	370	138	48	184
西 藏	Tibet	3	2	1	
陕 西	Shaanxi	346	205	76	65
甘 肃	Gansu	283	241	38	4
青 海	Qinghai	1	1		
宁 夏	Ningxia	17	12	3	2
新 疆	Xinjiang	156	74	38	44
新疆兵团	Xinjiang Corps				
黑龙江农垦	Heilongjiang Land Reclamation				

1-4 听力语言残疾康复
Rehabilitation of Persons with Hearing and Speech Disabilities

地 区	Region	新收训聋儿 Newly Trained Deaf Children	机构训练 Deaf Children Trained in Institutions	家庭训练 Deaf Children Trained in Families	在训聋儿数 Deaf Children Being Trained	培训家长 Parents Trained
		人 person	人 person	人 person	人 person	人 person
全 国	**Total**	**19659**	**15896**	**3764**	**31571**	**38646**
北 京	Beijing	187	186	1	332	498
天 津	Tianjin	56	49	7	139	134
河 北	Hebei	2346	1454	892	2870	2704
山 西	Shanxi	422	422		797	1027
内蒙古	Inner Mongolia	401	298	103	528	729
辽 宁	Liaoning	521	351	170	1043	968
吉 林	Jilin	332	222	110	409	904
黑龙江	Heilongjiang	436	348	88	647	618
上 海	Shanghai	135	61	74	381	384
江 苏	Jiangsu	1179	1078	101	2338	2309
浙 江	Zhejiang	485	472	13	802	737
安 徽	Anhui	1476	1407	69	2123	3477
福 建	Fujian	545	502	43	860	988
江 西	Jiangxi	644	534	110	931	1022
山 东	Shandong	1176	1019	157	2146	2465
河 南	Henan	2324	1883	441	3229	2928
湖 北	Hubei	791	749	42	940	942
湖 南	Hunan	962	800	162	1597	1754
广 东	Guangdong	1015	976	39	2237	4128
广 西	Guangxi	495	326	169	836	1063
海 南	Hainan	59	59		108	255
重 庆	Chongqing	206	153	53	403	686
四 川	Sichuan	974	683	291	1559	1856
贵 州	Guizhou	542	475	67	703	719
云 南	Yunnan	607	270	337	925	1298
西 藏	Tibet	4	4		12	4
陕 西	Shaanxi	423	379	44	965	1253
甘 肃	Gansu	385	287	98	542	449
青 海	Qinghai	132	116	16	177	208
宁 夏	Ningxia	53	51	2	151	413
新 疆	Xinjiang	195	183	12	528	1510
新疆兵团	Xinjiang Corps	35	14	21	66	62
黑龙江农垦	Heilongjiang Land Reclamation	32		32	32	64

1-4 续表 1 Continued 1

地 区	Region	本年度接受国家项目救助 Subsidized by State Projects in 2012		本年度接受地方项目救助 Subsidized by Local Projects in 2012	专业人员培训 Professionals Trained		
		接受人工耳蜗救助 Poor Deaf Children Subsidized by CDPF Rescuing Project through Cochlear Implantation	接受助听器救助 Poor Deaf Children Subsidized by CDPF Hearing Aids Rescuing Project			培训省级机构专业人员 Professionals of Institutions at Provincial Level	培训地市级机构专业人员 Professionals of Institutions at Prefectural/ City Level
		人 person	人 person	人 person	人 person	人 person	人 person
全 国	**Total**	**4000**	**4500**	**7326**	**7731**	**2181**	**2465**
北 京	Beijing	30		127	300	20	10
天 津	Tianjin	15	22	195	16	12	
河 北	Hebei	216	240	274	221	23	169
山 西	Shanxi	143	120	286	381	172	180
内蒙古	Inner Mongolia	74	95	226	90	41	32
辽 宁	Liaoning	139	140	18	266	131	115
吉 林	Jilin	82	110	52	256	43	173
黑龙江	Heilongjiang	116	150	10	81	15	23
上 海	Shanghai	16		166	154	71	
江 苏	Jiangsu	150	160	919	509	203	73
浙 江	Zhejiang	100	100	283	115	29	17
安 徽	Anhui	244	250	151	577	332	163
福 建	Fujian	131	100	410	197	51	85
江 西	Jiangxi	150	160	100	73	43	13
山 东	Shandong	300	320	659	338	29	103
河 南	Henan	395	360	244	394	116	49
湖 北	Hubei	185	210	166	61	18	28
湖 南	Hunan	210	240	121	77	6	36
广 东	Guangdong	250	188	1375	2029	437	995
广 西	Guangxi	128	200	99	53	25	6
海 南	Hainan	26	30	92			
重 庆	Chongqing	99	130	113	390	52	
四 川	Sichuan	200	300	510	201	17	40
贵 州	Guizhou	122	180	128	19	4	
云 南	Yunnan	100	200	124	292	42	57
西 藏	Tibet	8	15				
陕 西	Shaanxi	147	160	210	105	34	62
甘 肃	Gansu	100	130	32	6	2	2
青 海	Qinghai	20	25	69	73	5	6
宁 夏	Ningxia	15	30	20	40	40	
新 疆	Xinjiang	85	100	34	325	168	28
新疆兵团	Xinjiang Corps	2	25	17			
黑龙江农垦	Heilongjiang Land Reclamation	2	10				

1-4 续表 2 Continued 2

地 区	Region	培训县级机构专业人员 Professionals of Institutions at County Level	成年听力语言康复技术服务 Adults Received Hearing and Speech Rehabilitation Services	训练后走向 Directions in which Children have gone After Rehabilitation			
				普小 Ordinary Primary Schools	普幼 Ordinary Kindergartens	特殊教育学校(聋校) Special Education Schools (Schools for Deaf Students)	其他 Other Directions
		人 person	人次 person-time	人 person	人 person	人 person	人 person
全 国	**Total**	**2993**	**35216**	**1357**	**1618**	**2331**	**1966**
北 京	Beijing	270	135	13	53	18	39
天 津	Tianjin	4	2955	5	22	9	
河 北	Hebei	29	1388	57	122	180	247
山 西	Shanxi	29	2334	29	56	33	22
内蒙古	Inner Mongolia	17	789	16	12	23	22
辽 宁	Liaoning	20	957	14	41	21	23
吉 林	Jilin	40	534	8	47	14	20
黑龙江	Heilongjiang	43	85	6	25	67	25
上 海	Shanghai	83	3807	16	22	6	3
江 苏	Jiangsu	233	3350	44	87	119	166
浙 江	Zhejiang	69	2694	73	80	52	86
安 徽	Anhui	82	1608	183	72	348	133
福 建	Fujian	61	826	19	63	33	63
江 西	Jiangxi	17	523	30	23	18	
山 东	Shandong	206	1370	96	125	206	110
河 南	Henan	229	2123	129	171	206	176
湖 北	Hubei	15	611	34	30	49	54
湖 南	Hunan	35	898	82	82	88	46
广 东	Guangdong	597	2468	126	111	143	184
广 西	Guangxi	22	355	18	52	46	86
海 南	Hainan					2	20
重 庆	Chongqing	338	1018	18	35	19	39
四 川	Sichuan	144	897	77	51	261	119
贵 州	Guizhou	15	23	24	11	60	34
云 南	Yunnan	193	407	76	60	117	149
西 藏	Tibet		123				
陕 西	Shaanxi	9	606	58	87	148	71
甘 肃	Gansu	2	72	34	3	24	11
青 海	Qinghai	62	183	2		2	2
宁 夏	Ningxia		123	15	4		
新 疆	Xinjiang	129	838	13	34	17	8
新疆兵团	Xinjiang Corps		68	2		2	1
黑龙江农垦	Heilongjiang Land Reclamation						

1-5　听力语言康复机构
Rehabilitation Institutions of Hearing and Speech

地　区	Region	机构概况 Rehabilitation Institutions					
		累计建设 Rehab-institutions Established	省级 at Provincial Level	地市级 at Prefectural/City Level	县级 at County Level	本年新建 Established in 2012	本年注销 Rehab-institutions Cancelled Registration in 2012
		个 unit	个 unit	个 unit	个 unit	个 unit	个 unit
全　国	**Total**	**1044**	**32**	**355**	**656**	**190**	**188**
北　京	Beijing	18	1		17	3	
天　津	Tianjin	8	1	4	3		
河　北	Hebei	93	1	12	80	8	9
山　西	Shanxi	51	1	16	34	3	3
内蒙古	Inner Mongolia	23	1	17	5	6	7
辽　宁	Liaoning	44	1	21	22	6	4
吉　林	Jilin	20	1	9	10		
黑龙江	Heilongjiang	30	1	16	13	5	11
上　海	Shanghai	19	1		18	1	1
江　苏	Jiangsu	62	1	11	50	10	10
浙　江	Zhejiang	30	1	9	20	11	5
安　徽	Anhui	51	1	24	26	5	4
福　建	Fujian	28	1	12	15	6	5
江　西	Jiangxi	31	1	9	21	13	11
山　东	Shandong	85	1	26	58	30	25
河　南	Henan	81	1	28	52		
湖　北	Hubei	36	1	14	21	8	11
湖　南	Hunan	54	1	17	36	13	9
广　东	Guangdong	75	1	26	48	15	24
广　西	Guangxi	29	1	8	20	4	9
海　南	Hainan	4	1		3	4	
重　庆	Chongqing	12	1		11	1	
四　川	Sichuan	32	1	16	15	7	22
贵　州	Guizhou	24	1	8	15	11	4
云　南	Yunnan	19	1	14	4	6	1
西　藏	Tibet	1	1				
陕　西	Shaanxi	36	1	12	23	12	12
甘　肃	Gansu	18	1	11	6	1	
青　海	Qinghai	6	1	4	1		
宁　夏	Ningxia	6	1	3	2	1	1
新　疆	Xinjiang	16	1	8	7		
新疆兵团	Xinjiang Corps						
黑龙江农垦	Heilongjiang Land Reclamation	1	1				

1-5 续表 1 Continued 1

地 区	Region	机构概况 Rehabilitation Institutions					
		机构康复功能 Rehabilitation Services Provided by the Institutions					
		开展助听器验配 Providing the Service of Fitting Hearing-aids	开展人工耳蜗术后调试 Providing Adjustments After Cochlear Implantation Surgery	开展听力语言训练 Providing Training of Hearing and Speech	开展社区指导 Providing Guidance at Communities	开展听觉口语法 Providing Implementation of Hearing and Speech Training	开展成年听力语言康复服务 Providing Hearing and Speech Rehabilitation Service to Adults
		个 unit	个 unit	个 unit	个 unit	个 unit	个 unit
全 国	**Total**	**316**	**116**	**967**	**361**	**303**	**193**
北 京	Beijing	4	3	17	11	5	3
天 津	Tianjin	4	2	8	4	4	3
河 北	Hebei	16	4	93	33	20	25
山 西	Shanxi	10	1	51	10	14	4
内蒙古	Inner Mongolia	6	1	23	5	11	2
辽 宁	Liaoning	17	3	36	16	12	12
吉 林	Jilin	8	2	19	15	7	9
黑龙江	Heilongjiang	11	4	26	6	7	4
上 海	Shanghai	3	2	19	13	8	3
江 苏	Jiangsu	16	8	60	33	25	15
浙 江	Zhejiang	14	2	23	11	11	5
安 徽	Anhui	8	5	50	9	14	5
福 建	Fujian	13	5	22	15	4	4
江 西	Jiangxi	16	3	27	17	6	5
山 东	Shandong	27	9	82	30	35	12
河 南	Henan	28	18	71	20	20	12
湖 北	Hubei	11	4	32	7	9	6
湖 南	Hunan	16	8	51	13	12	9
广 东	Guangdong	21	10	71	34	27	11
广 西	Guangxi	9	3	27	8	7	6
海 南	Hainan	2	2	4	4		4
重 庆	Chongqing	1	1	9	6	3	1
四 川	Sichuan	17	6	28	14	13	12
贵 州	Guizhou	4	3	24	3	4	2
云 南	Yunnan	12	2	15	4	7	5
西 藏	Tibet	1	1	1		1	1
陕 西	Shaanxi	7	1	32	7		6
甘 肃	Gansu	5	1	18	4	3	2
青 海	Qinghai	2		6	2	2	
宁 夏	Ningxia	1		5	3	4	1
新 疆	Xinjiang	4	1	16	3	7	2
新疆兵团	Xinjiang Corps						
黑龙江农垦	Heilongjiang Land Reclamation	1					1

1-5 续表 2 Continued 2

地 区	Region	在岗专业人员 On-the-job Professionals				
		教师 Teachers	其中：个别化教师 Individualized Teachers	医技 Doctors and Technicians	其中：助听器验配师 Technicians That Check and Fit Hearing Aids	管理 Managerial Personnels
		人 person	人 person	人 person	人 person	人 person
全 国	**Total**	**9706**	**3627**	**1635**	**677**	**2309**
北 京	Beijing	262	108	35	11	44
天 津	Tianjin	84	44	9	5	18
河 北	Hebei	760	260	94	51	250
山 西	Shanxi	497	125	47	14	106
内蒙古	Inner Mongolia	264	102	54	11	81
辽 宁	Liaoning	475	135	48	28	104
吉 林	Jilin	216	66	32	16	45
黑龙江	Heilongjiang	287	58	27	10	60
上 海	Shanghai	136	64	9	4	25
江 苏	Jiangsu	607	291	89	38	158
浙 江	Zhejiang	191	67	32	20	39
安 徽	Anhui	414	196	34	17	97
福 建	Fujian	268	81	75	23	57
江 西	Jiangxi	173	68	79	35	51
山 东	Shandong	793	291	172	59	205
河 南	Henan	931	279	156	64	185
湖 北	Hubei	419	200	116	46	95
湖 南	Hunan	502	195	67	27	117
广 东	Guangdong	673	320	97	40	111
广 西	Guangxi	157	60	33	18	57
海 南	Hainan	46	15	15	8	11
重 庆	Chongqing	104	41	13	7	25
四 川	Sichuan	335	162	80	34	74
贵 州	Guizhou	213	70	27	9	41
云 南	Yunnan	172	52	31	16	32
西 藏	Tibet	6	4	2	2	1
陕 西	Shaanxi	431	163	66	29	101
甘 肃	Gansu	83	11	25	11	21
青 海	Qinghai	27	13	4	4	8
宁 夏	Ningxia	37	13	4	1	5
新 疆	Xinjiang	102	46	29	8	28
新疆兵团	Xinjiang Corps					
黑龙江农垦	Heilongjiang Land Reclamation			1	1	

1-6 肢体残疾康复
Rehabilitation of Persons with Physical Disability

地　区	Region	肢体残疾康复 Rehabilitation of Persons with Physical Disability					
		肢体残疾康复训练 Persons with Physical Disability Receiving Rehabilitation Training	脑瘫儿童机构康复训练 Systematic Rehabilitation Training in Institutions for Children with Cerebral Palsy	肢体残疾儿童社区、家庭康复训练 Children with Physical Disability Receiving Rehabilitation Training in Communities and Families	肢体残疾人社区、家庭康复训练 Persons with Physical Disability Receiving Rehabilitation Training in Communities and Families	贫困肢体残疾儿童矫治手术 Orthopedic Surgeries Conducted for Poor Children with Physical Disability	麻风畸残矫治手术 Orthopedic Surgeries Conducted for Persons with Leprosy-induced Disability
		人 person	人 person	人 person	人 person	人 person	例 case
全　国	**Total**	**357081**	**29522**	**24017**	**303542**	**6221**	**458**
北　京	Beijing	5142	262	124	4756		
天　津	Tianjin	4472	99	212	4161	23	
河　北	Hebei	18710	430	2540	15740	169	
山　西	Shanxi	9854	654	342	8858	345	
内蒙古	Inner Mongolia	5451	369	1083	3999	91	
辽　宁	Liaoning	16699	666	1131	14902	265	
吉　林	Jilin	7583	376	91	7116	117	
黑龙江	Heilongjiang	4553	363	367	3823	75	
上　海	Shanghai	5650	581	218	4851	7	
江　苏	Jiangsu	33419	4085	1345	27989	99	
浙　江	Zhejiang	5973	512	402	5059	35	
安　徽	Anhui	13438	451	535	12452	406	
福　建	Fujian	9691	1374	837	7480	33	
江　西	Jiangxi	15105	553	1497	13055	89	
山　东	Shandong	50839	2280	1054	47505	447	
河　南	Henan	19185	2931	1228	15026	356	
湖　北	Hubei	14172	1602	1187	11383	177	118
湖　南	Hunan	9530	1136	571	7823	205	30
广　东	Guangdong	31250	2699	1998	26553	81	38
广　西	Guangxi	5837	705	1021	4111	140	7
海　南	Hainan	105	52	14	39	63	
重　庆	Chongqing	8366	256	575	7535	122	
四　川	Sichuan	26161	4774	1533	19854	778	112
贵　州	Guizhou	1174	303	188	683	239	
云　南	Yunnan	7325	353	1221	5751	1167	53
西　藏	Tibet	120	49	31	40	46	
陕　西	Shaanxi	7293	210	590	6493	201	100
甘　肃	Gansu	7029	533	1206	5290	234	
青　海	Qinghai	1301	129	223	949	60	
宁　夏	Ningxia	4869	183	96	4590	59	
新　疆	Xinjiang	5136	514	463	4159	71	
新疆兵团	Xinjiang Corps	1036	25	94	917	21	
黑龙江农垦	Heilongjiang Land Reclamation	613	13		600		

1-6　续表　Continued

地　区	Region	肢体残疾康复、管理技术人员培训 Training for Managerial and Technical Personnel on Physical Disability Rehabilitation	国家级 at State Level	省级 at Provincial Level	地市级 at Prefectural/ city Level	县级 Level
		人 person	人 person	人 person	人 person	人 person
全　国	**Total**	**38835**	**108**	**2585**	**3990**	**32152**
北　京	Beijing	3586	1	1200		2385
天　津	Tianjin	607	2			605
河　北	Hebei	778	20		83	675
山　西	Shanxi	207	3	5	120	79
内蒙古	Inner Mongolia	255	2			253
辽　宁	Liaoning	4197	1		1180	3016
吉　林	Jilin	792	2		48	742
黑龙江	Heilongjiang	405	1		151	253
上　海	Shanghai	2786	2	353		2431
江　苏	Jiangsu	5770	4		117	5649
浙　江	Zhejiang	936	2		7	927
安　徽	Anhui	434	3	60	14	357
福　建	Fujian	397	2	80	100	215
江　西	Jiangxi	202	2		2	198
山　东	Shandong	6286	4		150	6132
河　南	Henan	675	1	80		594
湖　北	Hubei	270	3		4	263
湖　南	Hunan	637	3		191	443
广　东	Guangdong	2562	14	151	1378	1019
广　西	Guangxi	355	3	15		337
海　南	Hainan	156	2		150	4
重　庆	Chongqing	616	2	40		574
四　川	Sichuan	2588	8		110	2470
贵　州	Guizhou	266	2			264
云　南	Yunnan	1439	3	549	2	885
西　藏	Tibet	1	1			
陕　西	Shaanxi	308	3	52		253
甘　肃	Gansu	104	3		3	98
青　海	Qinghai	452	2			450
宁　夏	Ningxia	170	3			167
新　疆	Xinjiang	596	2		180	414
新疆兵团	Xinjiang Corps	1	1			
黑龙江农垦	Heilongjiang Land	1	1			
	Reclamation	2	2			

1-7 肢体残疾康复训练服务机构
Rehabilitation Institutions for Persons with Physical Disability

地 区	Region	机构合计 Rehabilitation Institutions	省级 at Provincial Level		
				残联办 Run by Disabled Persons' Federations	其他办 Run by Others
		个 unit	个 unit	个 unit	个 unit
全 国	**Total**	**1592**	**31**	**28**	**3**
北 京	Beijing	12	1	1	
天 津	Tianjin	5	1	1	
河 北	Hebei	73	1	1	
山 西	Shanxi	35	2	2	
内蒙古	Inner Mongolia	22			
辽 宁	Liaoning	55	1	1	
吉 林	Jilin	112	1	1	
黑龙江	Heilongjiang	37	1	1	
上 海	Shanghai	88	2	2	
江 苏	Jiangsu	98			
浙 江	Zhejiang	36	1	1	
安 徽	Anhui	48	1	1	
福 建	Fujian	92	1	1	
江 西	Jiangxi	24	1	1	
山 东	Shandong	224			
河 南	Henan	46	1	1	
湖 北	Hubei	43	1		1
湖 南	Hunan	40	2	1	1
广 东	Guangdong	204	1	1	
广 西	Guangxi	20	1	1	
海 南	Hainan				
重 庆	Chongqing	30	1	1	
四 川	Sichuan	49	1	1	
贵 州	Guizhou	10	1	1	
云 南	Yunnan	27	1	1	
西 藏	Tibet	1	1	1	
陕 西	Shaanxi	68	2	1	1
甘 肃	Gansu	21	1	1	
青 海	Qinghai	9	1	1	
宁 夏	Ningxia	11	1	1	
新 疆	Xinjiang	34	1	1	
新疆兵团	Xinjiang Corps	1			
黑龙江农垦	Heilongjiang Land Reclamation	17			

1-7　续表 1　Continued 1

地　区	Region	开展肢体残疾康复训练机构 Rehabilitation Institutions					
		地市级 at Prefectural/ City Level	残联办 Run by Disabled Persons' Federations	其他办 Run by Others	县级 at County Level	残联办 Run by Disabled Persons' Federations	其他办 Run by Others
		个 unit	个 unit	个 unit	个 unit	个 unit	个 unit
全　国	**Total**	**263**	**126**	**137**	**1298**	**593**	**705**
北　京	Beijing				11	2	9
天　津	Tianjin				4	3	1
河　北	Hebei	10	3	7	62	24	38
山　西	Shanxi	9	6	3	24	15	9
内蒙古	Inner Mongolia	4		4	18	13	5
辽　宁	Liaoning	15	8	7	39	15	24
吉　林	Jilin	8	5	3	103	24	79
黑龙江	Heilongjiang	16	2	14	20	4	16
上　海	Shanghai				86	7	79
江　苏	Jiangsu	24	9	15	74	31	43
浙　江	Zhejiang	8	8		27	17	10
安　徽	Anhui	10	4	6	37	3	34
福　建	Fujian	13	4	9	78	16	62
江　西	Jiangxi	5	2	3	18	5	13
山　东	Shandong	24	8	16	200	89	111
河　南	Henan	12	7	5	33	15	18
湖　北	Hubei	13	5	8	29	23	6
湖　南	Hunan	9	4	5	29	18	11
广　东	Guangdong	36	24	12	167	128	39
广　西	Guangxi	5	2	3	14	11	3
海　南	Hainan						
重　庆	Chongqing				29	4	25
四　川	Sichuan	12	10	2	36	29	7
贵　州	Guizhou	2		2	7		7
云　南	Yunnan	7	3	4	19	15	4
西　藏	Tibet						
陕　西	Shaanxi	3		3	63	27	36
甘　肃	Gansu	4	3	1	16	13	3
青　海	Qinghai	2	2		6	5	1
宁　夏	Ningxia	4	4		6	6	
新　疆	Xinjiang	6	2	4	27	16	11
新疆兵团	Xinjiang Corps				1		1
黑龙江农垦	Heilongjiang Land Reclamation	2	1	1	15	15	

1-7 续表 2 Continued 2

地区	Region	残联办机构在岗人员 Staff of Rehabilitation Institutions Owned by PWDs' Federations					
			省级 at Provincial Level				
				医技 Doctors and Technicians	教师 Teachers	管理 Managerial Personnels	其他 Other Staff Members
		人 person	人 person	人 person	人 person	人 person	人 person
全　国	**Total**	**8255**	**1041**	**785**	**49**	**118**	**89**
北　京	Beijing	87	19	19			
天　津	Tianjin	47	32	29		1	2
河　北	Hebei	327	12	7	1	2	2
山　西	Shanxi	349	142	136		6	
内蒙古	Inner Mongolia	68					
辽　宁	Liaoning	129	19	11	6	2	
吉　林	Jilin	448	9	6	3		
黑龙江	Heilongjiang	37	6	1	3	1	1
上　海	Shanghai	380	308	205		56	47
江　苏	Jiangsu	608					
浙　江	Zhejiang	495	2	2			
安　徽	Anhui	70	25	18	4	1	2
福　建	Fujian	136	20	13	3	1	3
江　西	Jiangxi	123	20	12	5	3	
山　东	Shandong	863					
河　南	Henan	417	27	21	3	2	1
湖　北	Hubei	297					
湖　南	Hunan	209	77	54	5	11	7
广　东	Guangdong	1600	11	6	5		
广　西	Guangxi	78	22	16		2	4
海　南	Hainan						
重　庆	Chongqing	24	11	5	2	1	3
四　川	Sichuan	427	90	71		19	
贵　州	Guizhou	9	9	8		1	
云　南	Yunnan	297	38	34			4
西　藏	Tibet	17	17	16		1	
陕　西	Shaanxi	351	75	55	5	3	12
甘　肃	Gansu	177	27	25		2	
青　海	Qinghai	25	6	3	1	1	1
宁　夏	Ningxia	54	12	10	1	1	
新　疆	Xinjiang	81	5	2	2	1	
新疆兵团	Xinjiang Corps						
黑龙江农垦	Heilongjiang Land Reclamation	25					

1-7　续表 3　Continued 3

地　区	Region	残联办机构在岗人员 Staff of Institutions Run by PWDs' Federations				
		地市级 at Prefectural/ City Level	医技 Doctors and Technicians	教师 Teachers	管理 Managerial Personnels	其他 Other Staff Members
		人 person	人 person	人 person	人 person	人 person
全　国	**Total**	**2403**	**1271**	**338**	**309**	**485**
北　京	Beijing					
天　津	Tianjin					
河　北	Hebei	207	132	2	20	53
山　西	Shanxi	96	46	12	8	30
内蒙古	Inner Mongolia					
辽　宁	Liaoning	52	17	12	14	9
吉　林	Jilin	51	25	14	9	3
黑龙江	Heilongjiang	16	10	1	3	2
上　海	Shanghai					
江　苏	Jiangsu	148	50	44	26	28
浙　江	Zhejiang	313	201	8	29	75
安　徽	Anhui	33	4	12	3	14
福　建	Fujian	74	38	22	11	3
江　西	Jiangxi	12	4	3	3	2
山　东	Shandong	109	79	10	9	11
河　南	Henan	167	119	13	23	12
湖　北	Hubei	72	34	6	11	21
湖　南	Hunan	31	8	17	3	3
广　东	Guangdong	734	368	112	88	166
广　西	Guangxi	14	7	4	2	1
海　南	Hainan					
重　庆	Chongqing					
四　川	Sichuan	132	42	34	21	35
贵　州	Guizhou					
云　南	Yunnan	12	5	1	3	3
西　藏	Tibet					
陕　西	Shaanxi					
甘　肃	Gansu	91	74	1	12	4
青　海	Qinghai	5		2	2	1
宁　夏	Ningxia	18	4	6	4	4
新　疆	Xinjiang	9	4	2	3	
新疆兵团	Xinjiang Corps					
黑龙江农垦	Heilongjiang Land Reclamation	7			2	5

1-7 续表 4 Continued 4

地 区	Region	残联办机构在岗人员 Staff of Institutions Run by PWDs' Federations				
		县级 at County Level	医技 Doctors and Technicians	教师 Teachers	管理 Managerial Personnels	其他 Other Staff Members
		人 person	人 person	人 person	人 person	人 person
全 国	**Total**	**4811**	**1655**	**869**	**1047**	**1240**
北 京	Beijing	68	52	3	13	
天 津	Tianjin	15	6	2	5	2
河 北	Hebei	108	26	21	30	31
山 西	Shanxi	111	52	13	22	24
内蒙古	Inner Mongolia	68	25	12	15	16
辽 宁	Liaoning	58	5	3	39	11
吉 林	Jilin	388	59	13	53	263
黑龙江	Heilongjiang	15	3	3	5	4
上 海	Shanghai	72	56	1	13	2
江 苏	Jiangsu	460	235	54	63	108
浙 江	Zhejiang	180	104	12	30	34
安 徽	Anhui	12	2	4	4	2
福 建	Fujian	42	14	5	17	6
江 西	Jiangxi	91	40	8	6	37
山 东	Shandong	754	300	93	155	206
河 南	Henan	223	108	40	48	27
湖 北	Hubei	225	80	47	44	54
湖 南	Hunan	101	35	26	21	19
广 东	Guangdong	855	232	225	203	195
广 西	Guangxi	42	13	6	12	11
海 南	Hainan					
重 庆	Chongqing	13	2	3	7	1
四 川	Sichuan	205	54	37	56	58
贵 州	Guizhou					
云 南	Yunnan	247	3	174	49	21
西 藏	Tibet					
陕 西	Shaanxi	276	101	48	67	60
甘 肃	Gansu	59	16	4	24	15
青 海	Qinghai	14	5	2	5	2
宁 夏	Ningxia	24	10	5	7	2
新 疆	Xinjiang	67	16	5	19	27
新疆兵团	Xinjiang Corps					
黑龙江农垦	Heilongjiang Land Reclamation	18	1		15	2

1-8　智力残疾康复

Rehabilitation of Persons with Intellectual Disability

地　区	Region	贫困智力残疾儿童康复训练 Poor Children with Intellectual Disability Receiving Rehabilitation Training	机构康复训练 Trained in Institutions	社区、家庭康复训练 Trained in Communities and Families	成年智力残疾人社区、家庭康复训练 Adults with Intellectual Disability Trained in Communities and Families
		人 person	人 person	人 person	人 person
全　国	**Total**	**115218**	**20043**	**95175**	**24968**
北　京	Beijing	490	361	129	1876
天　津	Tianjin	1707	209	1498	106
河　北	Hebei	8246	525	7721	670
山　西	Shanxi	4407	429	3978	132
内蒙古	Inner Mongolia	1923	476	1447	150
辽　宁	Liaoning	3857	713	3144	127
吉　林	Jilin	3387	319	3068	131
黑龙江	Heilongjiang	1949	373	1576	92
上　海	Shanghai	2806	634	2172	8209
江　苏	Jiangsu	11359	2104	9255	4285
浙　江	Zhejiang	2308	764	1544	1151
安　徽	Anhui	2128	448	1680	33
福　建	Fujian	5537	943	4594	830
江　西	Jiangxi	5181	200	4981	230
山　东	Shandong	4562	1893	2669	2325
河　南	Henan	11020	1675	9345	221
湖　北	Hubei	6376	735	5641	958
湖　南	Hunan	2040	858	1182	468
广　东	Guangdong	8070	2511	5559	1498
广　西	Guangxi	5519	620	4899	30
海　南	Hainan	47	40	7	10
重　庆	Chongqing	3334	310	3024	131
四　川	Sichuan	8543	877	7666	250
贵　州	Guizhou	540	253	287	9
云　南	Yunnan	2856	334	2522	564
西　藏	Tibet	71	39	32	
陕　西	Shaanxi	1019	423	596	197
甘　肃	Gansu	2411	336	2075	22
青　海	Qinghai	753	95	658	62
宁　夏	Ningxia	854	145	709	
新　疆	Xinjiang	1398	316	1082	42
新疆兵团	Xinjiang Corps	234	35	199	159
黑龙江农垦	Heilongjiang Land Reclamation	286	50	236	

1-8 续表 Continued

地区	Region	智力残疾康复、管理技术人员培训 Training for Managerial and Technical Personnel on Intellectual Disabilities Rehabilitation	国家级 at State Level	省级 at Provincial Level	地市级 at Prefectural/ City Level	县级 at County Level
		人次 person-time	人次 person-time	人次 person-time	人次 person-time	人次 person-time
全国	**Total**	**17138**	**110**	**915**	**1077**	**15036**
北京	Beijing	2987	1			2986
天津	Tianjin	59	3			56
河北	Hebei	642	3		105	534
山西	Shanxi	236	4	80	110	42
内蒙古	Inner Mongolia	172	3			169
辽宁	Liaoning	2159	3		139	2017
吉林	Jilin	388	3		18	367
黑龙江	Heilongjiang	358	3		151	204
上海	Shanghai	854	1			853
江苏	Jiangsu	2218	5	9	56	2148
浙江	Zhejiang	485	4		13	468
安徽	Anhui	169	4	90	13	62
福建	Fujian	164	4		9	151
江西	Jiangxi	114	3		2	109
山东	Shandong	1093	5	2	197	889
河南	Henan	366	8	98		260
湖北	Hubei	227	6		8	213
湖南	Hunan	485	5	45	12	423
广东	Guangdong	1056	6	532	88	430
广西	Guangxi	206	5	15	63	123
海南	Hainan	30	2			28
重庆	Chongqing	200	3	5		192
四川	Sichuan	943	1		30	912
贵州	Guizhou	62	3			59
云南	Yunnan	538	3	1		534
西藏	Tibet	1	1			
陕西	Shaanxi	203	4	38		161
甘肃	Gansu	59	4		3	52
青海	Qinghai	466	3			463
宁夏	Ningxia	6	4			2
新疆	Xinjiang	192	3		60	129
新疆兵团	Xinjiang Corps					
黑龙江农垦	Heilongjiang Land Reclamation					

1-9　智力残疾康复训练服务机构
Rehabilitation Institutions for Persons with Intellectual Disability

地　区	Region	机构合计 Rehabilitation Institutions for Persons with Intellectual Disability	省级 at Provincial Level	残联办 Run by Disabled Persons' Federations	其他办 Run by Others
		个 unit	个 unit	个 unit	个 unit
全　国	**Total**	**1206**	**29**	**25**	**4**
北　京	Beijing	29	1	1	
天　津	Tianjin	4	1	1	
河　北	Hebei	50	1	1	
山　西	Shanxi	37	2	2	
内蒙古	Inner Mongolia	19			
辽　宁	Liaoning	48	1	1	
吉　林	Jilin	27			
黑龙江	Heilongjiang	27	1	1	
上　海	Shanghai	118			
江　苏	Jiangsu	80	1	1	
浙　江	Zhejiang	51	1	1	
安　徽	Anhui	29	1	1	
福　建	Fujian	53	1	1	
江　西	Jiangxi	20	1	1	
山　东	Shandong	97			
河　南	Henan	37	1	1	
湖　北	Hubei	39	1		1
湖　南	Hunan	43	1	1	
广　东	Guangdong	203	1	1	
广　西	Guangxi	17	1	1	
海　南	Hainan	1	1		1
重　庆	Chongqing	32	1	1	
四　川	Sichuan	48	1	1	
贵　州	Guizhou	11			
云　南	Yunnan	15	1	1	
西　藏	Tibet	1	1	1	
陕　西	Shaanxi	16	2	1	1
甘　肃	Gansu	19	1	1	
青　海	Qinghai	8	1	1	
宁　夏	Ningxia	11	1	1	
新　疆	Xinjiang	15	1	1	
新疆兵团	Xinjiang Corps				
黑龙江农垦	Heilongjiang Land Reclamation	1	1		1

1-9 续表 1 Continued 1

地区	Region	机构 Intellectual Disability Rehabilitation Institutions					
		地市级 at Prefectural/ City Level	残联办 Run by PWDs' Federations	其他办 Run by Others	县级 at County Level	残联办 Run by PWDs' Federations	其他办 Run by Others
		个 unit	个 unit	个 unit	个 unit	个 unit	个 unit
全国	**Total**	**229**	**112**	**117**	**948**	**480**	**468**
北京	Beijing				28	1	27
天津	Tianjin				3	2	1
河北	Hebei	12	4	8	37	10	27
山西	Shanxi	8	7	1	27	9	18
内蒙古	Inner Mongolia	5	1	4	14	9	5
辽宁	Liaoning	11	6	5	36	11	25
吉林	Jilin	9	6	3	18	9	9
黑龙江	Heilongjiang	8	3	5	18	3	15
上海	Shanghai				118	93	25
江苏	Jiangsu	11	7	4	68	22	46
浙江	Zhejiang	7	7		43	22	21
安徽	Anhui	12	3	9	16	3	13
福建	Fujian	9	4	5	43	7	36
江西	Jiangxi	9	1	8	10	3	7
山东	Shandong	20	8	12	77	17	60
河南	Henan	11	5	6	25	10	15
湖北	Hubei	9	2	7	29	22	7
湖南	Hunan	9	2	7	33	12	21
广东	Guangdong	31	16	15	171	140	31
广西	Guangxi	6	4	2	10	4	6
海南	Hainan						
重庆	Chongqing				31	5	26
四川	Sichuan	12	10	2	35	28	7
贵州	Guizhou	3		3	8	1	7
云南	Yunnan	4	3	1	10	6	4
西藏	Tibet						
陕西	Shaanxi	4	1	3	10	7	3
甘肃	Gansu	7	2	5	11	7	4
青海	Qinghai	2	2		5	5	
宁夏	Ningxia	4	4		6	6	
新疆	Xinjiang	6	4	2	8	6	2
新疆兵团	Xinjiang Corps						
黑龙江农垦	Heilongjiang Land Reclamation						

1-9 续表 2 Continued 2

地 区	Region	残联办机构在岗人员 Staff of Rehabilitation Institutions Owned by PWDs' Federations	省级 at Provincial Level	医技 Doctors and Technicians	教师 Teachers	管理 Managerial Personnels	其他 Other Staff Members
		人 person	人 person	人 person	人 person	人 person	人 person
全 国	**Total**	**5360**	**484**	**167**	**184**	**67**	**66**
北 京	Beijing	47	15	2	13		
天 津	Tianjin	19	10		6	1	3
河 北	Hebei	126	4		1	1	2
山 西	Shanxi	153	24		19	3	2
内蒙古	Inner Mongolia	60					
辽 宁	Liaoning	111	27	3	10	1	13
吉 林	Jilin	88					
黑龙江	Heilongjiang	60	11	1	8	1	1
上 海	Shanghai	351					
江 苏	Jiangsu	366	8		6	1	1
浙 江	Zhejiang	255	2	2			
安 徽	Anhui	64	25	6	14	1	4
福 建	Fujian	84	11		8	1	2
江 西	Jiangxi	50	27	12	5	3	7
山 东	Shandong	335					
河 南	Henan	396	23	5	12	1	5
湖 北	Hubei	198					
湖 南	Hunan	109	21		10	9	2
广 东	Guangdong	1616	11		8	1	2
广 西	Guangxi	88	50	18	15	13	4
海 南	Hainan						
重 庆	Chongqing	21	5	2	2	1	
四 川	Sichuan	340	82	66		16	
贵 州	Guizhou	12					
云 南	Yunnan	102	27	3	15	5	4
西 藏	Tibet	3	3	1		1	1
陕 西	Shaanxi	78	30	14	2	2	12
甘 肃	Gansu	91	43	31	10	2	
青 海	Qinghai	27	6	1	3	1	1
宁 夏	Ningxia	47	9		8	1	
新 疆	Xinjiang	63	10		9	1	
新疆兵团	Xinjiang Corps						
黑龙江农垦	Heilongjiang Land Reclamation						

1-9 续表 3 Continued 3

地区	Region	残联办机构在岗人员 Staff of Rehabilitation Institutions Run by PWDs' Federations				
		地市级 at Prefectural/ City Level	医技 Doctors and Technicians	教师 Teachers	管理 Managerial Personnels	其他 Other Staff Members
		人 person	人 person	人 person	人 person	人 person
全国	**Total**	**1736**	**574**	**552**	**282**	**328**
北京	Beijing					
天津	Tianjin					
河北	Hebei	72	7	36	28	1
山西	Shanxi	70	36	12	13	9
内蒙古	Inner Mongolia	15	1	6	2	6
辽宁	Liaoning	40	2	23	12	3
吉林	Jilin	45	10	25	8	2
黑龙江	Heilongjiang	36		19	8	9
上海	Shanghai					
江苏	Jiangsu	118	12	58	27	21
浙江	Zhejiang	75	9	51	6	9
安徽	Anhui	20	4	8	3	5
福建	Fujian	49	5	25	9	10
江西	Jiangxi	9	2	3	2	2
山东	Shandong	69	9	40	12	8
河南	Henan	154	122	2	21	9
湖北	Hubei	19	11	1	3	4
湖南	Hunan	10	1	5	2	2
广东	Guangdong	750	304	171	88	187
广西	Guangxi	26	4	11	4	7
海南	Hainan					
重庆	Chongqing					
四川	Sichuan	87	21	36	14	16
贵州	Guizhou					
云南	Yunnan	11	2	3	3	3
西藏	Tibet					
陕西	Shaanxi	6			1	5
甘肃	Gansu	10	3	3	2	2
青海	Qinghai	5		2	2	1
宁夏	Ningxia	18	4	6	4	4
新疆	Xinjiang	22	5	6	8	3
新疆兵团	Xinjiang Corps					
黑龙江农垦	Heilongjiang Land Reclamation					

1-9 续表 4 Continued 4

地 区	Region	残联办机构在岗人员 Staff of Rehabilitation Agencies Run by Disabled Persons' Federations				
		县级 at County Level	医技 Doctors and Technicians	教师 Teachers	管理 Managerial Personnels	其他 Other Staff Members
		人 person	人 person	人 person	人 person	人 person
全 国	**Total**	**3140**	**656**	**908**	**749**	**827**
北 京	Beijing	32		26	6	
天 津	Tianjin	9	1	2	4	2
河 北	Hebei	50	11	5	14	20
山 西	Shanxi	59	21	13	13	12
内蒙古	Inner Mongolia	45	14	9	10	12
辽 宁	Liaoning	44		18	10	16
吉 林	Jilin	43	5	14	14	10
黑龙江	Heilongjiang	13	3	3	4	3
上 海	Shanghai	351	5	49	106	191
江 苏	Jiangsu	240	52	97	35	56
浙 江	Zhejiang	178	36	51	51	40
安 徽	Anhui	19	1	12	3	3
福 建	Fujian	24	5	4	10	5
江 西	Jiangxi	14	7	4	2	1
山 东	Shandong	266	75	63	41	87
河 南	Henan	219	106	43	39	31
湖 北	Hubei	179	51	45	48	35
湖 南	Hunan	78	18	22	16	22
广 东	Guangdong	855	167	282	202	204
广 西	Guangxi	12	2	5	4	1
海 南	Hainan					
重 庆	Chongqing	16	2	8	4	2
四 川	Sichuan	171	23	64	50	34
贵 州	Guizhou	12	5	3	4	
云 南	Yunnan	64	1	30	25	8
西 藏	Tibet					
陕 西	Shaanxi	42	15	9	7	11
甘 肃	Gansu	38	11	6	12	9
青 海	Qinghai	16	7	2	5	2
宁 夏	Ningxia	20	7	7	4	2
新 疆	Xinjiang	31	5	12	6	8
新疆兵团	Xinjiang Corps					
黑龙江农垦	Heilongjiang Land Reclamation					

1-10 精神病防治康复

Prevention and Rehabilitation of Mental Illness

地 区	Region	开展精防康复工作县(市、区) Counties/Cities/Districts where Prevention and Rehabilitation of Mental Illness have been Conducted	精神病人 People with Mental Illness	监护病人 People with Mental Illness under Guardianship	监护率 Guardian-ship Rate
		个 unit	万人 10,000 persons	万人 10,000 persons	%
全 国	**Total**	**2586**	**593.6**	**449.0**	**75.6**
北 京	Beijing	15	4.3	4.3	99.8
天 津	Tianjin	16	6.2	5.9	95.3
河 北	Hebei	170	25.7	22.4	87.3
山 西	Shanxi	64	10.1	8.1	80.5
内蒙古	Inner Mongolia	84	7.0	5.7	80.9
辽 宁	Liaoning	107	26.9	23.9	89.0
吉 林	Jilin	63	15.9	15.5	97.1
黑龙江	Heilongjiang	111	18.5	15.6	84.3
上 海	Shanghai	17	11.0	10.6	96.4
江 苏	Jiangsu	108	53.0	43.0	81.0
浙 江	Zhejiang	74	18.6	17.3	93.1
安 徽	Anhui	85	26.5	19.6	73.8
福 建	Fujian	84	12.6	11.0	87.7
江 西	Jiangxi	101	18.4	13.9	75.7
山 东	Shandong	132	40.0	33.9	84.8
河 南	Henan	156	51.9	20.7	39.9
湖 北	Hubei	92	34.3	22.3	65.2
湖 南	Hunan	120	32.0	24.1	75.5
广 东	Guangdong	127	40.7	28.9	71.0
广 西	Guangxi	91	12.1	9.4	77.7
海 南	Hainan	12	4.4	1.1	24.5
重 庆	Chongqing	40	18.0	14.4	80.3
四 川	Sichuan	143	41.2	32.4	78.8
贵 州	Guizhou	76	7.9	6.5	81.7
云 南	Yunnan	118	15.1	9.5	63.2
西 藏	Tibet				
陕 西	Shaanxi	110	20.5	11.8	57.4
甘 肃	Gansu	60	12.1	10.8	89.0
青 海	Qinghai	33	0.4	0.3	81.7
宁 夏	Ningxia	21	3.4	3.0	87.8
新 疆	Xinjiang	68	2.5	1.6	63.9
新疆兵团	Xinjiang Corps	6	1.0	0.7	70.1
黑龙江农垦	Heilongjiang Land Reclamation	82	1.4	0.7	45.3

1-10 续表 1 Continued 1

地 区	Region	显好病人 People with Mental Illness who have gotten Effective Treatment	显好率 Significant Improvement Rate	参与社会总人数 People with Mental Illness who have Participated into Social Life after Rehabilitation	参与率 Social Involvement Rate	肇事人次 People with Mental Illness who Caused Serious Troubles	肇事率 Violent Events Rate
		万人 10,000 persons	%	万人 10,000 persons	%	人次 person-time	%
全 国	**Total**	**301.8**	**67.2**	**236.4**	**52.6**	**8749**	**0.19**
北 京	Beijing	2.7	63.9	1.7	39.6	14	0.03
天 津	Tianjin	4.8	80.6	4.1	70.0	3	0.01
河 北	Hebei	14.7	65.5	11.8	52.4	177	0.08
山 西	Shanxi	5.7	70.0	4.5	55.2	45	0.06
内蒙古	Inner Mongolia	3.7	66.2	3.2	56.6	46	0.08
辽 宁	Liaoning	15.9	66.6	12.6	52.8	31	0.01
吉 林	Jilin	11.0	71.1	9.1	58.7	61	0.04
黑龙江	Heilongjiang	10.0	64.3	6.7	42.9	76	0.05
上 海	Shanghai	9.8	92.4	9.0	85.1	25	0.02
江 苏	Jiangsu	31.9	74.3	26.9	62.5	77	0.02
浙 江	Zhejiang	12.3	71.2	10.3	59.7	452	0.26
安 徽	Anhui	11.1	56.8	9.4	48.1	86	0.04
福 建	Fujian	7.9	71.6	6.1	55.4	109	0.10
江 西	Jiangxi	8.4	60.5	6.3	45.0	2328	1.67
山 东	Shandong	25.2	74.4	21.0	62.0	177	0.05
河 南	Henan	11.2	54.3	8.5	41.1	694	0.34
湖 北	Hubei	14.3	63.8	10.6	47.5	488	0.22
湖 南	Hunan	15.0	62.3	11.1	46.2	286	0.12
广 东	Guangdong	19.1	66.0	14.4	49.9	621	0.21
广 西	Guangxi	6.2	65.2	4.9	51.8	472	0.50
海 南	Hainan	0.3	27.5	0.1	12.6	35	0.33
重 庆	Chongqing	11.4	79.2	9.0	62.4	358	0.25
四 川	Sichuan	19.9	61.5	11.5	35.5	1208	0.37
贵 州	Guizhou	4.3	67.1	3.6	55.7	213	0.33
云 南	Yunnan	5.8	61.0	4.7	49.4	241	0.25
西 藏	Tibet						
陕 西	Shaanxi	7.8	65.9	6.4	54.8	164	0.14
甘 肃	Gansu	7.4	68.9	5.8	54.0	128	0.12
青 海	Qinghai	0.2	50.6	0.1	40.3		
宁 夏	Ningxia	2.1	69.6	1.7	57.5	92	0.30
新 疆	Xinjiang	0.8	51.2	0.5	34.4	12	0.08
新疆兵团	Xinjiang Corps	0.4	64.1	0.3	50.8	30	0.44
黑龙江农垦	Heilongjiang Land Reclamation	0.2	36.2	0.1	14.2		

1-10 续表 2 Continued 2

地区	Region	接受治疗的精神病患者 People with Mental Illness who have gotten Medical Treatment	接受康复训练 People with Mental Illness who have gotten Rehabilitation Training	精神康复机构 Rehabilitation Institutions for People with Mental Illness	其中：精神病人 People with Mental Illness who have gotten Rehabilitation Training in Those Institutions
		人 person	人 person	个 unit	人 person
全国	**Total**	**1865391**	**1079599**	**2198**	**538572**
北京	Beijing	21651	7991	14	3716
天津	Tianjin	13773	10776	13	8118
河北	Hebei	95921	62378	89	6582
山西	Shanxi	31016	16326	62	15999
内蒙古	Inner Mongolia	22126	8076	34	5080
辽宁	Liaoning	65426	42541	148	20748
吉林	Jilin	41033	50510	56	12323
黑龙江	Heilongjiang	24247	8912	39	7133
上海	Shanghai	65759	25131	147	3317
江苏	Jiangsu	179894	140037	109	43205
浙江	Zhejiang	98788	74474	60	16278
安徽	Anhui	78268	20834	52	11201
福建	Fujian	49527	41143	64	11177
江西	Jiangxi	67387	32362	81	28959
山东	Shandong	214486	126794	231	42285
河南	Henan	103559	75058	85	31460
湖北	Hubei	118106	54675	92	49213
湖南	Hunan	103694	39169	108	20615
广东	Guangdong	119691	60006	343	62537
广西	Guangxi	60210	20337	29	18869
海南	Hainan	2863	1055	1	279
重庆	Chongqing	81572	51343	40	18029
四川	Sichuan	85455	46501	103	37812
贵州	Guizhou	14523	17996	23	5989
云南	Yunnan	26749	8778	41	21545
西藏	Tibet			1	2
陕西	Shaanxi	44045	24657	57	23443
甘肃	Gansu	18313	5410	33	5180
青海	Qinghai	855	111	1	103
宁夏	Ningxia	5877	2553	9	1080
新疆	Xinjiang	5102	2240	24	3833
新疆兵团	Xinjiang Corps	2912	1425	6	1835
黑龙江农垦	Heilongjiang Land Reclamation	2563		3	627

1-10 续表 3 Continued 3

地 区	Region	贫困患者 People with Mental Illness Living in Poverty	接受医疗救助的贫困患者 Those who have gotten Medical Assistance	接受国家专项彩金免费服药项目医疗救助的贫困患者 Poor Patients who Received Free Medicines Funded by National Lottery Medical Assistance Project	接受国家专项彩金免费住院项目医疗救助的贫困患者 Poor Patients who Received Free Treatment in Hospital Funded by National Lottery Medical Assistance Project	接受其他项目医疗救助的贫困患者 Poor Patients who Received Medical Assistance Funded by Other Projects
		人 person	人 person	人 person	人 person	人 person
全 国	**Total**	**1433404**	**443723**	**141068**	**24941**	**277714**
北 京	Beijing	9742	5639	563	124	4952
天 津	Tianjin	7354	2995	1060	79	1856
河 北	Hebei	24268	6475	4896	978	601
山 西	Shanxi	15104	5945	3569	440	1936
内蒙古	Inner Mongolia	24055	3196	2313	370	513
辽 宁	Liaoning	75412	25522	4921	859	19742
吉 林	Jilin	59441	20374	8824	2633	8917
黑龙江	Heilongjiang	23614	4596	3795	688	113
上 海	Shanghai	14586	8790	818		7972
江 苏	Jiangsu	85890	44222	5000	1060	38162
浙 江	Zhejiang	38415	9874	2200	384	7290
安 徽	Anhui	99999	69864	9053	871	59940
福 建	Fujian	37859	12014	6224	997	4793
江 西	Jiangxi	80229	19612	7884	217	11511
山 东	Shandong	98287	24663	6421	1569	16673
河 南	Henan	61941	22855	6461	1494	14900
湖 北	Hubei	88474	14386	10300	1200	2886
湖 南	Hunan	76678	13730	4800	1000	7930
广 东	Guangdong	95712	36962	3556	645	32761
广 西	Guangxi	60654	10572	6681	1078	2813
海 南	Hainan	3947	1366	1174	69	123
重 庆	Chongqing	80436	11187	4233	654	6300
四 川	Sichuan	109861	19544	8872	1740	8932
贵 州	Guizhou	23920	4491	2702	974	815
云 南	Yunnan	40561	12328	5884	1088	5356
西 藏	Tibet					
陕 西	Shaanxi	47440	15217	6382	1724	7111
甘 肃	Gansu	21666	3773	2649	1000	124
青 海	Qinghai	1586	1357	751	130	476
宁 夏	Ningxia	10964	4046	3662	384	
新 疆	Xinjiang	7606	4634	3005	339	1290
新疆兵团	Xinjiang Corps	2668	1876	800	150	926
黑龙江农垦	Heilongjiang Land Reclamation	5035	1618	1615	3	

1-10 续表 4 Continued 4

地 区	Region	发现关锁病人 People with Mental Illness who were Found being Locked-up	解除关锁病人 Freed from Locked-up	培训精防康复管理、技术人员 Trained Managerial Personnels and Technicians of Prevention and Rehabilitation
		人 person	人 person	人 person
全 国	**Total**	**8354**	**5056**	**51032**
北 京	Beijing			941
天 津	Tianjin			1372
河 北	Hebei	300	160	3540
山 西	Shanxi	514	246	385
内蒙古	Inner Mongolia	363	129	789
辽 宁	Liaoning	74	47	1024
吉 林	Jilin	14	12	1398
黑龙江	Heilongjiang	50	27	207
上 海	Shanghai			8963
江 苏	Jiangsu	88	47	5525
浙 江	Zhejiang	92	47	5628
安 徽	Anhui	62	48	330
福 建	Fujian	171	94	1124
江 西	Jiangxi	937	464	274
山 东	Shandong	304	246	5765
河 南	Henan	1074	679	495
湖 北	Hubei	541	301	656
湖 南	Hunan	390	287	699
广 东	Guangdong	869	513	4615
广 西	Guangxi	44	34	262
海 南	Hainan	526	320	45
重 庆	Chongqing	142	116	1394
四 川	Sichuan	640	526	2593
贵 州	Guizhou	284	233	226
云 南	Yunnan	398	301	1006
西 藏	Tibet			
陕 西	Shaanxi	327	146	411
甘 肃	Gansu	91	25	1046
青 海	Qinghai	5		100
宁 夏	Ningxia	4	2	75
新 疆	Xinjiang	48	6	102
新疆兵团	Xinjiang Corps	2		42
黑龙江农垦	Heilongjiang Land Reclamation			

1-11　孤独症儿童康复训练
Rehabilitation Training for Children with Autism

地区	Region	孤独症儿童康复训练机构 Rehabilitation Institutions for Children with Autism	省级机构 at Provincial Level	地市级及以下其他机构 at Prefectual/City Level and Lower	机构内教师 Teachers Working in Those Institutions	省级机构内教师 at Provincial Level	地市级及以下其他机构内教师 at Prefectual/City Level and Lower
		个 unit	个 unit	个 unit	人 person	人 person	人 person
全　国	**Total**	**929**	**30**	**899**	**6679**	**291**	**6388**
北　京	Beijing	20	1	19	209	25	184
天　津	Tianjin	3	2	1	19	18	1
河　北	Hebei	32	1	31	133	1	132
山　西	Shanxi	11	1	10	66	15	51
内蒙古	Inner Mongolia	25		25	92		92
辽　宁	Liaoning	42	1	41	296	28	268
吉　林	Jilin	36	1	35	423	19	404
黑龙江	Heilongjiang	23	2	21	168	15	153
上　海	Shanghai	26	1	25	136	7	129
江　苏	Jiangsu	87	1	86	631	5	626
浙　江	Zhejiang	35	1	34	301	10	291
安　徽	Anhui	34	1	33	184	6	178
福　建	Fujian	55	1	54	445	12	433
江　西	Jiangxi	28	1	27	67	5	62
山　东	Shandong	98		98	907		907
河　南	Henan	75	1	74	345	9	336
湖　北	Hubei	28	1	27	199	11	188
湖　南	Hunan	32	1	31	178	12	166
广　东	Guangdong	102	1	101	1064	6	1058
广　西	Guangxi	11		11	117		117
海　南	Hainan	1	1		8	8	
重　庆	Chongqing	15	1	14	75	1	74
四　川	Sichuan	39	2	37	137	11	126
贵　州	Guizhou	16	1	15	272	24	248
云　南	Yunnan	5	1	4	19	15	4
西　藏	Tibet						
陕　西	Shaanxi	18	2	16	77	8	69
甘　肃	Gansu	10	1	9	41	3	38
青　海	Qinghai	5		5	3		3
宁　夏	Ningxia	11	1	10	29	8	21
新　疆	Xinjiang	6	1	5	38	9	29
新疆兵团	Xinjiang Corps						
黑龙江农垦	Heilongjiang Land Reclamation						

1-11 续表 1 Continued 1

地 区	Region	机构内在训儿童 Children with Autism Trained in Those Institutions	省级机构在训儿童 at Provincial Level	地市级及以下其他机构在训儿童 at City Level and Lower	贫困孤独症儿童救助 Poor Children with Autism Supported
		人 person	人 person	人 person	人 person
全 国	**Total**	**11119**	**1263**	**9856**	**6809**
北 京	Beijing	266	85	181	36
天 津	Tianjin	93	70	23	25
河 北	Hebei	260	10	250	271
山 西	Shanxi	230	40	190	216
内蒙古	Inner Mongolia	248		248	171
辽 宁	Liaoning	568	149	419	295
吉 林	Jilin	354	56	298	220
黑龙江	Heilongjiang	212	36	176	96
上 海	Shanghai	250	3	247	227
江 苏	Jiangsu	821	20	801	457
浙 江	Zhejiang	278		278	135
安 徽	Anhui	228	35	193	193
福 建	Fujian	849	47	802	652
江 西	Jiangxi	373	30	343	13
山 东	Shandong	900		900	464
河 南	Henan	901	116	785	343
湖 北	Hubei	348	60	288	224
湖 南	Hunan	291	60	231	261
广 东	Guangdong	2118	16	2102	1385
广 西	Guangxi	285	20	265	228
海 南	Hainan	40	40		46
重 庆	Chongqing	222	5	217	180
四 川	Sichuan	226	119	107	85
贵 州	Guizhou	205	50	155	147
云 南	Yunnan	34	13	21	32
西 藏	Tibet				
陕 西	Shaanxi	98	60	38	230
甘 肃	Gansu	27	7	20	55
青 海	Qinghai	57		57	13
宁 夏	Ningxia	103	36	67	48
新 疆	Xinjiang	215	61	154	61
新疆兵团	Xinjiang Corps	19	19		
黑龙江农垦	Heilongjiang Land Reclamation				

1-11 续表 2 Continued 2

地 区	Region	儿童训练后走向 Directions in which Children have gone After Rehabilitation					
		省级 at Provincial Level			地市级及以下 at Prefectual/ City Level and Lower		
		普幼及普小 Ordinary Kindergartens or Primary Schools	特殊教育学校 Special Education Schools	其他 Other Directions	普幼及普小 Ordinary Kindergartens or Primary Schools	特殊教育学校 Special Education Schools	其他 Other Directions
		人 person	人 person	人 person	人 person	人 person	人 person
全 国	**Total**	**150**	**24**	**123**	**688**	**625**	**1288**
北 京	Beijing	13		32	10	38	56
天 津	Tianjin	2	4				
河 北	Hebei	4	1		8	43	26
山 西	Shanxi			39	4		3
内蒙古	Inner Mongolia				31	16	32
辽 宁	Liaoning				82	77	21
吉 林	Jilin				27	16	31
黑龙江	Heilongjiang	4	1	13	33	9	6
上 海	Shanghai			1	13	80	66
江 苏	Jiangsu	3	5	1	56	35	58
浙 江	Zhejiang				14	20	34
安 徽	Anhui	2			23	41	20
福 建	Fujian	1	9	5	23	4	41
江 西	Jiangxi				44	61	89
山 东	Shandong				44	68	50
河 南	Henan			14	111	14	345
湖 北	Hubei				6	11	46
湖 南	Hunan	5		6	25	12	44
广 东	Guangdong	2	2		98	48	182
广 西	Guangxi					12	12
海 南	Hainan	18		4	2		
重 庆	Chongqing		2		2	2	26
四 川	Sichuan	39		8	7		22
贵 州	Guizhou	50			15	16	56
云 南	Yunnan						
西 藏	Tibet						
陕 西	Shaanxi				3		7
甘 肃	Gansu				4	1	12
青 海	Qinghai						1
宁 夏	Ningxia	6			3	1	2
新 疆	Xinjiang	1					
新疆兵团	Xinjiang Corps						
黑龙江农垦	Heilongjiang Land Reclamation						

1-12 辅助器具供应服务
Provision of Assistive Devices

地区	Region	辅助器具供应 Assistive Devices Provided	辅助器具供应品种 Categories of Assistive Devices Provided	矫形器装配 Orthotic Devices Fitted	国家彩金项目装配 Fitted for PWDs by the National Lottery Project			
						上肢矫形器 Orthoses for Upper Limbs	脊柱矫形器 Orthoses for Spinal Cord	下肢矫形器 Orthoses for Lower Limbs
		件 piece	种 category	例 case	例 case	例 case	例 case	例 case
全 国	**Total**	**1144774**	**760**	**40105**	**14372**	**1014**	**676**	**12682**
北 京	Beijing	5693	53	97	51		2	49
天 津	Tianjin	40289	85	365	341	4		337
河 北	Hebei	34167	350	434	413	45	3	365
山 西	Shanxi	37124	48					
内蒙古	Inner Mongolia	15561	34	116	103	2	7	94
辽 宁	Liaoning	27928	414	468	399	38	18	343
吉 林	Jilin	25539	120	348	200	6	11	183
黑龙江	Heilongjiang	10424	41	120	89	25	11	53
上 海	Shanghai	153299	371	18718				
江 苏	Jiangsu	83898	257	1918	1080	25	11	1044
浙 江	Zhejiang	27789	340	153	101	4	8	89
安 徽	Anhui	20956	200	799	601	32	6	563
福 建	Fujian	11635	309	417	406	18	14	374
江 西	Jiangxi	16499	40	1120	653	78	170	405
山 东	Shandong	82036	700	377	177	11	6	160
河 南	Henan	122542	140	2770	659	119	28	512
湖 北	Hubei	31254	100	623	605	12	6	587
湖 南	Hunan	82477	760	1599	1113	85	24	1004
广 东	Guangdong	50459	720	2526	1409	12	8	1389
广 西	Guangxi	16471	224	662	613	56	25	532
海 南	Hainan	1591	260					
重 庆	Chongqing	14313	400	199	109	1	3	105
四 川	Sichuan	49496	500	2348	2257	140	65	2052
贵 州	Guizhou	12640	95	66	65	9	4	52
云 南	Yunnan	37405	78	561	362	46	2	314
西 藏	Tibet	937	22	239				
陕 西	Shaanxi	53181	100	1352	1202	129	156	917
甘 肃	Gansu	18823	104	596	569	74	55	440
青 海	Qinghai	14999	125	501	423	28	32	363
宁 夏	Ningxia	24677	56	94	89	2		87
新 疆	Xinjiang	15851	221	476	240	13	1	226
新疆兵团	Xinjiang Corps	2261	10	43	43			43
黑龙江农垦	Heilongjiang Land Reclamation	2560	11					

1-12　续表 1　Continued 1

地　区	Region	假肢装配 Artificial Limbs Fitted	国家彩金项目装配 Fitted for PWDs by the National Lottery Project	大腿 Upper-knee Artificial Limbs Fitted	小腿 Lower-knee Artificial Limbs Fitted
		例 case	例 case	例 case	例 case
全　国	**Total**	**38961**	**27032**	**10629**	**12497**
北　京	Beijing	263	107	21	45
天　津	Tianjin	258	239	48	45
河　北	Hebei	970	894	384	420
山　西	Shanxi	725	677	336	338
内蒙古	Inner Mongolia	542	365	98	222
辽　宁	Liaoning	2028	1194	495	524
吉　林	Jilin	989	966	411	405
黑龙江	Heilongjiang	589	430	136	287
上　海	Shanghai	532			
江　苏	Jiangsu	2052	1245	463	527
浙　江	Zhejiang	1077	530	198	257
安　徽	Anhui	912	750	330	317
福　建	Fujian	674	568	206	232
江　西	Jiangxi	2624	1947	800	843
山　东	Shandong	1263	624	273	315
河　南	Henan	4309	1866	767	773
湖　北	Hubei	1910	1796	753	899
湖　南	Hunan	2949	1620	633	676
广　东	Guangdong	1702	1057	345	612
广　西	Guangxi	2329	2080	808	1126
海　南	Hainan	218	218	67	88
重　庆	Chongqing	300	294	156	129
四　川	Sichuan	2265	1781	745	859
贵　州	Guizhou	1139	791	344	406
云　南	Yunnan	1484	1245	437	625
西　藏	Tibet	155			
陕　西	Shaanxi	1473	1378	508	519
甘　肃	Gansu	1066	1037	361	409
青　海	Qinghai	480	393	120	198
宁　夏	Ningxia	216	203	115	72
新　疆	Xinjiang	1262	531	192	234
新疆兵团	Xinjiang Corps	106	106	44	62
黑龙江农垦	Heilongjiang Land Reclamation	100	100	35	33

1-12 续表 2 Continued 2

地 区	Region	膝离断 Knee From off 例 case	髋离断 Hip From off 例 case	功能性上肢 Functional Upper Limbs 例 case	装饰假手 Artificial Hands for Decoration Purpose 例 case
全 国	**Total**	**901**	**678**	**965**	**1362**
北 京	Beijing	3	4	32	2
天 津	Tianjin	30	30	1	85
河 北	Hebei	23	13	17	37
山 西	Shanxi	3			
内蒙古	Inner Mongolia	22	9	8	6
辽 宁	Liaoning	54	44	23	54
吉 林	Jilin	55	50	15	30
黑龙江	Heilongjiang	1		4	2
上 海	Shanghai				
江 苏	Jiangsu	28	28	102	97
浙 江	Zhejiang	30	29		16
安 徽	Anhui	22	11	50	20
福 建	Fujian	14	24	31	61
江 西	Jiangxi	53	25	27	199
山 东	Shandong	21	11	1	3
河 南	Henan	76	74	110	66
湖 北	Hubei	59	24	3	58
湖 南	Hunan	84	52	66	109
广 东	Guangdong	14	5	20	61
广 西	Guangxi	21	30	18	77
海 南	Hainan		1	26	36
重 庆	Chongqing	7	2		
四 川	Sichuan	65	35	36	41
贵 州	Guizhou	18	19	4	
云 南	Yunnan	25	51	31	76
西 藏	Tibet				
陕 西	Shaanxi	81	64	163	43
甘 肃	Gansu	45	22	104	96
青 海	Qinghai	17	6	29	23
宁 夏	Ningxia	9	7		
新 疆	Xinjiang	20	7	36	42
新疆兵团	Xinjiang Corps				
黑龙江农垦	Heilongjiang Land Reclamation	1	1	8	22

1-12　续表 3　Continued 3

地　区	Region	其他辅助器具供应 Other Assistive Devices Provided	国家彩金项目免费发放 Assistive Devices Provided to PWDs by the National Lottery Project	助视器 Vision-Aids	免费发放 Free of Charge	重度残疾人适配 Fitted for PWDs with Severe Disabilities	就学、就业适配 Fitted for PWDs of Schooling and Employovent
		件 piece	件 piece	件 piece	件 piece	件 piece	件 piece
全　国	**Total**	**1065708**	**296486**	**105455**	**167032**	**20818**	**3181**
北　京	Beijing	5333	551	313	138	41	59
天　津	Tianjin	39666	3966	2416	1550		
河　北	Hebei	32763	14717	6551	7429	602	135
山　西	Shanxi	36399	6562		6459	103	
内蒙古	Inner Mongolia	14903	3184	1090	1806	285	3
辽　宁	Liaoning	25432	15256	5907	7470	1854	25
吉　林	Jilin	24202	18189	9494	7457	1238	
黑龙江	Heilongjiang	9715	4868	1041	3512	290	25
上　海	Shanghai	134049					
江　苏	Jiangsu	79928	12218	6435	4702	856	225
浙　江	Zhejiang	26559	6289	1220	4478	548	43
安　徽	Anhui	19245	13300	6752	3711	2363	474
福　建	Fujian	10544	4006	770	2985	194	57
江　西	Jiangxi	12755	7100	1530	4826	695	49
山　东	Shandong	80396	10358	3684	6454	220	
河　南	Henan	115463	17216	6410	9302	1325	179
湖　北	Hubei	28721	18566	7315	10143	1108	
湖　南	Hunan	77929	24505	4048	19125	1122	210
广　东	Guangdong	46231	8078	1099	6241	262	476
广　西	Guangxi	13480	9640	5198	3540	773	129
海　南	Hainan	1373	605	15	455	135	
重　庆	Chongqing	13814	7793	5399	2394		
四　川	Sichuan	44883	9942	1639	7567	632	104
贵　州	Guizhou	11435	6295	2805	2971	450	69
云　南	Yunnan	35360	14355	3158	10443	647	107
西　藏	Tibet	543	481	26	421	34	
陕　西	Shaanxi	50356	31140	12189	15312	3297	342
甘　肃	Gansu	17161	10239	3941	5001	858	439
青　海	Qinghai	14018	2190	117	2040	19	14
宁　夏	Ningxia	24367	7445	2376	4675	379	15
新　疆	Xinjiang	14113	3540	1131	2065	344	
新疆兵团	Xinjiang Corps	2112	1432	1006	340	84	2
黑龙江农垦	Heilongjiang Land Reclamation	2460	2460	380	2020	60	

1-13 辅助器具供应服务机构

Assistive Devices Provision and Service Centers

地 区	Region	地市级机构 Assistive Devices Provision and Service Centers at Prefectural/city Level	本年度新建 Established in 2012	县级机构 Assistive Devices Provision and Service Centers at County Level	本年度新建 Established in 2012
		个 unit	个 unit	个 unit	个 unit
全 国	**Total**	**188**	**24**	**847**	**193**
北 京	Beijing			5	2
天 津	Tianjin			9	3
河 北	Hebei	9	1	52	10
山 西	Shanxi	7	1	36	1
内蒙古	Inner Mongolia	3		26	7
辽 宁	Liaoning	14		91	4
吉 林	Jilin	8		34	6
黑龙江	Heilongjiang	6	2	7	1
上 海	Shanghai			15	1
江 苏	Jiangsu	7		48	7
浙 江	Zhejiang	8		29	8
安 徽	Anhui	5		4	1
福 建	Fujian	11	5	32	12
江 西	Jiangxi	4	1	15	8
山 东	Shandong	14	2	50	9
河 南	Henan	9	1	27	6
湖 北	Hubei	5	1	25	10
湖 南	Hunan	13	1	71	28
广 东	Guangdong	19	1	57	9
广 西	Guangxi	7	2	16	4
海 南	Hainan				
重 庆	Chongqing			26	4
四 川	Sichuan	7	2	22	7
贵 州	Guizhou	2	1	11	5
云 南	Yunnan	9	2	41	18
西 藏	Tibet				
陕 西	Shaanxi	5		14	8
甘 肃	Gansu	7		58	8
青 海	Qinghai	2		5	1
宁 夏	Ningxia	1	1	4	1
新 疆	Xinjiang	3		13	4
新疆兵团	Xinjiang Corps	1			
黑龙江农垦	Heilongjiang Land Reclamation	2		4	

1-14 儿童残疾预防
Disability Prevention for Children

地 区	Region	残疾儿童筛查 Screening for Children with Disabilities						
		开展残疾儿童筛查工作县 Counties Which has Developed the Screening for Children with Disabilities	开展残疾儿童筛查工作的医疗卫生机构 Medical Care Institutions Which has Developed the Screening for Children with Disabilities	省级 at Provincial Level	地市级 at Prefectural/City Level	县级 at County Level	本年度新诊断0-6岁残疾儿童 Children with Disabilities Newly Diagnosed from 0-6 Years Old in 2012	视力残疾儿童 Children with Visual Disability
		个 unit	个 unit	个 unit	个 unit	个 unit	人 person	人 person
全 国	**Total**	**1091**	**1563**	**6**	**116**	**1441**	**48263**	**5617**
北 京	Beijing	10	22			22	444	14
天 津	Tianjin	14	6			6	318	18
河 北	Hebei	30	37		1	36	1283	146
山 西	Shanxi	59	79	5	21	53	1273	89
内蒙古	Inner Mongolia	7	17			17	123	7
辽 宁	Liaoning	28	20		9	11	380	34
吉 林	Jilin	17	10		1	9	294	34
黑龙江	Heilongjiang	37	17			17	388	17
上 海	Shanghai	17	264			264	1394	700
江 苏	Jiangsu	108	157		4	153	3482	470
浙 江	Zhejiang	41	116		3	113	796	28
安 徽	Anhui	59	34		3	31	4723	301
福 建	Fujian	11	12		1	11	362	26
江 西	Jiangxi	9	35			35	2662	985
山 东	Shandong	55	95			95	5536	317
河 南	Henan	10	9		2	7	892	68
湖 北	Hubei	40	72		6	66	1894	208
湖 南	Hunan	43	47		8	39	3864	402
广 东	Guangdong	29	157		41	116	2233	87
广 西	Guangxi	41	27			27	2921	146
海 南	Hainan	2					61	2
重 庆	Chongqing	38	76			76	3159	603
四 川	Sichuan	58	74			74	4352	403
贵 州	Guizhou	7	6			6	2250	320
云 南	Yunnan	29	28		1	27	955	52
西 藏	Tibet	4	1			1	45	
陕 西	Shaanxi	20	24			24	915	60
甘 肃	Gansu	59	28			28	516	53
青 海	Qinghai	11	39		1	38	301	12
宁 夏	Ningxia	7	9		1	8	266	11
新 疆	Xinjiang	4	3			3	39	
新疆兵团	Xinjiang Corps	84	34	1	5	28	127	3
黑龙江农垦	Heilongjiang Land Reclamation	103	8		8		15	1

1-14 续表 1 Continued 1

地 区	Region	本年度新诊断0-6岁残疾儿童 Children with Disabilities Newly Diagnosed from 0-6 Years Old in 2012					
		听力残疾儿童 Children with Hearing Disability	言语残疾儿童 Children with Speech Disability	肢体残疾儿童 Children with Physical Disability	智力残疾儿童 Children with Mental Retardation	精神残疾儿童 Children with Mental Disability	多重残疾儿童 Children with Multiple Disability
		人 person	人 person	人 person	人 person	人 person	人 person
全 国	**Total**	**6781**	**3623**	**15777**	**8824**	**2525**	**5116**
北 京	Beijing	107	5	83	113	67	55
天 津	Tianjin	48	20	108	105	12	7
河 北	Hebei	224	57	458	270	30	98
山 西	Shanxi	163	130	448	263	32	148
内蒙古	Inner Mongolia	24	19	44	9	1	19
辽 宁	Liaoning	52	26	180	52	27	9
吉 林	Jilin	13	7	170	38	8	24
黑龙江	Heilongjiang	79	11	134	79	40	28
上 海	Shanghai	88	18	444	92	43	9
江 苏	Jiangsu	565	170	825	404	310	738
浙 江	Zhejiang	213	41	168	217	46	83
安 徽	Anhui	894	343	1477	747	356	605
福 建	Fujian	57	35	81	82	14	67
江 西	Jiangxi	260	262	478	449	93	135
山 东	Shandong	747	452	2117	1240	341	322
河 南	Henan	131	36	323	145	40	149
湖 北	Hubei	233	226	810	261	49	107
湖 南	Hunan	553	405	1090	524	149	741
广 东	Guangdong	221	239	621	540	233	292
广 西	Guangxi	486	268	869	654	97	401
海 南	Hainan	6	4	24	17	5	3
重 庆	Chongqing	334	203	1265	603	100	51
四 川	Sichuan	543	284	1629	921	273	299
贵 州	Guizhou	338	141	617	328	85	421
云 南	Yunnan	148	59	502	107	4	83
西 藏	Tibet	5	4	35	1		
陕 西	Shaanxi	117	76	364	223	22	53
甘 肃	Gansu	69	51	148	79	22	94
青 海	Qinghai	27	17	121	80		44
宁 夏	Ningxia	20	7	71	131	10	16
新 疆	Xinjiang	2	2	18	5	2	10
新疆兵团	Xinjiang Corps	12	5	47	41	14	5
黑龙江农垦	Heilongjiang Land Reclamation	2		8	4		

1-14　续表 2　Continued 2

地　区	Region	儿童残疾预防宣传 Prevention of Children with Disability		残疾儿童家长学校 Schools for Training Parents of Children with Disabilities			
		发放儿童残疾预防宣传材料 Distributed Advocacy Materials	举办儿童残疾预防宣传活动 Advocacy Activities Holded	残疾儿童家长学校累计数 Total	省级 at Provincial Level	地市级 at Prefectural/ City Level	县级 at County Level
		份 piece	次 time	个 unit	个 unit	个 unit	个 unit
全　国	**Total**	**2236697**	**2927**	**1371**	**13**	**73**	**1285**
北　京	Beijing	15560	22	469			469
天　津	Tianjin	8805	14	1			1
河　北	Hebei	218698	227	34	1	4	29
山　西	Shanxi	47390	33	45	3	12	30
内蒙古	Inner Mongolia	22823	9	2	1		1
辽　宁	Liaoning	45510	25	10		7	3
吉　林	Jilin	12500	17	5		2	3
黑龙江	Heilongjiang	10474	36	8		1	7
上　海	Shanghai	134658	367	78	2		76
江　苏	Jiangsu	196493	277	57		3	54
浙　江	Zhejiang	89187	164	62		4	58
安　徽	Anhui	114866	162	38	1	2	35
福　建	Fujian	24500	13				
江　西	Jiangxi	46102	25	1			1
山　东	Shandong	242974	166	47		3	44
河　南	Henan	9410	11	2		1	1
湖　北	Hubei	183710	77	6			6
湖　南	Hunan	51608	46	17		4	13
广　东	Guangdong	81069	76	35	1	22	12
广　西	Guangxi	77285	64	3			3
海　南	Hainan	250	1				
重　庆	Chongqing	113256	48	34	3		31
四　川	Sichuan	149819	199	392		1	391
贵　州	Guizhou	20130	213	1			1
云　南	Yunnan	63748	53	4		1	3
西　藏	Tibet						
陕　西	Shaanxi	76940	63	2		2	
甘　肃	Gansu	108663	351				
青　海	Qinghai	12473	26	7			7
宁　夏	Ningxia	26550	30	11	1	4	6
新　疆	Xinjiang	7410	7				
新疆兵团	Xinjiang Corps	22416	90				
黑龙江农垦	Heilongjiang Land Reclamation	1420	15				

1-14 续表 3 Continued 3

地 区	Region	残疾儿童家长学校 Schools for Training Parents of Children with Disabilities							
		本年度开展家长学校活动 Activities Holded for Parents of Children with Disabilities in 2012	省级 at Provincial Level	地市级 at Prefectural/ City Level	县级 at County Level	本年度残疾儿童家长参与人数 Parents of Children with Disabilities Participating in 2012	省级 at Provincial Level	地市级 at Prefectural/ City Level	县级 at County Level
		次 time	次 time	次 time	次 time	人次 person time	人次 person time	人次 person time	人次 person time
全 国	**Total**	**1668**	**263**	**208**	**1197**	**63570**	**11135**	**8140**	**44295**
北 京	Beijing	200			200	9258			9258
天 津	Tianjin	1			1	25			25
河 北	Hebei	65	4	2	59	4243	350	235	3658
山 西	Shanxi	339	208	54	77	6016	3680	750	1586
内蒙古	Inner Mongolia	4	1		3	152	70		82
辽 宁	Liaoning	24		20	4	508		390	118
吉 林	Jilin	3			3	920			920
黑龙江	Heilongjiang	11		1	10	94		52	42
上 海	Shanghai	198	3		195	5868	350		5518
江 苏	Jiangsu	152		24	128	5376		680	4696
浙 江	Zhejiang	116		34	82	2892		1429	1463
安 徽	Anhui	115	30	2	83	9848	4500	65	5283
福 建	Fujian								
江 西	Jiangxi	2			2	300			300
山 东	Shandong	130		5	125	3939		369	3570
河 南	Henan	2		1	1	1400		1200	200
湖 北	Hubei	17			17	871			871
湖 南	Hunan	57		35	22	2243		1659	584
广 东	Guangdong	59	10	10	39	2870	1625	621	624
广 西	Guangxi	8			8	335			335
海 南	Hainan								
重 庆	Chongqing	70	6		64	1650	360		1290
四 川	Sichuan	49		1	48	3258		120	3138
贵 州	Guizhou	2			2	34			34
云 南	Yunnan	7		3	4	201		90	111
西 藏	Tibet								
陕 西	Shaanxi	8		8		320		320	
甘 肃	Gansu								
青 海	Qinghai	4			4	229			229
宁 夏	Ningxia	25	1	8	16	720	200	160	360
新 疆	Xinjiang								
新疆兵团	Xinjiang Corps								
黑龙江农垦	Heilongjiang Land Reclamation								

1-15　康复人才
Rehabilitation Professionals

地　区	Region	康复机构在岗人员 Staff of Rehabilitation Institutions	省级 Staff of Rehabilitation Institutions at Provincial Level	业务人员 Professionals	管理人员 Managerial Personnels	其他人员 Other Staff Members
		人 person	人 person	人 person	人 person	人 person
全　国	**Total**	**197649**	**10202**	**7116**	**1438**	**1648**
北　京	Beijing	2743	100	75	16	9
天　津	Tianjin	2008	161	138	12	11
河　北	Hebei	7327	488	352	55	81
山　西	Shanxi	8267	246	166	36	44
内蒙古	Inner Mongolia	3515	1430	856	350	224
辽　宁	Liaoning	7427	221	165	56	
吉　林	Jilin	7919	751	522	125	104
黑龙江	Heilongjiang	5334	379	231	52	96
上　海	Shanghai	3370	495	343	77	75
江　苏	Jiangsu	9635	73	52	14	7
浙　江	Zhejiang	4103	175	80	15	80
安　徽	Anhui	6108	96	59	13	24
福　建	Fujian	5697	107	66	10	31
江　西	Jiangxi	4495	366	263	23	80
山　东	Shandong	23600	37	22	5	10
河　南	Henan	10204	843	540	33	270
湖　北	Hubei	8815	165	125	21	19
湖　南	Hunan	10200	480	389	35	56
广　东	Guangdong	23253	330	206	37	87
广　西	Guangxi	4216	140	72	21	47
海　南	Hainan	130	88	65	13	10
重　庆	Chongqing	5673	65	24	38	3
四　川	Sichuan	7783	668	522	122	24
贵　州	Guizhou	7496	59	41	14	4
云　南	Yunnan	4406	129	91	10	28
西　藏	Tibet	62	54	35	11	8
陕　西	Shaanxi	6639	941	705	122	114
甘　肃	Gansu	1586	260	211	29	20
青　海	Qinghai	120	38	23	9	6
宁　夏	Ningxia	340	64	48	8	8
新　疆	Xinjiang	3990	694	583	43	68
新疆兵团	Xinjiang Corps	943				
黑龙江农垦	Heilongjiang Land Reclamation	245	59	46	13	

1-15 续表 1 Continued 1

地区	Region	康复机构在岗人员 Staff of Rehabilitation Institutions			
		地市级康复机构在岗人员 Staff of Rehabilitation Institutions at Prefectural/City Level	业务人员 Professionals	管理人员 Managerial Personnels	其他人员 Other Staff Members
		人 person	人 person	人 person	人 person
全国	**Total**	**66389**	**46871**	**8291**	**11227**
北京	Beijing				
天津	Tianjin	74	35	12	27
河北	Hebei	3283	2282	487	514
山西	Shanxi	4150	3259	478	413
内蒙古	Inner Mongolia	868	648	106	114
辽宁	Liaoning	1962	1132	334	496
吉林	Jilin	3798	2525	643	630
黑龙江	Heilongjiang	3392	2381	589	422
上海	Shanghai				
江苏	Jiangsu	1892	1091	397	404
浙江	Zhejiang	1476	862	349	265
安徽	Anhui	4171	3205	393	573
福建	Fujian	1544	1315	126	103
江西	Jiangxi	1952	1108	234	610
山东	Shandong	8024	5986	914	1124
河南	Henan	3556	2416	353	787
湖北	Hubei	3638	2837	415	386
湖南	Hunan	4640	3275	457	908
广东	Guangdong	5801	4084	650	1067
广西	Guangxi	1521	949	169	403
海南	Hainan	24	14	4	6
重庆	Chongqing				
四川	Sichuan	1455	917	216	322
贵州	Guizhou	3009	2107	485	417
云南	Yunnan	2384	1566	181	637
西藏	Tibet				
陕西	Shaanxi	825	500	104	221
甘肃	Gansu	436	331	63	42
青海	Qinghai	21	12	4	5
宁夏	Ningxia	117	80	12	25
新疆	Xinjiang	2031	1719	85	227
新疆兵团	Xinjiang Corps	242	193	7	42
黑龙江农垦	Heilongjiang Land Reclamation	103	42	24	37

1-15　续表 2　Continued 2

地　区	Region	康复机构在岗人员 Staff of Rehabilitation Institutions			
		县级康复机构在岗人员 Staff of Rehabilitation Institutions at County Level	业务人员 Professionals	管理人员 Managerial Personnels	其他人员 Other Staff Members
		人 person	人 person	人 person	人 person
全　国	**Total**	**121058**	**77999**	**16675**	**26384**
北　京	Beijing	2643	1911	375	357
天　津	Tianjin	1773	911	163	699
河　北	Hebei	3556	2258	724	574
山　西	Shanxi	3871	2447	436	988
内蒙古	Inner Mongolia	1217	805	174	238
辽　宁	Liaoning	5244	2816	743	1685
吉　林	Jilin	3370	1591	644	1135
黑龙江	Heilongjiang	1563	1052	201	310
上　海	Shanghai	2875	1740	539	596
江　苏	Jiangsu	7670	4796	924	1950
浙　江	Zhejiang	2452	1464	392	596
安　徽	Anhui	1841	1098	323	420
福　建	Fujian	4046	2614	645	787
江　西	Jiangxi	2177	1302	345	530
山　东	Shandong	15539	11807	1499	2233
河　南	Henan	5805	3991	755	1059
湖　北	Hubei	5012	3444	663	905
湖　南	Hunan	5080	3320	884	876
广　东	Guangdong	17122	11537	2588	2997
广　西	Guangxi	2555	1677	299	579
海　南	Hainan	18	10	4	4
重　庆	Chongqing	5608	3968	839	801
四　川	Sichuan	5660	3093	729	1838
贵　州	Guizhou	4428	1922	322	2184
云　南	Yunnan	1893	1204	264	425
西　藏	Tibet	8		1	7
陕　西	Shaanxi	4873	3327	681	865
甘　肃	Gansu	890	483	157	250
青　海	Qinghai	61	30	14	17
宁　夏	Ningxia	159	91	36	32
新　疆	Xinjiang	1265	767	169	329
新疆兵团	Xinjiang Corps	701	487	112	102
黑龙江农垦	Heilongjiang Land Reclamation	83	36	31	16

1-15 续表 3 Continued 3

地 区	Region	康复人才培训情况 Training for Staff of Rehabilitation Institutions					
		本年度举办康复管理人员培训班 Training Courses for Rehabilitation Managerial Staff in 2012	培训康复管理人员 Rehabilitation Managerial Staff Trained	本年度举办康复业务人员培训班 Training Courses for Rehabilitation Professionals in 2012	培训康复业务人员 Rehabilitation Professionals Trained	本年度举办社区康复协调员培训班 Training Courses for Community-Based Rehabilitation Coordinators in 2012	培训社区康复协调员 Community-Based Rehabilitation Coordinators Trained
		期 course	人 person	期 course	人 person	期 course	人 person
全 国	**Total**	**1785**	**25169**	**2553**	**50206**	**3313**	**185900**
北 京	Beijing	21	2750	12	550	57	6694
天 津	Tianjin	9	193	10	187	31	1306
河 北	Hebei	98	1034	110	1925	171	8086
山 西	Shanxi	71	683	59	1243	124	7034
内蒙古	Inner Mongolia	31	301	36	560	71	5877
辽 宁	Liaoning	134	1847	129	1921	187	10097
吉 林	Jilin	78	617	84	952	92	6288
黑龙江	Heilongjiang	39	200	50	630	171	2906
上 海	Shanghai	58	1046	67	3662	47	4363
江 苏	Jiangsu	99	2155	169	5794	210	15385
浙 江	Zhejiang	78	785	103	2121	91	6366
安 徽	Anhui	39	596	57	2377	85	5111
福 建	Fujian	63	686	35	1360	79	4677
江 西	Jiangxi	51	605	90	732	100	3785
山 东	Shandong	220	2424	286	6961	256	22365
河 南	Henan	34	344	33	1431	168	10720
湖 北	Hubei	32	453	42	992	243	5055
湖 南	Hunan	42	488	68	1706	125	5750
广 东	Guangdong	120	2031	210	5324	130	11403
广 西	Guangxi	36	811	39	1182	83	4658
海 南	Hainan	10	86	5	135	15	886
重 庆	Chongqing	41	444	55	1069	76	7192
四 川	Sichuan	77	891	465	1603	162	9134
贵 州	Guizhou	23	361	30	653	49	1994
云 南	Yunnan	98	1354	120	2772	156	6532
西 藏	Tibet	1	1	2	47	1	16
陕 西	Shaanxi	60	852	44	704	94	4593
甘 肃	Gansu	34	248	45	381	88	3138
青 海	Qinghai	36	287	32	399	44	740
宁 夏	Ningxia	11	235	17	400	13	709
新 疆	Xinjiang	28	302	36	374	80	2731
新疆兵团	Xinjiang Corps					2	155
黑龙江农垦	Heilongjiang Land Reclamation	13	59	13	59	12	154

2-1　学前教育阶段
Pre-school Rehabilitation and Education

地　区	Region	残疾人事业专项彩票公益金助学项目资助 Support of Educational Project Funded by Dedicated Welfare Lottery Fund in 2012	视力残疾 Children with Visual Disability	听力残疾 Children with Hearing Disability	言语残疾 Children with Speech Disability	肢体残疾 Children with Physical Disability
		人 person	人 person	人 person	人 person	人 person
全　国	**Total**	**10280**	**480**	**2700**	**678**	**1854**
北　京	Beijing	213	8	57	5	28
天　津	Tianjin	100	1	33	1	12
河　北	Hebei	600	11	147	27	125
山　西	Shanxi	324	13	80	26	71
内蒙古	Inner Mongolia	160	8	32	9	69
辽　宁	Liaoning	500	65	76	28	42
吉　林	Jilin	260	1	13	11	52
黑龙江	Heilongjiang	300	6	48	9	81
上　海	Shanghai					
江　苏	Jiangsu	650	11	278	22	85
浙　江	Zhejiang	400	54	64	53	60
安　徽	Anhui	300	3	95	17	38
福　建	Fujian	403	9	163	7	58
江　西	Jiangxi	300	20	90	26	35
山　东	Shandong	850	38	172	29	247
河　南	Henan	810	66	237	130	94
湖　北	Hubei	500	14	85	54	95
湖　南	Hunan	400	17	161	15	35
广　东	Guangdong	550	22	66	39	190
广　西	Guangxi	400	9	74	16	48
海　南	Hainan	80	1		3	6
重　庆	Chongqing	200	8	48	33	12
四　川	Sichuan	700	50	193	30	138
贵　州	Guizhou	260	11	61	15	68
云　南	Yunnan	260	3	90	25	19
西　藏	Tibet	30	13	4	2	2
陕　西	Shaanxi	200	2	167	4	
甘　肃	Gansu	150	6	15	9	70
青　海	Qinghai	70	3	11	8	23
宁　夏	Ningxia	60	4	17	6	16
新　疆	Xinjiang	200	1	117	18	9
新疆兵团	Xinjiang Corps	30	2	6	1	9
黑龙江农垦	Heilongjiang Land Reclamation	20				17

2-1 续表 Continued

地区	Region	智力残疾 Chidren with Intellectual Disability	精神残疾 Children with Psychiatric Disability	多重残疾 Children with Multi-disabilities	残疾人事业专项彩票公益金助学项目资助本年新入园 Preschool New Admission Funded by Dedicated Welfare Lottery Fund in 2012	其他残疾儿童学前教育助学项目资助 Support of Other Pre-School Educational Project for Disabled Children in 2012
		人 person	人 person	人 person	人 person	人 person
全国	**Total**	**2287**	**871**	**1410**	**4038**	**4429**
北京	Beijing	35	56	24	11	10
天津	Tianjin	49		4	66	
河北	Hebei	144	67	79	327	211
山西	Shanxi	74	9	51	113	81
内蒙古	Inner Mongolia	15	6	21	56	3
辽宁	Liaoning	107	131	51	223	
吉林	Jilin	111	54	18	84	
黑龙江	Heilongjiang	72	65	19	55	20
上海	Shanghai					
江苏	Jiangsu	146	40	68	223	159
浙江	Zhejiang	56	55	58	383	626
安徽	Anhui	43	13	91	103	106
福建	Fujian	86	54	26	295	171
江西	Jiangxi	40	30	59	67	10
山东	Shandong	209	18	137	395	395
河南	Henan	206	13	64	133	
湖北	Hubei	177	8	67	174	20
湖南	Hunan	92	15	65	213	152
广东	Guangdong	119	41	73	143	318
广西	Guangxi	136	40	77	221	64
海南	Hainan	16	52	2	9	
重庆	Chongqing	63	4	32	50	74
四川	Sichuan	170	41	78	179	1302
贵州	Guizhou	32	18	55	115	491
云南	Yunnan	21	36	66	133	30
西藏	Tibet		1	8	1	
陕西	Shaanxi	1		26	41	114
甘肃	Gansu	20	1	29	105	30
青海	Qinghai	10		15	40	12
宁夏	Ningxia	12		5	29	24
新疆	Xinjiang	14	2	39	47	
新疆兵团	Xinjiang Corps	10	1	1	4	6
黑龙江农垦	Heilongjiang Land Reclamation	1		2		

2-2　义务教育阶段未入学学龄残疾儿童少年

School-age Children with Disabilities Unable to Enter Schools

地　区	Region	未入学学龄残疾儿童少年 School-age Children with Disabilities Unable to Enter Schools	视力残疾 Children with Visual Disability	听力残疾 Children with Hearing Disability	言语残疾 Children with Speech Disability
		人 person	人 person	人 person	人 person
全　国	**Total**	**90960**	**5677**	**5754**	**5646**
北　京	Beijing	419		3	2
天　津	Tianjin	477	9	16	15
河　北	Hebei	1561	67	119	93
山　西	Shanxi	2435	126	173	163
内蒙古	Inner Mongolia	1471	57	59	86
辽　宁	Liaoning	3016	108	138	103
吉　林	Jilin	2710	76	125	145
黑龙江	Heilongjiang	927	42	52	24
上　海	Shanghai	45	3	2	
江　苏	Jiangsu	1498	59	130	27
浙　江	Zhejiang	918	26	67	14
安　徽	Anhui	3431	107	120	148
福　建	Fujian	1433	41	67	37
江　西	Jiangxi	5229	526	563	449
山　东	Shandong	3972	215	226	138
河　南	Henan	8345	425	657	623
湖　北	Hubei	2488	137	115	132
湖　南	Hunan	6401	315	244	394
广　东	Guangdong	4631	193	205	208
广　西	Guangxi	5750	321	312	501
海　南	Hainan	671	30	34	44
重　庆	Chongqing	1523	152	98	97
四　川	Sichuan	5017	393	335	353
贵　州	Guizhou	6912	949	733	593
云　南	Yunnan	5441	389	357	401
西　藏	Tibet	450	43	28	53
陕　西	Shaanxi	4874	417	356	240
甘　肃	Gansu	3329	179	186	171
青　海	Qinghai	794	38	48	37
宁　夏	Ningxia	942	42	36	57
新　疆	Xinjiang	3692	189	145	286
新疆兵团	Xinjiang Corps				
黑龙江农垦	Heilongjiang Land Reclamation	158	3	5	12

2-2 续表 Continued

地 区	Region	肢体残疾 Children with Physical Disability	智力残疾 Chidren with Intellectual Disability	精神残疾 Children with Psychiatric Disability	多重残疾 Children with Multi-disabilities
		人 person	人 person	人 person	人 person
全 国	**Total**	**28624**	**28163**	**3529**	**13567**
北 京	Beijing	100	196	22	96
天 津	Tianjin	175	233	2	27
河 北	Hebei	610	452	30	190
山 西	Shanxi	759	863	58	293
内蒙古	Inner Mongolia	459	510	43	257
辽 宁	Liaoning	1087	1143	148	289
吉 林	Jilin	864	1041	191	268
黑龙江	Heilongjiang	246	373	71	119
上 海	Shanghai	24	14		2
江 苏	Jiangsu	494	660	45	83
浙 江	Zhejiang	313	345	48	105
安 徽	Anhui	1015	1256	173	612
福 建	Fujian	382	625	70	211
江 西	Jiangxi	1176	1536	251	728
山 东	Shandong	1255	1440	211	487
河 南	Henan	3198	2607	121	714
湖 北	Hubei	842	790	82	390
湖 南	Hunan	2319	1740	156	1233
广 东	Guangdong	1269	1556	357	843
广 西	Guangxi	1728	1442	146	1300
海 南	Hainan	226	192	29	116
重 庆	Chongqing	405	559	59	153
四 川	Sichuan	1676	1473	225	562
贵 州	Guizhou	1786	1530	270	1051
云 南	Yunnan	1756	1423	100	1015
西 藏	Tibet	192	28	32	74
陕 西	Shaanxi	1436	1292	230	903
甘 肃	Gansu	1212	895	121	565
青 海	Qinghai	286	245	13	127
宁 夏	Ningxia	255	373	30	149
新 疆	Xinjiang	1028	1260	190	594
新疆兵团	Xinjiang Corps				
黑龙江农垦	Heilongjiang Land Reclamation	51	71	5	11

2-3　高中教育阶段
Senior High Education

地　区	Region	特殊教育普通高中学校(班) Special Education Senior High Schools/classes	盲普通高中 Senior High Schools for Blind Students	聋普通高中 Senior High Schools for Deaf Students	其他 Others	学生 Students: 招生 Newly Enrolled Studnets with Disabilities	学生 Students: 盲 Students with Visual Disability	学生 Students: 聋 Students with Hearing Disability
		个 unit	个 unit	个 unit	个 unit	人 person	人 person	人 person
全　国	**Total**	**186**	**22**	**121**	**43**	**2765**	**443**	**2322**
北　京	Beijing	2	1	1		8	8	
天　津	Tianjin	2	1	1		39	12	27
河　北	Hebei	12	1	11		296	119	177
山　西	Shanxi	5	1	4		140	17	123
内蒙古	Inner Mongolia	8		5	3	94	3	91
辽　宁	Liaoning	9	1	8		56		56
吉　林	Jilin	4		4		11		11
黑龙江	Heilongjiang	1		1				
上　海	Shanghai	1	1					
江　苏	Jiangsu	4		4		149		149
浙　江	Zhejiang	7	1	5	1	98	17	81
安　徽	Anhui	3		3		210		210
福　建	Fujian	20	3	10	7	191	22	169
江　西	Jiangxi	4		4		58		58
山　东	Shandong	23	1	16	6	365	21	344
河　南	Henan	5	1	3	1	123	52	71
湖　北	Hubei	7		6	1	179		179
湖　南	Hunan	12	2	9	1	258	32	226
广　东	Guangdong	7		4	3	42		42
广　西	Guangxi	10	4	6		30	6	24
海　南	Hainan	8			8	9	6	3
重　庆	Chongqing	2	1	1		84	70	14
四　川	Sichuan	10		4	6	58	10	48
贵　州	Guizhou	6		5	1	59	1	58
云　南	Yunnan							
西　藏	Tibet							
陕　西	Shaanxi	3	1	2		34		34
甘　肃	Gansu	2	1	1		120	30	90
青　海	Qinghai	7		2	5	15	14	1
宁　夏	Ningxia	1	1			11		11
新　疆	Xinjiang	1		1		28	3	25
新疆兵团	Xinjiang Corps							
黑龙江农垦	Heilongjiang Land Reclamation							

2-3 续表 1 Continued 1

地 区	Region	学生 Students					
		在校生 Students at Schools	盲 Students with Visual Disability	聋 Students with Hearing Disability	毕业生 Graduates	盲 Students with Visual Disability	聋 Students with Hearing Disability
		人 person	人 person	人 person	人 person	人 person	人 person
全 国	**Total**	**7043**	**1488**	**5555**	**1322**	**136**	**1186**
北 京	Beijing	16	16		4	4	
天 津	Tianjin	132	30	102	58	9	49
河 北	Hebei	382	45	337	92	19	73
山 西	Shanxi	372	37	335	101	9	92
内蒙古	Inner Mongolia	96	3	93	47	7	40
辽 宁	Liaoning	125		125	8		8
吉 林	Jilin	39		39	4		4
黑龙江	Heilongjiang						
上 海	Shanghai	86	58	28	4	4	
江 苏	Jiangsu	392		392	126		126
浙 江	Zhejiang	418	38	380	97	15	82
安 徽	Anhui	446	9	437	79		79
福 建	Fujian	521	109	412	141	8	133
江 西	Jiangxi	138		138	22		22
山 东	Shandong	888	111	777	108	19	89
河 南	Henan	243	29	214	72	4	68
湖 北	Hubei	287		287	103		103
湖 南	Hunan	313	18	295	37	5	32
广 东	Guangdong	134	25	109	27		27
广 西	Guangxi	225	48	177	30	1	29
海 南	Hainan	618	615	3	2	2	
重 庆	Chongqing	202	188	14	24	20	4
四 川	Sichuan	133	22	111	23		23
贵 州	Guizhou	161	3	158	49	2	47
云 南	Yunnan						
西 藏	Tibet						
陕 西	Shaanxi	115	8	107	8		8
甘 肃	Gansu	165	40	125	35	8	27
青 海	Qinghai	54		54			
宁 夏	Ningxia	284	36	248	11		11
新 疆	Xinjiang	58		58	10		10
新疆兵团	Xinjiang Corps						
黑龙江农垦	Heilongjiang Land Reclamation						

2-3　续表 2　Continued 2

地　区	Region	残疾人中等职业学校(班) Secondary Vocational Schools/classes for PWDs	教育部门办 Established by Education Administrative Departments	残联部门办 Established by Disabled Persons' Federations	其他 Others
		个 unit	个 unit	个 unit	个 unit
全　国	**Total**	**152**	**115**	**13**	**24**
北　京	Beijing	3	3		
天　津	Tianjin	1		1	
河　北	Hebei	3	2		1
山　西	Shanxi	3	3		
内蒙古	Inner Mongolia	4	1	1	2
辽　宁	Liaoning	6	4	1	1
吉　林	Jilin	5	5		
黑龙江	Heilongjiang	6	4		2
上　海	Shanghai	3	3		
江　苏	Jiangsu	15	14	1	
浙　江	Zhejiang	1		1	
安　徽	Anhui	9	5	1	3
福　建	Fujian	6	5		1
江　西	Jiangxi	2	2		
山　东	Shandong	17	13	1	3
河　南	Henan	7	7		
湖　北	Hubei	7	2	1	4
湖　南	Hunan	11	9	1	1
广　东	Guangdong	6	4	1	1
广　西	Guangxi	5	4		1
海　南	Hainan	2	2		
重　庆	Chongqing	4	3		1
四　川	Sichuan	7	6		1
贵　州	Guizhou	1	1		
云　南	Yunnan	6	5	1	
西　藏	Tibet				
陕　西	Shaanxi	8	5	1	2
甘　肃	Gansu	1	1		
青　海	Qinghai	1	1		
宁　夏	Ningxia				
新　疆	Xinjiang	2	1	1	
新疆兵团	Xinjiang Corps				
黑龙江农垦	Heilongjiang Land Reclamation				

2-3 续表 3 Continued 3

地 区	Region	残疾人中等职业学校(班)学生 Students of Secondary Vocational Schools/classes for PWDs			
		招生 Newly Enrolled Students	盲 Students with Visual Disability	聋 Students with Hearing Disability	肢残 Students with Physical Disability
		人 person	人 person	人 person	人 person
全 国	**Total**	**5609**	**1194**	**2024**	**2391**
北 京	Beijing	86	50	24	12
天 津	Tianjin				
河 北	Hebei	98	35	11	52
山 西	Shanxi	15		15	
内蒙古	Inner Mongolia	41	15	9	17
辽 宁	Liaoning	60	30	28	2
吉 林	Jilin	288	172	116	
黑龙江	Heilongjiang	70	1	59	10
上 海	Shanghai	46	7	39	
江 苏	Jiangsu	438	49	324	65
浙 江	Zhejiang	120		120	
安 徽	Anhui	258	61	130	67
福 建	Fujian	95	9	86	
江 西	Jiangxi				
山 东	Shandong	536	158	244	134
河 南	Henan	141	41	87	13
湖 北	Hubei	79		10	69
湖 南	Hunan	411	96	180	135
广 东	Guangdong	165	44	52	69
广 西	Guangxi	50		1	49
海 南	Hainan	7			7
重 庆	Chongqing	165	52	25	88
四 川	Sichuan	20	1	5	14
贵 州	Guizhou	10			10
云 南	Yunnan	219	89	91	39
西 藏	Tibet				
陕 西	Shaanxi	2056	228	322	1506
甘 肃	Gansu	30		30	
青 海	Qinghai				
宁 夏	Ningxia				
新 疆	Xinjiang	105	56	16	33
新疆兵团	Xinjiang Corps				
黑龙江农垦	Heilongjiang Land Reclamation				

2-3 续表 4 Continued 4

地区	Region	残疾人中等职业学校(班)学生 Students of Secondary Vocational Schools/classes for PWDs 在校学生 Students at Schools 人 person	盲 Students with Visual Disability 人 person	聋 Students with Hearing Disability 人 person	肢残 Students with Physical Disability 人 person
全 国	**Total**	**10442**	**2495**	**4978**	**2969**
北 京	Beijing	178	110	57	11
天 津	Tianjin	15			15
河 北	Hebei	84	31	7	46
山 西	Shanxi	36		36	
内蒙古	Inner Mongolia	147	98	12	37
辽 宁	Liaoning	262	204	56	2
吉 林	Jilin	621	340	281	
黑龙江	Heilongjiang	103	1	89	13
上 海	Shanghai	189	8	181	
江 苏	Jiangsu	944	136	602	206
浙 江	Zhejiang	488		488	
安 徽	Anhui	638	146	309	183
福 建	Fujian	120	10	101	9
江 西	Jiangxi				
山 东	Shandong	1397	370	733	294
河 南	Henan	268	44	207	17
湖 北	Hubei	132		26	106
湖 南	Hunan	1024	264	432	328
广 东	Guangdong	515	171	126	218
广 西	Guangxi	192	13	68	111
海 南	Hainan	13			13
重 庆	Chongqing	250	50	79	121
四 川	Sichuan	139	38	62	39
贵 州	Guizhou	7			7
云 南	Yunnan	614	89	325	200
西 藏	Tibet				
陕 西	Shaanxi	1487	208	594	685
甘 肃	Gansu	44	14	30	
青 海	Qinghai	9		3	6
宁 夏	Ningxia				
新 疆	Xinjiang	526	150	74	302
新疆兵团	Xinjiang Corps				
黑龙江农垦	Heilongjiang Land Reclamation				

2-3 续表 5 Continued 5

地区	Region	残疾人中等职业学校(班)学生 Students of Secondary Vocational Schools/classes for PWDs			
		毕业生 Graduates	盲 Students with Visual Disability	聋 Students with Hearing Disability	肢残 Students with Physical Disability
		人 person	人 person	人 person	人 person
全国	**Total**	**7354**	**1942**	**1395**	**4017**
北京	Beijing	75	35	29	11
天津	Tianjin	10			10
河北	Hebei	54	9	4	41
山西	Shanxi	17		17	
内蒙古	Inner Mongolia	91	71		20
辽宁	Liaoning	57	45	12	
吉林	Jilin	123	86	37	
黑龙江	Heilongjiang	13		13	
上海	Shanghai	51	7	44	
江苏	Jiangsu	234	25	125	84
浙江	Zhejiang	123		123	
安徽	Anhui	202	53	72	77
福建	Fujian	32	8	23	1
江西	Jiangxi	2			2
山东	Shandong	677	202	349	126
河南	Henan	126	51	58	17
湖北	Hubei	38	1		37
湖南	Hunan	254	77	98	79
广东	Guangdong	185	40	36	109
广西	Guangxi	71			71
海南	Hainan	1			1
重庆	Chongqing	3135	950	15	2170
四川	Sichuan	48	9	23	16
贵州	Guizhou	10			10
云南	Yunnan	276	74	132	70
西藏	Tibet				
陕西	Shaanxi	1269	127	123	1019
甘肃	Gansu	38	14	24	
青海	Qinghai				
宁夏	Ningxia				
新疆	Xinjiang	142	58	38	46
新疆兵团	Xinjiang Corps				
黑龙江农垦	Heilongjiang Land Reclamation				

2-3 续表 6 Continued 6

地 区 Region	残疾人中等职业学校(班)学生 Students of Secondary Vocational Schools/classes for PWDs			
	毕业生获得职业资格证书 Graduates Who were Issued Professional Qualification Certificates	盲 Students with Visual Disability	聋 Students with Hearing Disability	肢残 Students with Physical Disability
	人 person	人 person	人 person	人 person
全 国 Total	**5816**	**1689**	**731**	**3396**
北 京 Beijing	75	35	29	11
天 津 Tianjin				
河 北 Hebei	11	3		8
山 西 Shanxi				
内蒙古 Inner Mongolia	91	71		20
辽 宁 Liaoning	49	45	4	
吉 林 Jilin	86	86		
黑龙江 Heilongjiang				
上 海 Shanghai	23	7	16	
江 苏 Jiangsu	199	18	102	79
浙 江 Zhejiang	75		75	
安 徽 Anhui	185	53	55	77
福 建 Fujian	32	8	23	1
江 西 Jiangxi	2			2
山 东 Shandong	493	150	293	50
河 南 Henan	56	36	11	9
湖 北 Hubei	34			34
湖 南 Hunan	101	35	41	25
广 东 Guangdong	71	19	3	49
广 西 Guangxi				
海 南 Hainan	1			1
重 庆 Chongqing	3038	910		2128
四 川 Sichuan	14	2		12
贵 州 Guizhou	10			10
云 南 Yunnan	89	69	20	
西 藏 Tibet				
陕 西 Shaanxi	972	84	44	844
甘 肃 Gansu				
青 海 Qinghai				
宁 夏 Ningxia				
新 疆 Xinjiang	109	58	15	36
新疆兵团 Xinjiang Corps				
黑龙江农垦 Heilongjiang Land Reclamation				

2-4 高等教育
Higher Education

地 区	Region	高等特殊教育学院 Higher Special Education Institutions							
		机构 Institutions	录取残疾考生 Newly Enrolled Students	本科 Under-graduates	盲 Students with Visual Disability	聋 Students with Hearing Disability	专科(高职) Postsecondary Specialised College Students (Vocational College	盲 Students with Visual Disability	聋 Students with Hearing Disability
		个 unit	人 person	人 person	人 person	人 person	人 person	人 person	人 person
全 国	**Total**	**20**	**1134**	**460**	**109**	**351**	**674**	**222**	**452**
北 京	Beijing	1	20	12	5	7	8		8
天 津	Tianjin	2	20	11		11	9	4	5
河 北	Hebei		12	5	2	3	7	3	4
山 西	Shanxi		51	13	3	10	38		38
内蒙古	Inner Mongolia								
辽 宁	Liaoning	3	257	34	7	27	223	113	110
吉 林	Jilin	1	207	204	66	138	3	2	1
黑龙江	Heilongjiang		2	1	1		1		1
上 海	Shanghai								
江 苏	Jiangsu	3	127	65	2	63	62	24	38
浙 江	Zhejiang		78	27	3	24	51	6	45
安 徽	Anhui		24	10	1	9	14	1	13
福 建	Fujian	1	28	16	6	10	12	3	9
江 西	Jiangxi		10	6	1	5	4	2	2
山 东	Shandong	1	71	27	4	23	44	5	39
河 南	Henan	3	17	2		2	15		15
湖 北	Hubei		7	2		2	5	1	4
湖 南	Hunan		19	9	1	8	10	1	9
广 东	Guangdong	2	57				57	11	46
广 西	Guangxi	1	11	3		3	8		8
海 南	Hainan								
重 庆	Chongqing	1	9	9	7	2			
四 川	Sichuan		4	1		1	3	2	1
贵 州	Guizhou		63	2		2	61	27	34
云 南	Yunnan		38	1		1	37	17	20
西 藏	Tibet								
陕 西	Shaanxi	1							
甘 肃	Gansu		1				1		1
青 海	Qinghai								
宁 夏	Ningxia		1				1		1
新 疆	Xinjiang								
新疆兵团	Xinjiang Corps								
黑龙江农垦	Heilongjiang Land Reclamation								

2-4　续表 1　Continued 1

地　区	Region	普通高等院校 Ordinary Higher Education Institutions 残疾考生达到录取分数线 Students who Passed the Admission Line	录取人数 Students Enrolled	本科 Undergraduates	盲 Students with Visual Disability	聋 Students with Hearing Disability	肢残 Students with Physical Disability
		人 person	人 person	人 person	人 person	人 person	人 person
全　国	**Total**	**7613**	**7229**	**3538**	**310**	**384**	**2844**
北　京	Beijing	126	125	66	7	30	29
天　津	Tianjin	73	72	36	2	3	31
河　北	Hebei	432	397	192	34	35	123
山　西	Shanxi	183	183	61			61
内蒙古	Inner Mongolia	366	354	155	18	23	114
辽　宁	Liaoning	301	301	115	16	18	81
吉　林	Jilin	193	193	147	22	19	106
黑龙江	Heilongjiang	153	153	104	18	13	73
上　海	Shanghai	49	49	30	4	16	10
江　苏	Jiangsu	396	396	193			193
浙　江	Zhejiang	204	189	83	5	16	62
安　徽	Anhui	298	265	127	5	27	95
福　建	Fujian	240	229	103	7	7	89
江　西	Jiangxi	211	197	109	8	12	89
山　东	Shandong	388	367	222	19	29	174
河　南	Henan	400	400	206	31	14	161
湖　北	Hubei	227	225	95	5	15	75
湖　南	Hunan	237	231	115	14	14	87
广　东	Guangdong	305	280	99	11	5	83
广　西	Guangxi	197	189	80	16		64
海　南	Hainan	61	61	24	1		23
重　庆	Chongqing	182	179	105	14	6	85
四　川	Sichuan	357	316	145	10	10	125
贵　州	Guizhou	414	347	164	1	3	160
云　南	Yunnan	420	359	195	14	10	171
西　藏	Tibet	35	35	25		1	24
陕　西	Shaanxi	334	334	175	5	28	142
甘　肃	Gansu	272	272	73			73
青　海	Qinghai	134	134	89	6	2	81
宁　夏	Ningxia	131	116	53	6	9	38
新　疆	Xinjiang	252	239	145	11	18	116
新疆兵团	Xinjiang Corps	42	42	7		1	6
黑龙江农垦	Heilongjiang Land Reclamation						

2-4 续表 2 Continued 2

地 区	Region	普通高等院校 Ordinary Higher Education Institutions 录取残疾考生 Students Enrolled 专科(高职) Postsecondary Specialised College Students (Vocational College Students)	盲 Students with Visual Disability	聋 Students with Hearing Disability	肢残 Students with Physical Disability
		人 person	人 person	人 person	人 person
全 国	**Total**	**3691**	**261**	**465**	**2965**
北 京	Beijing	59	3	14	42
天 津	Tianjin	36	3	12	21
河 北	Hebei	205	28	34	143
山 西	Shanxi	122			122
内蒙古	Inner Mongolia	199	19	35	145
辽 宁	Liaoning	186	35	38	113
吉 林	Jilin	46	9	7	30
黑龙江	Heilongjiang	49	5	7	37
上 海	Shanghai	19	1	8	10
江 苏	Jiangsu	203		1	202
浙 江	Zhejiang	106	6	28	72
安 徽	Anhui	138	11	19	108
福 建	Fujian	126	5	33	88
江 西	Jiangxi	88	3	15	70
山 东	Shandong	145	12	21	112
河 南	Henan	194	30	15	149
湖 北	Hubei	130	7	42	81
湖 南	Hunan	116	5	8	103
广 东	Guangdong	181	13	13	155
广 西	Guangxi	109	7	16	86
海 南	Hainan	37	2	4	31
重 庆	Chongqing	74	9	8	57
四 川	Sichuan	171	12	22	137
贵 州	Guizhou	183	2	1	180
云 南	Yunnan	164	10	14	140
西 藏	Tibet	10	1	2	7
陕 西	Shaanxi	159	4	30	125
甘 肃	Gansu	199			199
青 海	Qinghai	45	2	4	39
宁 夏	Ningxia	63	9	5	49
新 疆	Xinjiang	94	7	7	80
新疆兵团	Xinjiang Corps	35	1	2	32
黑龙江农垦	Heilongjiang Land Reclamation				

3-1 城镇残疾人就业状况
Employment of PWDs in Urban Areas

地 区	Region	就业合计 Employed PWDs	集中就业 PWDs Employed in Collective Form	本年度新安排 Newly Employed in Collective Form in 2012	按比例就业 PWDs Employed by quota Scheme	本年度新安排 Newly Employed by Quota Scheme in 2012	公益性岗位就业 PWDs Employed Through Welfare Post
		人 person	人 person	人 person	人 person	人 person	人 person
全 国	**Total**	**4447807**	**1205493**	**101838**	**1191454**	**80098**	**113681**
北 京	Beijing	72969	6359	285	41183	1181	13009
天 津	Tianjin	34995	7560	643	22683	1511	394
河 北	Hebei	196283	51726	4603	83392	3464	5961
山 西	Shanxi	123451	39288	1836	24704	947	2701
内蒙古	Inner Mongolia	117464	17285	2016	20916	1759	3044
辽 宁	Liaoning	316421	101232	2994	80962	2334	1989
吉 林	Jilin	157204	41019	2798	25383	1534	2574
黑龙江	Heilongjiang	129495	32871	3387	24194	1274	8581
上 海	Shanghai	69379	17296	717	39410	1851	4790
江 苏	Jiangsu	304863	108480	6644	87662	6647	857
浙 江	Zhejiang	198512	87262	5908	67568	3710	4827
安 徽	Anhui	188527	46463	3971	25835	3987	10190
福 建	Fujian	122192	41377	3057	26082	2732	5168
江 西	Jiangxi	149082	32472	5789	16450	1087	5230
山 东	Shandong	248376	76665	6981	86506	7065	2967
河 南	Henan	306326	100578	13022	55220	8822	10725
湖 北	Hubei	233082	60863	4350	37309	2311	4659
湖 南	Hunan	274345	57747	4622	68087	2782	3351
广 东	Guangdong	198019	26370	3411	75407	7688	3484
广 西	Guangxi	80361	18444	1381	24758	1568	1357
海 南	Hainan	10236	1385	335	3603	194	250
重 庆	Chongqing	142695	52085	3253	39572	1062	3608
四 川	Sichuan	276553	52024	10875	67297	6128	3261
贵 州	Guizhou	77551	26704	1135	12755	1049	303
云 南	Yunnan	74187	28655	1996	22822	1048	606
西 藏	Tibet	1031	718	63	102	40	111
陕 西	Shaanxi	103709	23517	1892	33185	2131	2612
甘 肃	Gansu	108769	25745	1939	21331	1561	4787
青 海	Qinghai	7148	2474	410	1750	288	340
宁 夏	Ningxia	22637	4958	314	6046	387	458
新 疆	Xinjiang	70505	13894	995	32734	1541	993
新疆兵团	Xinjiang Corps	15731	1926	216	11112	372	199
黑龙江农垦	Heilongjiang Land Reclamation	15709	51		5434	43	295

3-1 续表 Continued

地 区	Region	本年度新安排 Newly Employed in 2012	个体及其他形式就业 PWDs Self-employed or Employed in Other Forms	本年度新安排 Newly Employed in 2012	辅助性就业 PWDs of Assistive Employment	本年度新安排 Newly Employed in 2012
		人 person	人 person	人 person	人 person	人 person
全 国	**Total**	**17712**	**1922783**	**122790**	**14396**	**6881**
北 京	Beijing	629	11960	803	458	9
天 津	Tianjin	169	4358	241		
河 北	Hebei	588	55129	4078	75	49
山 西	Shanxi	122	56575	2614	183	52
内蒙古	Inner Mongolia	429	75673	3684	546	396
辽 宁	Liaoning	497	132147	7713	91	91
吉 林	Jilin	73	88228	6912		
黑龙江	Heilongjiang	1613	63833	3111	16	4
上 海	Shanghai	281	7713	354	170	
江 苏	Jiangsu	260	107170	7128	694	375
浙 江	Zhejiang	583	36353	3451	2502	980
安 徽	Anhui	535	104971	6073	1068	403
福 建	Fujian	1184	48707	4751	858	612
江 西	Jiangxi	1168	93649	6617	1281	411
山 东	Shandong	382	81638	4917	600	305
河 南	Henan	1763	139016	17244	787	561
湖 北	Hubei	463	130095	4891	156	108
湖 南	Hunan	955	145072	3133	88	78
广 东	Guangdong	822	91733	4502	1025	479
广 西	Guangxi	285	35360	2210	442	255
海 南	Hainan	32	4996	322	2	
重 庆	Chongqing	221	47345	2513	85	85
四 川	Sichuan	833	151952	12041	2019	842
贵 州	Guizhou	95	37762	2143	27	27
云 南	Yunnan	131	22028	1440	76	76
西 藏	Tibet	17	87	47	13	13
陕 西	Shaanxi	642	43992	2831	403	166
甘 肃	Gansu	2147	56732	4135	174	77
青 海	Qinghai	236	2488	836	96	86
宁 夏	Ningxia	115	11075	721	100	58
新 疆	Xinjiang	224	22617	1114	267	261
新疆兵团	Xinjiang Corps	40	2400	124	94	22
黑龙江农垦	Heilongjiang Land Reclamation	178	9929	96		

3-2 农村残疾人就业状况
Employment of PWDs in Rural Areas

地 区	Region	实际就业 Employed PWDs	从事农业生产劳动 PWDs Engaged in Farming	从事其他形式就业 PWDs Employed in Other Forms
		万人 10,000 persons	万人 10,000 persons	万人 10,000 persons
全 国	**Total**	**1770.3**	**1389.9**	**380.4**
北 京	Beijing	4.5	3.0	1.5
天 津	Tianjin	6.7	4.8	2.0
河 北	Hebei	87.2	68.5	18.8
山 西	Shanxi	40.7	29.5	11.2
内蒙古	Inner Mongolia	28.0	22.8	5.3
辽 宁	Liaoning	40.1	29.1	11.0
吉 林	Jilin	30.6	25.5	5.0
黑龙江	Heilongjiang	24.5	20.1	4.4
上 海	Shanghai	2.6	0.4	2.2
江 苏	Jiangsu	69.9	52.4	17.5
浙 江	Zhejiang	31.1	20.5	10.5
安 徽	Anhui	108.0	86.1	21.9
福 建	Fujian	36.6	29.1	7.4
江 西	Jiangxi	55.6	41.9	13.7
山 东	Shandong	135.4	106.3	29.0
河 南	Henan	186.0	147.5	38.4
湖 北	Hubei	89.7	67.0	22.7
湖 南	Hunan	91.9	67.0	24.9
广 东	Guangdong	64.7	53.3	11.5
广 西	Guangxi	64.0	51.0	13.0
海 南	Hainan	6.5	5.5	0.9
重 庆	Chongqing	50.1	40.3	9.8
四 川	Sichuan	174.7	141.5	33.2
贵 州	Guizhou	77.3	61.1	16.2
云 南	Yunnan	103.4	88.4	15.0
西 藏	Tibet	3.0	2.9	0.1
陕 西	Shaanxi	72.5	54.3	18.2
甘 肃	Gansu	49.0	39.5	9.6
青 海	Qinghai	3.7	3.2	0.5
宁 夏	Ningxia	10.8	9.0	1.8
新 疆	Xinjiang	21.6	18.5	3.1
新疆兵团	Xinjiang Corps			
黑龙江农垦	Heilongjiang Land Reclamation			

3-3 城镇残疾人登记失业与职业培训
Unemployment Registration of PWDs in Urban Areas and Vocational Training

地区	Region	本年度城镇残疾人新登记失业 PWDs in Urban Areas who Registered as being Unemployed Newly Added in 2012	残疾人职业培训 Vocational Training for PWDs			
			职业培训基地 Vocational Training Base			本年度城镇职业培训 PWDs in Urban Areas Receiving Vocational Training in 2012
				残联兴办 Established by Disabled Persons' Federations	依托社会机构兴办 Established by Social Organizations	
		人 person	个 unit	个 unit	个 unit	人 person
全 国	**Total**	**45146**	**5271**	**1927**	**3344**	**298618**
北 京	Beijing	541	45	8	37	4111
天 津	Tianjin		24	13	11	1780
河 北	Hebei	1211	524	261	263	17274
山 西	Shanxi	679	300	72	228	7258
内蒙古	Inner Mongolia	1149	65	21	44	11637
辽 宁	Liaoning	1082	133	49	84	15586
吉 林	Jilin	7784	172	49	123	17058
黑龙江	Heilongjiang	535	73	23	50	10806
上 海	Shanghai	342	93	84	9	7846
江 苏	Jiangsu	1202	184	66	118	17636
浙 江	Zhejiang	5623	294	68	226	13251
安 徽	Anhui	1155	114	66	48	7647
福 建	Fujian	1030	378	172	206	6989
江 西	Jiangxi	1437	206	38	168	3992
山 东	Shandong	553	716	193	523	18319
河 南	Henan	1795	203	41	162	26010
湖 北	Hubei	986	253	200	53	4811
湖 南	Hunan	1571	172	74	98	5605
广 东	Guangdong	5537	111	47	64	14247
广 西	Guangxi	322	63	34	29	5384
海 南	Hainan		7	1	6	567
重 庆	Chongqing	1075	26	5	21	3184
四 川	Sichuan	2455	441	196	245	26075
贵 州	Guizhou	3926	115	8	107	4163
云 南	Yunnan	230	63	32	31	5771
西 藏	Tibet	139	1	1		56
陕 西	Shaanxi	1393	64	15	49	12210
甘 肃	Gansu	374	38	18	20	17827
青 海	Qinghai	69	81	26	55	2816
宁 夏	Ningxia	377	28	3	25	2874
新 疆	Xinjiang	430	282	42	240	4793
新疆兵团	Xinjiang Corps	144	2	1	1	1035
黑龙江农垦	Heilongjiang Land Reclamation					

4-1　城镇残疾人参加社会保险

Urban PWDs Covered by Social Insurance

地区	Region	城镇残疾职工参加社会保险合计 Urban Workers with Disabilities Covered by Social Insurance	参加养老保险 Covered by Pension Insurance	参加医疗保险 Covered by Medical Insurance	残疾居民参加社会保险 Disabled Residents Covered by Social Insurance	参加城镇居民医疗保险 Covered by Medical Insurance for Urban Residents	参加城镇居民社会养老保险 Covered by New Types of Pension Insurance
		万人 10,000 persons	万人 10,000 persons	万人 10,000 persons	万人 10,000 persons	万人 10,000 persons	万人 10,000 persons
全　国	**Total**	**280.9**	**173.4**	**164.9**	**1275.3**	**498.6**	**325.3**
北　京	Beijing	6.7	6.0	5.9	17.4	4.9	10.3
天　津	Tianjin	3.6	2.7	2.5	10.4	7.1	1.8
河　北	Hebei	9.3	5.3	4.6	63.7	15.1	12.5
山　西	Shanxi	8.5	3.4	4.1	51.7	11.9	12.5
内蒙古	Inner Mongolia	6.1	2.6	3.5	37.7	11.9	5.1
辽　宁	Liaoning	18.6	11.2	8.9	42.1	18.4	17.6
吉　林	Jilin	6.6	3.5	3.2	28.8	21.5	7.1
黑龙江	Heilongjiang	6.4	2.9	2.8	32.2	13.9	4.2
上　海	Shanghai	7.1	6.9	7.1	3.3	1.7	2.3
江　苏	Jiangsu	26.8	18.9	17.6	124.7	37.8	23.2
浙　江	Zhejiang	14.4	12.5	12.1	15.4	12.0	6.4
安　徽	Anhui	8.3	5.0	4.0	48.5	27.1	15.9
福　建	Fujian	4.8	2.7	2.8	25.7	11.5	6.2
江　西	Jiangxi	10.7	3.9	4.0	70.7	22.6	11.1
山　东	Shandong	19.0	13.2	12.1	62.3	14.9	22.5
河　南	Henan	24.9	11.4	10.3	199.1	38.7	26.0
湖　北	Hubei	15.9	7.5	8.3	54.1	27.9	21.4
湖　南	Hunan	19.3	12.3	9.9	52.4	25.1	19.9
广　东	Guangdong	13.6	9.0	8.8	40.2	28.8	7.3
广　西	Guangxi	4.3	2.2	2.5	35.9	13.4	3.6
海　南	Hainan	0.7	0.4	0.3	5.7	4.8	4.6
重　庆	Chongqing	7.5	5.6	5.0	26.9	17.1	11.1
四　川	Sichuan	11.1	7.7	7.6	63.4	28.7	22.0
贵　州	Guizhou	3.6	1.9	1.9	21.6	11.0	7.7
云　南	Yunnan	5.1	3.6	3.4	22.5	9.3	9.2
西　藏	Tibet	0.3	0.2	0.2	0.5	0.2	0.2
陕　西	Shaanxi	6.0	3.6	3.6	50.7	19.7	8.9
甘　肃	Gansu	2.8	1.7	1.5	29.7	19.8	11.5
青　海	Qinghai	0.4	0.3	0.2	1.6	1.0	0.5
宁　夏	Ningxia	0.9	0.7	0.6	8.4	4.0	4.6
新　疆	Xinjiang	4.8	2.9	3.3	19.9	9.2	7.5
新疆兵团	Xinjiang Corps	1.8	1.1	1.2	2.5	2.1	0.8
黑龙江农垦	Heilongjiang Land Reclamation	0.8	0.8	0.8	5.6	5.6	

4-1 续表 1 Continued 1

地 区	Region	残疾居民参加城镇居民社会养老保险 PWDs Covered by Payment in New Types of Pension Insurance						
		享受养老保金 PWDs Covered by the Insurance Pension	重度残疾人 Persons with Severe Disability	60周岁以下参保残疾人 PWDs under Age 60	重度残疾人 Persons with Severe Disability	全部或部分代缴 Paid by Subsidy Totally or Partially	其他残疾人 Other PWDs	全部或部分代缴 Paid by Subsidy Totally or Partially
		万人 10,000 persons	万人 10,000 persons	万人 10,000 persons	万人 10,000 persons	万人 10,000 persons	万人 10,000 persons	万人 10,000 persons
全 国	**Total**	**133.73**	**34.82**	**191.58**	**62.76**	**59.18**	**128.82**	**47.74**
北 京	Beijing			10.26	5.08	5.08	5.18	5.18
天 津	Tianjin	0.89	0.26	0.94	0.81	0.81	0.13	0.13
河 北	Hebei	4.20	1.26	8.34	1.88	1.88	6.46	1.76
山 西	Shanxi	7.62	0.83	4.92	1.04	0.78	3.88	0.48
内蒙古	Inner Mongolia	1.54	0.73	3.57	1.36	1.28	2.21	0.85
辽 宁	Liaoning	6.86	1.80	10.74	3.62	2.80	7.12	4.20
吉 林	Jilin	1.32	0.61	5.77	2.16	2.16	3.61	1.51
黑龙江	Heilongjiang	1.74	0.66	2.42	0.74	0.68	1.69	0.49
上 海	Shanghai	0.22	0.22	2.08	2.08	2.08		
江 苏	Jiangsu	14.62	2.30	8.54	2.97	2.83	5.57	0.76
浙 江	Zhejiang	2.63	0.66	3.75	1.71	1.26	2.04	0.86
安 徽	Anhui	6.66	3.33	9.19	3.14	2.84	6.04	0.63
福 建	Fujian	2.20	1.14	4.01	1.29	1.22	2.72	1.70
江 西	Jiangxi	5.74	0.63	5.39	1.28	1.18	4.11	2.93
山 东	Shandong	12.98	1.95	9.48	3.16	3.01	6.32	2.74
河 南	Henan	12.45	3.11	13.57	4.54	4.49	9.03	0.67
湖 北	Hubei	6.20	2.08	15.18	5.29	5.25	9.89	6.74
湖 南	Hunan	9.38	2.65	10.56	2.95	2.88	7.61	2.53
广 东	Guangdong	2.30	1.07	4.97	1.77	1.67	3.20	1.17
广 西	Guangxi	1.65	0.51	1.97	0.77	0.71	1.19	0.39
海 南	Hainan	1.58	0.26	2.97	0.43	0.43	2.54	
重 庆	Chongqing	5.23	1.48	5.84	1.65	1.65	4.19	3.44
四 川	Sichuan	5.32	1.71	16.65	3.79	3.43	12.87	0.88
贵 州	Guizhou	5.56	1.15	2.14	1.20	1.11	0.94	0.40
云 南	Yunnan	1.70	0.51	7.51	1.22	1.20	6.29	1.45
西 藏	Tibet	0.11	0.05	0.07	0.03	0.03	0.04	0.04
陕 西	Shaanxi	4.00	1.23	4.88	1.45	1.45	3.43	2.56
甘 肃	Gansu	4.21	0.79	7.31	3.21	2.95	4.10	0.46
青 海	Qinghai	0.48	0.03	0.06	0.03	0.03	0.03	0.02
宁 夏	Ningxia	2.22	1.23	2.38	1.10	1.09	1.28	0.87
新 疆	Xinjiang	1.80	0.55	5.67	0.79	0.73	4.89	1.80
新疆兵团	Xinjiang Corps	0.30	0.04	0.46	0.23	0.19	0.23	0.10
黑龙江农垦	Heilongjiang Land Reclamation							

4-1　续表 2　Continued 2

地　区	Region	城镇个体就业参加社会保险 PWDs in Urban Areas Self-employed and Covered by Social Insurance				
		参加社会保险 Self-employed and Covered by Social Insurance	参加养老保险 Self-employed and Covered by Pension Insurance	参加城镇职工养老保险 Covered by Pension Insurance for Urban Workers	参加城镇居民养老保险 Covered by Pension Insurance for Urban Residents	参加医疗保险 Self-employed and Covered by Medical Insurance
		万人 10,000 persons	万人 10,000 persons	万人 10,000 persons	万人 10,000 persons	万人 10,000 persons
全　国	**Total**	**109.78**	**59.81**	**17.79**	**39.46**	**46.50**
北　京	Beijing	1.42	1.33	1.33		1.42
天　津	Tianjin	0.01	0.01	0.01		0.01
河　北	Hebei	2.83	1.73	0.33	1.38	1.66
山　西	Shanxi	2.81	1.69	0.52	1.11	0.92
内蒙古	Inner Mongolia	2.21	1.47	0.61	0.81	0.96
辽　宁	Liaoning	3.66	1.52	0.68	0.80	1.47
吉　林	Jilin	3.53	1.33	0.55	0.78	1.56
黑龙江	Heilongjiang	3.19	1.04	0.38	0.65	1.02
上　海	Shanghai	0.12	0.06	0.06		0.11
江　苏	Jiangsu	11.96	4.99	1.43	3.26	3.81
浙　江	Zhejiang	1.88	1.45	0.72	0.64	1.17
安　徽	Anhui	8.96	3.39	0.72	2.56	2.58
福　建	Fujian	2.25	1.46	0.37	1.03	0.88
江　西	Jiangxi	3.44	1.72	0.41	1.31	1.74
山　东	Shandong	5.46	3.23	1.51	1.59	2.59
河　南	Henan	9.75	4.09	1.33	2.60	3.50
湖　北	Hubei	7.80	3.22	0.83	2.28	4.28
湖　南	Hunan	7.00	3.94	1.01	2.92	2.55
广　东	Guangdong	5.17	3.03	1.11	1.92	2.95
广　西	Guangxi	1.38	0.68	0.21	0.45	0.73
海　南	Hainan	0.23	0.18	0.05	0.12	0.18
重　庆	Chongqing	2.27	1.90	0.46	1.37	1.48
四　川	Sichuan	6.62	4.36	1.02	3.22	3.84
贵　州	Guizhou	1.61	0.47	0.13	0.34	0.98
云　南	Yunnan	1.23	0.86	0.20	0.64	0.69
西　藏	Tibet					
陕　西	Shaanxi	7.81	7.13	0.69	5.37	1.19
甘　肃	Gansu	1.56	1.08	0.14	0.93	0.67
青　海	Qinghai	0.10	0.07	0.03	0.03	0.05
宁　夏	Ningxia	0.51	0.46	0.10	0.35	0.18
新　疆	Xinjiang	2.17	1.39	0.44	0.91	0.81
新疆兵团	Xinjiang Corps	0.25	0.19	0.08	0.10	0.13
黑龙江农垦	Heilongjiang Land Reclamation	0.57	0.34	0.34		0.38

4-2 残疾人参加新型农村社会养老保险

PWDs Covered by New Types of Rural Pension Insurance

地 区	Region	参保残疾人 PWDs Covered by the Insurance	享受养老保金 PWDs Covered by the Insurance Pension	重度残疾人 Persons with Severe Disability	60周岁以下参保残疾人 PWDs under Age 60
		万人 10,000 persons	万人 10,000 persons	万人 10,000 persons	万人 10,000 persons
全 国	**Total**	**1333.81**	**507.45**	**136.13**	**826.36**
北 京	Beijing				
天 津	Tianjin	3.50	2.15	0.86	1.34
河 北	Hebei	114.50	35.56	7.94	78.94
山 西	Shanxi	58.54	28.80	3.59	29.74
内蒙古	Inner Mongolia	20.75	9.50	3.75	11.25
辽 宁	Liaoning	28.25	7.56	2.17	20.69
吉 林	Jilin	10.36	3.21	0.93	7.15
黑龙江	Heilongjiang	10.51	5.04	0.55	5.47
上 海	Shanghai	1.71	0.37	0.17	1.34
江 苏	Jiangsu	33.82	13.90	4.54	19.92
浙 江	Zhejiang	25.92	12.91	3.52	13.01
安 徽	Anhui	67.09	26.26	10.25	40.83
福 建	Fujian	34.09	14.92	6.07	19.17
江 西	Jiangxi	46.48	24.78	3.87	21.70
山 东	Shandong	101.95	37.81	14.60	64.14
河 南	Henan	121.31	57.31	15.36	64.00
湖 北	Hubei	79.88	36.61	7.81	43.27
湖 南	Hunan	78.21	31.36	5.22	46.85
广 东	Guangdong	50.34	21.27	5.22	29.07
广 西	Guangxi	45.60	18.23	3.79	27.37
海 南	Hainan	11.85	3.75	0.87	8.10
重 庆	Chongqing	22.33	10.64	2.50	11.68
四 川	Sichuan	142.45	28.21	9.25	114.24
贵 州	Guizhou	30.42	17.44	3.71	12.98
云 南	Yunnan	51.01	16.41	5.25	34.60
西 藏	Tibet	1.09	0.62	0.07	0.47
陕 西	Shaanxi	28.89	7.81	2.63	21.08
甘 肃	Gansu	79.76	23.47	6.60	56.29
青 海	Qinghai	2.17	0.71	0.16	1.46
宁 夏	Ningxia	13.56	5.22	3.56	8.34
新 疆	Xinjiang	17.48	5.60	1.31	11.87
新疆兵团	Xinjiang Corps				
黑龙江农垦	Heilongjiang Land Reclamation				

4-2　续表　Continued

地　区	Region	重度残疾人 Persons with Severe Disability	全部或部分代缴 Paid by Subsidy Totally or Partially	其他残疾人 Other PWDs	全部或部分代缴 Paid by Subsidy Totally or Partially
		万人 10,000 persons	万人 10,000 persons	万人 10,000 persons	万人 10,000 persons
全　国	**Total**	**236.56**	**224.62**	**589.80**	**149.96**
北　京	Beijing				
天　津	Tianjin	0.93	0.93	0.41	0.41
河　北	Hebei	15.31	15.31	63.64	20.21
山　西	Shanxi	10.76	8.93	18.98	2.06
内蒙古	Inner Mongolia	3.70	3.62	7.55	2.95
辽　宁	Liaoning	4.83	4.05	15.86	13.54
吉　林	Jilin	2.32	2.32	4.83	2.51
黑龙江	Heilongjiang	1.16	1.12	4.31	0.52
上　海	Shanghai	0.86	0.86		
江　苏	Jiangsu	5.27	4.85	14.64	1.57
浙　江	Zhejiang	4.52	4.35	8.49	4.34
安　徽	Anhui	12.81	12.28	28.01	7.13
福　建	Fujian	9.17	9.17	10.00	5.33
江　西	Jiangxi	5.94	5.55	15.76	2.92
山　东	Shandong	18.30	16.90	45.84	20.02
河　南	Henan	25.59	25.45	38.41	1.05
湖　北	Hubei	12.75	11.13	30.53	9.44
湖　南	Hunan	12.00	11.77	34.85	5.84
广　东	Guangdong	9.95	8.98	19.12	4.64
广　西	Guangxi	6.61	5.87	20.76	5.87
海　南	Hainan	1.98	1.98	6.12	
重　庆	Chongqing	4.58	4.58	7.10	4.92
四　川	Sichuan	22.66	21.95	91.58	3.20
贵　州	Guizhou	4.08	4.03	8.90	1.92
云　南	Yunnan	9.27	9.10	25.33	8.05
西　藏	Tibet	0.10	0.10	0.37	0.37
陕　西	Shaanxi	6.72	6.71	14.36	9.54
甘　肃	Gansu	16.71	15.31	39.58	3.02
青　海	Qinghai	0.94	0.89	0.51	0.24
宁　夏	Ningxia	3.24	3.20	5.10	2.12
新　疆	Xinjiang	3.49	3.35	8.38	5.74
新疆兵团	Xinjiang Corps				
黑龙江农垦	Heilongjiang Land Reclamation				

4-3 社会救助与社会福利

Social Relief and Welfare

地 区	Region	社会救助 Social Relief			
		城镇 in Urban Areas			农村 in Rural Areas
		已纳入最低生活保障范围 PWDs Covered by Basic Living Allowance System	集中供养 PWDs Living in Welfare Institutions	其他救助救济 Other Assistance and Relief	已纳入最低生活保障范围 PWDs Covered by Basic Living Allowance System
		万人 10,000 persons	万人 10,000 persons	万人 10,000 persons	万人 10,000 persons
全 国	**Total**	**266.54**	**12.19**	**68.10**	**803.99**
北 京	Beijing	4.75	0.03	0.50	2.34
天 津	Tianjin	3.30	0.03	1.48	2.21
河 北	Hebei	6.89	0.40	1.07	35.82
山 西	Shanxi	6.31	0.11	1.51	19.93
内蒙古	Inner Mongolia	9.39	0.37	4.53	21.30
辽 宁	Liaoning	16.36	0.48	1.98	18.79
吉 林	Jilin	13.64	0.63	1.85	15.93
黑龙江	Heilongjiang	15.60	0.33	2.00	13.03
上 海	Shanghai	1.37	0.01	5.10	0.50
江 苏	Jiangsu	8.95	0.74	4.38	23.79
浙 江	Zhejiang	3.01	0.45	1.35	15.71
安 徽	Anhui	9.23	0.58	0.88	34.49
福 建	Fujian	4.59	0.23	1.00	19.24
江 西	Jiangxi	10.67	1.06	1.52	25.73
山 东	Shandong	7.96	0.90	1.93	33.06
河 南	Henan	17.71	0.83	4.20	65.33
湖 北	Hubei	18.63	1.15	3.10	47.69
湖 南	Hunan	21.62	0.77	4.26	55.20
广 东	Guangdong	9.38	0.36	3.02	28.87
广 西	Guangxi	7.66	0.31	0.71	45.08
海 南	Hainan	2.07	0.02	0.74	4.49
重 庆	Chongqing	5.99	0.36	2.36	14.31
四 川	Sichuan	16.39	0.88	4.96	67.83
贵 州	Guizhou	6.18	0.31	0.92	41.59
云 南	Yunnan	7.50	0.29	1.92	57.32
西 藏	Tibet	0.42		0.06	2.96
陕 西	Shaanxi	6.98	0.30	5.94	30.74
甘 肃	Gansu	11.05	0.09	1.24	35.71
青 海	Qinghai	0.56	0.01	0.14	2.61
宁 夏	Ningxia	1.73	0.06	0.75	8.66
新 疆	Xinjiang	5.49	0.08	1.42	13.72
新疆兵团	Xinjiang Corps	2.08	0.02	0.86	
黑龙江农垦	Heilongjiang Land Reclamation	3.05	0.01	0.41	

4-3 续表 Continued

地区	Region	社会救助 Social Relief 农村 in Rural Areas 五保供养 PWDs Living in Welfare Institutions 万人 10,000 persons	社会救助 Social Relief 农村 in Rural Areas 其他救助救济 Other Assistance and Relief 万人 10,000 persons	社会福利 Social Welfare 享受生活补贴 PWDs with Living Subsidy 万人 10,000 persons	社会福利 Social Welfare 享受护理补贴 PWDs with Nursing Subsidy 万人 10,000 persons
全 国	**Total**	**68.47**	**193.16**	**239.11**	**36.32**
北 京	Beijing	0.09	1.40	12.39	0.88
天 津	Tianjin	0.36	1.90	5.38	0.02
河 北	Hebei	2.50	4.00	1.72	
山 西	Shanxi	2.89	5.21	0.85	
内蒙古	Inner Mongolia	1.15	7.99	13.84	3.78
辽 宁	Liaoning	2.35	3.06	0.50	0.20
吉 林	Jilin	0.94	1.41		
黑龙江	Heilongjiang	0.97	3.00	0.54	
上 海	Shanghai	0.01	0.67	1.58	0.35
江 苏	Jiangsu	2.10	10.22	17.47	6.79
浙 江	Zhejiang	0.67	8.49	14.66	3.30
安 徽	Anhui	3.18	5.63	19.40	0.77
福 建	Fujian	1.09	3.07	11.75	0.64
江 西	Jiangxi	2.59	3.87	0.18	
山 东	Shandong	3.14	6.93	13.88	1.24
河 南	Henan	6.01	12.89	4.05	
湖 北	Hubei	4.01	6.38	17.66	0.29
湖 南	Hunan	7.12	10.61	9.96	0.52
广 东	Guangdong	2.46	3.92	23.95	13.54
广 西	Guangxi	6.88	4.07	2.06	0.08
海 南	Hainan	0.15	0.99	0.18	2.39
重 庆	Chongqing	1.74	5.81		0.16
四 川	Sichuan	5.54	15.40	3.68	0.58
贵 州	Guizhou	1.35	7.74	1.12	
云 南	Yunnan	4.40	8.83	1.16	0.07
西 藏	Tibet	0.07	0.15	0.03	
陕 西	Shaanxi	2.03	37.19	57.11	0.09
甘 肃	Gansu	1.87	9.01	1.08	0.12
青 海	Qinghai	0.21	0.78	0.81	
宁 夏	Ningxia	0.15	1.32	1.34	
新 疆	Xinjiang	0.44	1.23	0.69	0.50
新疆兵团	Xinjiang Corps			0.09	
黑龙江农垦	Heilongjiang Land Reclamation				

4-4 托养服务

Fostering Service

地区	Region	寄宿制托养服务 Boarding Fostering Services				机构性质 Property of the Institutions		
		寄宿制托养服务机构合计 Boarding Fostering Institutions	省级 at Provincial Level	地市级 at Prefectural/ City Level	县级 at County Level	民办非企业 Private Non-profit Entity	事业单位 Public Institute	其他 Others
		个 unit	个 unit	个 unit	个 unit	个 unit	个 unit	个 unit
全国	**Total**	**3903**	**6**	**177**	**3720**	**1366**	**1107**	**1430**
北京	Beijing	89			89	49	39	1
天津	Tianjin	9			9	2	4	3
河北	Hebei	129	1	6	122	43	40	46
山西	Shanxi	80	1	5	74	25	33	22
内蒙古	Inner Mongolia	152		8	144	29	93	30
辽宁	Liaoning	180		11	169	61	37	82
吉林	Jilin	41		9	32	14	12	15
黑龙江	Heilongjiang	105		8	97	40	28	37
上海	Shanghai	184			184	8	27	149
江苏	Jiangsu	745		5	740	505	56	184
浙江	Zhejiang	823		20	803	192	312	319
安徽	Anhui	105		13	92	21	25	59
福建	Fujian	79	1	5	73	18	20	41
江西	Jiangxi	16	1	1	14	5	6	5
山东	Shandong	447		14	433	117	151	179
河南	Henan	45	1	4	40	27	13	5
湖北	Hubei	112		10	102	27	32	53
湖南	Hunan	99		8	91	44	17	38
广东	Guangdong	111		10	101	53	16	42
广西	Guangxi	15		1	14	6	7	2
海南	Hainan	3		1	2	2		1
重庆	Chongqing	36			36	7	14	15
四川	Sichuan	61		10	51	5	25	31
贵州	Guizhou	13			13	6		7
云南	Yunnan	26		6	20	10	11	5
西藏	Tibet							
陕西	Shaanxi	78		7	71	21	47	10
甘肃	Gansu	38		5	33	3	20	15
青海	Qinghai	34		2	32	9	11	14
宁夏	Ningxia	8		3	5	4	1	3
新疆	Xinjiang	16		2	14	6	6	4
新疆兵团	Xinjiang Corps	18		2	16	5	2	11
黑龙江农垦	Heilongjiang Land Reclamation	6	1	1	4	2	2	2

4-4　续表 1　Continued 1

地区	Region	寄宿制托养服务 Boarding Fostering Services				
		托养残疾人 PWDs in the Boarding Fostering Institutions	智力残疾人 Persons with Intellectual Disability	精神残疾人 Persons with Psychiatric Disability	其他类别残疾人 Persons with Other Disabilities	重度残疾人 Persons with Severe Disabilities
		人 person	人 person	人 person	人 person	人 person
全　国	**Total**	**112850**	**32712**	**30882**	**49256**	**29322**
北　京	Beijing	2041	457	876	708	202
天　津	Tianjin	162	59	49	54	40
河　北	Hebei	3655	801	1575	1279	401
山　西	Shanxi	1371	502	489	380	240
内蒙古	Inner Mongolia	3572	1065	528	1979	1137
辽　宁	Liaoning	8312	2903	2329	3080	1796
吉　林	Jilin	828	536	236	56	34
黑龙江	Heilongjiang	4347	1034	1008	2305	2252
上　海	Shanghai	5764	2521	1500	1743	1081
江　苏	Jiangsu	15593	6067	2741	6785	3772
浙　江	Zhejiang	11950	2184	3045	6721	5187
安　徽	Anhui	1943	486	466	991	525
福　建	Fujian	2691	776	1253	662	494
江　西	Jiangxi	845	285	181	379	172
山　东	Shandong	15662	4873	3818	6971	3490
河　南	Henan	3597	1089	794	1714	954
湖　北	Hubei	1277	541	409	327	206
湖　南	Hunan	3552	1275	1159	1118	673
广　东	Guangdong	5863	1582	1789	2492	929
广　西	Guangxi	1141	282	587	272	118
海　南	Hainan	546	99	267	180	
重　庆	Chongqing	1199	204	653	342	291
四　川	Sichuan	2117	511	845	761	298
贵　州	Guizhou	868	73	657	138	87
云　南	Yunnan	1343	119	780	444	118
西　藏	Tibet					
陕　西	Shaanxi	3609	801	1028	1780	757
甘　肃	Gansu	1826	475	414	937	428
青　海	Qinghai	4020	425	157	3438	3222
宁　夏	Ningxia	263	102	77	84	45
新　疆	Xinjiang	1792	468	343	981	267
新疆兵团	Xinjiang Corps	780	101	539	140	104
黑龙江农垦	Heilongjiang Land Reclamation	321	16	290	15	2

4-4 续表 2 Continued 2

地 区	Region	日间照料托养服务 Day-Care Fostering Service						本年度享受居家托养服务残疾人 PWDs Recieving Fostering Service at Home in 2012
		日间照料托养服务机构 Day-Care Fostering Institutions	托养残疾人 PWDs in the Institutions	智力残疾人 Persons with Intellectual Disability	精神残疾人 Persons with Psychiatric Disability	其他类别残疾人 Persons with Other Disabilities	重度残疾人 Persons with Severe Disabilities	
		个 unit	人 person	人 person	人 person	人 person	人 person	人 person
全 国	**Total**	**3372**	**73902**	**35140**	**17478**	**21284**	**9929**	**560127**
北 京	Beijing	257	1569	864	376	329	289	17584
天 津	Tianjin	70	1137	644	227	266	157	9985
河 北	Hebei	30	529	141	209	179	64	12102
山 西	Shanxi	41	556	152	151	253	223	8483
内蒙古	Inner Mongolia	60	482	157	51	274	184	14297
辽 宁	Liaoning	152	2681	1737	292	652	309	21813
吉 林	Jilin	25	203	65	23	115	94	13796
黑龙江	Heilongjiang	30	375	266	55	54	20	9346
上 海	Shanghai	430	13689	9990	2479	1220	68	17811
江 苏	Jiangsu	797	15175	6808	3247	5120	2784	58412
浙 江	Zhejiang	290	5149	1769	1419	1961	1709	42929
安 徽	Anhui	30	994	201	309	484	346	13075
福 建	Fujian	38	1152	649	133	370	151	17268
江 西	Jiangxi	2	113	69	26	18	18	9837
山 东	Shandong	105	2494	968	556	970	482	32922
河 南	Henan		160	60	35	65	59	12170
湖 北	Hubei	82	2832	1251	685	896	361	13472
湖 南	Hunan	44	1497	570	404	523	239	15814
广 东	Guangdong	442	12037	4474	3471	4092	1028	23952
广 西	Guangxi	26	1260	560	349	351	175	21228
海 南	Hainan	2	110	15	90	5	1	7688
重 庆	Chongqing	83	848	247	304	297	176	10689
四 川	Sichuan	185	4301	1768	1289	1244	278	45348
贵 州	Guizhou	2	50	14	5	31	18	11811
云 南	Yunnan	17	271	85	107	79	45	13457
西 藏	Tibet							7816
陕 西	Shaanxi	31	1870	800	375	695	264	18252
甘 肃	Gansu	14	711	292	208	211	66	13248
青 海	Qinghai	5	98	14	10	74	74	9730
宁 夏	Ningxia	33	906	248	452	206	189	11991
新 疆	Xinjiang	46	541	238	70	233	55	17820
新疆兵团	Xinjiang Corps	2	100	24	71	5	3	4820
黑龙江农垦	Heilongjiang Land Reclamation	1	12			12		1161

5-1　农村贫困残疾人扶持效果
Poverty Alleviation for PWDs in Rural Areas

地　区	Region	贫困残疾人扶持效果 Results of Assisting PWDs to Get Rid of Poverty				残疾人实用技术培训 Training on Applied Technologies for PWDs	
		本年扶持贫困残疾人户 Poor Households with Disabled Member Assisted in 2012	本年扶持贫困残疾人 PWDs Assisted in 2012	本年实际脱贫 Rural PWDs who Got Rid of Poverty in 2012	本年返贫 Reimpoverished PWDs in 2012	本年度培训残疾人 Training on Applied Technologies for PWDs in 2012	本年度培训投入经费 Fund for Training on Applied Technologies for PWDs in 2012
		万户 10,000 households	万人次 10,000 person-times	万人 10,000 persons	万人 10,000 persons	万人次 10,000 person-times	万元 10,000 Yuan
全　国	**Total**	**146.10**	**229.92**	**137.32**	**22.80**	**86.13**	**26104.0**
北　京	Beijing	0.41	0.51	0.36	0.12	0.54	47.6
天　津	Tianjin	1.42	1.71			0.29	82.6
河　北	Hebei	16.84	19.92	13.60	1.72	4.80	1588.8
山　西	Shanxi	5.99	9.48	4.04	1.34	2.09	691.5
内蒙古	Inner Mongolia	2.05	4.35	3.98	0.74	1.72	828.5
辽　宁	Liaoning	4.96	7.26	3.90	0.49	1.77	544.7
吉　林	Jilin	1.64	2.22	1.42	0.15	5.91	978.4
黑龙江	Heilongjiang	1.47	2.09	1.41	0.11	1.68	188.1
上　海	Shanghai	0.60	0.96	0.05		0.33	166.8
江　苏	Jiangsu	3.75	4.09	1.35	0.17	1.82	1093.7
浙　江	Zhejiang	14.14	17.69	1.88	0.52	2.16	1198.0
安　徽	Anhui	7.28	12.82	3.32	0.78	2.37	590.2
福　建	Fujian	2.28	3.29	1.68	0.19	9.28	1166.1
江　西	Jiangxi	2.56	4.02	6.77	0.44	0.72	387.8
山　东	Shandong	4.99	8.22	5.54	0.36	5.64	1789.6
河　南	Henan	6.22	17.61	9.70	0.96	6.36	1880.6
湖　北	Hubei	5.19	11.37	6.40	0.76	4.11	901.1
湖　南	Hunan	4.26	7.89	4.09	1.22	1.51	1265.3
广　东	Guangdong	3.14	6.16	3.69	0.20	2.01	944.4
广　西	Guangxi	1.80	3.78	8.66	0.60	3.23	738.1
海　南	Hainan	0.35	0.56	0.21	0.06	0.41	169.0
重　庆	Chongqing	3.90	5.60	8.22	1.55	1.85	736.1
四　川	Sichuan	14.74	23.34	12.96	2.48	8.72	2952.3
贵　州	Guizhou	7.78	13.28	7.52	1.55	1.36	588.5
云　南	Yunnan						1848.9
西　藏	Tibet	0.03	0.06	0.02		0.02	207.4
陕　西	Shaanxi	10.08	15.45	9.90	1.26	1.73	729.1
甘　肃	Gansu	7.28	10.75	10.18	2.40	4.52	769.1
青　海	Qinghai	1.06	1.32	0.74	0.22	0.62	172.2
宁　夏	Ningxia	1.36	1.54	1.13	0.16	0.70	161.4
新　疆	Xinjiang	1.79	2.65	0.82	0.17	2.09	370.1
新疆兵团	Xinjiang Corps	0.90	2.02	0.24	0.06	1.12	301.0
黑龙江农垦	Heilongjiang Land Reclamation	0.26	0.53	0.15		0.05	27.2

5-2 扶贫资金与残疾人扶贫贷款
Poverty Alleviation Fund and Loans

地 区	Region	扶贫资金 Poverty Alleviation Fund		残疾人扶贫贷款 Poverty Alleviation Fund and Loans		
				康复扶贫贴息贷款 Interest-subsidized Loans for Rehabilitation		
		省级财政投入 Poverty Alleviation Fund from the Provincial Budget	社会募集 Fund Raised From Society	本年度项目贷款实际落实 Actually Allocated Loans for Project in 2012	本年度项目贷款中央贴息实际落实 Interest Actually Allocated Subsidized by the Central Fiscal Budget for Project in 2012	本年度项目贷款扶持贫困残疾人 Poor PWDs Supported by Loans for Project in 2012
		万元 10,000 Yuan	万元 10,000 Yuan	万元 10,000 Yuan	万元 10,000 Yuan	人 person
全 国	**Total**	**14508.2**	**2723.0**	**57290.1**	**2771.2**	**23658**
北 京	Beijing	1732.0				
天 津	Tianjin	456.7				
河 北	Hebei	3.0	42.0	3460.0	173.0	1129
山 西	Shanxi	252.6		2800.0	120.0	1067
内蒙古	Inner Mongolia		30.0	1910.0	88.0	624
辽 宁	Liaoning	500.0	22.0	3200.0	160.0	1083
吉 林	Jilin		100.0	1550.0	75.3	222
黑龙江	Heilongjiang	46.0	4.3	2455.5	143.6	901
上 海	Shanghai					
江 苏	Jiangsu	540.0	273.9	1050.0	52.5	319
浙 江	Zhejiang	2296.0	1391.1	1410.8	70.0	823
安 徽	Anhui	553.9	2.4	2870.0	131.0	1038
福 建	Fujian	1171.8	31.0	2998.7	87.5	1338
江 西	Jiangxi	20.0	30.5	2860.0	143.0	812
山 东	Shandong	106.1	40.0	2280.0	114.0	748
河 南	Henan		3.6	3140.0	157.0	1854
湖 北	Hubei	68.8	12.0	2800.0	140.0	947
湖 南	Hunan	200.0	110.3	2570.0	128.5	729
广 东	Guangdong	201.2	95.4	1050.0	52.5	710
广 西	Guangxi	2831.2	43.8	330.6	16.5	39
海 南	Hainan	152.5		12.5		1
重 庆	Chongqing	2403.0	336.2	1750.0	87.5	633
四 川	Sichuan	448.1	33.1	2982.0	160.5	2144
贵 州	Guizhou	40.4	2.0	1163.0	58.0	115
云 南	Yunnan		36.0	2100.0	105.0	836
西 藏	Tibet					
陕 西	Shaanxi		10.0	3210.0	160.5	1310
甘 肃	Gansu	360.0	2.0	2640.0	132.0	880
青 海	Qinghai		0.2	1171.0	58.6	147
宁 夏	Ningxia		32.1	1336.0	66.8	1024
新 疆	Xinjiang	55.0	15.1	1670.0	63.0	1884
新疆兵团	Xinjiang Corps	70.0		400.0	20.0	275
黑龙江农垦	Heilongjiang Land Reclamation		24.1	120.0	7.0	26.0

5-2 续表 Continued

地区 Region	残疾人扶贫贷款 Poverty Alleviation Fund and Loans					
	康复扶贫贴息贷款 Interest-subsidized Loans for Rehabilitation			其他贷款 Other Loans		
	本年度到户贷款实际落实 Loans Actually Allocated to the Households in 2012	本年度到户贷款中央贴息实际落实 Interest Actually Allocated subsidized by the Central Fiscal Budget to the Households in 2012	本年度到户贷款扶持贫困残疾人 Poor PWDs Supported by Loans to the Households in 2012	残疾人贷款资金 Loans for PWDs	残疾人贷款贴息资金 Interest-subsidized Loans for PWDs	本年度扶持 Poor PWDs Supported by Loans in 2012
	万元 10,000 Yuan	万元 10,000 Yuan	人 person	万元 10,000 Yuan	万元 10,000 Yuan	人 person
全国 Total	**45332.4**	**3185.3**	**31083**	**55324.9**	**2707.9**	**11988**
北京 Beijing						
天津 Tianjin				9100.0	325.2	2610
河北 Hebei	2600.0	182.0	2009	737.8	9.8	346
山西 Shanxi	2401.9	166.0	1555	40.5	1.3	38
内蒙古 Inner Mongolia	2482.6	198.0	8163	125.0		25
辽宁 Liaoning	2300.0	161.0	1079			
吉林 Jilin	2328.8	160.2	1408			63
黑龙江 Heilongjiang	1813.7	122.0	933			
上海 Shanghai						
江苏 Jiangsu	750.0	52.5	437	268.0		126
浙江 Zhejiang	1400.0	70.0	323	29816.7	1475.0	2289
安徽 Anhui	1929.8	131.0	295	2.0		1
福建 Fujian	663.0	87.5	856	964.5	79.7	269
江西 Jiangxi	2043.0	143.0	313		5.0	
山东 Shandong	1700.0	119.0	467	1708.0	31.9	89
河南 Henan	2363.0	164.0	1253			
湖北 Hubei	2000.0	140.0	1820	247.0	16.0	126
湖南 Hunan	2750.0	192.5	1001	3645.0	182.3	1631
广东 Guangdong	750.0	52.5	150			
广西 Guangxi	849.6	59.5	548	630.0	15.5	366
海南 Hainan	5.0		1			1
重庆 Chongqing	1250.0	87.5	372			
四川 Sichuan	2396.9	160.5	1627	806.0	50.4	1557
贵州 Guizhou	1110.0	75.5	509	150.0	6.3	101
云南 Yunnan	1500.0	105.0	661	8.0	1.8	23
西藏 Tibet						
陕西 Shaanxi	2293.0	160.5	1100			
甘肃 Gansu	1200.0	84.0	600			
青海 Qinghai	835.0	58.5	355			
宁夏 Ningxia	717.1	50.2	384	9.0	0.1	63
新疆 Xinjiang	2100.0	147.0	2513	500.4	20.7	362
新疆兵团 Xinjiang Corps	800.0	56.0	351	6567.1	487.1	1902
黑龙江农垦 Heilongjiang Land Reclamation						

5-3 社会帮扶与残疾人扶贫基地建设

Social Assistance and Construction of Poverty Alleviation Bases

地区	Region	社会帮扶 Social Assistance for Needy PWDs		残疾人扶贫基地建设 Poverty Alleviation bases for PWDs		
		结对帮扶单位 Companies or Units who Assisted PWDs in One-to-one way	结对帮扶个人 Individuals who Assisted PWDs in One-to-one way	残疾人扶贫基地 Poverty Alleviation Bases for PWDs	安置残疾人就业 Providing Employment for Disabled Persons	扶持带动贫困残疾人 Supporting and Leading Disabled Persons
		个 unit	人 person	个 unit	人 person	户 household
全　国	**Total**	**64473**	**412649**	**5226**	**101963**	**257565**
北　京	Beijing	177	2137	121	3646	5190
天　津	Tianjin	184	403	154	2010	2559
河　北	Hebei	1245	7001	126	2115	7363
山　西	Shanxi	688	2964	305	5091	6746
内蒙古	Inner Mongolia	2680	6259	85	2229	3100
辽　宁	Liaoning	4066	21948	54	1018	2654
吉　林	Jilin	2062	4941	154	2232	7327
黑龙江	Heilongjiang	3243	4933	104	3387	2611
上　海	Shanghai	127	410	64	1504	3668
江　苏	Jiangsu	2062	11283	412	9651	13734
浙　江	Zhejiang	3680	13255	916	7464	29302
安　徽	Anhui	819	4428	59	1594	2922
福　建	Fujian	2555	4714	141	5211	5130
江　西	Jiangxi	2600	12286	149	1753	2397
山　东	Shandong	4233	18300	787	16054	41786
河　南	Henan	4679	101702	190	8767	12430
湖　北	Hubei	1061	5360	100	2791	12104
湖　南	Hunan	1531	11101	157	3876	14311
广　东	Guangdong	1082	11792	87	3820	5947
广　西	Guangxi	5648	7457	122	1057	11347
海　南	Hainan	16		9	117	449
重　庆	Chongqing	981	13283	56	933	1771
四　川	Sichuan	5573	25180	316	5306	25823
贵　州	Guizhou	969	18246	62	544	4421
云　南	Yunnan	2016	19695	80	735	3520
西　藏	Tibet	4	30			
陕　西	Shaanxi	1402	6934	210	3283	12277
甘　肃	Gansu	5187	65172	43	1806	8516
青　海	Qinghai	339	774	31	1121	993
宁　夏	Ningxia	316	1360	24	685	3185
新　疆	Xinjiang	1991	5721	98	1918	3570
新疆兵团	Xinjiang Corps	1148	2885	8	100	346
黑龙江农垦	Heilongjiang Land Reclamation	109	695	2	145	66

5-4 农村贫困残疾人危房改造

House Renovation for Poor PWDs in Rural Areas

地 区	Region	本年度危房改造实际完成 Houses Renovated for PWDs in 2012	本年度危房改造项目受益贫困残疾人 Poor PWDs who Benefited by House Renovation Project in 2012	本年度投入资金 Fund Input in Houses Renovation in 2012	省级投入资金 Fund from the Provincial Budgets	地市级投入资金 Fund from the Prefectural/ City Level Budgets	县级投入资金 Fund from the County Level Budgets
		户 household	人 person	万元 10,000 Yuan	万元 10,000 Yuan	万元 10,000 Yuan	万元 10,000 Yuan
全 国	**Total**	**132368**	**157074**	**118588.1**	**60232.7**	**16199.8**	**42155.6**
北 京	Beijing	792	859	501.4	89.7	157.8	253.9
天 津	Tianjin	101	127	205.0	131.5		73.5
河 北	Hebei	5410	6586	4750.9	1738.8	1225.8	1786.3
山 西	Shanxi	4860	5594	2369.5	990.0	665.0	714.5
内蒙古	Inner Mongolia	7685	8595	8774.6	2043.8	2704.7	4026.1
辽 宁	Liaoning	1790	2228	568.3		205.9	362.4
吉 林	Jilin	2365	2715	1653.9	849.3	383.8	420.8
黑龙江	Heilongjiang	1687	2177	1680.3	331.8	627.5	721.0
上 海	Shanghai	355	355	218.5	2.9		215.6
江 苏	Jiangsu	1072	1247	518.0	200.0	3.3	314.7
浙 江	Zhejiang	4496	5603	4029.9	106.9	142.9	3780.1
安 徽	Anhui	3887	4775	2336.6	1461.4	12.0	863.2
福 建	Fujian	2849	5274	3862.3	1479.4	587.7	1795.2
江 西	Jiangxi	4416	5267	1175.9	916.7	129.8	129.4
山 东	Shandong	4918	6452	5150.2	2052.4	1733.2	1364.6
河 南	Henan	5200	8133	1622.5	1297.0	106.5	219.0
湖 北	Hubei	1753	2364	857.7	677.4	42.0	138.3
湖 南	Hunan	4725	5657	2460.1	299.1	160.6	2000.4
广 东	Guangdong	2630	2992	2643.7	970.2	969.9	703.6
广 西	Guangxi	12964	15823	12247.6	8394.2	1318.5	2534.9
海 南	Hainan	1406	1671	1483.6	612.8	24.0	846.8
重 庆	Chongqing	4847	5295	5722.0	1638.0		4084.0
四 川	Sichuan	5161	5560	5559.2	2624.7	372.8	2561.7
贵 州	Guizhou	3267	3587	1259.3	536.4	182.2	540.7
云 南	Yunnan	6411	6857	8966.6	6861.7	667.1	1437.7
西 藏	Tibet	500	514	300.0	300.0		
陕 西	Shaanxi	2923	3815	1754.1	400.0	702.0	652.0
甘 肃	Gansu	10235	12771	10851.3	6000.0	1336.2	3515.1
青 海	Qinghai	2346	2593	2759.8	2404.8	30.3	324.7
宁 夏	Ningxia	1560	1714	2006.2	1687.1	10.0	309.1
新 疆	Xinjiang	15214	15276	8902.2	2284.3	1468.3	5149.6
新疆兵团	Xinjiang Corps	3799	3849	11298.5	10850.5	224.0	224.0
黑龙江农垦	Heilongjiang Land Reclamation	744	749	98.6		6.0	92.6

6-1 地、州、盟(不含地级市)专门协会建立情况
Establishment of Special Associations in Prefectures

地 区	Region	盲人协会 Associations of Persons with Visual Disability Established	聋人协会 Associatins of Persons with Hearing Disability Established	肢残人协会 Association of Persons with Physical Disability Established	智力残疾人及亲友协会 Associations of Persons with Intellectual Disability and Their Relatives and Friends Established	精神残疾人及亲友协会 Associations of Persons with Ppsychiatric Disability and Their Relatives and Friends Established	备注 Remarks
		个 unit	个 unit	个 unit	个 unit	个 unit	个 unit
全 国	**Total**	**60**	**59**	**64**	**58**	**58**	**3**
北 京	Beijing						
天 津	Tianjin						
河 北	Hebei						
山 西	Shanxi						
内蒙古	Inner Mongolia	4	4	4	3	3	1
辽 宁	Liaoning						
吉 林	Jilin	1	1	1	1	1	
黑龙江	Heilongjiang	1	1	1	1	1	
上 海	Shanghai						
江 苏	Jiangsu						
浙 江	Zhejiang						
安 徽	Anhui	1	1	1	1	1	
福 建	Fujian						
江 西	Jiangxi						
山 东	Shandong						
河 南	Henan						
湖 北	Hubei	1	1	1	1	1	
湖 南	Hunan	3	3	3	3	3	
广 东	Guangdong						
广 西	Guangxi						
海 南	Hainan		1	1	1	1	
重 庆	Chongqing						
四 川	Sichuan	5	5	5	5	5	
贵 州	Guizhou	4	4	4	4	4	
云 南	Yunnan	8	8	8	8	8	
西 藏	Tibet	1		1			
陕 西	Shaanxi						
甘 肃	Gansu	3	3	3	3	3	
青 海	Qinghai	6	6	6	6	6	
宁 夏	Ningxia						
新 疆	Xinjiang	12	12	12	11	11	1
新疆兵团	Xinjiang Corps	10	9	13	10	10	1
黑龙江农垦	Heilongjiang Land Reclamation						

6-2　市(含地级市)专门协会建立情况

Establishment of Special Associations in Cities

地　区	Region	盲人协会 Associations of Persons with Visual Disability Established	聋人协会 Associatins of Persons with Hearing Disability Established	肢残人协会 Association of Persons with Physical Disability Established	智力残疾人及亲友协会 Associations of Persons with Intellectual Disability and Their Relatives and Friends Established	精神残疾人及亲友协会 Associations of Persons with Ppsychiatric Disability and Their Relatives and Friends Established	备注 Remarks
		个 unit	个 unit	个 unit	个 unit	个 unit	个 unit
全　国	**Total**	**284**	**284**	**285**	**275**	**275**	**8**
北　京	Beijing						
天　津	Tianjin						
河　北	Hebei	11	11	11	11	11	
山　西	Shanxi	9	9	10	9	9	
内蒙古	Inner Mongolia	8	8	8	6	6	2
辽　宁	Liaoning	14	14	14	14	14	
吉　林	Jilin	8	8	8	8	8	
黑龙江	Heilongjiang	12	12	12	12	12	
上　海	Shanghai						
江　苏	Jiangsu	13	13	13	13	13	
浙　江	Zhejiang	11	11	11	8	8	3
安　徽	Anhui	16	16	16	15	15	1
福　建	Fujian	9	9	9	8	8	1
江　西	Jiangxi	6	6	6	6	6	
山　东	Shandong	17	17	17	15	15	1
河　南	Henan	18	18	18	18	18	
湖　北	Hubei	12	12	12	12	12	
湖　南	Hunan	12	12	12	12	12	
广　东	Guangdong	21	21	21	21	21	
广　西	Guangxi	14	14	14	14	14	
海　南	Hainan	2	2	2	2	2	
重　庆	Chongqing						
四　川	Sichuan	17	17	17	17	17	
贵　州	Guizhou	5	5	5	5	5	
云　南	Yunnan	8	8	8	8	8	
西　藏	Tibet						
陕　西	Shaanxi	10	10	10	10	10	
甘　肃	Gansu	12	12	12	12	12	
青　海	Qinghai	1	1	1	1	1	
宁　夏	Ningxia	5	5	5	5	5	
新　疆	Xinjiang	4	4	4	4	4	
新疆兵团	Xinjiang Corps						
黑龙江农垦	Heilongjiang Land Reclamation	9	9	9	9	9	

6-3 市辖区专门协会建立情况

Establishment of Special Associations in Districts under Cities

地区	Region	盲人协会 Associations of Persons with Visual Disability Established	聋人协会 Associatins of Persons with Hearing Disability Established	肢残人协会 Association of Persons with Physical Disability Established	智力残疾人及亲友协会 Associations of Persons with Intellectual Disability and Their Relatives and Friends Established	精神残疾人及亲友协会 Associations of Persons with Ppsychiatric Disability and Their Relatives and Friends Established	备注 Remarks
		个 unit	个 unit	个 unit	个 unit	个 unit	个 unit
全 国	**Total**	**839**	**838**	**840**	**809**	**810**	**24**
北 京	Beijing	14	14	14	14	14	
天 津	Tianjin	16	16	16	16	16	
河 北	Hebei	36	36	36	35	35	1
山 西	Shanxi	18	18	18	16	16	2
内蒙古	Inner Mongolia	18	18	18	18	18	
辽 宁	Liaoning	60	60	60	60	60	
吉 林	Jilin	23	22	23	22	22	
黑龙江	Heilongjiang	68	68	68	68	68	
上 海	Shanghai	16	16	16	16	16	
江 苏	Jiangsu	57	57	57	56	57	
浙 江	Zhejiang	32	32	32	20	21	10
安 徽	Anhui	35	35	36	34	33	
福 建	Fujian	25	25	25	20	20	5
江 西	Jiangxi	12	12	12	12	12	
山 东	Shandong	53	53	53	52	52	
河 南	Henan	51	51	51	51	51	
湖 北	Hubei	34	34	34	29	29	5
湖 南	Hunan	34	34	34	34	34	
广 东	Guangdong	54	54	54	54	54	
广 西	Guangxi	34	34	34	34	34	
海 南	Hainan	4	4	4	4	4	
重 庆	Chongqing	20	20	20	19	19	1
四 川	Sichuan	39	39	39	39	39	
贵 州	Guizhou	10	10	10	10	10	
云 南	Yunnan	12	12	12	12	12	
西 藏	Tibet						
陕 西	Shaanxi	25	25	25	25	25	
甘 肃	Gansu	17	17	17	17	17	
青 海	Qinghai	4	4	4	4	4	
宁 夏	Ningxia	7	7	7	7	7	
新 疆	Xinjiang	11	11	11	11	11	
新疆兵团	Xinjiang Corps						
黑龙江农垦	Heilongjiang Land Reclamation						

6-4 县(含县级市)专门协会建立情况
Establishment of Special Associations in Counties

地 区	Region	盲人协会 Associations of Persons with Visual Disability Established	聋人协会 Associatins of Persons with Hearing Disability Established	肢残人协会 Association of Persons with Physical Disability Established	智力残疾人及亲友协会 Associations of Persons with Intellectual Disability and Their Relatives and Friends Established	精神残疾人及亲友协会 Associations of Persons with Ppsychiatric Disability and Their Relatives and Friends Established	备注 Remarks
		个 unit	个 unit	个 unit	个 unit	个 unit	个 unit
全 国	**Total**	**1906**	**1892**	**1924**	**1841**	**1842**	**43**
北 京	Beijing	2	2	2	2	2	
天 津	Tianjin	3	3	3	3	3	
河 北	Hebei	135	135	135	134	134	1
山 西	Shanxi	80	80	80	79	78	2
内蒙古	Inner Mongolia	82	82	82	76	76	6
辽 宁	Liaoning	44	44	44	44	44	
吉 林	Jilin	40	40	40	40	40	
黑龙江	Heilongjiang	64	64	64	64	64	
上 海	Shanghai	1	1	1	1	1	
江 苏	Jiangsu	49	49	49	49	49	
浙 江	Zhejiang	56	56	58	44	43	10
安 徽	Anhui	50	48	53	47	48	
福 建	Fujian	58	58	58	50	50	8
江 西	Jiangxi	61	60	61	60	59	
山 东	Shandong	89	84	87	80	80	2
河 南	Henan	108	108	108	108	108	
湖 北	Hubei	62	58	61	54	54	1
湖 南	Hunan	80	79	80	77	77	2
广 东	Guangdong	69	69	69	68	68	
广 西	Guangxi	75	75	75	75	75	
海 南	Hainan	15	15	15	15	15	
重 庆	Chongqing	18	18	18	17	17	1
四 川	Sichuan	113	112	114	112	112	1
贵 州	Guizhou	71	70	72	70	70	
云 南	Yunnan	108	108	112	102	102	5
西 藏	Tibet	1					
陕 西	Shaanxi	83	83	83	77	79	
甘 肃	Gansu	69	69	69	69	69	
青 海	Qinghai	37	37	37	37	36	
宁 夏	Ningxia	13	13	13	12	12	1
新 疆	Xinjiang	83	83	83	80	80	3
新疆兵团	Xinjiang Corps						
黑龙江农垦	Heilongjiang Land Reclamation	87	89	98	95	97	

7-1 盲人按摩
Blind Massage

地 区	Region	保健按摩人员本年度培训 Blind Health-care Masseurs Trained in 2012	医疗按摩人员本年度培训 Blind Therapeutical Masseurs Trained in 2012	按摩机构 Institutions of Blind Massage	
				医疗按摩机构 Therapeutical Blind Massage Clinics	保健按摩机构 Health-care Blind Massage Houses
		人 person	人 person	人 person	人 person
全 国	**Total**	**16514**	**4925**	**848**	**12887**
北 京	Beijing	509	98	2	489
天 津	Tianjin	36	25	4	159
河 北	Hebei	785	782	55	364
山 西	Shanxi	402	95	49	354
内蒙古	Inner Mongolia	272	142	29	205
辽 宁	Liaoning	635	138	22	1067
吉 林	Jilin	843	598	36	262
黑龙江	Heilongjiang	281	72	23	207
上 海	Shanghai	403	8		115
江 苏	Jiangsu	668	87	19	753
浙 江	Zhejiang	327	205	21	932
安 徽	Anhui	566	77	89	226
福 建	Fujian	854	166	4	273
江 西	Jiangxi	286	47	64	307
山 东	Shandong	665	284	81	1153
河 南	Henan	1193	624	86	444
湖 北	Hubei	596	62	41	720
湖 南	Hunan	1220	254	17	456
广 东	Guangdong	506	195	6	697
广 西	Guangxi	628	126	7	156
海 南	Hainan	183	75	2	120
重 庆	Chongqing	581	75	29	610
四 川	Sichuan	1131	60	36	1028
贵 州	Guizhou	368	17	3	329
云 南	Yunnan	564	83	11	623
西 藏	Tibet	22			17
陕 西	Shaanxi	1008	288	68	284
甘 肃	Gansu	236	64	26	182
青 海	Qinghai	270	58	1	146
宁 夏	Ningxia	289	22		104
新 疆	Xinjiang	149	98	9	77
新疆兵团	Xinjiang Corps	38		7	26
黑龙江农垦	Heilongjiang Land Reclamation			1	2

7-1　续表　Continued

地　区	Region	盲人医疗按摩人员专业技术职务任职资格评审 Vocational Qualification Appraisal for the Blind Therapeutical Masseurs		盲人保健按摩人员就业 Employed Blind Health-care Masseurs	盲人医疗按摩人员就业 Employed Blind Therapeutical Masseurs	扶持特困盲人按摩师就业 Employed Blind Masseurs in Poverty Assisted in 2012
		中级 Middle Level Blind Therapeutical Masseurs	初级 Junior Level Blind Therapeutical Masseurs			
		人 person	人 person	人 person	人 person	人 person
全　国	**Total**	**551**	**1655**	**24962**	**2805**	**8078**
北　京	Beijing	5	18	1641	165	31
天　津	Tianjin			502	22	44
河　北	Hebei	14	146	826	410	320
山　西	Shanxi	2	13	321	62	174
内蒙古	Inner Mongolia			420	120	288
辽　宁	Liaoning	71	84	646	115	160
吉　林	Jilin			747	228	416
黑龙江	Heilongjiang	49	52	418	40	137
上　海	Shanghai			365	21	
江　苏	Jiangsu	28	63	916	43	198
浙　江	Zhejiang	86	228	1805	72	216
安　徽	Anhui	62	102	842	71	283
福　建	Fujian	54	129	1384	158	298
江　西	Jiangxi	40	111	610	30	197
山　东	Shandong		167	1054	208	659
河　南	Henan	9	9	776	172	941
湖　北	Hubei	42	158	1188	147	629
湖　南	Hunan	31	102	917	177	816
广　东	Guangdong			2335	83	143
广　西	Guangxi	35	113	799	11	248
海　南	Hainan	8	28	150	2	14
重　庆	Chongqing		1	1014	184	137
四　川	Sichuan			2336	49	487
贵　州	Guizhou		10	1018	18	307
云　南	Yunnan		6	506		311
西　藏	Tibet			16		
陕　西	Shaanxi		22	501	86	210
甘　肃	Gansu			236	57	145
青　海	Qinghai	2	29	258	8	220
宁　夏	Ningxia			271	19	20
新　疆	Xinjiang		55	125	24	18
新疆兵团	Xinjiang Corps	9	4	14	3	11
黑龙江农垦	Heilongjiang Land Reclamation	4	5	5		

8-1 宣传文化
Publicity and Culture

地 区	Region	宣传 Publicity					
		省级 at Provincial Level					
		中央级媒体采用稿件 Articles Used by Central Media	主要新闻媒体刊播稿件 Articles Used by Major Media	报纸专版 Features in Newspapers	广播电台残疾人专题栏目 Radio Broadcast Special Programs on Disability	电视手语栏目 Sign Language TV Programmes	电视公益广告片 Advertisement for Public Interest on TV
		件 piece	件 piece	个 unit	个 unit	个 unit	个 unit
全 国	**Total**	**745**	**10554**	**168**	**38**	**30**	**48**
北 京	Beijing	150	420	61	7	1	13
天 津	Tianjin	6	1820	6	1	1	
河 北	Hebei		613	3	1	1	2
山 西	Shanxi		302	5	1		
内蒙古	Inner Mongolia	16	41			1	
辽 宁	Liaoning	26	466	23	1	1	5
吉 林	Jilin	5	306	1		1	
黑龙江	Heilongjiang	36	380	3	1	1	1
上 海	Shanghai	8	50	1	1	2	3
江 苏	Jiangsu	16	270	8	1	2	3
浙 江	Zhejiang	5	67	1	1	1	5
安 徽	Anhui	30	505	3	1	1	1
福 建	Fujian	2	3	8	1	1	
江 西	Jiangxi	16	40	5	2	1	
山 东	Shandong	10	680	4	1	1	1
河 南	Henan	5	100	3	1	1	1
湖 北	Hubei	14	1300		1	1	
湖 南	Hunan	10	22			1	3
广 东	Guangdong	3	80	3	1	1	
广 西	Guangxi		98	5	1	1	
海 南	Hainan				3		
重 庆	Chongqing	35	70	5	1	1	1
四 川	Sichuan	10	90	1	5	1	
贵 州	Guizhou						
云 南	Yunnan		253	13	1	1	1
西 藏	Tibet		25				
陕 西	Shaanxi	227	398			1	2
甘 肃	Gansu	50	510	2	1	1	
青 海	Qinghai	5	430		1	1	2
宁 夏	Ningxia	10	660	1	1	1	
新 疆	Xinjiang	50	260	3	1	1	1
新疆兵团	Xinjiang Corps		290			1	3
黑龙江农垦	Heilongjiang Land Reclamation		5				

8-1 续表 1 Continued 1

地 区 Region	宣传 Publicity					
	省级 at Provincial Level		地市级 at Prefectural/City Level			
	报纸公益广告 Advertisement for Public Interest on Newspaper	新促会 Societies for Promoting News Relating to PWDs	主要新闻媒体刊播稿件 Articles Used by Major Media	报纸专版 Features in Newspapers	广播电台残疾人专题栏目 Radio Broadcast Special Programs on Disability	电视手语栏目 Sign Language TV Programmes
	个 unit	个 unit	件 piece	个 unit	个 unit	个 unit
全 国 Total	**53**	**28**	**44398**	**1375**	**468**	**184**
北 京 Beijing		1	886	76	9	2
天 津 Tianjin		1	283	13	10	3
河 北 Hebei	1		3241	74	12	11
山 西 Shanxi			1512	17	11	1
内蒙古 Inner Mongolia		1	1294	10	17	7
辽 宁 Liaoning	3	1	6137	33	9	9
吉 林 Jilin		1	1484	21	16	4
黑龙江 Heilongjiang		1	323	12	24	3
上 海 Shanghai		1	249	20	10	13
江 苏 Jiangsu	10	1	2300	145	27	14
浙 江 Zhejiang	5	1	4027	34	16	14
安 徽 Anhui	3	1	2156	28	12	14
福 建 Fujian	1	1	600	33	8	11
江 西 Jiangxi		1	612	6	3	4
山 东 Shandong		1	3221	42	12	7
河 南 Henan	2	1	396	219	58	3
湖 北 Hubei		1	1120	130	14	3
湖 南 Hunan	5	1	3087	94	31	1
广 东 Guangdong		1	1317	22	16	6
广 西 Guangxi		1	668	19	10	4
海 南 Hainan		1	15		1	1
重 庆 Chongqing	1	1	506	53	7	5
四 川 Sichuan		1	1691	133	38	5
贵 州 Guizhou		1	291	5	2	2
云 南 Yunnan		1	1323	28	9	7
西 藏 Tibet			9			
陕 西 Shaanxi	1	1	832	11	7	15
甘 肃 Gansu		1	2586	26	42	9
青 海 Qinghai	1	1	151	25	8	
宁 夏 Ningxia		1	324	21	5	2
新 疆 Xinjiang	5	1	1078	20	24	4
新疆兵团 Xinjiang Corps	15		564	5		
黑龙江农垦 Heilongjiang Land Reclamation			115			

8-1 续表 2 Continued 2

地区	Region	宣传 Publicity			文化 Culture		
		地市级 at Prefectural/City Level			省级 at Provincial Level		
		电视公益广告片 Advertisement for Public Interest on TV	报纸公益广告 Advertisement for Public Interest on Newspaper	新促会 Societies for Promoting News Relating to PWDs	公共图书馆盲文及盲人有声读物图书室 Reading Rooms with Braille and Audio Reading Materials in Public Library	残疾人文化周 Culture Week for PWDs	残疾人文化艺术类比赛及展览 Cultural or Art Competitions and Exhibitions of PWDs
		个 unit	个 unit	个 unit	个 unit	场次 time	次 time
全国	**Total**	**255**	**453**	**115**	**48**	**122**	**154**
北京	Beijing	5	6		5	17	43
天津	Tianjin	1	2	2	2	1	3
河北	Hebei	16	15	6	1	11	12
山西	Shanxi	2	3	3	2	2	4
内蒙古	Inner Mongolia	3	3	2	1	1	2
辽宁	Liaoning	16	20	3	1	1	1
吉林	Jilin	8	11	5	5	3	1
黑龙江	Heilongjiang	10	21	3	1	1	2
上海	Shanghai		4	1	1	12	5
江苏	Jiangsu	39	153	9	1	5	15
浙江	Zhejiang	16	21	10	1	1	5
安徽	Anhui	7	22	3	1	1	2
福建	Fujian	4	4	7	2	1	1
江西	Jiangxi	6	3		1	2	3
山东	Shandong	7	10	7	1	1	5
河南	Henan	1		13	3	1	5
湖北	Hubei	9	28		1	1	4
湖南	Hunan	16	57	4	5	6	6
广东	Guangdong	26	4	9	2	20	3
广西	Guangxi	3	2	1	1	1	1
海南	Hainan				1		
重庆	Chongqing	2	5	1	1	1	1
四川	Sichuan	24	40			12	10
贵州	Guizhou	3	3	5			
云南	Yunnan	2	1	9	1	1	1
西藏	Tibet					2	
陕西	Shaanxi	12	5	3	1	1	2
甘肃	Gansu	7	5	6	1	1	9
青海	Qinghai				1	10	3
宁夏	Ningxia	6	5		1	1	1
新疆	Xinjiang	4		3	3	2	3
新疆兵团	Xinjiang Corps					1	1
黑龙江农垦	Heilongjiang Land Reclamation					1	

8-1　续表 3　Continued 3

地　区	Region	文化 Culture 省级 at Provincial Level 残疾人艺术团 PWDs' Performing Art Troupes 个 unit	地市级 at Prefectural/City Level 公共图书馆盲文及盲人有声读物图书室 Reading Rooms with Braille and Audio Reading Materials in Public Library 个 unit	残疾人文化周 Culture Week for PWDs 场次 time	残疾人文化艺术类比赛及展览 Cultural or Art Competitions and Exhibitions of PWDs 次 time	残疾人艺术团 PWDs' Performing Art Troupes 个 unit
全　国	**Total**	**25**	**431**	**1660**	**971**	**263**
北　京	Beijing	1	14	120	94	38
天　津	Tianjin	3	19	12	38	14
河　北	Hebei		15	107	40	6
山　西	Shanxi		10	43	24	6
内蒙古	Inner Mongolia		16	43	24	7
辽　宁	Liaoning		18	91	55	9
吉　林	Jilin	5	9	73	21	5
黑龙江	Heilongjiang	1	23	23	33	11
上　海	Shanghai	1	24	97	85	32
江　苏	Jiangsu	1	17	68	87	16
浙　江	Zhejiang	1	13	18	22	12
安　徽	Anhui		18	63	20	10
福　建	Fujian	1	27	16	32	5
江　西	Jiangxi	1	9	10	11	6
山　东	Shandong	1	20	35	22	9
河　南	Henan	1	15	81	32	2
湖　北	Hubei	1	8	56	38	5
湖　南	Hunan		25	100	99	24
广　东	Guangdong	1	19	73	23	9
广　西	Guangxi		6	13	5	3
海　南	Hainan	1		7		
重　庆	Chongqing		13	84	26	8
四　川	Sichuan	1	38	33	29	3
贵　州	Guizhou		11	64	12	1
云　南	Yunnan	1	10	73	16	10
西　藏	Tibet			2		
陕　西	Shaanxi	1	17	30	15	4
甘　肃	Gansu	1	5	27	25	1
青　海	Qinghai		2	10	4	1
宁　夏	Ningxia		5	10	11	2
新　疆	Xinjiang	1	5	59	21	4
新疆兵团	Xinjiang Corps			17	3	
黑龙江农垦	Heilongjiang Land Reclamation			102	4	

9-1 体 育

Sports

地 区	Region	省级 at Provincial Level					
		残疾人群众体育健身活动 Massive Sports and Fitness Activities for PWDs	残疾人群众体育健身活动参加人数 Participation in Massive Sports and Fitness Activities for PWDs	残疾人群众体育活动示范点 Sports Activity Demonstration Sites for PWDs	残疾人体育健身指导员 Coaches for Fitness Activity for PWDs	残疾人体育比赛 Sports Events for PWDs	参赛残疾人运动员 Disabled Athletes who Participated in the Sports Events
		次 time	人次 person-time	个 unit	人 person	次 time	人次 person-time
全 国	**Total**	**218**	**49384**	**351**	**2836**	**80**	**12574**
北 京	Beijing	8	4532	35	850	5	362
天 津	Tianjin	8	4000	13	165	9	2300
河 北	Hebei	15	630	27	52	10	660
山 西	Shanxi	2	380	1	132	1	162
内蒙古	Inner Mongolia						
辽 宁	Liaoning				137		
吉 林	Jilin	2	5800	10	76		
黑龙江	Heilongjiang	1	500		10		
上 海	Shanghai	25	4100	58	120	20	3900
江 苏	Jiangsu	5	2560	11	150	1	400
浙 江	Zhejiang	5	1500	1	20	1	800
安 徽	Anhui				85	1	227
福 建	Fujian	30	2800	30	50	1	200
江 西	Jiangxi	3	650	1	40	1	218
山 东	Shandong	1	50	11	78	1	45
河 南	Henan	2	1200	5	50	2	200
湖 北	Hubei	10	1500	25	240	1	80
湖 南	Hunan	6	312	5	28	4	721
广 东	Guangdong	10	1200	22	54	2	200
广 西	Guangxi			2	39	2	305
海 南	Hainan						
重 庆	Chongqing	2	1800	10	5	1	39
四 川	Sichuan	2	7000	5	10	2	500
贵 州	Guizhou	1	80	10		2	245
云 南	Yunnan	2	920	8	95		
西 藏	Tibet						
陕 西	Shaanxi	49	4000	25	189	8	280
甘 肃	Gansu	15	1900	28	47	2	410
青 海	Qinghai	4	1000	3	11	3	320
宁 夏	Ningxia	3	320	5	100		
新 疆	Xinjiang	6	600				
新疆兵团	Xinjiang Corps	1	50		3		
黑龙江农垦	Heilongjiang Land Reclamation						

9-1　续表　Continued

地　区	Region	省级 at Provincial Level			地市级 at Prefectural/City Level			
		残疾人体育训练基地 Sports Training Bases for PWDs	残疾人体育训练基地在编人员 Full-time Staff at Sports Training Bases for PWDs	聘任教练员 Stable Coaches	残疾人体育活动 Sports Activity of PWDs	残疾人体育活动参加残疾人 Participants with Disabilities in Sports Activity of PWDs	残疾人群众体育活动示范点 Sports Activity Demonstration Sites for PWDs	残疾人体育健身指导员 Coaches for Fitness Activity for PWDs
		个 unit	人 person	人 person	次 time	人次 person-time	个 unit	人 person
全　国	**Total**	**200**	**525**	**700**	**3953**	**525485**	**1040**	**6616**
北　京	Beijing	10	65	28	1391	66594	68	455
天　津	Tianjin	3	42	14	156	6832	31	435
河　北	Hebei	16	50	53	107	10106	56	456
山　西	Shanxi			18	73	2047	18	130
内蒙古	Inner Mongolia	3	18	6	42	1152	8	12
辽　宁	Liaoning	28	50	25	100	41837	40	358
吉　林	Jilin	16	46	10	56	5057	128	234
黑龙江	Heilongjiang	3		8	13	2043		140
上　海	Shanghai	5	16	160	610	266402	148	518
江　苏	Jiangsu	1	20	31	71	5722	92	58
浙　江	Zhejiang	4	50	20	74	6205	66	311
安　徽	Anhui	1	3	15	84	4102	41	56
福　建	Fujian	15	38	58	51	3425	23	251
江　西	Jiangxi	2	8	13	13	815	4	9
山　东	Shandong	4	36	12	82	5018	35	309
河　南	Henan	6	6	20	88	7314	18	426
湖　北	Hubei	10	10	24	180	6630	6	36
湖　南	Hunan	8	8	16	103	6757	36	140
广　东	Guangdong	9		27	103	10206	18	123
广　西	Guangxi	1		6	22	2559	8	249
海　南	Hainan				5	400	1	1
重　庆	Chongqing	5	5	15	278	26863	74	76
四　川	Sichuan	5	5	30	59	4913	58	1529
贵　州	Guizhou	4	8	11	14	1078	2	2
云　南	Yunnan			18	41	11454	15	58
西　藏	Tibet							
陕　西	Shaanxi	25	25	12	61	3386	23	73
甘　肃	Gansu	9	9	26	27	8332	9	96
青　海	Qinghai	1	1	5	2	346		1
宁　夏	Ningxia	2	2	5	9	390	10	48
新　疆	Xinjiang	4	4	12	31	6365	4	14
新疆兵团	Xinjiang Corps			2	7	1135		12
黑龙江农垦	Heilongjiang Land Reclamation							

10-1 法规体系
Legal System

地 区	Region	省级修订《残疾人保障法实施办法》Revision of the Implementation Method of the Law on the Protection of PWDs	制定或修改关于残疾人的专门法规、规章 Laws and Regulations Enacted or Reviewed Specially for PWDs	省级 at Provincial Level	地市级 at Prefectural/ City Level	制定或修改保障残疾人权益的规范性文件 Regulations Enacted Or Reviewed Directly Related to PWDs	省级 at Provincial Level	地市级 at Prefectural/ City Level	县级 at County Level
		个 unit	个 unit	个 unit	个 unit	个 unit	个 unit	个 unit	个 unit
全 国	**Total**	**12**	**30**	**5**	**25**	**706**	**61**	**109**	**536**
北 京	Beijing								
天 津	Tianjin	1				10	7		3
河 北	Hebei		4	1	3	36	6	5	25
山 西	Shanxi					19		4	15
内蒙古	Inner Mongolia	1				6	1		5
辽 宁	Liaoning		1		1	12		5	7
吉 林	Jilin		1		1	30		3	27
黑龙江	Heilongjiang		1		1	6		2	4
上 海	Shanghai					1			1
江 苏	Jiangsu	1				50		6	44
浙 江	Zhejiang		2		2	43	2	3	38
安 徽	Anhui					21	1	7	13
福 建	Fujian					26	3	7	16
江 西	Jiangxi		2		2	26		5	21
山 东	Shandong	1	3	1	2	51		7	44
河 南	Henan	1	2		2	23		11	12
湖 北	Hubei	1	1		1	26		2	24
湖 南	Hunan					21		2	19
广 东	Guangdong					20	2	9	9
广 西	Guangxi	1				9		2	7
海 南	Hainan					1			1
重 庆	Chongqing					36	1		35
四 川	Sichuan	1				61	3	4	54
贵 州	Guizhou		1	1		9	1		8
云 南	Yunnan	1				10		1	9
西 藏	Tibet					2	1		1
陕 西	Shaanxi	1	1		1	8		2	6
甘 肃	Gansu	1	2	1	1	119	22	18	79
青 海	Qinghai		1	1		14	11	1	2
宁 夏	Ningxia		7		7	6		3	3
新 疆	Xinjiang	1	1		1	4			4
新疆兵团	Xinjiang Corps								
黑龙江农垦	Heilongjiang Land Reclamation								

10-2 执法检查
Inspections on Law Enforcement

地 区	Region	人大执法检查或专题调研 Inspections and Investigations by Officials of People's Congresses	省级 at Provincial Level	地市级 at Prefectural/City Level	县级 at County Level
		次 time	次 time	次 time	次 time
全 国	**Total**	**923**	**33**	**159**	**731**
北 京	Beijing	5			5
天 津	Tianjin	17	1		16
河 北	Hebei	76	1	10	65
山 西	Shanxi	55	1	10	44
内蒙古	Inner Mongolia	13		2	11
辽 宁	Liaoning	32		8	24
吉 林	Jilin	14	1	3	10
黑龙江	Heilongjiang	19	1	6	12
上 海	Shanghai	3	1		2
江 苏	Jiangsu	47	1	7	39
浙 江	Zhejiang	62	1	9	52
安 徽	Anhui	39	1	8	30
福 建	Fujian	41	1	7	33
江 西	Jiangxi	24	1	2	21
山 东	Shandong	77	5	10	62
河 南	Henan	32	1	12	19
湖 北	Hubei	35	1	7	27
湖 南	Hunan	42	1	5	36
广 东	Guangdong	20	1	3	16
广 西	Guangxi	15	1	5	9
海 南	Hainan	5	1	2	2
重 庆	Chongqing	28	1		27
四 川	Sichuan	48	1	7	40
贵 州	Guizhou	23	1	2	20
云 南	Yunnan	23	1	1	21
西 藏	Tibet	1	1		
陕 西	Shaanxi	20	1	4	15
甘 肃	Gansu	52	1	9	42
青 海	Qinghai	14	1	2	11
宁 夏	Ningxia	12	1	2	9
新 疆	Xinjiang	14	1	2	11
新疆兵团	Xinjiang Corps	15	1	14	
黑龙江农垦	Heilongjiang Land Reclamation				

10-2 续表 Continued

地区	Region	政协视察或专题调研 Inspections and Investigations by Officials of People's Political Consultative Conferences	省级 at Provincial Level	地市级 at Prefectural/City Level	县级 at County Level
		次 time	次 time	次 time	次 time
全国	**Total**	**810**	**12**	**111**	**687**
北京	Beijing	5			5
天津	Tianjin	2			2
河北	Hebei	69	1	9	59
山西	Shanxi	33		4	29
内蒙古	Inner Mongolia	14			14
辽宁	Liaoning	33		10	23
吉林	Jilin	17		4	13
黑龙江	Heilongjiang	16	1	2	13
上海	Shanghai	5	3		2
江苏	Jiangsu	46		9	37
浙江	Zhejiang	68		6	62
安徽	Anhui	54		12	42
福建	Fujian	33		2	31
江西	Jiangxi	27	2	3	22
山东	Shandong	57		5	52
河南	Henan	28		4	24
湖北	Hubei	35		8	27
湖南	Hunan	43		3	40
广东	Guangdong	14	1	7	6
广西	Guangxi	7		3	4
海南	Hainan	8		5	3
重庆	Chongqing	30	1		29
四川	Sichuan	53	1	5	47
贵州	Guizhou	9	1	1	7
云南	Yunnan	24		1	23
西藏	Tibet				
陕西	Shaanxi	14			14
甘肃	Gansu	41		5	36
青海	Qinghai	4		1	3
宁夏	Ningxia	7		1	6
新疆	Xinjiang	14	1	1	12
新疆兵团	Xinjiang Corps				
黑龙江农垦	Heilongjiang Land Reclamation				

10-3　法制宣传
Publicity on Laws

地　区	Region	普法宣传教育活动 Activities for Laws Publicity and Education	省级 at Provincial Level	地市级 at Prefectural/ City Level	县级 at County Level	普法宣传教育活动参加人数 Participatients of Activities for Laws Publicity and Education	省级 at Provincial Level	地市级 at Prefectural/ City Level	县级 at County Level
		次 time	次 time	次 time	次 time	人 person	人 person	人 person	人 person
全　国	**Total**	**8925**	**74**	**789**	**8062**	**928274**	**18671**	**117570**	**792033**
北　京	Beijing	66	2		64	12470	700		11770
天　津	Tianjin	49	2		47	2534	210		2324
河　北	Hebei	325	2	43	280	45143	2000	5734	37409
山　西	Shanxi	170	1	36	133	28055	55	2544	25456
内蒙古	Inner Mongolia	178		27	151	18153		2340	15813
辽　宁	Liaoning	216	3	31	182	20734	160	3329	17245
吉　林	Jilin	180	2	17	161	20896	550	4072	16274
黑龙江	Heilongjiang	152	1	22	129	14103	20	3043	11040
上　海	Shanghai	86	5		81	11435	800		10635
江　苏	Jiangsu	481	1	24	456	52176	60	3596	48520
浙　江	Zhejiang	178	2	20	156	20280	200	2010	18070
安　徽	Anhui	297	1	35	261	14185	20	1743	12422
福　建	Fujian	251	3	20	228	21648	834	3790	17024
江　西	Jiangxi	132	1	17	114	12084	76	806	11202
山　东	Shandong	277	2	52	223	31353	1800	8566	20987
河　南	Henan	228		36	192	49478		6103	43375
湖　北	Hubei	246	4	32	210	36623	600	4894	31129
湖　南	Hunan	243	1	25	217	14306	120	1404	12782
广　东	Guangdong	227	1	63	163	17721	2500	4524	10697
广　西	Guangxi	212	13	19	180	56550	1579	5185	49786
海　南	Hainan	25	3	3	19	1758	111	60	1587
重　庆	Chongqing	225	2		223	69757	180		69577
四　川	Sichuan	559	4	64	491	81719	280	1687	79752
贵　州	Guizhou	2674	1	14	2659	28594	1500	1013	26081
云　南	Yunnan	294	1	18	275	30492	1200	706	28586
西　藏	Tibet	46	1	20	25	11192	850	6358	3984
陕　西	Shaanxi	146	1	22	123	14064	70	2951	11043
甘　肃	Gansu	184	3	41	140	63259	396	3972	58891
青　海	Qinghai	66	7	7	52	5739	315	324	5100
宁　夏	Ningxia	45		10	35	2696		273	2423
新　疆	Xinjiang	253	1	27	225	65391	320	12695	52376
新疆兵团	Xinjiang Corps	154	1	30	123	50761	300	22825	27636
黑龙江农垦	Heilongjiang Land Reclamation	60	2	14	44	2925	865	1023	1037

10-3 续表 Continued

地 区	Region	残疾人工作者法律培训班 Training Courses for Laws	省级 at Provincial Level	地市级 at Prefectural/ City Level	县级 at County Level	法律培训班参加人数 Trainees of Laws Courses	省级 at Provincial Level	地市级 at Prefectural/ City Level	县级 at County Level
		次 time	次 time	次 time	次 time	人 person	人 person	人 person	人 person
全 国	**Total**	**1576**	**27**	**193**	**1356**	**87922**	**2287**	**16387**	**69248**
北 京	Beijing	24	1		23	2301	401		1900
天 津	Tianjin	20	2		18	1158	150		1008
河 北	Hebei	104	1	14	89	4663	47	983	3633
山 西	Shanxi	80	1	24	55	4225	150	1108	2967
内蒙古	Inner Mongolia	42		3	39	1882		113	1769
辽 宁	Liaoning	87	1	22	64	7754	120	4490	3144
吉 林	Jilin	50	2	4	44	2480	140	237	2103
黑龙江	Heilongjiang	28	1	4	23	1030	3	316	711
上 海	Shanghai	22			22	3465			3465
江 苏	Jiangsu	79		8	71	4761		580	4181
浙 江	Zhejiang	61		6	55	4206		764	3442
安 徽	Anhui	56		8	48	1880		484	1396
福 建	Fujian	57	2	4	51	4447	58	610	3779
江 西	Jiangxi	46	1	7	38	1982	65	147	1770
山 东	Shandong	136	2	14	120	5498	200	1153	4145
河 南	Henan	79		9	70	4971		1415	3556
湖 北	Hubei	67	1	8	58	3254	70	804	2380
湖 南	Hunan	78	1	7	70	2912	120	514	2278
广 东	Guangdong	39		11	28	2057		566	1491
广 西	Guangxi	41	2	2	37	2672	95	132	2445
海 南	Hainan	7	1	1	5	495	45	72	378
重 庆	Chongqing	41	1		40	3856	60		3796
四 川	Sichuan	111	1	10	100	5512	4	600	4908
贵 州	Guizhou	32	1	3	28	1893	100	164	1629
云 南	Yunnan	43	1	3	39	1935	180	201	1554
西 藏	Tibet	2		2		76		76	
陕 西	Shaanxi	19	1	3	15	1769	70	339	1360
甘 肃	Gansu	45	1	9	35	2319	99	225	1995
青 海	Qinghai	15		2	13	373		24	349
宁 夏	Ningxia	22		3	19	483		176	307
新 疆	Xinjiang	39	1	2	36	1515	50	94	1371
新疆兵团	Xinjiang Corps								
黑龙江农垦	Heilongjiang Land Reclamation	4	1		3	98	60		38

10-4 法律救助
Legal Aid

地 区	Region	建立残疾人法律救助协调组织 Legal Assistance and Coordination Organization for PWDs			
		建立残疾人法律救助工作协调机构 Legal Assistance and Coordination Organization for PWDs	省级 at Provincial Level	地市级 at Prefectural/ City Level	县级 at County Level
		个 unit	个 unit	个 unit	个 unit
全 国	**Total**	**1188**	**25**	**188**	**975**
北 京	Beijing	8	1		7
天 津	Tianjin	17	1		16
河 北	Hebei	129	1	11	117
山 西	Shanxi	24	1	7	16
内蒙古	Inner Mongolia	40		2	38
辽 宁	Liaoning	62	1	13	48
吉 林	Jilin	32	1	4	27
黑龙江	Heilongjiang	9	1	3	5
上 海	Shanghai	6	1		5
江 苏	Jiangsu	52	1	8	43
浙 江	Zhejiang	40		2	38
安 徽	Anhui	28	1	3	24
福 建	Fujian	44	1	7	36
江 西	Jiangxi	18	1	2	15
山 东	Shandong	39		8	31
河 南	Henan	65	1	17	47
湖 北	Hubei	78	1	17	60
湖 南	Hunan	68	1	11	56
广 东	Guangdong	33	1	6	26
广 西	Guangxi	17	1	6	10
海 南	Hainan				
重 庆	Chongqing	41	1		40
四 川	Sichuan	85	1	15	69
贵 州	Guizhou	37	1	6	30
云 南	Yunnan				
西 藏	Tibet				
陕 西	Shaanxi	23		9	14
甘 肃	Gansu	77	1	15	61
青 海	Qinghai	55	1	8	46
宁 夏	Ningxia	8		2	6
新 疆	Xinjiang	46	1	2	43
新疆兵团	Xinjiang Corps	2	1	1	
黑龙江农垦	Heilongjiang Land Reclamation	5	1	3	1

10-4 续表 1 Continued 1

地区	Region	残疾人法律救助工作站 Legal Assistance Station for PWDs			
		残疾人法律救助工作站 Legal Assistance Station for PWDs	省级 at Provincial Level	地市级 at Prefectural/City Level	县级 at County Level
		个 unit	个 unit	个 unit	个 unit
全　国	**Total**	**811**	**14**	**126**	**671**
北　京	Beijing	4			4
天　津	Tianjin	17	1		16
河　北	Hebei	129	1	11	117
山　西	Shanxi	27		6	21
内蒙古	Inner Mongolia	27		3	24
辽　宁	Liaoning	42	1	14	27
吉　林	Jilin	8		3	5
黑龙江	Heilongjiang	5		1	4
上　海	Shanghai	5	1		4
江　苏	Jiangsu	52	1	9	42
浙　江	Zhejiang	32		3	29
安　徽	Anhui	13			13
福　建	Fujian	36		5	31
江　西	Jiangxi	23	1	2	20
山　东	Shandong	37		6	31
河　南	Henan	43		5	38
湖　北	Hubei	36	1	6	29
湖　南	Hunan	68	1	11	56
广　东	Guangdong	8		3	5
广　西	Guangxi	25	1	7	17
海　南	Hainan	2			2
重　庆	Chongqing	14			14
四　川	Sichuan	43	1	9	33
贵　州	Guizhou	15		2	13
云　南	Yunnan	2	1	1	
西　藏	Tibet				
陕　西	Shaanxi	1			1
甘　肃	Gansu	76	1	15	60
青　海	Qinghai				
宁　夏	Ningxia	4	1	1	2
新　疆	Xinjiang	16	1	2	13
新疆兵团	Xinjiang Corps	1		1	
黑龙江农垦	Heilongjiang Land Reclamation				

10-4　续表 2　Continued 2

地　区	Region	残疾人法律救助工作站 Legal Assistance Station for PWDs			
		残疾人法律救助工作站办理的案件 Cases Handled by the Legal Assistance Stations for PWDs	省级 at Provincial Level	地市级 at Prefectural/City Level	县级 at County Level
		件 case	件 case	件 case	件 case
全　国	**Total**	**6453**	**610**	**1405**	**4438**
北　京	Beijing	155			155
天　津	Tianjin	461	107		354
河　北	Hebei	1101	22	559	520
山　西	Shanxi	174		93	81
内蒙古	Inner Mongolia	46		6	40
辽　宁	Liaoning	210	12	92	106
吉　林	Jilin	45		6	39
黑龙江	Heilongjiang	27		20	7
上　海	Shanghai	14			14
江　苏	Jiangsu	180	1	29	150
浙　江	Zhejiang	331		19	312
安　徽	Anhui	193			193
福　建	Fujian	292		31	261
江　西	Jiangxi	102	12	17	73
山　东	Shandong	278		103	175
河　南	Henan	202		26	176
湖　北	Hubei	600	257	89	254
湖　南	Hunan	348	12	56	280
广　东	Guangdong	32		20	12
广　西	Guangxi	145	13	63	69
海　南	Hainan	2			2
重　庆	Chongqing	522			522
四　川	Sichuan	313	4	99	210
贵　州	Guizhou	32		2	30
云　南	Yunnan	7	6	1	
西　藏	Tibet				
陕　西	Shaanxi				
甘　肃	Gansu	495	160	41	294
青　海	Qinghai				
宁　夏	Ningxia	31	1	10	20
新　疆	Xinjiang	98	3	6	89
新疆兵团	Xinjiang Corps	17		17	
黑龙江农垦	Heilongjiang Land Reclamation				

10-4 续表 3 Continued 3

地 区	Region	残疾人法律援助中心(工作站) Legal Aid Centers (Station) for PWDs			
		残疾人法律援助中心(工作站) Legal Aid Centers (Station) for PWDs	省级 at Provincial Level	地市级 at Prefectural/ City Level	县级 at County Level
		个 unit	个 unit	个 unit	个 unit
全 国	**Total**	**2979**	**29**	**326**	**2624**
北 京	Beijing	17	1		16
天 津	Tianjin				
河 北	Hebei	186	1	11	174
山 西	Shanxi	120		10	110
内蒙古	Inner Mongolia	102	1	12	89
辽 宁	Liaoning	115	1	14	100
吉 林	Jilin	66	1	8	57
黑龙江	Heilongjiang	119	1	13	105
上 海	Shanghai	18	1		17
江 苏	Jiangsu	115	1	13	101
浙 江	Zhejiang	98	1	11	86
安 徽	Anhui	113	1	15	97
福 建	Fujian	93	1	9	83
江 西	Jiangxi	94	1	9	84
山 东	Shandong	153	1	17	135
河 南	Henan	165	1	17	147
湖 北	Hubei	92	1	11	80
湖 南	Hunan	118	1	13	104
广 东	Guangdong	123	1	21	101
广 西	Guangxi	119	1	14	104
海 南	Hainan	17		2	15
重 庆	Chongqing	41	1		40
四 川	Sichuan	136	1	15	120
贵 州	Guizhou	88	1	8	79
云 南	Yunnan	135	1	15	119
西 藏	Tibet	8	1	7	
陕 西	Shaanxi	106	1	9	96
甘 肃	Gansu	96	1	15	80
青 海	Qinghai	55	1	8	46
宁 夏	Ningxia	24	1	5	18
新 疆	Xinjiang	86	1	8	77
新疆兵团	Xinjiang Corps	158	1	15	142
黑龙江农垦	Heilongjiang Land Reclamation	3		1	2

10-4　续表 4　Continued 4

地　区	Region	残疾人法律援助中心(工作站)办理的案件 Cases Handled by Legal Aid Centers(Stations)	省级 at Provincial Level	地市级 at Prefectural/City Level	县级 at County Level
		残疾人法律法律援助中心(工作站) Legal Aid Center(Station) for PWDs			
		件 case	件 case	件 case	件 case
全　国	**Total**	**24550**	**328**	**5307**	**18915**
北　京	Beijing	323	42		281
天　津	Tianjin				
河　北	Hebei	2626	27	1223	1376
山　西	Shanxi	753		434	319
内蒙古	Inner Mongolia	370	1	73	296
辽　宁	Liaoning	1016	1	236	779
吉　林	Jilin	413	11	73	329
黑龙江	Heilongjiang	642	5	149	488
上　海	Shanghai	228	2		226
江　苏	Jiangsu	1038	1	163	874
浙　江	Zhejiang	1069	15	171	883
安　徽	Anhui	1180	14	202	964
福　建	Fujian	1104	8	194	902
江　西	Jiangxi	906	13	95	798
山　东	Shandong	1454		377	1077
河　南	Henan	705		232	473
湖　北	Hubei	1187	126	230	831
湖　南	Hunan	857	6	68	783
广　东	Guangdong	529	12	157	360
广　西	Guangxi	629	4	101	524
海　南	Hainan	63		10	53
重　庆	Chongqing	1403			1403
四　川	Sichuan	1186	4	183	999
贵　州	Guizhou	238	1	14	223
云　南	Yunnan	1596	10	189	1397
西　藏	Tibet	2		2	
陕　西	Shaanxi	452	13	180	259
甘　肃	Gansu	1077	5	70	1002
青　海	Qinghai	197	4	15	178
宁　夏	Ningxia	264	1	178	85
新　疆	Xinjiang	844	2	186	656
新疆兵团	Xinjiang Corps	139		99	40
黑龙江农垦	Heilongjiang Land Reclamation	60		3	57

10-5 参政议政

PWDs Participating in the Administration and Discussion of State Affairs

地区	Region	人大代表和政协委员 Disabled deputies of People's Congresses and Committee Members of People's Political Consultative Conferences			
		人大代表 Disabled Deputies of the People's Congresses	省级 at Provincial Level	地市级 at Prefectural/City Level	县级 at County Level
		人 person	人 person	人 person	人 person
全　国	**Total**	**1849**	**37**	**218**	**1594**
北　京	Beijing	29	1		28
天　津	Tianjin	27			27
河　北	Hebei	100	4	14	82
山　西	Shanxi	78	2	5	71
内蒙古	Inner Mongolia	87		6	81
辽　宁	Liaoning	76	2	8	66
吉　林	Jilin	58	1	6	51
黑龙江	Heilongjiang	54	3	5	46
上　海	Shanghai	9	1		8
江　苏	Jiangsu	91		15	76
浙　江	Zhejiang	169	3	23	143
安　徽	Anhui	71	2	6	63
福　建	Fujian	47		6	41
江　西	Jiangxi	20		1	19
山　东	Shandong	78	1	6	71
河　南	Henan	51		8	43
湖　北	Hubei	101		33	68
湖　南	Hunan	121	1	11	109
广　东	Guangdong	46	1	14	31
广　西	Guangxi	29	1	5	23
海　南	Hainan	5	1		4
重　庆	Chongqing	57			57
四　川	Sichuan	124	2	8	114
贵　州	Guizhou	84	2	7	75
云　南	Yunnan	81	2	5	74
西　藏	Tibet	4		3	1
陕　西	Shaanxi	49	1	11	37
甘　肃	Gansu	24	1	3	20
青　海	Qinghai	29	4	2	23
宁　夏	Ningxia	10		2	8
新　疆	Xinjiang	32	1	2	29
新疆兵团	Xinjiang Corps	8		3	5
黑龙江农垦	Heilongjiang Land Reclamation				

10-5　续表 1　Continued 1

地　区	Region	人大代表和政协委员 Disabled Deputies of People's Congresses and Committee Members of People's Political Consultative Conferences			
		政协委员 Disabled Committee Members of People's Political Consultative Conferences	省级 at Provincial Level	地市级 at Prefectural/City Level	县级 at County Level
		人 person	人 person	人 person	人 person
全　国	**Total**	**3408**	**71**	**455**	**2882**
北　京	Beijing	26	1		25
天　津	Tianjin	18	1		17
河　北	Hebei	257	6	21	230
山　西	Shanxi	161	3	12	146
内蒙古	Inner Mongolia	118	2	15	101
辽　宁	Liaoning	184	2	35	147
吉　林	Jilin	104	2	13	89
黑龙江	Heilongjiang	144	3	19	122
上　海	Shanghai	23	2		21
江　苏	Jiangsu	165	2	22	141
浙　江	Zhejiang	208	3	34	171
安　徽	Anhui	136	4	24	108
福　建	Fujian	116	3	11	102
江　西	Jiangxi	80		33	47
山　东	Shandong	173	1	20	152
河　南	Henan	91		14	77
湖　北	Hubei	131		29	102
湖　南	Hunan	172	1	18	153
广　东	Guangdong	126	2	33	91
广　西	Guangxi	70	1	8	61
海　南	Hainan	29	2		27
重　庆	Chongqing	84	1		83
四　川	Sichuan	193	5	24	164
贵　州	Guizhou	108	5	8	95
云　南	Yunnan	151	1	11	139
西　藏	Tibet	7	3	4	
陕　西	Shaanxi	109	2	10	97
甘　肃	Gansu	97	5	15	77
青　海	Qinghai	36	5	5	26
宁　夏	Ningxia	25	1	6	18
新　疆	Xinjiang	61	2	8	51
新疆兵团	Xinjiang Corps	5		3	2
黑龙江农垦	Heilongjiang Land Reclamation				

10-5 续表 2 Continued 2

地区	Region	协助提出建议、议案和提案 PWDs Assisting to Put Forward Proposals and Motions		办理人大政协建议、提案 Handling Proposals of Peoples' Congresses and Motions of People's Political Consultative Conferences	
		协助人大代表提出议案、建议 Proposals Put Forward at People's Congresses with Assistance of PWDs	协助政协委员提出提案 Motions Put forward at People's Political Consultative Conferences with Participation of PWDs	办理人大建议 Proposals of Peoples' Congresses Handled	办理政协提案 Motions of People's Political Consultative Conferences Handled
		件 case	件 case	件 case	件 case
全 国	**Total**	**569**	**1202**	**488**	**947**
北 京	Beijing		3	1	3
天 津	Tianjin	2	1	2	6
河 北	Hebei	29	58	24	40
山 西	Shanxi	34	78	23	32
内蒙古	Inner Mongolia	22	55	6	30
辽 宁	Liaoning	16	52	21	37
吉 林	Jilin	19	30	6	18
黑龙江	Heilongjiang	10	27	11	27
上 海	Shanghai	1	6	5	9
江 苏	Jiangsu	30	52	36	61
浙 江	Zhejiang	58	75	51	72
安 徽	Anhui	15	41	16	40
福 建	Fujian	19	48	17	46
江 西	Jiangxi	34	52	18	39
山 东	Shandong	21	72	40	60
河 南	Henan	12	35	11	38
湖 北	Hubei	35	56	31	48
湖 南	Hunan	38	70	32	48
广 东	Guangdong	33	51	42	63
广 西	Guangxi	6	25	5	17
海 南	Hainan	7	17	5	10
重 庆	Chongqing	34	37	15	27
四 川	Sichuan	30	61	20	39
贵 州	Guizhou	12	27	6	20
云 南	Yunnan	16	36	10	16
西 藏	Tibet		1		3
陕 西	Shaanxi	6	16	4	23
甘 肃	Gansu	13	53	8	33
青 海	Qinghai	6	1	5	2
宁 夏	Ningxia	1	15	3	12
新 疆	Xinjiang	9	42	12	27
新疆兵团	Xinjiang Corps	1	9	2	1
黑龙江农垦	Heilongjiang Land Reclamation				

10-6 无障碍环境建设
Accessible Environment Building

地 区	Region	无障碍建设与管理法规、政府令 Regulations and Decrees on Accessible Environment Building and Management	无障碍建设领导协调组织 Leading and Coordinating Bodies for Building Accessible Environment	系统开展无障碍建设市、县、区 Cities and Counties that Systematic Accessibility Construction has been Carried out	地市级 at Prefectural/City Level	县级 at County Level
		个 unit	个 unit	个 unit	个 unit	个 unit
全 国	**Total**	**438**	**1194**	**1084**	**165**	**919**
北 京	Beijing	2	13	16		16
天 津	Tianjin	9	17	16	16	
河 北	Hebei	43	128	183	11	172
山 西	Shanxi	16	43	66	11	55
内蒙古	Inner Mongolia	2	21			
辽 宁	Liaoning	6	39	5	4	1
吉 林	Jilin	12	22	12	4	8
黑龙江	Heilongjiang	3	15			
上 海	Shanghai	5	27	17		17
江 苏	Jiangsu	22	76	56	8	48
浙 江	Zhejiang	21	30	26	2	24
安 徽	Anhui	10	23	76	16	60
福 建	Fujian	24	57			
江 西	Jiangxi	7	29	58	11	47
山 东	Shandong	33	68	6	5	1
河 南	Henan	25	32	52	5	47
湖 北	Hubei	6	24			
湖 南	Hunan	19	32	6	6	
广 东	Guangdong	28	33	6	6	
广 西	Guangxi	10	33	126	14	112
海 南	Hainan	6	9	2	2	
重 庆	Chongqing	6	30	38		38
四 川	Sichuan	22	111	35	7	28
贵 州	Guizhou	14	16	26	2	24
云 南	Yunnan	18	37	74	5	69
西 藏	Tibet		2			
陕 西	Shaanxi	13	29	43	3	40
甘 肃	Gansu	39	69	101	15	86
青 海	Qinghai	1	55	11	3	8
宁 夏	Ningxia	5	17	23	5	18
新 疆	Xinjiang	9	43	2	2	
新疆兵团	Xinjiang Corps		5			
黑龙江农垦	Heilongjiang Land Reclamation	2	9	2	2	

10-6 续表 Continued

地区	Region	贫困残疾人家庭无障碍改造 Accessibility Renovation for Homes of Poor Disabled Persons	省级 at Provincial Level	地市级 at Prefectural/City Level	县级 at County Level	无障碍建设检查 Inspections on Accessibility	无障碍培训 Training on Accessibility
		个 unit	个 unit	户 household	户 household	次 time	人次 person-time
全 国	**Total**	**141471**	**20549**	**10333**	**110589**	**3354**	**33511**
北 京	Beijing	11559			11559	237	4699
天 津	Tianjin	1487			1487	60	484
河 北	Hebei	1357		160	1197	142	950
山 西	Shanxi	1873		200	1673	51	646
内蒙古	Inner Mongolia	7167		1100	6067	72	123
辽 宁	Liaoning	12147		812	11335	227	3720
吉 林	Jilin	1598			1598	23	353
黑龙江	Heilongjiang	2634		110	2524	43	99
上 海	Shanghai	2848	450		2398	235	2469
江 苏	Jiangsu	17893		300	17593	168	5668
浙 江	Zhejiang	4112	300		3812	190	811
安 徽	Anhui	2228		400	1828	179	333
福 建	Fujian	2130		184	1946	93	1812
江 西	Jiangxi	1191		20	1171	28	135
山 东	Shandong	11278	3243	1565	6470	264	1284
河 南	Henan	1552		519	1033	132	366
湖 北	Hubei	1482		718	764	125	667
湖 南	Hunan	2234		120	2114	57	566
广 东	Guangdong	4718	103	2645	1970	94	1422
广 西	Guangxi	5251		3	5248	198	541
海 南	Hainan	500		50	450	30	113
重 庆	Chongqing	4960			4960	59	662
四 川	Sichuan	27348	14388	400	12560	184	3303
贵 州	Guizhou	1694	1100	249	345	57	168
云 南	Yunnan	697			697	86	466
西 藏	Tibet	200		100	100	6	
陕 西	Shaanxi	1680		10	1670	21	281
甘 肃	Gansu	1178		40	1138	73	54
青 海	Qinghai	1985	965		1020	29	60
宁 夏	Ningxia	1922		350	1572	29	219
新 疆	Xinjiang	2070		30	2040	141	848
新疆兵团	Xinjiang Corps	348		248	100	17	
黑龙江农垦	Heilongjiang Land Reclamation	150			150	4	189

10-7　残疾人机动轮椅车燃油补贴

Subsidy for Petrol Used by Motorized Wheelchairs of Disabled Persons

地　区	Region	残疾人机动轮椅车燃油补贴 Subsidy for Petrol Used by Motorized Wheelchairs of Disabled Persons	省级 at Provincial Level	地市级 at Prefectural/City level	县级 at County Level
		人 person	人 person	人 person	人 person
全　国	**Total**	**554349**	**35935**	**41735**	**476679**
北　京	Beijing	18475			18475
天　津	Tianjin	16075			16075
河　北	Hebei	12803		30	12773
山　西	Shanxi	17159		1594	15565
内蒙古	Inner Mongolia	17095		1019	16076
辽　宁	Liaoning	13682		50	13632
吉　林	Jilin	14103			14103
黑龙江	Heilongjiang	16314		619	15695
上　海	Shanghai	28297	14159		14138
江　苏	Jiangsu	22438		350	22088
浙　江	Zhejiang	15914	6000	1693	8221
安　徽	Anhui	26369		4467	21902
福　建	Fujian	13025		1163	11862
江　西	Jiangxi	16446		2514	13932
山　东	Shandong	21514		268	21246
河　南	Henan	51683		11859	39824
湖　北	Hubei	35527		3143	32384
湖　南	Hunan	26954		1168	25786
广　东	Guangdong	31407		6936	24471
广　西	Guangxi	13997			13997
海　南	Hainan	5734	373	349	5012
重　庆	Chongqing	3988			3988
四　川	Sichuan	22977	35	87	22855
贵　州	Guizhou	21524	11633	820	9071
云　南	Yunnan	12955			12955
西　藏	Tibet	2411		1525	886
陕　西	Shaanxi	8834		184	8650
甘　肃	Gansu	13976		545	13431
青　海	Qinghai	3715	3715		
宁　夏	Ningxia	14648		846	13802
新　疆	Xinjiang	10784		5	10779
新疆兵团	Xinjiang Corps	1990		483	1507
黑龙江农垦	Heilongjiang Land Reclamation	1536	20	18	1498

10-8 残疾人信访工作
Complaints by Letter and Visit

地区	Region	来信 Complaint Letter					
		总计 Subtotal	涉法涉诉类 Complaints Related with Legal Lawsuit	康复类 Rehabilitation	教育类 Education	就业类 Employment	扶贫类 Poverty Alleviation
		件 case	件 case	件 case	件 case	件 case	件 case
全国	**Total**	**55498**	**2695**	**7953**	**2780**	**8077**	**10723**
北京	Beijing	7186	377	731	165	595	1632
天津	Tianjin	224	30	12	1	20	17
河北	Hebei	1309	160	208	113	333	234
山西	Shanxi	1776	68	495	137	319	198
内蒙古	Inner Mongolia	1047	40	86	99	190	263
辽宁	Liaoning	971	42	81	27	225	145
吉林	Jilin	826	40	140	44	158	153
黑龙江	Heilongjiang	1010	126	79	63	158	173
上海	Shanghai	1124	71	75	18	82	82
江苏	Jiangsu	1254	50	194	33	172	144
浙江	Zhejiang	1331	121	73	42	188	406
安徽	Anhui	2306	73	295	90	284	434
福建	Fujian	1097	95	103	59	178	194
江西	Jiangxi	718	24	143	33	132	80
山东	Shandong	1114	51	119	57	145	314
河南	Henan	669	31	95	33	111	125
湖北	Hubei	3151	145	340	72	385	489
湖南	Hunan	7877	243	1396	360	1504	2066
广东	Guangdong	2939	78	494	260	418	852
广西	Guangxi	1853	138	502	83	330	161
海南	Hainan	380	26	40	30	55	64
重庆	Chongqing	305	20	26	21	34	22
四川	Sichuan	4637	271	436	140	661	779
贵州	Guizhou	1390	23	262	54	131	230
云南	Yunnan	1401	53	217	141	109	326
西藏	Tibet	221	1	58	34	56	40
陕西	Shaanxi	1984	69	278	212	305	349
甘肃	Gansu	1844	152	322	134	259	198
青海	Qinghai	91	13	13	9	7	27
宁夏	Ningxia	163	2	37	19	15	10
新疆	Xinjiang	2582	51	510	135	393	413
新疆兵团	Xinjiang Corps	627	11	73	51	97	96
黑龙江农垦	Heilongjiang Land Reclamation	91		20	11	28	7

10-8 续表 1 Continued 1

地 区	Region	来信 Complaint Letter				
		社会保障类 Social Security	文化体育类 Culture and Sports	机动车轮椅类 Motor Vehicle and Wheelchair	意见建议类 Opinions and Suggestions	其他类 Others
		件 case	件 case	件 case	件 case	件 case
全 国	**Total**	**10065**	**799**	**4665**	**1358**	**6383**
北 京	Beijing	1573	129	401	37	1546
天 津	Tianjin	101	1	1	1	40
河 北	Hebei	129	21	33	34	44
山 西	Shanxi	286	35	131	52	55
内蒙古	Inner Mongolia	180	6	83	33	67
辽 宁	Liaoning	292		36	21	102
吉 林	Jilin	170	7	89	2	23
黑龙江	Heilongjiang	286	3	42	40	40
上 海	Shanghai	283	18	92	179	224
江 苏	Jiangsu	247	19	55	54	286
浙 江	Zhejiang	285	10	43	36	127
安 徽	Anhui	689	51	169	94	127
福 建	Fujian	248	12	116	26	66
江 西	Jiangxi	120	11	72	32	71
山 东	Shandong	201	26	80	30	91
河 南	Henan	60	12	40	77	85
湖 北	Hubei	440	7	455	28	790
湖 南	Hunan	1097	99	558	213	341
广 东	Guangdong	525	24	144	43	101
广 西	Guangxi	233	24	252	18	112
海 南	Hainan	69	9	48	9	30
重 庆	Chongqing	64	4	14	15	85
四 川	Sichuan	757	41	250	84	1218
贵 州	Guizhou	281	20	320	12	57
云 南	Yunnan	342	3	85	11	114
西 藏	Tibet	16		12	4	
陕 西	Shaanxi	290	98	279	24	80
甘 肃	Gansu	281	20	307	17	154
青 海	Qinghai	11		3		8
宁 夏	Ningxia	39	1	20		20
新 疆	Xinjiang	292	56	383	109	240
新疆兵团	Xinjiang Corps	155	32	51	23	38
黑龙江农垦	Heilongjiang Land Reclamation	23		1		1

10-8 续表 2 Continued 2

地 区	Region	来访 Complaint Visit					
		总计 Subtotal	涉法涉诉类 Complaints Related with Legal Lawsuit	康复类 Rehabilitation	教育类 Education	就业类 Employment	扶贫类 Poverty Alleviation
		人次 person-time	人次 person-time	人次 person-time	人次 person-time	人次 person-time	人次 person-time
全 国	**Total**	**343957**	**16139**	**59194**	**18510**	**48527**	**58911**
北 京	Beijing	5574	836	370	176	525	762
天 津	Tianjin	2222	317	127	96	208	258
河 北	Hebei	8466	743	1786	540	1742	1417
山 西	Shanxi	15787	357	3168	926	1983	2327
内蒙古	Inner Mongolia	5888	58	914	584	743	1387
辽 宁	Liaoning	16130	1194	1867	573	1808	3588
吉 林	Jilin	4835	248	561	342	806	976
黑龙江	Heilongjiang	4674	374	570	272	930	635
上 海	Shanghai	3780	264	280	145	387	484
江 苏	Jiangsu	5206	131	575	231	910	594
浙 江	Zhejiang	9745	353	1545	649	1129	1600
安 徽	Anhui	16014	511	1723	697	2185	3217
福 建	Fujian	8953	3115	1574	330	843	902
江 西	Jiangxi	6775	272	1157	316	2121	1066
山 东	Shandong	5763	189	585	297	862	1091
河 南	Henan	7793	152	1085	357	1171	1237
湖 北	Hubei	22818	1699	2685	868	3229	3255
湖 南	Hunan	32494	1753	4927	1781	5270	5713
广 东	Guangdong	14273	299	2711	818	2455	2029
广 西	Guangxi	17058	265	4052	759	1780	2080
海 南	Hainan	2760	118	363	211	273	959
重 庆	Chongqing	4824	150	554	190	834	409
四 川	Sichuan	35032	1359	5935	1981	5077	6239
贵 州	Guizhou	9433	166	2760	375	1148	1389
云 南	Yunnan	22653	308	4834	1577	2412	3978
西 藏	Tibet	346		13	83	14	98
陕 西	Shaanxi	24678	391	5655	1316	3151	5274
甘 肃	Gansu	8215	280	1571	515	917	1871
青 海	Qinghai	564	26	79	21	98	189
宁 夏	Ningxia	2108	47	476	182	238	366
新 疆	Xinjiang	15007	128	3725	1058	2315	2677
新疆兵团	Xinjiang Corps	2803	34	375	218	476	760
黑龙江农垦	Heilongjiang Land Reclamation	1286	2	592	26	487	84

10-8 续表 3 Continued 3

地 区	Region	来访 Complaint Visit 社会保障类 Social Security	文化体育类 Culture and Sports	机动车轮椅类 Motor Vehicle and Wheelchair	意见建议类 Opinions and Suggestions	其他类 Others
		人次 person-time	人次 person-time	人次 person-time	人次 person-time	人次 person-time
全 国	**Total**	**60731**	**4951**	**34324**	**5718**	**36952**
北 京	Beijing	722	75	376	116	1616
天 津	Tianjin	564	18	77	6	551
河 北	Hebei	853	168	558	136	523
山 西	Shanxi	2907	364	1547	302	1906
内蒙古	Inner Mongolia	963	66	652	49	472
辽 宁	Liaoning	2427	215	2562	481	1415
吉 林	Jilin	605	34	779	24	460
黑龙江	Heilongjiang	1056	89	319	80	349
上 海	Shanghai	593	60	352	289	926
江 苏	Jiangsu	1050	22	885	66	742
浙 江	Zhejiang	2256	73	880	141	1119
安 徽	Anhui	4525	166	1604	264	1122
福 建	Fujian	1121	37	699	90	242
江 西	Jiangxi	748	84	542	151	318
山 东	Shandong	904	100	171	120	1444
河 南	Henan	1339	131	1586	146	589
湖 北	Hubei	4965	125	2904	167	2921
湖 南	Hunan	7339	538	2912	669	1592
广 东	Guangdong	2743	198	1838	194	988
广 西	Guangxi	2969	120	1769	177	3087
海 南	Hainan	268	48	315	26	179
重 庆	Chongqing	1205	39	575	67	801
四 川	Sichuan	5270	535	2898	1109	4629
贵 州	Guizhou	979	136	1240	87	1153
云 南	Yunnan	4158	228	2473	157	2528
西 藏	Tibet	96	38	4		
陕 西	Shaanxi	4291	797	1491	117	2195
甘 肃	Gansu	1562	161	910	71	357
青 海	Qinghai	60	4	44		43
宁 夏	Ningxia	465	19	102	74	139
新 疆	Xinjiang	1084	216	1125	250	2429
新疆兵团	Xinjiang Corps	560	47	134	89	110
黑龙江农垦	Heilongjiang Land Reclamation	84		1	3	7

11-1 省(自治区、直辖市)级残联

Disabled Persons' Federations in Provinces, Autonomous Regions and Municipalities

地区	Region	省市县乡残联实有人员 Actual Total Staff of Disabled Persons' Federations at Provincial,City, County and Township Level	省级残联机关 Disabled Persons' Federations at Provincial Level		省级残联事业单位 Affiliated Institutions at Provincial Level		
			实有人员 Actual Staff	残疾人干部 Staff with Disability	单位 Institutions	实有人员 Actual Total Staff	残疾人 Persons with Disability
		人 person	人 person	人 person	个 unit	人 person	人 person
全 国	**Total**	**119731**	**1555**	**128**	**156**	**5905**	**257**
北 京	Beijing	1432	59	11	11	252	
天 津	Tianjin	893	44	4	9	168	29
河 北	Hebei	5488	52	4	4	143	5
山 西	Shanxi	5196	62	4	8	229	7
内蒙古	Inner Mongolia	3244	33		4	73	2
辽 宁	Liaoning	4177	45	6	6	345	14
吉 林	Jilin	3109	44	5	5	215	14
黑龙江	Heilongjiang	2758	44	5	2	60	2
上 海	Shanghai	1224	45	4	7	171	12
江 苏	Jiangsu	5127	52	4	6	135	7
浙 江	Zhejiang	5348	44	4	6	206	
安 徽	Anhui	3386	48	3	4	137	6
福 建	Fujian	2609	40	4	4	78	8
江 西	Jiangxi	4020	65	2	6	118	
山 东	Shandong	6740	54	3	2	154	6
河 南	Henan	8743	51	6	3	132	5
湖 北	Hubei	3768	52	2	4	46	1
湖 南	Hunan	5354	46	3	6	90	5
广 东	Guangdong	7436	52	6	5	326	40
广 西	Guangxi	3277	60	4	5	121	5
海 南	Hainan	852	40	3	2	58	2
重 庆	Chongqing	1983	43		3	143	5
四 川	Sichuan	11374	50	5	2	600	
贵 州	Guizhou	3393	45	3	2	78	2
云 南	Yunnan	3543	53	5	8	226	27
西 藏	Tibet	200	30	2	2	74	3
陕 西	Shaanxi	5301	57	3	7	720	9
甘 肃	Gansu	3818	83	10	10	524	20
青 海	Qinghai	1333	37	2	2	22	2
宁 夏	Ningxia	1021	52	5	2	79	
新 疆	Xinjiang	3071	53	5	5	164	17
新疆兵团	Xinjiang Corps	300	13	1	3	14	1
黑龙江农垦	Heilongjiang Land Reclamation	213	7		1	4	1

11-1 续表 Continued

地区	Region	干部队伍综合培训情况 Training of Staff 省级举办综合培训班 Provincial-level General Training Courses	参加省级综合培训人次 Trainees on Provincial-level Training Courses	省级举办残疾人干部培训班 Provincial-level Training Courses for Staff with Disability	参加省级残疾人干部培训人次 Trainees on Provincial-level Training Courses for Staff with Disability	参加全国培训人次 Trainees on State-level Training Courses	参加全国残疾人干部培训人次 Trainees on Stats-level Training Courses for Staff with Disability
		期 course	人次 person-time	期 course	人次 person-time	人次 person-time	人次 person-time
全 国	**Total**	**130**	**14718**	**44**	**2358**	**1096**	**140**
北 京	Beijing	5		3			
天 津	Tianjin	2	130	5	350	5	1
河 北	Hebei	1	52	1	4	1	
山 西	Shanxi	1	40				2
内蒙古	Inner Mongolia	5	700	3	200		
辽 宁	Liaoning	3	130	1		1	1
吉 林	Jilin	2	263	1	80	30	1
黑龙江	Heilongjiang	1	180			2	
上 海	Shanghai	43	7570	5	550		
江 苏	Jiangsu	2	59	2	100		
浙 江	Zhejiang	2	100			12	54
安 徽	Anhui	1	265	1	72	302	10
福 建	Fujian	11					
江 西	Jiangxi	1	236	2	50	136	35
山 东	Shandong	2	188			13	
河 南	Henan	6	180			20	3
湖 北	Hubei	2		2			
湖 南	Hunan	3		1		15	
广 东	Guangdong	5	750	1	50	30	2
广 西	Guangxi	10	680	2	120	160	
海 南	Hainan	1					
重 庆	Chongqing	1	50				
四 川	Sichuan	6		6			
贵 州	Guizhou		500		20	95	12
云 南	Yunnan	1	40			1	1
西 藏	Tibet						
陕 西	Shaanxi	2	1220	3	230		
甘 肃	Gansu			2	150	20	
青 海	Qinghai	3	540			40	
宁 夏	Ningxia	2	415	2	122	180	2
新 疆	Xinjiang	4	350	1	260	10	15
新疆兵团	Xinjiang Corps					1	
黑龙江农垦	Heilongjiang Land Reclamation	2	80			22	1

11-2 地市级残联

Disabled Persons' Federations in Cities and Prefectures

地 区	Region	残联 Disabled Persons' Federations	残联机关 Disabled Persons' Federations					
			配备了残疾人领导干部的残联 Disabled Persons' Federations whose Leadership Include PWDs	实有人员 Actual Staff	残疾人领导干部 Leaders with Disability	残疾人干部 Ordinary Staff with Disability	建立残疾人人才库的残联 Disabled Persons' Federations that have Established Data base of Talents with Disabilities	残疾人人才库人库 PWDs Enrolled in the Data Base of Talents with Disabilities
		个 unit	个 unit	人 person	人 person	人 person	个 unit	人 person
全 国	**Total**	**360**	**232**	**5288**	**251**	**376**	**228**	**14497**
北 京	Beijing							
天 津	Tianjin							
河 北	Hebei	11	11	229	12	10	11	785
山 西	Shanxi	11	9	164	9	11	7	640
内蒙古	Inner Mongolia	12	7	189	7	18	9	244
辽 宁	Liaoning	14	14	287	15	24	14	1616
吉 林	Jilin	10	5	202	5	11	9	512
黑龙江	Heilongjiang	13	8	178	8	11	13	606
上 海	Shanghai							
江 苏	Jiangsu	13	7	283	8	19	10	772
浙 江	Zhejiang	11	9	257	12	14	8	805
安 徽	Anhui	16	7	170	7	8	8	586
福 建	Fujian	9	9	126	9	11	5	306
江 西	Jiangxi	11	7	139	7	11	7	793
山 东	Shandong	17	14	371	14	24	12	1237
河 南	Henan	18	12	284	13	16	18	1049
湖 北	Hubei	13	4	169	6	11	4	289
湖 南	Hunan	14	11	223	11	13	8	817
广 东	Guangdong	21	12	337	16	24	10	173
广 西	Guangxi	15	13	159	13	15	9	93
海 南	Hainan	3		31		4	1	19
重 庆	Chongqing							
四 川	Sichuan	21	11	256	11	20	14	1343
贵 州	Guizhou	9	8	120	8	10	4	109
云 南	Yunnan	16	12	205	14	19	8	155
西 藏	Tibet	7	4	70	6	9		
陕 西	Shaanxi	10	6	223	6	13	3	456
甘 肃	Gansu	15	14	228	14	23	15	393
青 海	Qinghai	8	2	70	2	3	6	183
宁 夏	Ningxia	5	3	62	4	2	2	36
新 疆	Xinjiang	14	11	185	12	20	4	368
新疆兵团	Xinjiang Corps	14	2	49	2	2	5	106
黑龙江农垦	Heilongjiang Land Reclamation	9		22			4	6

11-2　续表　Continued

地　区	Region	事业单位　Affiliated Institutions			干部队伍综合培训情况　Training of Cadre			
		单位 Institutions	实有人员 Actual Total of Staff	残疾人 Persons with Disability	地市级举办综合培训班 City-level General Training Courses	参加地市级培训人次 Trainees on City-level General Training Courses	地市级举办残疾人干部培训班 City-level Training Courses for Staff with Disability	参加地市级残疾人干部培训人次 Trainees on City-level Training Courses for Staff with Disability
		个 unit	人 person	人 person	期 course	人次 person-time	期 course	人次 person-time
全　国	**Total**	**634**	**7280**	**426**	**964**	**58577**	**400**	**15811**
北　京	Beijing							
天　津	Tianjin							
河　北	Hebei	20	344	16	38	2885	18	662
山　西	Shanxi	34	443	34	26	1978	16	1083
内蒙古	Inner Mongolia	19	108	7	16	1142	5	259
辽　宁	Liaoning	33	426	31	123	9389	92	3245
吉　林	Jilin	23	212	10	27	1178	18	649
黑龙江	Heilongjiang	25	199	10	20	3676	11	284
上　海	Shanghai							
江　苏	Jiangsu	31	418	13	21	1361	7	248
浙　江	Zhejiang	24	388	20	17	1267	11	656
安　徽	Anhui	19	105	4	53	2346	9	513
福　建	Fujian	23	184	11	12	405	1	30
江　西	Jiangxi	16	81	6	28	537	6	38
山　东	Shandong	40	537	64	50	1964	22	827
河　南	Henan	43	736	23	29	1159	14	706
湖　北	Hubei	28	206	11	18	293	7	202
湖　南	Hunan	28	165	7	30	3122	18	1330
广　东	Guangdong	71	1827	91	139	10032	26	1385
广　西	Guangxi	26	156	7	38	731	8	87
海　南	Hainan	4	37	3	1	61		
重　庆	Chongqing							
四　川	Sichuan	25	159	11	136	6855	71	2292
贵　州	Guizhou	9	45	4	5	123	3	
云　南	Yunnan	22	87	9	27	2717	1	128
西　藏	Tibet	4	17	1				
陕　西	Shaanxi	16	139	10	37	2879	5	272
甘　肃	Gansu	20	104	9	28	1272	13	618
青　海	Qinghai	6	30		9	269	8	155
宁　夏	Ningxia	6	41	4	12	245	4	40
新　疆	Xinjiang	12	61	7	23	678	5	79
新疆兵团	Xinjiang Corps	7	25	3				
黑龙江农垦	Heilongjiang Land Reclamation				1	13	1	23

11-3 县(县级市、市辖区)级残联

Disabled Persons' Federations in Counties, County-Level Cities and Districts under Cities

地区	Region	残联 Disabled Persons' Federations	残联机关 Disabled Persons' Federations				
			配备了残疾人干部的残联 Disabled Persons' Federations with Disabled Staff	实有人员 Actual Staff	残疾人干部 Ordinary Staff with Disability	建立残疾人人才库的残联 Disabled Persons' Federations that have Established Data base of Talents with Disabilities	残疾人人才库入库 PWDs Enrolled in the Data Base of Talents with Disabilities
		个 unit	个 unit	人 person	人 person	个 unit	人 person
全国	**Total**	**3099**	**1624**	**26725**	**2207**	**1723**	**77335**
北京	Beijing	16	13	217	24	10	535
天津	Tianjin	19	13	135	21	18	528
河北	Hebei	172	172	1455	189	132	7546
山西	Shanxi	119	97	1667	130	96	3243
内蒙古	Inner Mongolia	106	53	928	94	63	1205
辽宁	Liaoning	103	100	756	113	99	3047
吉林	Jilin	70	28	902	40	49	1305
黑龙江	Heilongjiang	132	37	628	39	129	3920
上海	Shanghai	17	11	183	25	12	216
江苏	Jiangsu	106	62	1166	73	75	5984
浙江	Zhejiang	86	59	956	69	50	1905
安徽	Anhui	109	25	780	33	55	5547
福建	Fujian	84	39	430	46	49	1233
江西	Jiangxi	104	49	762	80	55	1892
山东	Shandong	151	59	1759	77	90	11592
河南	Henan	166	94	2390	117	123	2939
湖北	Hubei	100	40	976	54	32	917
湖南	Hunan	125	76	1417	103	46	2309
广东	Guangdong	130	47	1165	57	17	316
广西	Guangxi	111	45	709	67	32	737
海南	Hainan	19	7	135	8	4	10
重庆	Chongqing	39	20	289	29	23	2076
四川	Sichuan	180	88	1364	112	107	4301
贵州	Guizhou	86	68	744	114	46	979
云南	Yunnan	129	84	1141	138	102	1992
西藏	Tibet	7	1	9	2		
陕西	Shaanxi	110	61	1089	96	37	5528
甘肃	Gansu	86	81	1014	123	46	2302
青海	Qinghai	46	11	261	11	17	137
宁夏	Ningxia	21	13	171	18	10	259
新疆	Xinjiang	95	57	757	87	61	2609
新疆兵团	Xinjiang Corps	152	11	190	15	21	171
黑龙江农垦	Heilongjiang Land Reclamation	103	3	180	3	17	55

11-3　续表　Continued

地　区	Region	事业单位 Affiliated Institutions			干部队伍综合培训情况 Training of Cadre	
		单位 Institutions	实有人员 Actual Total of Staff	残疾人 Persons with Disability	县级举办综合培训班累计 County-level General Training Courses	参加县级培训 Trainees on County-level General Training Courses
		个 unit	人 person	人 person	期 course	人次 person-time
全　国	**Total**	**2182**	**11671**	**900**	**6229**	**323059**
北　京	Beijing	27	273	28	61	5623
天　津	Tianjin	26	201	21	80	3759
河　北	Hebei	92	596	37	420	21046
山　西	Shanxi	149	718	52	286	15817
内蒙古	Inner Mongolia	41	167	24	188	12886
辽　宁	Liaoning	86	428	33	286	16481
吉　林	Jilin	68	391	15	139	6898
黑龙江	Heilongjiang	69	244	33	162	5845
上　海	Shanghai	20	167	19	45	4431
江　苏	Jiangsu	125	778	45	344	22572
浙　江	Zhejiang	104	613	47	324	16093
安　徽	Anhui	46	252	28	211	12595
福　建	Fujian	118	290	37	191	7761
江　西	Jiangxi	50	253	14	203	6603
山　东	Shandong	85	553	60	452	22254
河　南	Henan	151	1203	46	253	13785
湖　北	Hubei	96	452	30	156	6268
湖　南	Hunan	119	654	27	215	9318
广　东	Guangdong	165	965	54	161	8619
广　西	Guangxi	89	286	35	195	13606
海　南	Hainan	11	65	7	24	1384
重　庆	Chongqing	45	185	22	115	8199
四　川	Sichuan	80	465	36	522	25524
贵　州	Guizhou	37	172	21	107	6695
云　南	Yunnan	86	249	33	317	11553
西　藏	Tibet					
陕　西	Shaanxi	74	506	30	312	11315
甘　肃	Gansu	49	154	18	186	10086
青　海	Qinghai	16	70	6	54	3117
宁　夏	Ningxia	6	48	1	44	1448
新　疆	Xinjiang	51	270	40	176	11478
新疆兵团	Xinjiang Corps	1	3	1		
黑龙江农垦	Heilongjiang Land Reclamation					

11-4 乡(镇、街道)残联

Disabled Persons' Federations in Townships (Towns, Streets)

地区	Region	乡(镇、街道)已建残联 Disabled Persons' Federations Established in Townships (Towns, Streets)	残联机关 Disabled Persons' Federation			
			实有人员 Actual Staff	专职残联理事长 Full-time Presidents	兼职残联理事长 Part-time Presidents	残疾人专职委员 Full-time Workers on Disability
		个 unit	人 person	人 person	人 person	人 person
全国	**Total**	**39378**	**61307**	**13049**	**19839**	**49367**
北京	Beijing	300	631	259	42	995
天津	Tianjin	241	345	241		252
河北	Hebei	2264	2669	783	1481	2275
山西	Shanxi	1463	1913	567	678	1827
内蒙古	Inner Mongolia	1057	1746	214	704	1100
辽宁	Liaoning	1510	1890	583	811	1640
吉林	Jilin	895	1143	206	689	873
黑龙江	Heilongjiang	1279	1405	184	846	1871
上海	Shanghai	218	658	2	216	1719
江苏	Jiangsu	1346	2295	816	349	1481
浙江	Zhejiang	1337	2884	808	302	1197
安徽	Anhui	1293	1894	248	700	1524
福建	Fujian	1101	1461	210	652	1733
江西	Jiangxi	1479	2602	463	882	3320
山东	Shandong	1833	3312	972	406	2324
河南	Henan	2351	3947	1021	1091	3109
湖北	Hubei	1212	1867	161	588	2518
湖南	Hunan	2395	2759	809	1247	2306
广东	Guangdong	1608	2764	566	772	1549
广西	Guangxi	1234	1786	204	791	1465
海南	Hainan	225	486	47	88	289
重庆	Chongqing	1005	1323	359	513	1110
四川	Sichuan	4334	8480	877	2676	4007
贵州	Guizhou	1471	2189	478	624	1789
云南	Yunnan	1354	1582	648	517	1653
西藏	Tibet					
陕西	Shaanxi	1536	2567	402	595	1884
甘肃	Gansu	1374	1711	787	587	1435
青海	Qinghai	403	843	14	206	492
宁夏	Ningxia	225	568	12	153	188
新疆	Xinjiang	1029	1581	108	633	1326
新疆兵团	Xinjiang Corps	6	6			7
黑龙江农垦	Heilongjiang Land Reclamation					109

11-4 续表 Continued

地 区	Region	干部队伍综合培训情况 Training of Staff		志愿者助残情况 Volunteer	
		乡镇级举办综合培训班 Township-level General Training Courses	参加乡镇级培训人次 Trainees on Township-level Training	志愿者登记在册 Registered Volunteer	受助残疾人 PWDs Helped by Volunteers
		期 course	人次 person-time	万人 10,000 persons	万人 10,000 persons
全 国	**Total**	**21796**	**374649**	**193.4**	**569.2**
北 京	Beijing	319	22457	1.8	30.1
天 津	Tianjin	199	4977	10.2	7.2
河 北	Hebei	1073	12666	16.2	57.6
山 西	Shanxi	1037	24418	1.6	4.5
内蒙古	Inner Mongolia	338	5765	0.5	4.1
辽 宁	Liaoning	982	18757	3.8	7.7
吉 林	Jilin	318	4583	6.9	12.2
黑龙江	Heilongjiang	203	2490	15.2	20.9
上 海	Shanghai	198	19383	0.8	2.8
江 苏	Jiangsu	1264	29698	8.2	70.3
浙 江	Zhejiang	809	22256	7.0	16.9
安 徽	Anhui	685	13777	1.0	3.4
福 建	Fujian	336	4461	3.9	12.4
江 西	Jiangxi	884	8494	2.5	8.0
山 东	Shandong	1994	40462	13.8	25.5
河 南	Henan	896	8017	11.8	139.7
湖 北	Hubei	511	5013	2.8	8.8
湖 南	Hunan	369	7254	8.8	22.7
广 东	Guangdong	773	14328	29.8	5.3
广 西	Guangxi	622	8340	5.4	8.4
海 南	Hainan	62	595	0.5	0.6
重 庆	Chongqing	564	8822	1.4	25.6
四 川	Sichuan	3977	38607	14.7	33.3
贵 州	Guizhou	374	2953	3.3	3.8
云 南	Yunnan	524	14772	0.9	6.4
西 藏	Tibet				
陕 西	Shaanxi	1265	11500	11.3	13.7
甘 肃	Gansu	629	11965	5.9	10.7
青 海	Qinghai	76	997	0.2	0.5
宁 夏	Ningxia	110	1721	2.3	1.6
新 疆	Xinjiang	405	5121	0.8	4.3
新疆兵团	Xinjiang Corps			0.1	0.1
黑龙江农垦	Heilongjiang Land Reclamation				

11-5 村(社区)残疾人组织

Disabled Persons' Federations in Villages and Communities

地 区	Region	已建残协 Associations of PWDs Established		残协情况 Associations		
		村 in Villages	社区 in Communities	已建残疾人活动室 Entertainment Rooms for PWDs Established	村 in Villages	社区 in Communities
		个 unit	个 unit	个 unit	个 unit	个 unit
全 国	**Total**	**536952**	**70186**	**385657**	**328211**	**57446**
北 京	Beijing	3716	2042	3434	1890	1544
天 津	Tianjin	3518	1335	4122	2899	1223
河 北	Hebei	48413	2993	51102	48124	2978
山 西	Shanxi	23425	1770	13651	12422	1229
内蒙古	Inner Mongolia	10500	1767	6821	5251	1570
辽 宁	Liaoning	11453	3888	15034	11221	3813
吉 林	Jilin	9280	1496	7201	6006	1195
黑龙江	Heilongjiang	7246	2162	4600	2973	1627
上 海	Shanghai	1682	3515	5005	1694	3311
江 苏	Jiangsu	15837	4694	18692	14307	4385
浙 江	Zhejiang	22163	2839	17693	15003	2690
安 徽	Anhui	11827	2088	6469	5146	1323
福 建	Fujian	14626	2004	7601	6444	1157
江 西	Jiangxi	15618	2216	10432	8753	1679
山 东	Shandong	65883	4704	49124	45339	3785
河 南	Henan	43591	3345	27844	24882	2962
湖 北	Hubei	20878	2930	10875	8850	2025
湖 南	Hunan	36548	3014	22387	19926	2461
广 东	Guangdong	18585	5215	7883	4314	3569
广 西	Guangxi	14197	1588	6820	5823	997
海 南	Hainan	2137	324	570	418	152
重 庆	Chongqing	8842	1854	7063	5418	1645
四 川	Sichuan	43463	4638	32615	28523	4092
贵 州	Guizhou	15525	1159	7743	6890	853
云 南	Yunnan	12155	1370	5705	4784	921
西 藏	Tibet					
陕 西	Shaanxi	26301	1777	13368	12116	1252
甘 肃	Gansu	16086	1121	13754	12631	1123
青 海	Qinghai	4266	344	1332	1166	166
宁 夏	Ningxia	1759	391	848	592	256
新 疆	Xinjiang	7421	1508	5776	4406	1370
新疆兵团	Xinjiang Corps	11	92	90		90
黑龙江农垦	Heilongjiang Land Reclamation		3	3		3

11-5　续表　Continued

地　区	Region	残协情况 Associations			志愿者助残情况 Volunteers	
		残疾人专职委员选聘情况 Full-time Workers on Disability			志愿者登记在册 Registered Volunteers	受助残疾人 PWDs Assisted by Volunteers
		残疾人专职委员 Full-time Workers on Disability	村 in Villages	社区 in Communities		
		人 person	人 person	人 person	万人 10,000 person	万人 10,000 person
全　国	**Total**	**517959**	**461718**	**56241**	**182.1**	**550.3**
北　京	Beijing	4568	3050	1518	1.4	6.7
天　津	Tianjin	4669	3490	1179	9.4	7.3
河　北	Hebei	51406	48413	2993	13.7	50.5
山　西	Shanxi	24364	22730	1634	1.9	3.5
内蒙古	Inner Mongolia	12077	10320	1757	0.3	2.4
辽　宁	Liaoning	15369	11519	3850	5.1	17.9
吉　林	Jilin	10505	8961	1544	8.3	15.6
黑龙江	Heilongjiang	5808	2714	3094	10.2	11.6
上　海	Shanghai	3658	2087	1571	1.4	2.8
江　苏	Jiangsu	19236	14922	4314	10.4	43.5
浙　江	Zhejiang	15333	13592	1741	3.7	17.4
安　徽	Anhui	12117	10102	2015	1.8	8.0
福　建	Fujian	16538	14895	1643	3.3	11.8
江　西	Jiangxi	12722	11239	1483	7.2	14.1
山　东	Shandong	59106	55489	3617	15.4	24.4
河　南	Henan	44580	41639	2941	14.9	169.0
湖　北	Hubei	12840	11005	1835	2.7	11.6
湖　南	Hunan	34266	31906	2360	11.3	26.1
广　东	Guangdong	21919	18304	3615	13.7	5.1
广　西	Guangxi	15881	14351	1530	5.2	7.9
海　南	Hainan	2451	2260	191	0.7	1.3
重　庆	Chongqing	10579	8648	1931	4.0	26.0
四　川	Sichuan	31879	29905	1974	10.8	32.0
贵　州	Guizhou	11066	10339	727	1.3	1.7
云　南	Yunnan	12616	11551	1065	0.6	2.8
西　藏	Tibet					
陕　西	Shaanxi	26487	24919	1568	14.8	11.4
甘　肃	Gansu	17128	16063	1065	5.7	13.3
青　海	Qinghai	2882	2740	142	0.1	0.4
宁　夏	Ningxia	1528	1266	262	1.3	1.1
新　疆	Xinjiang	4320	3299	1021	1.5	2.6
新疆兵团	Xinjiang Corps	61		61	0.1	0.2
黑龙江农垦	Heilongjiang Land Reclamation				0.0	0.4

12-1 残疾人综合服务设施
Comprehensive Service Facilities for PWDs

地 区	Region	已投入使用项目 Projects in Operation			
		本年度新投入使用项目 Projects Getting into Operation in 2012			
		项目个数 Number of Projects	建设用地面积 Area Covered by the Project Construction	建设规模 Construction Area	总投资 Total Investment
		个 unit	平方米 square meter	平方米 square meter	万元 10,000 Yuan
全 国	**Total**	**98**	**426360**	**329586**	**117959.7**
北 京	Beijing	1	1664	4781	2914.8
天 津	Tianjin	2	1795	2200	1709.0
河 北	Hebei	6	9413	11431	4334.0
山 西	Shanxi	3	8403	11499	2141.0
内蒙古	Inner Mongolia	4	2450	1650	314.0
辽 宁	Liaoning	9	217360	114953	44111.0
吉 林	Jilin	2	1500	980	191.0
黑龙江	Heilongjiang				
上 海	Shanghai				
江 苏	Jiangsu	8	49017	33833	10400.0
浙 江	Zhejiang	2	4740	6040	1801.0
安 徽	Anhui	6	11900	10760	1815.0
福 建	Fujian	2	1882	4700	830.0
江 西	Jiangxi	1	600	1200	240.8
山 东	Shandong	2	2396	4800	3450.0
河 南	Henan	9	14064	10414	2534.0
湖 北	Hubei	3	5301	5418	1380.0
湖 南	Hunan	4	6182	6696	1850.0
广 东	Guangdong	5	7624	23232	4589.0
广 西	Guangxi	6	11468	10098	1922.7
海 南	Hainan				
重 庆	Chongqing	4	14195	29699	13570.0
四 川	Sichuan	6	26228	13679	6749.1
贵 州	Guizhou	2	4860	4800	592.0
云 南	Yunnan	2	738	4965	306.0
西 藏	Tibet				
陕 西	Shaanxi				
甘 肃	Gansu	2	4800	4500	8160.0
青 海	Qinghai	1	8000	90	500.0
宁 夏	Ningxia	1	1600	1600	578.6
新 疆	Xinjiang	3	4931	3931	680.0
新疆兵团	Xinjiang Corps				
黑龙江农垦	Heilongjiang Land Reclamation	2	3250	1636	296.6

12-1　续表 1　Continued 1

地　区	Region	已投入使用项目 Projects in Operation			
		累计已投入使用项目 Accumulated Projects in Operation			
		项目个数 Number of Projects	建设用地面积 Area Covered by the Project Construction	建设规模 Construction Area	总投资 Total Investment
		个 unit	平方米 square meter	平方米 square meter	万元 10,000 Yuan
全　国	**Total**	**1971**	**4440280**	**3557583**	**962140.7**
北　京	Beijing	1	1664	4781	2914.8
天　津	Tianjin	23	105221	82485	39607.0
河　北	Hebei	150	249642	151931	29363.7
山　西	Shanxi	47	117133	101403	26927.0
内蒙古	Inner Mongolia	63	78240	52483	8330.8
辽　宁	Liaoning	128	382657	252181	81898.7
吉　林	Jilin	39	49717	56503	13016.4
黑龙江	Heilongjiang	99	109659	64891	12942.5
上　海	Shanghai	7	271054	55903	52010.8
江　苏	Jiangsu	64	223478	206072	84520.4
浙　江	Zhejiang	56	438758	342442	114007.5
安　徽	Anhui	67	105030	98371	18254.8
福　建	Fujian	71	85085	129586	43840.9
江　西	Jiangxi	18	16404	25056	5426.3
山　东	Shandong	138	501783	290773	64212.8
河　南	Henan	135	256334	181445	28532.8
湖　北	Hubei	56	64763	73970	14436.5
湖　南	Hunan	87	133673	149580	21295.9
广　东	Guangdong	73	362738	363136	97041.0
广　西	Guangxi	92	61253	107566	14649.0
海　南	Hainan	7	6117	7909	2804.0
重　庆	Chongqing	27	56130	79666	24114.2
四　川	Sichuan	71	160011	139843	39421.7
贵　州	Guizhou	58	45686	49554	8281.0
云　南	Yunnan	120	121870	126369	20478.1
西　藏	Tibet				
陕　西	Shaanxi	66	108094	94570	24466.6
甘　肃	Gansu	92	109963	95559	31680.6
青　海	Qinghai	31	23452	13001	3745.0
宁　夏	Ningxia	18	50791	27676	6377.6
新　疆	Xinjiang	51	111282	120284	25606.6
新疆兵团	Xinjiang Corps	10	19393	8102	1307.0
黑龙江农垦	Heilongjiang Land Reclamation	6	13204	4490	628.6

12-1 续表 2 Continued 2

地 区	Region	在建项目 Projects under Construction			
		项目个数 Number of Projects	建设用地面积 Area Covered by the Project Construction	建设规模 Construction Area	总投资 Total Investment
		个 unit	平方米 square meter	平方米 square meter	万元 10,000 Yuan
全 国	**Total**	**204**	**1533814**	**1231921**	**418847.6**
北 京	Beijing	3	12922	21706	18911.2
天 津	Tianjin				
河 北	Hebei	5	3705	8109	1490.0
山 西	Shanxi	12	45892	49490	35432.5
内蒙古	Inner Mongolia	8	50891	51148	16060.0
辽 宁	Liaoning	1	7035	3047	3420.8
吉 林	Jilin	5	14703	12521	2267.0
黑龙江	Heilongjiang	5	5242	3642	465.0
上 海	Shanghai	1	3500	5541	4100.0
江 苏	Jiangsu	13	199225	228341	85487.9
浙 江	Zhejiang	16	72624	72464	21859.1
安 徽	Anhui	8	34396	36968	2510.4
福 建	Fujian	4	4322	15860	22350.0
江 西	Jiangxi				
山 东	Shandong	11	108870	58249	24406.3
河 南	Henan	11	112003	143920	26519.0
湖 北	Hubei	14	52014	77292	17698.5
湖 南	Hunan	3	15185	12718	2960.0
广 东	Guangdong	10	198422	143036	48058.5
广 西	Guangxi	10	242287	40354	8085.8
海 南	Hainan	4	12671	5500	5693.0
重 庆	Chongqing	7	61961	45614	13470.7
四 川	Sichuan	10	41064	27577	5889.0
贵 州	Guizhou	7	21700	15573	3470.3
云 南	Yunnan	8	67859	33549	6616.5
西 藏	Tibet				
陕 西	Shaanxi	5	37525	39710	13517.0
甘 肃	Gansu	3	1608	2572	357.0
青 海	Qinghai	1	800	1000	700.0
宁 夏	Ningxia	1	14140	3000	555.0
新 疆	Xinjiang	18	91250	73422	26497.2
新疆兵团	Xinjiang Corps				
黑龙江农垦	Heilongjiang Land Reclamation				

12-1 续表 3 Continued 3

地 区	Region	筹建项目 Projects under Discussion and Preparation 项目个数 Number of Projects	建设用地面积 Area Covered by the Project Construction	建设规模 Construction Area	总投资 Total Investment
		个 unit	平方米 square meter	平方米 square meter	万元 10,000 Yuan
全 国	**Total**	**176**	**1261688**	**1013068**	**315885.3**
北 京	Beijing	1	3888	4693	5000.0
天 津	Tianjin	1	14476	13456	4200.0
河 北	Hebei	2	5814	3574	512.2
山 西	Shanxi	11	40758	27402	7618.5
内蒙古	Inner Mongolia	1	10845	7700	3000.0
辽 宁	Liaoning	2	1680	3080	620.0
吉 林	Jilin				
黑龙江	Heilongjiang	4	1750	1900	423.0
上 海	Shanghai				
江 苏	Jiangsu	6	84337	66250	29775.4
浙 江	Zhejiang	12	79429	140696	74731.3
安 徽	Anhui	9	34827	24812	5755.0
福 建	Fujian	5	9906	33910	11306.0
江 西	Jiangxi	4	49669	59019	20591.1
山 东	Shandong	6	32150	38955	4670.0
河 南	Henan	7	21600	17087	4791.2
湖 北	Hubei	15	52556	37210	8386.8
湖 南	Hunan	9	47598	35860	5124.5
广 东	Guangdong	12	456161	122647	36459.2
广 西	Guangxi				
海 南	Hainan	8	10966	15907	6545.0
重 庆	Chongqing	4	22600	16400	6550.0
四 川	Sichuan	18	82464	128197	27738.0
贵 州	Guizhou	11	77509	78770	25587.2
云 南	Yunnan	4	13333	10295	1080.0
西 藏	Tibet				
陕 西	Shaanxi	6	24858	70681	15748.2
甘 肃	Gansu	4	5498	6167	1559.0
青 海	Qinghai	5	3001	7500	3274.0
宁 夏	Ningxia	2	33948	3540	1059.8
新 疆	Xinjiang	7	40067	37360	3780.0
新疆兵团	Xinjiang Corps				
黑龙江农垦	Heilongjiang Land Reclamation				

12-2 残疾人康复设施

Rehabilitation Service Facilities for PWDs

地 区	Region	已投入使用项目 Projects in Operation			
		本年度新投入使用项目 Projects Getting into Operation in 2012			
		项目个数 Number of Projects	建设用地面积 Area Covered by the Project Construction	建设规模 Construction Area	总投资 Total Investment
		个 unit	平方米 square meter	平方米 square meter	万元 10,000 Yuan
全 国	**Total**	**22**	**60634**	**78809**	**22838.2**
北 京	Beijing				
天 津	Tianjin				
河 北	Hebei				
山 西	Shanxi	2	3931	3659	1050.0
内蒙古	Inner Mongolia				
辽 宁	Liaoning	1	7000	22636	4109.0
吉 林	Jilin	3	8851	20362	8408.0
黑龙江	Heilongjiang				
上 海	Shanghai				
江 苏	Jiangsu	1	2000	2000	400.0
浙 江	Zhejiang	1	10000	3340	1500.0
安 徽	Anhui				
福 建	Fujian				
江 西	Jiangxi	1	50	50	10.0
山 东	Shandong				
河 南	Henan				
湖 北	Hubei				
湖 南	Hunan				
广 东	Guangdong	4	7100	7300	1015.2
广 西	Guangxi				
海 南	Hainan				
重 庆	Chongqing				
四 川	Sichuan	7	20001	16861	5716.0
贵 州	Guizhou	1	1200	1200	500.0
云 南	Yunnan				
西 藏	Tibet				
陕 西	Shaanxi				
甘 肃	Gansu				
青 海	Qinghai				
宁 夏	Ningxia				
新 疆	Xinjiang	1	500	1400	130.0
新疆兵团	Xinjiang Corps				
黑龙江农垦	Heilongjiang Land Reclamation				

12-2　续表 1　Continued 1

地　区	Region	已投入使用项目 Projects in Operation 累计已投入使用项目 Accumulated Projects in Operation 项目个数 Number of Projects	建设用地面积 Area Covered by the Project Construction	建设规模 Construction Area	总投资 Total Investment
		个 unit	平方米 square meter	平方米 square meter	万元 10,000 Yuan
全　国	**Total**	**231**	**823896**	**670069**	**191917.2**
北　京	Beijing	3	8423	13221	8273.7
天　津	Tianjin	8	7379	9550	2444.7
河　北	Hebei	5	17813	12096	1678.1
山　西	Shanxi	31	101396	68646	16693.4
内蒙古	Inner Mongolia	2	4005	4005	430.0
辽　宁	Liaoning	12	21508	41541	7101.9
吉　林	Jilin	6	10942	22186	8611.0
黑龙江	Heilongjiang	3	1478	4246	307.0
上　海	Shanghai				
江　苏	Jiangsu	36	86724	86963	28539.9
浙　江	Zhejiang	14	167091	109304	35100.9
安　徽	Anhui	2	920	1892	699.0
福　建	Fujian	3	15069	12507	2376.5
江　西	Jiangxi	3	1550	3850	190.0
山　东	Shandong	10	29911	22629	2840.0
河　南	Henan	5	59982	49912	7164.0
湖　北	Hubei	6	10717	12077	1196.0
湖　南	Hunan	10	5733	7102	978.0
广　东	Guangdong	33	61563	63032	16180.8
广　西	Guangxi	2	3486	2260	335.0
海　南	Hainan	1	667	400	400.0
重　庆	Chongqing	3	1990	3713	930.0
四　川	Sichuan	21	175491	98369	44196.5
贵　州	Guizhou	2	1200	1200	500.0
云　南	Yunnan				
西　藏	Tibet	1	3513	3513	927.1
陕　西	Shaanxi	4	17528	10884	2003.7
甘　肃	Gansu	2	2145	1500	660.0
青　海	Qinghai	1	5051	1592	830.0
宁　夏	Ningxia				
新　疆	Xinjiang	2	620	1880	330.0
新疆兵团	Xinjiang Corps				
黑龙江农垦	Heilongjiang Land Reclamation				

12-2 续表 2 Continued 2

地 区	Region	在建项目 Projects under Construction			
		项目个数 Number of Projects	建设用地面积 Area Covered by the Project Construction	建设规模 Construction Area	总投资 Total Investment
		个 unit	平方米 square meter	平方米 square meter	万元 10,000 Yuan
全 国	**Total**	**67**	**672033**	**553632**	**148282.7**
北 京	Beijing				
天 津	Tianjin				
河 北	Hebei	1	9463	13883	3470.0
山 西	Shanxi	7	26987	19510	5083.0
内蒙古	Inner Mongolia	1	3000	3000	1200.0
辽 宁	Liaoning	2	7728	10747	3046.5
吉 林	Jilin	2	16700	9500	2159.5
黑龙江	Heilongjiang				
上 海	Shanghai				
江 苏	Jiangsu	7	26709	52359	21380.0
浙 江	Zhejiang	4	24090	48340	18140.0
安 徽	Anhui	2	31380	22918	3584.0
福 建	Fujian				
江 西	Jiangxi	4	10920	9700	1751.0
山 东	Shandong	6	135187	127442	33607.0
河 南	Henan	2	11208	12500	3300.0
湖 北	Hubei	1	6170	11000	3200.0
湖 南	Hunan	1	3985	6435	450.0
广 东	Guangdong	9	30092	54254	11376.8
广 西	Guangxi	2	10983	8340	1718.8
海 南	Hainan				
重 庆	Chongqing	1	1920	3500	301.9
四 川	Sichuan	3	9682	7705	2962.0
贵 州	Guizhou	1	1000	800	120.0
云 南	Yunnan	1	3962	8000	1600.0
西 藏	Tibet				
陕 西	Shaanxi	3	12307	10150	2200.0
甘 肃	Gansu	4	258894	87504	17723.0
青 海	Qinghai				
宁 夏	Ningxia	2	27666	21044	7849.2
新 疆	Xinjiang				
新疆兵团	Xinjiang Corps	1	2000	5000	2060.0
黑龙江农垦	Heilongjiang Land Reclamation				

12-2　续表 3　Continued 3

地　区	Region	筹建项目 Projects under Discussion and Preparation			
		项目个数 Number of Projects	建设用地面积 Area Covered by the Project Construction	建设规模 Construction Area	总投资 Total Investment
		个 unit	平方米 square meter	平方米 square meter	万元 10,000 Yuan
全　国	**Total**	**60**	**767412**	**419424**	**165503.2**
北　京	Beijing				
天　津	Tianjin				
河　北	Hebei	1	333333	51310	39000.0
山　西	Shanxi	4	10153	10360	2408.0
内蒙古	Inner Mongolia	1	18000	20800	4700.0
辽　宁	Liaoning				
吉　林	Jilin				
黑龙江	Heilongjiang				
上　海	Shanghai				
江　苏	Jiangsu	4	43613	36898	16400.0
浙　江	Zhejiang	1	13353	8000	3600.0
安　徽	Anhui	3	22024	14000	3755.0
福　建	Fujian	1	901	8259	3225.0
江　西	Jiangxi	1	2011	2310	556.0
山　东	Shandong	3	69680	28000	10301.0
河　南	Henan	6	34949	16100	2950.0
湖　北	Hubei	5	32890	16324	5310.3
湖　南	Hunan				
广　东	Guangdong	8	88785	70960	40096.9
广　西	Guangxi	7	33881	47041	10449.0
海　南	Hainan				
重　庆	Chongqing	5	33615	37000	11703.0
四　川	Sichuan	4	17533	20063	5644.0
贵　州	Guizhou				
云　南	Yunnan				
西　藏	Tibet				
陕　西	Shaanxi	6	12690	32000	5405.0
甘　肃	Gansu				
青　海	Qinghai				
宁　夏	Ningxia				
新　疆	Xinjiang				
新疆兵团	Xinjiang Corps				
黑龙江农垦	Heilongjiang Land Reclamation				

12-3 残疾人托养设施
Fostering Service Facilities for PWDs

地 区	Region	已投入使用项目 Projects in Operation 本年度新投入使用项目 Projects Getting into Operation in 2012 项目个数 Number of Projects	建设用地面积 Area Covered by the Project Construction	建设规模 Construction Area	总投资 Total Investment
		个 unit	平方米 square meter	平方米 square meter	万元 10,000 Yuan
全 国	**Total**	**24**	**142546**	**99123**	**15126.0**
北 京	Beijing				
天 津	Tianjin				
河 北	Hebei	2	18266	5504	1315.0
山 西	Shanxi				
内蒙古	Inner Mongolia	1	2000	2000	100.0
辽 宁	Liaoning	2	13000	34500	319.0
吉 林	Jilin	1	3345	3352	1400.0
黑龙江	Heilongjiang				
上 海	Shanghai				
江 苏	Jiangsu	5	65169	21573	5350.0
浙 江	Zhejiang	1	2000	2000	400.0
安 徽	Anhui				
福 建	Fujian				
江 西	Jiangxi				
山 东	Shandong	1	15000	7608	2500.0
河 南	Henan				
湖 北	Hubei	1	620	186	120.0
湖 南	Hunan				
广 东	Guangdong	1	1000	2000	400.0
广 西	Guangxi				
海 南	Hainan				
重 庆	Chongqing				
四 川	Sichuan				
贵 州	Guizhou				
云 南	Yunnan				
西 藏	Tibet				
陕 西	Shaanxi	7	17440	14930	1880.0
甘 肃	Gansu	1	1625	2389	495.0
青 海	Qinghai				
宁 夏	Ningxia				
新 疆	Xinjiang				
新疆兵团	Xinjiang Corps				
黑龙江农垦	Heilongjiang Land Reclamation	1	3081	3081	847.0

12-3　续表 1　Continued 1

地　区	Region	已投入使用项目 Projects in Operation 累计已投入使用项目 Accumulated Projects in Operation 项目个数 Number of Projects	建设用地面积 Area Covered by the Project Construction	建设规模 Construction Area	总投资 Total Investment
		个 unit	平方米 square meter	平方米 square meter	万元 10,000 Yuan
全　国	**Total**	**155**	**715540**	**431282**	**126435.6**
北　京	Beijing				
天　津	Tianjin	15	19550	8729	3258.7
河　北	Hebei	3	25119	10304	2315.0
山　西	Shanxi	1	5986	2000	400.0
内蒙古	Inner Mongolia	2	7440	3320	270.0
辽　宁	Liaoning	16	89352	48712	10083.5
吉　林	Jilin	1	3345	3352	1400.0
黑龙江	Heilongjiang	3	7840	10818	3346.8
上　海	Shanghai				
江　苏	Jiangsu	20	188344	84951	37537.0
浙　江	Zhejiang	16	88667	45400	18900.0
安　徽	Anhui				
福　建	Fujian	2	16386	7451	550.0
江　西	Jiangxi	1	17264	500	60.0
山　东	Shandong	10	58335	23463	10805.0
河　南	Henan	4	16333	11186	1942.2
湖　北	Hubei	12	37496	19006	3285.0
湖　南	Hunan	11	4250	4622	957.0
广　东	Guangdong	6	7355	20026	12256.0
广　西	Guangxi				
海　南	Hainan				
重　庆	Chongqing	1	70	68	197.9
四　川	Sichuan	4	6806	7932	2800.5
贵　州	Guizhou	1	1500	2000	40.0
云　南	Yunnan				
西　藏	Tibet				
陕　西	Shaanxi	20	92522	90338	8494.0
甘　肃	Gansu	3	10037	10801	1302.0
青　海	Qinghai				
宁　夏	Ningxia				
新　疆	Xinjiang	1	3023	3023	888.0
新疆兵团	Xinjiang Corps				
黑龙江农垦	Heilongjiang Land Reclamation	2	8521	13281	5347.0

12-3 续表 2 Continued 2

地 区	Region	在建项目 Projects under Construction 项目个数 Number of Projects	建设用地面积 Area Covered by the Project Construction	建设规模 Construction Area	总投资 Total Investment
		个 unit	平方米 square meter	平方米 square meter	万元 10,000 Yuan
全 国	**Total**	**49**	**454872**	**301134**	**95871.0**
北 京	Beijing				
天 津	Tianjin	1	1508	1600	600.0
河 北	Hebei	1	3333	19400	5438.0
山 西	Shanxi	1	1667	2000	400.0
内蒙古	Inner Mongolia	1	2920	2920	800.0
辽 宁	Liaoning	5	60564	51497	29400.0
吉 林	Jilin	2	2500	5700	2900.0
黑龙江	Heilongjiang				
上 海	Shanghai				
江 苏	Jiangsu	14	155302	119202	30710.0
浙 江	Zhejiang				
安 徽	Anhui				
福 建	Fujian	3	6693	12087	3648.0
江 西	Jiangxi	2	14119	8750	1190.0
山 东	Shandong	3	94656	26846	10690.0
河 南	Henan	5	43421	19665	3858.0
湖 北	Hubei				
湖 南	Hunan	2	24710	5910	980.0
广 东	Guangdong	1	12000	7073	807.0
广 西	Guangxi	1	3300	3000	600.0
海 南	Hainan				
重 庆	Chongqing	1	9834	3860	1200.0
四 川	Sichuan	1	3500	1500	200.0
贵 州	Guizhou				
云 南	Yunnan				
西 藏	Tibet				
陕 西	Shaanxi	3	10664	6124	1400.0
甘 肃	Gansu				
青 海	Qinghai	1	2680	2000	650.0
宁 夏	Ningxia				
新 疆	Xinjiang	1	1500	2000	400.0
新疆兵团	Xinjiang Corps				
黑龙江农垦	Heilongjiang Land Reclamation				

12-3 续表 3 Continued 3

地 区	Region	筹建项目 Projects under Discussion and Preparation			
		项目个数 Number of Projects	建设用地面积 Area Covered by the Project Construction	建设规模 Construction Area	总投资 Total Investment
		个 unit	平方米 square meter	平方米 square meter	万元 10,000 Yuan
全 国	**Total**	**50**	**625457**	**210791**	**65565.8**
北 京	Beijing				
天 津	Tianjin				
河 北	Hebei	1	1232	2000	400.0
山 西	Shanxi	3	11500	11000	3199.0
内蒙古	Inner Mongolia				
辽 宁	Liaoning	3	8100	8800	1800.0
吉 林	Jilin				
黑龙江	Heilongjiang	1	4000	10000	2000.0
上 海	Shanghai				
江 苏	Jiangsu	5	31187	23820	3750.0
浙 江	Zhejiang	1	4662	5671	5671.0
安 徽	Anhui	1	6666	3000	420.0
福 建	Fujian	2	22034	13150	3529.0
江 西	Jiangxi				
山 东	Shandong	1	1000	1000	200.0
河 南	Henan	4	26300	8317	1450.0
湖 北	Hubei	4	13620	10720	1987.0
湖 南	Hunan	2	143256	27439	11969.9
广 东	Guangdong	4	287065	25000	9778.9
广 西	Guangxi	4	21185	16062	3101.0
海 南	Hainan				
重 庆	Chongqing	3	8190	10000	5576.0
四 川	Sichuan	1	5000	1800	1000.0
贵 州	Guizhou	1	4000	2000	1400.0
云 南	Yunnan				
西 藏	Tibet	1	4200	3813	1140.0
陕 西	Shaanxi	8	22260	27200	7194.0
甘 肃	Gansu				
青 海	Qinghai				
宁 夏	Ningxia				
新 疆	Xinjiang				
新疆兵团	Xinjiang Corps				
黑龙江农垦	Heilongjiang Land Reclamation				

13-1 残疾人事业信息化建设

Informationzation on the Work for PWDs

地 区	Region	门户网站 Websites	省级 at Provincial Level	地市级 at Prefectural/City Level	县级 at County Level	省级网站本年度发稿量 Articles Published by Provincial-level Websites of Disabled Persons' Federations	各级信息化专业人才 IT Professionals
		个 unit	个 unit	个 unit	个 unit	篇 sheet	人 person
全 国	**Total**	**1540**	**33**	**272**	**1235**	**69888**	**4948**
北 京	Beijing	17	1		16	2638	29
天 津	Tianjin	14	1		13	797	57
河 北	Hebei	36	1	10	25	2875	248
山 西	Shanxi	72	1	11	60	1484	191
内蒙古	Inner Mongolia	36	1	8	27	800	149
辽 宁	Liaoning	67	1	14	52	5316	196
吉 林	Jilin	45	1	9	35	1100	130
黑龙江	Heilongjiang	27	1	7	19	848	184
上 海	Shanghai	18	1		17	3231	48
江 苏	Jiangsu	112	1	13	98	6641	224
浙 江	Zhejiang	95	1	11	83	6000	144
安 徽	Anhui	75	1	16	58	9600	159
福 建	Fujian	94	1	9	84	2679	151
江 西	Jiangxi	40	1	6	33	479	167
山 东	Shandong	85	1	17	67	1500	210
河 南	Henan	25	1	8	16	705	236
湖 北	Hubei	45	1	10	34	3572	141
湖 南	Hunan	76	1	13	62	2100	188
广 东	Guangdong	73	1	21	51	2838	289
广 西	Guangxi	116	1	14	101	1500	210
海 南	Hainan	2	1	1		40	43
重 庆	Chongqing	39	1		38	1293	87
四 川	Sichuan	105	1	17	87	300	279
贵 州	Guizhou	23	1	6	16	829	125
云 南	Yunnan	51	1	10	40	2200	212
西 藏	Tibet	1	1			75	17
陕 西	Shaanxi	59	1	10	48	1875	159
甘 肃	Gansu	35	1	14	20	2414	129
青 海	Qinghai	7	1	3	3	499	69
宁 夏	Ningxia	13	1	4	8	1210	37
新 疆	Xinjiang	34	1	9	24	1050	132
新疆兵团	Xinjiang Corps	2	1	1		500	181
黑龙江农垦	Heilongjiang Land Reclamation	1	1			900	127

13-1 续表 Continued

地 区	Region	本年度信息工作培训情况 Training for Web Technology and Management in 2012			
		省级 at Provincial Level		地市级 at Prefectural/City Level	
		举办信息工作培训班 Training Course for Web Technology and Management	参加信息工作培训班 Participants of Training Course	举办信息工作培训班 Training Course for Web Technology and Management	参加信息工作培训班 Participants of Training Course
		期 course	人次 person-time	期 course	人次 person-time
全 国	**Total**	**44**	**3007**	**342**	**9113**
北 京	Beijing	3	150		
天 津	Tianjin	1	1		
河 北	Hebei	2	108	13	335
山 西	Shanxi			9	165
内蒙古	Inner Mongolia	1	130	9	132
辽 宁	Liaoning	4	148	65	2077
吉 林	Jilin	2	90	11	399
黑龙江	Heilongjiang			5	163
上 海	Shanghai	6	400		
江 苏	Jiangsu			24	1147
浙 江	Zhejiang	1	35	6	353
安 徽	Anhui	1	150	12	252
福 建	Fujian	2	260	9	202
江 西	Jiangxi	1	260	10	113
山 东	Shandong	1	150	21	440
河 南	Henan			11	258
湖 北	Hubei	1	100	9	351
湖 南	Hunan	1	150	7	130
广 东	Guangdong	1	36	22	610
广 西	Guangxi	1	130	8	109
海 南	Hainan	1	50		
重 庆	Chongqing	1	55		
四 川	Sichuan	1	30	43	798
贵 州	Guizhou	2	90	6	279
云 南	Yunnan	1	74	6	111
西 藏	Tibet	1	35	1	20
陕 西	Shaanxi	3	100	8	182
甘 肃	Gansu	1	130	10	165
青 海	Qinghai	1	80	7	96
宁 夏	Ningxia	1	30	5	122
新 疆	Xinjiang	1	20	4	78
新疆兵团	Xinjiang Corps				
黑龙江农垦	Heilongjiang Land Reclamation	1	15	1	26

5

分省统计报告

Statistical Report of Provinces

2012年北京市残疾人事业发展统计公报

2012年，在中国残联的指导和北京市委、市政府的领导下，全市残联系统深入贯彻落实科学发展观，紧紧围绕残疾人“两个体系”建设，全面推进残疾人社会融合，不断提高残疾人社会保障和服务水平，圆满完成了全年各项目标任务，推动首都残疾人事业迈上了新的台阶。

一、康复

2012年，通过实施一批重点康复工程，使各类别残疾人得到不同程度的康复。康复服务质量全面提升，积极探索机构康复、社区康复、家庭康复相结合的新模式，开展了康复知识大讲堂、辅具知识进社区、千名康复员进家庭等活动，创建了13所家庭康复培训学校。积极开展残疾预防，与市卫生局、市妇幼保健院共同开展了发育迟缓儿童残疾预防干预、脑瘫儿童早期监测和儿童发育干预示范中心试点建设项目。积极推动康复机构、辅具机构建设，北京康复中心一期工程建成，康复医院改建取得突破性进展。8个区县、332个街乡镇建立了辅助器具服务机构，为残疾人提供个性化辅助器具评估与适配服务。研发出具有国际领先水平的第三代智能假肢产品，进一步提升了辅具服务水平，“人人享有康复服务”目标基本实现，质量有所提升。

全年完成白内障复明手术10356例；为667名贫困白内障患者免费施行复明手术，全年为362名低视力患者配用助视器，培训低视力儿童家长25名，有效开展家庭康复训练。对920名盲人进行定向行走训练。

加强市级聋儿康复机构建设，完善聋儿康复网络。共对332名聋儿进行了听力语言康复训练，规范聋儿家长学校，开展家庭训练，共培训聋儿家长498名；培养各类专业人员300人。

大力推广“社会化、综合性、开放式”精神病防治康复工作。2011年，在15个区县开展精神病防治康复工作，对42927名重性精神病患者进行综合防治康复，监护率达到99.79%，显好率达到63.74%，社会参与率达到39.47%，肇事率0.03%；对5639名贫困精神病患者进行医疗救助。

建立了1个市级孤独症儿童康复训练机构，有85名孤独症儿童进行了康复训练。

深入开展辅助器具供应服务，全面推进普及型假肢装配，截止到2012年底，累计建立辅助器具供应服务机构5个，为残疾人减免费用装配普及型假肢263例，供应各类辅助器具5693件，装配矫形器97例。

全年开展肢体残疾康复训练服务的机构达到12个，对5142名肢体残疾人进行了康复训练，其中：脑瘫儿童系统康复训练262人，肢体残疾儿童社区、家庭康复124人，成年肢体残疾人社区、家庭康复4756人。

全年开展智力残疾康复训练服务的机构达到29个；对490名智力残疾儿童进行了康复训练，不同程度地开展了智力残疾儿童早期康复训练与服务。

在全市16个区县开展了社区康复工作，累计建立社区康复站3601个，已开展社区康复服务社区5517个，配备了4225名社区康复协调员。

二、教育

通过媒体宣传、筹办论坛、电视访谈、微博互动、典型示范等多种形式，大力倡导和宣传融合教育理念。会同教育部门制定了《北京市中小学融合教育行动计划》、《关于进一步加强随班就读工作的指导意见》、《北京市残疾儿童少年送教上门管理办法》，完成了全市1722所中小学无障碍设施情况摸底调查，在全市部署了融合教育示范区和示范校创建活动。启动“康教结合”试点工作，对全市978所幼儿园进行残疾儿童学前教育调查，积极探索残疾儿童学前教育模式。开展适龄未入学残疾儿童少年调查，建立了未入学残疾儿童少年台账制度，为450名重度和多重残疾儿童提供了送教上门服务。

开办特殊教育普通高中2所，在校生16人；其中聋高中1所，在校生0人；盲高中1所，在校生16人。残疾人中等职业教育机构有3个，在校生178人，毕业生75人，其中获得职业资格证书75人。

高等特殊教育学院 1 所，有 125 名残疾人被普通高等院校录取，20 名残疾人进入特殊教育学院学习。

未入学适龄残疾儿童少年总数 419 人，其中视力残疾 0 人，听力残疾 3 人，言语残疾 2 人，智力残疾 100 人，肢体残疾 196 人，精神残疾 22 人，多重残疾 96 人。

三、就业

依法推动机关、事业单位、国有企业安排残疾人就业岗位预留、定向招录制度的落实，会同市国资委出台了《关于推动北京市国有及国有控股企业安排残疾人就业指导意见》。通过开展网上审核、加强宣传等措施，进一步加大残疾人就业审核工作力度。通过对超比例安置单位给予奖励、对就业残疾人给予保险补贴，以及为企业进行无障碍改造、为聋人就业企业配备手语翻译等措施，积极促进残疾人按比例就业。对应届残疾大学毕业生实行就业评估、指导、推介一条龙跟踪服务，就业率达到 98% 以上。第六次残疾人职业技能大赛首次纳入全市职工职业技能大赛，参赛人数创历史新高，900 余人次取得国家职业资格证书。以“爱立方”为品牌，残疾人职业康复劳动产品首次走进文博会，成功入选北京礼物。市残联、市质监局共同制定了国内第一部《盲人保健按摩服务规范》和《保健按摩操作规范》，填补了同行业空白。

城镇新安排 2907 残疾人就业。其中，集中就业残疾人 285 人，按比例安排残疾人就业 1181 人，公益性岗位就业 629 人，个体及其它形式就业 803 人，辅助性就业 458 人，全市城镇实际在业人数 72969 人；45101 农村残疾人稳定实现就业，其中从事农业生产劳动 29654 人。

职业培训基地 45 个，其中残联兴办 8 个，本年度城镇职业培训人数 4111 人。

培训盲人保健按摩 509 人；医疗按摩人员 98，保健按摩机构达到 489 个，医疗按摩机构达到 2 个；有 5 人通过医疗按摩人员中级职称评审，18 人通过医疗按摩人员初级职称评审。

四、社会保障

在实现政策全覆盖基础上，加大宣传和落实力度，努力做到应保尽保、不留死角。为全市所有持证残疾人参保意外伤害险，残疾人遭受意外伤害可获最高 6 万元的保险赔付。认真落实“九养”政策，为 9.9 万名残疾人发放养老助残券，为 1782 名残疾人配发小帮手电子服务器。为机构托养残疾人和居家养护残疾人提供阳光家园资助，为 2314 户遭受意外灾害的特殊困难残疾人家庭给予临时救助，积极做好 7•21 特大灾害和 11•3 延庆雪灾中遭受严重损失的扶贫助残基地、职业康复站、温馨家园灾后恢复重建工作，为残疾人基本生活、基本医疗、基本养老、基本住房等各方面提供了可靠保障。

城镇残疾职工参加社会保险人数达到 67167 人，其中参加养老保险人数 59652 人，参加医疗保险人数 59382 人；城镇残疾居民参加医疗保险达到 48794 人；城乡 70891 名残疾人纳入最低生活保障范围；城镇已纳入最低生活保障 47477 人，城镇集中供养和其他救助救济 5338 人；农村已纳入最低生活保障 23414 人，五保供养和其他救助救济 14881 人。

寄宿制托养机构 89 个，托养残疾人 2041 人；日间照料托养机构合计 257 人，托养残疾人 1569 人；本年度享受居家托养服务残疾人 17584 人。

五、扶贫

2012 年扶持贫困残疾人户 4109 户，扶持 5064 人，接受实用技术培训的残疾人 5350 人次，投入培训经费 47.64 万元，市级财政投入扶贫资金 1732 万元。

结对帮扶单位 177 个，结对帮扶个人 2137 人；建立残疾人扶持基地 121 个，安置残疾人就业 3646 人，扶持带动残疾人 5190 户。

完成 792 户农村贫困残疾人危房改造，投入危房资金 501.36 万元，受益残疾人 859 人。

六、宣传文化

抓住党的十八大、市第十一次党代会、全国助残日、国际残疾人日等重大政治事件和重大节日契机，加强整体策划，全方位、立体式做好宣传工作。成功举办全国助残日残疾人优秀文化成果展，回良玉、邓朴方、郭金龙、张海迪等领导莅临参观，给予高度评价。十八大期间，《北京新闻》播出长达 7 分钟“更多残疾人走出家门参与社会”新闻，《北京日报》四天连发专版，集中展示我市残疾人事业发展成就；中央电视台新闻联播、人民日报、北京电视台、新华网等40余家媒体在黄金时间、显著位置，对全国助残日、国际残疾人日系列活动进行了广泛、深入地报道。开通北京残联官方微博，在第三批上线单位中各项排名位居前列。与梅兰芳大剧院、国家大剧院、中国美术馆、中央电视台、中国儿童艺术剧院等公共文化机构开展公益合作，牵手残疾人走进高雅艺术殿堂，共享首都文化建设成果。推行音乐治疗和心理咨询服务，让更多的残疾人在文化娱乐活动中愉悦身心，回归社会。送文化下基层，建立了12个区县流动图书馆，基层演出达100场。残疾人手工艺品首次走进党代会和国际论坛展示，“爱立方”品牌社会影响力得到提升。北京市残疾人艺术团成为第一批“北京市优秀文化品牌团队”，并代表市政府参加了北京——莫斯科友好城市国际残疾人日演出，首都残疾人工作在国内外的影响力进一步扩大。

我市残联的新闻稿件被中央媒体采用150件，主要新闻媒体刊播稿件数420件，报刊专版61个，残疾人专题广播节目7个，电视手语新闻栏目1个，建立了市级残疾人事业新闻宣传促进会1个。各区县残联的新闻稿件被主要新闻媒体刊播数达到886件，报刊专版76个，残疾人专题广播节目9个，电视手语新闻栏目2个。

市和区县两级残联在公共图书馆设立盲文及盲人有声读物阅览室已分别达到5和14个，举办残疾人文化周17和120个，举办残疾人文化艺术类比赛及展览分别是43和94个，已成立北京市残疾人艺术团队1个，区县成立残疾人艺术团38个。

七、体育

体育工作取得新成效。在全市范围内建立的“残疾人体育健身示范点”，起到良好示范作用。推广轮椅舞蹈、轮椅健身操、太极柔力球、太平鼓等残疾人群众性体育项目，推动基层残疾人文化体育工作活跃开展。选送25名优秀运动员、教练员进入国家队参加伦敦残奥会，取得4金、6银、3铜的可喜成绩，为国家和北京市争得了荣誉。

市级残疾人体育健身活动8次，参加人数4532人，残疾人体育示范点35个，残疾人体育健身指导员850人，残疾人体育比赛5次，参与的残疾人运动员362人次，残疾人体育训练基地10个，聘任教练员28人。

各区县残联举办残疾人体育健身活动1391次，66594人参加活动，残疾人体育示范点68个，残疾人体育健身指导员455人。

八、维权

残疾人合法权益得到切实维护。依托公、检、法、司等部门和机构，不断完善残疾人法律救助工作联席会制度，并在温馨家园建立了47个法律服务工作站，为残疾人提供法律政策咨询、代书、调解等法律服务1.6万人次，诉讼、仲裁代理33件，为残疾人挽回直接经济损失380多万元。

县级以上人大执法检查和政协视察、专题调研各5次；开展普法宣传教育活动66次，参加人数12470人；开展法律培训班24次，参加人数2301人；建立残疾人法律救助协调机构8个；建立残疾人法律救助工作站4个，办理案件155件；建立残疾人法律援助中心（工作站）17个，办理案件323件；协助残联系统人大代表、政协委员提出议案、建议、提案3件，办理议案、建议、提案4件。

无障碍建设与管理法规、政府令2个；无障碍建设领导协调组织13个；系统开展无障碍建设区县16个；贫困残疾人家庭无障碍改造11559户，无障碍检查237次，无障碍培训4699人次，残疾人机动轮椅车燃油补贴18475人。

市区两级残联共处理残疾人群众来信7186件，接待残疾人群众来访5574人次，其中集体访4批次，32人次。

九、组织建设

基层组织建设取得新成效。基层残联组织换届工作基本完成，一批年富力强、政治素质好、残疾人认可的同志进入班子，整体素质进一步提高。开展了基层组织建设调研，研究制定了加强残疾人干部队伍建设的意见。加强与组织部门的协调、对区县工作的指导，在区县残联领导班子建设、残疾人干部队伍配备、街乡镇残联组织建设和基层残疾人工作者队伍建设等方面取得了新的突破。我市街道（乡、镇）均建立了温馨家园，提前实现了“十二五”规划提出的“每个街道、乡镇至少建成一个示范残疾人温馨家园”目标。

2012年，我会领导班子配备了1名驻会肢体残疾人副理事长，1名盲人理事，2名肢体残疾人驻会理事，1名智力残疾人亲友理事以及1名驻会聋人理事。全市13个区县残联机关配备了残疾人干部。

在残疾人专职委员选聘方面，街道（乡镇）选聘残疾人专职委员995名；社区（村）选聘残疾人专职委员4568名。

残联干部综合培训工作取得较好成绩。全市残联实有人员已达1432人，干部培训工作取得新进展。

全市共建立各类残疾人专门协会80个，其中盲人协会16个、聋人协会16个、肢残人协会16个、智力残疾人及亲友协会16个、精神残疾人及亲友协会16个。

十、服务设施建设

残疾人服务设施建设得到全面发展。截止到2012年底，已竣工并投入使用的残疾人综合服务设施共计1个，在建项目共计3个，筹建项目共计1个。其中已竣工并投入使用的残疾人综合服务设施总占地面积0.17万平方米，总建设规模0.48万平方米，总投资0.29亿元；

已竣工并投入使用的康复设施共计3个，已竣工并投入使用的康复设施总占地面积0.84万平方米，总建设规模1.32万平方米，总投资0.83亿元。

十一、事业统计与信息化

信息化服务水平不断提高。为方便我市残疾人就近就便享受免费上网服务，我市启动了残疾人免费上网项目。启动了残疾人服务“一卡通”建设项目，建立了基于GIS的数据空间展示系统，实现了残疾人实时、动态全程服务管理。在全市各区县的大力支持下圆满完成新一轮残疾人状况监测工作。

统计队伍建设进一步加强，各级残联共有17名专、兼职统计人员从事残疾人事业统计工作，统计人员业务素质培养普遍得到重视，市级残联举办培训班1期，参加培训的人员达到40人次。

全市残联系统全面推进网站建设。经过改版，我市建成了全站无障碍的公众服务网站，有16个区县残联网站已开通。这为今后残联系统网站集群服务奠定了基础，残联系统网上信息服务正在逐步覆盖全市。2012年市区县两级残联共开设网站技术培训班3期，培训各级残联信息员达150人次。

全市各级残联共有29名专业技术人员从事信息化工作；建立市级残联局域网1个，网上办公(OA)系统1个。

2012 年天津市残疾人事业发展统计公报

2012 年，在市委、市政府的领导和中国残联的指导以及全社会的大力支持下，天津市残联全面完成“十二五”中期任务，加快健全两个体系，切实改善残疾人物质和文化生活，积极推进残疾人康复、教育、就业、扶贫、盲人按摩、维权、文化体育、社会保障、组织建设、服务设施和信息化建设等工作，努力增强为残疾人服务的能力，大力改善残疾人物质和文化生活状况，把中央和市委、市政府关于促进残疾人事业发展、加快推进残疾人社会保障体系和服务体系建设等一系列重大决策部署落到实处，全面完成了年度残疾人工作各项任务，得到了中央和市领导同志的充分肯定。现根据 2012 年度残疾人事业统计数据和实际情况，进行分析，并公报如下:

一、残疾人康复工作力度加大

积极推进残疾人社区康复工作。截至 2012 年底，在 13 个市辖区和 3 个县开展了社区康复工作，有 1611 个社区已建立康复站。目前，有社区康复协调员 4055 人，比 2011 年增加 1.1%；为 235878 名生活在社区的残疾人建立了社区康复服务档案，到 2012 年底，累计有 191667 人接受了社区康复服务，是 2011 年的 4 倍。从图 1-1 看，“十二五”期间，社区康复工作水平显著提高。

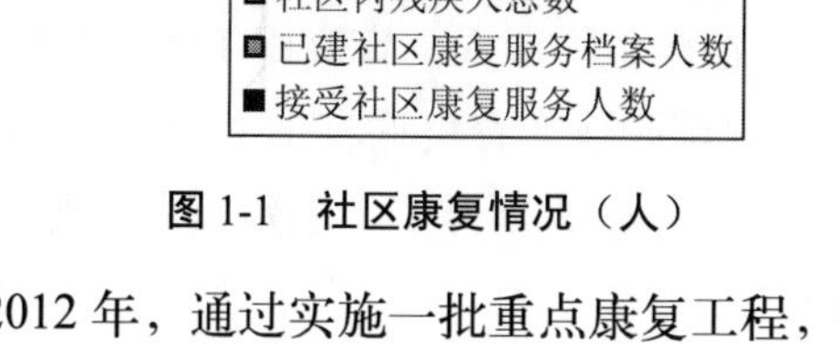

图 1-1　社区康复情况（人）

2012 年，通过实施一批重点康复工程，使各类别残疾人得到不同程度的康复。全年完成白内障复明手术 5744 例，为 1168 例贫困白内障患者免费施行复明手术。全年为 1868 名低视力患者配用助视器，比 2011 年增长 2 倍。培训低视力儿童家长 138 名，比 2011 年增长 79.2%。有效开展家庭康复训练。对 1256 名盲人进行定向行走训练，训练人数大大提高，康复范围不断扩大。

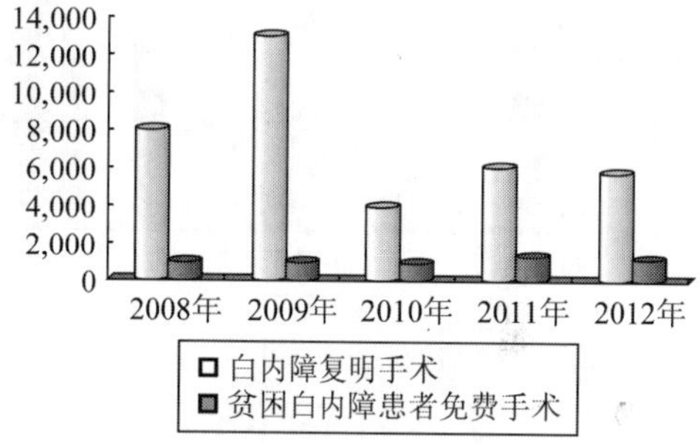

图 2　白内障复明手术情况（例）

加强省级聋儿康复机构建设，完善聋儿康复网络。2012 年对新收训 56 名聋儿进行了听力语言训练，比 2011 年增长了 21.7%。其中机构康复训练人数 49 名，比 2011 年增加 36.1%。家庭康复训练人数 7 名。共对 139 名聋儿进行了听力语言康复训练，比 2011 年增长 25.2%。规范聋儿家长学校，开展家庭训练，共培训聋儿家长 134 名，比 2011 年增长 60%；培养各类专业人员 16 人，是 2011 年的 4 倍。受训聋儿有 27 名进入普幼普小，有 9 名进入聋校；开展成年听力语言康复技术服务，聋人接受服务 2955 人次，是 2011 年的 2 倍。机构康复功能，依然主要集中在听力语言训练和社区指导上；助听器验配、人工耳蜗、成年听力语言康复等由于技术含量较大，主要集中在市聋儿康复中心开展。

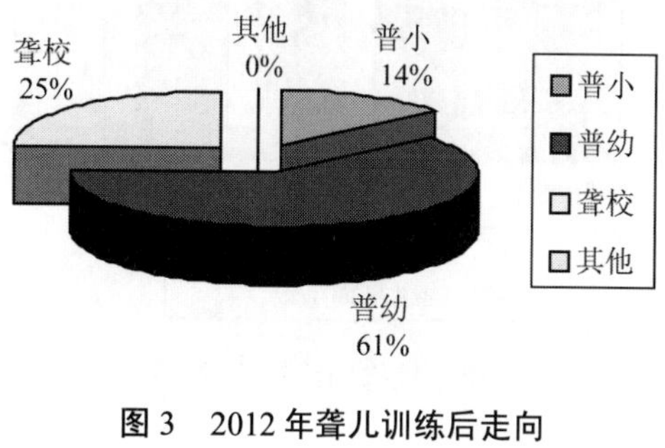

图 3　2012 年聋儿训练后走向

大力推广“社会化、综合性、开放式”精神病防治康复工作。2012 年，在 16 个区县开展精神病防治康复工作，覆盖总人口数达到 984.4 万人。对 62155 名精神病患者进行综合防治康复，监护率达到 95.3%，显好率达到 76.8%，社会参与率达到 66.7%、无关锁病人。接受治疗的精神病患者 13773 人。接受康复训练的精神病人数 10776 人，其中在精神康复机构训练的 8118 人。对 2995 名贫困精神病患者进行医疗救助，占贫困患者的 40.7%。建立了 2 个省级孤独症儿童康复训练机构，有 70 名孤独症儿童进行了康复训练，是 2011 年的 2 倍。

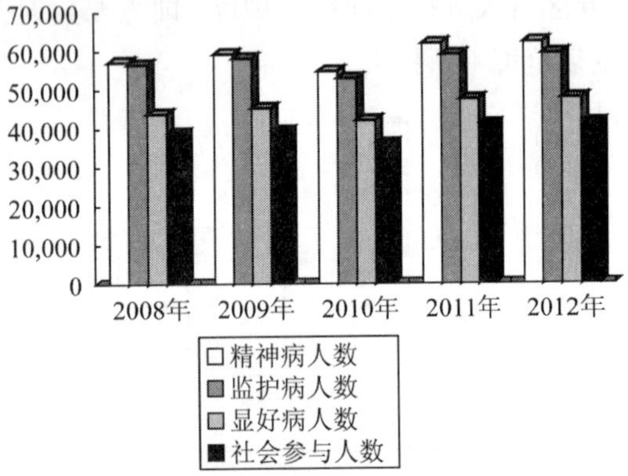

图 4　精神病防治康复工作情况（人）

全年开展肢体残疾康复训练服务的机构达到 5 个,完成 23 例贫困肢体残疾儿童矫治手术、装配了矫形器等辅助器具，进行了术后康复训练。对 4472 名肢体残疾人进行了康复训练,比 2011 年增长 3 倍，其中：脑瘫儿童机构康复训练 99 人,比 2011 年增长 50%, 肢体残疾儿童社区、家庭康复 212 人，是 2011 年的 3.5 倍，成年肢体残疾人社区、家庭康复 4161 人，是 2011 年的 4 倍。

全年开展智力残疾康复训练服务的机构达到 4 个；对 1707 名智力残疾儿童进行了康复训练，是 2011 年的 6 倍，不同程度地开展了智力残疾儿童早期康复训练与服务。

图 5　智力残疾康复机构训练与社区、家庭训练对比

深入开展残疾人辅助器具供应服务，全面推进普及型辅助假肢装配工作，截止到 2012 年底，累计建立辅助器具供应服务机构 9 个，为残疾人装配假肢 258 例，比 2011 年增长 70.8%。全市辅助器具供应品种 85 种 40289 件，较 2011 年增长 5.6%，装配矫形器 365 例，是 2011 年的 3.6 倍。国家彩金项目为残疾人免费发放 3966 件。残疾人辅助器具管理水平和供应服务水平有所提高，使更多贫困残疾人得以恢复和改善肢体功能，生活自理。从 2012 年与近几年辅助器具各个指标对比上看，辅助器具供应呈增加趋势。

开展残疾儿童筛查工作县 14 个，开展残疾儿童筛查工作的医疗卫生机构 6 个，本年度新诊断 0-6 岁残疾儿童 318 人，发放儿童残疾预防宣传材料 8805 份，举办儿童残疾预防宣传活动 14 次，建立残疾儿童家长学校 1 个，本年度开展家长学校活动 1 次，参与 25 人次。

二、残疾人教育工作进展良好

2012 年，为接受各阶段教育的残疾学生发放助学金，残疾人整体素质有所提高。全市各特教学校义务教育阶段对残疾学生继续实施“三免一补”（免交杂费、教科书费、住宿费，补贴生活费）政策，实现义务教育阶段免费教育。未入学学龄残疾儿童少年总数 477 人，其中视力残疾 9 人，听力残疾 16 人，言语残疾 15 人，智力残疾 233 人，肢体残疾 175 人，精神残疾 2 人，多重残疾 27 人。

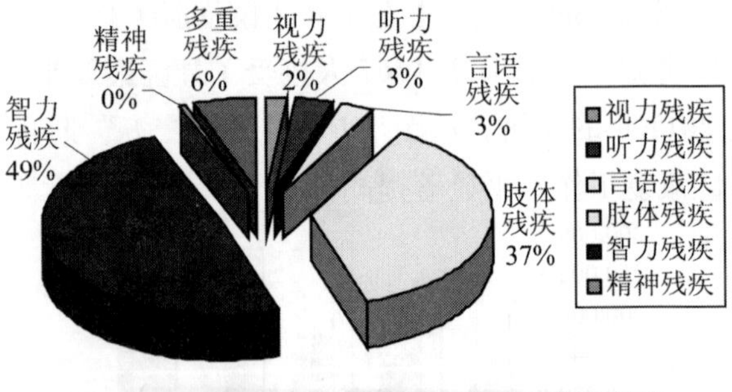

图 6　2012 年度未入学学龄残疾儿童少年分类

2012 年，残疾人特殊教育事业发展较稳定。开办特殊教育普通高中 2 所，在校生 132 人；其中聋高中 1 所，在校生 102 人；盲高中 1 所，在校生 30 人。残疾人中等职业教育机构有 1 个，在校生 15 人。高等特殊教育学院 2 所,有 72 名残疾人被普通高等院校录取。

三、残疾人就业工作稳步推进

2012年，各区县残疾人城镇集中就业人数有所增加，本年度新增643人；按比例就业依然是残疾人主要就业形式，2012年新增1511人；个体就业及其他形式就业2012年新增241人。到2012年底，全市城镇累计安排残疾人就业34995人，其中公益性岗位就业394人，2012年新增169人，是2011年的2倍。

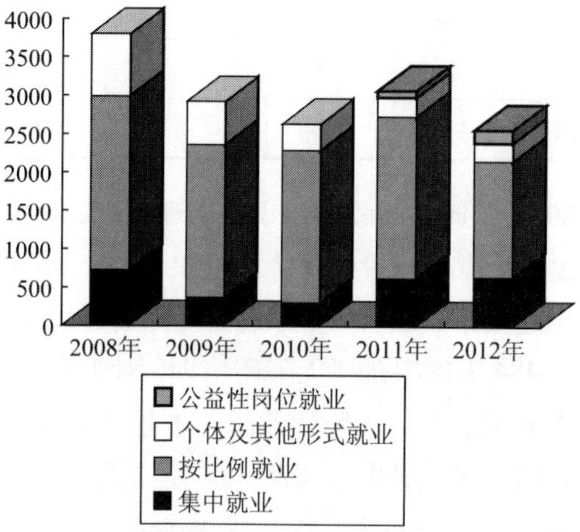

图7 近几年城镇残疾人本年度新增就业状况（人）

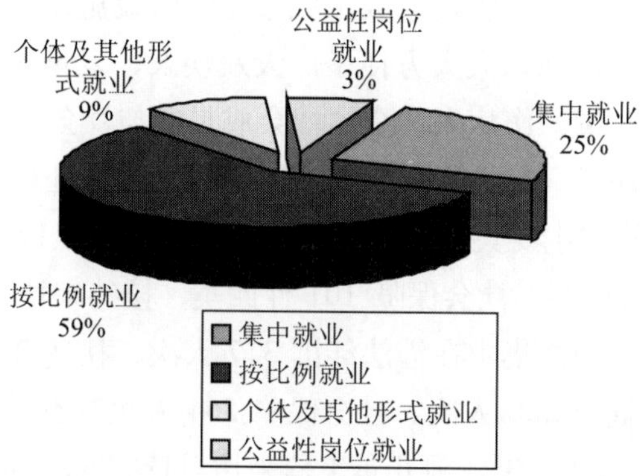

图8 2012年城镇残疾人四种就业形式本年度新增就业情况

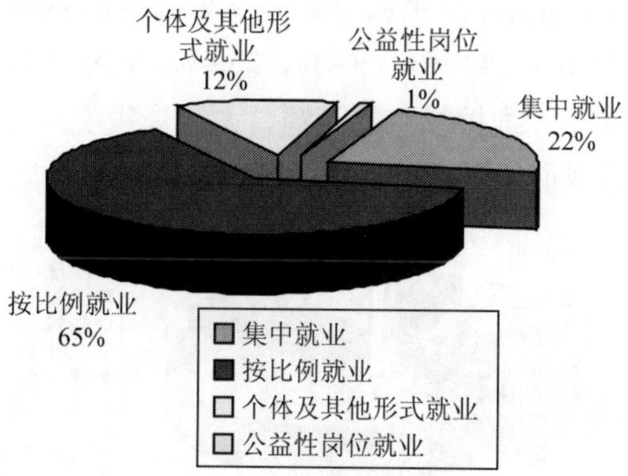

图9 2012年城镇残疾人四种就业形式累计就业情况

到2012年底，农村残疾人实际就业67258人。农村残疾人主要从事农业生产劳动，有47684人，占总数的71%，较2011年有所增加。

截止2012年底，全市城乡残疾人就业合计102253人，突破了10万大关。

职业培训基地24个,其中残联兴办13个，本年度城镇职业培训人数1780人。培训盲人保健按摩36人；医疗按摩人员25人，保健按摩机构达到159个，医疗按摩机构达到4个，较2011年有所增加。

四、残疾人社会保障工作逐步完善

随着我市生活保障制度的不断规范和完善，更多的残疾人得到扶助，2012年，城乡55122名残疾人纳入最低生活保障范围，实现了“应保尽保”；为进一步改善残疾人家庭的生活状况，在低保这一最基本的保障措施基础上给予生活救助，城镇已纳入最低生活保障32973人，城镇集中供养和其他救助救济15111人；农村已纳入最低生活保障22149人，农村五保供养和其他救助救济22600人。

在城镇，残疾人参加社会保险，特别是通过多种形式就业后参加社会保险的人数较2011年有所增加，2012年城镇残疾职工参加社会保险人数达到35997人，其中参加养老保险人数26759人，参加医疗保险人数25483人；城镇残疾居民参加医疗保险达到71136人。

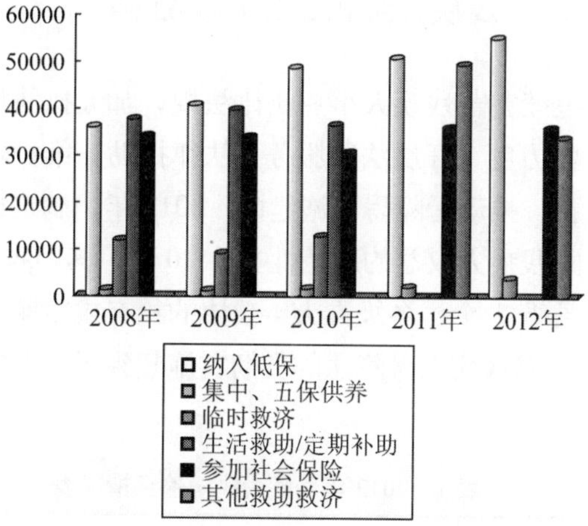

图10 残疾人社会保障情况（人）

截止2012年，建立了寄宿制托养机构9个，托养残疾人162人；日间照料托养机构合计70个，托养残疾人1137人；本年度享受居家托养服务残疾人9985人。

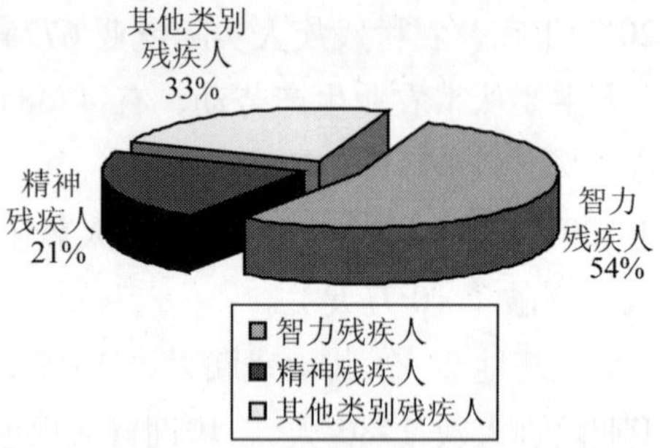

图 11　2012 年在托养服务机构中托养的残疾人情况

五、残疾人扶贫工作成效显著

加大扶持力度，加强实用技术培训，扩大扶贫成果，扶贫效果显著。2012 年，扶持残疾人户 14216 户，扶持 17077 人次，无脱贫人次，无返贫人员。接受实用技术培训的残疾人 2884 人次，投入培训经费 82.6 万元。积极动员机关、企事业单位、志愿者组织及党员、干部、学生、街坊邻里等社会各界，采取多种形式，进行“帮、包、带、扶”，并充分发挥工会、共青团、妇联等团体和组织在残疾人扶贫工作中的作用，结对帮扶单位 184 个，结对帮扶个人 403 人；建立残疾人扶贫基地 154 个，安置残疾人就业 2010 人，扶持带动残疾人 2559 户。

农村贫困残疾人危房改造成绩显著。2012 年完成 101 户农村贫困残疾人危房改造，投入危房改造资金 205 万元，受益残疾人 127 人。

六、残疾人维权工作切实加强

继续完善残疾人事业法律法规，加大执法检查和监督力度，开展法律服务、法律援助，维护残疾人权益，推动无障碍设施建设。2012 年，制定或修改保障残疾人权益的规范性文件 10 个，其中省级 7 个、县级 3 个；各级人大、政协的检查或专题调研 19 次，对残疾人保障法的贯彻实施起到了重要的推动作用。

表 1　2012 年残疾人执法检查情况表

级别	人大执法检查或专题调研	政协视察或专题调研
省级	1	0
县级	16	2

已建立残疾人法律救助工作协调机构 17 个；建立残疾人法律救助工作站 17 个，2012 年办理案件 461 件，其中，省级 107 件、县级 354 件。2012 年残联协助人大代表、政协委员提出议案、建议、提案 3 件，办理议案、建议、提案 8 件，残疾人参政议政工作得到加强。

表 2　2012 年残疾人法制宣传教育和法律工作者培训班情况表

级别	法制宣传教育		残疾人工作者法律培训	
	普法宣传教育活动		法律培训班	
	次数	人数	个数	人数
省级	2	210	2	150
县级	47	2324	18	1008

2012 年颁布无障碍建设与管理法规、政府令 9 个；建立无障碍建设领导协调组织 17 个；系统开展无障碍建设市、县 16 个；进行无障碍建设检查 60 次，有 484 人次参加了无障碍培训，对 1487 户贫困残疾人家庭进行了无障碍改造。本年度发放残疾人机动轮椅车燃油补贴 16075 人。全市大多数新建主要城市道路、公共建筑物、居住建筑大都建设了相应的无障碍设施，同时加强了无障碍改造和对已建无障碍设施的管理，我市城市无障碍设施建设得到进一步加强，大大方便了广大残疾人、老年人、妇女、儿童、伤病人和全体社会成员参与社会生活。

2012 年，全市各级残联信访部门共处理来信 224 件，主要集中在涉法涉诉 30 件、扶贫 17 件、就业 20 件、社会保障 101 件四类；接待来访 2222 人次，同样集中在涉法涉诉 317 人次、扶贫 258 人次、就业 208 人次、社会保障 564 人次四类。整体来看，2012 年较前几年来信来访总量有所增加，其中，涉法涉诉、扶贫、就业、社会保障四类分别占总的来信量的 13.4%、7.6%、8.9%、45.1%,占来访量的 14.3%、11.6%、9.4%、25.4%；残疾人基本生活、就业、维护权利等问题，尤其是残疾人生活，仍然是我们迫切要解决的重大问题。

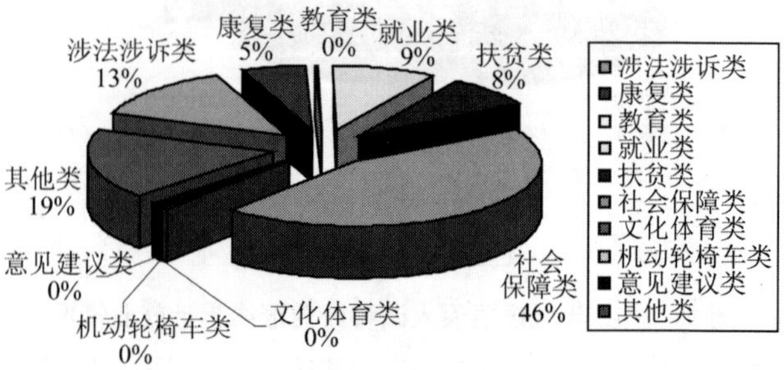

图 12　2012 年残疾人来信（件）情况

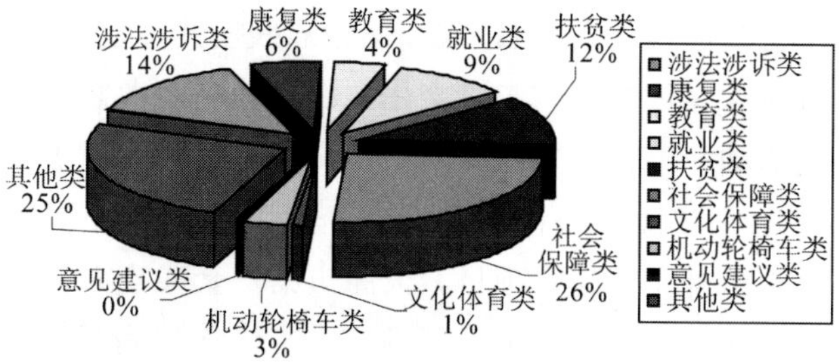

图 13　2012 年残疾人来访（人次）情况

七、宣传文化体育工作广泛深入

2012 年，中央级媒体采用稿件 6 件，省级主要新闻媒体刊播稿件数 1820 件，省级报纸专版 6 个，省级广播电台残疾人专题节目 1 个，省级电视手语栏目 1 个，省级残疾人事业新闻宣传促进会 1 个；地市级主要新闻媒体刊播稿件数 283 件，地市级报纸专版 13 个，地市级广播电台残疾人专题节目 10 个，地市级电视手语栏目 3 个，地市级电视公益广告片 1 个，地市级报纸公益广告 2 个，建立地市级新促会 2 个。

省级公共图书馆设立盲文及盲人有声读物阅览室已达到 2 个，举办残疾人文化周 1 场次，举办残疾人文化艺术类比赛及展览分别是 3 次，已成立残疾人艺术团队 3 个。

地市级公共图书馆设立盲文及盲人有声读物阅览室已达到 19 个，举办残疾人文化周 12 场次，举办残疾人文化艺术类比赛及展览分别是 38 次，已成立残疾人艺术团队 14 个。

省级残疾人群众体育健身活动 8 次，参加人数 4000 人，残疾人体育示范点 13 个，残疾人体育健身指导员 165 人，残疾人体育比赛 9 次，参与的残疾人运动员 2300 人次，残疾人体育训练基地 3 个，聘任教练员 14 人。

地市级残疾人体育健身活动 156 次，参加 6832 人次，残疾人体育示范点 31 个，残疾人体育健身指导员 435 人。

八、残疾人组织建设工作进一步健全

天津市共有各类残疾人 57 万，其中持证残疾人 21 万，占残疾人总数的 37%。截至 2012 年底，全市残联系统实有人员共有 893 人，其中：市残联机关工作人员 44 名、直属单位工作人员 168 名，区县残联机关工作人员 135 名、直属单位工作人员 201 名，乡镇（街道）残联工作人员 345 名。全市 241 个街道（乡镇）已配备残疾人专职委员 252 人，有专职理事长 241 名、无兼职理事长，基本建立了“一办三站一岗（残联办公室、残疾人康复站、服务站（社）、志愿者助残联络站、残疾人维权岗），形成了多层次、多项目的残疾人服务载体和服务工作网络，为残疾人服务的能力显著增强。市及区县残联全部建立了残疾人人才库，有 651 名残疾人入库，其中，市级 123 人，区县级 528 人。目前，已有 3518 个村建立了残协，建立了 2899 个残疾人活动室，选聘了 3490 个残疾人专职委员；1335 个社区建立了残协，建立了 1223 个残疾人活动室，选聘了 1179 个残疾人专职委员。

随着志愿者队伍的不断壮大，越来越多的残疾人得到不同程度的帮助。目前，全市已登记在册助残志愿者共 101978 人，受助残疾人共计 71657 人。

九、残疾人信息化建设工作稳步提高

残疾人信息化建设队伍不断壮大，市及区县残联至少配备了一名统计人员，全系统共有统计人员 27 人，其中 7 人获得了统计从业资格证书；有信息化专业技术人员 57 人，全系统工作人员计算机知识水平较往年有所提高。

目前，市残联及 13 个区县残联建立了门户网站。市残联门户网站全年发稿量 797 篇，是 2011 年的 2 倍。加大信息化基础设施建设和技术保障工作，提高信息化安全投入。2012 年，全系统计算机拥有量 542 台，较 2011 年增长 7.3%；全年信息化建设投入 114.3 万元。其中：硬件投入 60.6 万元，软件投入 23.8 万元，系统运行维护费 29.9 万元；用于信息化安全的投入 2.9 万元。

总之，2012 年我市全面完成了残疾人事业“十二五”年度任务，在完善和落实残疾人事业法规政策、保障残疾人合法权益、健全残疾人社会保障和服务体系、改善残疾人物质和文化生活状况、发展残疾人体育运动等方面取得了新进展，推动我市残疾人事业发展继续走在全国前列。国家和本市残疾儿童抢救性康复项目深入开展。全面提高了康复服务水平。为各教育阶段残疾学生和贫困残疾人家庭子女发放了助学金；对适龄重度残疾儿童少年积极开展送教上门服务，义务教育向学前教育和职业教育两头延伸。进一步加大落实促进残疾人就业和自主创业政策力度，加强残疾人就业援助和服务，我市肢体残疾人李振环被国务院命名为全国就业创业优秀个人。农村残疾人就业和扶贫开发工作取得切实成效。全市残疾人法律救助机制进一步健全，残疾人法律援助范围进一步扩大，大力推广基层残疾人诉求表达和信访代理机制，加强残疾人信访事项办理结果反馈及监督制度的落实，强化解决残疾人矛盾纠纷和困难问题的力度，切实维护了残疾人权益和社会和谐稳定。河东区和滨海新区大港申报为第二批全国“阳光家园”示范区，全市残疾人托养服务水平进一步提高。紧紧围绕推动残疾人事业科学发展和重要节点，开展了广泛深入的宣传活动和丰富多彩的文化助残活动。人民日报以《给残疾人一双隐形的翅膀》为题，天津日报以《特别的爱给特别的你》为题，对我市发展残疾人事业、改善残疾人民生情况进行了大篇幅报道；我市报送的广播节目《为明眼人指路的盲人》获第十届全国各地广播电台残疾人专题节目展播一等奖。编印了《社会主义核心价值观教育简明读本》，在残疾人和残疾人工作者中开展社会主义核心价值体系教育，举办了第四届残疾人歌唱大赛、第十届残疾儿童艺术节、残疾人文化月、“走进文化中心，共享艺术盛宴”等活动，丰富了残疾人的精神文化生活；天津市残疾儿童艺术节被评为 2012 年度天津市最受市民欢迎的精神文明建设项目。天津市第一套残疾人轮椅广播健身操向全国进行了推广；市残联和滨海新区塘沽残联共同承办了全国轮椅广播健身操训练营活动；成功举办了我市第二届“残疾人健身周”活动暨第三届“体彩杯”全民健身运动会残疾人组比赛。组队参加了一系列国际国内赛事，取得了较好成绩。中国残联先后确定和平区、河东区为全国残疾人文化体育工作示范创建单位，滨海新区汉沽、市残疾人文体中心为全国助残健身工程示范创建单位。进一步升级市残联计算机网络系统，实现了与中国残联残疾人基础数据库的平滑对接和与兄弟省区市残联的信息共享。我市残疾人事业信息化和统计工作受到了中国残联信息中心的通报表扬。我们将进一步增强信心，再接再厉，认真解决工作中存在的问题，推动我市残疾人工作不断再上新台阶。

2012年河北省残疾人事业发展统计公报

2012年，在中国残联和省委、省政府的领导下，我省各级残联以科学发展观为指导，深入贯彻落实党的十八大精神和国务院29号文件及残疾人事业发展“十二五”规划，以构建残疾人公共服务体系为目标，以“十项助残工程”为中心任务，紧紧围绕加快发展残疾人事业的大事、要事和残疾人“三最”问题，实施重点突破、带动整体提升，残疾人事业实现了历史性发展和跨越。

一、残疾人康复工作

社区康复服务覆盖面稳步扩大：全省有37个市辖区、138个县（市）共28018个社区（村）开展了社区康复服务工作，占社区（村）总数的56.15%；有16002个社区已建康复服务站，比2011年增加了8.68%；社区康复协调员累计达37044人，比2011年增加了5.59%；接受过培训的社区康复协调员累计达33344人；为1564600名社区内的残疾人建立了社区康复服务档案，占社区残疾人总数的40.04%，到2012年底，累计299852人接受过社区康复服务，比2011年增加了42.54%。

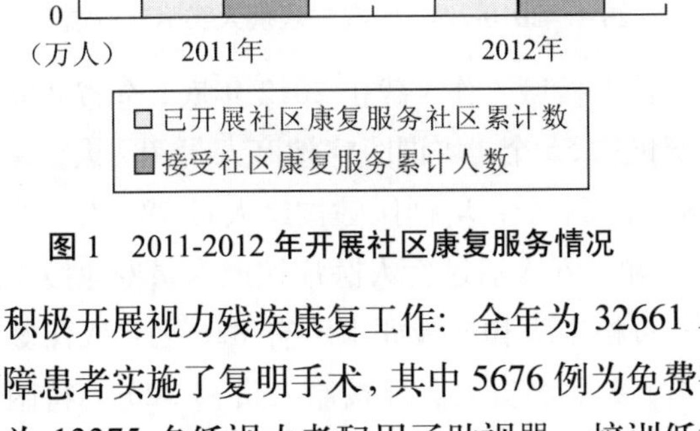

图1　2011-2012年开展社区康复服务情况

积极开展视力残疾康复工作：全年为32661名白内障患者实施了复明手术，其中5676例为免费手术；为13375名低视力者配用了助视器，培训低视力儿童家长2322人，配用助视器人数和培训家长人数远高于2011年；对6272名盲人进行了定向行走训练，远高于2011年的474名，并培训定向行走指导师146名。

认真做好听力语言、肢体和智力残疾康复工作：截止2012年底，我省共建成听力语言残疾康复机构93个；全年完成聋儿听力语言康复训练2346名，培训聋儿家长2704名；274名聋儿接受了地方项目救助；培训专业人员221名；成年听力语言康复技术服务1388人次。截止2012年底，开展肢体残疾康复训练服务机构73个，完成肢体残疾康复训练18710人，培训康复管理、技术人员778人次。开展智力残疾康复训练服务机构50个，有8246名贫困智力残疾儿童得到康复训练，培训管理、技术人员644人次。

大力推进精神病防治康复工作：全省有170个县（市、区）开展了精神病防治康复工作，覆盖总人口5549.9万，有257166名精神病患者，其中22.4万名精神病患者受到监护，显好病人数为14.7万人；有9.6万名精神病患者接受了康复治疗，6.2万人接受了康复训练；全省共有精神病康复机构89个，机构内精神病人数为6582人；在24268名贫困患者中有5874人接受了国家专项彩金服药救助项目医疗救助和国家专项彩金住院救助项目医疗救助，601人接受了其他项目医疗救助；培训精防康复管理、技术人员3540人；年度投入工作经费3425600元。到2012年底，孤独症儿童康复机构达32个，机构内有老师133人，有260名孤独症儿童在机构内接受康复训练。

加强残疾人辅助器具供应服务和机构建设：截止2012年底，全省市、县级残联共建辅助器具供应机构累计61个，其中市级9个，县级52个；全省各类辅助器具供应34167件，其中矫形器装配434例（国家彩金项目残疾人矫形器装配413例），装配普及型假肢970例（国家彩金项目残疾人假肢装配894例，其中大腿384例，小腿420例，膝离断23例，髋离断13例，功能性上肢17例，装饰假手37例），发放其他辅助器具32763件（国家彩金项目残疾人免费发放14717件）。

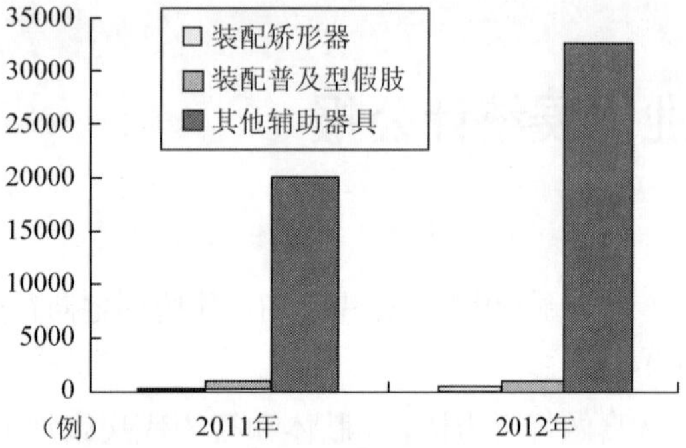

图 2　2011-2012 年辅助器具供应情况

积极做好残疾预防工作：到 2012 年底，全省有 30 个县、区的 37 个医疗卫生机构开展了残疾儿童筛查工作。本年度新诊断 0-6 岁残疾儿童 1283 人，其中视力残疾 146 人，听力残疾 224 人，言语残疾 57 人，肢体残疾 458 人，智力残疾 270 人，精神残疾 30 人，多重残疾 98 人。全省共发放残疾预防宣传材料 218698 份，举办儿童残疾预防宣传活动 227 次。全省共有残疾儿童家长学校 34 个，本年度开展家长学校活动 65 次，残疾儿童家长参与人数达到 4243 人次。

加强康复人才培养：截止 2012 年底，康复机构在岗人员总数为 7327 人，其中省级 488 人、市级 3283、县级 3556 人。2012 年共举办康复管理人员培训班 98 期，培训康复管理人员 1034 人；举办康复业务人员培训班 110 期，培训康复业务人员 1925 人；举办社区康复协调员培训班 171 期，培训社区康复协调员 8086 人。

二、残疾人教育、就业工作

积极发展残疾人教育：2012 年，我省有 600 名学前残疾儿童接受专项彩票公益金助学项目资助，327 名学前残疾儿童接受专项彩票公益金助学项目资助新入园，211 名学残疾儿童接受了其他学前教育助学项目资助。

截止 2012 年底，全省有统计的未入学学龄残疾儿童少年总数为 1561 人。全省开办特殊教育普通高中 12 所，在校学生 382 人，毕业生 92 人。2012 年，全省有 397 名残疾学生被普通高等院校录取，有 12 名残疾学生进入特殊教育学院学习。

截止 2012 年底，全省有残疾人中等职业教育机构 3 个，在校生 84 人，有 54 人毕业，其中 11 人获得职业资格证书。

残疾人就业状况稳定：2012 年，城镇新安排 12782 名残疾人就业，其中集中就业 4603 人、按比例就业 3464 人、公益性岗位就业 588 人、个体及其他形式就业 4078 人，辅助性就业 49 人。到 2012 年底，城镇残疾人实际就业人数为 196283 人，还有 27570 名城镇残疾人未就业。城镇本年新登记失业 1211 人。农村实际就业 872365 人，其中从事农业生产劳动 684720 人，占 78.49%；农村其他形式就业 187645 人，占 21.51%；还有 183062 名农村残疾人未就业。全省共有残疾人职业培训基地 524 个，2012 年对 17274 名城镇残疾人进行了职业培训。

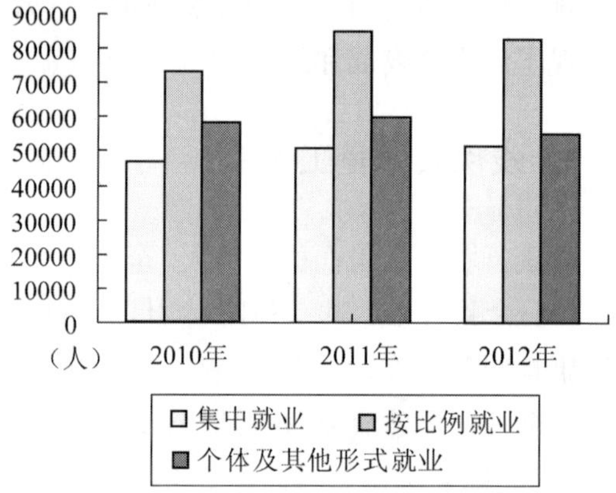

图 3　2010-2012 年城镇残疾人累计实际就业情况

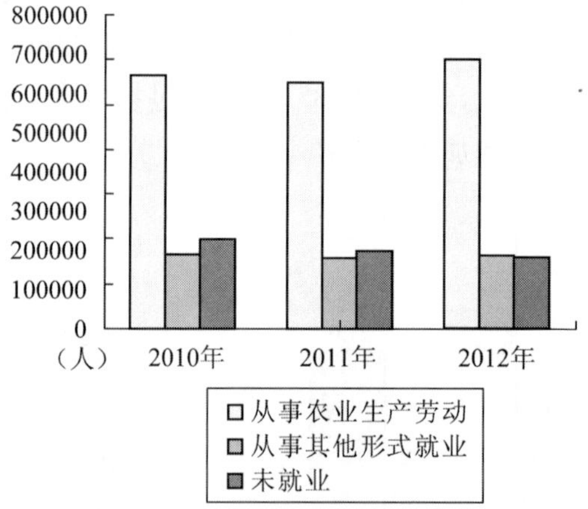

图 4　2010-2012 年农村残疾人实际就业情况

盲人按摩工作：截止 2012 年底，全省共有医疗按摩机构 55 个，培训医疗按摩人员 782 人；保健按摩机构 364 个，培训保健按摩人员 785 人；分别有 14 人和 146 人通过盲人医疗按摩人员专业技术职务任职资格中级和初级评审；有 826 名盲人保健按摩人员、410 名盲人医疗按摩人员和 320 名特困盲人按摩师就业。

三、社会保障工作

截止 2012 年底，全省 172 个县（市、区）全部开展了城镇居民养老保险工作，符合参保条件的居民 155862 人，实际参保 125382 人，其中 12622 名重度残疾人已享受养老保险金待遇。在 60 周岁以下的参保残疾人中，有 18763 名重度残疾人，其中 9414 名残疾人获得全额代缴，9349 名残疾人获得部分代缴；有 64615 名非重度残疾人参保，其中 2610 人获得全额代缴，14964 人获得部分代缴。

截止 2012 年底，全省 172 个县（市、区）全部开展了新农保工作，符合参保条件的农村残疾人为 1344044 人，实际参保 1145000 人，共中 79427 名重度残疾人已享受新农保待遇。在 60 周岁以下的参保残疾人中，有 153050 名重度残疾人，其中 66377 名残疾人获得全额代缴，86673 名残疾人获得部分代缴；有 636389 名非重度残疾人参保，其中 30726 人获得全额代缴，171414 人获得部分代缴。

截止 2012 年底，城镇残疾职工参加社会保险累计达 93450 人，城镇残疾居民参加社会保险累计 637091 人，城镇个体就业参加社会保险 28332 人。城镇中，68949 名残疾人已纳入最低生活保障范围，4030 人纳入集中供养，10673 人得到其他救助救济。农村中，358182 名残疾人已纳入最低生活保障范围，25010 人纳入五保供养，40013 人得到其他救助救济。17157 名残疾人享受生活补贴。

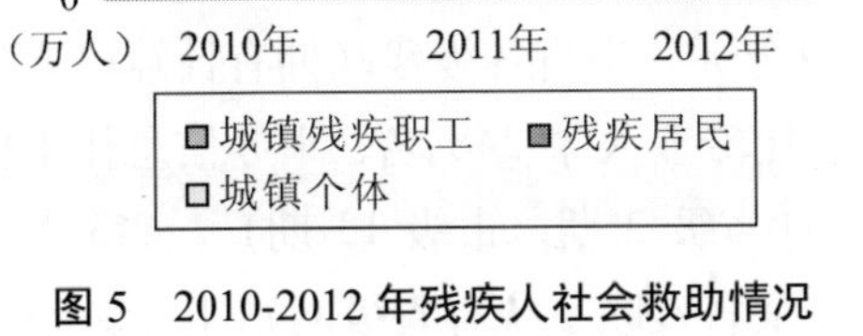

图 5　2010-2012 年残疾人社会救助情况

到 2012 年底，全省寄宿制托养服务机构达 129 个，3655 名残疾人在机构内托养；日间照料托养服务机构 30 个，529 名残疾人在机构内托养；居家托养服务托养 12102 名残疾人，占托养总人数的 74.31%。

四、残疾人扶贫工作

截止 2012 年底，全省农村共有贫困残疾户 465194 户，贫困残疾人 731747 人。2012 年共扶持农村贫困残疾人 168411 户，199230 名残疾人。其中 135999 名残疾人脱贫，有 17243 人返贫。47969 人次农村残疾人接受了实用技术培训，投入培训经费 1588.8 万元。1245 个单位和 7001 名个人对贫困残疾人结对帮扶。2012 年，全省共投入 4750.9 万元，其中省级投入 1738.8 万元，市级投入 1225.8 万元，县级投入 1786.3 万元，对 5410 户农村贫困残疾人进行了危房改造，使 6586 名残疾人受益。

2012 年，126 个残疾人扶贫基地安置 2115 名残疾人就业，扶持带动 7363 名残疾人。

五、残疾人宣传文体工作

2012 年，全省主要新闻媒体刊播稿件 3854 件，其中省级 613 件、市级 3241 件；报纸专版 77 个，其中省级 3 个、市级 74 个；有广播电台残疾人专题节目 13 个，其中省级 1 个、市级 12 个；电视手语栏目 12 个，其中省级 1 个、市级 11 个；电视公益广告片 18 个，其中省级 2 个、市级 16 个；报纸公益广告 16 个，其中省级 1 个、市级 15 个。

全省共建成公共图书馆盲文及盲人有声读物图书室 16 个，其中省级 1 个、市级 15 个；全省共举办残疾人文化活动周 118 场次；举办残疾人文化艺术类比赛及展览 52 次，其中省级 12 次、市级 40 次；有 6 个市级残疾人艺术团队。

2012 年举办省级群众体育健身活动 15 次，630 人次参加了体育健身活动。有省级残疾人群众体育活动示范点 27 个，残疾人体育健身指导员 52 人，残疾人体育训练基地 16 个，残疾人体育训练基地在编人员 50 人，聘任教练员 53 人。省级举办体育比赛 10 次，参赛残疾人运动员 660 人次。市级组织 107 次残疾人体育活动，10106 人次参加体育活动。全省共有市级群众残疾人体育活动示范点 56 个，残疾人体育健身指导员 456 人。

六、残疾人维权工作

继续完善残疾人法规和规章：省残联制定或修改关于残疾人的专门法规、规章 1 个，制定或修改保障残疾人权益的规范性文件 6 个；市级制订或修改关于残疾人的专门法规、规章 3 个，制定或修改保障残疾人权益的规范性文件 5 个；县级制定或修改保障残疾人权益的规范性文件 25 个。

加大执法力度和法制宣传：2012 年，全省各级人大执法检查或专题调研 76 次，其中省级 1 次、市级 10 次、县级 65 次；各级政协视察或专题调研 69 次，其中省级 1 次、市级 9 次、县级 59 次。各级残联组织的普法宣传教育活动 325 次，45143 人参加；举办残疾人工作者法律培训班 104 个，4663 人参加培训。

积极开展法律服务和法律援助工作，维护残疾人合法权益：全省共建立残疾人法律救助工作协调机构 129 个，其中省级 1 个、市级 11 个、县级 117 个。全省共有法律救助工作站 129 个，其中省级 1 个、市级 11 个、县级 117 个；办理法律救助案件 1101 件，其中省级 22 件、市级 559 件、县级 520 件。全省共有残疾人法律援助中心（工作站）186 个，其中省级 1 个、市级 11 个、县级 174 个；办理援助案件 2626 件，其中省级 27 件、市级 1223 件、县级 1376 件。

各级残联积极发挥参政议政作用：截止 2012 年底，全省残联系统共有各级人大代表 100 人，其中省级 4 人、市级 14 人、县级 82 人；政协委员 257 人，其中省级 6 人、市级 21 人、县级 230 人；协助人大代表提出议案、建议 29 件，其中市级 4 件、县级 25 件；协助政协委员提出提案 58 件，其中省级 4 件、市级 8 件、县级 46 件；残联办理人大建议 24 件，其中市级 4 件、县级 20 件；残联办理政协提案 40 件，其中省级 2 件、市级 11 件、县级 27 件。

无障碍工作继续推进：全省 11 个设区市、172 个县（市、区）全部系统开展了无障碍建设工作。全省共出台无障碍建设与管理法规、政府令 43 个，其中省级 1 个、市级 4 个、县级 38 个；全省共成立无障碍建设领导协调组织 128 个，其中省级 1 个、市级 11 个、县级 116 个；省、市、县有关部门进行无障碍检查 142 次；全省 950 人参加了无障碍培训；为 1357 户贫困残疾人家庭进行了无障碍改造。

全省共为 12803 名残疾人发放了机动轮椅车燃油补贴。

各级残联派出大量人员下访，把问题解决在基层，确保了社会稳定。2012 年各级残联共处理残疾人来信 1309 件，来访 8466 人次，有效地维护了残疾人的合法权益。

七、残疾人组织更加健全

截止 2012 年底，省、市、县、乡（镇、街道）全部建立了残联组织，市、县级残联全部配备了残疾人领导干部；全省各级残联共有残疾人工作者 5488 名。全省 172 个县（市、区）残联全部规范化达标。在 2264 个乡（镇、街道）残联中，有专职残联理事长 783 人，占乡（镇、街道）残联总数的 34.58%，兼职理事长 1481 人，有残疾人专职委员 2275 人。

截止 2012 年底，全省 48413 个村（含农村社区）全部建立了残疾人协会，配备了残疾人专职委员；2993 个社区全部建立了残疾人协会，配备了残疾人专职委员。全省 48124 个村（含村社区）建立了残疾人活动室，2978 个城市社区建立了残疾人活动室。积极开展志愿者助残活动，助残志愿者登记在册人数达到 137206 人，受助残疾人达 504982 人。

为提高残联干部队伍素质，2012 年全省各级残联共举办综合培训班 1532 期，36649 人次参加了培训；举办残疾人干部培训班 19 期，666 人次参加了培训。

八、事业统计与信息化建设

全省共有统计人员 213 名，153 人具有统计从业资格证书，占统计人员总数的 71.8%；本年度举办省级统计培训班 1 期，52 名统计人员参加了培训，市级举办统计培训班 14 期，407 人参加了培训。

全省各级残联本年度信息化建设共投入 304.6 万元，其中硬件投入 220.0 万元，软件投入 43.6 万元，系统运行维护费 41.0 万元；用于信息化安全的投入 11.9 万元。全省各级残联拥有计算机 1226 台，共有信息化专业人才 248 名，举办信息化工作培训班 15 期（省级 2 期、市级 13 期），443 人次参加了培训；全省残联系统有省级网站 1 个、市级网站 10 个、县级网站 25 个；省级网站当年发稿 2875 篇。

九、综合服务设施建设

截止到 2012 年底，全省已竣工并投入使用的各级残疾人综合服务设施共计 150 个，在建项目共计

5 个，筹建项目共计 2 个。其中已竣工并投入使用的各级残疾人综合服务设施总占地面积 24.96 万平方米，总建设规模 15.19 万平方米，总投资 2.94 亿元;

已竣工并投入使用的各级康复设施共计 5 个，在建项目共计 1 个，筹建项目共计 1 个。其中已竣工并投入使用的各级康复设施总占地面积 17813 平方米，总建设规模 12096 平方米，总投资 1678.10 万元;

已竣工并投入使用的各级托养设施共计 3 个，在建项目共计 1 个，筹建项目共计 1 个，其中已竣工并投入使用的各级托养设施总占地面积 25119 平方米，总建设规模 10304 平方米，总投资 2315 万元。

2012 年山西省残疾人事业发展统计公报

2012 年，在省委、省政府的坚强领导和中国残联的正确指导下，全省各级残联认真学习贯彻落实党的十七届六中全会、十八大和省第十次党代会精神，以邓小平理论、“三个代表”重要思想、科学发展观为指导，以目标责任考核为抓手，以残疾人社会保障和服务体系建设为重点，以为残疾人服务为中心，科学谋划事业发展，狠抓各项工作落实，圆满完成了年度工作任务。

一、康复工作

2012 年，康复工作紧紧围绕残疾人“人人享有康复服务”目标这一主线，不断推进康复机构规范化建设，康复救助政策不断完善，康复项目顺利实施，大批残疾人得到康复救助。

视力残疾康复 全年完成白内障复明手术 29124 例，其中为 7046 名贫困白内障患者免费施行复明手术；全年为 56 名低视力患者配用助视器，培训低视力儿童家长 3829 名，有效开展家庭康复训练。对 6364 名盲人进行定向行走训练。

听力语言残疾康复 加强聋儿康复机构建设，完善聋儿康复网络，共对 797 名聋儿进行了听力语言康复训练，培养各类专业人员 381 人。规范聋儿家长学校，开展家庭训练，共培训聋儿家长 1027 名。

肢体残疾康复 全年开展肢体残疾康复训练服务的机构达到 35 个,对 345 名贫困肢体残疾儿童实施矫治手术、装配了矫形器等辅助器具，进行了术后康复训练；对 9854 名肢体残疾人进行了康复训练，其中：脑瘫儿童机构康复训练 654 人,肢体残疾儿童社区、家庭康复 342 人，成年肢体残疾人社区、家庭康复 8858 人。

智力残疾康复 全年开展智力残疾康复训练服务的机构达到 37 个；对 4407 名智力残疾儿童进行了康复训练，不同程度地开展了智力残疾儿童早期康复训练与服务。

精神病防治康复和孤独症儿童康复 在 64 个县（市、区）开展精神病防治康复工作，对 100626 名重性精神病患者进行综合防治康复，监护率达到 80.52%，显好率达到 56.33%，社会参与率达到 44.48%，肇事率 0.04%；解除关锁 246 人；对 5945 名贫困精神病患者进行医疗救助。

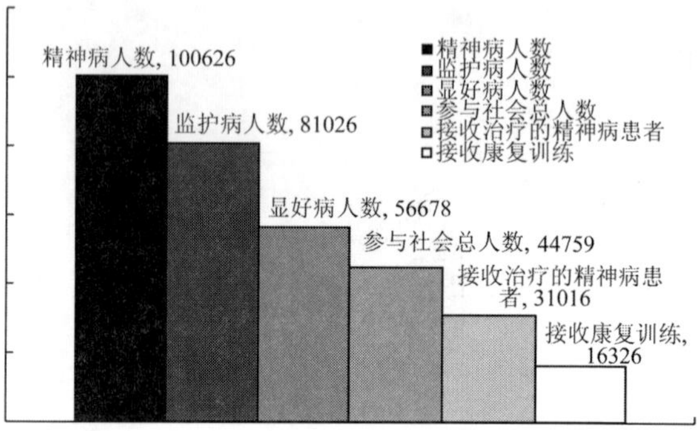

图 1　2012 年精神病防治康复情况（单位：人）

省级孤独症儿童康复训练机构，有 40 名孤独症儿童进行了康复训练。在其它康复训练机构训练孤独症儿童 190 名。

辅助器具供应 深入开展辅助器具供应服务，全面推进普及型假肢装配，截止到 2012 年底，累计建立辅助器具供应服务机构 43 个，为残疾人减免费用装配普及型假肢 725 例，供应辅助器具 37124 件。

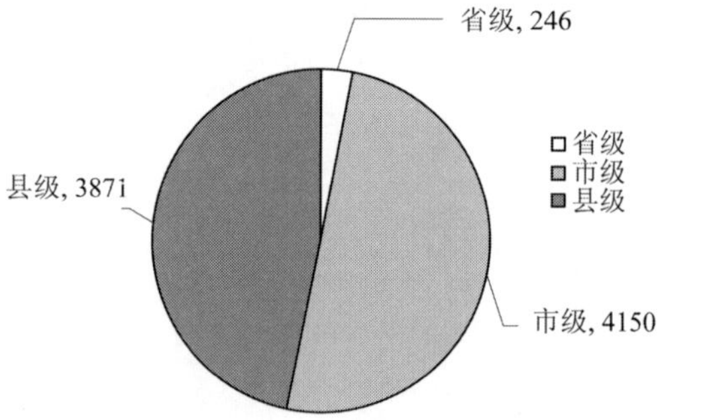

图 2　2012 年康复机构在岗人员情况（单位：人）

社区康复 在 23 个市辖区和 87 个县（市）开展了社区康复工作，累计建立社区康复站 4971 个，配备 16586 名社区康复协调员。

加大各市康复协调员培训力度，省残联举办 9 期社区康复协调员市（县）级师资等培训班，组织 100 名基层康复技术人员到省直康复机构进修。各市、县培训社区康复协调员 5600 名、康复管理干部和专业技术人员 1162 名。

二、教育工作

残疾人的教育工作受到了全社会的高度重视，残疾人受教育的权利得到了保障。通过实施彩票公益金助学项目，对198名残疾大学生每人资助5000元，对102名残疾人家庭子女大学生每人资助3000元，“交通银行—残疾青少年助学计划”资助了200名残疾高中生，每人1000元。使用78万元专项彩票公益金资助了308名学前年龄段的残疾儿童。我省4名特教学校教师获得“交通银行--特教园丁奖”荣誉。

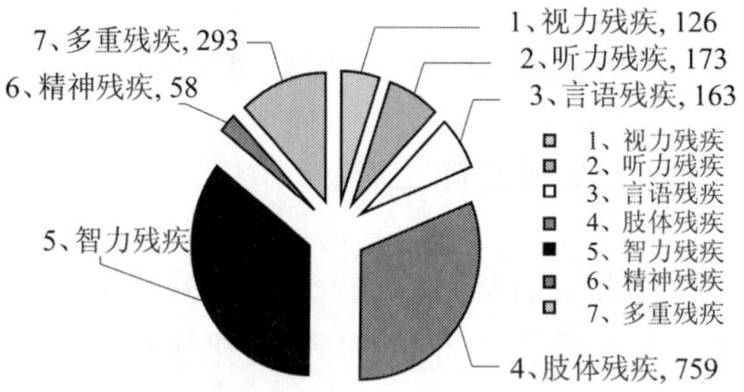

图3 2012年未入学学龄残疾儿童少年情况（单位：人）

全省开办特殊教育普通高中5所，在校生372人。其中：聋高中4所，在校生335人；盲高中1所，在校生37人。全省残疾人中等职业教育机构3个，在校生36人，毕业生17人。有183名残疾人被普通高等院校录取，51名残疾人进入特殊教育学院学习。

全省未入学适龄残疾儿童少年总数2435人。其中：视力残疾126人，听力残疾173人，言语残疾163人，智力残疾759人，肢体残疾863人，精神残疾58人，多重残疾293人。

三、就业工作

就业 继续实施了“城镇百万残疾人就业工程”，开展了以“帮扶到人、岗位到手、政策到位、服务到家”为主题的2012年全省就业援助月活动，进一步加大残疾人就业工作力度。城镇新安排5571名残疾人就业。其中，集中就业残疾人1836人，按比例安排残疾人就业947人，公益性岗位就业122人，个体及其它形式就业2614人，辅助性就业52人。全省城镇实际在业人数123451人。406923名农村残疾人稳定实现就业，其中：从事农业生产劳动294641人，其他形式就业112282人。

职业培训 组织我省选手参加全国残疾人岗位精英职业技能及盲文基础能力竞赛，获得了优秀作品奖和团结协作奖。全省残疾人职业培训基地300个,其中残联兴办72个，依托社会机构兴办228个；本年度城镇职业培训人数7235人。

盲人按摩 全省保健按摩机构354个，医疗按摩机构49个，全年培训盲人保健按摩人员402人、医疗按摩人员95人。组织了全国盲人医疗按摩人员资格考试和全省盲人医疗按摩资格评审，有2人通过医疗按摩人员中级职称评审，13人通过医疗按摩人员初级职称评审。

四、社会保障工作

残疾人的社会保障工作得到全面加强。按照重点保障和特殊扶助的要求，2012年我省实现了符合低保条件的残疾人“应保尽保”。参加城乡居民养老保险的人数进一步加大。城镇残疾职工参加社会保险人数达到85263人，其中：参加养老保险人数34477人，参加医疗保险人数41122人。城镇残疾居民参加医疗保险达到119075人。城乡262391名残疾人纳入最低生活保障范围，其中：城镇已纳入最低生活保障63095人，农村已纳入最低生活保障199296人。城镇集中供养和其他救助救济16223人。五保供养和其他救助救济80973人。

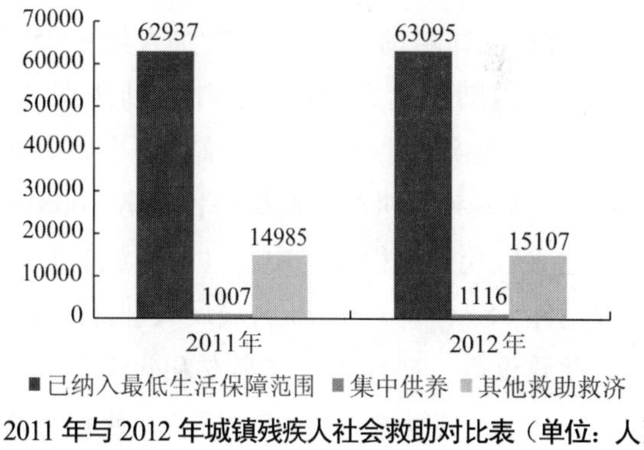

图4 2011年与2012年城镇残疾人社会救助对比表（单位：人）

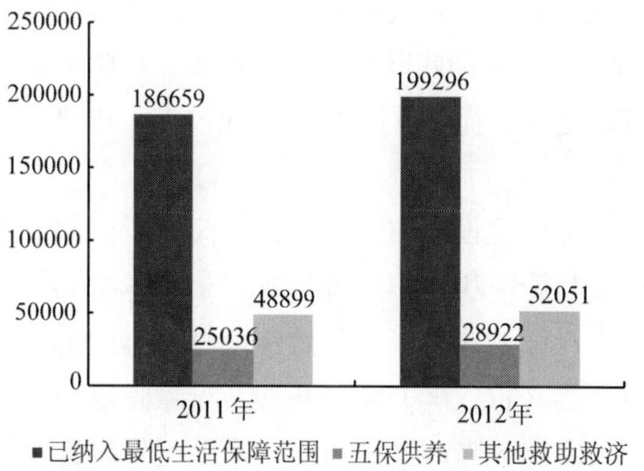

图5 2011年与2012年农村残疾人社会救助对比表（单位：人）

全省寄宿制托养机构 80 个，托养残疾人 1371 人；日间照料托养机构合计 41 人，托养残疾人 556 人；本年度享受居家托养服务残疾人 8483 人。

五、扶贫工作

本年度扶持贫困残疾人户 59879 户，扶持 94844 人，脱贫 40381 人。接受实用技术培训的残疾人 20866 人次，投入培训经费 691.47 万元。

结对帮扶单位 688 个，结对帮扶个人 2964 人；建立残疾人扶持基地 305 个，安置残疾人就业 5091 人，扶持带动残疾人 6746 户。

完成 4860 户农村贫困残疾人危房改造，投入资金 2369.50 万元，受益残疾人 5594 人。

六、维权工作

2012 年全力推进法制建设，积极开展残疾人法律援助和法律服务活动，扎实开展贫困残疾人家庭无障碍改造工作，积极维护残疾人合法权益。

法制建设 开展了《无障碍环境建设条例》我省实施办法立法准备工作，地市级制定或修改了保障残疾人权益的规范性文件 4 件；县级以上人大执法检查或专题调研 55 次，政协视察和专题调研 33 次。开展普法宣传教育活动 170 次，参加人数 28055 人； 开展法律培训班 80 次，参加人数 4225 人。

法律救助 建立残疾人法律救助协调机构 24 个； 建立残疾人法律救助工作站 27 个，办理案件 174 件；为残疾人进行了法律咨询服务 10081 人次。

建立残疾人法律援助中心（工作站）120 个，办理案件 753 件，对 1678 名残疾人进行法律援助。

参政议政 残疾人及其亲友和残疾人工作者当选为省、市、县级人大代表的 78 人；残疾人及其亲友和残疾人工作者被推荐为省、市、县级政协委员的 161 人。协助残联系统人大代表、政协委员提出议案、建议、提案 112 件，办理议案、建议、提案 55 件。

无障碍建设 市、县（市、区）政府制定无障碍建设与管理法规、政府令 16 个； 全省 43 个市、县（市、区）建立了无障碍建设领导协调组织；66 个市、县（市、区）系统开展了无障碍建设；贫困残疾人家庭无障碍改造 1873 户，无障碍建设检查 51 次，无障碍培训 646 人次 。

为 17159 名符合条件的残疾人发放了残疾人机动轮椅车燃油补贴。

来信来访 各级残联共处理残疾人来信 1776 件，接待残疾人来访 15787 人次，其中：集体访 19 批次，195 人次。

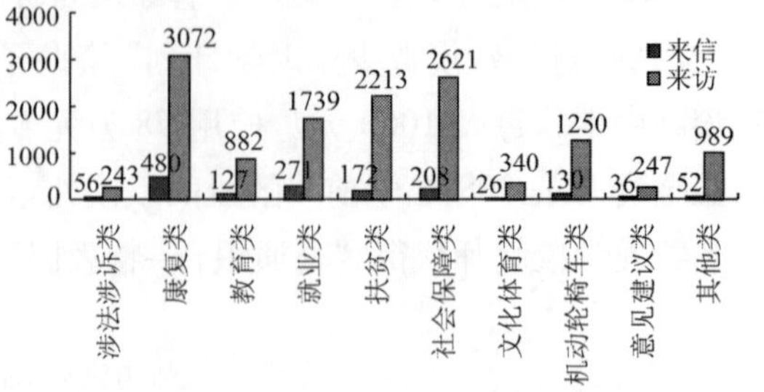

图 6 2012 年残疾人来信来访（县级）情况（单位：人、件）

七、宣传文体工作

2012 年，各级残联进一步加大残疾人事业宣传力度，以面向基层为重点开展文化体育活动、推动残疾人文化体育服务体系建设开展文化体育工作。

宣传工作 举办“山西省残疾人事业好新闻评选”和“广播电台残疾人专题节目展播”活动，选送 14 件作品参加全国评选。组织 2010 年-2011 年“山西省残疾人事业好新闻奖”评选，评出一、二、三等奖作品。省级主要报刊媒体刊登稿件数 302 篇；报纸专版 5 个；开办残疾人专题广播节目 1 个；地市级主要新闻媒体刊播稿件数 1512 件，报刊专版 17 个，残疾人专题广播节目 11 个，电视手语新闻栏目 1 个，建立地市级新促会 3 个。

文化工作 制定出台《山西省关于加强残疾人文化建设的意见》文件。省级和地市级公共图书馆设立盲文及盲人有声读物阅览室已达到 2 个和 10 个，举办残疾人文化周活动 2 次和 43 次，举办残疾人文化艺术类比赛及展览分别是 4 次和 24 次。我省省级图书馆和所有已建成完工的市级图书馆均全部建立了盲人图书室，没有市级图书馆的市在市政府所在区的县级图书馆建立了盲人图书室。

体育工作 举办省级残疾人体育健身活动 2 次，参加人数 400 人；建设残疾人群众体育活动示范点 1 个，培训残疾人体育健身指导员 132 人，组织残疾人体育比赛 1 次，参与的残疾人运动员 162 人次，聘任教练员 18 人。

地市级残疾人体育示范点 18 个，组织残疾人体育健身活动 73 次，参加人数 2047 人。

先后组队参加了全国特教学校盲人跳绳，盲人乒乓球，全国聋人田径、乒乓球、游泳等比赛，参赛人数47人，获得2个第一名、1个第二名、3个第三名以及其它名次。

在2012年伦敦残奥会上，我省盲人柔道运动员李小东、周倩分获1银、1铜。

八、组织建设工作

2012年，全省残疾人组织建设工作以加强基层残疾人组织建设为主线，以实施“强基育人工程”为抓手，各项工作稳步推进。

组织建设 按照《基层残疾人组织规范化建设（33条）达标验收方案》，完成了对基层残疾人组织规范化建设达标验收。全省市县出台了专职委员管理办法，两级残联对专职委员培训达1万多人次，通过财政支出和政府购买公益性岗位落实残疾人专职委员待遇的达80%。

在残疾人专职委员选聘方面，1463个乡镇（街道）中，选聘残疾人专职委员1827名；25467个社区（村）中，选聘残疾人专职委员24364名。

队伍建设 各级残联领导班子基本上都配备了残疾人理事长或副理事长。省残联配备了驻会盲人理事；11个市级残联中，有9个市残联领导班子配备了残疾人理事长或副理事长；119个县级残联中，有97个县级残联机关配备了残疾人干部。全省市县乡残联实有人员已达5196人。干部培训工作取得新进展。

专门协会 全省共建立各类残疾人专门协会533个。其中：盲人协会107个、聋人协会107个、肢残人协会108个、智力残疾人及亲友协会104个、精神残疾人及亲友协会103个、智力残疾人及亲友协会和精神残疾人及亲友协会二者合一的4个。

截止12月底，全省残疾人证录入数为746556条，发放证件705916个，发证率达到94.6%。

九、统计工作

统计队伍建设进一步加强，各级残联共有137名专、兼职统计人员从事残疾人事业统计工作，统计人员业务素质培养普遍得到重视，省级残联举办培训班1期，参加培训的人员达到80人次；市级残联举办培训班10期，参加培训的人员达到178人次。地方残联全面推进网站建设，目前省残联已开通了门户网站，有11个市级残联网站和60个县级残联网站也已开通，网站总数比去年增加18个。这为今后残联系统网站集群服务奠定了基础，残联系统网上信息服务正在逐步覆盖全省。市级残联开设网站技术培训班9期，培训各级残联信息员达165人次。各级残联共有191名专业技术人员从事信息化工作。

十、基础设施建设工作

截止到2012年底，已竣工并投入使用的各级残疾人综合服务设施共计47个，在建项目共计12个，筹建项目共计11个。其中：已竣工并投入使用的各级残疾人综合服务设施总占地面积11.71万平方米，总建设规模10.14万平方米，总投资2.69亿元。

已竣工并投入使用的各级康复设施共计31个，在建项目共计7个，筹建项目共计4个。其中：已竣工并投入使用的各级康复设施总占地面积10.14万平方米，总建设规模6.86万平方米，总投资1.67亿元。

已竣工并投入使用的各级托养设施共计1个，在建项目共计1个，筹建项目共计3个，其中：已竣工并投入使用的各级托养设施总占地面积0.60万平方米，总建设规模0.20万平方米，总投资0.04亿元；

十一、残疾人状况监测工作

配合全国监测办进行2011年度问卷数据计算机录入和质量评估，完成《2011年新一轮全国残疾人状况监测山西数据分析报告》和《2011年山西省残疾人小康实现程度评估报告》课题研究。

十二、各市残疾人工作生动活泼、锐意进取，创新争优氛围更加浓厚

太原市积极推进《太原市残疾人保障办法》修订工作。大同市协调城区政府通过公益岗位安置的办法解决了取缔残疾人机动轮椅车非法营运遗留问题。朔州市在怀仁县兴建了占地200亩的市残疾人扶贫基地。忻州市努力营造创业带动就业的良好氛围，被省政府授予“全省就业工作先进集体”荣誉

称号。阳泉市对城乡二级以上残疾人实施特殊救助，形成了长效机制。晋中市利用市级彩票公益金，对 200 名高中阶段残疾学生进行资助。吕梁市年初由市政府分管领导和各县（市、区）政府分管领导签订“残疾人事业目标管理责任书”，年中督导，年底考评。长治市被确定为“十二五”残疾儿童随报及早期康复工作试点市。晋城市残联被市政府表彰为“创业型城市创建工作先进集体”。临汾市积极创建“儿童康复无盲点市”。运城市残联在全国农村贫困残疾人信息管理系统培训班上介绍了凯盛项目扶贫经验。

在各级政府的大力支持下，在各级残联的共同努力下，在全社会的大力帮助下，残疾人事业虽然得到了快速发展，但残疾人事业滞后于经济社会发展的局面尚未根本改变，残疾人总体状况与社会平均水平差距较大的局面尚未根本改变，残疾人社会保障体系和服务体系不健全的问题仍然相当突出，残疾人事业城乡和区域发展不平衡的问题仍然相当突出。

推进残疾人事业又好又快发展，实现残疾人达小康目标，必须健全残疾人社会保障和服务体系，努力提高残疾人社会保障水平，切实保障残疾人基本生存权。以重度残疾人和贫困残疾人为重点，逐步建立完善生活补贴和护理补贴制度。解决好残疾人社会福利制度建设、农村残疾人扶贫开发和危房改造等基本需求问题，使发展成果更多更公平地惠及每一个残疾人。有效扩大公共服务供给，着力保障残疾人的发展权。重视残疾人人力资源的开发，千方百计促进残疾人就业，努力增加残疾人收入，缩小残疾人收入与社会平均水平的差距。以残疾儿童为重点，建立完善免费抢救性康复制度，加快普及残疾人基本康复服务。以促进残疾人全面发展为着眼点，不断提高残疾人受教育水平，丰富残疾人精神文化生活，促进残疾人充分参与社会。努力推进制度定型，为残疾人社会保障和服务体系长远发展打下基础。推动建立与经济发展和政府财力增长相适应的残疾人基本公共服务财政支出增长机制，建立政府主导、社会参与、公办民办并举的服务供给模式。

2012年内蒙古自治区残疾人事业发展统计公报

2012年全区残疾人工作按照自治区党委、政府的统一部署和中国残联的工作安排，以实施残疾人事业“十二五”发展纲要为重要契机，以深入贯彻落实中央7号、自治区党委6号和国办19号文件为根本要求，以构建残疾人社会保障体系和服务体系基本框架为主线，以全面实施残疾人五个专项工程为重点，全面提升残疾人工作整体水平，残疾人生活状况得到不断改善，重点难点工作有了新的突破。

一、残疾人康复工作

全区各类康复机构在岗人员总数达3515人。22个市辖区和81个旗县（市）全部开展了社区康复工作，累计建立社区康复站2017个，配备社区康复协调员9831名，为4.2万名残疾人开展社区康复服务。举办康复管理人员、业务人员、社区康复协调员培训班138次，累计培训各类康复人员6738人次。在7个旗县区开展了“十二五”残疾儿童随报及早期康复试点工作。

全年完成白内障复明手术10928例，其中为贫困白内障患者免费实施复明手术5749例；为1228名低视力患者配用助视器，培训低视力儿童家长162名；对2038名盲人进行定向行走训练。

各级听力语言康复机构有23所，系统开展助听器验配、人工耳蜗术后调试、听力语言训练、社会康复指导等各类康复服务，机构内在岗专业技术人员达264人。全年对528名听力残疾儿童开展听力语言康复训练，培训聋儿家长729名。

开展肢体残疾康复训练服务的机构有22所，在岗专业技术人员68人。全年为91名贫困肢体残疾儿童实施矫治手术，装配了矫形器等辅助器具，并开展术后康复训练；对5451名肢体残疾人进行了康复训练，其中：脑瘫儿童系统康复训练369人，肢体残疾儿童社区、家庭康复1083人，成年肢体残疾人社区、家庭康复3999人。

开展智力残疾康复训练服务的机构有19所，在岗专业技术人员60人。全年为1923名智力残疾儿童不同程度地开展了早期康复训练与服务。

全区投入111.6万元大力推广“社会化、综合性、开放式”精神病防治康复工作，目前已有84个旗县（市区）开展精神病防治康复工作。全年为2.4万名贫困精神病患者提供不同程度的医疗救助，对6.9万余名重性精神病患者进行综合防治康复，监护率达到80.88%，显好率达到53.50%，社会参与率达到45.74%，肇事率降至0.07%。全区建立孤独症儿童康复机构25所，机构内在岗教师92名，为248名孤独症儿童提供康复训练服务。

深入开展辅助器具供应服务，全面推进普及型假肢装配，截止到2012年底，累计建立辅助器具供应服务机构29个，为残疾人供应辅助器具1.6万件，减免费用装配普及型假肢542例，装配矫形器116例。

二、残疾人教育工作

开办特殊教育普通高中8所，在校生96人。开办残疾人中等职业教育机构4所，在校生147人，应届毕业生91人全部获得职业资格证书。残疾人接受高等教育规模继续扩大，共有354名残疾考生被普通高等院校录取，上线残疾考生录取率达到100%。为160名残疾儿童提供了学前教育资助。

未入学适龄残疾儿童少年总数1471人，其中视力残疾57人，听力残疾59人，言语残疾86人，智力残疾459人，肢体残疾510人，精神残疾43人，多重残疾257人。

三、残疾人就业工作

城镇新安排8284名残疾人就业。其中，集中就业残疾人2016人，按比例安排残疾人就业1759人，公益性岗位就业429人，个体及其它形式就业3684人，辅助性就业396人，全区城镇实际在业残疾人达到11.7万名。农村牧区28万余名残疾人实现稳定就业，其中从事农牧业生产劳动的22.8万人。

全区建立残疾人职业培训基地65个，其中残联兴办21个，全年为1.2万名城镇残疾人提供职业技术培训。

2012 年，新培训盲人保健按摩人员 272 名，医疗按摩人员 142 名，注册保健按摩机构 205 所，医疗按摩机构 29 所。

四、残疾人社会保障工作

全区城镇残疾职工参加社会保险达 6.1 万余人，其中参加养老保险 2.6 万人，参加医疗保险 3.5 万人。城镇残疾居民参加医疗保险达 11.9 万人。城乡共有 30.7 万名残疾人纳入最低生活保障范围，其中城镇 9.4 万人，农村牧区 21.3 万人。9.14 万名残疾人享受五保供养和其他救助救济。率先在全国实行城乡贫困残疾人生活困难补贴制度和重度残疾人护理补贴制度。

全区建成残疾人寄宿制托养机构 152 个，托养残疾人 3572 人。建立残疾人日间照料托养机构合计 60 所，托养残疾人 482 人。全年共有 1.43 万名残疾人享受居家托养服务。

五、残疾人扶贫工作

自治区党委、政府印发了《关于贯彻落实〈中国农村扶贫开发纲要(2011-2020 年)〉的实施意见》，全区共扶持贫困残疾人家庭 2 万余户，扶持残疾人 4.3 万人，帮助 3.9 万名残疾人实现脱贫。为残疾人提供实用技术培训 1.7 万人次，投入培训经费 828.5 万元。2680 个结对帮扶单位，6259 名结对帮扶个人为残疾人提供了社会帮扶。建立残疾人扶贫基地 85 个，安置 2229 名残疾人就业，扶持带动 3100 户残疾人家庭。

全年投入危房资金 8774.58 万元，完成农村牧区贫困残疾人危房改造 7685 户， 8596 名残疾人受益。

六、残疾人宣传、文化、体育工作

2012 年，中央媒体采用稿件 16 件，自治区主要新闻媒体刊播稿件数 41 件，盟市主要新闻媒体刊播稿件数 1294 件，开设电视手语新闻栏目 8 个，设立残疾人报刊专版 10 个，开办残疾人专题广播节目 17 个，建立新促会 3 个。成立自治区级残疾人图书馆 1 所，盟市公共图书馆设立盲文及盲人有声读物阅览室已达到 16 个。举办残疾人文化周活动 44 场次。成功举办了第二届中韩残疾人及残疾人工作者摄影展和自治区第三届残疾人文艺汇演。市、县两级残联举办残疾人文化艺术类比赛及展览 24 场次，成立残疾人艺术团队 7 个。建立残疾人体育训练基地 3 所，聘任教练员 6 人。建立残疾人体育示范点 8 个，选聘残疾人体育健身指导员 12 人。各地开展残疾人体育健身活动 42 次，参与残疾人 1152 人次。

七、残疾人维权工作

修订了《内蒙古自治区实施<中华人民共和国残疾人保障法>办法》。县级以上人大针对残疾人工作执法检查或专题调研 13 次，政协针对残疾人工作视察和专题调研 14 次。全区开展普法宣传教育活动 178 次，参与人数 1.82 万人次。开展法律培训班 42 次，参加人数 1981 人次。建立残疾人法律救助协调机构 40 个。建立残疾人法律救助工作站 27 个，办理案件 46 件。建立残疾人法律援助中心（工作站）102 个，办理案件 370 件。 协助残联系统人大代表、政协委员提出议案、建议、提案 77 件，办理议案、建议、提案 36 件。

自治区建设厅、经信委、残联联合印发了《关于贯彻落实<无障碍环境建设条例>的通知》。成立无障碍建设领导协调组织 21 个。完成贫困残疾人家庭无障碍改造 7167 户，为 1.7 万名残疾人发放机动轮椅车燃油补贴。

各级残联共处理残疾人群众来信 1047 件，接待残疾人群众来访 5888 人次。

八、残疾人组织建设工作

2012 年，全区各级残联实有工作人员 3244 人。12 个盟市中，7 个盟市残联领导班子配备了残疾人理事长或副理事长。106 个旗县（市、区）残联中，53 个旗县（市、区）残联机关配备了残疾人干部。

在残疾人专职委员选聘方面，1059 个乡镇（苏木、街道）中，选聘残疾人专职委员 1100 名。1.2 万个社区（嘎查、村）中，选聘残疾人专职委员 1.2 万名。

全区建立各类残疾人专门协会 551 个，其中盲人协会、聋人协会、肢残人协会各 112 个，智力残疾人及亲友协会、精神残疾人及亲友协会各 103 个，智力残疾人及亲友协会和精神残疾人及亲友协会二者合一的 9 个。

九、残疾人事业信息化建设工作

全区残疾人事业统计队伍建设进一步加强，各级残联共有 122 名专、兼职统计人员，且统计人员业务素质培养普遍得到重视。自治区残联举办培训班 1 期，参加培训的人员达到 170 人次，盟市级举办培训班 8 期，参加培训的人员达到 202 人次。

各级残联全面推进网站建设，除自治区残联门户网站外，已有 8 个盟市和 27 个旗县（市、区）开通残联门户网站，为今后残联系统网站集群服务奠定了基础。各级残联从事信息化工作的专业技术人员达 149 名，各级残联组织开展信息工作培训班 10 期，培训各级残联信息员 262 人次。

2013 年，自治区残联将按照中国残联和自治区党委、政府的工作部署，深入学习贯彻党的十八大关于“健全残疾人社会保障和服务体系，切实保障残疾人权益”的要求，深入贯彻落实党中央、国务院及自治区党委、政府关于加快残疾人事业发展的各项方针政策，认真实施残疾人事业“十二五”规划纲要，进一步推进和完善残疾人专项工程，加快残疾人社会保障和服务体系建设，推动残疾人事业与经济社会协调发展。

2012年辽宁省残疾人事业发展统计公报

2012年在省委、省政府重视关怀和中国残联悉心指导下，辽宁省残联坚持以科学发展观统领全局，牢牢抓住国家加快社会建设，着力保障和改善民生及高度重视残疾人事业的战略机遇期，紧紧围绕《辽宁省残疾人事业“十二五”发展纲要》，以组织实施全省“残疾人十大民生工程”为载体，圆满完成年度任务指标。残疾人生活状况进一步改善，“两个体系”建设取得显著成果，残疾人幸福指数不断提升，残疾人事业在更高的起点上又好又快地发展。

一、康复

2012年，以“人人享有康复服务”为目标，进一步完善全省康复服务网络建设。全省有62个市辖区、44个县（市）开展了社区康复服务，已开展康复服务的社区（村）11752个,占社区（村）总数的85%。社区康复协调员12921名，本年新增754名。已建社区康复站的社区10097个，本年新增377个。全省共1132878人建立了社区康复服务档案，占全省残疾人总数的55.7%，比上年度增长3.2%。317339人次的残疾人享受了社区康复，比2011年增长了178%。

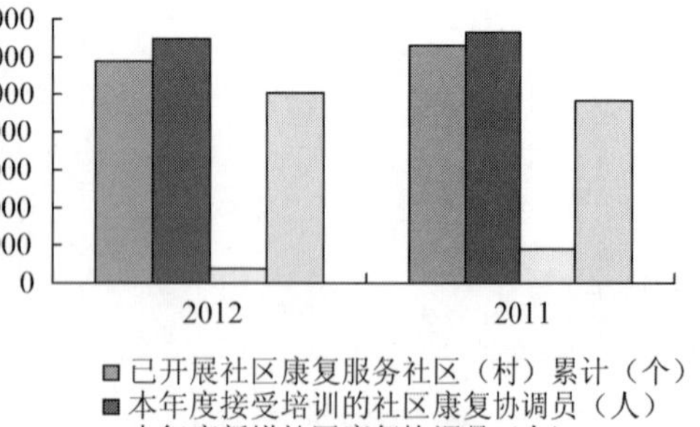

图1 2012年度全省社区康复情况

实施白内障复明手术20719例，其中，免费施行白内障复明手术的贫困患者7418名，占全年白内障手术总数的35.8%。低视力患者配用助视器人数为5926名，比上年度增长414.4%。培训低视力儿童家长1610名，比上年度增长362.6%。对6525名盲人进行定向行走训练，比上年度增长1126.5%。

新收训聋儿521名，其中，机构训练351名，占新收训聋儿67%。家庭训练170名，占新收训聋儿33%。在训聋儿数1043名。培训聋儿家长968名。培训专业人员266人，比上年度增长57%。接受地方项目救助18人。为957名成年人提供康复语言技术服务。累计建设机构44个，在岗专业人员475名，比去年增长140%。

精神康复机构148个，培训精防康复管理、技术人员1024名；孤独症儿童康复训练机构42个，在训儿童375名。

在107个县（市、区）开展精神病防治康复工作，对269033名精神病患者进行综合防治康复，监护率89%，显好率59%，社会参与率47%，肇事率0.011%，解除关锁47人，对25522贫困精神病患者进行医疗救助。

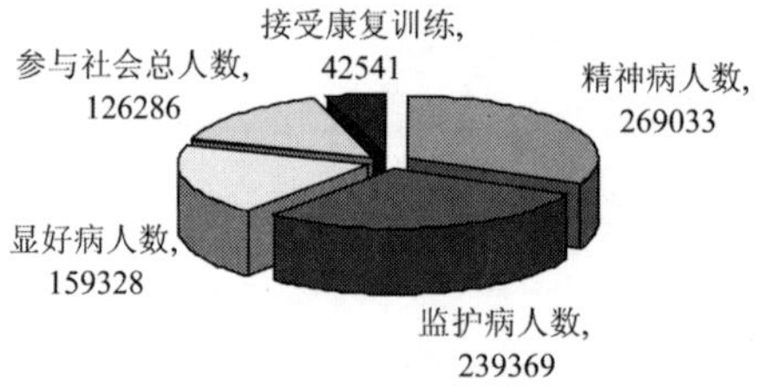

图2 2012年度全省精神病人康复情况（单位：人）

肢体残疾康复训练服务机构55个，机构在岗人员129名；肢体残疾康复16699人，比上年度增长141.8%，其中，脑瘫儿童系统康复训练666人，肢体残疾儿童社区、家庭康复训练1131人，成年肢体残疾人社区、家庭康复训练14902名。

智力残疾儿童康复3857人，比上年度增长152%；培训康复管理、技术人员2158人；智力残疾康复训练服务机构48个，残联办机构在岗人员111人，比上年度增长5.7%。

注重康复人才培养，举办康复管理人员培训班134期，培训1847人；举办康复业务人员培训班129期，培训1921人；举办社区康复协调员培训班187期，培训10097人。

深入开展辅助器具供应服务，全面推进普及型假肢装配工作。截止年底，全省累计建立辅助器具供应服务机构 105 个，辅助器具供应品种 414 个，计 27928 件，装配矫形器 468 例，装配假肢 2028 例，装配其它辅助器具 25432 件，为残疾人免费发放 15256 件。

二、教育

2012 年，残疾人教育服务体系逐步健全， 残疾人受教育水平不断提高。投资 4 亿余元的省残疾中等职业技术学校新校区主体已基本完成，并升格为辽宁特殊教育职业学院。当年学校共招收学历教育学生 347 人，在校学生达到 550 人。

全省残疾人事业专项彩票公益金助学项目资助 500 名家庭经济困难的残疾儿童，比上年度增加了 411 人。专项彩票公益金项目资助新入园残疾儿童 223 人，比上年度增加 208 人。

未入学适龄残疾儿童少年总数 3016 人，其中视力残疾 108 人，听力残疾 138 人，言语残疾 103 人，智力残疾 1143 人，肢体残疾 1087 人，精神残疾 148 人，多重残疾 289 人。

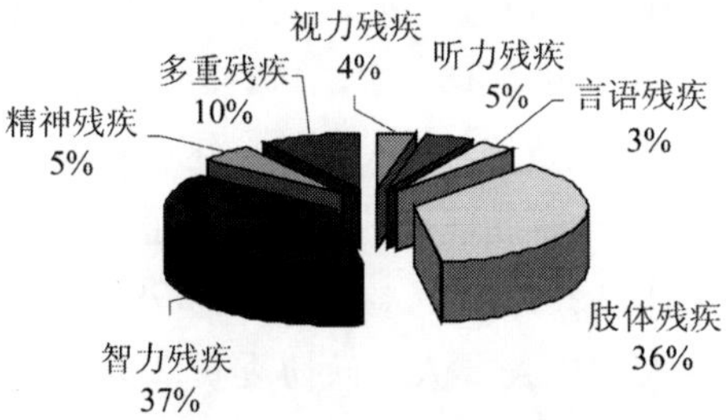

图 3　2012 年度未入学学龄残疾儿童少年分类

特殊教育普通高中学校（班）9 个，在校生 125 人。残疾人中等职业学校（班）6 个，在校生 262 人，毕业生 57 人，获得职业资格证书 49 人。残疾人中等职业技术学校招生 60 名。301 名达到录取分数线的残疾人被普通高等院校录取，257 名残疾人被高等特殊教育学院录取，上线残疾考生录取率 100%。

三、就业

2012 年，我省强化了残疾人职业技能培训，促进更多的残疾人稳定就业。城镇 316421 残疾人实现就业，其中，集中就业残疾人 101232 人；按比例安排就业残疾人 80962 人；公益性岗位就业 1989 人；残疾人个体就业和多种形式灵活就业 132147 人，是残疾人就业的主要形式，占整个就业比例的 41%。未就业人数比上年度下降了 6.3%。农村残疾人就业人数稳定增长， 401293 名残疾人实现就业，其中，从事农业生产劳动 290800 人，比上年度增长 2.6%；其它形式就业的是 110493 人，比上年度增长 3.7%；未就业人数比上年度下降了 3.3%。

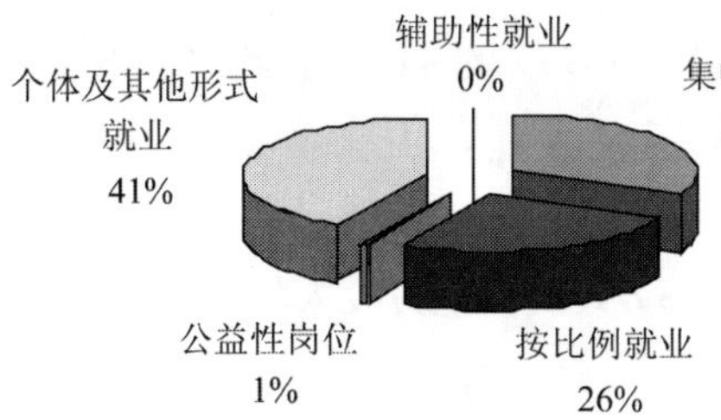

图 4　2012 年度全省城镇残疾人就业情况

残疾人职业培训基地 133 个，其中，残联开办 49 个，依托社会机构开办 84 个。培训城镇残疾人 15586 人次，培训人次比上年度增长 9.5%。盲人医疗按摩人员专业技术职务任职资格评审中，71 人通过中级、84 人通过初级评审；646 名盲人按摩人员就业，扶持 160 名特困盲人按摩师就业。

四、社会保障

2012 年，全省残疾人随着社会保障制度不断改善，残疾人社会保障水平进一步提高。城镇残疾职工参加社会保险已达 186018 人，其中，参加养老保险人数 111635 人，比上年度增长 27%，参加医疗保险人数 89447 人，比上年度增长 55.6%。城镇残疾居民参加社会保险 420982 人，其中，参加城镇居民医疗保险 183770 人，比上年度增长 33%。参加新型农村合作医疗 502367 人，比上年度增长 48%。城镇个体就业残疾人参加社会保险 36625 人，其中，参加养老保险 15209 人，参加医疗保险 14707 人。城镇纳入最低生活保障残疾人 163624 名。农村纳入最

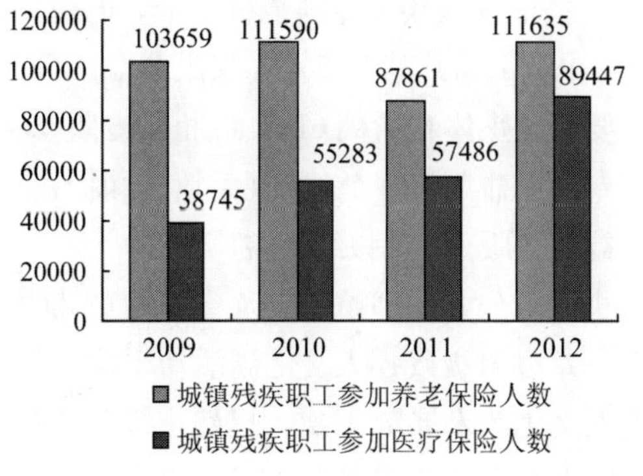

图 5　2012 年全省城镇残疾职工参加社会保险情况
（单位：人）

低生活保障残疾人187909名,其中,五保供养23485人,临时救济30633人,享受生活补贴4994人,享受护理补贴1987人。

五、扶贫开发

2012年,扶持72567名残疾人,占全省农村贫困残疾人总数173977的41.7%,其中,本年扶持了49598户残疾人家庭,占全省农村残疾人家庭120212总数的41%,使38978人脱贫;实用技术培训残疾人17697人次,地方投入培训经费544.74万元。

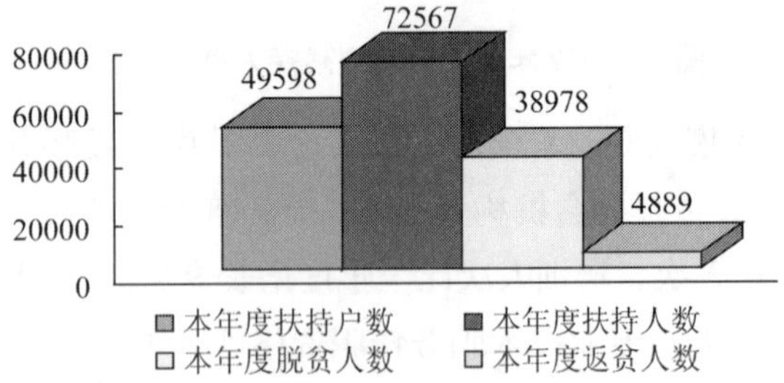

图6 2012年度全省残疾人扶持情况

省级财政投入扶贫资金500万元,康复扶贫贴息贷款项目实际落实3200万,比上年度增长1.6%,扶持残疾人1083名。本年度危房改造实际完成1790户,危房改造项目受益残疾人2228名,投入资金568.3万元。建立残疾人扶持基地54个,安排残疾人就业1018名,扶持带动2654名贫困残疾人就业。结对帮扶贫困残疾人的单位和个人分别达到4066个和21948人。

六、宣传文化 、体育

2012年,进一步丰富残疾人文化服务,残疾人体育工作取得显著成绩。中央级媒体采用稿件26件,省级主要新闻媒体刊播稿件466件,报刊专版有23个,广播电视残疾人专题节目1个,电视手语栏目1个,电视公益广告片5个,报纸公益广告3个。市级主要新闻媒体刊播稿6137件,报刊专版33个,残疾人专题广播节目9个,电视手语新闻栏目9个,电视公益广告版16个,报纸公益广告20个。

已建省级公共图书馆盲文及盲人有声读物图书室1个,举办省级残疾人文化周活动1次,举办省级残疾人文化艺术展览1次。已建市级公共图书馆盲文及盲人有声读物图书室18个,举办市级残疾人文化周活动91次,举办省级残疾人文化艺术展览55次,建立市级残疾人艺术团队9个。

建立省级残疾人体育训练基地28个,在编工作人员50人。市级组织残疾人体育活动100次,41837人次参加,比上年度增长34%。市级残疾人群众体育活动示范点40个,残疾人体育健身指导员358人。

七、维权

2012年,全省各级残联充分发挥残疾人法律救助站的作用,以各级司法行政部门、法律援助机构提供的法律服务和法律援助为主导,以有关部门、残联、社会力量等提供的法律救助为补充的残疾人法律救助体系已经基本形成。

省级举办普法宣传教育活动3次,160人参加。举办法律培训班1次,120人参加。建立残疾人法律救助协调机构1个,办理案件12件。建立残疾人援助中心(工作站)1个,办理案件1件;市级举办普法宣传教育活动31次,3329人参加。举办法律培训班22次,4490人参加。建立残疾人法律救助工作站14个,办理案件92件。建立残疾人援助中心(工作站)14个,办理案件236件;县级举办普法宣传教育活动182次,17245人参加。举办法律培训班64次, 3144人参加。建立残疾人法律救助工作站27个,办理案件106件。建立残疾人援助中心(工作站)100个,办理案件779件。

省级人大代表2人,政协委员2人,残联协助政协委员提出议案2件,残联办理人大建议1件,办理政协提案2件。

市级人大代表8人,政协委员35人,残联协助人大代表和政协委员提出议案、建议分别为3件和21件,残联办理人大建议13次,办理政协提案21次。县级人大代表66人,政协委员147人,残联协助人大代表和政协委员提出议案、建议分别为13次和29次,残联办理人大建议7次,办理政协提案14次。

无障碍建设法规、标准进一步完善。省、市、县(市、区)无障碍建设检查分别是9次、112次和106次,无障碍培训人次分别为350、1848和1522。市级完成贫困残疾人家庭无障碍改造812户,县级完成11335户,比上年度增加56.3%。

全省共处理残疾人来信971件,接待来访16130人次,其中,个人访14441人次,集体访122批次、1689人次。

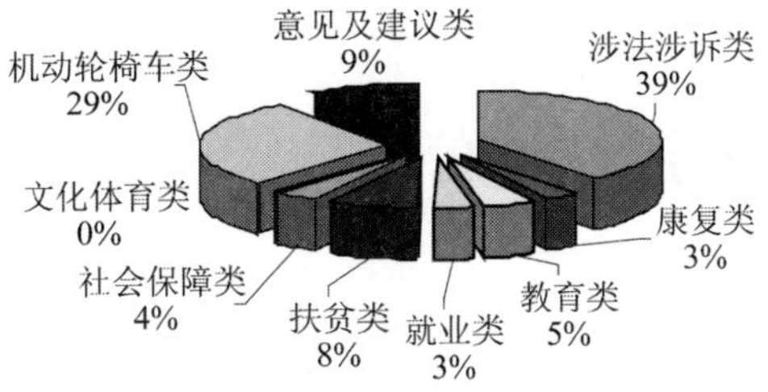

图 7　2012 年度全省信访人次

八、组织建设

2012 年，省级及 14 个市残联理事会已有残疾人领导干部 21 人，县（市、区）配备了残疾人干部或聘用残疾人 113 人。积极推进乡镇（街道）、村（社区）专职委员配备工作，全省已建乡镇（街道）残联 1510 个，村已建残协 11453 个，城市社区已建残协 3888 个。全省基层残疾人组织规范化建设全部达标。

我省街道、乡镇残联配备专职理事长 583 人、兼职理事长 811 人，配备残疾人专职委员 1641 人，村（社区）配备残疾人专职委员 15369 人，其中，村（含农村社区）11519 人，城市社区 3850 人。志愿者登记在册总数为 50832 人，受助残疾人总数为 179152 人。

九、信息化建设

2012 年，统计队伍建设进一步加强。全省 128 名专、兼职统计人员从事残疾人事业统计工作，各级残联重视统计人员业务能力培养，省级举办 1 期培训班，20 人参训；市级举办 20 期培训班，420 人参训，培训次数比上年度增长 5 期，增加人数 206 人次。

加大对基层网站的建设力度。市级残联建立网站 14 个，县级残联建立网站 52 个，网站总数比上年度增加 19 个。省及各市举办信息工作培训班 69 次，2225 人参训。省级网站全年发稿量 5316 篇。

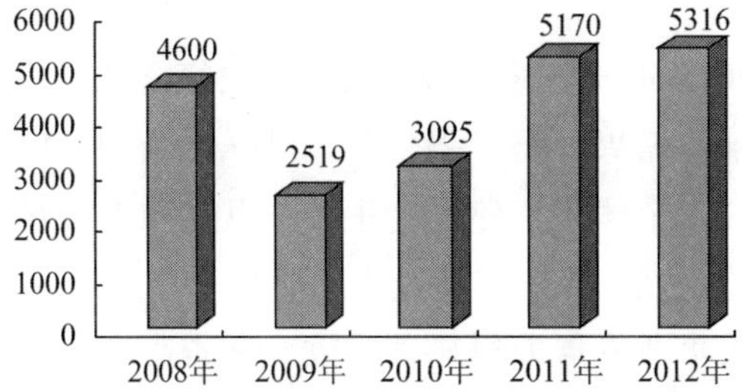

图 8　2012 年度省级网站当年发稿量（单位：篇）

信息化建设投入 349 万余元，其中，硬件投入 202 余万元，软件投入为 97.3 万元，系统运行维护费近 50 万元。信息化安全投入为 32.6 万元。信息化专业人才 196 名。计算机数量 1703 台，比上年度增长 10.2%。省级服务器 14 台。

从整体统计数据分析，2012 年全省残疾人事业各项任务指标基本完成，呈现积极向上的发展态势和卓有成效的工作局面。有 85%以上的残疾人参加了城镇医疗保险和新农合医疗保险。残疾人教育基础设施明显改善，残疾人家庭无障碍改造数量和质量明显提高，残疾人社会保障水平不断提高，残疾人服务持续改善。

2013 年全省残疾人工作将继续紧紧围绕我省经济社会发展大局，全面落实党的十八大对发展残疾人事业的要求，加快推进残疾人社会保障体系和服务体系建设，进一步改善残疾人生产、生活状况，不断加强各级残联思想、组织和队伍建设，在全面建成小康社会和建设富庶文明幸福新辽宁进程中迈出新步伐。

2012 年吉林省残疾人事业发展统计公报

2012 年，吉林省残疾人工作围绕全省“科学发展、加快振兴、富民强省”总目标，以加快推进残疾人“两个体系”建设为主线，以加强农村残疾人工作为重点，统筹实施残疾人事业“十二五”规划，残疾人事业发展取得显著成效，全省残疾人生产生活状况得到明显改善。

一、康复工作

围绕残疾人“人人享有康复服务”目标，继续推进康复服务体系建设，组织实施国家残疾人事业专项彩票公益金康复项目和“七彩梦行动计划”及吉林省“互助关爱助残工程”，等各类康复救助工程（项目），推进残疾人康复工作全面开展。

（一）视力残疾康复。全年完成白内障复明手术 1.5 万例; 为 2,947 名贫困白内障患者免费施行复明手术，全年为 7,254 名低视力患者配用助视器，培训低视力儿童家长 2,604 名，有效开展家庭康复训练。对 4,493 名盲人进行定向行走训练。

（二）听力语言康复。加强省级聋儿康复机构建设，完善聋儿康复网络。共对 409 名聋儿进行了听力语言康复训练，规范聋儿家长学校，开展家庭训练，共培训聋儿家长 904 名；培养各类专业人员 256 人。

本年度接受国家人工耳蜗项目救助 82 人，接受国家助听器项目救助 110 人，接受地方听力康复项目救助 52 人。

听力语言残疾儿童训练后走向所占比例为，普小 9.0%，普幼 52.8%，特教学校（聋校）15.7%，其他 22.5%。

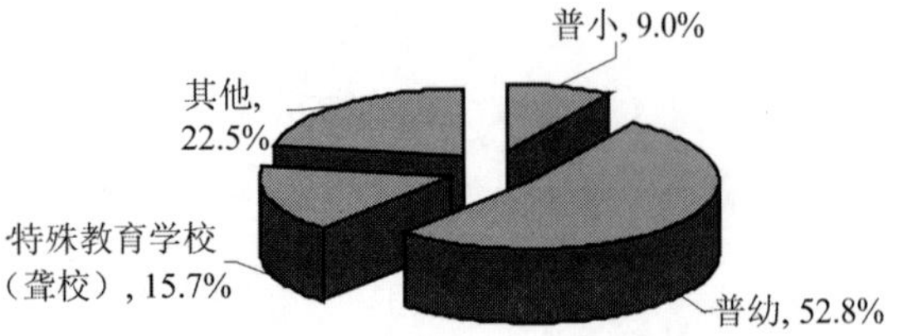

图1 2012年吉林省听力语言残疾儿童训练后走向

（三）精防康复和孤独症儿童康复。大力推广“社会化、综合性、开放式”精神病防治康复工作。2012 年，在全省范围内开展精神病防治康复工作，对 15.9 万精神病患者进行综合防治康复，监护率达到 97.1%，显好率达到 71.1%，社会参与率达到 58.7%，肇事率 0.4‰；解除关锁 12 人；对 2 万名贫困精神病患者进行医疗救助。

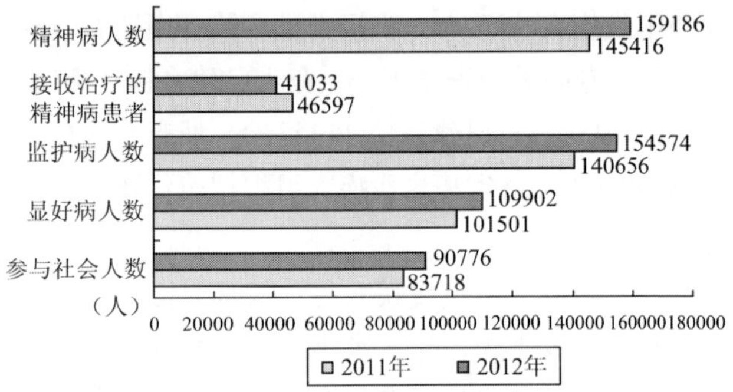

图2 2012年与2011年吉林省精防康复情况对比

全省共有孤独症儿童康复训练机构 36 家，其中本年度新增 4 家，在训儿童 354 名。有 220 名贫困孤独症儿童得到了康复救助。据测算，还有大量贫困家庭孤独症儿童没有条件接受正规机构训练。

（四）肢体与智力残疾康复。全年开展肢体残疾康复训练服务的机构达到 112 个,对 117 名贫困肢体残疾儿童实施矫治手术、装配了矫形器等辅助器具，进行了术后康复训练；对 7,583 名肢体残疾人进行了康复训练，其中: 脑瘫儿童系统康复训练 376 人,肢体残疾儿童社区、家庭康复 91 人，成年肢体残疾人社区、家庭康复 7,116 人。

全年开展智力残疾康复训练服务的机构达到 27 个；对 3,387 名智力残疾儿童进行了康复训练，不同程度地开展了智力残疾儿童早期康复训练与服务。

（五）辅助器具供应服务。深入开展辅助器具供应服务，全面推进普及型假肢装配，截止到 2012 年底，累计建立辅助器具供应服务机构 42 个，为残疾人减免费用装配普及型假肢 989 例，供应辅助器具 2.5 万件。

（六）社区康复服务。在 30 个市辖区（含开发区）和 40 个县（市）开展了社区康复工作，累计建立社区康复站2,744个，配备8,161名社区康复协调员。开展家长学校工作的残疾人康复机构达到28家，培训家长320人次。

（七）康复人才。截止2012年底，全省康复机构在岗人数为7,919人，全年由各地残联主办的各类培训班254期，培训7,857名各类康复人才。

二、教育情况

特殊教育普通高中4所，在校生39人；残疾人中等职业教育机构有5个，在校生621人，当年毕业生123人，其中获得职业资格证书86人。共有193名残疾人被普通高等院校录取，207名残疾人进入特殊教育学院学习。

未入学适龄残疾儿童少年总数2,710人，其中视力残疾76人，听力残疾125人，言语残疾145人，智力残疾1,041人，肢体残疾864人，精神残疾191人，多重残疾268人。未入学儿童总人数增加842人。

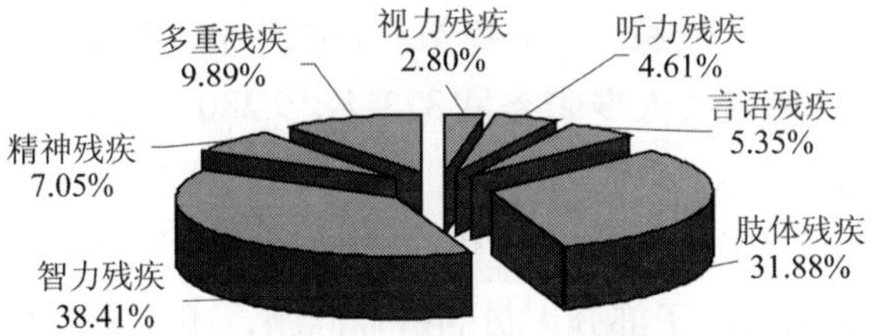

图3　2012年吉林省残疾未入学儿童少年情况

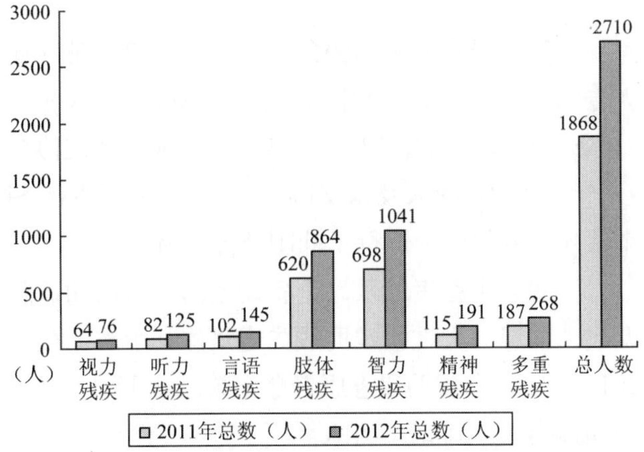

图4　2012年与2011年残疾儿童少年未入学情况对比

三、就业培训

（一）城乡残疾人就业情况。2012年城镇新安排1.1万残疾人就业。其中，集中就业残疾人2,798人，按比例安排残疾人就业1,534人，公益性岗位就业73人，个体及其它形式就业6,912人，全省城镇实际在业残疾人15.7万人，个体及其他形式就业仍为残疾人就业主渠道；30.6万农村残疾人实现稳定就业，其中从事农业生产劳动25.5万人。职业培训基地172个，其中残联兴办49个，依托社会机构兴办123个，本年度城镇职业培训人数1.7万人。

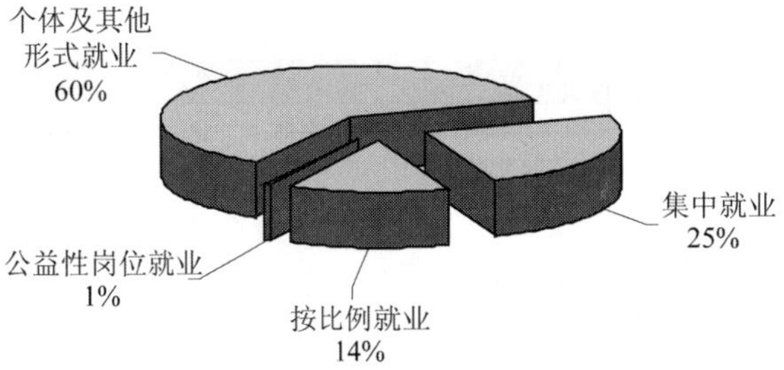

图5　2012年城镇残疾人新增就业情况

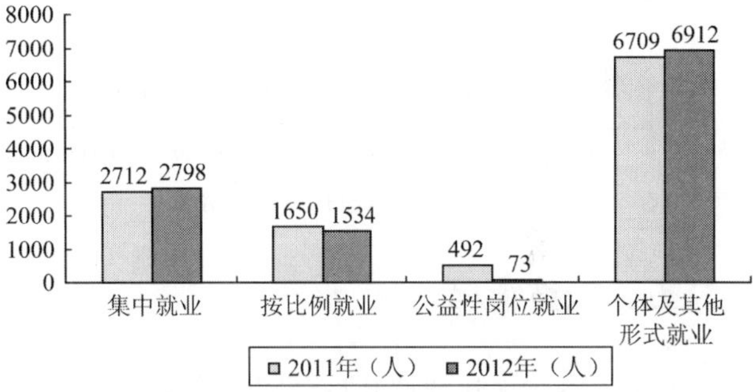

图6　2012年与2011年吉林省城镇残疾人新增就业情况对比

（二）盲人按摩。培训盲人保健按摩人员843人；医疗按摩人员598人，保健按摩机构达到262个，医疗按摩机构达到36个；有975名盲人按摩人员实现就业，其中保健按摩人员747人，医疗按摩人员228人，全省各级残联扶持416名特困盲人按摩师实现就业。

四、社会保障

（一）社会保险。全省城镇残疾职工参加社会保险人数达到6.6万人，其中参加养老保险人数3.5万人，参加医疗保险人数3.2万人；城镇残疾居民参加医疗保险达到21.5万人。

（二）社会救助。2012年全省城乡共有29.6万名残疾人纳入最低生活保障范围；城镇已纳入最低生活保障13.6万人，城镇集中供养0.6万人，其他救助救济1.9万人。

农村已纳入最低生活保障15.9万人，农村五保供养0.9万人，其他救助救济1.4万人。

（三）托养服务。全省寄宿制托养机构全年托养残疾人828人；日间照料托养机构合计25个，托养残疾人 203 人；本年度享受居家托养服务残疾人 1.4 万人。

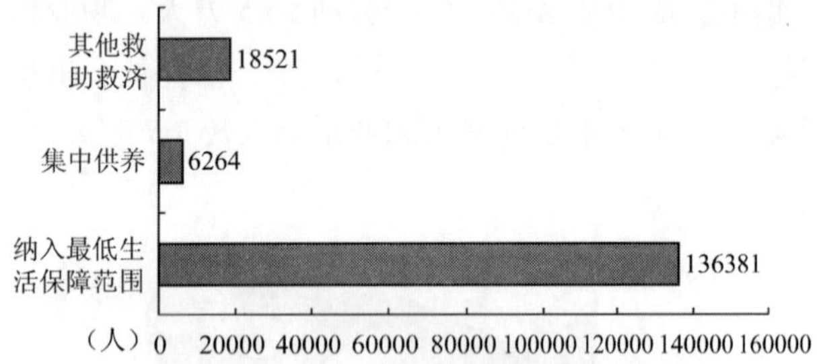

图7 2012年城镇社会救助情况

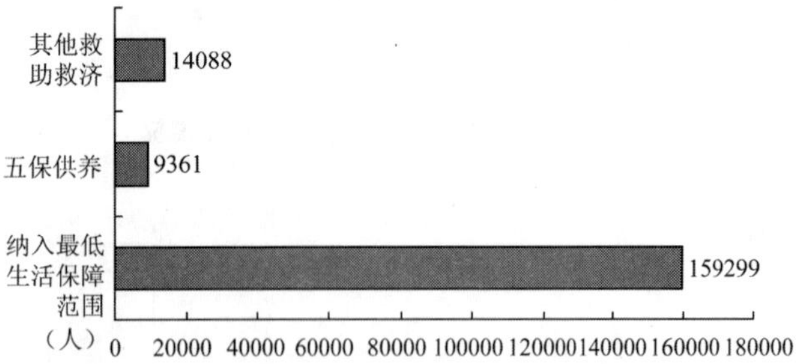

图8 2012年农村社会救助情况

五、扶贫情况

本年度全省各级残联扶持贫困残疾人 1.6 万户，2.2 万人，其中脱贫 1.4 万人，接受实用技术培训的残疾人达 5.9 万人次，投入培训经费 978.4 万元。

开展社会帮扶活动，其中结对帮扶单位 2,062 个，结对帮扶个人 4,941 人；建立残疾人扶持基地 154 个，安置残疾人就业 2,232 人，扶持带动残疾人 7,327 户残疾人脱贫致富。

六、法律维权

（一）残疾人法规政策及执法检查。2012 年，有 4 个市（州），27 个县（区）制定或修改了保障残疾人权益的专门法规或规范性文件；县级以上人大执法检查或专题调研 14 次，政协视察和专题调研 17 次。

（二）残疾人法制宣传与法律救助。全年开展普法宣传教育活动 180 次，参加人数 2.1 万人；开办法律培训班 50 次，参加人数 2,480 人；建立残疾人法律救助协调机构 32 个；建立残疾人法律救助工作站 8 个，办理案件 45 件；建立残疾人法律援助中心（工作站）66 个，办理案件 413 件。

（三）残疾人参政议政。全省残联协助各级人大代表、政协委员提出议案、建议、提案 49 件,办理议案、建议、提案 24 件。

（四）无障碍建设与残疾人机动轮椅车燃油补贴。截止 2012 年底，全省各级政府成立无障碍建设领导协调组织 22 个；系统开展无障碍建设市、县有 12 个；贫困残疾人家庭无障碍改造 1,598 户，无障碍检查 23 次，无障碍培训 353 人次 ，残疾人机动轮椅车燃油补贴 1.4 万人。

（五）残疾人信访。2012 年，全省各级残联共处理残疾人群众来信 826 件，接待残疾人群众来访 4,835 人次，其中集体访 49 批次，727 人次。

七、组织建设

（一）残联组织。全省各级残联实有人员 3,109 人，通过培训教育使干部素质得到进一步提高。残疾人干部配备工作进一步加强，全省 9 个市（州）残联领导班子中已有 5 个配备了残疾人领导干部。全省各级残联残疾人人才库得到进一步充实和完善。

（二）残疾人专职委员。全省有 895 个乡镇（街道）选聘残疾人专职委员 873 名；9,280 个社区（村）选聘残疾人专职委员 10,505 名。选聘残疾人专职委员不仅为广大残疾人提供了大量就近服务的社会公益岗位,解决了部分人员的就业问题，还为基层推进“残疾人社会保障体系和服务体系”建设提供必要的人员保障。

（三）残疾人专门协会。全省共建立各类残疾人专门协会 357 个，其中盲人协会 72 个、聋人协会 71 个、肢残人协会 72 个、智力残疾人及亲友协会 71 个、精神残疾人及亲友协会 71 个。全省共有 54 个残疾人专门协会进行了社团登记注册。

（四）志愿者助残。全省助残志愿者活动蓬勃发展，涌现一大批扶残助残先进集体和个人。截止 2012 年底，全省助残志愿者登记数已达 15.2 万人，受助残疾人达到 27.8 万人。

八、宣传文化

（一）宣传。各级新闻媒体采访报道了大量涉及残疾人等社会弱势群体的相关新闻、专题节目。省和地市级主要新闻媒体刊播稿件 1,790 件，报刊专版 22 个，残疾人专题广播节目 16 个,电视手语新闻栏目 5 个,投放各类公益广告 19 个。我省推荐的作品《草根英雄刘凤英》（吉林市人民广播电台）荣获全国第十届“各地人民广播电台残疾人专题节目展播”评选一等奖。

（二）文化。残疾人的文化事业发展势头良好。借助第八届东北亚博览会平台成功举办首届残疾人优秀作品（产品）展示（展销）活动，进一步营造了全社会关心、支持、帮助残疾人的良好社会氛围。

省和地市级公共图书馆设立盲文及盲人有声读物阅览室达到 14 个，举办残疾人文化周活动 76 场（次），举办残疾人文化艺术类比赛及展览 22 个，全省已成立 10 个残疾人艺术团队。

九、残疾人体育

积极开展残疾人体育活动。我省残疾人运动员付彦龙在伦敦残疾人奥林匹克运动会上斩获我省首枚残奥会金牌，实现了我省残奥体育的历史性突破。

全省各地开展残疾人体育健身活动 58 次，参加人数为 1.1 万人；建立残疾人体育示范点 138 个，选聘残疾人体育健身指导员 310 人;建立省级残疾人体育训练基地 16 个。

十、服务设施

已竣工并投入使用的各级残疾人综合服务设施共计 39 个，在建项目共计 5 个。其中已竣工并投入使用的各级残疾人综合服务设施总占地面积 5 万平方米，总建设规模 5.7 万平方米，累计投资 1.3 亿元。

已竣工并投入使用的各级康复设施共计 6 个，在建项目共计 2 个。其中已竣工并投入使用的各级康复设施总占地面积 1.1 万平方米，总建设规模 2.2 万平方米，累计投资 8,611 万元.

已竣工并投入使用的各级托养设施共计 1 个，在建项目共计 2 个，其中已竣工并投入使用的各级托养设施总占地面积 3,345 平方米，总建设规模 3,352 平方米，累计投资 1,400 万元。

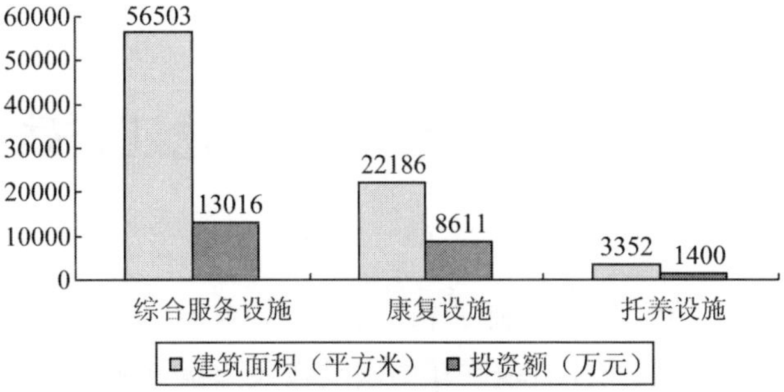

图9　吉林省残疾人综合服务设施建设情况

2012 年 5 月落成并投入使用的吉林省残疾人康复中心是吉林省委、省政府深入贯彻落实中央 7 号文件精神，全面推进残疾人“两个体系”建设的又一成果。省康复中心的建成对于指导并辐射带动全省残疾人康复服务工作具有深远意义。

从全省范围看，我省各类残疾人服务设施数量少、规模小、功能弱，今后仍需进一步加强。特别是加强专业化的康复和托养机构设施建设，提高为残疾人的服务能力。

十一、统计与信息化

（一）残疾人事业统计。全省各级残联统计队伍建设进一步加强，共有 86 名专、兼职统计人员从事残疾人事业统计工作，统计人员业务素质培养普遍得到重视，统计数据质量逐年提高，全省举办统计人员培训班 11 期，284 人次参加培训。

（二）信息化。全省各级残联全面推进信息公开，目前省残联及各市州残联全面开通了公众网站，35 个县级残联开通网站,网站总数比去年增加 4 个。全省各级残联共有 130 名专兼职技术人员从事信息化工作。举办信息工作培训班 13 期，培训各级残联信息员 489 人次。省残联网站全年发稿 1,100 件，网站点击率逐年增加，网上信息服务能力逐年加强。

信息化手段的不断增强使我省残联组织管理残疾人事务的能力得到较大提升。但也应当看到长期以来我省残联信息化建设资金投入严重不足，还缺乏覆盖全省的残疾人基础数据库和综合服务系统，需要在今后的工作中加快推进。

2012 年黑龙江省残疾人事业发展统计公报

2012 年是实施“十二五”规划承上启下的重要一年，黑龙江省残联在中国残联大力指导和省委、省政府的高度重视下，深入贯彻落实《黑龙江省残疾人事业“十二五”发展纲要》，加快推进残疾人社会保障体系和服务体系建设，残疾人事业蓬勃发展，残疾人生活进一步改善。

一、残疾人康复工作

2012 年，紧紧围绕“人人享有康复服务”目标，通过实施一批重点康复工程，为残疾人提供有效的康复服务。

社区康复 在 68 个市辖区和 64 个县（市）开展了社区康复工作，累计建立社区康复站 1258 个，配备 4319 名社区康复协调员，2012 年共有 2.8 万名残疾人得到康复服务。

视力残疾康复 全年完成白内障复明手术 12217 例，为 4300 名贫困白内障患者免费施行复明手术，为 1141 名低视力患者配用助视器，培训低视力儿童家长 824 名，对 4676 名盲人进行定向行走训练。

听力语言残疾康复 加强省级聋儿康复机构建设，完善聋儿康复网络。2012 年对 647 名聋儿进行了听力语言康复训练，培训聋儿家长 618 名，培养各类专业人员 81 人；实施贫困聋儿人工耳蜗、助听器抢救性康复项目，人工耳蜗项目资助贫困聋儿 10 名，助听器项目资助贫困聋儿 81 名。

智力残疾康复 全省共有开展智力残疾康复训练机构 27 个，对 1949 名 0—14 岁的智力残疾儿童进行了康复训练，不同程度地开展了智力残疾儿童早期康复训练与服务。

肢体残疾康复 2012 年开展肢体残疾康复训练服务的机构达到 37 个；对 75 名贫困肢体残疾儿童实施矫治手术；对 4553 名肢体残疾儿童进行了康复训练，其中：脑瘫儿童系统康复训练 363 人,肢体残疾儿童社区、家庭康复 367 人，成年肢体残疾人社区、家庭康复 3823 人。

精神病防治康复 2012 年，在 111 个县（市、区）开展精神病防治康复工作，对 18.5 万重性精神病患者进行综合防治康复，监护率达到 84.3%，显好率达到 54.2%，社会参与率达到 36.2%，肇事率 0.04%；解除关锁 27 人；对 4596 名贫困精神病患者进行医疗救助。

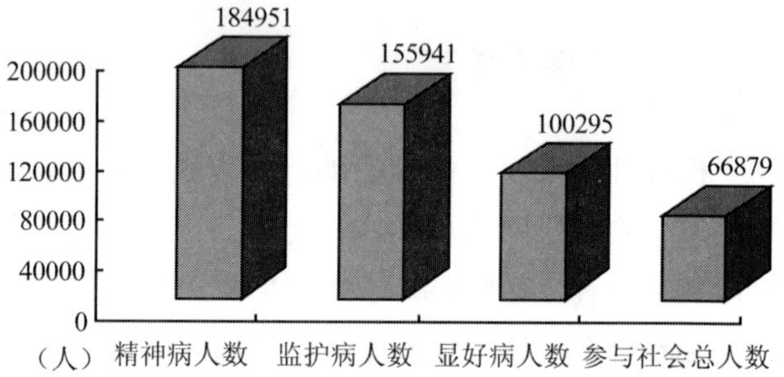

图1 2012年全省精神病防治康复工作

建立了 2 个省级、21 个地市级及以下孤独症儿童康复训练机构，在省级机构训练 36 名，在地市级及以下其他机构训练 176 名。

辅助器具供应服务 深入开展辅助器具供应服务，全面推进普及型假肢装配，2012 年，为残疾人减免费用装配普及型假肢 589 例，供应辅助器具 10424 件，装配矫形器 120 例。

康复人才 全省各类康复机构共有在岗人员 5334 人。2012 年，全省共举办各类康复人才培训班 260 期，培训康复人才 3736 人次。

二、残疾人教育工作

继续完善残疾人教育体系，提高义务教育普及水平，落实残疾人教育救助政策。

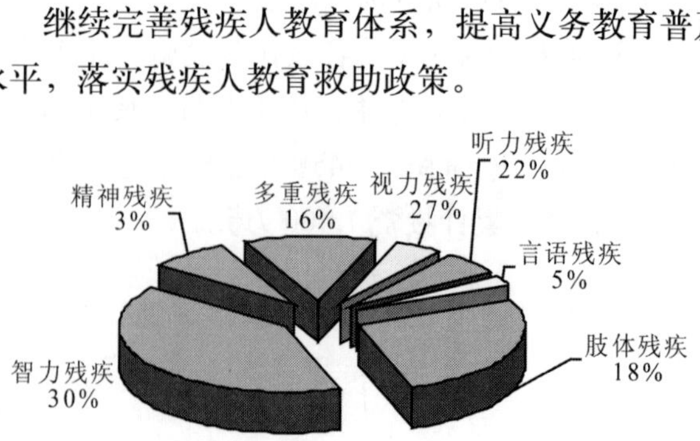

图2 2012年未入学学龄残疾儿童少年按残疾类别分类

义务教育 未入学学龄残疾儿童少年总数 927

人，其中视力残疾 42 人，听力残疾 52 人，言语残疾 24 人，肢体残疾 246 人，智力残疾 373 人，精神残疾 71 人，多重残疾 119 人。

中高等教育 有 153 名残疾人被普通高等院校录取，2 名残疾人进入特殊教育学院学习。

三、残疾人就业工作

紧紧围绕"十二五"发展纲要确定的任务，大力加强残疾人就业工作的力度，就业人数逐步增加。

就业状况 2012 年，城镇新安排残疾人就业 9389 人，其中，集中就业残疾人 3387 人，按比例安排残疾人就业 1274 人，公益性岗位就业 1613 人，个体及其它形式就业 3111 人，全国城镇实际在业人数 13.0 万人；24.5 万农村残疾人稳定实现就业，其中从事农业生产劳动 20.1 万人。

职业培训 职业培训基地 73 个,其中残联兴办 23 个，本年度城镇职业培训人数 1.1 万人。

盲人按摩 2012 年,培训盲人保健按摩 281 人；医疗按摩人员 72，保健按摩机构达到 207 个，医疗按摩机构达到 23 个；有 49 人和 52 人通过医疗按摩人员中级和初级职称评审。

四、残疾人扶贫工作

扶贫效果及资金投入 本年度扶持贫困残疾人户 1.5 万户，扶持 2.1 万人，脱贫 1.4 万人，返贫 0.1 万人，接受实用技术培训的残疾人 1.7 万人次，全年投入培训经费 188.1 万元。

2012 年，结对帮扶单位 3243 个，结对帮扶个人 4933 人；建立残疾人扶持基地 104 个，安置残疾人就业 3387 人，扶持带动残疾人 2611 人。

农村贫困残疾人危房改造 2012 年完成 1687 户农村贫困残疾人危房改造，投入危房资金 1680.25 万元，2117 名残疾人受益。

五、残疾人社会保障工作

截至 2012 年底，城镇残疾职工参加社会保险人数达到 6.4 万人，其中参加养老保险人数 2.9 万人，参加医疗保险人数 2.8 万人；城镇残疾居民参加医疗保险达到 13.9 万人；城乡 28.6 万名残疾人纳入最低生活保障范围；城镇已纳入最低生活保障 15.6 万人，城镇集中供养和其他救助救济 2.3 万人；农村已纳入最低生活保障 13.0 万人，五保供养和其他救助救济 4.0 万人。

六、残疾人托养服务机构建设工作

截至 2012 年底，残疾人寄宿制托养服务机构 105 个，托养残疾人规模达到 4347 人；日间照料托养服务机构 30 个，托养残疾人 375 人；本年度享受居家托养服务残疾人 9346 人。

七、残疾人维权工作

不断完善残疾人事业法规体系和残疾人维权工作机制，扩大残疾人法律服务覆盖面，依法保障残疾人合法权益。

法制建设 2011 年，全省开展县级以上人大执法检查或专题调研 19 次，政协视察和专题调研 16 次。各级残联积极组织开展残疾人普法宣传教育活动，全年共组织参与普法宣传教育活动 152 次，比上年度增加 10 次。各级残联积极与当地普法办、司法局联系，举办残疾人工作者法律培训班 28 次，培训人数 1030 人。

法律救助 截至 2012 年底，建立残疾人法律救助工作协调机构 9 个，其中省级 1 个、市（地）3 个、县（市、区）3 个。建立残疾人法律救助工作站 5 个，办理案件 27 件。建立残疾人法律援助中心（工作站）119 个，办理案件 642 件。

参政议政 我省残疾人人大代表、政协委员共有 198 人，协助提出议案、提案 37 件，办理建议 38 件，充分发挥了残疾人参政议政的权利。

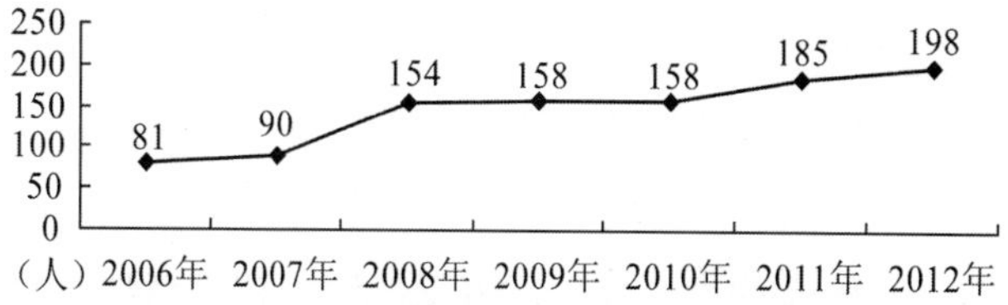

图 3 近年来我省残疾人人大代表、政协委员情况

无障碍设施建设 截至 2012 年底，共有无障碍建设领导协调组织 15 个，开展 43 次无障碍建设检查，贫困残疾人家庭无障碍改造 2634 户，培训 99 人次，1.6 万名残疾人获得机动轮椅车燃油补贴。

残疾人信访 各级残联共处理残疾人群众来信 1010 件，接待残疾人群众来访 4674 人次，其中集体访 5 批次，30 人次。

八、残疾人宣传文体工作

促进残疾人特殊艺术和竞技体育发展，不断丰富、活跃残疾人群众文化体育生活。

宣传文化 2012 年，中央及媒体采用稿件数 36 件，省及地市级主要新闻媒体刊播残疾人事业稿件数 603 件，开辟报刊专版 15 个。开展残疾人专题广播节目 25 个，电视手语新闻栏目 4 个。公共图书馆设立盲文及盲人有声读物阅览室达到 24 个，举办残疾人文化艺术类比赛及展览 35 次，成立 12 个残疾人艺术团队。

体育 2012 年，全省共举办残疾人体育健身活动 14 次，2,543 名残疾人参加活动。拥有残疾人体育健身指导员 150 人。建有省级残疾人体育训练基地 3 个，聘任教练员 8 人。

九、残疾人组织建设工作

继续加强残疾人组织建设，发挥政府联系残疾人的桥梁和纽带作用。

组织建设 截至 2012 年底，省残联配备了驻会肢残、盲人、聋人理事，全省 13 个市（地）中有 8 个市（地）配备了残疾人理事长或副理事长,132 个县（市、区）中 37 个县（市、区）残联机关配备了残疾人干部。

在残疾人专职委员选聘方面，1331 个乡镇（街道）中，选聘残疾人专职委员 1279 名。1.1 万个社区（村）中，选聘残疾人专职委员 5808 名。

专门协会 省、市（地）、县（市、区）三级专门协会均已建立健全，组建率达 100%。

十、残疾人事业统计与信息化建设

加强统计队伍建设，提高信息化基础建设水平，为残疾人事业服务能力进一步增强。

事业统计 省、市（地）、县（市、区）残联共有统计员 155 人，其中 20 人有统计从业资格证书。2012 年全省残联系统共举办统计人员培训班 4 期，72 人参加培训。

信息化建设 各级残联全面推进网站建设，目前共开通 1 个省级残联、7 个地市级残联、19 个县级残联网站。2012 年省残联网站发稿 848 篇，建有局域网 1 个、网上办公（OA）系统 1 个。全省各级残联系统拥有计算机 818 台。

十一、分析总结

2012 年，我省残联紧紧围绕残疾人社会保障体系和服务体系建设，全面实施残疾人事业“十二五”发展纲要确定的各项工作任务,各级政府加大了对残疾人事业的重视程度，对残疾人事业给予特殊扶持，我省残疾人事业发展取得了一定的成绩。但是，由于我省经济发展相对薄弱，资金投入相对欠缺，残疾人事业的发展还存在着亟待解决的问题和不足，这些问题需要在今后的工作中加以改进。

2012 年上海市残疾人事业发展统计公报

在 2012 年，上海市残联系统以学习实践科学发展观为统领，认真贯彻《中共上海市委 上海市人民政府关于加快推进本市残疾人事业发展的实施意见》精神，按照中国残联的工作要求和市委、市政府对残疾人工作的总体部署，着力推进“两个体系”建设，提高残疾人社会保障和公共服务水平，各方面工作取得新成效。

一、康复工作

本市制定出台了社区康复、视力残疾康复、听力语言康复、肢体残疾康复、智力残疾康复、精神病防治康复、辅助器具服务、儿童残疾预防、康复人才建设、残疾人养护服务等 10 个上海市残疾人康复“十二五”配套实施方案，进一步细化工作目标，明确具体措施，有序推进残疾人康复“十二五”工作。成功召开“2012 国际康复无障碍生活博览会暨国际康复无障碍学术大会”，近 3000 人观展，中国残疾人联合会主席团主席张海迪出席“中途之家”康复论坛并发表重要讲话。圆满完成 2012 年市政府实事项目——“为 1 万名残疾人补贴提供个性化辅助器具适配服务”，截至 2012 年底，共适配服务 12907 人，超额完成 29%。

为不断满足残疾人日益增加的康复需求，本市调整了一系列救助政策，包括提高脑瘫、孤独症儿童康复救助补贴标准、提高残疾人健康体检补贴标准、提高贫困肢体残疾人安装假肢矫形器补贴标准等。不断深化脊髓损伤者“中途之家”康复服务内涵，注册伤友已近 500 人，在全市全面推广“中途之家”护理用品配发工作。全市 17 个区（县）均开展残疾儿童筛查工作，建立各级残疾儿童家长学校 78 家。截至 2012 年底，累计建立社区康复服务档案 333008 人，接受社区康复服务累计达 323571 人。

2012 年度共完成白内障复明手术 50907 例，其中贫困白内障免费手术 3004 例。低视力者配用助视器 4178 名，培训低视力儿童家长 1062 人，盲人定向行走训练 1939 人。新收训聋儿 135 人，其中机构训练 61 人，家庭训练 74 人，培训聋儿家长 384 人。监护精神病人 106299 人，其中显好病人数为 98177 人。智力儿童康复训练 2806 人，其中机构康复训练 634 人，社区、家庭康复训练 2172 人。肢体残疾康复训练 5650 人，其中成年肢体残疾人社区、家庭康复 4851 人。全年完成辅助器具适配服务 153299 件，其中安装假肢 532 例、矫形器 18718 例、其他辅助器具 134049 件。

二、教育工作

2012 年，本市重新调整未入学适龄残疾儿童少年调查工作机制，进一步强化市、区县两级部门和单位之间的沟通联系，建立信息通报与反馈制度，对发现的未入学适龄残疾儿童少年及时响应、及时妥善解决就学困难。据统计，2012 年未入学适龄残疾儿童少年 45 人，同比 2011 年 112 人减少 59.82%。2012 年，全市特殊教育普通高中教育、中等职业教育相比 2011 年教育机构数未发生变化，在校残疾学生总数略有减少。

三、就业培训工作

2012 年，本市促进残疾人就业工作继续以分散按比例就业、集中就业为主，自主创业、非正规就业等多种就业途径共同推进。本市在继续强化实施超比例安置残疾人就业奖励、开展残疾人职业技能培训扶持、提升残疾人劳动服务机构就业服务能力、推动残疾人职业康复援助基地发展等既有残疾人就业促进政策的同时，积极会同相关部门研究加大残疾人就业扶持的政策和举措。在产业结构转型的关键时期，切实稳定残疾人就业岗位，逐步提高残疾人劳动性收入水平。2012 年，本市残疾人就业主要数据与 2011 年相比呈现基本持平。

四、社会保障

2012 年，在本市实施城镇居民社会养老保险的同时，制定实施了重度残疾人参加城镇居民社会养老保险代缴政策。此项政策实施后，本市通过为重度残疾人代缴城镇居民社会养老保险（每人每年1100元）和新型农村社会养老保险（每人每年900元）个人缴费、为重残人员代缴城镇居民基本医疗保险、为农村困难残疾人实施参加新型农村社会养老保险和新型农村合作医疗缴费补贴，完善了残疾人参加社会保险的帮扶机制，实现了全市城乡残疾人的社会养老、医疗保险制度全覆盖。2012年，本市为20792名重度残疾人代缴城镇居民社会养老保险，其中全额代缴19554人；为8555名重度残疾人代缴新型农村社会养老保险，其中全额代缴7839人。

五、维权信访

着力规范初信初访办理，从源头上预防新增重复信访，在“事要解决”上下功夫，确保信访矛盾的有效化解，全年受理来信535件，接待来访392人次；加强区县残疾人法律救助站建设，完善全市残疾人法律救助网络，推进残疾人法律援助和法律救助工作，降低残疾人享受法律救助服务的门槛、增加服务内容、扩大服务范围，积极开展残疾人法律援助、救助服务，先后为276人次提供法律服务，办理法律援助案2件，维护了残疾人的合法权益；加强信息化建设，完善无障碍电子地理信息系统，开展助盲语音服务播报器使用培训，稳步推进信息无障碍建设工作；保障残疾人最直接的利益，认真做好惠及残疾人的实事项目，及时发放残疾人机动轮椅车燃油补贴，惠及14159人，提高型家庭无障碍改造共惠及450户；推动《无障碍环境建设条例》实施，举办了“无障碍环境建设业务培训班”，区县残联专职干部、督导队长及部分队员共530余人参加。

六、宣传文体

认真贯彻落实中国残联等11个部委《关于加强残疾人文化建设的意见》，推动残疾人文化艺术繁荣发展。组织开展第二十二次“全国助残日”暨第十三次“上海助残周”活动，各媒体共播出电视广播报道20余条，刊登文字和图片报道100余篇，进一步加大了残疾人事业宣传，扩大了残疾人事业的社会影响。加强区县残疾人文化艺术活动指导力度，扩大残疾人群众文化体育活动覆盖面和参与率。努力打造一区一品，塑造残疾人文化体育品牌项目。组织开展2012年上海市残疾人文化活动月系列活动，以快乐读书月、文化助残月、无障碍影视月、交流展演月等不同主题贯穿全年，鼓励、吸纳残疾人广泛参与，提升残疾人文化活动的覆盖面,促进残疾人均等享有社会公共文化服务。拓展残疾人艺术培训内容，开办舞台表演、语言、舞台造型妆等艺术类培训；首推残疾人社会艺术水平考级工作，本市已有5名听障残疾人通过中国舞蹈家协会舞蹈八级考试。开展“我读书、我快乐、我阳光”上海市残疾人读书系列活动，在全市举办“阅读改变生活”上海市残疾人读书励志讲坛、“上海市残疾人读书达人大赛”、“上海市残疾人优秀读书组织评选”等主题活动，并荣获上海市第十四届读书节“优秀活动项目”。本市首家无障碍电影院挂牌，开设无障碍电影专场，满足残疾人个性化文化需求，2012年底全市已有2个区县率先推出无障碍电影专场；成立无障碍电影志愿者讲解员队伍，并与广播新闻中心联合制作无障碍电影公益广告,呼吁全社会对残疾人个性化文化需求的关注。举办“第八届上海市残疾人文艺汇演”，选拔优秀艺术人才，促进特殊艺术创作。组团参加第十一届中国国际合唱节，精彩亮相2012上海旅游节，积极参与社会公共文化活动，提升残疾人特殊艺术影响力。各区县结合“文化进社区”，因地制宜开展了多种形式的文化和健身活动，形成“月月有主题、周周有活动”的浓厚氛围。

2012年，上海残疾人事业发展得到中央及市级媒体的关注，其中中央级媒体采用稿件数8件，本市各级主要新闻媒体刊播稿件数299件，刊播残疾人事业电视公益广告3个。巩固发展残疾人事业专栏专刊，目前上海公共媒体宣传残疾人事业的固定专版、专栏和专题主要有：《新民晚报》的《阳光天地》专版（随报发行）；电视台《时事传真》、都市广播《同一片蓝天下》、内部刊物《灵芝草》四个专栏专刊。

2012年，市区两级公共图书馆设有盲文有声读物图书室共计25个；残疾人文化周期间，市级举办残疾人文化活动12场，区县级举办残疾人文化活动97场。2012年，全市及区县共举办各类残疾人文化艺术类比赛展览80次，设立各级残疾人艺术团队33个，成为广大残疾人展示特殊艺术才能、集中参与活动的重要平台。

2012年江苏省残疾人事业发展统计公报

2012年，全省各级残联围绕服务“民生幸福工程”和实施“残疾人幸福生活推进计划”，以高度的责任感和紧迫感，埋头苦干，锐意进取，奋力推进各项工作任务的落实，为全面建成更高水平小康社会、开启江苏基本实现现代化新征程作出了新的贡献。

一、康复

2012年全省残疾人康复工作围绕一条主线——实现残疾人“人人享有康复服务”目标；完善“两个体系”——康复政策保障体系和康复服务体系；贯彻落实《关于将部分康复项目纳入基本医疗保障范围的实施办法》。各地认真贯彻落实全省残疾人“人人享有康复服务”工作推进会精神，大力普及残疾人康复服务。康复项目进医保工作进展明显，13个省辖市全部制定了实施办法，48个县（市、区）已制定实施细则，11个县（市）残联康复中心被认定为定点康复机构，已和人社部门、新农合结算系统联网，儿童抢救性康复和辅具项目实现即时结报，全面完成了年度任务。

全省在59个市辖区和49个县（市）开展了社区康复工作；在1.94万个社区中，已开展社区康复服务的社区有1.67万个，占85.70%；累计建立社区康复站1.45万个，配备1.94万名社区康复协调员；共有53个残疾人康复机构开展了家长学校工作。

全省开展视力残疾康复机构总数达49个，巩固白内障无障碍省创建成果，全省白内障无障碍“发现一例，复明一例”机制成熟运行，全年完成白内障复明手术6万例；为1.72万名贫困白内障患者免费施行复明手术，全年为6501名低视力患者配用助视器，对8081名盲人进行定向行走训练。

推进听力语言康复机构规范化管理，完善基层服务网络。加强省级聋儿康复机构建设，完善聋儿康复网络。已建省级听力语言康复机构1个，基层听力语言康复机构61个。全省共对2338名聋儿进行了听力语言康复训练，接受地方项目救助的聋儿有919名；培训各类专业人员509人；与省财政厅联合制定下发《关于印发国家残疾儿童康复救助“七彩梦行动计划”江苏省实施方案的通知》，指导各地做好国家贫困残疾儿童抢救性康复项目，全年为173名听障儿童植入人工耳蜗并进行康复训练。

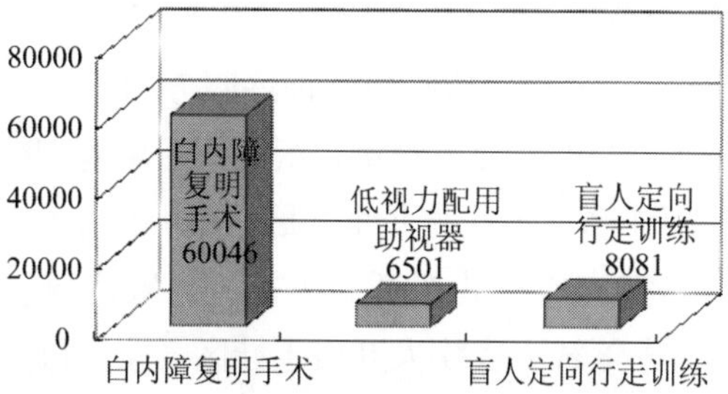

图1　2012年白内障复明手术、低视力康复、盲人定向行走训练开展情况（单位：例、人）

大力推广“社会化、综合性、开放式”精神病防治康复工作。2012年在108个县（市、区）开展精神病防治康复工作，对53.04万名精神病患者进行综合防治康复，监护率达到81.01%，显好率达到60.18%，社会参与率达到50.63%，肇事率0.01%；解除关锁47人；对4.42万名贫困精神病患者进行医疗救助，截至2012年底全省共有109个精神康复机构。

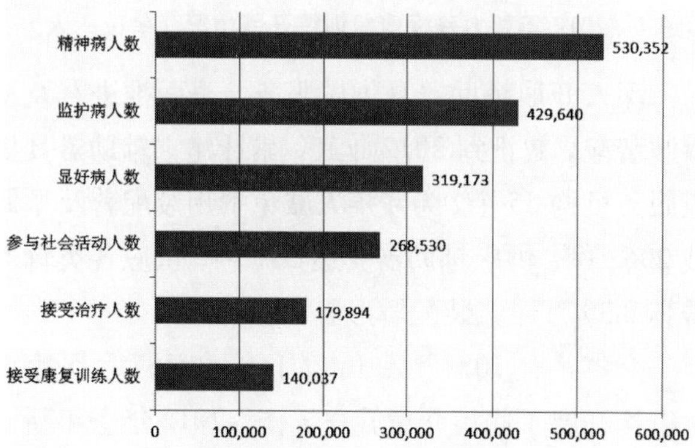

图2　2012年精神病人监护和救助情况（单位：人）

建立了1个省级孤独症儿童康复训练机构，20名孤独症儿童在其中进行康复训练。基层共有86个孤独症儿童康复训练机构，在训孤独症儿童共计801人。

全年开展肢体残疾康复训练服务的机构达到98个，对33419名肢体残疾人进行了康复训练，其中：脑瘫儿童机构康复训练4085人，肢体残疾儿童社区、家庭康复训练 1345 人，成年肢体残疾人社区、家庭康复训练 27989 人，全年共完成贫困肢体残疾儿童矫治手术 99 例。

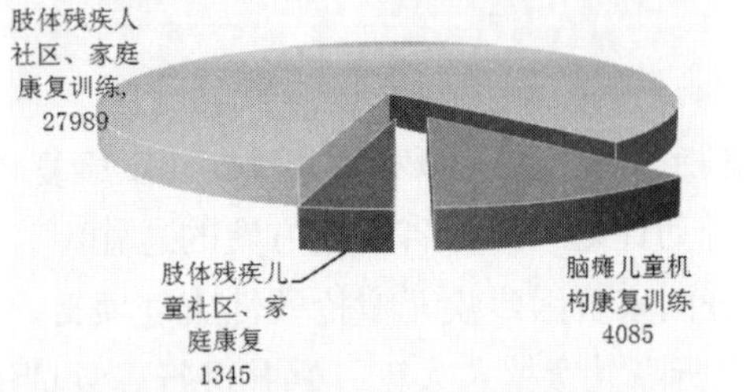

图 3　2012 年肢体残疾康复训练情况（单位：人）

全年开展智力残疾康复训练服务的机构达到 80 个；对 11359 名智力残疾儿童进行了康复训练，其中为 2104 名智力残疾儿童开展了机构康复训练，为 9255 名智力残疾儿童开展了社区、家庭康复，为 4285 名成年智力残疾人开展了社区、家庭康复，不同程度地开展了智力残疾儿童早期康复训练与服务。全年各类智力残疾康复管理、技术人员培训达 2218 人次。

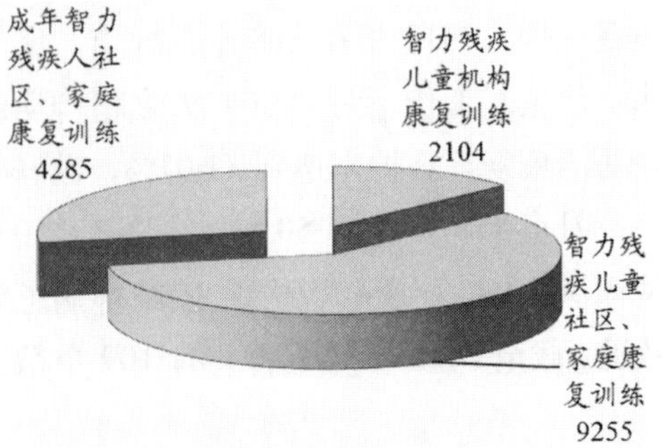

图 4　2012 年智力残疾康复训练开展情况（单位：人）

深入开展辅助器具供应服务，全面推进普及型假肢装配，截止到 2012 年底，累计建立辅助器具供应服务机构 55 个，为残疾人减免费用装配普及型假肢 2052 例，供应辅助器具达 257 种，供应各类辅助器具 8.39 万件，装配矫形器 1918 例。

全省共有 108 个县（市、区）和 157 个医疗卫生机构开展了残疾儿童筛查工作，2012 年全年新诊断 0-6 岁残疾儿童 3482 名；全省共举办了 277 次儿童残疾预防宣传活动，发放儿童残疾预防宣传材料 19.65 万份；全省共有 57 个残疾儿童家长学校，全年共开展 152 次家长学校活动，残疾儿童家长参与人数达 5376 人次，共培训聋儿家长 2309 名，训低视力儿童家长 1203 名，有效开展家庭康复训练。

截至 2012 年底，我省共有康复机构在岗人员 9635 人，全省全年共举办康复管理人员培训班 99 期，培训康复管理人员 2155 人；举办康复业务人员培训班 169 期，培训康复业务人员 5794 人；举办康复社区康复协调员培训班 210 期，培训社区康复协调员 15385 人。

二、教育

2012 年，残疾人受教育权进一步得到保障，残疾人义务教育和高中教育免费、高中大学残疾学生教育专项补贴等全省性残疾人特殊保障普惠性政策得到全面落实，残疾人教育工作跨上新台阶。全年共有 650 名儿童接受了残疾人事业彩票公益金助学项目资助，其中 223 名儿童受资助新入园。我省各地多渠道争取资金支持，对 159 名残疾儿童给予学前教育资助。

全省已开办特殊教育普通高中 4 所，在校生 392 人。残疾人中等职业教育机构 15 个，在校生 944 人，2012 年度毕业生 234 人，其中获得职业资格证书 199 人。高等特殊教育学院 3 所，有 396 名残疾人被普通高等院校录取，127 名残疾人进入特殊教育学院学习。

截止到 2012 年底，全省有未入学适龄残疾儿童少年 1498 人，其中视力残疾 59 人，听力残疾 130 人，言语残疾 27 人，肢体残疾 494 人，智力残疾 660 人，精神残疾 45 人，多重残疾 83 人。

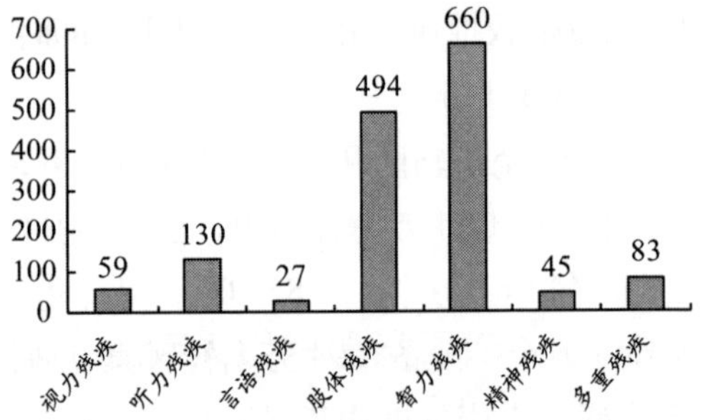

图 5　2012 年未入学学龄残疾儿童情况（单位：人）

三、就业

全省各级残联围绕省政府 2012 年重点助残实事项目多渠道、多层次、多形式安排残疾人就业，组织各种类型的职业培训。城镇新安排 2.11 万名残疾人就业。其中，集中就业残疾人 6644 人，按比例安排残疾人就业 6647 人，公益性岗位就业 260 人，个体及其它形式就业 7128 人，辅助性就业 375 人，全省城镇实际在业人数 30.49 万人；69.90 万农村残疾人实现稳定就业，其中从事农业生产劳动 52.38 万人。

建立残疾人创业基地，采取扶持政策鼓励残疾人创业和自谋职业，全省残疾人职业培训基地达184个，其中残联兴办66个，依托社会机构兴办118个。抓好残疾人就业培训工作，全年共有1.76万城镇残疾人接受了职业培训。

进一步推动盲人保健按摩行业规范化管理。2012年度培训盲人保健按摩人员668名；盲人医疗按摩人员87名，保健按摩机构达到753个，医疗按摩机构达到19个；在专业技术职务资格评审中，分别有28人和63人通过医疗按摩人员中级和初级职称评审。

四、社会保障

为加快推进残疾人社会保障体系和服务体系建设，进一步改善残疾人状况，促进残疾人平等参与社会生活、共享改革发展成果，残疾人参加新型农村和城镇居民社会养老保险工作继续推进。我省有33.82万残疾人参加了新型农村社会养老保险，在参保的残疾人中有4.54万重度残疾人领取养老金待遇，5.27万60岁以下重度残疾人参保，其中4.85万得到了政府的参保扶助（全部代缴3.26万人，部分代缴1.59万人），1.57万非重度残疾人享受了全额或部分代缴的优惠政策。在推行的城镇居民社会养老保险工作中我省有23.16万残疾人参保，享受养老金待遇的人数达到14.62万人。在参保的残疾人中有2.30万重度残疾人领取养老金待遇，60岁以下的重度残疾人中有2.83万得到了政府的参保扶助（全部代缴2.15万人，部分代缴0.68万人），0.76万非重度残疾人享受了全额或部分代缴的优惠政策。

城镇残疾职工参加社会保险人数达到26.75万人，其中参加养老保险人数18.87万人，参加医疗保险人数17.62万人；有37.80万残疾居民参加了城镇居民医疗保险，有121.75万残疾居民参加了新型农村合作医疗；城乡32.73万名残疾人纳入最低生活保障范围；城镇已纳入最低生活保障8.95万人，城镇集中供养和其他救助救济5.12万人；农村已纳入最低生活保障23.78万人，五保供养和其他救助救济12.32万人。2012年共有17.47万和6.79万符合条件的城乡残疾人分别享受了稳定的生活补贴和护理补贴。

残疾人托养服务工作稳步推进，托养服务体系取得新成绩。2012年末全省已建成各类托养服务机构1050个，在托养服务机构中托养及享受居家托养服务残疾人达8.92万人。

五、扶贫开发

2012年，我省残疾人扶贫工作紧紧围绕年初制定的扶贫工作目标，制定残疾人扶贫基地星级分类管理办法，继续做好残疾人扶贫基地建设、康复扶贫贷款、危房改造等残疾人扶贫工作，进一步完善扶贫措施，使贫困残疾人生活状况、收入水平、发展能力得到不断改善和提高。2012年共扶持贫困残疾人户3.75万户，扶持残疾人4.09万人，脱贫1.35万人次，接受实用技术培训的残疾人达1.82万人次，投入培训经费1093.70万元。

2012年全省共有结对帮扶单位2062个，结对帮扶个人1.13万人。建立残疾人扶贫基地412个，安置残疾人就业9651人，扶持带动残疾人1.37万人。完成1072户农村贫困残疾人危房改造，投入危房资金518.04万元，受益残疾人1247人。

六、宣传文化

2012年残疾人事业宣传工作紧密围绕事业大局，广泛宣传全国及江苏残疾人事业发展成就，大力繁荣基层残疾人文化生活，认真贯彻落实《关于加强残疾人文化建设的意见》精神，截至2012年底，省级宣传文化工作中，中央媒体采用稿件16件，主要新闻媒体刊播稿件数270件，省级共开辟报刊专版8个，残疾人专题广播节目1个，电视手语新闻栏目2个，电视公益广告片3个，省级残疾人事业新闻宣传促进会1个；地市级主要新闻媒体刊播稿件数2300件，共开辟地市级报刊专版145个，残疾人专题广播节目27个，电视手语新闻栏目14个，电视公益广告片39个，建立地市级新促会9个。

我省省级和地市级公共图书馆设立盲文及盲人有声读物阅览室分别达到1和17个，共举办5个省级和68个地市级残疾人文化周，共举办了15次省级和87次地市级残疾人文化艺术类比赛及展览。第三届“残疾人文化周”活动圆满成功，第八届全省残疾人艺术汇演精彩纷呈，参演节目63个、演职人员近千名，涌现出一批优秀节目。

七、体育

积极推进残疾人群众体育健身工作。组织省级残疾人群众体育健身活动5次，参加人数2560人，建设残疾人群众体育活动示范点11个，配备残疾人体育健身指导员150人，组织省级残疾人体育比赛1次，参与的残疾人运动员400人次，省级残疾人体育训练基地1个，聘任教练员达31人。

在伦敦残奥会上，我省残疾人运动员17人、24人次获18枚金牌，8人、9人次获9枚银牌，3人获3枚铜牌， 2人破2项世界纪录，继雅典、北京残奥会之后，金牌数和奖牌数连续三次位居全国各省区市第一。

各地深入开展残疾人体育工作。地市级组织残疾人体育活动71次，参加人数5722人次，设立残疾人体育示范点92个，配备残疾人体育健身指导员58人。

八、维权

2012年我省残疾人法制建设取得重大突破。经过不懈努力和多方争取，《江苏省残疾人保障条例》列入2012年省人大立法计划，2012年11月29日，省十一届人大常委会第三十一次会议审议通过了条例，2013年3月1日起正式施行，使我省近年来实施的一系列助残政策制度通过法律确定下来。2012年全省有6个地市制定或修改了保障残疾人权益的规范性文件；全省县级以上人大执法检查或专题调研47次，政协视察和专题调研46次。全省开展普法宣传教育活动481次，参加人数5.22万人；举办法律工作者培训班79次，参加人数4761人。

截止到2012年底，我省建立残疾人法律救助协调机构52个； 建立残疾人法律救助工作站52个，办理案件180件；建立残疾人法律援助中心（工作站）115个，办理案件1038件；有力地促进了法律救助和法律援助工作。

残疾人参政议政工作得到加强，各级残联协助人大代表、政协委员提出议案、建议、提案82件，办理议案、建议、提案97件。

无障碍建设法规、标准进一步完善。全省共有11个地市、11个县（市、区）出台了无障碍建设与管理办法；省本级、11个市、64个县（市、区）成立了无障碍建设领导协调组织；56个县（市、区）系统开展无障碍建设；为17893户贫困残疾人家庭实施了无障碍改造，全省开展无障碍检查168次，无障碍培训5668人次；为2.24万残疾人发放了残疾人机动轮椅车燃油补贴。

各级残联共处理残疾人群众来信1254件，接待残疾人群众来访5206人次，其中集体来访28批次，646人次。

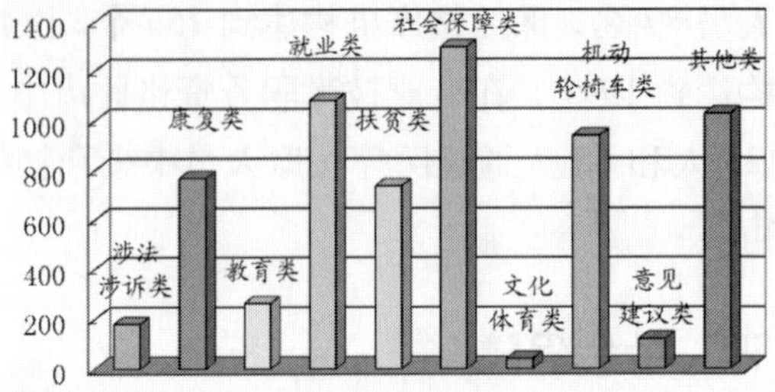

图6　2012年全省信访情况（单位：件）

九、组织建设

基层组织规范化建设进一步巩固，残疾人组织建设“强基育人”工程有效实施。乡镇（街道）残联换届工作基本完成，乡镇（街道）、社区（村）残疾人专职委员配备工作全面完成， 2012年全省13个地市级残联中，7个领导班子配备了残疾人理事长或副理事长。106个县级残联中，62个县级残联机关配备了残疾人干部。在残疾人专职委员选聘方面，1346个乡镇（街道）中，选聘残疾人专职委员1481名；15837个村（含农村社区）和4694个城市社区中，选聘残疾人专职委员19236名。

全省省市县乡残联实有人员已达5127人。干部培训工作取得新进展，各级残联共举办培训班376期，培训机关干部、协会干部及残疾人专职委员2.43万人次，对提高残联系统干部队伍素质起到了重要作用。

全省共建立省级以下各类残疾人专门协会594个，其中盲人协会119个、聋人协会119个、肢残人协会119个、智力残疾人及亲友协会118个、精神残疾人及亲友协会119个，各级各类残疾人专门协会活动日益活跃。

十、信息化建设

截至2012年底，江苏省残疾人人口基础信息数据库累计采集、收录3513317人残疾人实名信息，残疾人各类需求信息2105253条。残疾人人口基础信息数据库和业务工作平台为残疾人社会保障体系和服务体系建设提供进一步支持和保障。

2012 年全年省残联门户网站共录入信息 6641 条，加大“两个体系”建设、残疾人“人人享有康复服务”等重点工作的宣传报道。大力宣传残疾人事业发展成就，成功承办全国残疾人社会福利政策与服务研讨会暨第六届中国残疾人事业发展论坛。

残疾人事业统计队伍建设进一步加强，全省各级残联共有 139 名专、兼职统计人员从事残疾人事业统计工作，统计人员业务素质培养普遍得到重视，省级残联举办培训班 1 期，36 人参加培训；地市级举办培训班 14 期，366 人参加了培训。

地方残联全面推进网站建设，目前省级残联、13 个地市级残联和 98 个县级残联已全部开通了公众服务网站，为残联系统网站集群服务奠定了基础，残联系统网上信息服务正在逐步覆盖全省。地方残联也积极举办各类信息工作培训班，2012 年省级及地市级残联共开设网站技术培训班 24 期，培训各级残联信息员达 1147 人次，各级残联共有 224 名专业技术人员从事信息化工作。

2012年浙江省残疾人事业发展统计公报

2012年，全省残疾人工作继续保持良好发展势头，全面实施残疾人事业发展“十二五”规划取得新进展，保障与服务体系建设取得新突破，广大残疾人得到新实惠。

一、康复

2012年，进一步完善并实施残疾人康复工程，使各类别残疾人得到不同程度的康复。全年完成白内障复明手术3.46万例；为1.90万名贫困白内障患者免费施行复明手术，培训低视力儿童家长966名，有效开展家庭康复训练。对5790名盲人进行定向行走训练。

加强省级聋儿康复机构建设，完善聋儿康复网络。共对802名聋儿进行了听力语言康复训练，规范聋儿家长学校，开展家庭训练，共培训聋儿家长737名；共为8705名听力残疾人免费适配助听器；培养各类专业人员115人。

全年开展肢体残疾康复训练服务的机构达到36个，为残疾人减免费用装配普及型假肢1077例，对35名贫困肢体残疾儿童实施矫治手术、装配了矫形器等辅助器具，进行了术后康复训练；对5973名肢体残疾人进行了康复训练，其中：肢体残疾儿童社区、家庭康复402人，成年肢体残疾人社区、家庭康复5059人。

全年开展智力残疾康复训练服务的机构达到51个；对2308名智力残疾儿童进行了康复训练，不同程度地开展了智力残疾儿童早期康复训练与服务。

深入开展辅助器具供应服务，全面推进普及型假肢装配，截止到2012年底，累计建立辅助器具供应服务机构37个，供应辅助器具2.78万件，装配矫形器153例。

在32个市辖区和54个县（市）开展了社区康复工作，累计建立社区康复站0.99万个，配备1.08万名社区康复协调员。

二、教育

2012年，按照“省办盲校，市办聋校，县办培智学校”要求，全力推进特殊教育体系建设，积极筹建浙江特殊教育职业学院，全年开办特殊教育普通高中7所，在校生418人。其中聋高中5所，在校生380人；盲高中1所，在校生38人。残疾人中等职业教育机构1个，在校生488人，毕业生123人，其中获得职业资格证书75人。有78名残疾人进入特殊教育学院学习。

未入学适龄残疾儿童少年总数918人，其中视力残疾26人，听力残疾67人，言语残疾14人，智力残疾313人，肢体残疾345人，精神残疾48人，多重残疾105人。

三、就业

2012年，继续组织实施“万名残疾人就业创业”计划，加大就业工作考核力度，全年城镇新安排1.46万名残疾人就业。其中，集中就业残疾人0.41万人，按比例安排残疾人就业0.42万人，公益性岗位就业583人，个体及其他形式就业0.35万人，辅助性就业0.25万人，城镇实际在业人数19.85万人；农村残疾人稳定实现就业31.07万人，其中从事农业生产劳动20.52万人。

职业培训基地294个，其中残联兴办68个，本年度城镇职业培训人数1.33万人。

四、社会保障

2012年，继续推进“残疾人共享小康工程”，组织实施残疾人基本生活保障工程、残疾人托（安）养工程，健全残疾人社会保障体系，全年城镇残疾职工参加医疗保险人数12.07万人；城镇残疾居民参加医疗保险达到11.96万人；其中，城镇已纳入最低生活保障3.38万人，城镇集中供养和其他救助救济1.80万人；农村已纳入最低生活保障21.6万人，五保供养和其他救助救济9.16万人。

寄宿制托养机构823个，托养残疾人1.52万人；日间照料托养机构290个，托养残疾人0.27万人；本年度享受居家托养服务残疾人5.5万人。

五、扶贫

2012年，组织各地开展残疾人扶贫脱困和残疾人事业结对帮扶工作，全年度扶持贫困残疾人户14.14万户，扶持17.69万人，脱贫1.88万人，返贫0.52万人，接受实用技术培训的残疾人2.16万人次，投入培训经费1,198.02万元。

结对帮扶单位0.37万个，结对帮扶个人1.33万人；建立残疾人扶贫基地916个，安置残疾人就业0.75万人，扶持带动残疾人家庭2.93万户。

完成0.45万户农村贫困残疾人家庭危房改造，投入资金4269万元，受益残疾人0.56万人。

六、维权

2012年，重视残疾人维权工作，健全残疾人维权组织，全年制定或修改了保障残疾人权益的规范性文件省级2件、市级3件；县级以上人大执法检查或专题调研62次，政协视察和专题调研68次。

开展普法宣传教育活动178次，参加人数2.03万人；

举办法律培训班61次，参加人数0.42万人；

建立残疾人法律救助协调机构40个；

建立残疾人法律救助工作站32个，办理案件331件；

建立残疾人法律援助中心（工作站）98个，办理案件1069件； 协助残联系统人大代表、政协委员提出议案、建议、提案133件，办理议案、建议、提案123件。

无障碍建设与管理法规、政府令21个；无障碍建设领导协调组织30个；系统开展无障碍建设市、县26个；贫困残疾人家庭无障碍改造0.41万户，无障碍检查0.02万次，无障碍培训0.08万人次 ，残疾人机动轮椅车燃油补贴1.59万人。

各级残联共处理残疾人群众来信0.13万件，接待残疾人群众来访0.97万人次，其中集体访36批次、0.06万人次。

七、宣传文化

2012年，进一步健全残疾人事业宣传文化工作机制，充分发挥残疾人艺术团体的作用，全省省级中央媒体采用稿件49件，主要新闻媒体刊播稿件数120件，报刊专版3个，残疾人专题广播节目1个，电视手语新闻栏目1个，省级残疾人事业新闻宣传促进会1个。

市级主要新闻媒体刊播稿件数4027件，报刊专版34个，残疾人专题广播节目16个，电视手语新闻栏目14个，建立市级新促会11个。

省级和市级公共图书馆设立盲文及盲人有声读物阅览室已达到1个和13个，举办残疾人文化周1个和18个，举办残疾人文化艺术类展览22个，已成立残疾人艺术团队1个和12个。

八、体育

2012年，以参加伦敦残奥会为契机，全面推进残疾人体育工作，全年开展省级残疾人体育健身活动5次，参加人数0.15万人，残疾人体育比赛1次，参与的残疾人运动员800人次，残疾人体育训练基地5个。

市级残疾人体育健身活动74次，参加人数0.62万人，残疾人体育示范点66个。

九、组织建设

2012年，认真贯彻中央7号文件及省委3号文件，进一步推动残疾人基层组织建设，全省11个市级残联中，7个领导班子配备了残疾人副理事长。89个县级残联中，62个配备了残疾人干部。

在残疾人专职委员选聘方面，0.13万个乡镇（街道）中，选聘残疾人专职委员0.12万名；2.50万个村（社区）中，选聘残疾人专职委员1.53万名。

残联干部综合培训工作取得较好成绩。全省市县乡残联实有人员已达0.53万人，干部培训工作取得新进展。

全省共建立各类残疾人专门协会471个，其中盲人协会100个、聋人协会100个、肢残人协会102个、智力残疾人及亲友协会73个、精神残疾人及亲友协会73个、智力残疾人及亲友协会和精神残疾人及亲友协会二者合一的23个。

十、信息化

2012年，继续加强残联信息化工作，推进“一网、两库、三平台”建设。统计队伍建设进一步加强，全省各级残联共有82名专（兼）职统计人员从事残疾人事业统计工作，统计人员业务素质培养普遍得到重视，省级残联举办培训班 2 期，参加培训的人员达到 120 人次；市级举办培训班 22 期，参加培训的人员达到 658 人次。

全面推进网站建设，目前省残联已开通了公众服务网站，有 11 个市级残联网站和 83 个县级残联网站也已开通。这为今后残联系统网站集群服务奠定了基础，残联系统网上信息服务正在逐步覆盖全省。积极举办各类信息工作培训班，2012 年省级及市级残联开设网站技术培训班 7 期，培训各级残联信息员达 388 人次。

十一、综合服务设施

2012 年，充分利用贯彻中央 7 号、省委 3 号文件以及各地创建“爱心城市”之机，全面推进残疾人综合服务设施建设。截止到 2012 年底，全省在建各级残疾人综合服务设施项目共计 16 个，筹建项目共计 12 个。其中已竣工并投入使用的各级残疾人综合服务设施总建设规模 69.03 万平方米，总投资 22.74 亿元。

已竣工并投入使用的各级康复设施共计 33 个，在建项目共计 4 个，筹建项目共计 7 个。其中已竣工并投入使用的各级康复设施总建设规模 24.04 万平方米，总投资 6.14 亿元。

全省已竣工并投入使用的各级托养设施共计 2 个，在建项目 2 个，筹建项目共计 2 个，其中已竣工并投入使用的各级托养设施总建设规模 3.51 万平方米，总投资 1.89 亿元。

2012年安徽省残疾人事业发展统计公报

2012年，我省残疾人事业在省委、省政府的坚强领导下，深入贯彻落实科学发展观，以“创先争优，迎接十八大”为契机，扎实推进工作，残疾人事业取得新发展，各项工作取得新成就，广大残疾人得到新实惠。

一、康复

2012年，会同卫生等部门，超额完成贫困残疾人康复民生工程任务，直接受益残疾人87366人。其中，首次将6651名残疾儿童抢救性康复纳入省政府民生工程，投入资金7220万元，人均受助1.1万元；投入1170万元，为1.16万名贫困白内障患者免费施行复明手术；投入3450万元，对6.99万名贫困精神病患者给予服药补贴。全年为1840名贫困精神残疾人每人提供4000元住院救助，为3788名低视力患者配用助视器，培训低视力儿童家长619名，有效开展家庭康复训练，对3853名盲人进行定向行走训练。

加强省级聋儿康复机构建设与管理，进一步完善聋儿康复网络，提升康复服务能力。全年共对2123名聋儿进行了听力语言康复训练；继续开设聋儿家长学校，开展家庭训练，共培训聋儿家长3477名；培养各类专业人员577人。

大力推广“社会化、综合性、开放式”精神病防治康复工作。在85个市县开展精神病防治康复工作，对26.54万重性精神病患者进行综合防治康复，监护率达到73.79%，显好率达到41.93%，社会参与率达到35.52%，肇事率0.03%；解除关锁48人。

建立了1个省级孤独症儿童康复训练机构，有35名孤独症儿童进行了康复训练。

进一步加强全省残疾人辅助器具中心机构建设，与全省16个地市签订成立辅具中心责任状，其中，合肥、淮北、阜阳、滁州、铜陵等市已经挂牌开展服务。到2012年底，累计建立辅助器具供应服务机构9个，为残疾人减免费用装配普及型假肢912例，供应辅助器具2.10万件，装配矫形器799例。

全年开展肢体残疾康复训练服务的机构达到48个，对406名贫困肢体残疾儿童实施矫治手术、装配了矫形器等辅助器具，进行了术后康复训练；对13438名肢体残疾人进行了康复训练，其中：脑瘫儿童系统康复训练451人，肢体残疾儿童社区、家庭康复535人，成年肢体残疾人社区、家庭康复12452人。

全年开展智力残疾康复训练服务的机构达到29个；对2128名智力残疾儿童进行了康复训练，不同程度地开展了智力残疾儿童早期康复训练与服务。

社区康复工作稳步推进。全省43个市辖区和56个县（市）开展了社区康复工作，累计建立社区康复站0.38万个，配备0.66万名社区康复协调员。

二、教育

2012年累计开办特殊教育普通高中3所，在校生446人；残疾人中等职业教育机构有9个，在校生638人，毕业生202人，其中获得职业资格证书185人。全年共有265名残疾人被普通高等院校录取，24名残疾人进入特殊教育学院学习。省残工委协同各部门落实特教学校学生人均经费不低于普教5倍的政策，并会同省教育厅、财政厅印发高校残疾学生资助办法，提高救助标准。

未入学适龄残疾儿童少年总数3431人，其中视力残疾107人，听力残疾120人，言语残疾148人，智力残疾1015人，肢体残疾1256人，精神残疾173人，多重残疾612人。

三、就业

2012年残疾人就业工作力度加大，举办各类技能培训100余期，1万多名残疾人接受免费技能培训。会同省人社厅成功举办第五届全省残疾人职业技能竞赛。联合各级人社、工商联等部门，举办50多场就业供需招聘会，城镇新安排1.50万残疾人就业。其中，集中就业残疾人0.40万人，按比例安排残疾人就业0.40万人，公益性岗位就业535人，个体及其它形式就业0.61万人，辅助性就业0.11万人；

城镇实际在业人数 18.85 万人；108.00 万农村残疾人稳定实现就业，其中从事农业生产劳动 86.13 万人。

2012 年，全省共有职业培训基地 114 个，其中残联兴办 66 个，本年度城镇职业培训人数 0.76 万人。

盲人按摩事业稳定发展，按摩机构数量迅速增长。2012 年度培训盲人保健按摩 566 人，医疗按摩人员 77 人，保健按摩机构达到 226 个，医疗按摩机构达到 89 个；有 62 人和 102 人通过医疗按摩人员中级和初级职称评审。

四、社会保障

2012 年，抓住实施新农保、城居保政策全覆盖机遇，加大工作力度，为 117.6 万残疾人争取到代缴保费的政策优待。2012 年，城镇残疾职工参加社会保险人数达到 8.34 万人，其中参加养老保险人数 5.00 万人，参加医疗保险人数 4.04 万人；城镇残疾居民参加医疗保险达到 27.05 万人；城乡 43.72 万名残疾人纳入最低生活保障范围；城镇已纳入最低生活保障 9.23 万人，城镇集中供养和其他救助救济 1.46 万人；农村已纳入最低生活保障 34.49 万人，五保供养和其他救助救济 8.81 万人。

残疾人托养服务工作稳步推进。寄宿制托养机构 105 个，托养残疾人 0.19 万人；日间照料托养机构合计 30 个，托养残疾人 0.10 万人；本年度享受居家托养服务残疾人 1.31 万人。

2012 年，继续实施贫困重度残疾人生活特别救助民生工程，全省各级财政投入 2.77 亿元，对低保内 42 万人名一级、二级残疾人给予每人每年 660 元救助，并建立救助标准年增 10%机制。

五、扶贫开发

2012 年度扶持贫困残疾人户 7.28 万户，扶持 12.82 万人，脱贫 3.32 万人，返贫 0.78 万人；接受实用技术培训的残疾人 2.37 万人次，投入培训经费 590.19 万元。

全省结对帮扶单位 0.08 万个，结对帮扶个人 0.44 万人；建立残疾人扶持基地 59 个，安置残疾人就业 0.16 万人，扶持带动残疾人 0.29 万户。

完成 0.39 万户农村贫困残疾人危房改造，投入危房改造资金 2,336.60 万元，受益残疾人 0.48 万人。

六、维权

2012 年，配合省人大开展《残疾人保障法》以及我省《残疾人保障条例》贯彻情况检查，有力促进法规政策的落实。制定或修改了保障残疾人权益的规范性文件省级 1 件、地市级 7 件； 县级以上人大执法检查或专题调研 39 次，政协视察和专题调研 54 次。开展普法宣传教育活动 297 次，参加人数 1.42 万人；举办法律培训班 56 次，参加人数 0.19 万人；建立残疾人法律救助协调机构 28 个；建立残疾人法律救助工作站 13 个，办理案件 193 件；建立残疾人法律援助中心（工作站）113 个，办理案件 1180 件；协助残联系统人大代表、政协委员提出议案、建议、提案 56 件，办理议案、建议、提案 56 件。

无障碍建设法规、标准进一步完善。全省共出台 10 个省、地市、县级无障碍建设与管理法规、规章，共建立无障碍建设领导协调组织 23 个；系统开展无障碍建设市、县 76 个；贫困残疾人家庭无障碍改造 0.22 万户，无障碍检查 0.02 万次，无障碍培训 0.03 万人次，残疾人机动轮椅车燃油补贴 2.64 万人。

各级残联共处理残疾人群众来信 2300 多件，接待残疾人群众来访 1.60 万人次，其中集体访 39 批次，600 多人次。

七、宣传文体

2012 年，全省残疾人事业宣文工作成绩显著。成功举办了第三届省特奥会；在伦敦残奥会上，我省残疾运动员刘美丽、王键、康国锋获得 1 金 2 铜的好成绩；组织参加中国残联好新闻评选和广播节目展播，荣获全国优秀组织奖。

2012 省及中央媒体采用稿件 30 件，主要新闻媒体刊播稿件数 505 件，报刊专版 3 个，残疾人专题广播节目 1 个，电视手语新闻栏目 1 个，省级残疾人事业新闻宣传促进会 1 个；地市级主要新闻媒体刊播稿件数 2156 件，报刊专版 28 个，残疾人专题广播节目 12 个，电视手语新闻栏目 14 个，建立地市级新促会 3 个。省级和地市级公共图书馆设立盲文及盲人有声读物阅览室已达到 1 和 18 个，举办残疾人文化周 1 和 63 个，举办残疾人文化艺术类比赛及展览分别是 2 和 20 个，已成立残疾人艺术团队 0 和 10 个。

全省共有残疾人体育健身指导员 85 人，举办残疾人体育比赛1次，参与的残疾人运动员227人次，残疾人体育训练基地1个，聘任教练员15人。地市级残疾人体育健身活动84次，参加人数0.41万人，残疾人体育示范点 41 个，残疾人体育健身指导员56人。

八、组织建设

2012年认真贯彻执行省委、省政府关于各级残联换届指导意见。到2012年底，我省95%以上县、乡残联完成换届，60%以上县级残联成立党组。16个地市级残联（含直辖市的县、区）中，7 个的领导班子配备了残疾人理事长或副理事长。109 个县级残联中，25个县级残联机关配备了残疾人干部。在残疾人专职委员选聘方面，0.15万个乡镇（街道）中，选聘残疾人专职委员0.15万名；1.39万个社区（村）中，选聘残疾人专职委员1.21万名。残联干部综合培训工作取得较好成绩。全国省市县乡残联实有人员已达0.34人，干部培训工作取得新进展。

全省共建立各类各级残疾人专门协会 503 个，其中盲人协会102个、聋人协会100个、肢残人协会106个、智力残疾人及亲友协会97个、精神残疾人及亲友协会97个、智力残疾人及亲友协会和精神残疾人及亲友协会二者合一的1个。

九、综合服务设施建设

到2012年底，已竣工并投入使用的各级残疾人综合服务设施共计67个，在建项目共计8个，筹建项目共计 9 个。其中已竣工并投入使用的各级残疾人综合服务设施总占地面积 10.50 万平方米，总建设规模9.84 万平方米，总投资1.83亿元；

已竣工并投入使用的各级康复设施共计 2 个，在建项目共计2个，筹建项目共计3个。其中已竣工并投入使用的各级康复设施总占地面积0.09万平方米，总建设规模0.19万平方米，总投资0.07亿元；

安徽省精神残疾人托养（康复）中心5000平方米项目开工建设，安徽省特殊中专学校 2.2 万平方米一期项目综合楼封顶并开始内装。

十、信息化建设

2012年统计队伍建设进一步加强，各级残联共有 130 名专、兼职统计人员从事残疾人事业统计工作，统计人员业务素质培养普遍得到重视，省级残联举办培训班1期，参加培训的人员达到150人次；地市级举办培训班12期，参加培训的人员达到156人次。

全省各级残联全面推进网站建设，16个省辖市全部开通门户网站，58个县级残联网站也已开通，网站总数比去年增加6个。这为今后残联系统网站集群服务奠定了基础。各地残联积极举办各类信息工作培训班，2012年省级及地市级残联开设网站技术培训班13期，培训各级残联信息员达402人次。

各级残联共有 159 名专业技术人员从事信息化工作；省级残联共建立局域网1个，网上办公（OA）系统1个。

全省残疾人综合业务管理系统已承载本省残疾人基本信息达 380 多万条。为加强数据库管理，推动政府有关部门数据共享机制建设，2012年省残联会同省民政、财政、卫生、统计等部门制定《关于加强残疾人基础信息数据库建设的意见》，对数据库建设、数据更新、开发、统计分析等，提出工作要求，为数据库的横向开发、数据交换共享与应用奠定政策基础。

2012年福建省残疾人事业发展统计公报

2012年，福建省残疾人工作在省委、省政府的正确领导和中国残联的精心指导下，全面实施《福建省残疾人事业“十二五”发展纲要》，以改善残疾人生活、提高为残疾人服务能力为出发点和落脚点，开拓创新，扎实推进，残疾人事业科学发展、跨越发展取得明显成效。

一、残疾人康复工作

2012年,通过中央和省级重点康复项目的实施，以及各地实施的配套项目，全省投入10854万元使12.1万名残疾人得到康复服务,大力推进残疾人“人人享有康复服务”。

全年完成白内障复明手术1.77万例，其中超额完成省委、省政府为民办实事“光明行动”项目任务,为1.26万名贫困白内障患者免费施行复明手术。创新低视力康复工作，启动“福乐视康行动”等新项目，为749名低视力患者配用助视器，比2011年增长61%；培训低视力儿童家长946名，比2011年增加5.3倍。对4255名盲人进行定向行走训练。

加强省级聋儿康复机构建设，完善聋儿康复网络。共对860名聋儿进行了听力语言康复训练，规范聋儿家长学校，开展家庭训练，共培训聋儿家长988名；加强聋儿康复人才队伍建设，培养各类专业人员197人，比上年增长121%。

大力推广“社会化、综合性、开放式”精神病防治康复工作。在84个市县开展精神病防治康复工作，对12.56万重性精神病患者进行综合防治康复，监护率达到87.68%，显好率达到62.80%，社会参与率达到48.58%，肇事率0.09%；解除关锁94人；对1.2万名贫困精神病患者进行医疗救助，比2011年增加近1倍人数。全省救助贫困孤独症儿童652名，有849名孤独症儿童在机构内进行康复训练，37名孤独症儿童进入普幼、普小及特殊教育学校就学。

深入开展辅助器具供应服务，全面推进普及型假肢装配。截止到2012年底，累计建立县级以上残疾人辅助器具供应服务机构44个，为残疾人减免费用装配普及型假肢674例,供应辅助器具1.16万件，装配矫形器417例；辅助器具供应品种由2011年的148种增至309种，为残疾人提供更趋个性化的服务。

全省开展肢体残疾康复训练服务的机构达92个,为33名贫困肢体残疾儿童实施矫治手术，装配矫形器等辅助器具，并进行术后康复训练；对9691名肢体残疾人进行了康复训练，其中：脑瘫儿童系统康复训练1374人,肢体残疾儿童社区、家庭康复837人，成年肢体残疾人社区、家庭康复7480人。

全年开展智力残疾康复训练服务的机构达53个；对5537名智力残疾儿童进行了康复训练,其中：智力残疾儿童机构康复训练943人，智力残疾儿童社区、家庭康复4594人。

在25个市辖区和58个县（市）开展了社区康复工作，累计建立社区康复站3760个，配备9429名社区康复协调员。省级安排825万元支持苏区、老区县165个社区建设规范康复室。2012年新增接受社区康复残疾人16.5万人,较上一年度增长2倍。

积极配合卫生等部门开展残疾儿童筛查工作。2012年，全省新诊断0-6岁残疾儿童362名。积极开展儿童残疾预防宣传,共发放宣传材料2.45万份。

二、残疾人教育工作

全省未入学适龄残疾儿童少年总数1433人,比2011年减少131%，其中以智力残疾、肢体残疾和多重残疾儿童人数居多，占总数的85%。

全省已开办特殊教育普通高中20所，在校生521人，其中：聋高中10所，在校生412人；盲高中3所，在校生109人。残疾人中等职业教育机构有6个，在校生120人，毕业生32人，其中获得职业资格证书32人。高等特殊教育学院建有1所。全省参加2012年高考的残疾考生有240人达到录取分数线，其中229人被普通高等院校录取，录取率达95.42%。

2012年，全省有698名学龄前残疾儿童接受残疾人事业专项彩票公益金助学项目资助，比2011年增长3倍；171名学龄前残疾儿童获其他助学项目资助。

继续实施“双百扶残助学计划”等项目，全省安排1954.3万元，资助贫困残疾学生和残疾人子女8722名。

三、残疾人就业工作

开展“城镇百万残疾人就业工程”等活动，省级以上安排8000万元扶贫贷款额度全额贴息扶持残疾人就业创业。全省城镇实际在业人数12.22万人，本年度城镇新安排1.23万名残疾人就业，其中:集中就业残疾人3057人，按比例安排残疾人就业2732人，公益性岗位就业1184人，个体及其它形式就业4751人，辅助性就业612人。36.58万农村残疾人稳定实现就业，其中从事农业生产劳动的农村残疾人占80%。

全省63个残疾人就业服务机构规范化建设验收达标，省残疾人劳动就业服务中心为全国第二个通过考评验收的省级机构。全省现有残疾人职业培训基地378个,其中残联兴办172个。全年培训残疾人25694人（次），省级盲按、计算机等技能培训班常年举办。

盲人按摩事业稳定发展。本年度培训盲人保健按摩854人，盲人医疗按摩166人，分别有54人和129人通过医疗按摩人员中级和初级职称评审。全省277个盲人按摩机构中,有保健按摩机构273个，医疗按摩机构4个。全省现有盲人按摩就业人员1542名，其中盲人保健按摩人员占90%。

四、社会保障工作

2012年,全省残疾人社会保障状况进一步改善。城镇残疾职工参加社会保险人数达到4.81万人，其中参加养老保险人数2.74万人，参加医疗保险人数2.84万人；城镇残疾居民参加医疗保险达到11.54万人；城乡23.83万名残疾人纳入最低生活保障范围；城镇已纳入最低生活保障4.58万人，城镇集中供养和其他救助救济1.22万人；农村已纳入最低生活保障19.24万人，五保供养和其他救助救济4.15万人。继续实施“全省重度残疾人困难补助金制度”，已有23.7万名贫困重度残疾人受益。

进一步落实残疾人参加保险补助制度，参加城乡社会养老保险的残疾人达57.8万人，其中政府对农村、城镇重度残疾人参保最低档个人缴费分别给予补贴100%和50%。继续推进残疾人意外伤害保险工作，补助近21万名残疾人参保。

全省已建寄宿制残疾人托养机构79个，托养残疾人2691人；日间照料托养机构38个，托养残疾人1152人；本年度享受居家托养服务残疾人1.73万人。省启能研究指导中心被中国残联评为“阳光家园”示范机构。

五、残疾人扶贫开发工作

坚持项目带动、品牌带动，帮助残疾人脱贫致富。实施省委、省政府为民办实事“残疾人就业扶助项目”，为6000名残疾人提供创业就业和开展种植养殖提供每户5000元资助。继续实施“福乐助残扶贫攻坚工程”，对全省221个省级扶贫重点村扶持1326户残疾人发展生产及安排残疾人家庭危房改造5000人。

各级残联不断加大扶贫和培训力度，共扶持贫困残疾人户2.28万户，扶持3.29万人，脱贫1.68万人，返贫1927人，比2011年减少23%；全年投入培训经费1166.14万元，接受实用技术培训的残疾人9.28万人次，比2011年增长近4倍。通过扶持，绝大多数受助残疾人掌握了技能，实现了脱贫。

结对帮扶单位2555个，结对帮扶个人4714人；建立残疾人扶持基地141个，安置残疾人就业5211人，扶持带动残疾人5130户。

完成2849户农村贫困残疾人危房改造，投入危房改造资金3,862.34万元，受益残疾人5274人，比2011年增长56%。

六、残疾人宣传文化工作

残疾人文化发展重长效，省残联联合省委宣传部等10个部门出台了我省《关于加强残疾人文化建设的实施意见》，各地将残疾人文化纳入城乡公共文化服务体系建设大局，开展一系列残疾人喜闻乐见的文化活动。

创新宣传模式，开展了“法制宣传周”、“闽台残疾人文化周”、“体育健身周”、“慈善助残周”四个季度主题周活动，全省联动，不断掀起残疾人事业宣传热潮。省级中央媒体采用稿件2件，主要新闻媒体刊播稿件数3件，报刊专版8个，残疾人专题广播节目1个，电视手语新闻栏目1个，省级残疾人事业新闻宣传促进会1个。市级主要新闻媒体刊播稿件数600件，报刊专版33个，残疾人专题广播节目8个，电视手语新闻栏目11个，建立市级新促会7个。

省级公共图书馆设立盲文及盲人有声读物阅览室2个，市级已设立27个，比2011年增加13个。在全省范围建设"福乐书屋"，逐步解决残疾人读书难的问题。省残疾人文化活动中心每周定期开放，为残疾人提供免费服务；省残疾人艺术团开展下基层、进高校等公益巡演22场。市级残联举办残疾人文化周16场次，举办残疾人文化艺术类比赛及展览32次，全省已建立市级残疾人艺术团队5个。

七、残疾人体育生活

残疾人体育工作创佳绩。我省12名残疾人运动员及5名教练员、领队参加第十四届伦敦残奥会，取得3金、1银、2铜及打破3项世界纪录、1项残奥会纪录、4项亚洲纪录的好成绩。省委、省政府再次对参赛人员按照奥运会参赛人员同等标准进行表彰奖励，省残联首次荣立集体三等功。圆满承办全国聋人田径锦标赛，来自全国各省（市、区）近400人参会。成功举办全省残疾人青少年田径锦标赛、残疾人体育训练营等活动。

在全省范围建设"福乐健身站"，残疾人体育健身指导员、分级员等队伍得到发展，全省残疾人体育工作新机制已初现端倪。省级举办残疾人体育健身活动30次，参加人数2800人；建立残疾人体育示范点30个，残疾人体育健身指导员50人；残疾人体育训练基地15个，聘任教练员58人。市级举办残疾人体育健身活动51次，参加人数3425人；建立残疾人体育示范点23个，残疾人体育健身指导员251人。

八、残疾人维权工作

全面宣传贯彻《福建省实施<残疾人保障法>办法》。省人大常委会组织对6个设区市开展我省首次大范围的《残疾人保障法》执法检查，有力推进残疾人权益保障工作。市级制定或修改保障残疾人权益的规范性文件7件；县级以上人大执法检查或专题调研41次，政协视察和专题调研33次。

全省开展普法宣传教育活动251次，参加人数2.16万人；开展法律培训班57次，参加人数4447人；建立残疾人法律救助协调机构44个；建立残疾人法律救助工作站36个，办理案件292件；建立残疾人法律援助中心（工作站）93个，办理案件1104件；协助残联系统人大代表、政协委员提出议案、建议、提案67件，办理议案、建议、提案63件。

全省已制定县级以上无障碍建设与管理法规、政府令24个，建立无障碍建设领导协调组织57个。省残联与省委宣传部、法制办等8个部门联合开展"全省无障碍督查月活动"，对全省100多个医院、机场、车站等公共服务场所无障碍设施进行督查。省残联为8个设区市残联配发了无障碍汽车。2012年，为全省2130户贫困残疾人实施家庭无障碍改造，为1.3万名残疾人发放机动轮椅车燃油补贴。

多措并举推进残疾人信访维权工作。建立全省残疾人服务专线"968891"，畅通残疾人利益诉求和服务咨询渠道。组织"全省残联领导干部接访下访专项活动"，积极化解矛盾。各级残联共处理残疾人群众来信1097件，接待残疾人群众来访8753人次，其中集体访31批次，789人次，比2011年来信、来访数量明显减少。

九、残疾人组织建设

省残联高度重视协管工作，联合省委组织部出台《关于在残联换届工作中进一步加强残联领导班子和干部队伍建设的意见》。9个设区市残联党组全部成立，84个县级残联全部实现机构单列；9个设区市残联全部配备了残疾人领导干部，84个县级残联中，39个县级残联机关配备了残疾人干部。全省7个设区市、79个县（市、区）和所有乡镇（街道）残联已完成换届。

组织规范化建设有力推进。开展全省残疾人组织建设"强基育人"工程，97%的县级残联实现了规范达标。1001个乡镇（街道）、14628个村、2004个社区成立了残联（残协）。1105个乡镇（街道）中，选聘残疾人专职委员1733名；1.68万个社区（村）中，选聘残疾人专职委员1.65万名。

省、市、县、乡残联共有编制1487名，实有人员达2609人。全省残联新增残疾人就业、康复、辅具、托养等服务机构36个、增编84名。出台《福建省残疾人联络员管理办法》，明确将乡镇、街道残疾人联络员列入人事部门管理范围，使省残联人才队伍建设进入规范化轨道。

残联干部综合培训工作取得新进展。全省残联系统共举办乡镇级以上综合培训班550期,培训1.26万人次。

省级五个残疾人专门协会圆满完成换届。全省9个设区市均已建立五个残疾人专门协会，其中14个协会已进行社团登记; 26个市辖区和58个县（含县级市）也全部建立五个专门协会，其中133个协会已进行社团登记。

成立了由首批17支志愿服务队组成的“福建省福乐助残志愿服务联盟”，志愿助残服务活动更加活跃、广泛，全年受助残疾人达23.14万人。

十、残疾人综合服务设施建设

以“全省残疾人服务设施建设年”作为残联年度工作主题，成效显著。新建10所省级公办“福乐家园”，省级补助共2000万元，带动市、县两级投资11611万元，全省残疾人服务设施规模将增加约4.6万平方米。

一批建设项目重大突破。总建筑面积8915 m^2、投资近5000万元的省“福乐幼儿园”二期项目前期工作进展顺利，建成后将达到全国三级康复机构标准，招生可达500人，规模名列全国前茅。总建筑面积6928m^2、投资5680万元的省残疾人游泳康复馆经省政府批准已正式立项建设，建成后可承接全国残疾人游泳比赛和我省残疾人运动员日常训练，将步入全国省级残疾人体育设施先进行列。

省、厦门市“福乐幼儿园”规范运作，泉州、漳州、南平等市“福乐幼儿园”建设也已启动。全省评选了首批9家“福乐盲按店”、30家“福乐健身站”及第二批35家“福乐种养基地”并予以补助。

省级安排200万元扶持10个原中央苏区县、老区县残疾人服务大楼无障碍改造。各级残疾人就业、康复、辅助器具、托养等服务设施建设得到推进。

十一、信息化建设

信息化平台建设取得新成效。“海西助残”综合业务管理系统进一步完善，加强数据采集并实现“实名制、直通车”，随时核查、统计，规范程序，透明操作。截止至2012年12月31日，残疾人基础信息库数据量达87.2万条,其中残疾人享受到政府、残联的各项优惠政策达18.1万人次,采集数比增2.9倍；其中残疾人需求更新数为72.6万人，比增1.07倍。

2012年，全省各级残联投入信息化建设经费248万元，信息化安全意识进一步提高，用于信息安全设备的投入比上一年增长47.27%。全省残联系统共有151名专业技术人员从事信息化工作。

注重加强与纵向、横向部门(单位)的沟通协作，实现数据交换共享。2012年，我省与省城乡居民养老保险中心实现了全省所有残疾人参加养老保险的数据交换，获得全省残疾人实际参保25.3万人的数据。

省残联门户网站“残疾人在线”全年访问量达88.9万人次，比上年同期增长37.04%，在残疾人事业新闻宣传、政务公开、信息服务等方面发挥了重要作用。9个地市级残联网站和84个县级残联网站已全部开通，残联系统网上信息服务逐步覆盖全省。省、市级残联共开办网站技术培训班11期，培训各级残联信息员达462人次。

统计队伍建设进一步加强，各级残联共有105名专、兼职统计人员从事残疾人事业统计工作。统计人员业务素质培养普遍得到重视，省级残联举办培训班1期，参加培训的人员达到40人次；地市级举办培训班7期，参加培训的人员达到180人次。

2012 年江西省残疾人事业发展统计公报

2012 年，是我省经济社会全面快速发展的一年。一年来，在省委省政府和中国残联信息中心的正确领导下，全省残联深入贯彻落实科学发展观，坚持以完善残疾人社会保障和服务体系建设为目标，以实施民生工程残疾人项目为重点，认清形势抓机遇，开拓创新谋发展，残疾人工作取得了较大成效，残疾人事业统计又上一新台阶。

一、残疾人康复工作取得良好成效

2012 年，通过实施一批重点康复工程，使各类别残疾人得到不同程度的康复。全年完成白内障复明手术 1.81 万例；其中为 4600 名贫困白内障患者免费施行复明手术，全年为 1697 名低视力患者配用助视器，培训低视力儿童家长 460 名，有效开展家庭康复训练。对 4754 名盲人进行定向行走训练。

加强省级聋儿康复机构建设，完善聋儿康复网络。共对 931 名聋儿进行了听力语言康复训练，规范聋儿家长学校，开展家庭训练，共培训聋儿家长 1022 名；培养各类专业人员 73 人。

大力推广“社会化、综合性、开放式”精神病防治康复工作。在 101 个市县开展精神病防治康复工作，对 18.36 万重性精神病患者进行综合防治康复，监护率达到 75.72%，显好率 45.79%，社会参与率 34.09%，肇事率 1.27%；解除关锁 464 人；对 1.96 万名贫困精神病患者进行医疗救助。

建立了 1 个省级孤独症儿童康复训练机构，有 30 名孤独症儿童进行了康复训练。开展宣传普及教育，为麻风患者回归社会营造良好社会氛围。

深入开展辅助器具供应服务，全面推进普及型假肢装配。截止到 2012 年底，累计建立辅助器具供应服务机构 19 个，为残疾人减免费用装配普及型假肢 2624 例，供应辅助器具 1.65 万件，装配矫形器 1120 例。

全年开展肢体残疾康复训练服务的机构达到 24 个,对 89 名贫困肢体残疾儿童实施矫治手术、装配了矫形器等辅助器具，进行了术后康复训练；对 15105 名肢体残疾人进行了康复训练，其中：脑瘫儿童系统康复训练 553 人,肢体残疾儿童小区、家庭康复 1497 人,成年肢体残疾人小区、家庭康复 13055 人。

全年开展智力残疾康复训练服务的机构 20 个；对 5181 名智力残疾儿童进行了康复训练，不同程度地开展了智力残疾儿童早期康复训练与服务。

在 23 个市辖区和 77 个县（市）开展了小区康复工作，累计建立小区康复站 3600 个，配备 1.31 万名社区康复协调员。

二、残疾人教育工作全面深入开展

开办特殊教育普通高中 4 所，在校生 138 人；其中聋高中 4 所，在校生 138 人；残疾人中等职业教育机构有 2 个，毕业生 2 人，其中获得职业资格证书 2 人。有 197 名残疾人被普通高等院校录取，10 名残疾人进入特殊教育学院学习。

未入学适龄残疾儿童少年总数 5229 人，其中视力残疾 526 人，听力残疾 563 人，言语残疾 449 人，智力残疾 1176 人，肢体残疾 1536 人，精神残疾 251 人，多重残疾 728 人。

三、残疾人就业工作稳定推进

城镇新安排 1.51 万残疾人就业。其中，集中就业残疾人 5800 人，按比例安排残疾人就业 1100 人，公益性岗位就业 1168 人，个体及其它形式就业 6600 人，辅助性就业 0.13 万人，全国城镇实际在业人数 14.91 万人；55.64 万农村残疾人稳定实现就业，其中从事农业生产劳动 41.91 万人。

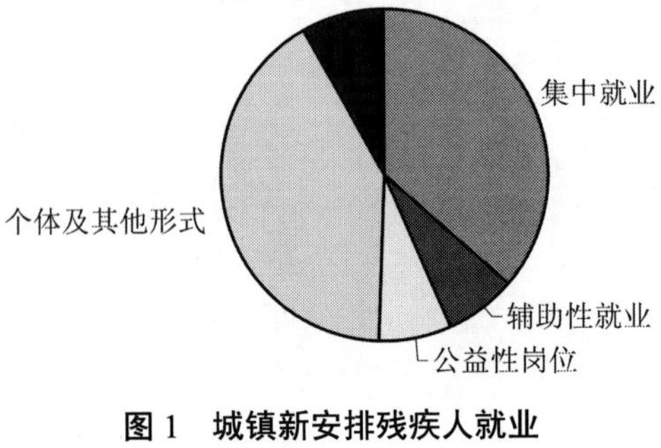

图 1　城镇新安排残疾人就业

举办职业培训基地 206 个,其中残联兴办 38 个,本年度城镇职业培训人数 400 人。

培训盲人保健按摩 286 人;医疗按摩人员 47,保健按摩机构达到 307 个,医疗按摩机构达到 64 个;分别有 40 人和 111 人通过医疗按摩人员中级和初级职称评审。

四、残疾人社会保障逐步完善

城镇残疾职工参加社会保险人数 10.72 万人,其中参加养老保险人数 3.93 万人,参加医疗保险人数 3.98 万人;城镇残疾居民参加医疗保险 22.63 万人;城乡 36.41 万名残疾人纳入最低生活保障范围;城镇已纳入最低生活保障 10.67 万人,城镇集中供养和其它救助救济 2.58 万人;农村已纳入最低生活保障 25.73 万人,五保供养和其它救助救济 6.46 万人。

寄宿制托养机构 16 个,托养残疾人 800 人;日间照料托养机构合计 2 人,托养残疾人 100 人;本年度享受居家托养服务残疾人 9800 人。

五、残疾人扶贫工作成效突出

本年度扶持贫困残疾人户 25600 户,扶持 40200 人,脱贫 6.77 万人,返贫 4400 人,接受实用技术培训的残疾人 7200 人次,投入培训经费 3878100 元。

结对帮扶单位 2600 个,结对帮扶个人 12300 人;建立残疾人扶持基地 149 个,安置残疾人就业 1800 人,扶持带动残疾人 2400 户。

完成农村贫困残疾人危房改造 4400 户,投入危房资金 1,175.92 万元,受益残疾人 5300 人。

六、残疾人维权工作力度增大

制定或修改了关于残疾人的专门法规、规章地市级 2 件;制定或修改了保障残疾人权益的规范性文件地市级 5 件;县级以上人大执法检查或专题调研 24 次,政协视察和专题调研 27 次。

开展普法宣传教育活动 132 次,参加人数 12100 人;开展法律培训班 46 次,参加人数 2000 人;建立残疾人法律救助协调机构 18 个;建立残疾人法律救助工作站 23 个,办理案件 102 件; 建立残疾人法律援助中心(工作站)94 个,办理案件 906 件;协助残联系统人大代表、政协委员提出议案、建议、提案 86 件,办理议案、建议、提案 57 件。

制定或完善无障碍建设与管理法规、政府令 7 个;建立无障碍建设领导协调组织 29 个;开展无障碍建设市、县 58 个;贫困残疾人家庭无障碍改造 1200 户,无障碍培训 100 人次,残疾人机动轮椅车燃油补贴 16400 人。

各级残联共处理残疾人群众来信 700 件,接待残疾人群众来访 6800 人次,其中集体访 23 批次,200 人次。

七、宣传文化体育 作进一步加强

省级中央媒体采用稿件 16 件,主要新闻媒体刊播稿件数 40 件,报刊专版 5 个,残疾人专题广播节目 2 个,电视手语新闻栏目 1 个,省级残疾人事业新闻宣传促进会 1 个;地市级主要新闻媒体刊播稿件数 612 件,报刊专版 6 个,残疾人专题广播节目 3 个,电视手语新闻栏目 4 个。

省级和各设区市公共图书馆设立盲文及盲人有声读物阅览室共 10 个,举办残疾人文化周活动 12 次,举办残疾人文化艺术类比赛及展览 14 个,已成立残疾人艺术团队 7 个。

省本级开展残疾人体育健身活动 3 次,参加人数 600 人;残疾人体育示范点 1 个,残疾人体育健身指导员 40 人,残疾人体育比赛 1 次,参与的残疾人运动员 218 人次,残疾人体育训练基地 2 个,聘任教练员 13 人。设区市开展残疾人体育健身活动 13 次,参加人数 800 人,残疾人体育示范点 4 个,残疾人体育健身指导员 9 人。

八、残疾人组织建设进一步健全

2012 年,各级残联领导班子基本上都配备了残疾人理事长或副理事长。11 个设区市残联中,7 个的领导班子配备了残疾人理事长或副理事长。104 个县级残联中,49 个县级残联机关配备了残疾人干部。

在残疾人专职委员选聘方面,1600 个乡镇(街道)中,选聘残疾人专职委员 3300 名;17800 个小区(村)中,选聘残疾人专职委员 12700 名。

残联干部综合培训工作取得较好成绩。全省市县乡残联实有人员已达 4000 人,干部培训工作取得新进展。

随着志愿者队伍的不断壮大,越来越多的残疾人得到不同程度的帮助。目前，全省已登记在册助残志愿者共 25452 人，受助残疾人共计 79911 人。

九、残疾人工作信息化建设扎实有效

统计队伍建设进一步加强。各级残联共有 129 名专、兼职统计人员从事残疾人事业统计工作，统计人员业务素质培养普遍得到重视，省级残联举办培训班 1 期，培训人员 35 人次；地市级举办培训班 9 期，培训人员 267 人次。

地方残联全面推进网站建设。目前省残联已开通了公众服务网站，有 6 个设区市残联网站和 33 个县级残联网站也已开通，网站总数比去年增加 4 个，为今后残联系统网站集群服务奠定了基础，残联系统网上信息服务正在逐步覆盖全省。设区市残联积极举办各类信息工作培训班，2012 年省残联及设区市残联开设网站技术培训班 11 期，培训各级残联信息员 373 人次。

各级残联共有 167 名专业技术人员从事信息化工作；省级残联共建立局域网 1 个，网上办公（OA）系统 1 个。

十、综合服务设施不断完善

截止到 2012 年底，已竣工并投入使用的各级残疾人综合服务设施共计 18 个，筹建项目共计 4 个。其中已竣工并投入使用的各级残疾人综合服务设施总占地面积 16400 平方米，总建设规模 25100 平方米，总投资 5400 万元；

已竣工并投入使用的各级康复设施共计 3 个，在建项目共计 4 个，筹建项目共计 1 个。其中已竣工并投入使用的各级康复设施总占地面积 1600 平方米，总建设规模 3800 平方米，总投资 0.02 亿元；

已竣工并投入使用的各级托养设施共计 1 个，在建项目共计 2 个，其中已竣工并投入使用的各级托养设施总占地面积 17300 平方米，总建设规模 500 平方米，总投资 0.01 亿元；

十一、民生工程投入逐年增强

2012 年，省政府进一步加大对我省残疾人民生工程的投入力度，全年共为近 18 万残疾人提供康复服务，其中为 114279 万名残疾人建立康复档案，为 17385 名残疾人配发了假肢等辅助器具，为 21401 名精神病患者提供了免费服药，为 476 名贫困残疾儿童提供了抢救性康复救助，为 2747 名残疾人提供了免费白内障复明手术；全年共为 3584 名残疾人提供了公益性岗位，8582 名农家书屋残疾人管理员，为 7057 名残疾人提供了相应的职能技术培训服务。

2012年山东省残疾人事业发展统计公报

2012年，在山东省委、省政府的关心重视下，全省残联系统围绕中心、服务大局，以推动落实省政府为民办实事项目为总抓手，扎实工作，锐意进取，圆满完成了年度工作任务。

一、康复

视力残疾康复：全省视力残疾康复机构78个，在岗人员2104人。全年共完成白内障复明手术5.82万例，为2.68万名贫困白内障患者免费施行复明手术，为2795名低视力患者配用助视器，培训低视力儿童家长513名，对6432名盲人进行定向行走训练。

听力言语残疾康复：全省听力语言康复机构85个，在岗人员1170人。对2146名聋儿进行了听力语言康复训练，开展家庭训练，共培训聋儿家长2465名，培养各类专业人员338人，开展成年听力语言康复技术服务1370人次。

肢体残疾康复：全省肢体残疾康复训练机构224个，其中残联办97个，残联办机构在岗人员863人。全年对50839名肢体残疾人进行了康复训练，其中：脑瘫儿童康复训练2280人，肢体残疾儿童社区、家庭康复1054人，成年肢体残疾人社区、家庭康复47505人。对447名贫困肢体残疾儿童实施矫治手术。

智力残疾康复：全省智力残疾康复训练机构97个，其中残联办25个，残联办机构在岗人员335人。对4562名智力残疾儿童进行了康复训练，2669名智力残疾儿童和2325名成年智力残疾人得到了社区、家庭康复训练。全年培训康复管理、技术人员1093人次。

精神残疾康复：全省132个县（市、区）开展了精神病防治康复工作，对39.95万重性精神病患者进行综合防治康复，监护率达到84.82%，显好率达到63.10%，社会参与率达到52.62%，肇事率0.04%。对2.47万名贫困精神病患者进行医疗救助。全省孤独症儿童康复训练机构98个，机构内教师907人，在训儿童900人，救助贫困孤独症儿童464人。

辅助器具供应：全省辅助器具供应服务机构64个，供应各类辅助器具8.20万件，假肢装配1263例，矫形器装配377例。

社区康复：全省共有145个县（市、区）（含开发区）开展了社区康复工作，累计建立社区康复站4.06万个，配备4.97万名社区康复协调员。开展家长学校工作的残疾人康复机构60个，培训家长2824人次。

二、教育培训就业

义务教育：截止2012年底，全省未入学适龄残疾儿童少年总数3972人，其中视力残疾215人，听力残疾226人，言语残疾138人，智力残疾1255人，肢体残疾1440人，精神残疾211人，多重残疾487人。

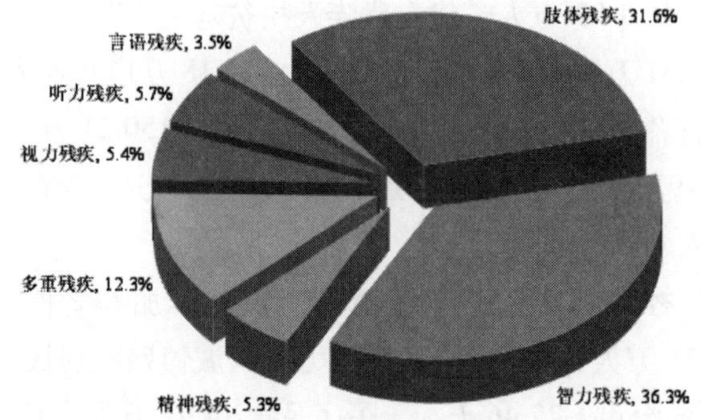

图1　2012年底全省未入学适龄各类残疾儿童分类

高等教育：全省有特殊教育普通高中23所，在校生888人。其中：聋高中16所、在校生777人；盲高中1所、在校生111人。残疾人中等职业教育机构17个，在校生1397人、毕业生677人，其中获得职业资格证书493人。高等特殊教育学院1所。367名残疾学生被普通高等院校录取。

职业培训：全省共有职业培训基地716个，其中193个为残联兴办，本年度城镇职业培训1.83万人。

就业：本年度全省城镇新安排残疾人就业19650人，其中：集中就业残疾人6981人、按比例安排残疾人就业7065人、公益性岗位就业382人、个体及其它形式就业4917人、辅助性就业305人。城镇实际在业残疾人24.84万人，135.38万农村残疾人稳定实现就业，其中从事农业生产劳动106.35万人。

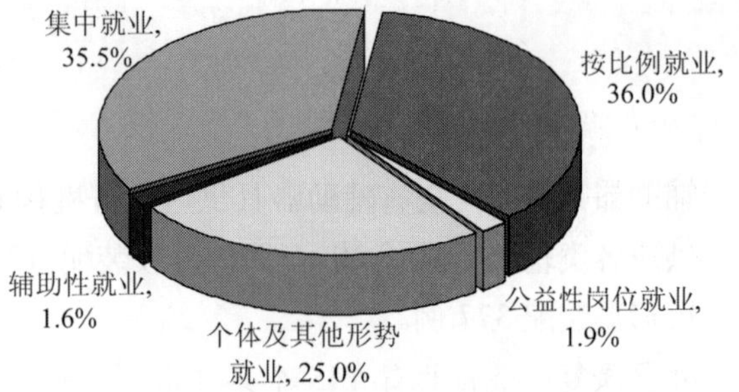

图2　2012年全省城镇新安排残疾人就业比例

盲人按摩：全省有盲人保健按摩机构1153个、医疗按摩机构81个。本年度培训盲人保健按摩人员665人、医疗按摩人员284人。167人通过医疗按摩人员初级职称评审。

三、扶贫和社会保障

扶贫：2012年度全省共扶持贫困残疾人户4.99万户、扶持8.22万人、脱贫5.54万人、返贫0.36万人。投入经费1789.64万元，使5.64万残疾人接受了实用技术培训。组建结对帮扶单位4233个，结对帮扶1.83万人。建立残疾人扶贫基地787个，安置1.61万残疾人就业，扶持带动了4.18万户残疾人。全省各级共投入了危房改造专项资金5150.21万元，对4918户农村贫困残疾人进行了危房改造，受益残疾人6452人。

社会保障：全省城镇残疾职工参加养老保险13.21万人、医疗保险12.11万人。城镇残疾居民参加养老保险22.46万人、医疗保险14.91万人。城镇个体就业残疾人参加养老保险3.23万人、医疗保险2.59万人。共有7.96万城镇残疾人纳入最低生活保障，集中供养和其他救助救济2.83万人。农村居民参加新型农村社会养老保险101.95万人、新型农村合作医疗保险161.38万人。33.06万农村残疾人纳入最低生活保障，五保供养和其他救助救济10.07万人。

托养：全省有寄宿制托养机构447个、托养1.57万残疾人。日间照料托养机构105个、托养0.25万残疾人。本年度有3.29万残疾人享受居家托养服务。

四、政策法规与维权

法规体系和政策文件：2012年，我省修订了《残疾人保障法》实施办法。市级制定或修改了关于残疾人的专门法规、规章2个，市级残联参与制定或修改保障残疾人权益的规范性文件7个。县级残联参与制定或修改保障残疾人权益的规范性文件44个。县级及以上人大开展执法检查或专题调研77次、政协视察和专题调研57次。

法制宣传：全省开展普法宣传教育活动277次、参加人数3.14万人。开展法律培训班136次、参加人数0.55万人。

法律救助：全省共建立残疾人法律救助协调机构39个。建立残疾人法律救助工作站37个、办理案件278件。 建立残疾人法律援助中心（工作站）153个、办理案件1454件。

无障碍建设：全省各级共出台33个无障碍建设与管理法规或政府令，有68个无障碍建设领导协调组织，6个市、县系统开展了无障碍建设。各级共开展无障碍专项检查264次、1284人参加了无障碍培训。全年对1.13万户贫困残疾人家庭进行了无障碍改造。发放残疾人机动轮椅车燃油补贴2.15万人。

信访：各级残联共处理残疾人来信1114件，接待残疾人来访5763人次，其中集体访共6批、55人。

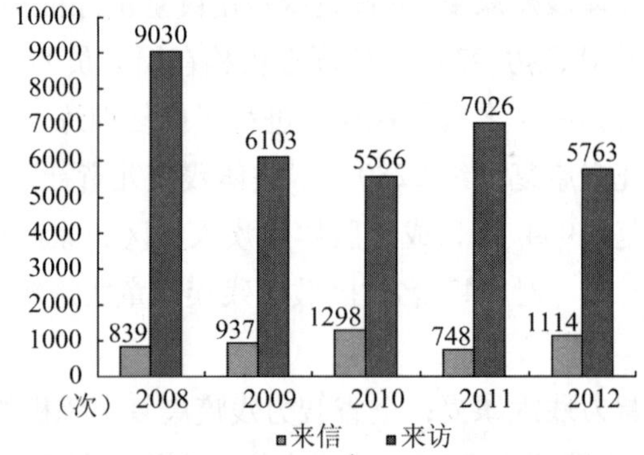

图3　2008-2012年全省残疾人来信、来访情况

五、文化体育

宣传文化：截止2012年底，省、市两级共开播残疾人专题广播节目13个、电视手语新闻栏目8个、报刊专版46个，21个公共图书馆设立盲文及盲人有声读物阅览室。各级共举办残疾人文化周36个、残疾人文化艺术类比赛及展览27个。全省已成立10个残疾人艺术团，省级和7个地市建立了残疾人事业新闻宣传促进会，全省主要新闻媒体全年共刊播与残疾人相关的稿件3901件。

体育：全省共有残疾人体育训练基地4个，聘任教练员12人。地市级组织残疾人体育活动82次，参加人数8018人，残疾人体育示范点35个，残疾人体育健身指导员309人。在2012年伦敦残奥会上，我省14名运动员获得2枚金牌、7枚银牌、2枚铜牌，1人创1项世界纪录、3人4次破3项残奥会纪录。

六、组织建设

组织队伍：截止2012年底，全省省、市、县、乡四级残联机关和事业单位共有编制4296个，实有人员6740人。14个市级残联领导班子配备了残疾人，59个县级残联机关配备了残疾人干部。选聘乡镇（街道）残疾人专职干事2324人、村（社区）残疾人专职委员5.91万人。

干部培训：省、市、县、乡四级残联本年度共举办综合类培训班2498期、培训6.49万人。省、市两级举办残疾人干部培训班22期、培训827人。

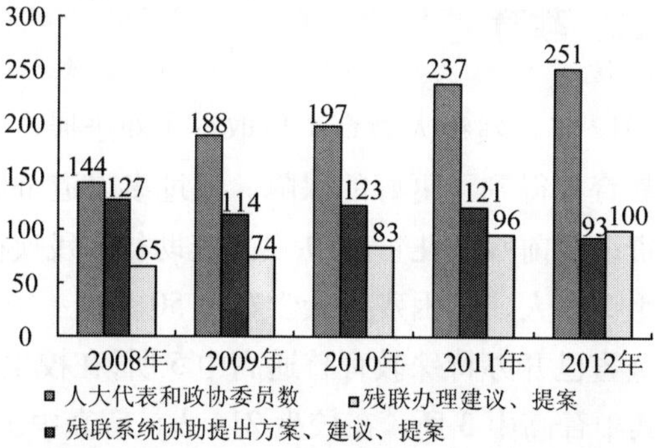

图4　2008-2012年全省残疾人参政议政情况

参政议政：在县级及以上残疾人及其亲友和残疾人工作者中，共有人大代表78人、政协委员173人。残联系统协助人大代表、政协委员提出议案、建议、提案93件，办理建议、提案100件。

专门协会：市、县两级共建立各类残疾人专门协会767个，其中盲人协会159个、聋人协会154个、肢残人协会157个、智力残疾人及亲友协会147个、精神残疾人及亲友协会147个、智力残疾人及亲友协会和精神残疾人及亲友协会二者合一的3个。

七、信息化与统计

信息化建设：截止2012年底，全省各级残联共有210名专业技术人员从事信息化工作，年度投入信息化经费433.71万元。除省残联外，17个市和67个县级残联开通了门户网站，完成了省、市两级残联门户网站的信息无障碍改造工作。省、市两级残联共举办各类信息工作培训班22期，培训各级残联信息员590人。

统计工作：各级残联共有160名专、兼职统计人员从事残疾人事业统计工作。省、市两级残联共举办统计业务培训班19期，培训369人次。2012年，全省开展了“走千家、访万户，察实情、摸实底”大调研活动，对160万持证残疾人进行入户调查，占持证残疾人总数的94%，基本摸清了持证残疾人的生活状况和各方面需求。继续在全省的38个样本县（市、区）开展残疾人状况监测工作，对2095名残疾人进行了入户监测。

2012年河南省残疾人事业发展统计公报

2012年，是极不平凡的一年，也是河南省残疾人事业快速发展的一年。在省委、省政府的正确领导下，全省残疾人工作按照年初提出的“突出一个中心，抓好五项重点，办好五件实事”的总体要求，经过全省上下共同努力，全面提升了各项业务水平，也有力推动了全省残疾人事业务实发展，各项工作再创佳绩，残疾人生活状况得到了新的改善。现将2012年残疾人事业各项指标统计公报如下：

一、康复

2012年，我省按照全省残疾人事业“十二五”发展规划，全面完成了康复年度任务。通过实施一批重点康复工程，使各类别残疾人得到不同程度的康复。

全年完成白内障复明手术2.5万例；为1.2万余名贫困白内障患者免费施行复明手术，为14402名低视力患者配用助视器，培训低视力儿童家长4843名，有效开展家庭康复训练。对8695名盲人进行定向行走训练。

加强省级聋儿康复机构建设，完善聋儿康复网络。共对3229名聋儿进行了听力语言康复训练，规范聋儿家长学校，开展家庭训练，共培训聋儿家长2928名；培养各类专业人员394人。

大力推广“社会化、综合性、开放式”精神病防治康复工作。2012年，在156个市县开展精神病防治康复工作，对51.9万重性精神病患者进行综合防治康复，监护率达到39.9%，显好率达到21.7%，社会参与率达到16.4%，肇事率0.1%；解除关锁679人；对2.3万名贫困精神病患者进行医疗救助。

建立了1个省级孤独症儿童康复训练机构，有116名孤独症儿童进行了康复训练。

深入开展辅助器具供应服务，全面推进普及型假肢装配，截止到2012年底，累计建立辅助器具供应服务机构36个，为残疾人减免费用装配普及型假肢4309例，供应辅助器具12.3万件，装配矫形器2770例。

全年开展肢体残疾康复训练服务的机构达到46个，对356名贫困肢体残疾儿童实施矫治手术、装配了矫形器等辅助器具，进行了术后康复训练；对19185名肢体残疾人进行了康复训练，其中：脑瘫儿童系统康复训练2931人,肢体残疾儿童社区、家庭康复1228人，成年肢体残疾人社区、家庭康复15026人。

全年开展智力残疾康复训练服务的机构达到37个；对11020名智力残疾儿童进行了康复训练，不同程度地开展了智力残疾儿童早期康复训练与服务。

在57个市辖区和103个县（市）开展了社区康复工作，累计建立社区康复站4.8万个，配备3万余名社区康复协调员。

二、教育

2012年，残疾人教育工作取得了新进展，残疾人受教育权得到了更好的保障。通过多渠道争取资金，资助学前残疾儿童810名，资助贫困残疾在校高中生230人，贫困残疾大学新生50人。

全省已开办特殊教育普通高中5所，在校生243人；其中聋高中3所，在校生214人；盲高中1所，在校生29人。残疾人中等职业教育机构有7个，在校生268人，毕业生126人，其中获得职业资格证书56人。高等特殊教育学院3所,有400名残疾人被普通高等院校录取，17名残疾人进入特殊教育学院学习。

截止到2012年底，全省有未入学适龄残疾儿童少年8345人，其中视力残疾425人，听力残疾657人，言语残疾623人，智力残疾3198人，肢体残疾2607人，精神残疾121人，多重残疾714人。

三、就业

残疾人就业培训成效显著。省委、省政府将残疾人就业培训工作继续列入2012年全省“十项民生工程”、“八项举措”，经过不懈努力，圆满完成了省委、省政府下达的培训就业任务。

截止 2012 年底，全省城镇新安排 4.14 万残疾人就业。其中，集中就业残疾人 1.3 万人，按比例安排残疾人就业 0.9 万人，公益性岗位就业 1763 人，个体及其它形式就业 1.7 万人，辅助性就业 0.1 万人，全省城镇实际在业人数 30.6 万人；186 万农村残疾人稳定实现就业，其中从事农业生产劳动 147.5 万人。

职业培训基地 203 个，其中残联兴办 41 个，本年度城镇职业培训人数 2.6 万人。

培训盲人保健按摩 1193 人；医疗按摩人员 624，保健按摩机构达到 444 个，医疗按摩机构达到 86 个；通过医疗按摩人员中级和初级职称评审各 9 人。

四、社会保障

为加快推进残疾人社会保障体系和服务体系建设，进一步改善残疾人状况，促进残疾人平等参与社会生活、共享社会发展成果，2012 年，省政府与 18 个省辖市政府签订了《残疾人“两个体系”建设目标责任书》，明确了 2012 年我省残疾人“两个体系”建设主要工作任务。省人大审议通过了《关于修改河南省〈残疾人保障法〉实施办法的决定》，在残疾人社会保障和服务等方面取得了重大突破。

截至 2012 年底，全省城镇残疾职工参加社会保险人数达到 24.9 万人，其中参加养老保险人数 11.4 万人，参加医疗保险人数 10.3 万人；城镇残疾居民参加医疗保险达到 38.7 万人；城乡 83.1 万名残疾人纳入最低生活保障范围；城镇已纳入最低生活保障 17.7 万人，城镇集中供养和其他救助救济 5 万余人；农村已纳入最低生活保障 65.3 万人，五保供养和其他救助救济 18.9 万人。

寄宿制托养机构 45 个，托养残疾人 0.4 万人；本年度享受居家托养服务残疾人 1.2 万人。

五、扶贫

2012 年，通过制定出台扶贫政策文件、实施助残扶贫项目、加强农村残疾人扶贫基地建设，强化残疾人培训成效等一系列措施，使贫困残疾人生活状况得到不断改善和提高。

2012 年，全省扶持贫困残疾人户 6.2 万户，扶持 17.6 万人，脱贫 9.7 万人，返贫 0.9 万人，接受实用技术培训的残疾人 6.4 万人次，投入培训经费 1,880.6 万元。

2012 年全省共有结对帮扶单位 4700 个，结对帮扶个人 10.2 万人；建立残疾人扶持基地 190 个，安置残疾人就业 0.9 万人，扶持带动残疾人 1.2 万户。

完成 5000 余户农村贫困残疾人危房改造，投入危房资金 1,622.5 万元，受益残疾人 8100 人。

六、维权

2012 年，我省残疾人维权工作紧紧围绕残疾人事业法制建设、残疾人权益保障、信访等各项工作的有效开展，切实加大维权工作力度，特别是《河南省实施〈中华人民共和国残疾人保障法〉办法》的颁布实施，对残疾人事业的全面进步起到了重要的促进作用。

2012 年，我省地市级制定或修改了关于残疾人的专门法规、规章 2 件；制定或修改了保障残疾人权益的规范性文件地市级 11 件；县级以上人大执法检查或专题调研 32 次，政协视察和专题调研 28 次。

大力开展普法宣传教育，2012 年全省开展普法宣传教育活动 228 次，参加人数 4.95 万人；开展法律培训班 79 次，参加人数 0.50 万人；建立残疾人法律救助协调机构 65 个；建立残疾人法律救助工作站 43 个，办理案件 202 件；建立残疾人法律援助中心（工作站）165 个，办理案件 705 件； 协助残联系统人大代表、政协委员提出议案、建议、提案 47 件，办理议案、建议、提案 49 件。

无障碍建设法规、标准进一步完善。全省共出台无障碍建设与管理法规、政府令 25 个；成立无障碍建设领导协调组织 32 个；系统开展无障碍建设市、县 52 个；为 0.2 万户贫困残疾人家庭进行无障碍改造，开展无障碍检查 100 次，无障碍培训 400 人次，为 5.2 万残疾人发放了机动轮椅车燃油补贴。

全省各级残联共处理残疾人群众来信 700 件，接待残疾人群众来访 7800 人次，其中集体访 93 批次，600 人次。

七、宣传、文化、体育

2012 年，按照我省残疾人事业“十二五”发展规划的有关任务目标，大力宣传残疾人工作亮点，打造舆论热点，丰富和活跃基层残疾人文化生活，推动残疾人体育协调发展，为残疾人事业发展提供了强有力的舆论支持，为广大残疾人参与文化体育生活提供了更好的服务。

宣传文化 2012 年省级中央媒体采用稿件 5 件，主要新闻媒体刊播稿件数 100 件，报刊专版 3 个，残疾人专题广播节目 1 个，电视手语新闻栏目 1 个，省级残疾人事业新闻宣传促进会 1 个；

地市级主要新闻媒体刊播稿件数 396 件，报刊专版 219 个，残疾人专题广播节目 58 个，电视手语新闻栏目 3 个，建立地市级新促会 13 个。

省级和地市级公共图书馆设立盲文及盲人有声读物阅览室分别达到 3 个和 15 个，举办残疾人文化周分别为 1 个和 81 个，举办残疾人文化艺术类比赛及展览分别是 5 和 32 个，已成立残疾人艺术团队分别为 1 和 2 个。

体育 省级残疾人体育健身活动 2 次，参加人数 1200 人，残疾人体育示范点 5 个，残疾人体育健身指导员 50 人，残疾人体育比赛 2 次，参与的残疾人运动员 200 人次，残疾人体育训练基地 6 个，聘任教练员 20 人。

地市级残疾人体育健身活动 88 次，参加人数 7300 人，残疾人体育示范点 18 个，残疾人体育健身指导员 426 人。

八、组织建设

2012 年，我省以“强基育人”工程为抓手，全面推进基层组织建设，以换届为契机，进一步加强残联领导班子建设和干部队伍建设，以规范化建设为目标，切实加强志愿助残服务工作，以严格规范管理为手段，切实加强残疾人证核发工作，以活跃专门协会为核心，创新社会组织服务管理，圆满完成了各项年度工作任务。

基层组织规范化建设进一步巩固。18 个地市级残联（含直辖市的县、区）中，12 个的领导班子配备了残疾人理事长或副理事长。166 个县级残联中，94 个县级残联机关配备了残疾人干部。

在残疾人专职委员选聘方面，0.24 万个乡镇（街道）中，选聘残疾人专职委员 0.31 万名；4.69 万个社区（村）中，选聘残疾人专职委员 4.46 万名。

残联干部综合培训工作取得较好成绩。全省残联实有人员已达 8700 人，干部培训工作取得新进展。

全省共建立各类残疾人专门协会 885 个（含开发区），其中盲人协会 177 个、聋人协会 177 个、肢残人协会 177 个、智力残疾人及亲友协会 177 个、精神残疾人及亲友协会 177 个。

九、信息化建设

2012 年，各级残联共有 190 名专、兼职统计人员从事残疾人事业统计工作，统计人员业务素质得到提高，省级残联举办培训班 1 期，参加培训的人员达到 40 人次；地市级举办培训班 16 期，参加培训的人员达到 253 人次。

地方残联全面推进网站建设，目前省残联已全部开通了公众服务网站，有 8 个地市级残联网站和 16 个县级残联网站也已开通，网站总数比去年增加 1 个。这为今后残联系统网站集群服务奠定了基础，残联系统网上信息服务正在逐步覆盖全国。地方残联也积极举办各类信息工作培训班，2012 年省级及地市级残联开设网站技术培训班 11 期，培训各级残联信息员达 258 人次。

各级残联共有 236 名专业技术人员从事信息化工作；省残联建立局域网 1 个。

十、服务设施

截至 2012 年底，全省已竣工并投入使用的各级残疾人综合服务设施共计 135 个，在建项目共计 11 个，筹建项目共计 7 个。其中已竣工并投入使用的各级残疾人综合服务设施总占地面积 25.6 万平方米，总建设规模 18.1 万平方米，总投资 2.9 元；

全省已竣工并投入使用的各级康复设施共计 5 个，在建项目共计 2 个，筹建项目共计 6 个。其中已竣工并投入使用的各级康复设施总占地面积 6 万平方米，总建设规模 5 平方米，总投资 0.7 亿元；

全省已竣工并投入使用的各级托养设施共计 4 个，在建项目共计 5 个，筹建项目共计 4 个，其中已竣工并投入使用的各级托养设施总占地面积 1.6 万平方米，总建设规模 1.1 万平方米，总投资 0.2 元。

2012年湖北省残疾人事业发展统计公报

2012年，湖北省残联在省委省政府的高度重视下，在中国残联的正确指导下，全省残联系统深入贯彻实施《湖北省残疾人事业"十二五"发展纲要》，以重点项目为抓手，加快推进残疾人"两个体系"试验区建设，实现"十二五"时期良好开局，残疾人事业实现快速发展态势，各方面工作取得新成效，广大残疾人获得更多实惠。

一、康复

2012年，通过科学制定"十二五"残疾人康复实施方案，紧紧围绕逐步实现残疾人人人享有康复服务的目标，以0-6岁残疾儿童抢救性康复和辅助器具适配为重点，实施系列康复服务工程，努力加快残疾人康复保障与服务体系建设，全力推进康复机构和康复人才队伍建设，圆满完成年度各项康复工作任务。

在39个市辖区和59个县（市）开展了社区康复工作，累计已建社区康复站的社区总数4567个，配备7284名社区康复协调员。

开展视力残疾康复机构总数达到14个，完成白内障复明手术30000例；为7456名贫困白内障患者免费施行复明手术；为7297名低视力患者配用助视器，培训低视力儿童家长7304名，有效开展家庭康复训练。对6668名盲人进行定向行走训练。

推进听力语言康复机构规范化管理，完善基层服务网络。已建设省级听力语言康复机构1个，市县级听力语言康复机构35个。年度新收训聋儿791名，在训聋儿940名；规范聋儿家长学校，开展家庭训练，共培训聋儿家长942名；开展各级各类听力语言康复专业技术人员培训，共培训专业人员61人；为166名贫困成年听力残疾人免费验配助听器，各级康复机构共为611名成年听力残疾人提供技术服务。

大力推广"社会化、综合性、开放式"精神病防治康复工作。在92个县（市、区）开展精神病防治康复工作，对342651重性精神病患者进行综合防治康复，监护率达到65.2%，显好率达到41.6%，社会参与率达到30.9%，肇事率0.001%；解除关锁301人；对14386名贫困精神病患者进行医疗救助。

建立了28个孤独症儿童康复训练机构；348名孤独症儿童在各级机构进行了康复训练。

开展肢体残疾康复训练服务机构达43个，其中，省级康复机构1个，地市级、县级康复机构42个；培训各级各类肢体残疾康复人员270人次；全省共对14172名肢体残疾者实施康复训练；实施救助项目资助1602名脑瘫儿童进行机构康复训练，资助177名贫困肢体残疾儿童实施矫治手术。

为麻风畸残者实施矫治手术118例，开展宣传普及教育，为麻风患者回归社会营造良好社会氛围。

开展智力残疾康复训练服务的机构39个，其中，省级康复机构1个，地市级、县级康复机构38个；培训各级各类智力残疾康复人员227人次；全省共对6376名智力残疾人进行康复训练；实施救助项目资助735名智力残疾儿童进行机构康复训练，同时培训儿童家长。

加强残疾人辅助器具服务体系建设，深入开展辅助器具供应服务，为残疾人减免费用供应辅助器具31254件，其中装配假肢1910例、矫形器623例，验配助视器28721件。

二、教育

2012年，特殊教育进一步完善，残疾人受教育权得到了更好保障，进一步提高了残疾人素质和平等参与社会的能力。

残疾人事业专项彩票公益金助学项目，为全省家庭经济困难的残疾儿童享受普惠性学前教育提供资助674人次。各地也积极多渠道争取资金支持，对20名残疾儿童给予学前教育资助。

已开办特殊教育普通高中班（部）7个，在校生287人；其中聋高中6个，在校生287人。残疾人中等职业学校（班）7个，在校生132人，毕业生38人，其中34人获得职业资格证书。全省有225

名残疾人被普通高等院校录取，7 名残疾人进入特殊教育学院学习。

截止到 2012 年底，全省有未入学适龄残疾儿童少年 2488 人，其中视力残疾儿童 137 人，听力残疾儿童 115 人，言语残疾儿童 132 人，智力残疾儿童 790 人，肢体残疾儿童 842 人，精神残疾儿童 82 人，多重残疾儿童 390 人。

三、就业

2012 年，残疾人就业工作在保持就业局势稳定的基础上实现新突破。城镇新增 233082 名残疾人就业，其中，集中就业残疾人 60863 人，按比例安排残疾人就业 37309 人，公益性岗位就业 4659 人，个体就业及其它形式灵活就业 130095 人，辅助性就业 156 人。全省 897459 名农村残疾人实现稳定就业，其中 670002 人从事农业生产劳动。

全省残疾人职业培训基地达到 253 个，其中残联兴办 200 个，依托社会机构兴办 53 个，4811 人次城镇残疾人接受了职业培训。

盲人按摩事业稳定发展，按摩机构迅速增长。2012 年度培训盲人保健按摩人员 596 名、盲人医疗按摩人员 62 名；保健按摩机构达到 720 个，医疗按摩机构达到 41 个；在专业技术职务资格评审中，分别有 42 人和 158 人通过医疗按摩人员中级和初级职称评审。

四、社会保障

以推进政府为残疾人办实事为抓手，积极创新工作方式方法，着力提高残疾人社会保障水平,2012 年全省残疾人社会保障状况保持平稳。残疾人参加新型农村和城镇居民社会养老保险工作实现了全覆盖，已有 74561 名城镇残疾人参加了城镇居民社会养老保险，参保率 46.9%。在 60 岁以下的参保残疾人中有 52933 名重度残疾人，其中 41564 名得到了政府的参保扶助，有 98874 名非重度残疾人也享受了全额或部分代缴的优惠政策。领取养老金待遇的人数达到 62048 人。

新型农村社会养老保险方面，共有 798761 名残疾人参加了新型农村社会养老保险，参保率 66.3%。在 60 周岁以下的参保残疾人中有重度残疾人 127450 名，其中 111250 名得到了政府的参保扶助（全部代缴 105674 人，部分代缴 5576 人），有 305259 名非重度残疾人也享受了全额或部分代缴的优惠政策。享受养老金待遇的人数达到 366052 人。

城镇残疾职工参加社会保险人数达到 74561 人，城镇残疾居民参加基本医疗保险达到 279372 人，城乡 663244 名残疾人纳入最低生活保障范围；城镇集中供养残疾人和农村五保供养残疾人分别达到 11547 人和 40124 人；94833 名城乡残疾人获得其他救助救济，176590 名和 2908 名符合条件的城乡残疾人分别享受了稳定的生活补贴和护理补贴。

2012 年，省残联把“阳光家园计划”作为重点工程在全省残联系统整体谋划、全面铺开，残疾人托养服务工作稳步推进。残疾人寄宿制托养服务机构达到 112 个，其中事业单位 32 个，民办非企业 27 个，其他性质的 53 个，托养残疾人 1277 人。残疾人日间照料机构达到 82 个，为 2832 名残疾人提供托养服务。接受居家托养服务的残疾人达到 13472 人。

五、扶贫开发

2012 年，残疾人扶贫工作稳中求进，贫困残疾人生产生活状况得到进一步改善。11716 名贫困残疾人得到扶持，其中 64049 人通过扶贫开发实际脱贫；接受实用技术培训的残疾人达到 41072 人次。

康复扶贫贴息贷款扶持 947 名农村残疾人,1061 个单位和 5360 名个人对贫困残疾人开展结对帮扶。残疾人扶持基地达到 100 个，安置 2791 名残疾人就业，扶持带动 12104 名残疾人。

完成 1753 户农村贫困残疾人危房改造，各地投入危房资金 8577024 元，2364 名残疾人受益。

六、宣传文化

2012 年，残疾人事业宣传工作通过培育典型，广泛宣传，使残疾人参与社会达到新水平。圆满组织以“加强残疾人文化服务保障残疾人文化权益”为主题的第二十二次全省助残日活动，出台了《关于加强志愿助残工作的实施意见》，组织了“身边的感动”先进事迹报告演出团赴全省各地巡回报告活动；举办了“0－6 岁残疾儿童抢救性康复工程”总结颁奖晚会演出活动；承办并组织了一系列丰富多彩的残疾人各类文艺汇演活动。

中央级媒体采用稿件数 14 件。省级主要新闻媒体刊播稿件数 1300 件，残疾人广播电专题节目 1 个，电视手语节目 1 个，建立省级新促会 1 个。地市级主要新闻媒体刊播稿件数 1120 件，报纸专版 130 个，残疾人广播电专题节目 14 个，电视手语节目 3 个，电视公益广告片 9 个，报纸公益广告 28 个。

省级公共图书馆设立盲文及盲人有声读物图书室 1 个，残疾人艺术团队 1 个；地市级公共图书馆设立盲文及盲人有声读物图书室 8 个，残疾人艺术团队 5 个。省、地市级残联积极开展了残疾人文化艺术周和残疾人文化艺术类比赛及展览活动。

七、体育

承办国际特奥会特奥东亚区暨澳门特殊奥运会第二十城市邀请赛；输送 5 名残疾人运动员参加第 14 届伦敦残奥会，获得 1 金 3 银 2 铜。

积极组织残疾人参加健身活动。省级组织残疾人体育健身活动 10 次，参加人数 1500 人；地市级组织残疾人体育健身活动 180 次，参加人数 6630 人。

八、维权

2012 年，争取人大立法支持，推动《湖北省实施〈中华人民共和国残疾人保障法〉办法》修订出台。新修订的《实施办法》在残疾人社会保障、事业经费保障、就业保障金征收、文化生活建设、特殊岗位津贴、无障碍环境几个方面实现重大突破。出台并推动实施了《湖北省残疾人事业十二五发展纲要》，维权组织建设得到加强，残疾人事业法律法规体系进一步完善，残疾人维权工作全面开展。

2012 年，地市级制定或修改了关于残疾人的专门法规、规章 1 件、制定或修改保障残疾人权益的规范性文件 2 件。全省县级以上人大进行《残疾人保障法》执法检查 35 次；政协进行视察和专题调研 35 次。全省开展普法宣传教育活动 246 次，3784 人参加；举办法律工作者培训班 67 个，3254 人参加。

截至 2012 年底，全省成立残疾人法律救助工作协调机构 78 个，建立残疾人法律救助工作站 36 个，办理案件 630 件。建立残疾人法律援助中心（工作站）92 个，办理案件 1187 件，有力地促进了法律救助和法律援助工作。

残疾人参政议政工作得到加强，各级残联协助人大代表、政协委员提出议案、建议、提案 91 件，办理议案、建议、提案 79 件。

无障碍建设法规、标准进一步完善。全省共出台了 6 个地市、县级无障碍建设与管理法规、规章；24 个市、县、区系统开展无障碍建设；全省开展无障碍建设检查 125 次，无障碍培训 667 人次；为 1482 个贫困残疾人家庭实施了无障碍改造；为 35527 名残疾人发放了残疾人机动轮椅车燃油补贴。

全省各级残联共处理残疾人群众来信 3151 件，接待残疾人群众来访 21818 人次，其中集体访 59 批次、911 人次。

九、组织建设

2012 年，在全面实施残疾人基层组织、基本队伍、基础设施建设“三基”工程中，着力推进残疾人组织建设“强基育人”工程，残疾人基层组织建设得到不断发展。13 个地市级残联领导班子中有 4 个配备了残疾人理事长或副理事长； 40 个县级残联机关配备了残疾人干部；已建乡镇（街道）残联 1212 个，已建率达到 95.7%，选聘残疾人专职委员 2518 名；已建社区（村）残协 20878 个，已建率达到 84.7%，选聘残疾人专职委员 12840 名。

全省市县乡残联实有人员已达 3768 人。各级残联共举办培训班 185 期，培训机关干部、协会干部及残疾人专职委员 7073 人次。

全省共建立市级以下各类残疾人专门协会 587 个，其中盲人协会、聋人协会、肢残人协会、智力残疾人及亲友协会、精神残疾人及亲友协会均为 117 个。

十、服务设施建设

加强项目规范化管理，制定完善了残疾人基础服务设施建设管理办法，实行项目绩效评估，切实发挥项目效益，残疾人基础服务设施建设步伐明显加快，，服务残疾人的能力得到提升。截至 2012 年底，全省已竣工并投入使用的各级残疾人综合服务设施 56 个，总占地面积 62362 平方米，总建设规模平方 73970.47 平方米，总投资 13436.54 万元；已竣工并投入使用的各级残疾人康复设施 6 个，总占地面积 10716 平方米，总建设规模 12077 平方米，总投资 1196 万元；已竣工并投入使用的各级残疾人托养服务设施 12 个，总占地面积 37496 平方米，总建设规模 19006 平方米，总投资 3285 万元。

十一、信息化建设

信息化专业人才和统计队伍进一步加强。全省各级残联共有 112 名统计人员人事残疾人统计工作。统计人员业务素质培养普遍得到重视。省级残联举办培训班 1 期，参加培训的人员达到 300 人次；地市残联举办培训班 11 期，参加培训的人员达到 189 人次；各级残联共有 141 名专业技术人员从事信息化工作。

网站建设全面推进，目前省残联已开通了公众服务网站，10 个地市级残联网站和 34 个县级残联网站已开通，网站总数比去年增加 6 个。2012 年，全省共举办信息培训班 10 期，培训各类残联信息员 451 人次。

2012年湖南省残疾人事业发展统计公报

2012年湖南省残疾人工作圆满完成各项任务指标，残疾人各项工作全面发展，残疾人得到不同程度的服务和不同类别的保障。根据2012年度残疾人事业统计数据及综合实际情况，公报如下:

一、残疾人康复工作取得进展

2012年我省残疾人康复工作全面提升，康复工作以康复项目为重点，以康复机构为依托，争取各类资金投入残疾人康复，加大社区康复办度，加强各级各类残疾人康复机构建设。

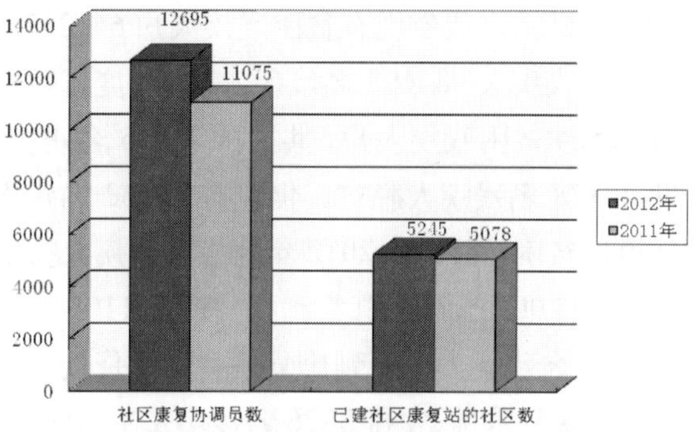

图1　社区康复情况(人、个)

截止到2012年底，在全省14个市州所属125个县区12607个社区村开展社区康复服务，已建成5245个社区康复站，有12695名各级社区康复协调员，本年度新增社区康复协调员3170名。到2012年底全省共建立11个家长学校，已登记家长学员861名，增强了社区康复力量。

2012年全省有15606名白内障患者免费手术，比2011年增加4%，为4925名低视力患者配用助视器，全省有24个视力残疾康复机构（其中地市级视力残疾康复机构4个，县区20个）。

全省有聋儿康复机构54个（其中省级1个，地市级17个，县区36个），新收训聋儿926名，比上年度增加4.7%，截止12月15日，“七彩梦行动计划”已为240名聋儿患者免费配发助听器，完成人工耳蜗手术210例。

加大精神残疾康复机构建设，2012年省残联共投入60万元，支持精神康复工、农、娱疗站的建设项目，已建成22个精神残疾康复机构。全省有孤独症儿童康复机构32个（其中省级1个，地市及以下其他机构31个，在训孤独症儿童291名）。

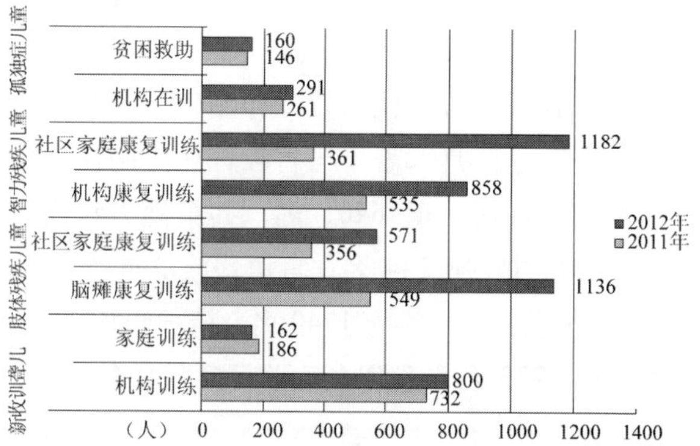

图2　残疾儿童康复情况

全省有肢体残疾康复机构40个，比2011年增加9个，全年有515名脑瘫儿童实施国家康复救助项目，为205名贫困残疾儿童进行了矫治手术，为30名麻风畸残患者进行了免费手术，现有智力残疾儿童康复机构43个，较上年增加了10个，500名智力残疾儿童得到了“国家彩票公益金”救助。

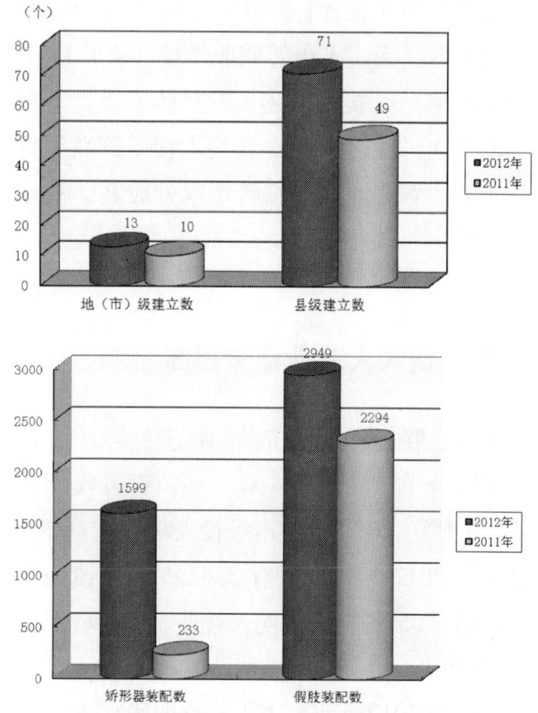

图3　辅助器具服务机构建立情况

2012年“国家彩票公益金”项目为我省残疾人

免费发放 24505 件各类辅助器具，全省共建设各级各类辅助器具服务机构 84 个（基中地市 13 个，县区 71 个），解决了部分残疾人辅助器具配发难题。

二、残疾人教育工作全面发展

全省残疾人基本享受到平等教育的权利，2012 年全省有 613 名各阶段教育的残疾学生享受残疾人事业彩票公益金助学项目的资助。全省特殊教育学校对义务教育阶段的学生实施“三免一补”政策（免交杂费、教科书费、住宿费、补贴生活费），省残联教就部经过认真部署，与省教育厅协调在全省共筛查未入学残疾儿童 6401 名，其中视力残疾儿童 315 名，听力残疾 244 名，言语残疾 394 名，肢体残疾 2319 名，智力残疾 1740 名，精神残疾 156 名，多重残疾 1233 名，我省未入学残疾儿童数偏多。

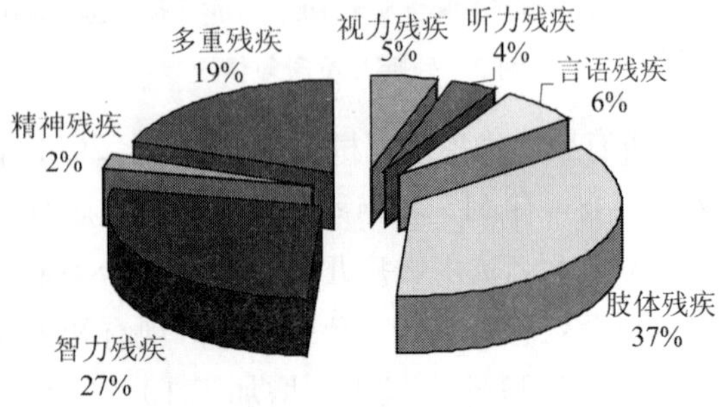

图 4　未入学残疾儿童情况

全省有特殊教育普通高中学校（班）12 个，共招生 258 名，残疾人中等职业学校（班）11 个，共招生 411 名，为提高残疾人的整体素质打下良好基础。2012 年全省有 19 名残疾人接受到高等特殊教育，全年达到普通高等院校录取分数名，被录取人数 231 名。

三、残疾人就业稳步提高

省残联联合省人力资源和社会保障厅、省财政厅共同出台了《湖南省实施“城镇百万残疾人就业工程”方案》，2012 年省本级投入项目配套资金 450 万元，到 2012 年底我省有 274345 名城镇残疾人就业，有 918705 名农村残疾人就业，年度培训城镇残疾人 5605 名。

截止到 2012 年底，本年度收取残疾人就业保障金 389746399.00 元，比 2011 年增加 13.7%,全省有残疾人职业培训基地 172 个,其中残联办 74 个。

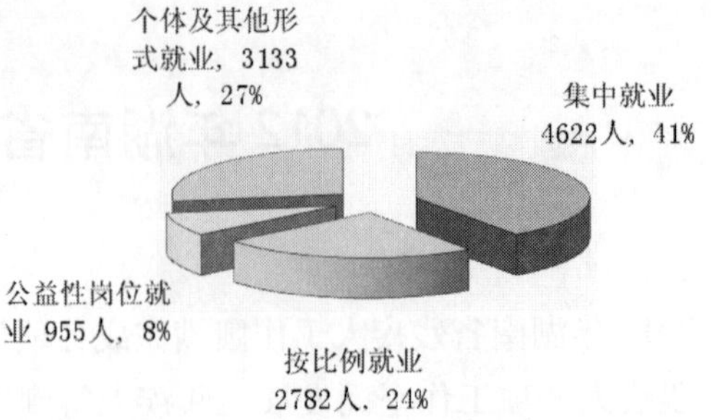

图 5　新增城镇残疾人就业状况

全省盲人医疗按摩机构 17 个，保健按摩机构 456 个，本年度共培训保健按摩人员 1220 名，全省盲人按摩机构共安排 1910 名盲人就业，其中中级专业技术人员 31 名，初级 102 名。

四、残疾人扶贫工作成绩显著

省残联加大对贫困残疾人扶贫力度，效果明显。统计数据显示，我省现有贫困残疾人户 647257 户，共有贫困残疾人 984695 名残疾人，本年度省残联共扶持 42564 贫困残疾人户，共扶持 78925 名残疾人，帮助 40878 名残疾人脱贫，但也有 12162 名残疾人重新返回贫困。省财政 2012 年共投入残疾人扶贫资金 2000000.00 元，社会募集到扶贫资金 1103000 元，共有 729 名残疾人享受到康复扶贫贴息贷款，全省有 157 个扶贫基地，安排 3876 名残疾人在基地就业。

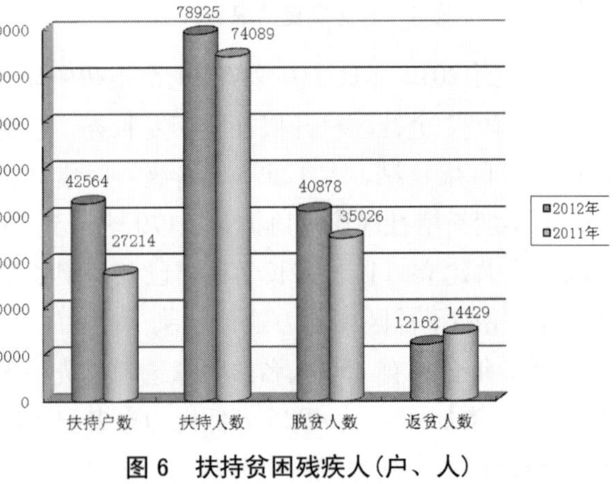

图 6　扶持贫困残疾人（户、人）

2012 年完成 4725 户残疾人危房改造，受益残疾人 5627 人，有 11101 人参与结对帮扶残疾人，有 1531 个结对帮扶单位。

五、残疾人社会保障体系逐步完善

中央提出加大对民生的投入，让老百姓享受到改革开放的成果，为了落实中央政策，各地出台了系列的保障民生政策，在提高贫困门槛后，数据显示，我省共有216218名城镇残疾人纳入最低生活保障，55166名农村残疾人纳入最低生活保障，全省有38个县区，6个地市出台残疾人生活补贴政策文件，有99630名残疾享受生活补贴。

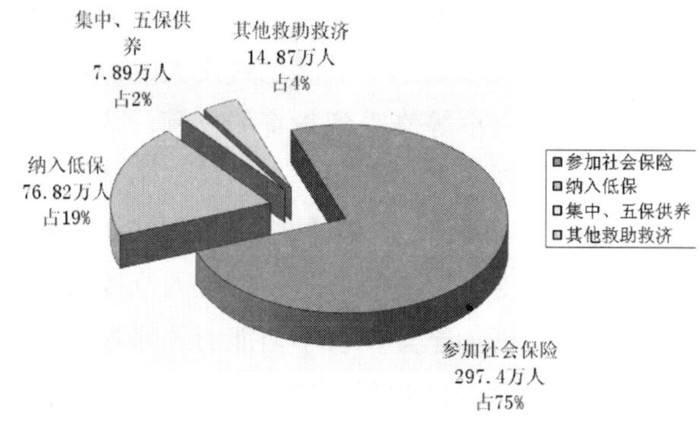

图7　社会救助情况

在省残联推动下，残疾人托养机构不断增加，各类托养投入经费大幅提高，全省现有99个寄宿制托养服务机构，其中地市8个，县区91个，托养残疾人数3552名，其中托养智力残疾人1275名，精神残疾1159名，其他类别残疾人1118名，重度残疾人673名，日间照料托养服务机构44个，托养残疾人1497名。本年度享受居家托养服务残疾人15814名。

六、残疾人宣传文体工作不断加强

2012年中央媒体采用稿件10件，主要原因新闻媒体刊稿稿件22件，电视手语栏目1个，电视公益广告片57个。

省级公共图书馆及盲人有声读物图书室5个，举办残疾人文化周6场次。

全省残疾人体育训练基地8个，省级举办4次残疾人体育比赛，有721名残疾人运动员参赛，地市本年度举办103次残疾人体育活动，共有6757名残疾人参加体育活动，全省体育训练基地有在编人员8人，有残疾人体育健身指导员168名。数据显示，我省在残疾人文化及体育方面的投入远远不能满足残疾人参与文化及体育活动的要求，这也是我省残疾人体育近年不能出成绩的决定因素之一。

七、残疾人维权工作效果明显

维护残疾人维益是残疾人工作的出发点和落脚点。省残联维护残疾人权益，加大残疾人保障法执法检查和监督力度，加强法律服务和法律救助，推动无障碍设施建设。

2012年省人大执法调查调研1次，有省级人大、政协各1人，成立省级无障碍建设领导协调组织1个。市州制定或修改保障残疾人权益规范性文件2个，人大执法检查或专题调研5次，政协视察或专题调研3次，建立残疾人法律救助协调机构68个，残疾人法律救助站68个，共办理案件124件，共有地市级人大代表17名，政协委员20名，出台无障碍建设与管理法规、政府令3个，成立无障碍建设领导协调组织6个，无障碍建设检查15次，改造无障碍残疾人家庭2114户，有25786名残疾人享受机动轮椅车燃油补贴。

2012年省残联接收残疾人来信132封，来访1011人次，其中个体上访865人次，集体上访13批次，从数据上看，上访人数和上访批次比2011年略有增加，上访原因主要集中在以下几方面：康复维权15%，教育5%，就业16%，扶贫18%，社会保障23%，机动轮椅车9%，数据体现残疾人扶贫、社会保障、康复等还有很多问题迫切需要解决。

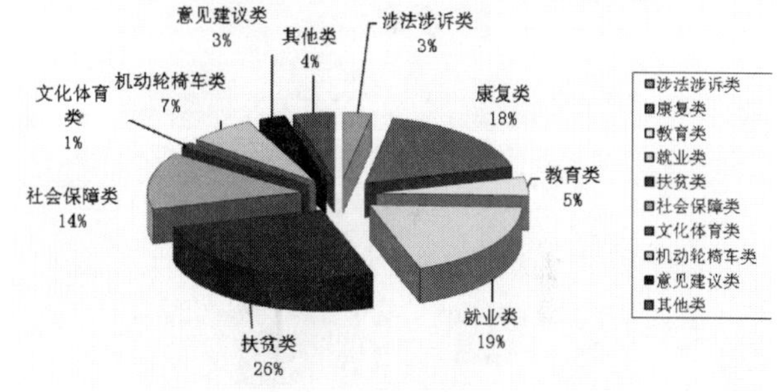

图8　2012年残疾人来信（件）情况

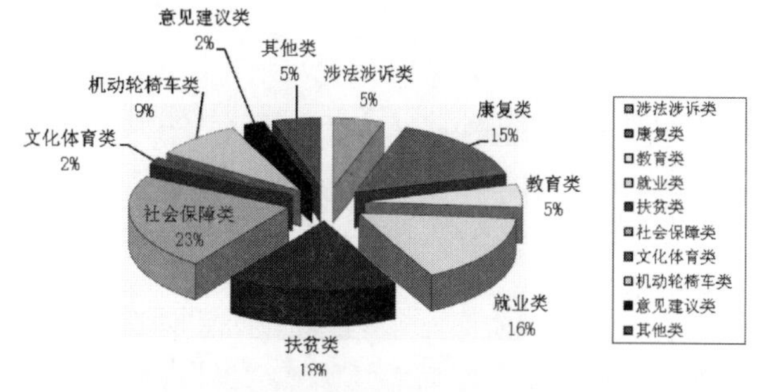

图9　2012年残疾人来访（人次）情况

八、残疾人组织正在健全

省残联系统坚决贯彻落实编制，市、县、乡残联实有工作人员5354人，14个市州125个县区建立残联，其中有12个市州残联配备残疾人领导干部，有 76 个县区残联配备了残疾人领导干部。

全省2401个乡镇已有2395个建立残联，有2155名工作人员，有 809 个乡镇配备专职理事长，已建残联乡镇中有专职委员 2306 名，形成了比较完善、多层次的组织领导机构。有 22387 个村（社区）建立残疾人活动室，34266 人被聘为村（社区）残疾人专职委员。

全省共有注册志愿者 200897 名，受助残疾人达 487865 人。

九、残疾人信息化建设扎实开展

残疾人事业数据统计工作稳步推进，做到数据支撑有公信力，为出台残疾人政策决策提供可靠数据。全省各级有 157 名统计员，其中有统计从业登记证书的 39 人，举办一次统计业务培训班，185 人接受培训。

省残联系统建立门户网站 76 个，举办一期信息工作培训班，150 人接受培训。

2012 年，湖南省残疾人工作紧紧围绕省委省政府《关于促进残疾人事业发展的实施意见》下功夫，残疾人工作呈稳步上升态势，残疾人“两个体系”的建设正在完善，发展中我们也还有很多需要解决的问题，残疾人康复远不能满足残疾人的需求，残疾人还不能完全平等享受到教育的权利，残疾人就业总会遇到歧视，大多数残疾人生活得不到保障。我们将进一步增强信心，相信在 2015 年我省残疾人都能“人人享受到康复服务”，“人人享受有适度保障”，就业更加充分，有学习能力的残疾儿童接受义务教育比例达到 85%，残疾人发展水平居我国中部省份前例。实现“政策法规体系完善，保障机制健全，服务体系完备，参与环境和谐，残疾人全面发展”。

2012年广东省残疾人事业发展统计公报

2012年是实施残疾人事业“十二五”规划的关键年。一年来，广东紧紧围绕“加快转型升级，建设幸福广东”的核心任务，紧扣残疾人社会保障体系和服务体系建设主线，全面开展残疾人康复、教育、就业、扶贫、社会保障、托养、维权、文化、体育等各项工作，取得了新的成就。

一、残疾人康复

2012年，通过实施一批重点康复工程，使各类别残疾人得到不同程度的康复。

1. 视力康复：全年完成白内障复明手术8.9万例，其中贫困白内障患者免费施行复明手术2.3万例；全年为1442名低视力患者配用助视器，培训低视力儿童家长122人，盲人定向行走训练4664人。

2. 听力言语康复：加强聋儿康复机构建设，完善聋儿康复网络。全省开展聋儿语训的机构（部、班）共75个，开展聋儿听力语言康复训练2237人，培训聋儿家长4128人，培养各类专业人员2029人。

3. 肢体康复：全年开展肢体残疾康复训练服务的机构达到204个，康复训练肢体残疾人31250人，其中：脑瘫儿童系统康复训练2699人、肢体残疾儿童社区、家庭康复1998人、成年肢体残疾人社区、家庭康复26553人。免费为81名贫困肢体残疾儿童实施矫治手术、装配矫形器等辅助器具以及术后康复训练。

4. 智力康复：全年开展智力残疾康复训练服务的机构203个；不同程度地开展了智力残疾儿童早期康复训练与服务，全年共康复训练智力残疾儿童8070人。

5. 精神康复：大力推广“社会化、综合性、开放式”精神病防治康复工作。2012年，在127个市县开展精神病防治康复工作，医疗救助3.7万名贫困精神病患者，对40.7万重性精神病患者进行综合防治康复，监护率达到70.97%，社会参与率达到35.40%，肇事率0.15%。全省共有孤独症儿童训练机构102家，在训孤独症儿童2118人，其中救助贫困孤独症儿童1385人。

6. 辅助器具供应：深入开展辅助器具供应服务，全面推进普及型假肢装配，截止到2012年底，累计建立辅助器具供应服务机构76个，为残疾人减免费用装配普及型假肢1702例，供应辅助器具5.1万件，装配矫形器2526例。

7. 社区康复工作：在58个市辖区和67个县(市)开展了社区康复工作，累计建立社区康复站7817个，配备18409名社区康复协调员。

二、残疾人教育

1. 学前康复教育阶段：本年度接受彩票公益金助学项目资助的学前残疾儿童550人，彩票公益金资助新入园残疾儿童143人，残疾儿童其他学前教育助学资助318人。

2. 义务教育阶段：全年登记未入学适龄残疾儿童少年总数4631人，其中视力残疾193人，听力残疾205人，言语残疾208人，智力残疾1269人，肢体残疾1556人，精神残疾357人，多重残疾843人。

3. 高中阶段教育：共开办特殊教育普通高中7所，在校生134人。残疾人中等职业教育机构有6个，在校生515人，毕业生185人，其中获得职业资格证书71人。

4. 高等教育阶段：开办高等特殊教育学院2所；全年有280名残疾人被普通高等院校录取，57名残疾人进入特殊教育学院学习。

三、残疾人培训、就业与扶贫

1. 残疾人培训：全省共有职业培训基地111个，其中残联兴办47个，社会机构兴办64个，城镇职业培训1.4万人。培训盲人保健按摩506人，医疗按摩195人。

2. 残疾人就业：2012年城镇实际在业人数19.8万人，农村残疾人在业64.7万人，其中从事农业生产劳动53.3万人。2012年城镇新安排1.7万残疾人就业，其中，集中就业残疾人3411人、按比例安排残疾人就业 7688 人、公益性岗位就业 822 人、个体及其它形式就业 4502 人、辅助性就业 1025 人。

3. 残疾人扶贫： 本年度扶持贫困残疾人户 3.1 万户，共扶持 6.2 万人，脱贫 3.7 万人，投入培训经费 944.4 万元，2.万多人次残疾人接受实用技术培训。截止年底共建立残疾人扶持基地 87 个，安置残疾人就业 0.4 万人，扶持带动残疾人 0.6 万户。全年完成 2630 户农村贫困残疾人危房改造，受益残疾人 2992 人。

四、残疾人社会保障与托养

1. 社会保障： 2012 年底城镇残疾居民参加社会保险人数达到 40.2 万人，农村残疾人参加社会保险人数达到 149 万人。纳入最低生活保障范围共 38.3 万名残疾人，其中城镇已纳入最低生活保障 9.4 万人、农村已纳入最低生活保障 28.9 万人。城镇集中供养和其他救助救济残疾人 3.4 万人、农村五保供养和其他救助救济残疾人 6.4 万人。

2. 残疾人托养： 全省共有寄宿制托养机构 111 个，托养残疾人 0.6 万人；日间照料托养机构合计 442 个，托养残疾人 1.2 万人；本年度享受居家托养服务残疾人 2.4 万人。

五、残疾人宣传文化与体育

1. 宣传： 2012 年我省主要新闻媒体刊播残疾人事业活动稿件 1397 件，其中省级以上刊物刊载 80 件，地市级刊物刊载 1317 件。截止 2012 年底，全省共有报纸专版 25 个，残疾人广播专题节目 17 个，电视手语栏目 7 个。

2. 文化： 省级和地市级公共图书馆设立盲文及盲人有声读物阅览室已达到 21 个，举办残疾人文化周活动 93 次，举办残疾人文化艺术类比赛及展览 26 次，已成立 10 个残疾人艺术团队。

3. 体育： 残疾人群众性的体育活动广泛开展，全年举办省级群众体育活动 10 次，参加人数 1200 人，举办地级市群众体育活动 103 次，参加人数 10206 人。

六、残疾人法制建设与维权

1. 残疾人法规体系建设： 2012 年全省各级残联参与、制定、修改有关残疾人的法规、规章、政策性的文件共 20 个，其中省级 2 个，地市级 9 个，县区级 9 个。开展人大政协执法检查、专题调研 34 次，其中省级 2 次，地市级 10 次，县区级 22 次；协助人大代表、政协委员提出议案、提案、建议共 84 件，其中省级 4 件，地市级 31 件，县区级 49 件.

2. 残疾人法律宣传与救助： 2012 年组织普法宣传教育活动 227 次，参加人数 1.8 万人。组织残疾人工作者法律培训班 39 个，参加人数 2057 人。全省 21 个地级市均成立了残疾人法律援助服务中心，全年办理案件 157 件；101 个区县级残联成立了残疾人法律援助服务中心，全年办理案件 360 件。

3. 残疾人无障碍建设： 截止 2012 年底全省建立无障碍建设领导协调组织 33 个；颁布无障碍建设与管理法规、政府令 28 个；系统开展无障碍建设示范市 6 个；贫困残疾人家庭无障碍改造 0.47 万户，发放残疾人机动轮椅车燃油补贴 3.14 万人。

4. 残疾人信访工作： 全年各级残联信访部门共处理残疾人来信 2939 件，其中省级 144 件，地市级 466 件，区县级 2329 件；来访 1.43 万人次，其中个人访 1.37 万人次，集体访 60 批次，566 人次。

七、残疾人事业组织建设

截止 2012 年底，省、市、县、乡级残联实有人员 7436 人。全省有 12 个地级以上市残联班子配备了残疾人领导，47 个县（市、区）配备了残疾人干部；全省 1609 个乡（镇、街道）均建立了残联，建设率达到 100%；专职残联理事长 566 人，兼职残联理事长 772 人。全省 25095 个村（社区）中已建残协 23800 个，建设率为 94.8%。全省共选聘 23468 名残疾人专职委员，其中乡镇街道 1549 名，村社区 21919 名。全省建立各类残疾人专门协会 718 个，其中盲人协会 144 个、聋人协会 144 个、肢残人协会 144 个、智力残疾人及亲友协会 143 个、精神残疾人及亲友协会 143 个。全省登记注册的助残志愿者 13.7 万名。

八、残疾人事业统计与信息化

截止 2012 年底，全省县区级以上残联有专兼职统计工作人员 177 人，其中有统计从业资格 34 人，占 19.2%，地级以上市举办统计人员培训班 20 期，

354 人参加了培训，效果良好。全省共有各级残联门户网站 73 个，其中省级 1 个，地市级 21 个，区县级 51 个；举办信息化工作培训班 23 期， 646 人参加了培训；省级残联网站全年发稿量 2838 篇。2012 年全省各级残联信息化建设共投入 935 万元，其中硬件投入占 53.3%，软件投入占 32.9%，系统运行维护费占 13.8%；全省各级残联共有信息化专业人才 289 人，为我省残疾人事业信息化建设做出了努力。

九、残疾人服务设施建设

截止到 2012 年底，各级残疾人综合服务设施中已竣工并投入使用的设施 73 个，在建项目 10 个，筹建项目 12 个。各级康复设施中已竣工并投入使用的设施 33 个，在建项目 9 个，筹建项目 8 个。各级托养设施中已竣工并投入使用的设施 6 个，在建项目 1 个，筹建项目 4 个。

其中已竣工并投入使用的各级残疾人综合服务设施总占地面积 36.27 万平方米，总建设规模 36.31 万平方米，总投资 9.7 亿元；已竣工并投入使用的各级康复设施总占地面积 6.16 万平方米，总建设规模 6.30 万平方米，总投资 1.6 亿元；已竣工并投入使用的各级托养设施总占地面积 0.74 万平方米，总建设规模 2.00 万平方米，总投资 1.23 亿元。

2012 年广西壮族自治区残疾人事业发展统计公报

2012 年，广西残疾人工作以科学发展观为指导，深入贯彻落实中央、自治区关于促进残疾人事业发展重大部署，全面推进残疾人社会保障和服务体系建设，创新残疾人工作，夯实残疾人工作基础，促进残疾人事业迈上新台阶。

一、全面开展社区康复活动，大力推进城市和农村残疾人“人人享有康复服务”目标的实现

2012 年，通过实施一批重点康复工程，使各类别残疾人得到不同程度的康复。全年有 36 个市辖区、75 个县（市）、6209 个社区（村）开展了社区康复服务工作，社区康复协调员达 9571 人，已建社区康复站社区达 2353 个。截至 2012 年底，有 64294 名残疾人得到就地就近的社区康复服务，新增 22040 名。

在视力残疾康复方面，全年共完成白内障复明手术 25975 例（其中 12144 名贫困白内障患者获免费手术），低视力配用助视器 4358 例，培训低视力儿童家长 1211 人，盲人定向行走训练 2571 名。

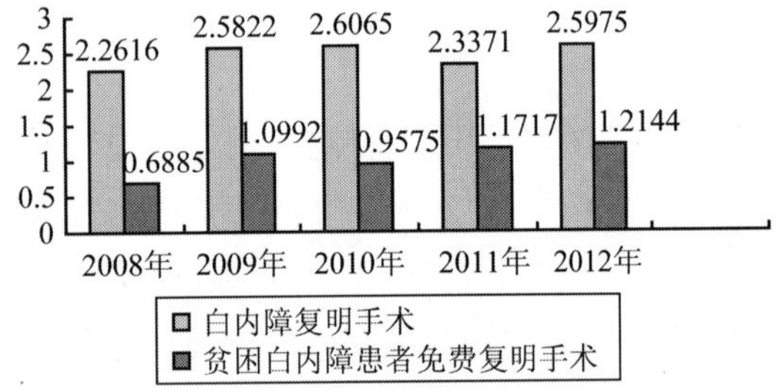

图 1　2008-2012 年广西白内障复明手术人数情况
（单位：万人）

在听力言语康复方面，全年新收训聋儿 4495 名（其中机构训练 326 人、家庭训练 169 人），培训聋儿家长 1063 名。2012 年聋儿语训机构累计建设数已达 29 个。在岗专业人员中，教师类达 157 人、医技类达 33 人、管理类达 57 人。

在精神病防治康复和孤独症儿童康复方面，全区开展精神病防治康复工作的县（市、区）达 91 个，覆盖总人口高达 3832 万人，其中，精神病人数 121418 人，监护病人数 94374 人，显好病人数 61501 人，接受治疗的精神病患者达 60210 人，接受康复训练人数为 20337 人，精神病康复机构合计达 29 个，在机构康复精神病人数为 18869 人。全区共有贫困患者 60654 人，其中接受医疗救助的贫困患者为 10572 人。孤独症儿童康复训练机构 11 个，在机构内接受康复训练的儿童为 285 人。

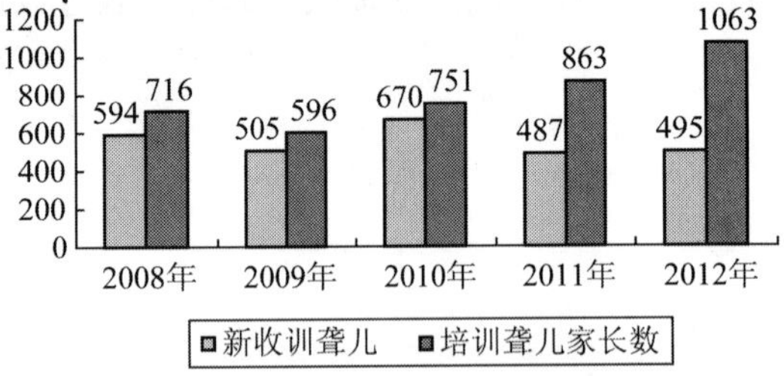

图 2　2008-2012 年广西听力言语康复训练情况
（单位：人）

在肢体残疾康复方面，全年肢体残疾康复训练数达 5837 人，其中肢体残疾儿童社区、家庭康复训练数为 1021 人，成年肢体残疾人社区、家庭康复训练数为 4111 人。全区开展肢体残疾康复训练服务机构达 20 个，其中残联系统办 14 个、其他办 6 个。

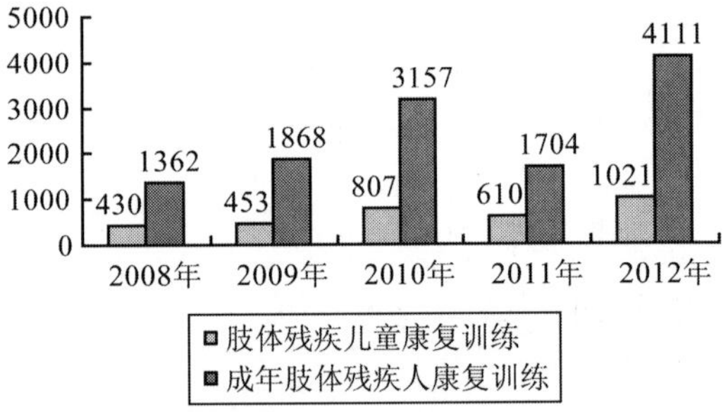

图 3　2008-2012 年广西肢体残疾康复训练情况
（单位：人）

在智力残疾康复方面，有 5519 名贫困智力残疾儿童接受训练（其中机构康复训练数 620 人，社区、家庭康复训练数 4899 人）。

全区开展智力残疾康复训练服务机构数合计达 17 个，其中残联系统办 9 个、其他办 8 个。

在辅助器具供应服务方面，全年辅助器具供应件数达 16471 件，供应品种为 224 种，免费发放的辅助器具件数为 9640 件。全年矫形器装配总例数为 662 例，普及型假肢装配总例数为 2329 例（其中：

大腿 808 例,小腿 1126 例,膝离断 21 例,髋离断 30 例,功能性上肢 18 例,装饰假手 77 例）。

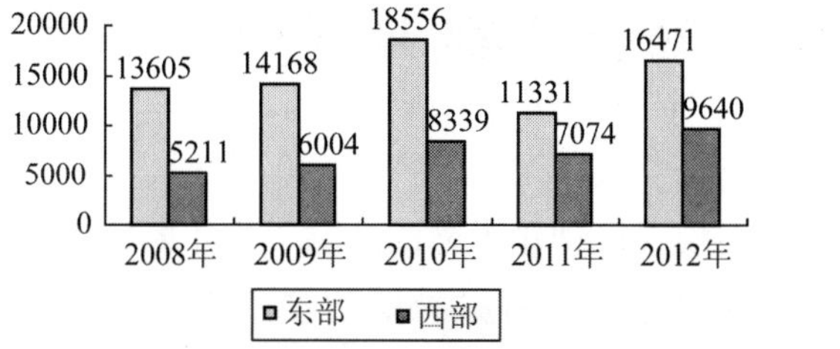

图 4　2008-2012 年广西辅助器具供应情况
（单位：人）

二、以扶残助学为“引擎”，推动我区特殊教育事业上台阶

对 685 名残疾儿童给予学前教育资助，其中，接受残疾人事业专项彩票公益金助学项目资助为 400 人，残疾人事业专项彩票公益金助学项目资助新入园为 221 人，其他残疾儿童学前教育助学项目资助 64 人。

已开办特殊教育普通高中班（部）10 个，在校生 225 人，其中聋高中 6 个，在校生 177 人；盲高中 4 个，在校生 48 人。残疾人中等职业学校（班）5 个，在校学生 192 人，其中：盲人 13 人，聋人 68 人，肢残 111 人，毕业生 71 人，肢残 71 人。高等特殊教育学院，在校生 11 人；普通高等院校，在校生 189 人。

截止到 2012 年底，全区未入学学龄残疾儿童少年 5750 人，其中视力残疾 321 人，听力残疾 312 人，言语残疾 501 人，肢体残疾 1728 人，智力残疾 1442 人，精神残疾 146 人，多重残疾 1300 人。

三、贯彻落实《残疾人就业条例》，促进就业工作迈出新步伐

贯彻落实《残疾人就业条例》，进一步完善政策法规体系，提高就业服务水平，全面推动残疾人就业工作纵向发展。全区城镇残疾人就业在岗 80361 人（集中就业合计 18444 人，按比例就业合计 24758 人，公益性岗位就业 1357 人，个体及其他形式就业合计 35360 人）；农村残疾人实际就业人数 640088 人（从事农业生产劳动 510182 人、从事其他形式就业 129906 人）。职业培训基地数 63 个。

盲人按摩事业发展迅速，全年培训盲人医疗按摩人员 628 人；盲人医疗按摩机构达 7 个，保健按摩机构 156 个；全区共计安排了 248 名特困盲人按摩师就业。

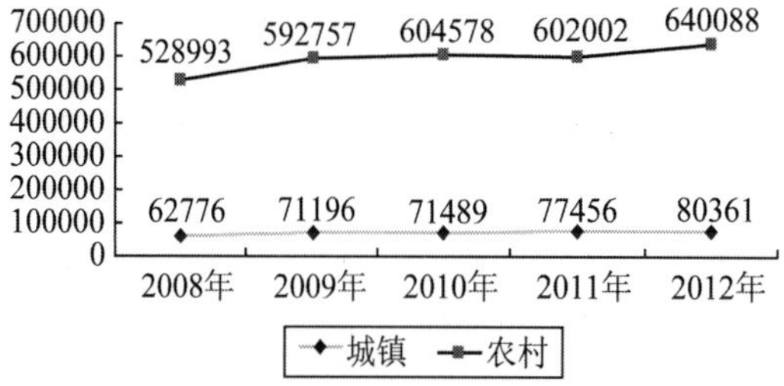

图 5　2008-2012 年广西残疾人就业状况
（单位：人）

残疾人社会保障工作进展顺利。全区参加社会保险的残疾人合计共 2652423 人（城镇残疾职工参加社会保险 43281 人，城镇残疾居民参加社会保险 358646 人，城镇个体就业参加社会保险 13761 人，农村残疾居民参加社会保险 2236746 人）。全区城镇和农村共有 527367 名残疾人已纳入最低生活保障范围。城镇残疾人中有 3066 人享受集中供养、7077 人享受各种救济；农村残疾人中有 68848 人享受五保供养、40746 人享受临时救济。

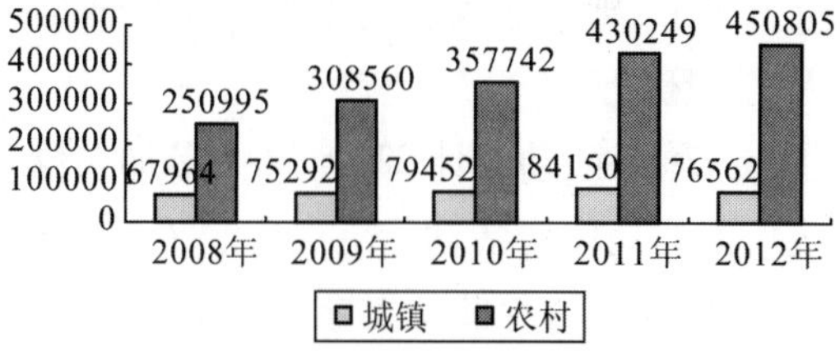

图 6　2008-2012 年广西残疾人纳入最低生活保障情况
（单位：人）

四、以新农村建设为契机，探索扶贫工作新模式

结合建设社会主义新农村，大力推进残疾人扶贫开发；把残疾人扶贫纳入“整村推进”范围，加大“帮包带扶”工作力度；开展以农村实用技术为主的培训，提高贫困残疾人生产劳动能力和技能。2012 年接受实用技术培训的残疾人达 32260 人次。

全年残疾人实用技术培训 32260 人次，对贫困残疾人开展结对帮扶的单位和个人分别达到 5648 个和 7457 人。建有残疾人扶贫基地 122 个，安置残疾人就业 1057 人和扶持带动残疾人 11347 人。

在农村贫困残疾人危房改造过程中，“扶残安居工程”成为广西残疾人事业的一个新亮点，各级纷纷把实施农村贫困残疾人危房改造列入“为民办实事”项目，纳入社会主义新农村建设和全面建设小康社会大局，作为构建和谐社会的重要举措强力

推进，取得了显著成效，产生了良好效益。实际完成危房改造 12964 户，受益贫困残疾人达 15823 人。

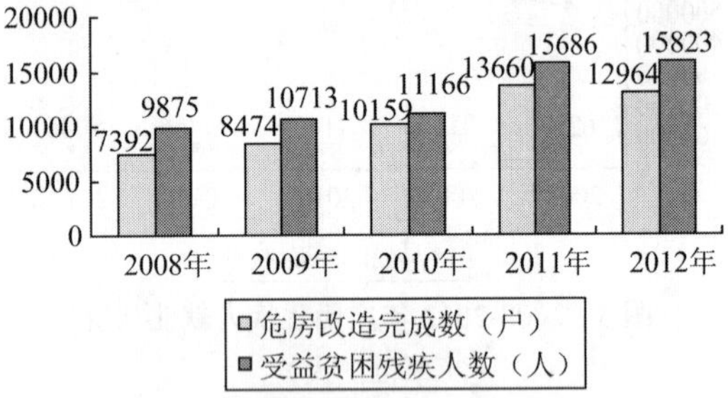

图 7　2008-2012 年农村贫困残疾人危房改造情况（单位：户、人）

五、以丰富残疾人文化生活为出发点，提升宣传文体工作活力

残疾人事业宣传工作进一步加强，社会舆论环境进一步改善。自治区、设区市开设报纸专栏 24 个、广播残疾人专题节目 11 个、电视手语栏目 5 个，残疾人事业新闻宣传促进会 2 个，盲文及盲人有声读物阅览室 7 个、残疾人文化艺术类比赛及展览 6 个、残疾人艺术团队 3 个。

残疾人体育活动共计 22 个，其中参加人数 2559 人。残疾人群众体育活动示范点自治区和设区市共有 10 个，残疾人体育健身指导员 288 人。

六、深入实施“扶残维权工程”，加强维权工作力度

修订《残疾人保障法》实施办法 1 部，制订或修改保障残疾人权益的规范性文件 9 个。

各级残联积极发挥参政议政作用，全区残联系统人大代表 29 人，政协委员 70 人，协助人大代表提出议案、建议 6 件，协助政协委员提出提案 25 件；办理人大建议 5 件，办理政协提案 17 件。

在法制宣传方面，全区各级残联共进行了 212 次普法宣传教育活动，举办了 41 个法律工作者培训班，参加人数 2672 人。

在法律救助方面，自治区、市、县三级共成立了 144 个残疾人法律救助工作站或残疾人法律援助中心（工作站），办理了 774 件案件。

在社会各界的关心关注下，全年没有发生侵害残疾人合法权益大案要案。

全区无障碍改造工作稳步推进，为残疾人日常生活和正常出行提供了便利，为残疾人参与经济社会生活创造了条件，提高了残疾人生活质量。全区无障碍建设与管理法规、政府令 10 个；无障碍建设领导协调组织 33 个；系统开展无障碍建设市、县 126 个；贫困残疾人家庭无障碍改造 5251 户，无障碍检查 190 次，无障碍培训 540 人次 。

残疾人机动轮车燃油补贴工作不断完善，补贴范围不断扩大，补贴补贴力度不断加强，全区为 13997 名残疾人提供机动轮椅车燃油补贴。

残疾人信访工作起到了为政府分忧、为残疾人解难的作用。全年各级残联共接待残疾人来访 17058 人次，处理残疾人来信 1853 件（次），解决了一些久拖不决的问题，维护了残疾人的合法权益和社会的稳定。

七、规范基层残疾人组织建设

加强基层残疾人组织规范化建设。全区 1234 个乡（镇、街道）建立健全了残联组织，配备专职理事长 204 名、兼职理事长 791 名、残疾人专职委员 1465 名；全区 15785 个社区（村）都已建立残协，共选聘 15881 名残疾人专职委员。

全区残联系统实有人员 3277 人。县（市、区）残联全部实现了规范化建设。

专门协会工作日益受到重视，协会在推动“三个活跃”中的作用日益显现。全区 14 个市级、109 个县级残联建立了五个残疾人专门协会。

八、信息化建设稳步推进

统计队伍建设进一步加强，各级残联共有 141 名专、兼职统计人员从事残疾人事业统计工作，统计人员业务素质培养普遍得到重视。自治区级残联举办培训班 1 期，参加培训的人员达到 20 人次；设区市举办培训班 14 期，参加培训的人员达到 191 人次。

各级残联全面推进网站建设，目前我区 14 个设区市及 101 个县级已开通残联网站。各级残联共有 210 名专业技术人员从事信息化工作。这为今后残联系统网站集群服务奠定了基础，残联系统网上信息服务正在逐步覆盖全区。基层残联也积极举办各类信息工作培训班，2012 年自治区及设区市残联开设网站技术培训班 9 期，培训各级残联信息员达 239 人次。

残联系统网站已逐步成为服务于社会和广大残疾人的电子政务信息服务平台，在政务公开、新闻宣传、信息服务等方面发挥了重要窗口作用。

九、基础服务设施建设力度进一步加大

截止到2012年底，已竣工并投入使用的各级残疾人综合服务设施共计92个，在建项目共计10个。其中已竣工并投入使用的各级残疾人综合服务设施总占地面积6.13万平方米，总建设规模10.76万平方米，总投资1.46亿元。已竣工并投入使用的各级康复设施共计2个，在建项目共计2个，筹建项目共计7个。其中已竣工并投入使用的各级康复设施总占地面积0.35万平方米，总建设规模0.23万平方米，总投资0.03亿元。在建托养设施1个，筹建共计4个。

2012年海南省残疾人事业发展统计公报

2012年在海南省委、省政府的领导和中国残联的指导下，我省各级残联学习贯彻“十八大”精神，围绕残疾人“两个体系”建设，认真组织实施“十二五”发展纲要各项任务目标，残疾人生活状况得到进一步提升，残疾人事业取得显著发展。

一、康复服务

我省围绕残疾人“人人享有康复服务”目标，加强残疾人康复服务工作，通过实施康复项目工程，使各类残疾人得到不同程度的康复。

在全省11个县（市）、市辖区开展了社区康复工作，建立一批社区康复站，为残疾人社区康复创造便捷的服务条件，全省配备了1342名社区康复协调员，累计有6047名残疾人得到康复服务。

在全社会的积极参与下，共完成白内障复明手术4779例，其中，为贫困白内障患者免费手术3587例，占手术完成总数的三分之二以上，脱盲率达99.2%；为159名低视力患者配用助视器，开展家庭康复训练，培训低视力儿童家长21名；对810名盲人进行定向行走训练。

继续推进听力语言康复机构建设，已建听力语言康复机构省级1个，县级3个；本年度新收训聋儿59名，在训聋儿108名，培训聋儿家长255名，本年度接受地方项目救助人数有92名；实施贫困聋儿人工耳蜗、助听器抢救性康复项目，完成国家“七彩梦”聋儿抢救性康复“人工耳蜗”8名、“助听器”30名的项目任务。开展“成人助听行动”，为465名成年人免费验配助听器。

大力开展精神病防治康复工作。在海口市、儋州市等10多个市县开展精神病防治康复工作，对精神病患者进行综合防治康复，监护率达到24.49%，显好率达到6.73%，社会参与率达到3.09%，肇事率0.08%；解除关锁320人；组织实施国家专项彩金服药、住院救助项目和其他项目医疗救助，为1366名精神病患者提供医疗救助。

已建立省级孤独症儿童康复训练机构1个，机构内在训儿童40名。全年开展智力残疾康复训练服务的机构有1个，培训各级各类智力残疾康复人员30名，对47名0-14岁的智力残疾儿童进行了康复训练，并对家长开展培训。

通过机构、社区、家庭相结合的方式对105名肢体残疾人进行了康复训练，其中，脑瘫儿童系统康复训练52人,肢体残疾儿童社区、家庭康复14人，成年肢体残疾人社区、家庭康复 39 人。本年度为63名贫困肢体残疾儿童实施矫治手术，装配了矫形器等辅助器具，进行了术后康复训练。

深入开展辅助器具供应服务，本年度组织供应各类残疾人用品用具1591件；为500名贫困肢体残疾人免费装配普及型假肢。

开展残疾儿童筛查工作的市县有2个，并举办了儿童残疾预防宣传活动。

举办康复人才培训班10期，培训康复管理、康复业务等康复人才1107人次。

二、教育助学

加大残疾人受教育权的保障力度，但残疾人受教育程度偏低。

全省已开办的残疾人中等职业学校（班）有2个，在校生13人，毕业生1人，其中，1人获得职业资格证书。本年度接受残疾人事业专项彩票公益金助学项目资助的残疾儿童有89名，开展各教育阶段残疾学生或贫困残疾人子女学生资助工作，全省共有760名贫困残疾学生及低保残疾人子女学生受益。组织实施“通向明天——残疾青少年助学计划”，对获得“交通银行特教园丁奖”、“交通银行残疾大学生励志奖”称号的教师和学生进行奖励，对40名高中教育阶段残疾在校生和20名残疾大学新生进行资助。

我省特教学校发展滞后，残疾儿童少年上学仍十分困难。截止到2012年底，全省有未入学适龄残疾儿童少年671人，其中，视力残疾儿童30人，听力残疾儿童34人，言语残疾儿童44人，智力残疾儿童192人，肢体残疾儿童226人，精神残疾儿童29人，多重残疾儿童116人。

三、劳动就业

采取优惠和扶持保护措施，多渠道、多层次、多种形式，促进残疾人实现就业。2012 年，全省城镇新安排 1385 名残疾人就业。其中，集中就业残疾人 335 名，按比例安排残疾人就业 194 名，公益性岗位就业残疾人 32 名，个体就业及其它形式灵活就业残疾人 322 名；全省城镇实际在业人数 10236 人；农村有 64843 名残疾人实现稳定就业，其中，55442 人从事农业生产劳动。

全省残疾人职业培训基地有达到 7 个，其中，残联兴办 1 个，依托社会机构兴办 6 个，接受了职业培训的城镇残疾人达 567 人次。

盲人按摩事业规范有序。全年培训盲人保健按摩人员共 183 名，盲人医疗按摩人员 75 名；建立的医疗按摩机构 2 个，保健按摩机构达到 120 个；出台《海南省盲人医疗按摩人员从事医疗按摩资格证书管理实施细则》，全年为 50 名盲人按摩人员进行高级保健按摩师资格鉴定。在专业技术职务资格评审中，分别有 8 人和 28 人通过医疗按摩人员中级和初级职称评审；盲人保健、医疗按摩师实现就业达 166 人。

四、社会保障

我省残疾人社会保障状况明显改善。残疾人新型农村和城镇居民社会养老保险试点工作继续推进，有一大批残疾人获得了社会保障。由于我省残疾人社会保障起步晚，滞后于经济社会的发展，残疾人社会保障在供给与需求上矛盾仍然突出。

2012 年，全省试点地区有 100019 名农村残疾人参加了新型农村合作医疗；有 118511 名残疾人参加了新型农村社会养老保险，参保率 93.4%。60 岁以下参保人数为 80983 人，其中，有 19798 名重度残疾人享受了全额或部分代缴的优惠政策。本年度，农村领取养老金待遇人数为 37528 名，其中，重度残疾人 8706 名。

城镇残疾居民参加基本医疗保险达 47716 人；参加社会养老保险达 45542 人，参保率 85%。60 周岁以下参保人数为 29703，其中，有 4327 名重度残疾人得到了政府的参保扶助。本年度，城镇享受养老金待遇的人数达到 15839 人，其中，重度残疾人 2580 名。2012 年度，全省城镇残疾职工参加社会保险人数达到 6560 人，其中，参加养老保险人数为 3553 名，参加医疗保险人数为 3367 名。

全省城乡有 65563 名残疾人纳入最低生活保障范围；城镇集中供养残疾人和农村五保供养残疾人分别达到 222 人和 1503 人；有 17257 名城乡残疾人获得其他方式的救助救济，25742 名符合条件的城乡残疾人分别享受了稳定的生活补贴和护理补贴。

实施“阳光家园”计划，残疾人托养服务工作取得成效。全省残疾人寄宿制托养服务机构达到 3 个，其中，民办非企业 2 个，其他性质的 1 个，托养了一大批残疾人，建立残疾人日间照料机构 2 个，为残疾人提供托养服务；全省接受居家托养服务的残疾人达到 7688 人；为 23658 名一级重度残疾人发放每月不低于 100 元的生活补助。三亚市残联被中国残联授予首批“阳光家园”全国示范机构。

五、扶贫开发

残疾人扶贫工作有所进展，取得一定成效，贫困残疾人生产生活状况得到进一步改善。2012 年，有 5596 名贫困残疾人得到扶持，其中,2098 人通过扶贫开发实际脱贫；接受实用技术培训的残疾人达到 4084 人次。

我省在三亚、琼中、保亭等市县建立残疾人扶贫基地 9 个，安置残疾人就业，扶持带动 449 名残疾人。

残疾人居住环境不断改善。完成 1406 户农村贫困残疾人危房改造，受益残疾人达 1671 名。

六、宣文体育

动员新闻媒体大力宣传残疾人事业，反映残疾人生活，宣传扶残助残先进典型，全省共刊播残疾人事业新闻稿件共 670 篇（条），大力营造有利于残疾人事业发展的社会环境。完成第十届各地人民广播电台残疾人节目展播活动和 2010—2011 年度残疾人事业好新闻作品的推荐参评工作。搭建了“海南省公共卫生联播网残疾人事业宣传平台”，加大了扶残助残宣传力度，普及残疾预防等知识。2012 年，全省共开辟残疾人专题广播节目 4 个，电视手语栏目 1 个；建立省级盲人有声读物图书室 1 个；地市级盲人有声读物图书室 2 个；开展形式多样的社区文化活动，丰富残疾人文化娱乐生活，组织残疾人文化活动 7 场次。

积极开展残疾人体育工作。组织地市级残疾人体育活动 5 次，参加人数达 400 人次；培训残疾人体育健身指导员 4 人。截止 2012 年底，省级残疾人体育训练基地累计已达 10 个，残疾人体育训练基地在编人员有 10 人，并聘请了 28 名教练员。

七、法制维权

残疾人事业法律法规体系逐步完善，加强残疾人维权工作力度，积极维护残疾人的合法权益。2012 年，制定或修改保障残疾人权益的规范性文件县级有 1 件，全省县级以上人大进行《残疾人保障法》执法检查 5 次；政协进行视察和专题调研 8 次。全省开展普法宣传教育活动 25 次，参加人数达 1758 人次；举办法律工作者培训班 7 个，参加人数达 495 人。

2012 年，建立了县级残疾人法律救助工作站 2 个，办理案件 2 件；建立残疾人法律援助中心（工作站）17 个，办理案件 63 件，切实为残疾人提供了法律救助服务。

残疾人参政议政工作逐步加强，本年度各级残联协助人大代表、政协委员提出议案、建议、提案 24 件，办理建议、提案 15 件。

地市级出台无障碍建设与管理法规、政府令 6 个；地市、县级建立无障碍建设领导协调组织 9 个；为 500 户贫困残疾人家庭进行了无障碍改造；全省开展无障碍建设检查 30 次，无障碍培训 113 人次；为 5734 名残疾人发放了残疾人机动轮椅车燃油补贴。

2012 年，全省各级残联共处理残疾人群众来信 380 件，接待残疾人群众来访 2760 人次，其中集体访 21 批次、248 人次。

八、组织建设

残疾人基层组织规范化建设逐步完善。2012 年，全省乡镇（街道）残联建设率达到 97%，选聘残疾人专职委员 289 名；已建社区（村）残协 2137 个，选聘残疾人专职委员 2451 名。

全省市县乡残联队伍不断充实，实有人员达 852 人，残疾人干部配备工作有所加强，省残联领导班子中配备了 1 名残疾人副理事长，13 个县级以上残联机关配备了残疾人干部；加强残联干部培训工作，各级残联共举办培训班 26 期，培训机关干部、协会干部及残疾人专职委员 1445 人次，残联系统干部队伍素质有所提升。

2012 年，成立的省级以下各类残疾人专门协会达 109 个，其中，盲人协会 21 个、聋人协会 22 个、肢残人协会 22 个、智力残疾人及亲友协会 22 个、精神残疾人及亲友协会 22 个。全省市、市辖区、县（含县级市）专门协会已建比例达 100%，

九、综合服务设施

市县残疾人综合服务设施项目建设有所进展，但部分已建成的残疾人综合服务设施存在局限性，如建筑面积不足、功能单一、硬件设施陈旧等，还不具备综合服务能力。

截止 2012 年底，全省已投入使用和累计投入使用的项目有 6 个，有 4 个在建项目，8 个项目正在筹建。

十、信息化建设

省残联网站改版后，注重政策信息发布，页面浏览量逐步提升，同时加强网站的无障碍建设力度，为更多的残疾人提供信息服务，省残联网站在政务公开、新闻宣传、信息服务等方面发挥了重要窗口作用，在 2012 年度全国残联系统网站评测中进入了前 10 名。

市县网站建设仍然滞后，截止 2012 年底，仅海口市、定安县残联开通残联网站。

2012 年重庆市残疾人事业发展统计公报

2012 年，重庆市残疾人工作认真贯彻落实党的十八大、市第四次党代会精神，深入贯彻落实科学发展观，重视和加强改善残疾人民生，加快推进残疾人社会保障和服务“两个体系”建设，进一步夯实了残疾人事业发展基础，进一步完善了涉及残疾人切身利益的政策体系，进一步让残疾人得到了更多实惠，全市残疾人工作迈上了新的台阶。

一、残疾人康复工作

加大残疾人康复救助力度，进一步扩大康复服务范围。为 16821 名白内障患者实施复明手术（其中，免费手术 8188 名）、为 2789 名低视力患者配用助视器，对 1140 名盲人进行定向行走训练；对 403 名聋儿、3334 名智力残疾儿童、222 名孤独症儿童、8366 名肢体残疾人进行康复训练；对 122 名贫困肢体残疾儿童实施矫治手术；对 11187 名贫困精神病患者进行医疗救助；为残疾人装配普及型假肢 300 例、矫形器 199 例，为老年听力残疾人免费佩戴助听器 394 人，供应其它辅助器具 8415 件。

加强人才队伍建设，进一步提高康复服务能力。举办市级培训班 6 期，培训康复人才 737 人（康复技术骨干 250 人，其他康复人才 487 人）；区县逐级培训康复业务人员、康复协调员 8261 人次；选派康复人才参加中国残联培训 50 人次；承办“2012 年全国听障儿童康复专业技术人员轮训班”，参训 130 余人。

实施标准化工作管理，进一步规范康复机构建设。制定下发《重庆市区县辅助器具展示厅建设管理规范》、《重庆市残疾儿童康复救助定点机构基本标准》《重庆市社区康复站建设管理规范》等文件。新增国家定点康复机构 10 个，新建残疾人康复示范社区 100 个、示范性残疾人社区康复站 78 个、区县辅助器具展示厅 10 个、市级低视力康复部 6 个，在 10 个区县开展居家康复服务试点，对 4 个区县“人人享有康复服务”进行初评，对 7 个区县创建“市级残疾人社区康复示范区县”进行验收。

二、残疾人教育工作

残疾人特殊教育不断加强。截止到 2012 年底，全市共开办特殊教育普通高中 2 所，在校生 202 人；其中聋高中 1 所，在校生 14 人；盲高中 1 所，在校生 188 人。残疾人中等职业教育机构有 4 个，在校生 250 人，毕业生 3135 人，其中获得职业资格证书 3038 人。高等特殊教育学院 1 所,有 179 名残疾人被普通高等院校录取，9 名残疾人进入特殊教育学院学习。

三、残疾人就业工作

残疾人就业覆盖面不断扩大。2012 年全市通过多种形式新安排城镇残疾人就业 7134 人。其中，集中就业残疾人 3253 人，按比例安排残疾人就业 1062 人，公益性岗位就业 221 人，个体及其它形式就业 2513 人，辅助性就业 85 人，全市城镇实际在业人数 14.27 万人；50.07 万农村残疾人稳定实现就业，其中从事农业生产劳动 40.32 万人。

开展残疾人职业技能培训，兴办职业培训基地 26 个,其中残联兴办 5 个，本年度城镇职业培训人数 3184 人。

盲人按摩事业稳定发展，按摩机构迅速增长。2012 年培训盲人保健按摩人员 581 人；医疗按摩人员 75，保健按摩机构达到 610 个，医疗按摩机构达到 29 个。

四、社会保障工作

34.8 万名残疾人参加了城乡居民基本养老保险，6.1 万名残疾人参加了城镇职工养老保险；63.3 万名残疾人参加了新型城乡居民合作医疗，5 万名残疾人参加了城镇职工医疗保险。

城乡 20.3 万名残疾人纳入最低生活保障范围；2.1 万名残疾人得到城镇集中供养或农村五保供养；8.2 万名城乡残疾人获得其他救助救济；3 个区出台了重度残疾人护理补贴制度，受益残疾人达 2572

人。

推进残疾人托养服务工作，采取多种形式建立残疾人托养服务机构和日间照料站（所），完成“阳光家园计划”任务。截止2012年底，全市共建立寄宿制托养机构36个，托养残疾人1199人；日间照料托养机构合计83个，托养残疾人848人；享受居家托养服务残疾人1.07万人。

五、残疾人扶贫开发工作

2012年全市加大扶持残疾人力度，开展残疾人扶贫工作。全市共扶持贫困残疾人5.6万人，接受实用技术培训的残疾人1.85万人次。

2012年全市加大资金投入，完成4847户农村贫困残疾人危房改造，投入危房资金5722万元，受益残疾人5295人。建立残疾人扶持基地56个，安置残疾人就业933人，扶持带动残疾人1771户。结对帮扶单位981个，结对帮扶个人1.33万人。

六、残疾人宣传文化工作

残疾人文体工作不断丰富。2012年全市共有残疾人报刊专版58个，残疾人专题广播节目8个，电视手语新闻栏目6个。在各级公共图书馆设立盲文及盲人有声读物阅览室已达到14个，建立残疾人“文化进社区”活动点470个，举办残疾人文化周85场次，举办残疾人文化艺术类比赛及展览27次，已成立残疾人艺术团队8个，残疾人体育活动参加人数2.69万人次。

七、残疾人维权工作

继续完善残疾人法律法规，开展法律服务、法律援助和法制宣传，维护残疾人合法权益。截止2012年底，全市制定或修改保障残疾人权益的规范性文件36个，其中省级1个，区县35个；各级人大执法检查或专题调研28次，政协视察和专题调研30次，检查范围逐渐扩大，对残疾人保障法的贯彻和实施起到了重要的推动作用

全市开展普法宣传教育活动225次，参加人数6.98万人；开展法律培训班41次，参加人数3856人；建立残疾人法律救助协调机构41个；建立残疾人法律救助工作站14个，办理案件522件；建立残疾人法律援助中心（工作站）41个，办理案件1403件；协助人大代表、政协委员提出议案、建议、提案71件，办理议案、建议、提案42件。

无障碍建设法规、标准进一步完善。截止2012年底，全市建立无障碍建设领导协调组织30个；系统开展无障碍建设区县38个；贫困残疾人家庭无障碍改造4960户，无障碍检查59次，无障碍培训662人次，残疾人机动轮椅车燃油补贴3988人。

2012年，全市各级残联信访部门共处理来信305件，接待残疾人群众来访4824人次。总体看来，2012年信访总量有所减少。

八、残疾人组织建设工作

2012年，全市基层残疾人组织规范化建设逐步完善，县（区）、乡（镇、街道）、村（社区）三级网络整体推进。40个区县残联全部达到了基层残疾人组织规范化建设验收标准。全市1005个乡镇（街道）中，选聘残疾人专职委员1110名；1.07万个社区（村）中，选聘残疾人专职委员1.06万名，切实增强了为残疾人服务的力量。

全市建立各类残疾人专门协会188个，其中盲人协会38个、聋人协会38个、肢残人协会38个，智力残疾人及亲友协会36个、精神残疾人及亲友协会36个、智力残疾人及亲友协会和精神残疾人及亲友协会二者合一的2个。

九、残疾人综合服务设施建设

残疾人综合服务设施建设得到进一步发展，为基层残疾人工作更好地开展提供了基础条件。截止到2012年底，全市已竣工并投入使用的各级残疾人综合服务设施共计27个，在建项目共计7个，筹建项目共计4个，其中已竣工并投入使用的各级残疾人综合服务设施总占地面积5.61万平方米，总建设规模7.97万平方米，总投资2.41亿元；已竣工并投入使用的各级康复设施共计3个，在建项目共计1个，筹建项目共计5个，其中已竣工并投入使用的各级康复设施总占地面积0.2万平方米，总建设规模0.37万平方米，总投资0.09亿元；已竣工并投入使用的各级托养设施共计1个，在建项目共计1个，筹建项目共计3个，其中已竣工并投入使用的各级托养设施总占地面积0.01万平方米，总建设规模0.01万平方米，总投资0.02亿元。

十、残疾人事业统计与信息化建设

统计队伍建设进一步加强。全市各级残联共有53名专、兼职统计人员从事残疾人事业统计工作，统计人员业务素质培养普遍得到重视，省级残联举办培训班1期，参加培训的人员50人次。

全面推进网站建设，目前全市共开通各级残联门户网站39个，其中省级1个，区县级38个。2012年省级残联开设网站技术培训班1期，培训各级残联信息员达55人次。各级残联共有87名专业技术人员从事信息化工作；省级残联共建立局域网1个，网上办公（OA）系统1个。

2012年四川省残疾人事业发展统计公报

2012年，是残疾人事业“十二五”发展的关键之年。在省委、省政府的领导下，在中国残联的指导和支持下，在全社会的关爱下，我省残疾人事业延续了良好的发展势头，各方面工作取得了新进步、新成效，残疾人得到了更多的实惠。现根据我省2012年度残疾人事业统计数据和实际情况，进行分析，并公报如下：

一、康复

1.积极推进残疾人社区康复工作。截至2012年底，共在28个市辖区和100个县开展了社区康复工作；有6772个社区已建立康复站，配备的社区康复员总数达到16148名，比上年增长25.2%。

2.大力完善视力康复机构和人员，通过实施一批重点康复工程，使各类视力残疾人得到不同程度的康复。截至2012年底，全省视力残疾康复机构的总数为21个，在岗人员总数达到217名，其中专业技术人员145名，专业技术人员所占比例达到了66.8%；2012年，在全省范围内实施白内障复明手术45000例，其中共为22870名贫困白内障患者免费实施手术，免费手术数比上年增加43.4%；盲人定向行走指导师总数达到69名，共进行盲人定向行走训练7353人次。

3.加强全省聋儿康复网络建设，大力充实聋儿康复机构专业人员。2012年共培养聋儿康复专业人员201人，截至年底，全省聋儿康复机构的在岗教师总计达335名；全年共对1559名聋儿进行了听力语言康复训练；培训聋儿家长1856名。

4.肢体残疾康复工作成效显著。截至年底，全省的肢体残疾康复训练服务机构数达到49个；全年共对778名贫困肢体残疾儿童实施了矫治手术、装配了矫形器等辅助器具，并进行了术后康复训练；对26161名肢体残疾人进行了康复训练，其中：脑瘫儿童系统康复训练4774人,肢体残疾儿童社区、家庭康复1533人，成年肢体残疾人社区、家庭康复19854人。

5.稳步推进智力残疾康复工作。截至年底，全省的智力残疾康复训练服务机构数达到48个，比上年增加了28个；全年共对8543名智力残疾儿童进行了康复训练，不同程度地开展了智力残疾儿童早期康复训练与服务。

6.大力推广“社会化、综合性、开放式”精神病防治康复工作。2012年，共在143个市县开展精神病防治康复工作，对41.2万重性精神病患者进行综合防治康复，监护率达到78.8%，显好率达到48.4%，社会参与率达到28%，肇事率仅为0.3%；解除关锁526人；对1.9万名贫困精神病患者进行了医疗救助。

7.2012年，新建了2个省级孤独症儿童康复训练机构，全省各级孤独症儿童康复训练机构增加到39个，配备专业教师137名；全年共对226名孤独症儿童进行了康复训练。

8.深入开展辅助器具供应服务，全面推进普及型假肢装配。截至2012年底，全省已累计建立辅助器具供应服务机构29个，比上年增加7个；全年共为残疾人减免费用装配普及型假肢2265例，供应辅助器具49496件，装配矫形器2348例。

9.实施全省残联系统康复人才培养规划，加强康复人才队伍建设。截至2012年底，全省康复机构在岗人员总数达到7783名，其中：省级668名，地市级1455名，县级5660名。

二、教育

2012年，我省残疾人受教育权得到了更好地保障，进一步提高了残疾人整体素质和平等参与社会的能力。

1.本年度，残疾人事业专项彩票公益金助学项目共为我省家庭经济困难的残疾儿童享受普惠性学前教育提供资助700人次；全省各地也积极多渠道争取资金支持，对1302名残疾儿童提供了学前教育资助。

2.截至2012年底，全省特殊教育普通高中共有10所，在校生133人；残疾人中等职业教育机构共有7个，在校生139人，毕业生48人，其中获得职业资格证书14人；全年共有316名残疾人被普通高等院校录取，4名残疾人进入特殊教育学院学习。

3.截至2012年底，全省未入学适龄残疾儿童少年总数为5017人，其中：视力残疾393人，听力残疾335人，言语残疾353人，智力残疾1676人，肢体残疾1473人，精神残疾225人，多重残疾562人。

三、就业

1.2012年，全省残疾人就业工作取得稳步进展。城镇新增3.1万名残疾人就业，其中：集中就业残疾人10875名，按比例安排残疾人就业6128名，公益性岗位就业833名，个体及其它形式就业12041名，辅助性就业2019名。全省城镇实际在业人数达到27.7万名；农村实际在业人数达到174.7万名，其中从事农业生产劳动的人数为141.5万名。

2.截至2012年底，全省残疾人职业培训基地达到441个,其中残联兴办196个。本年度共有2.6万名城镇残疾人接受了职业培训。

3.2012年共培训盲人保健按摩人员1131名，医疗按摩人员60名；保健按摩机构达到1028个，医疗按摩机构达到36个。

四、社会保障

2012年度全省残疾人社会保障状况保持平稳，残疾人参加新型农村和城镇居民社会养老保险工作实现了全覆盖。

1.截至2012年底，已有28.7万名城镇残疾人参加了城镇居民医疗保险；已有22万名城镇残疾人参加了城镇居民养老保险，参保率达到了68.2%，在60岁以下的参保残疾人中有3.8万名重度残疾人，其中3.4万享受了全额代缴的优惠政策。在新型农村社会养老保险方面，已有234.3万名农村残疾人参加了新型农村合作医疗保险；已有142.5万名农村残疾人参加了新型农村社会养老保险，参保率达到了82.7%，在60岁以下的参保农村残疾人中有22.7万名重度残疾人，其中21.8万享受了全额代缴的优惠政策。

2.已有城乡84.2万名残疾人纳入最低生活保障范围。其中：城镇已纳入最低生活保障16.4万名，城镇集中供养和其他救助救济5.8万名；农村已纳入最低生活保障67.8万名，五保供养和其他救助救济20.9万名。

3.全省共建立寄宿制托养机构61个，托养残疾人2177名；日间照料托养机构合计185个，托养残疾人4301名；本年度享受居家托养服务的残疾人总计达到4.5万名。

五、扶贫开发

2012年,全省残疾人扶贫开发工作进一步推进，贫困残疾人生产生活状况得到进一步改善。

1.本年度共扶持贫困残疾人家庭14.7万户，扶持残疾人23.3万名，脱贫13万名；接受实用技术培训的残疾人共计8.7万人次。

2.已建立结对帮扶单位5573个，全年共结对帮扶残疾人2.5万名；已建立残疾人扶持基地316个，全年共安置残疾人就业5306名，扶持带动残疾人家庭2.6万户。

3.2012年，全省共投入危房改造资金5559.2万元，完成5161户农村贫困残疾人家庭危房改造，受益残疾人5560名。

六、维权

2012年，全省残疾人维权组织建设得到加强，残疾人事业法律法规体系得以进一步完善。

1.2012年，修订了四川省《残疾人保障法》实施办法；制定或修改了保障残疾人权益的规范性文件省级3件、地市级4件、县级54件；县级以上人大进行执法检查和专题调研共计48次，政协视察和专题调研53次。

2.全年共开展普法宣传教育活动559次，参加人数8.2万；开展法律培训班111次，参加人数0.6万。

3.截至2012年底，全省已建立残疾人法律救助协调机构85个；建立残疾人法律救助工作站43个，全年共办理案件313件；建立残疾人法律援助中心（工作站）136个，全年共办理案件1186件；全年共协助残联系统人大代表、政协委员提出议案、建议、提案91件，办理议案、建议、提案59件。

4.全省共出台无障碍建设与管理法规、政府令22个；共有35个市、县系统开展了无障碍建设；全年共开展无障碍建设检查184次；无障碍培训3303人次；为1.29万户贫困残疾人家庭实施了无障碍改造；为 2.3 万名残疾人发放了机动轮椅车燃油补贴。

5.2012 年，全省各级残联共处理残疾人群众来信 0.5 万件，接待残疾人群众来访 3.5 万人次，其中集体访 31 批次，473 人次。

七、宣传文化

2012 年，通过举办全省首届电视手语大赛，圆满组织第二十二次全国助残日活动等，残疾人事业的社会影响力和关注度得到快速提升，营造了有利于残疾人事业发展的舆论环境。残疾人文化生活更加丰富活跃，残疾人受到社会广泛关注并更加全面地参与到社会生活当中。

1.省级主要新闻媒体全年刊播稿件数 90 件，共开辟残疾人专题广播节目 5 个，电视手语新闻栏目 1 个，省级已建立残疾人事业新闻宣传促进会；地市级主要新闻媒体刊播稿件数 1691 件，共开辟报刊专版 133 个，残疾人专题广播节目 38 个，电视手语新闻栏目 5 个。

2.全省已设立公共图书馆盲文及盲人有声读物阅览室 38 个；全年共举办 45 场残疾人文化周活动；举办残疾人文化艺术类比赛及展览 39 场。

3.全省已成立残疾人艺术团队 4 个，其中包括新成立的省级艺术团：四川省残疾人艺术团。

八、体育

1.2012 年，共组织省级残疾人群众体育健身活动 2 次，7000 人次参加；已建立省级残疾人群众体育示范点 5 个，培训省级残疾人体育健身指导员 10 名；组织全省残疾人体育比赛 2 次，参赛运动员达 500 人次；现有 5 个省级残疾人体育训练基地，聘任教练员 30 名。

2.共组织地市级残疾人体育健身活动 59 次，4913 人次参加；已建立地市级残疾人体育示范点 58 个，培训地市级残疾人体育健身指导员 1529 名。

九、组织建设

1.截至 2012 年底，省残联领导班子配备了残疾人理事长和副理事长；全省有 11 个地市级残联的领导班子配备了残疾人理事长或副理事长；有 88 个县级残联机关配备了残疾人干部。

2.全省已建乡镇（街道）残联 4334 个，已建率达 92.9%，选聘残疾人专职委员 4007 名；已建村（社区）残协 4.4 万个，已建率达 91.5%，选聘残疾人专职委员 3.2 万名。

3.全省省、市、县、乡级残联实有人员已达 1.1 万名；残联干部综合培训工作取得较好成绩，省残联全年共举办残疾人干部培训班 6 期，地市级残联共举办残疾人干部培训班和综合培训班 207 期，县级残联共举办各类综合培训班 522 期，各级残联培训班共培训机关干部、协会干部及残疾人专职委员 7.3 万人次。

4.全省已建立省级以下各类残疾人专门协会 869 个。市级专门协会已建比例为 100%，市辖区专门协会已建比例 97.5%；县（含县级市）级专门协会已建比例为 79.6%。

十、信息化

1.2012 年，全省统计队伍建设进一步加强。全省各级残联共有 176 名专、兼职统计人员从事残疾人事业统计工作，统计人员业务素质培养普遍得到重视，省级残联举办培训班 1 期，参加培训的人员达到 30 人次；地市级举办培训班 20 期，参加培训的人员达到 540 人次。

2.全面推进网站建设。省残联已开通无障碍公众服务网站，有 17 个地市级残联网站和 87 个县级残联网站也已开通，网站总数比去年增加 22 个。这为今后残联系统网站集群服务奠定了良好的基础。

3.截止 2012 年底，全省各级残联共有 279 名专业技术人员从事信息化工作。

十一、服务设施建设

全省残疾人服务设施建设得到全面发展。

截至 2012 年底，已竣工并投入使用的各级残疾人综合服务设施共计 71 个，总占地面积 16 万平方米，总建设规模 14 万平方米，总投资 3.9 亿元；

已竣工并投入使用的各级康复设施共计 21 个，总占地面积 17.6 万平方米，总建设规模 9.8 万平方米，总投资 4.4 亿元；

已竣工并投入使用的各级托养设施共计 4 个，总占地面积 0.7 万平方米，总建设规模 0.8 万平方米，总投资 0.3 亿元。

2012年贵州省残疾人事业发展统计公报

2012年是全面实施残疾人事业发展“十二五”纲要重要的一年，在省委、省政府的领导下，在中国残联的指导下，在相关部门的支持下，贵州省残疾人联合会按照年初工作安排，着力加强促进残疾人事业发展的制度建设、民生建设、文化建设、基础建设、环境建设和机关建设，全面完成各项工作任务，为“十二五”残疾人事业又好又快更好更快发展打下了良好基础。根据残疾人事业统计数据和实际情况公报如下:

一、康复

2012年，通过实施一批重点康复工程，使各类别残疾人得到不同程度的康复。全年完成白内障复明手术15258例,比去年增加40%；为8451名贫困白内障患者免费施行复明手术，全年为2891名低视力患者配用助视器，培训低视力儿童家长402名，有效开展家庭康复训练。对2788名盲人进行定向行走训练。加强省级聋儿康复机构建设，完善聋儿康复网络。共对703名聋儿进行了听力语言康复训练，规范聋儿家长学校，开展家庭训练，共培训聋儿家长719名。

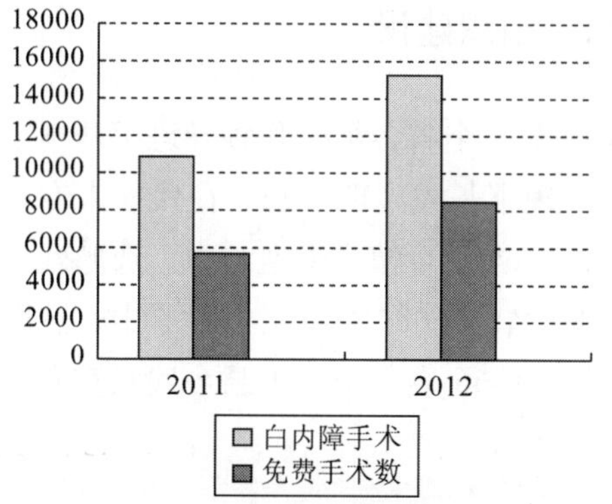

图1 2012与2011年贫困白内障手术、免费数比较

大力推广“社会化、综合性、开放式”精神病防治康复工作，在76个市县开展精神病防治康复工作，对7.9万重性精神病患者进行综合防治康复，监护率达到81.7%，显好率达到54.8%，社会参与率达到45.5%，肇事率0.3%；解除关锁233人；对4491名贫困精神病患者进行医疗救助。全省共培育了16个孤独症儿童康复训练机构对205名孤独症儿童进行了康复训练。深入开展辅助器具供应服务，全面推进普及型假肢装配，截止到2012年底，累计建立辅助器具供应服务机构13个，为残疾人装配矫形器66例，减免费用装配普及型假肢1139例，供应其他辅助器具11435件。全年开展肢体残疾康复训练服务的机构达到10个,对239名贫困肢体残疾儿童实施矫治手术并进行了术后康复训练；对1174名肢体残疾人进行了康复训练，其中：脑瘫儿童系统康复训练303人,肢体残疾儿童社区、家庭康复188人，成年肢体残疾人社区、家庭康复683人。全年开展智力残疾康复训练服务的机构达到11个；对540名智力残疾儿童进行了康复训练，不同程度地开展了智力残疾儿童早期康复训练与服务。在10个市辖区和62个县（市）开展了社区康复工作，累计建立社区康复站891个，配备5947名社区康复协调员。

二、教育就业

开办特殊教育普通高中6所，在校生161人；有347名残疾人被普通高等院校录取，63名残疾人进入特殊教育学院学习。城镇新安排4449残疾人就业。其中，集中就业残疾人1135人，按比例安排残疾人就业1049人，公益性岗位就业95人，个体及其它形式就业2143人，辅助性就业27人，全国城镇实际在业人数7.76万人；77.29万农村残疾人稳定实现就业，其中从事农业生产劳动61.11万人。本年度城镇职业培训人数4163人。培训盲人保健按摩368人；医疗按摩人员17，保健按摩机构达到329

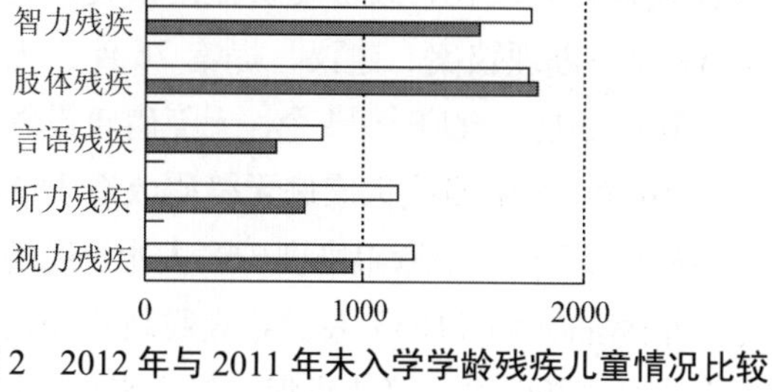

图2 2012年与2011年未入学学龄残疾儿童情况比较

个，医疗按摩机构达到 3 个；有 10 人通过医疗按摩人员初级职称评审。

三、社会保障

城镇残疾职工参加社会保险人数达到 3.6 万人，其中参加养老保险人数 1.9 万人，参加医疗保险人数 1.9 万人；城镇残疾居民参加医疗保险达到 11 万余人；城乡 47.8 万名残疾人纳入最低生活保障范围；城镇已纳入最低生活保障 6.2 万人，城镇集中供养和其他救助救济 1.2 万人；农村已纳入最低生活保障 41.6 万人，五保供养和其他救助救济 9.1 万人。寄宿制托养机构 13 个，托养残疾人 868 人；日间照料托养机构合计 2 个，托养残疾人 50 人；本年度享受居家托养服务残疾人 1.2 万人。

四、扶贫

本年度扶持贫困残疾人户 7.8 万户，扶持 13.3 万人，脱贫 7.5 万人，返贫 1.6 万人，接受实用技术培训的残疾人 1.4 万人次，投入培训经费 588.5 万元。结对帮扶单位 969 个，结对帮扶个人 1.8 万人；建立残疾人扶持基地 62 个，安置残疾人就业 544 人，扶持带动残疾人 4421 户。完成 3267 户农村贫困残疾人危房改造，投入危房资金 1,259.3 万元，受益残疾人 3587 人。

五、维权

制定或修改了关于残疾人的专门法规、规章省级 1 件；制定或修改了保障残疾人权益的规范性文件省级 1 件；县级以上人大执法检查或专题调研 23 次，政协视察和专题调研 9 次。开展普法宣传教育活动 2674 次，参加人数 2.9 万人；全省开展法律培训班 32 次，参加人数 1893 人，是去年的 1.8 倍；建立残疾人法律救助协调机构 37 个；建立残疾人法律援助中心（工作站）88 个，办理案件 238 件；协助残联系统人大代表、政协委员提出议案、建议、提案 39 件，办理议案、建议、提案 26 件。无障碍建设与管理法规、政府令 14 个；无障碍建设领导协调组织 16 个；贫困残疾人家庭无障碍改造 1694 户，无障碍检查 57 次，无障碍培训 168 人次，残疾人机动轮椅车燃油补贴 11633 人。各级残联共处理残疾人群众来信 1390 件，接待残疾人群众来访 9433 人次，其中集体访 37 批次，638 人次。

六、宣传文化

采用主题宣传模式，第一季度以“关注残疾人民生”为主题，第二季度以“全国助残日”为契机，以“文化助残”为主题，第三季度以伦敦残奥会举办和“残疾人文化周”活动为载体，以“发展残疾人文化”为主题，第四季度以“国际助残日”为契机，以“残疾人两个体系建设快速推进”为主题。市州级主要新闻媒体刊播稿件数 291 件，报刊专版 5 个，残疾人专题广播节目 2 个，电视手语新闻栏目 2 个。市州级公共图书馆设立盲文及盲人有声读物阅览室已达到 11 个，举办残疾人文化周活动 64 场，举办残疾人文化艺术类比赛及展览 12 个，已成立残疾人艺术团队 1 个。

七、体育

积极支持、配合 2012 年伦敦残奥会我省残疾人运动员参与组团、集训和比赛，最终我省参赛运动员获两个第四名、一个第五、一个第六名。与省体育局联合举办了 2012 年贵州省残疾人（20 周岁以下）田径锦标赛和游泳锦标赛（18 周岁以下），48 人次打破 23 项田径省纪录，破创游泳省纪录 52 项。派出 6 名运动员参加了 2012 年全国聋人羽毛球锦标赛，获 1.5 枚金牌、1 枚银牌、3 枚铜牌。

八、组织建设

2012 年，全省各级残联领导班子基本上都配备了残疾人理事长或副理事长。在残疾人专职委员选聘方面，1564 个乡镇（街道）中，选聘残疾人专职委员 1789 名；16684 个社区（村）中，选聘残疾人专职委员 11066 名。全省市县乡残联实有人员已达 3393 人。

九、信息化

省残联制定《贵州省残联系统统计工作评价暂行办法》，并开展了年度评价。成立了省残联信息统计工作小组，规范了统计工作流程。今年我省残疾人工作 37 项主要数据指标编入省统计局、国家统计局贵州调查总队编制的《2012 年贵州省统计年鉴》，这是我省残疾人事业发展数据首次纳入我省官方权威数据发布体系，为残疾人事业更好地融入全省经济社会总体发展奠定了基础。全年省级及市州级残联开设网站技术培训班 8 期，培训各级残联信息员达 369 人次，各级残联共有 125 名专业技术人员从事信息化工作，省级网站全年发稿量 829 篇。

2012年云南省残疾人事业发展统计公报

2012年党的十八大开启了全面建成小康社会新的伟大征程。在云南省委、省政府的正确领导下，全省残联认真贯彻落实省第九次党代会的决策部署，奋发有为、真抓实干，积极推进残疾人社会保障体系和服务体系建设，残疾人事业保持良好的发展势头，各方面工作取得新成效，广大残疾人得到新实惠。

一、残疾人康复

2012年云南省残疾人康复工作围绕实现残疾人“人人享有康复服务”目标，加强社区康复、白内障无障碍建设、重点救助项目、康复人才培养等重点工作，取得了一定实效。

实施“光明工程”，免费为6万例白内障患者实施复明手术，是2012年省政府十件惠民实事、好事之一。为贯彻实施好省委、省政府的安排部署，将“情系衣食父母，服务黎民百姓”的惠民阳光普照到每位需要救助的残疾人家庭，各级残联积极行动，精心组织，狠抓落实，将实施“光明工程”白内障患者的筛查工作作为2012年的首要任务和重要工作来抓。完成259,898名眼疾患者的筛查，121,582名眼疾患者筛查信息数据库的录入。做到不漏查、不漏报，确保每一名贫困白内障患者都能得到康复救助,全年完成白内障复明手术6.34万例；其中贫困白内障患者手术6.1万例。为评估“光明工程”的实施效能，省残联组织16个州（市）随机抽取了3,869名筛查对象进行筛查转运满意度调查，满意率达到98%以上。全面超额完成了“光明工程”白内障患者筛查任务，确保了省政府惠民实事任务目标的完成，给贫困白内障患者带来了实实在在的利益。

截止到2012年底，全省已有11个市辖区、93个县（市）中的6,861个社区开展了残疾人社区康复工作，全省共有8,904名社区康复协调员接受培训，建立了39.61万人的康复服务档案，有11.23万人接受社区康复服务，上述数据相比2011年均有大幅增长，其中接受社区康复服务人数增长106%，社区康复覆盖面进一步扩大。

2012年为4,191名低视力患者配用助视器，培训低视力儿童家长1,003名，有效开展家庭康复训练。对2,593名盲人进行定向行走

训练，上述数据相比2011年均有大幅增长，分别增长427.17%、368.69%、98.09%。

加强省级聋儿康复机构建设，完善聋儿康复网络。共对925名聋儿进行了听力语言康复训练，规范聋儿家长学校，开展家庭训练，共培训聋儿家长1,298名；培养各类专业人员292人，上述数据相比2011年均有大幅增长，分别增长29.73%、73.99%、734.29%。

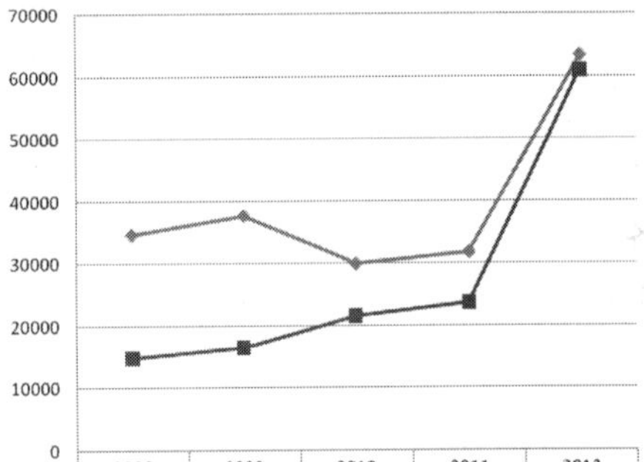

	2008	2009	2010	2011	2012
白内障复明手术	34724	37730	29991	31831	63415
其中贫困白内障患者手术	14861	16571	21638	23749	61038

图1 2008-2012年云南省白内障复明手术完成情况（例）

大力推广“社会化、综合性、开放式”精神病防治康复工作。2012年，在全省118个市县开展精神病防治康复工作，覆盖人口3,494.1万人，对9.52万重度精神病患者进行综合防治康复，监护率达到63.17%，显好率达到38.51%，社会参与率达到31.24%，肇事率0.16‰；解除关锁301人；对12,328名贫困精神病患者进行医疗救助。

深入开展辅助器具供应服务，全面推进普及型假肢装配，截止到2012年底，累计建立辅助器具供应服务机构52个，为残疾人减免费用装配普及型假肢1,484例，供应辅助器具37,405件，装配矫形器561例。

全年开展肢体残疾康复训练服务的机构达到27个,对1,167名贫困肢体残疾儿童实施矫治手术、装配了矫形器等辅助器具，进行了术后康复训练；对

7,325 名肢体残疾人进行了康复训练，其中：脑瘫儿童系统康复训练 353 人,肢体残疾儿童社区、家庭康复 1,221 人，成年肢体残疾人社区、家庭康复 5,751 人。上述数据相比 2011 年均有大幅增长，分别增长 17.39%、127.63%。

全年开展智力残疾康复训练服务的机构达到 15 个；对 2,856 名 0—14 岁的智力残疾儿童进行了康复训练，不同程度地开展了智力残疾儿童早期康复训练与服务。

二、残疾人教育

残疾人受教育权利得到更好的保障。通过实施彩票公益金、交通银行等助学项目，逐步建立残疾人教育服务机制。加强残疾人教育服务体系建设，提高残疾人受教育质量。制定并下发《残疾人事业专项彩票公益金助学项目（学前阶段）云南省实施方案》,安排下达彩票公益金助学项目资金 78 万元。积极推进省华夏中专搬迁新建工作，完成省华夏中专搬迁新建开工奠基仪式。昭通、临沧将特殊教育学校建设纳入重点工作,积极推动特殊教育的发展。各地积极采取措施提高残疾儿童少年义务教育普及水平，多渠道帮助贫困残疾人家庭子女接受教育。

全省特教学校已经发展到 30 所,残疾儿童义务教育入学率达 88.71%。未入学适龄残疾少年儿童总数 5,441 人，其中视力残疾 389 人，听力残疾 357 人，言语残疾 401 人，智力残疾 1,423 人，肢体残疾 1,756 人，精神残疾 100 人，多重残疾 1,015 人。

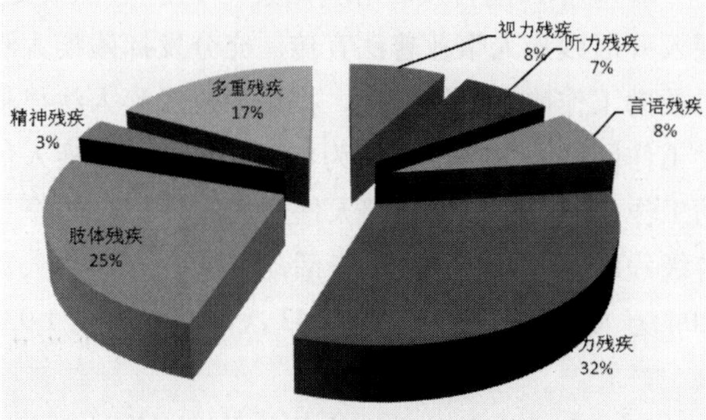

图 2　未入学残疾儿童残疾类别分布图

2012 年全省有 420 名残疾学生达到普通高等院校录取分数线,其中录取 359 人,录取率为 85.48%; 38 名残疾人进入特殊教育学院学习。

全省残疾人中等职业教育机构有 6 个，在校生 614 人，毕业生 276 人，其中获得职业资格证书 89 人。

三、残疾人就业与扶贫

2012 年云南省组织实施了残疾人就业和职业培训实名制统计管理。贯彻实施《云南省残疾人就业保障金征收使用管理办法》，建立残疾人就业保障金征收管理制度，有 26,008 个用人单位参加按比例安排残疾人就业审核，安排残疾人就业 10,250 人。积极探索残疾人实用技术培训和职业技能培训，加强残疾人就业服务，营造有利社会环境，有效地促进了残疾人就业和创业。2012 年，城镇新安排 4,691 名残疾人就业。其中，集中就业残疾人 1996 人，按比例安排残疾人就业 1,048 人，公益性岗位就业 606 人，个体及其它形式就业 1,440 人，辅助性就业 76 人，全省城镇实际在业人数 7.42 万人；103.43 万农村残疾人稳定实现就业，其中从事农业生产劳动 88.42 万人

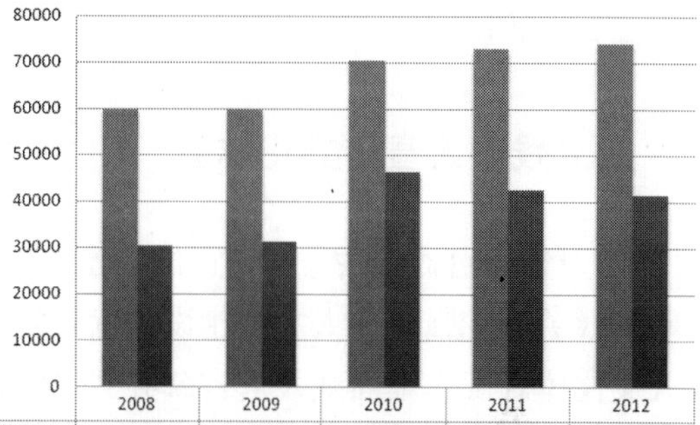

	2008	2009	2010	2011	2012
■就业人数合计	60057	60073	70347	72942	74187
■未就业人数合计	30464	31276	46421	42670	41364

图 3　2008-2012 年城镇残疾人就业情况（人）

职业培训基地 63 个,其中残联兴办 32 个，本年度城镇职业培训人数 5,771 人。

培训盲人保健按摩 564 人;医疗按摩人员 83 人,保健按摩机构达到 623 个,医疗按摩机构达到 11 个;有 6 人通过医疗按摩人员初级职称评审;扶持特困盲人按摩师就业 311 人。

城镇残疾职工参加社会保险人数达到 5.13 万人，其中参加养老保险人数 3.57 万人，参加医疗保险人数 3.36 万人；城镇残疾居民参加医疗保险达到 9.33 万人；城乡 64.81 万名残疾人纳入最低生活保障范围；城镇已纳入最低生活保障 7.5 万人，城镇集中供养和其他救助救济 2.21 万人；农村已纳入最低生活保障 57.32 万人。

寄宿制托养机构 26 个，托养残疾人 1,343 人；日间照料托养机构合计 17 个，托养残疾人 271 人；

本年度享受居家托养服务残疾人 13,457 人。

2012 年云南省农村残疾人扶贫显著加强。省残联与省财政厅联发《关于云南省“十二五”农村贫困残疾人实用技术培训项目实施办法的通知》，帮助残疾人脱贫致富。与省委组织部共同下发《云南省农村基层党组织助残扶贫工程实施办法》，与省商务厅联合下发《云南省万村千乡市场工程助残扶贫项目》。2011 年和 2012 年共投入中央彩票公益金残疾人危房改造项目经费 2,550 万元，为 11,000 户贫困残疾人家庭实施了危房改造。建立县级以上残疾人扶贫示范基地 80 个，加强了扶贫基地建设。

2012 年度扶持贫困残疾人户 5.59 万户，扶持 7.38 万人，脱贫 3.38 万人，返贫 2.03 万人，接受实用技术培训的残疾人 4.63 万人次。

结对帮扶单位 2,016 个，结对帮扶个人 19,695 人；建立残疾人扶贫基地 80 个，安置残疾人就业 735 人，扶持带动残疾人 3,520 人。

完成 6,411 户农村贫困残疾人危房改造，受益残疾人 6,857 人。

四、残疾人宣传文化体育

2012 年云南省残联与省委宣传部等 12 部门共同印发《关于加强残疾人文化建设的意见》，将残疾人文化体育工作全面纳入全省公共文化体育服务体系，在为残疾人提供均等文化体育服务的同时，广泛开展个性化服务，对残疾人文化创业、体育健身等给予特别扶持。与省体育局共同制定《云南省第十届残疾人运动会暨第四届特殊奥林匹克运动会竞赛规程总则方案》，确定了全省 6 个残疾人群众体育示范点，在全省范围进行了残疾人青少年体育苗子选拔工作。

2012 年云南省残联继续开展“全国助残日”活动、残疾人文化周、残疾人体育健身周、残疾人文化进社区等群众性残疾人文化体育活动，推进残疾人体育健身指导员培训和自强健身示范点建设。文山、怒江等地积极开展富有地方特色的残疾人文化体育活动。在伦敦残奥会上，我省共有 27 名运动员参赛，共获得 9 枚金牌、8 枚银牌、7 枚铜牌，打破两项个人世界纪录和一项团体世界纪录，金牌和奖牌总数在西部省份中位居第一。为全省各族人民赢得了巨大荣誉。

2012 年省级主要新闻媒体刊播残疾人事业稿件数 253 件，报刊专版 13 个，残疾人专题广播栏目 1 个，电视手语新闻栏目 1 个，建立省级新促会 1 个；地市级主要新闻媒体刊播稿件数 1,323 件，报刊专版 28 个，残疾人专题广播栏目 9 个，电视手语新闻栏目 7 个，建立地市级新促会 9 个。

省级和地市级公共图书馆设立盲文及盲人有声读物阅览室已达到 11 个，举办残疾人文化周 74 场次，举办残疾人文化艺术类比赛及展览 17 个，已成立残疾人艺术团队 11 个。

省残联开展残疾人体育健身活动 2 次，参加人数 920 人，残疾人体育示范点 8 个，残疾人体育健身指导员 95 人，残疾人体育训练基地 1 个，聘任教练员 18 人。

地市级残联开展残疾人体育健身活动 41 次，参加人次 11,454 人，建立残疾人体育示范点 15 个，培训残疾人体育健身指导员 58 人。

五、残疾人维权

为落实修订后的《中华人民共和国残疾人保障法》，《云南省残疾人保障条例》于 2012 年 7 月 29 日经云南省第十一届人民代表大会常务委员会第三十二次会议审议通过，自 2012 年 10 月 1 日起施行。条例的实施对于切实保障残疾人政治、经济、社会和文化权利产生了重要的影响。全省各级政府共制定或修改了保障残疾人权益的规范性文件 10 件；县级以上人大执法检查或专题调研 23 次，政协视察和专题调研 24 次。

2012 年云南省残联落实国家“六五”普法规划，深入开展残疾人事业普法宣传。充分发挥残疾人法律救助工作协调机制作用，推动形成残疾人法律救助工作网络。以解决问题为本，扎实做好残疾人信访工作，解决了一批残疾人信访案件。2012 年全省各级残联开展普法宣传教育活动 294 次，参加人数 3.04 万人；开展法律培训班 43 次，参加人数 1,935 人。

2012 年全省建立残疾人法律救助工作站 2 个，办理案件 7 件；建立残疾人法律援助中心（工作站）135 个，办理案件 1,596 件。

在各级人大、政协中共有 81 名残疾人人大代表、151 名残疾人政协委员。各级残联协助人大代表、政协委员向各级人大、政协会议共提出议案提案 52 件，办理议案提案 26 件。

2012 年全省颁布无障碍建设与管理法规、政府令 18 个，成立无障碍建设领导协调组织 37 个，系统开展无障碍建设市、县达 74 个，贫困残疾人家庭无障碍改造 697 户，开展无障碍建设检查 86 次；2012 年共向 12,955 名残疾人发放残疾人机动轮椅车燃油补贴。

2012 年全省各级残联共受理残疾人群众来信 1,401 件，接待残疾人群众来访 2.27 万人次，其中集体访 24 批次，350 人次。

六、残疾人组织建设

全省共有各类残疾人 288.3 万人。全省各级残联共有工作人员 3，543 人；所有的县级残联均已计划单列并实现规范化建设达标；全省建有乡（镇、街道）残联 1,354 个，共配备乡镇、街道残联理事长和选聘残疾人专职委员数 1,582 人；在 12,341 个村和 1,377 个社区建立残协 13,525 个，选聘残疾人专职委员 12,616 人。

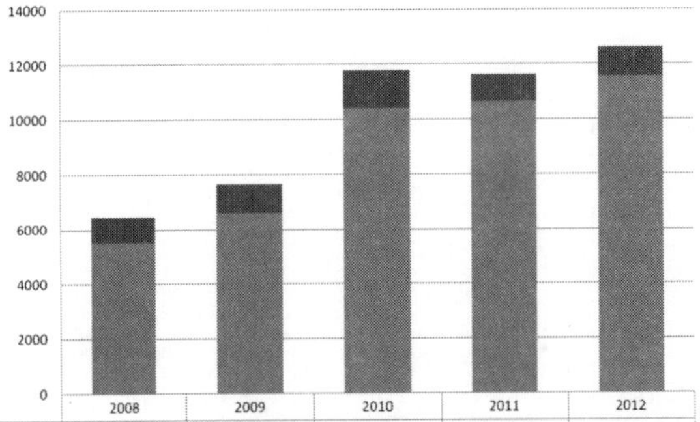

	2008	2009	2010	2011	2012
城市社区	958	1040	1379	989	1065
村（含农村社区）	5510	6605	10400	10631	11551

图 4　2008-2012 年城乡社区（村）残疾人专职委员聘用情况（人）

全省共建立各类残疾人专门协会 682 个，其中盲人协会 137 个、聋人协会 137 个、肢残人协会 141 个、智力残疾人及亲友协会 131 个、精神残疾人及亲友协会 131 个、智力残疾人及亲友协会和精神残疾人及亲友协会二者合一的 5 个。

七、信息化建设工作

2012 年 8 月云南省残联在 2011 年中国残联开展县级残联工作人员信息技术培训的基础上，联合大理学院对未参加中残联信息技术培训的 16 个州（市）残联、56 个非国家扶贫开发工作重点县残联的工作人员开展了一次面向基层残联，以提高基层残联工作人员信息技术应用水平为目的的培训，是省残联首次委托高等院校对基层残联工作人员进行的业务培训。通过培训，极大地提高了云南省基层残联信息技术人员的信息化技术应用水平，提升了专业素养，增强了他们履行工作职责的能力，为今后云南省残疾人信息化建设工作的开展打下了坚实的人才基础。

为实施好云南省“光明工程”白内障患者筛查工作，摸清云南省白内障患者的底数，为今后省政府实施“光明工程”提供基础数据，省残联投入 36.6 万元开发了“光明工程”白内障患者筛查数据库管理系统。该系统于 2012 年 5 月 20 日正式投入使用，7 月 20 日验收完毕，截止 2012 年 12 月 25 日，系统共录入筛查数据 122,311 条，手术数据 54,772 条，为保障“光明工程”顺利实施做出了重要贡献。

统计队伍建设进一步加强，2012 年全省各级残联共有 142 名专、兼职统计人员从事残疾人事业统计工作，统计人员业务素质培养普遍得到重视，省残联举办培训班 1 期，参加培训人员 50 人次；地市级举办培训班 12 期，参加人员 214 人次。

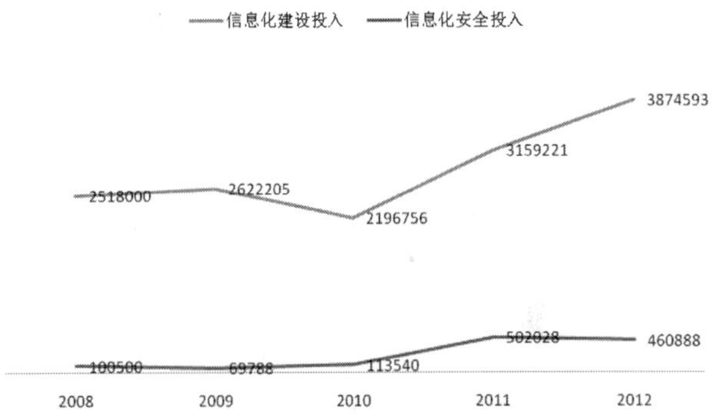

图 5　2008-2012 年信息化建设资金投入情况（元）

全省各级残联全面推进网站建设，截止到 2012 年底，全省各级残联共计建设网站 51 个。2012 年，全省各级残联共举办网站技术培训班 7 期，培训人员 185 人次。各级残联共有 212 名专业技术人员从事信息化工作。截止 2012 年底，各级残联配备了 1,559 台计算机，投入信息化建设经费达 387.46 万元。

2012 年，虽然全省残疾人工作取得了较大的进展，但是与广大残疾人的需求相比，仍然存在很大的差距。在工作中还存在不少困难和问题：一是残疾人事业由于基础较薄弱，在总体上与全省经济社会的快速发展还有不相适应的地方。二是基层组织建设和服务能力仍然比较薄弱，部分县级残联由于经费投入不足，许多工作难以有效开展。三是残疾人康复服务需求量较大，其中多数为贫困残疾人，由于康复经费投入始终处在较低水平，使残疾人得不到切实的康复服务。四是信息化建设工作急需加强，以适应残疾人事业发展需要。这些问题，都有待我们在今后的工作中努力加以解决。

云南省残疾人事业伴随着改革开放和社会主义现代化进程蓬勃发展，取得了长足的发展。在全面建成小康社会的新征途上，残疾人事业必将谱写新的辉煌篇章。我们将在以习近平同志为总书记的党中央领导下，进一步解放思想，锐意创新，求真务实，团结奋斗，奋力开创残疾人事业科学发展、和谐发展、跨越发展的新局面，为实现全面建成小康社会的宏伟目标做出新的更大贡献!

2012 年西藏自治区残疾人事业发展统计公报

2012 年，在自治区党委、政府的坚强领导下，在中国残联的大力指导下，全区广大残疾人工作者团结一心，扎实工作，全面完成了《西藏自治区“十二五”时期残疾人事业发展纲要》确定的年度工作任务。

一、康复

2012 年，我区制定了《关于印发<西藏自治区残疾人康复“十二五”实施方案>9 项康复工作实施方案的通知》、《西藏自治区残疾儿童康复救助“七彩梦行动计划”实施方案》等文件，积极开展各项康复服务工作；成立了“三星白内障手术中心”和“三星盲人定向行走训练中心”；继续实施康复人才百千万工程、贫困残疾儿童抢救性康复工程、贫困肢体残疾儿童矫治手术工程、百万贫困白内障复明工程。

我区全年完成了贫困白内障患者免费复明手术 1056 例，为 66 名低视力患者配用助视器，对 106 名盲人进行定向行走训练；对 46 名贫困肢体残疾儿童实施矫治手术、装配了矫形器等辅助器具并进行了术后康复训练，对 120 名肢体残疾人进行了康复训练，其中：脑瘫儿童系统康复训练 49 人,肢体残疾儿童社区、家庭康复 31 人，成年肢体残疾人社区、家庭康复 40 人；对 71 名智力残疾儿童进行了康复训练；不同程度地开展了智力残疾儿童早期康复训练与服务。在 1 个市辖区和 9 个县开展了社区康复工作；截止 2012 年底，为残疾人减免费用装配普及型假肢 155 例，供应辅助器具 937 件，装配矫形器 239 例。

二、教育

继续开展残疾人特殊教育和残疾儿童随班就读工作；组织开展首届特殊教育骨干教师培训工作；全年有 35 名残疾人被普通高等院校录取，截止 2012 年底，我区未入学适龄残疾儿童少年总数 450 人，其中视力残疾 43 人，听力残疾 28 人，言语残疾 53 人，智力残疾 192 人，肢体残疾 28 人，精神残疾 32 人，多重残疾 74 人。

三、就业

城镇新安排 1031 名残疾人就业。其中，集中就业残疾人 718 人，按比例安排残疾人就业 102 人，公益性岗位就业 17 人，个体及其它形式就业 87 人，辅助性就业 13 人，全区城镇实际在业人数 1000 人；2.98 万农村残疾人稳定实现就业，其中从事农业生产劳动 2.90 万人。

职业培训基地 1 个,其中残联兴办 1 个，本年度城镇职业培训人数 56 人。

培训盲人保健按摩 22 人；保健按摩机构达到 17 个。

四、社会保障

城镇残疾职工参加社会保险人数达到 0.32 万人，其中参加养老保险人数 0.19 万人，参加医疗保险人数 0.20 万人；城镇残疾居民参加医疗保险达到 0.22 万人；城乡 3.38 万名残疾人纳入最低生活保障范围；城镇已纳入最低生活保障 0.42 万人，城镇集中供养和其他救助救济 0.06 万人；农村已纳入最低生活保障 2.96 万人，五保供养和其他救助救济 0.22 万人。本年度享受居家托养服务残疾人 7816 人。

五、扶贫

本年度扶持贫困残疾人户 340 户，扶持 604 人，脱贫 241 人，返贫 31 人，接受实用技术培训的残疾人 159 人次，投入培训经费 207.36 万元。

完成 500 户农村贫困残疾人危房改造，投入危房资金 300.00 万元，受益残疾人 514 人。

六、维权

制定和修改了保障残疾人权益的规范性文件 1 件；县级以上人大执法检查或专题调研 1 次。

开展普法宣传教育活动 46 次，参加人数 1.12 万人； 开展法律培训班 2 次，参加人数 76 人；建立残疾人法律援助中心（工作站）8 个，办理案件 2 件； 协助残联系统人大代表、政协委员提出议案、建议、提案 1 件，办理议案、建议、提案 3 件。

无障碍建设领导协调组织 2 个；贫困残疾人家庭无障碍改造 200 户，残疾人机动轮椅车燃油补贴 2411 人。

各级残联共处理残疾人群众来信 221 件，接待残疾人群众来访 346 人次，其中集体访 21 批次。

七、宣传文化

2012 年，自治区主要新闻媒体刊播稿件数 25 件；地市级主要新闻媒体刊播稿件数 9 件；举办省级残疾人文化周及地市级残疾人文化周各 2 场次。

八、组织建设

2012 年，4 个地市级残联的领导班子配备了残疾人理事长或副理事长。1 个县级残联机关配备了残疾人干部。

全区共建立各类残疾人专门协会 3 个，其中盲人协会 2 个、肢残人协会 1 个。

九、信息化

统计队伍建设进一步加强，全区各级残联共有 15 名专、兼职统计人员从事残疾人事业统计工作，统计人员业务素质培养普遍得到重视，省级残联举办培训班 1 期，参加培训的人员达到 35 人次；地市级举办培训班 2 期，参加培训的人员达到 20 人次。

2012 年省级及地市级残联开设网站技术培训班 2 期，培训各级残联信息员达 55 人次。

各级残联共有 17 名专业技术人员从事信息化工作。

2012 年陕西省残疾人事业发展统计公报

2012 年，省残联坚持以“科学发展、富民强省”为主题，以创建全国残疾人“两个体系”建设试验区为抓手，加强领导，狠抓落实，全面完成了各项目标任务，全省残疾人事业呈现出良好的发展势头，实现了工作思路转变和工作重心调整，成为广大残疾人得到实惠最多的时期。

一、康复

2012 年，紧紧围绕“人人享有康复服务”目标，通过实施一批重点康复工程，为残疾人提供了有效的康复服务。大力加强残疾人社区康复示范站建设，积极推进残疾人社区康复工作；积极推进残疾人康复机构规范化建设；加强康复人才队伍建设，大力宣传和普及康复知识。

社区康复工作实现全覆盖，累计建立社区康复站 1198 个，配备社区康复协调员 7317 名。

开展视力残疾康复机构总数达到 39 个，全年完成白内障复明手术 15618 例；为 10349 名贫困白内障患者免费施行复明手术，全年为 9661 名低视力患者配用助视器，培训低视力儿童家长 145 名，有效开展家庭康复训练。对 3659 名盲人进行定向行走训练。

图 1 2008-2012 年全省白内障复明手术完成情况（例）

加强聋儿康复机构建设，完善聋儿康复网络。建设省级听力语言康复机构 1 个，市级听力语言康复机构 12 个，县级听力语言康复机构 23 个。共对 965 名聋儿进行了听力语言康复训练，规范聋儿家长学校，开展家庭训练，共培训聋儿家长 1253 名；培养各类专业人员 105 人。

大力推广“社会化、综合性、开放式”精神病防治康复工作。2012 年，全省所有市县精神病防治康复工作实现全覆盖，对 20.49 万名重性精神病患者进行综合防治康复，监护率达到 57.39%，显好率达到 37.84%，社会参与率达到 31.47%，肇事率 0.08%；解除关锁病人 146 名；对 1.52 万名贫困精神病患者进行了医疗救助。

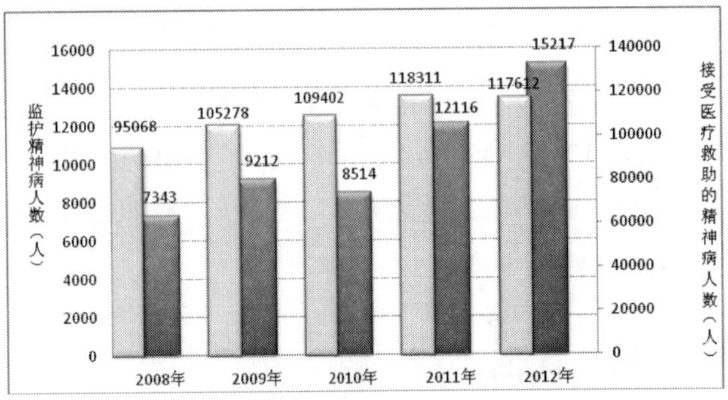

图 2 2008-2012 年全省精神病人监护和救助情况

建立了 2 个省级孤独症儿童康复训练机构，60 名孤独症儿童进行了康复训练。

全年为麻风畸残者实施矫治手术 100 例，开展宣传普及教育，为麻风患者回归社会营造良好社会氛围。

全年开展肢体残疾康复训练服务的机构达到 68 个,对 201 名贫困肢体残疾儿童实施矫治手术、装配了矫形器等辅助器具,进行了术后康复训练;对 7293 名肢体残疾人进行了康复训练，其中：脑瘫儿童系统康复训练 210 人,肢体残疾儿童社区、家庭康复 590 人，成年肢体残疾人社区、家庭康复 6493 人。

全年开展智力残疾康复训练服务的机构达到 16 个；对 1019 名智力残疾儿童进行了康复训练，不同程度地开展了智力残疾儿童早期康复训练与服务。

深入开展辅助器具供应服务，全面推进普及型假肢装配，截止到 2012 年底，各市县累计建立辅助器具供应服务机构 19 个。全年为残疾人减免费用供应辅助器具 5.32 万件，其中装配普及型假肢 1473 例，装配矫形器 1352 例。

二、教育

开办特殊教育普通高中 3 所，在校生 115 人。

残疾人中等职业教育机构有 8 个，在校生 1487 人，毕业生 1269 人，其中获得职业资格证书 972 人。高等特殊教育学院 1 所,2012 年全省有 334 名残疾人被普通高等院校录取。

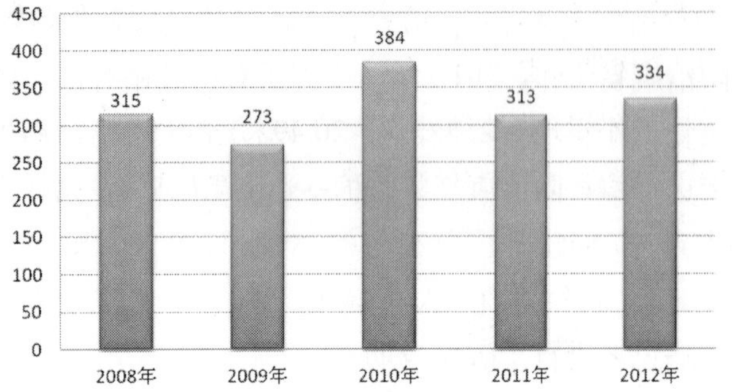

图 3　2008-2012 年高等院校录取残疾考生情况（人）

未入学适龄残疾儿童少年总数 4874 人，其中视力残疾 417 人，听力残疾 356 人，言语残疾 240 人，智力残疾 1436 人，肢体残疾 1292 人，精神残疾 230 人，多重残疾 903 人。

三、就业

实施“城镇百万残疾人就业工程”，促进残疾人多渠道、多层次、多形式就业。城镇新安排 7899 名残疾人就业。其中，集中就业残疾人 1892 人，按比例安排残疾人就业 2131 人，公益性岗位就业 642 人，个体及其它形式就业 2831 人，辅助性就业 403 人，全国城镇实际在业人数 10.37 万人；72.48 万农村残疾人稳定实现就业，其中从事农业生产劳动 54.31 万人。

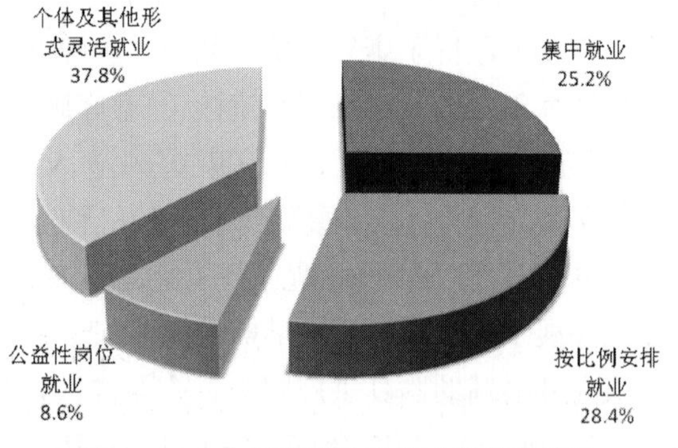

图 4　2012 年城镇残疾人新安排就业情况

职业培训基地 64 个,其中残联兴办 15 个，本年度城镇职业培训 1.22 万人。

培训盲人保健按摩 1008 人；医疗按摩人员 288 名，保健按摩机构达到 284 个，医疗按摩机构达到 68 个；有 22 人通过医疗按摩人员初级职称评审。

四、社会保障

城乡残疾人社会养老保险实现全覆盖。参保重度残疾人享受到省财政全额补贴最低缴费标准、中度或轻度残疾人享受市、县财政适当补贴缴费标准的特惠政策。逐步健全残疾人基本医疗保险制度。将符合规定的残疾人医疗康复项目纳入了医疗保险支付范围及大病救助范围。城镇残疾职工参加社会保险人数达到 5.97 万人，其中参加养老保险人数 3.57 万人，参加医疗保险人数 3.57 万人；城镇残疾居民参加医疗保险达到 19.70 万人；城乡 37.72 万名残疾人纳入最低生活保障范围；城镇已纳入最低生活保障 6.98 万人，城镇集中供养和其他救助救济 6.23 万人；农村已纳入最低生活保障 30.74 万人，五保供养和其他救助救济 39.22 万人。

出台了《陕西省“阳光家园计划——智力、精神和重度残疾人托养服务项目（2012-2015 年）”实施意见》。全省共有残疾人寄宿制托养机构 78 个，托养残疾人 3609 名；日间照料托养机构合计 31 个，托养残疾人 1870 名；本年度享受居家托养服务残疾人 1.83 万人。

五、扶贫开发

出台了《关于贯彻农村残疾人扶贫开发纲要（2011-2020 年）的实施意见》、《陕西省农村残疾人扶贫基地建设指导意见》。通过帮包带扶、移民搬迁、科技扶贫等多种形式，本年度扶持贫困残疾人 10.08 万户，扶持 15.45 万人，脱贫 9.90 万人，返贫 1.26 万人，接受实用技术培训的残疾人 1.73 万人次，投入培训经费 729.10 万元。

结对帮扶单位 1402 个，结对帮扶个人 6934 名；建立残疾人扶持基地 210 个，安置残疾人就业 3283 人，扶持带动残疾人 1.23 万户。

完成 2923 户农村贫困残疾人危房改造，投入危房资金 1,754.07 万元，受益残疾人 3815 名。

六、宣传文化

文体生活更加活跃。采取文化周集中大规模活动与经常性活动相结合的办法力推文化建设。成立省残疾人作家协会。举办省首届残疾人文学艺术精品展。省级中央媒体采用稿件 227 件，主要新闻媒体刊播稿件数 398 件，电视手语新闻栏目 1 个，省级残疾人事业新闻宣传促进会 1 个。

地市级主要新闻媒体刊播稿件数 832 件，报刊专版 11 个，残疾人专题广播节目 7 个，电视手语新闻栏目 15 个，建立地市级新促会 3 个。

在全国首家印发了《陕西省各级公共图书馆盲人阅览室建设指导意见》，省级和地市级公共图书馆设立盲文及盲人有声读物阅览室已达到 18 个，举办残疾人文化周 31 个，举办残疾人文化艺术类比赛及展览 17 个，成立残疾人艺术团队 5 个。

七、体育

在伦敦第十四届残奥会上，我省 8 名运动员参赛。获得 3 金 2 银 1 铜、两个第四名，第五、六、七、八名各一个，创参加残奥会历史最好成绩。省委、省政府发出贺电并召开了庆功表彰大会。

省级残疾人体育健身活动 49 次，参加人数 4000 人，残疾人体育示范点 25 个，残疾人体育健身指导员 189 人，残疾人体育比赛 8 次，参与的残疾人运动员 280 人次，残疾人体育训练基地 25 个，聘任教练员 12 人。

地市级残疾人体育健身活动 61 次，参加人数 3386 人，残疾人体育示范点 23 个，残疾人体育健身指导员 73 人。

八、维权

残疾人事业法律体系进一步完善，残疾人维权工作全面开展。新修订的《陕西省实施<中华人民共和国残疾人保障法>办法》正式施行，省人大法工委、省政府残工委召开宣传贯彻《陕西省实施<中华人民共和国残疾人保障法>办法》大会。

制定或修改了关于残疾人的专门法规、规章地市级 1 件；制定或修改了保障残疾人权益的规范性文件地市级 2 件；县级以上人大执法检查或专题调研 20 次，政协视察和专题调研 14 次。开展普法宣传教育活动 146 次，参加人数 1.41 万人；开展法律培训班 19 次，参加人数 1769 人。

全省建立残疾人法律救助协调机构 23 个；建立残疾人法律救助工作站 1 个；建立残疾人法律援助中心（工作站）106 个，办理案件 452 件；协助残联系统人大代表、政协委员提出议案、建议、提案 22 件，办理议案、建议、提案 27 件。

无障碍建设与管理法规、政府令 13 个；无障碍建设领导协调组织 29 个；系统开展无障碍建设市、县 43 个；贫困残疾人家庭无障碍改造 1680 户，无障碍检查 21 次，无障碍培训 281 人次，残疾人机动轮椅车燃油补贴 8834 人。

各级残联共处理残疾人群众来信 1984 件，接待残疾人群众来访 2.47 万人次，其中集体访 22 批次，200 人次。

九、组织建设

全面发展残疾人组织建设工作，在 18 个县（区）、102 个乡（镇、街道）、1009 个村（社区）开展创建“全省残疾人工作示范县（区）、乡（镇、街道）、村（社区）”活动。

多层次、多渠道、多形式对残疾人工作者进行了分类分级培训，基本形成了机构健全规范、队伍稳定实干、服务功能完善的残疾人组织网络，省市县乡残联实有人员已达 5301 人。6 个地市级残联的领导班子配备了残疾人理事长或副理事长，61 个县级残联机关配备了残疾人干部。

出台了《关于进一步加强农村（社区）残疾人专职委员队伍建设的实施意见》。1603 个乡镇（街道）中，选聘残疾人专职委员 1884 名；28193 个社区（村）中，选聘残疾人专职委员 2.65 万名。

省级以下共建立各类残疾人专门协会 580 个，其中盲人协会 118 个、聋人协会 118 个、肢残人协会 118 个、智力残疾人及亲友协会 112 个、精神残疾人及亲友协会 114 个。

十、服务设施建设

截止到 2012 年底，已竣工并投入使用的各级残疾人综合服务设施共计 66 个，在建项目共计 5 个，筹建项目共计 6 个。其中已竣工并投入使用的各级残疾人综合服务设施总占地面积 10.81 万平方米，总建设规模 9.46 万平方米，总投资 2.45 亿元；已竣工并投入使用的各级康复设施共计 4 个，在建项目共计 3 个，筹建项目共计 6 个。其中已竣工并投入使用的各级康复设施总占地面积 1.75 万平方米，总建设规模 1.09 万平方米，总投资 0.20 亿元；已竣工并投入使用的各级托养设施共计 20 个，在建项目共计 3 个，筹建项目共计 8 个，其中已竣工并投入使用的各级托养设施总占地面积 9.25 万平方米，总建设规模 9.03 万平方米，总投资 0.85 亿元。

十一、事业统计与信息化建设

统计队伍建设进一步加强。各级残联共有 133 名专、兼职统计人员从事残疾人事业统计工作，统计人员业务素质培养普遍得到重视，省级残联举办培训班 1 期，参加培训的人员达到 30 人次；地市级举办培训班 7 期，参加培训的人员达到 162 人次。

全面推进网站建设。省级残联已开通了公众服务网站，并完成了省残联门户网站的升级改版工作。11 个地市级残联及杨陵区残联全部建成网站,46 个县级残联网站也已开通，网站总数比去年增加 16 个。这为今后残联系统网站集群服务奠定了基础，残联系统网上信息服务正在逐步覆盖。各级残联共有 159 名专业技术人员从事信息化工作。省级及地市级残联开设网站技术培训班 11 期，培训各级残联信息员达 282 人次。

2012年甘肃省残疾人事业发展统计公报

2012年，在省委省政府的正确领导、中国残联的有力指导和社会各界的大力支持下，各级残联组织紧紧围绕全省工作大局，抢抓机遇、乘势而为，凝心聚力、创新进取，全面完成年初确定的各项残疾人工作任务，全省残疾人事业呈现亮点纷呈、多点突破、快速发展、强劲跨越的良好局面。

一、康复

社区康复：全省86个县（区、市）的4397个村（社区）开展了社区康复工作，康复协调员总数为7813人，有30万名残疾人接受了社区康复服务。

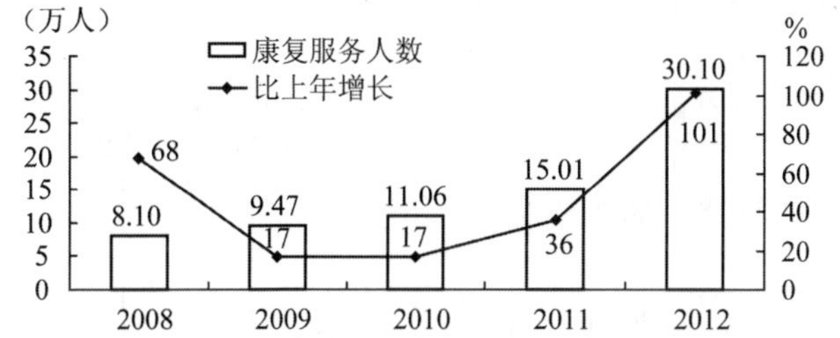

图1 2008-2012年接受社区康复服务残疾人数及增长速度

视力康复：全省全年实施白内障复明手术11126例，其中贫困白内障患者免费手术数7295例；为4988名低视力者配用了助视器；为2601名盲人进行了定向行走训练。

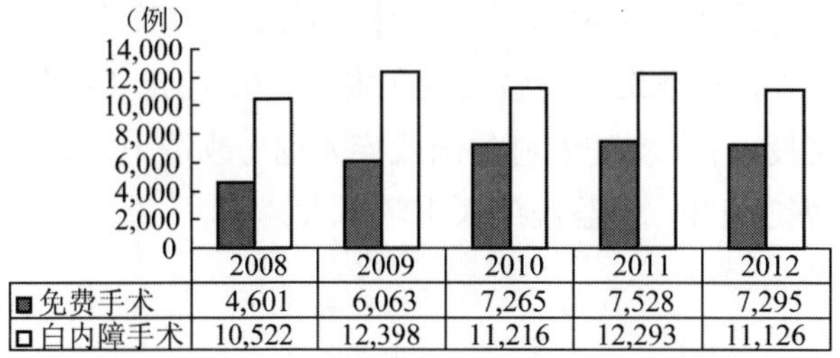

图2 2008-2012年全省实施白内障手术数量

听力语言康复：全省各级聋儿语训机构在训聋儿542名，其中年度新收训385名，有34名聋儿经过训练进入普小，3名进入普幼，24名进入特教学校；全年培训家长449人。

肢体康复：全年有7029名肢体残疾人接受了康复训练，其中脑瘫儿童机构康复533人，比上年增长43%，肢体残疾儿童社区、家庭康复1206人，成年肢体残疾人社区、家庭康复5290人。

智力康复：全年有2411名智力残疾人接受了康复训练，其中智力残疾儿童机构康复336人，增长53%，社区、家庭康复2075人，成年智力残疾人社区、家庭康复22人。

精神病及孤独症康复：全省有60个县（区、市）开展了精神病防治康复工作，精神病康复机构33个，精神病患者120993人，监护107709人，显好74177人，参与社会58142人，肇事128人；有18313名患者接受治疗，5410名接受了康复训练；贫困患者21666名，其中接受医疗救助3773人。有27名孤独症儿童在康复训练机构接受治疗。

辅具服务：全年全省各级辅助器具服务机构供应辅具104种18823件，其中装配假肢1066例，装配矫形器596例，供应其他辅助器具17161件，增长31%。

表1 2012年康复训练服务机构（个）

级别	类别				
	视力	听力语言	肢体	智力	辅助器具
省 级	1	1	1	1	1
市州级	4	11	4	7	7
县 级	10	6	16	11	58
合 计	15	18	21	19	66

二、教育

学前教育：全年有180名学前残疾儿童接受了学前教育助学项目资助，比上年增长128%，其中150名残疾儿童接受了中国残联彩票公益金助学项目资助。

义务教育：全省未入学学龄残疾儿童少年有3329人，比上年减少23%，其中视力残疾179人，听力残疾186人，言语残疾171人，肢体残疾1212人，智力残疾895人，精神残疾121人，多重残疾565人。

高中教育：有40名视力和125名听力残疾学生在两所特教高中就读。

高等教育：2012年全省有273名残疾考生进入

高等院校学习，其中普通高等院校录取 272 人，特殊教育学院录取 1 人。

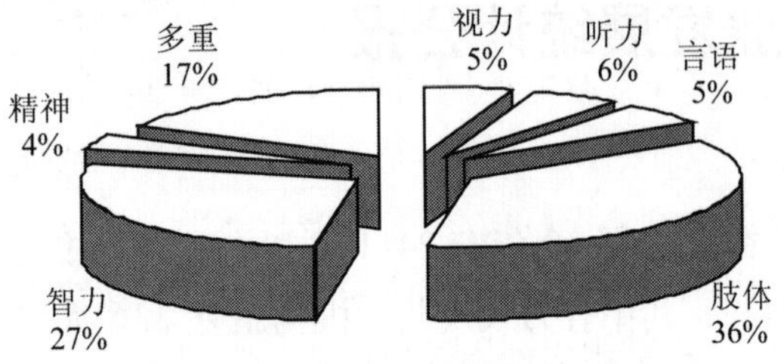

图 3　2012 年全省未入学残疾儿童类别比例

三、就业

就业培训：截止 2012 年底，全省城镇残疾人就业 108769 人，年度新增就业 9859 人；农村残疾人就业 490132 人，其中从事农业生产劳动 394576 人，其他形式就业 95556 人。全省 38 个职业培训基地当年培训残疾人 17827 人。

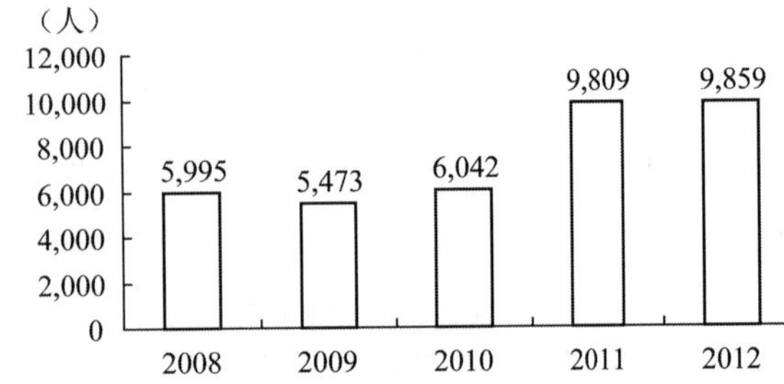

图 4　2008-2012 年城镇残疾人新增就业人数

盲人按摩：全省有医疗按摩机构 26 个，保健按摩机构 182 个，年度培训保健按摩人员 236 人、医疗按摩人员 64 人，盲人保健按摩人员就业 236 人，增长 17%。

四、社会保障

城乡低保：2012 年全省有 46.76 万城乡残疾人纳入低保，其中城镇 11.05 万，农村 35.71 万。

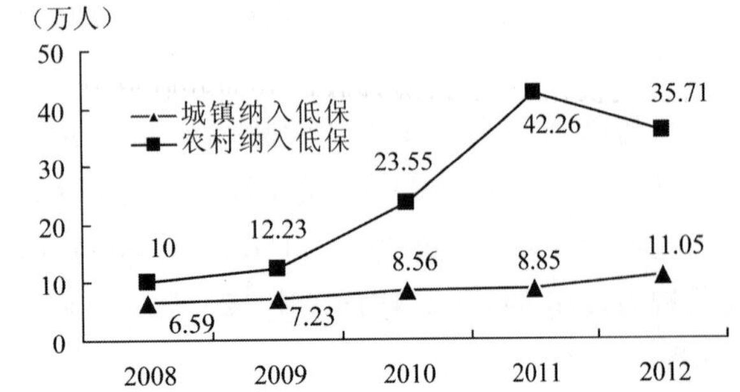

图 5　2008-2012 年全省城乡残疾人纳入低保人数

社会保险：有 2.82 万城镇残疾职工参加了社会保险，其中养老保险 1.69 万人，医疗保险 1.47 万人；有 29.72 万城镇残疾居民参加了社会保险，比上年增长 31%，其中医疗保险 19.83 万，养老保险 11.52 万；有 1.56 万城镇个体就业人员参加了医疗和养老保险；135.48 万农村残疾人参加了新农合，增长 52%，79.76 万参加了新农保。

托养服务：有 2537 名残疾人在全省 52 所托养机构接受寄宿制或日间托养照料服务，增长 27%，有 13248 名残疾人接受居家托养服务。

五、扶贫

资金投入：全省全年共扶持 10.18 万残疾人脱贫。省级年度财政扶贫资金投入 360 万元，比上年增长 11%；康复扶贫贷款项目资金实际落实 3840 万元，其中项目贷款 2640 万元，扶持 880 名贫困残疾人，到户贷款 1200 万元，扶持 600 名贫困残疾人。地方投入实用技术培训资金 769 万元，增长 53%，培训 4.5 万残疾人，增长 22%。

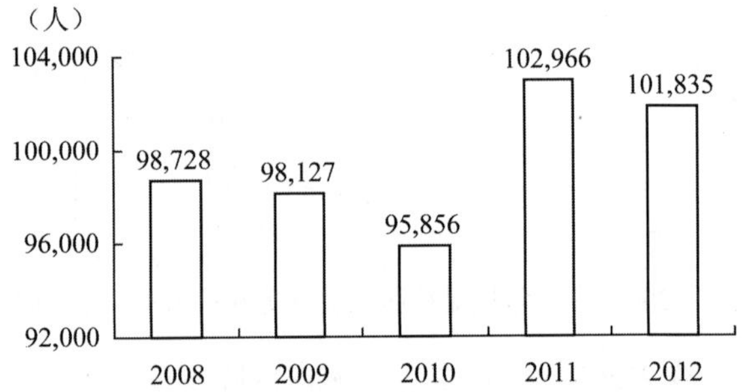

图 6　2008-2012 年扶持脱贫残疾人数

社会帮扶：结对帮扶单位 5187 个，增长 43%；结对帮扶个人 65172 人，增长 59%。全省 43 个扶贫基地扶持带动 8516 名残疾人，比上年增长 75%。

危房改造：全省共投入资金 1.09 亿元（不含中央投入），实施农村贫困残疾人危房改造 10235 户，增长 41%，受益残疾人 12771 人。

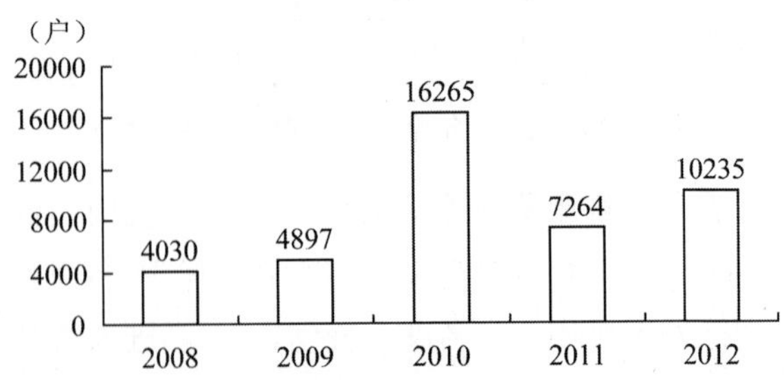

图 7　2008—2012 年危改户数

六、宣传文体

宣传文化：全年省市主要新闻媒体刊播残疾人

事业稿件3096件，增长47%，报纸专版28个，增长27%，电台专题节目43个，增长30%；举办残疾人文化艺术比赛及展览34次，残疾人艺术团队2个。

体育活动：省市举办残疾人体育活动42次，增长75%，参加人数10232人；残疾人体育活动示范点37个，增长28%；举办省级体育比赛2次，参赛运动员410人；省级训练基地9个，教练员26人。

七、维权

法律维权：全省各级人大执法检查52次，比上年增长37%，政协专题调研41次，减少10%，举办普法活动184次，增长7%。全省建立各级残疾人法律救助工作协调机构77个，增长67%，建立法律救助工作站76个，办理案件495件；建立法律援助中心96个，办理案件1077件。

表2 2012年全省各级残疾人法律救助情况

级　别	法律救助协调机构（个）	法律救助		法律援助	
		工作站（个）	办理案件（件）	工作站（个）	办理案件（件）
省　级	1	1	160	1	5
市州级	15	15	41	15	70
县　级	61	60	294	80	1002
合　计	77	76	495	96	1077

参政议政：全省共有24名人大代表和97名政协委员，各级残联协助提出议案、建议及提案66件。

无障碍建设：全省共有101个市县系统开展无障碍建设工作，有10个电视台开播手语栏目，省市建设公共图书馆盲文及盲人有声读物图书室6个，对1178户残疾人家庭实施无障碍改造。

信访：各级残联接待残疾人来信来访10059人次，其中来信1844件，增长44%；来访8215人次，下降11%。为近1.4万名残疾人发放机动轮椅车燃油补贴。

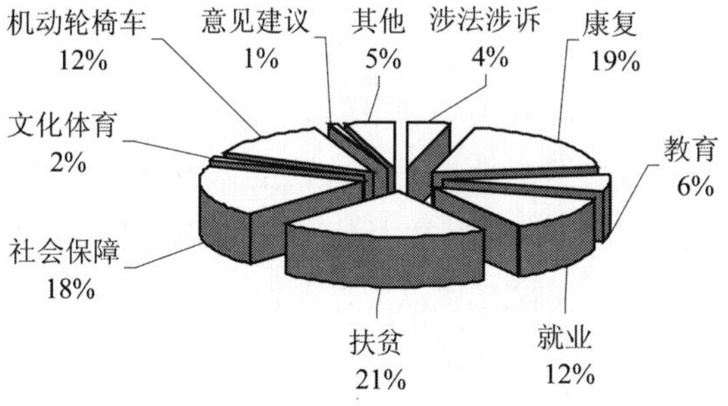

图8 2012年全省信访类别比例

八、组织建设

机构与队伍：截止2012年底，省市县乡四级残联有编制3038个，实有人员3818人，直属事业单位有79个，编制544人。省市县残联共有203名残疾人干部。86个县级残联全部达标，1374个乡（镇、街道）全部建立残联，17207个村（社区）全部建立残协，选聘了18563名残疾人专职委员。

培训工作：全年各级残联举办综合培训班214期，培训11358人次；有2845名优秀残疾人被收入残疾人人才库。

协会工作：全省各级专门协会全部建立。志愿者登记注册11.60万人，受助残疾人23.97万人。

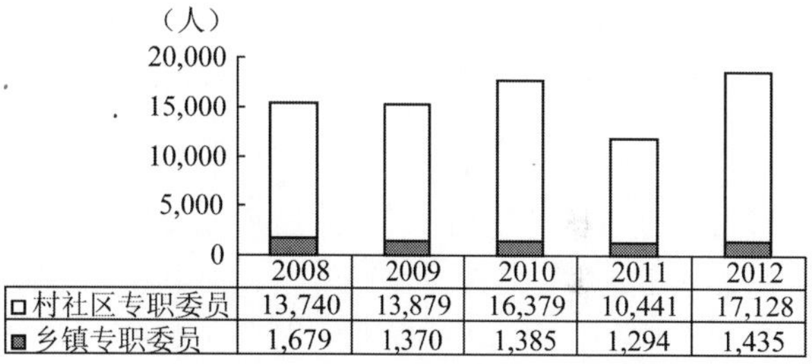

图9 2008-2012年全省专职委员数量

九、信息化建设

网站建设：2012年全省投入信息化建设资金176.88万元，其中硬件投入148.66万元，软件投入16.21万元，系统维护费用12.01万元。全省14个市州级残联和20个县级残联已开通残联网站。

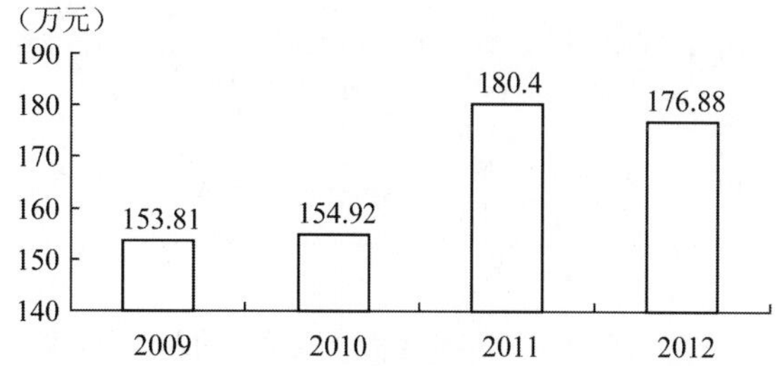

图10 2009-2012年全省残联信息化建设资金

信息发布：省级残联网站全年刊登信息稿件

2414 篇，比上年度增长 21%。省市残联举办信息工作培训班 11 期，培训 295 名残联干部。

数据库建设：截至 2012 年底，全省残疾人人口基础数据库共采集 53.77 万残疾人的基础数据信息，采集率为 28.9%，比上年增长了 6 个百分点，覆盖全省 86 个县区市。完成“省残疾人无障碍信息网络服务管理平台”建设和“省残疾人综合业务数据库”软件开发。

2012年青海省残疾人事业发展统计公报

2012年，在省委、省政府的坚强领导和中国残联的有力指导下，青海省残联以残疾人“两个体系”建设为核心任务，全力推进《青海省残疾人事业“十二五”规划》和年度计划，全面完成了各项业务指标，残疾人生产生活状况进一步改善，残疾人事业实现新发展。

一、康复

通过实施一批重点康复工程，使各类别残疾人得到不同程度的康复。全年完成白内障复明手术0.25万例，其中，0.24万名贫困白内障患者；为246名低视力患者配用助视器，培训低视力儿童家长97名，有效开展家庭康复训练。对1152名盲人进行定向行走训练。

加强省级聋儿康复机构建设，完善聋儿康复网络。共对177名聋儿进行了听力语言康复训练，规范聋儿家长学校，开展家庭训练，共培训聋儿家长208名；培养各类专业人员73人。

大力推广“社会化、综合性、开放式”精神病防治康复工作。在33个市县开展精神病防治康复工作，对0.39万重性精神病患者进行综合防治康复，监护率达到81.72%，显好率达到41.33%，社会参与率达到32.92%，肇事率0.00%；对0.14万名贫困精神病患者进行医疗救助。

深入开展辅助器具供应服务，全面推进普及型假肢装配，截止到2012年底，累计建立辅助器具供应服务机构7个，为残疾人减免费用装配普及型假肢480例，供应辅助器具1.5万件，装配矫形器501例。

全年开展肢体残疾康复训练服务的机构达到9个,对60名贫困肢体残疾儿童实施矫治手术、装配了矫形器等辅助器具,进行了术后康复训练;对1301名肢体残疾人进行了康复训练，其中：脑瘫儿童系统康复训练129人,肢体残疾儿童社区、家庭康复训练223人，成年肢体残疾人社区、家庭康复训练949人。

全年开展智力残疾康复训练服务的机构达到8个；对753名智力残疾儿童进行了康复训练。

在4个市辖区和42个县（市）开展了社区康复工作，累计建立社区康复站0.05万个，配备0.19万名社区康复协调员。

二、教育

残疾人受教育权利得到了更好保障，进一步提高了残疾人素质和平等参与社会的能力。

开办特殊教育普通高中7所，在校生54人；其中聋高中2所。残疾人中等职业教育机构有1个，在校生9人。有134名残疾人被普通高等院校录取。

未入学适龄残疾儿童少年总数794人，其中视力残疾38人，听力残疾48人，言语残疾37人，智力残疾286人，肢体残疾245人，精神残疾13人，多重残疾127人。

三、就业

城镇新安排0.19万残疾人就业。其中，集中就业残疾人0.04万人，按比例安排残疾人就业0.03万人，公益性岗位就业236人，个体及其它形式就业0.08万人，辅助性就业0.01万人，全国城镇实际在业人数0.71万人;3.65万农村残疾人稳定实现就业，其中从事农业生产劳动3.20万人。

职业培训基地81个,其中残联兴办26个，本年度城镇职业培训人数0.28万人。

培训盲人保健按摩270人；医疗按摩人员58，保健按摩机构达到146个，医疗按摩机构达到1个；有2人和29人通过医疗按摩人员中级和初级职称评审。

四、社会保障

城镇残疾职工参加社会保险人数达到0.42万人，其中参加养老保险人数0.27万人，参加医疗保险人数0.24万人；城镇残疾居民参加医疗保险达到0.95万人；城乡3万多名残疾人纳入最低生活保障范围。

寄宿制托养机构 34 个，托养残疾人 0.40 万人；日间照料托养机构合计 5 人,托养残疾人 0.01 万人；本年度享受居家托养服务残疾人 0.97 万人。

五、扶贫开发

扶持贫困残疾人户 1.06 万户，扶持 1.32 万人，脱贫 0.74 万人，返贫 0.22 万人，接受实用技术培训的残疾人 0.62 万人次，投入培训经费 172.24 万元。

结对帮扶单位 0.03 万个，结对帮扶个人 0.08 万人；建立残疾人扶持基地 31 个，安置残疾人就业 0.11 万人，扶持带动残疾人 0.10 万户。

完成 0.23 万户农村贫困残疾人危房改造，投入危房资金 2,759.78 万元，受益残疾人 0.26 万人，通过农牧民定居工程等渠道，改造贫困残疾人危房 0.13 万户。

六、宣传文化

省级中央媒体采用稿件 5 件，主要新闻媒体刊播稿件数 430 件，残疾人专题广播节目 1 个，电视手语新闻栏目 1 个，省级残疾人事业新闻宣传促进会 1 个。

地市级主要新闻媒体刊播稿件数 151 件，报刊专版 25 个，残疾人专题广播节目 8 个。

省级和地市级公共图书馆设立盲文及盲人有声读物阅览室已达到 1 和 2 个，举办残疾人文化周 10 和 10 次，举办残疾人文化艺术类比赛及展览分别是 3 和 4 个，已成立残疾人艺术团队 1 个。

七、体育

省级残疾人体育健身活动 4 次，参加人数 0.10 万人；残疾人体育示范点 3 个；残疾人体育比赛 3 次，参与的残疾人运动员 320 人次；残疾人体育训练基地 1 个。

地市级残疾人体育健身活动 2 次，参加人数 0.03 万人。

八、维权

制定或修改了关于残疾人的专门法规、规章省级 1 件；制定或修改了保障残疾人权益的规范性文件省级 11 件、地市级 1 件；县级以上人大执法检查或专题调研 14 次，政协视察和专题调研 4 次。

开展普法宣传教育活动 66 次，参加人数 0.57 万人；开展法律培训班 15 次，参加人数 0.04 万人；建立残疾人法律救助协调机构 55 个；建立残疾人法律援助中心（工作站）55 个，办理案件 197 件； 协助残联系统人大代表、政协委员提出议案、建议、提案 7 件，办理议案、建议、提案 7 件。

无障碍建设与管理法规、政府令 1 个；无障碍建设领导协调组织 55 个；系统开展无障碍建设市、县 11 个；贫困残疾人家庭无障碍改造 0.20 万户，无障碍培训 0.01 万人次 ， 残疾人机动轮椅车燃油补贴 0.37 万人。

各级残联共处理残疾人群众来信 0.01 万件，接待残疾人群众来访 0.06 万人次。

九、组织建设

8 个地市级残联（含直辖市的县、区）中，2 个领导班子配备了残疾人理事长或副理事长。46 个县级残联中，11 个县级残联机关配备了残疾人干部。

在残疾人专职委员选聘方面，0.04 万个乡镇（街道）中，选聘残疾人专职委员 0.05 万名；0.46 万个社区（村）中，选聘残疾人专职委员 0.29 万名。

残联干部综合培训工作取得较好成绩。全国省市县乡残联实有人员已达 0.13 人，干部培训工作取得新进展。

十、服务设施建设

截止到 2012 年底，已竣工并投入使用的各级残疾人综合服务设施共计 31 个，在建项目共计 1 个，筹建项目共计 5 个。其中已竣工并投入使用的各级残疾人综合服务设施总占地面积 2.35 万平方米，总建设规模 1.30 万平方米，总投资 0.37 亿元；已竣工并投入使用的各级康复设施共计 1 个，总占地面积 0.51 万平方米，总建设规模 0.16 万平方米，总投资 0.08 亿元；在建的各级托养设施共计项目共计 1 个。

十一、信息化建设

统计队伍建设进一步加强，各级残联共有 60 名专、兼职统计人员从事残疾人事业统计工作，统计人员业务素质培养普遍得到重视，省级残联举办培训班1期，参加培训的人员达到80人次；地市级举办培训班8期，参加培训的人员达到127人次。

地方残联全面推进网站建设，目前1个省级残联已全部开通了公众服务网站，有3个地市级残联网站和3个县级残联网站也已开通，网站总数比去年增加1个。这为今后残联系统网站集群服务奠定了基础，残联系统网上信息服务正在逐步覆盖全国。地方残联也积极举办各类信息工作培训班，2012年省级及地市级残联开设网站技术培训班8期，培训各级残联信息员达176人次。

各级残联共有69名专业技术人员从事信息化工作；省级残联建立局域网1个。

2012 年宁夏回族自治区残疾人事业发展统计公报

2012 年自治区残疾人工作在自治区党委、政府的正确领导下，在中国残联的指导下，全区残疾人工作者坚持“以残疾人为本，服务为先”的理念，以“十二五”规划为目标任务，大力推进两个体系建设，全面完成了年度工作任务，取得了显著成绩。

一、康复

（一）社区康复

2012 年，我区紧紧围绕残疾人“人人享有康复服务”目标，大力推进残疾人社区康复工作。全区 22 个县（市、区）全部开展社区康复服务，已开展社区康复服务的社区（村）累计 736 个，其中已建康复站的社区（村）477 个。社区康复协调员总数 1371 人。

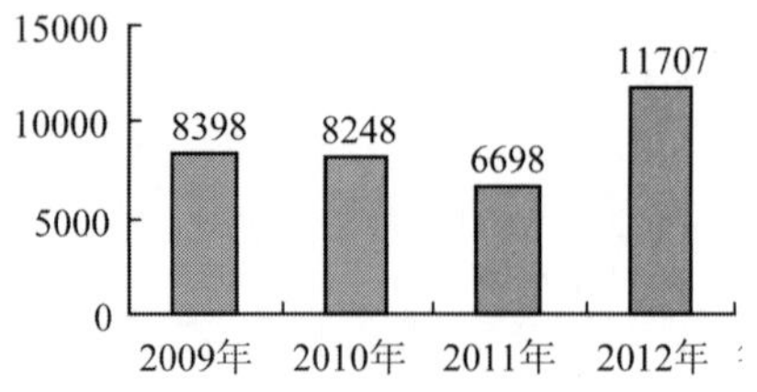

图 1　接受社区康复服务人数（人）

（二）视力残疾康复

本年度白内障复明手术 2629 例，其中贫困白内障患者免费手术 1884 例，低视力者配用助视器 2071 人，盲人定向行走训练 1127 人。

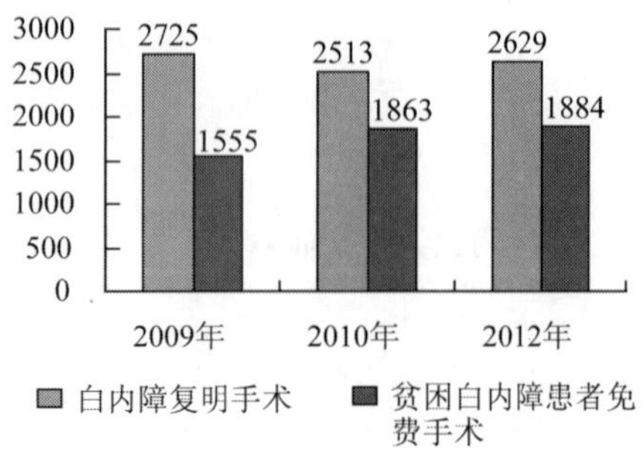

图 2　白内障复明手术统计分析（例）

（三）听力语言残疾康复

本年度在训聋儿 151 人，其中新收训聋儿 53 人，培训家长 413 人，接受地方项目救助 20 人。开展成年听力语言康复技术服务 123 人次。

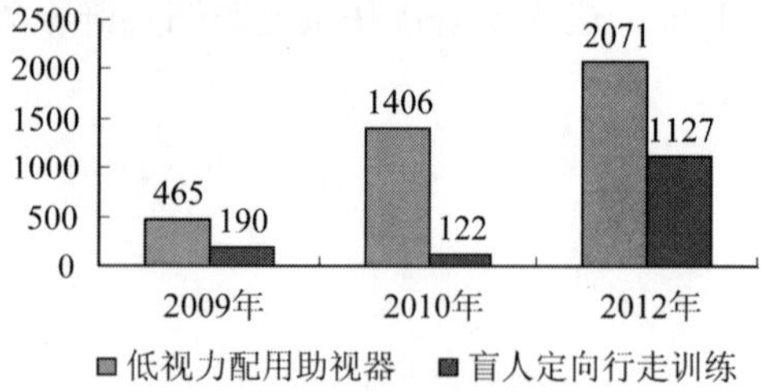

图 3　视力残疾康复情况（人）

（四）肢体残疾康复

本年度肢体残疾康复 4869 人，其中脑瘫儿童机构康复训练 183 人，肢体残疾儿童社区、家庭康复 96 人，成年肢体残疾人社区、家庭康复 4590 人。贫困肢体残疾儿童矫治手术 59 例，康复管理技术人员培训 170 人次。开展肢体残疾康复训练服务机构 11 个。

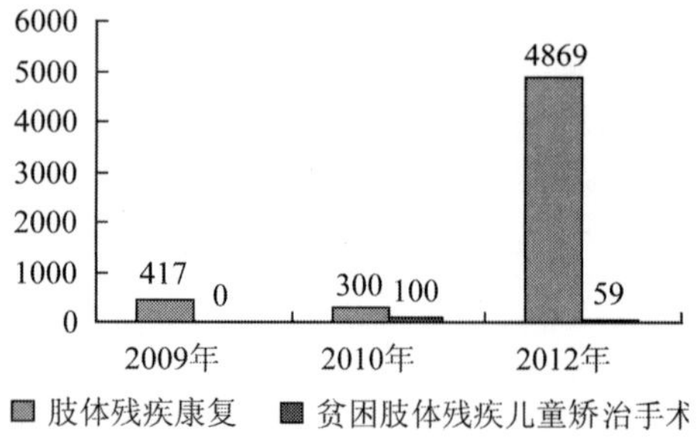

图 4　肢体残疾康复情况（人、例）

（五）智力残疾康复

本年度智力残疾儿童康复 854 人，其中智力残疾儿童机构康复训练 145 人，社区、家庭康复 709 人。开展智力残疾康复训练服务机构 11 个。

（六）精神残疾康复

精神病防治康复开展工作县（市、区）21 个，覆盖总人口 661.8 万，精神病人数 34374 人，监护病人数 30174 人，显好病人数 21013 人，参与社会总人数 17346 人，肇事人次 92 次，接受治疗的精神病患者 5877 人，接受康复训练 2553 人。精神病康复机构数 9 个，其中病人数 1080 人。贫困患者 10964 人，其中接受医疗救助的贫困患者 4046 人，接受国家专项彩金服药救助项目医疗救助的贫困患者 3662 人，接受国家专项彩金住院救助项目医疗救助的贫困患者 384 人。发现关锁病人 4 人，解除关锁病人

2 人。培训精防康复管理、技术人员 75 人。年度工作经费投入 150 万元。

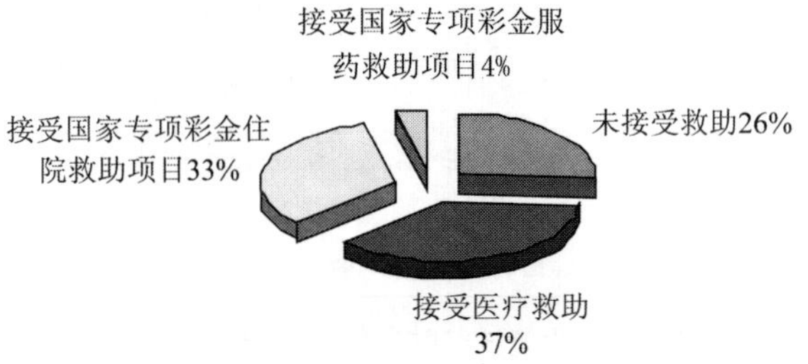

图 5　2012 年度贫困精神患者救助情况

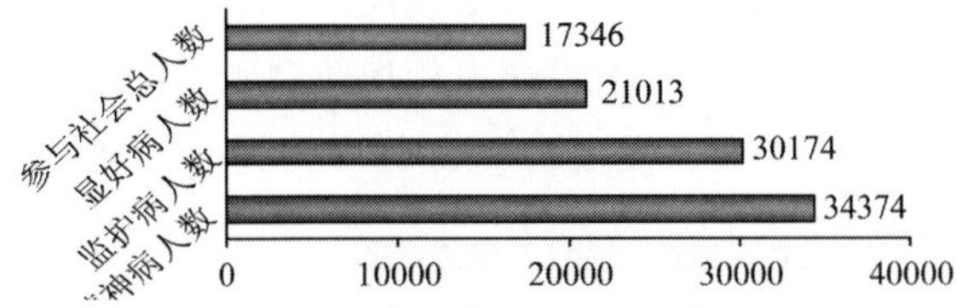

图 6　2012 年度精神防治工作情况（人）

孤独症儿童康复训练机构 11 个，机构内教师人数 29 人，机构内在训儿童 103 人，贫困孤独症儿童救助 48 人，

（七）辅助器具供应

本年度供应各类辅具 24677 件。矫形器装配 94 例，其中国家彩金项目装配 89 例，占 95%。假肢装配 216 例，其中国家彩金项目装配 203 例，占 94%。其他辅助器具供应 24367 件，其中国家彩金项目免费发放 7445 件，占 31%。

表 1　辅助器具供应情况

名　　称	2009 年	2010 年	2011 年	2012 年
矫形器装配总例数	43	66	106	94
国家彩金项目残疾人矫形器装配例数	0	0	106	89
假肢装配总例数	265	281	373	216
国家彩金项目残疾人假肢装配例数	0	0	348	203
其他辅助器具供应总件数	7651	6656	6082	24367

（八）儿童残疾预防

本年度开展残疾儿童筛查县（市、区）7 个，本年度新诊断 0—6 岁残疾儿童 266 人，发放儿童残疾预防宣传材料 26550 份，举办儿童残疾预防宣传活动 30 次。设立残疾儿童家长学校累计 11 个，开展活动 25 次，家长参与 720 人次。

（九）康复人才

康复机构在岗人员 340 人，其中自治区级 64 人，地市级 117 人，县级 159 人。本年度举办康复管理人员培训班 11 期，培训康复管理人员 235 人；举办康复业务人员培训班 17 期，培训康复业务人员 400 人；举办康复协调员培训班 13 期，培训康复协调员 709 人。

二、教育

（一）学前教育康复阶段

本年度接受残疾人事业专项彩票公益金助学项目资助 60 人，残疾人事业专项彩票公益金助学项目资助新入园 29 人，其他残疾儿童学前教育助学项目资助 24 人。

（二）义务教育阶段

未入学学龄残疾儿童少年 942 人，其中视力残疾 42 人，听力残疾 36 人，言语残疾 57 人，肢体残疾 255 人，智力残疾 373 人，精神残疾 30 人，多重残疾 149 人。

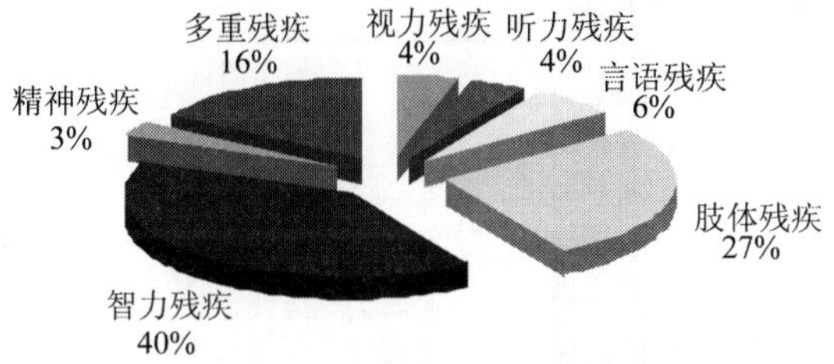

图 7　未入学学龄残疾儿童少年情况

（三）高中教育阶段

特殊教育普通高中学校 1 所，在校生 284 人，其中盲 36 人，占 12.7%；聋 248 人，占 87.3%。

（四）高等教育阶段

普通高等院校录取残疾学生 116 人，其中盲 15 人，聋 14 人，肢体 87 人。

三、就业

（一）城乡残疾人就业状况

1. 城镇残疾人就业状况

累计就业人数 22637 人，其中集中就业合计 4958 人，按比例就业合计 6046 人，公益性岗位就业 458 人，个体及其他形式就业合计 11075 人，辅助性就业 100 人。未就业合计 9910 人。

2. 农村残疾人就业状况

累计就业人数 108403 人，其中从事农业生产劳动 90042 人，占 83%；其他形式就业 18361 人，占

17%。未就业合计27632人。

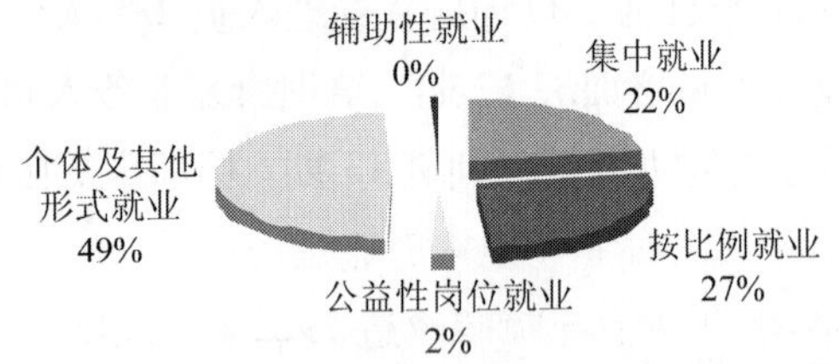

图8　城镇残疾人就业状况

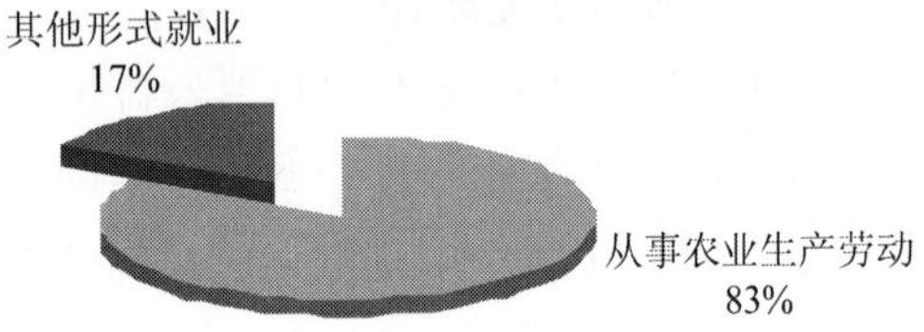

图9　农村残疾人就业状况

（二）盲人按摩

累计开设保健按摩机构104个。本年度培训保健按摩人员289人，医疗按摩人员22人。盲人保健按摩人员就业271人，盲人医疗按摩人员就业19人，扶持特困盲人按摩师就业20人。

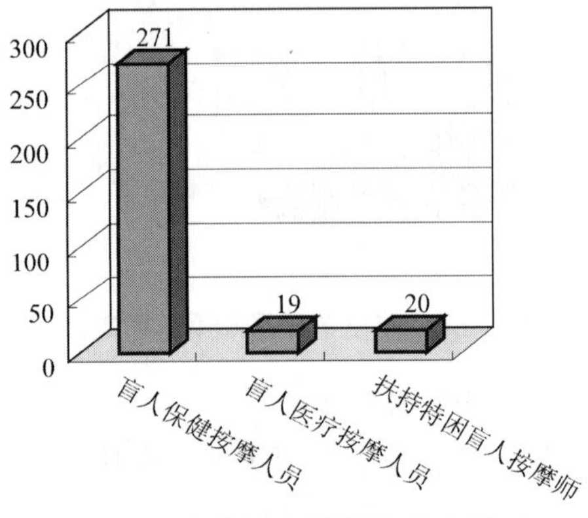

图10　盲人按摩就业情况（人）

四、扶贫

农村贫困残疾人户73155户，本年度扶持残疾人户13630户；贫困残疾人92154人，低收入残疾人18580人，本年度扶持残疾人15380人次。本年度脱贫残疾人11340人次，脱贫12%。本年度返贫人数1567人。本年度实用技术培训6969人次，各地投入经费共计161万元。

本年度康复扶贫贴息项目贷款1336万元，中央贴息66.8万元，扶持残疾人1024人。本年度到户贷款717万元，中央贴息50.2万元，扶持残疾人384人。

本年度联系社会结对帮扶单位316个，结对帮扶残疾人1360人。

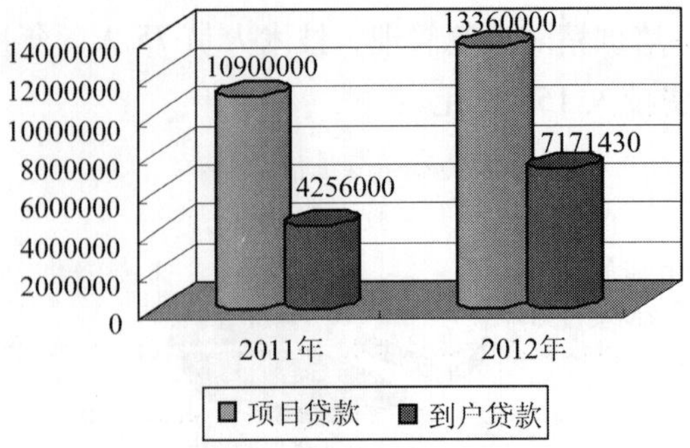

图11　康复扶贫贴息贷款情况（元）

累计建设残疾人扶贫基地24个，本年度安置残疾人就业685人，扶持带动残疾人3185人。

本年度农村贫困残疾人危房改造1560户，受益残疾人1714人，投入资金2006.2万元。

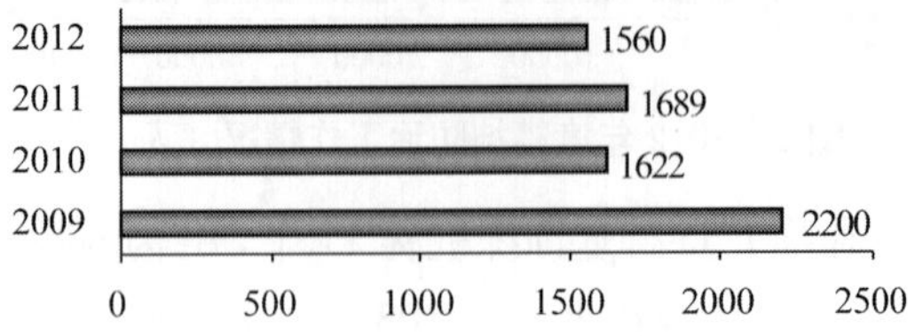

图12　贫困残疾人危房改造情况（户）

五、社会保障

城镇残疾职工参加社会保险人数合计9354人，城镇残疾居民参加社会保险人数合计84012人。符合参保条件的残疾居民54366人，实际参保45391人，参保率83.5%。其中符合参加社会养老保险的重度残疾人10994人，获得全额代缴和部分代缴10947人，代缴率99.6%。

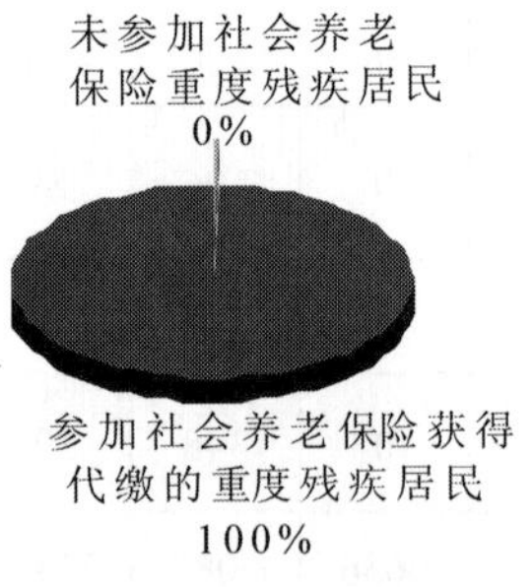

图13　城镇重度残疾居民参加社会养老保险情况

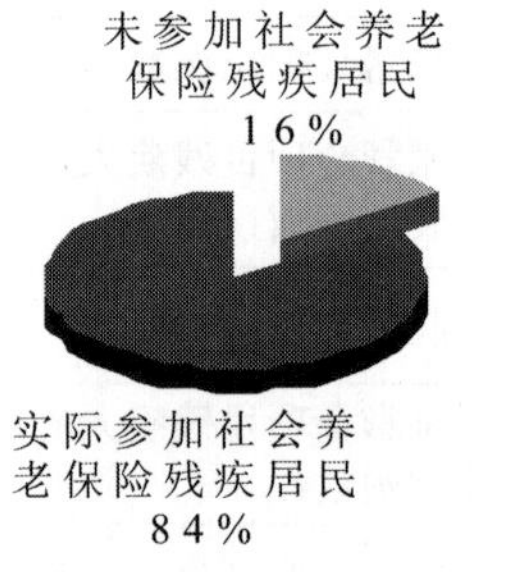

图14　城镇残疾居民参加社会养老保险情况

农村居民参加新型农村合作医疗人数972278人，农村居民参加新型农村社会养老保险135592人，参保率84%；其中符合参加新型农村社会养老保险的重度残疾人32392人，获得全额代缴和部分代缴31977人，代缴率98.7%。

城镇已纳入最低生活保障范围17328人，集中供养567人，其他救助救济7533人。

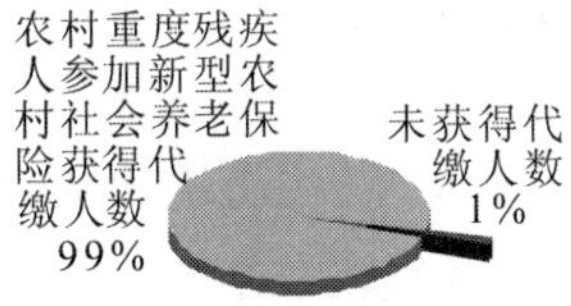

图 15 农村重度残疾人参加新型新型农村社会养老保险情况

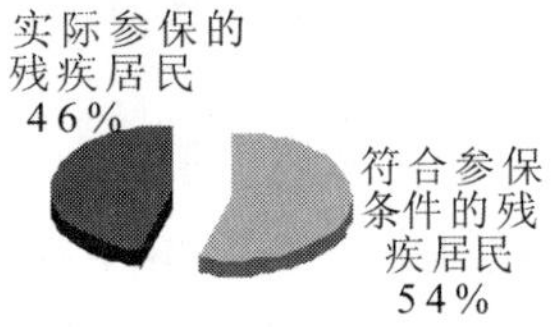

图 16 农村残疾居民参加农村社会养老保险情况

农村已纳入最低生活保障范围 86623 人，五保供养 1515 人，其他救助救济 13241 人。

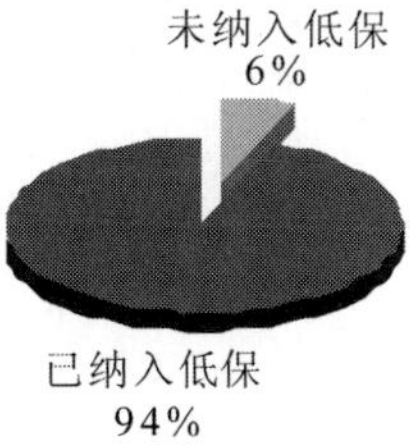

图 17 农村贫困残疾人享受低保情况

本年度享受生活补贴的人数 13378 人。

六、托养服务

设立寄宿制托养服务机构 8 个，托养残疾人数 263 人；设立日间照料托养服务机构 33 个，托养残疾人 906 人。本年度享受居家托养服务残疾人 11991 人。

七、体育宣传文化

（一）体育

区、市级残联举办残疾人群众体育健身活动 12 次，参加人数 710 人次。设立残疾人群众体育活动示范点 15 个，残疾人体育训练基地 2 个。聘请残疾人体育健身指导员 148 名。

（二）宣传

区、市级残联本年度中央级媒体采用稿件数 10 件，主要新闻媒体刊播稿件数 984 件，报纸专版 22 个，广播电台残疾人专题节目 6 个，电视手语栏目 3 个，电视公益广告片 6 个，报纸公益广告 5 个。

（三）文化

全区建立公共图书馆盲文及盲人有声读物图书室 6 个，举办残疾人文化周 11 场次，残疾人文化艺术类的比赛及展览 12 次，成立残疾人艺术团队 2 个。

八、维权

（一）维权

本年度全区人大执法检查或专题调研 12 次，政协视察或专题调研 7 次，开展普法宣传教育活动 45 次，建立残疾人法律救助工作站 4 个，残疾人法律援助中心（工作站）24 个，办理案件 179 件。全区选举残疾人参政议政的人大代表 10 人、政协委员 25 人。全区系统开展无障碍建设市、县 23 个，开展贫困残疾人家庭无障碍改造 1922 户，残疾人机动轮椅车燃油补贴 14648 人。

（二）信访

自治区级来信 13 件，来访 418 人次；地市级来信 42 件，来访 309 人次；县级来信 108 件，来访 1381 人次。

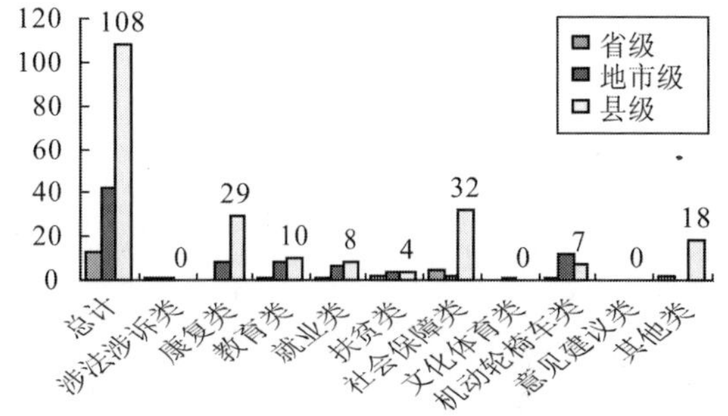

图 18 来信情况统计（件）

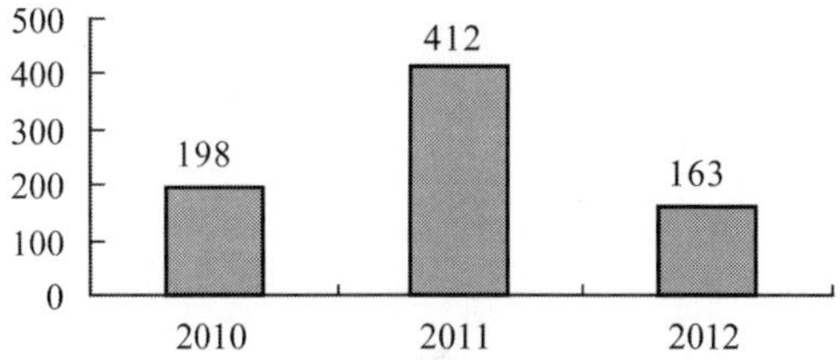

图 19 来信情况统计分析（件）

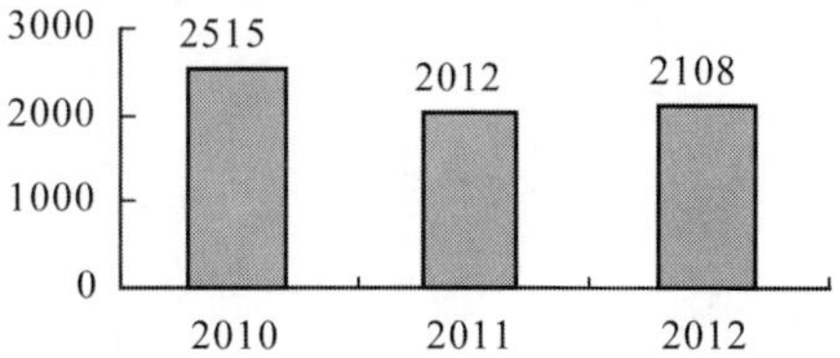

图 20 上访情况统计分析（次）

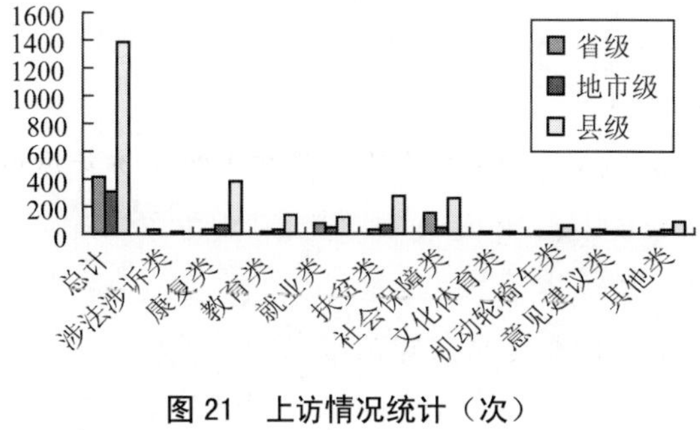

图 21 上访情况统计（次）

九、组织建设

28 个区、市、县（区、市）残联编制 489 人，实有人员 1021 人，其中有 17 个残联配备了残疾人领导干部。225 个乡（镇、街道）全部设立残联，志愿者登记注册 23175 人，受助残疾人 15823 人；村（社区）应建残协 2013 个，已建残协 1759 个，完成 87%。志愿者登记注册 13334 人，受助残疾人 11353 人。自治区残联举办干部队伍综合培训 2 期，地市级举办 12 期，县级举办 44 期，总计 58 期，参加培训 2108 人。5 个地级市残联全部建立残疾人专门协会，其中有 4 个进行了社团登记。22 个县（市、区），其中有 20 个建立了残疾人专门协会，16 个进行了社团登记。截止 2012 年底，全区已办理残疾人证 19.8 万本，办证率 46%。

十、信息化建设与事业统计

全区残联共有统计人员 23 人，其中有统计从业资格证书 9 人。本年度区、市级残联举办统计业务培训 6 期，236 人参加了培训。

4 个地市级、8 个县级残联开通了门户网站，本年度区、市级残联举办信息工作培训班 6 期，152 人参加了培训。自治区残联网站发稿量 1210 篇。

全区残联计算机数量 360 台。本年度投入信息化建设经费 70 万元。

2012 年新疆维吾尔自治区残疾人事业发展统计公报

2012 年自治区残联认真贯彻落实党的十八大和自治区党委八届四次全委（扩大）会议精神，努力实现新疆残疾人事业跨越发展，通过自治区组织民生工程中的富民安居工程、儿童康复救助、白内障复明、阳光家园托养工程和自治区残联大力实施扶贫就业基地建设、光明工程、农村基层党组织助残扶贫、爱心天使助学基金、贫困残疾人康复救助关爱、社区康复建设、儿童助听、阳光助行、肢体残疾假肢装配、残疾人驾驶机动燃油补贴等惠残工程，改善了残疾人的生存状况；残疾人康复、教育、就业、扶贫、社会保障、文化宣传体育、权益保障、无障碍环境建设、基层设施建设、慈善捐助、信息化建设、理论研究和援疆工作都取得了新成绩。现根据 2012 年度残疾人事业统计数据和实际情况，进行分析，并公报如下:

一、康复

2012 年，通过实施一批重点康复工程，使各类别残疾人得到不同程度的康复。全年完成白内障复明手术 1.3 万例，为 0.6 万名贫困白内障患者免费施行复明手术，由图 1-1 可以看出实施贫困白内障患者免费复明手术人数逐年递增，自治区残联每年都在加大对此项目的投资力度，使更多残疾人恢复光明。全年为 1415 名低视力患者配用助视器，培训低视力儿童家长 145 名，有效开展家庭康复训练。对 656 名盲人进行定向行走训练。

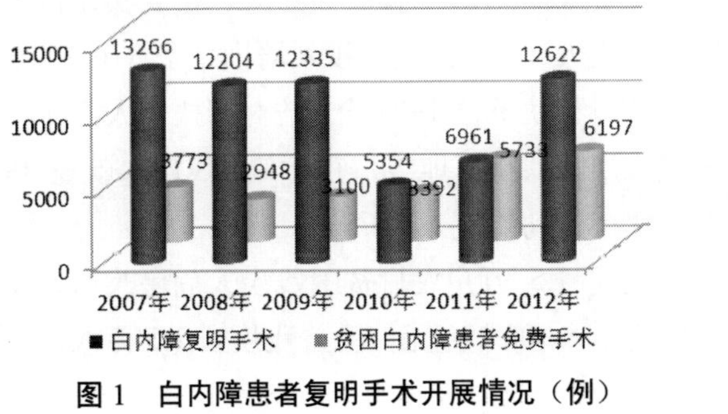

图 1 白内障患者复明手术开展情况（例）

自治区残联加强省级聋儿康复机构建设，完善聋儿康复网络。共对 528 名聋儿进行了听力语言康复训练，规范聋儿家长学校，开展家庭训练，共培训聋儿家长 1510 名；培养各类专业人员 325 人。

大力推广“社会化、综合性、开放式”精神病防治康复工作。2012 年，在 68 个市县开展精神病防治康复工作，对 2.5 万名重性精神病患者进行综合防治康复，监护率达到 63.9%，显好率达到 32.7%，社会参与率达到 22.0%，肇事率 0.05%；解除关锁 6 人；对 4634 名贫困精神病患者进行医疗救助。

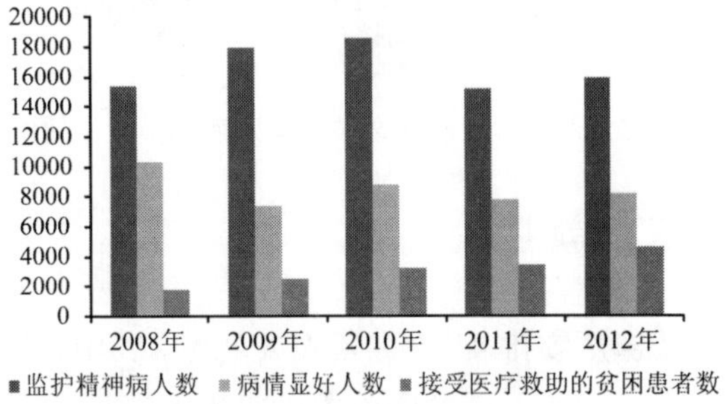

图 2 精神病防治康复工作情况（人）

自治区残联康复中心建有 1 个省级孤独症儿童康复训练机构，对 61 名孤独症儿童进行了康复训练。

深入开展辅助器具供应服务，全面推进普及型假肢装配，截止到 2012 年底，累计建立辅助器具供应服务机构 16 个，为残疾人装配普及型假肢 1262 例，供应辅助器具 1.6 万件，装配矫形器 476 例。

全年开展肢体残疾康复训练服务的机构达到 34 个，对 71 名贫困肢体残疾儿童实施矫治手术、装配了矫形器等辅助器具，进行了术后康复训练；对 5136 名肢体残疾人进行了康复训练，其中：脑瘫儿童系统康复训练 514 人，肢体残疾儿童社区、家庭康复 463 人，成年肢体残疾人社区、家庭康复 4159 人。

全年开展智力残疾康复训练服务的机构达到 15 个；对 1398 名智力残疾儿童进行了康复训练，不同程度地开展了智力残疾儿童早期康复训练与服务。

在 10 个市辖区和 79 个县（市）开展了社区康复工作，累计建立社区康复站 1374 个，配备 3388 名社区康复协调员。

二、教育

开办特殊教育聋普通高中 1 所，在校生 58 人。

残疾人中等职业教育机构 2 个，在校生 526 人，毕业生 142 人，其中获得职业资格证书 109 人。有 239 名残疾人被普通高等院校录取。

未入学适龄残疾儿童少年总数 3692 人，其中视力残疾 189 人，听力残疾 145 人，言语残疾 286 人，肢体残疾 1028 人，智力残疾 1260 人，精神残疾 190 人，多重残疾 594 人。

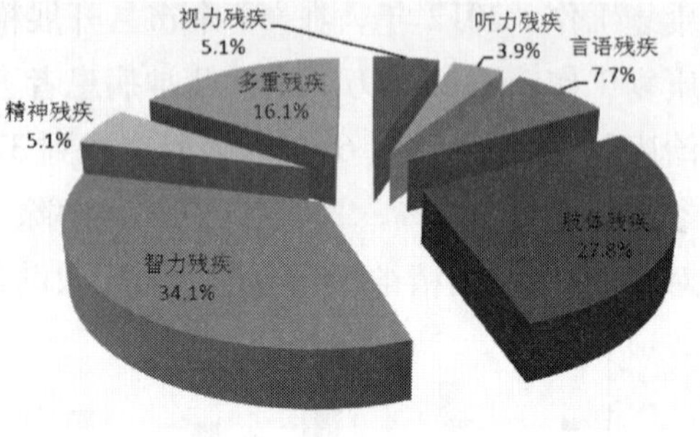

图 3 未入学残疾儿童中各类残疾儿童所占比例

三、就业

城镇新安排 4141 名残疾人就业。其中，集中就业残疾人 995 人，按比例安排残疾人就业 1541 人，公益性岗位就业 224 人，个体及其它形式就业 1114 人，辅助性就业 267 人，全疆城镇实际在业人数 7.0 万人；21.6 万农村残疾人稳定实现就业，其中从事农业生产劳动 18.5 万人。

职业培训基地 282 个,其中残联兴办 42 个，本年度城镇职业培训人数 4793 人。

培训盲人保健按摩 149 人；医疗按摩人员 98，保健按摩机构达到 77 个，医疗按摩机构达到 9 个；有 55 人通过医疗按摩人员中级和初级职称评审。

四、社会保障

城镇残疾职工参加社会保险人数达到 4.8 万人，其中参加养老保险人数 3.0 万人，参加医疗保险人数 3.3 万人；城镇残疾居民参加医疗保险达到 9.2 万人。城镇居民符合参加社会养老保险条件的残疾居民人数 12.2 万，实际参加社会养老保险人数 7.5 万，参保率 61.5%；城镇居民 60 周岁以下参加社会养老保险的重度残疾人 0.8 万人，其中 0.7 万人获得全额或部分代缴，重度残疾人代缴率达到 91%。农村居民参加新型农村合作医疗人数 25.4 万人，农村居民符合参加新型农村社会养老保险人数 22.5 万人，实际参保人数 17.5 万，参保率 78%；农村居民 60 周岁以下参加新型农村养老保险的重度残疾人 3.5 万人，其中 3.3 万人获得全额或部分代缴，代缴率达到 94%。

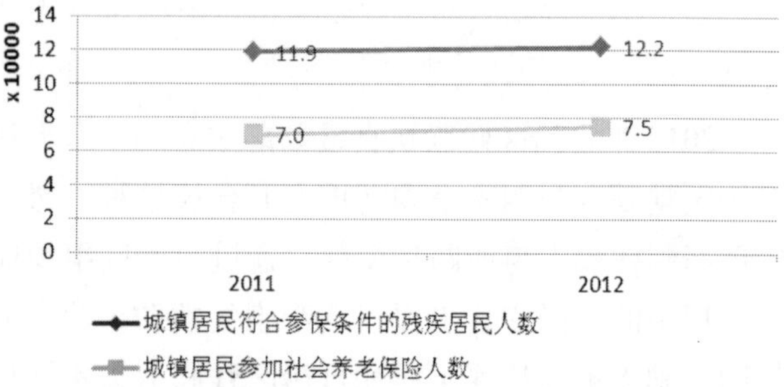

图 4 城镇居民参加社会养老保险情况（万人）

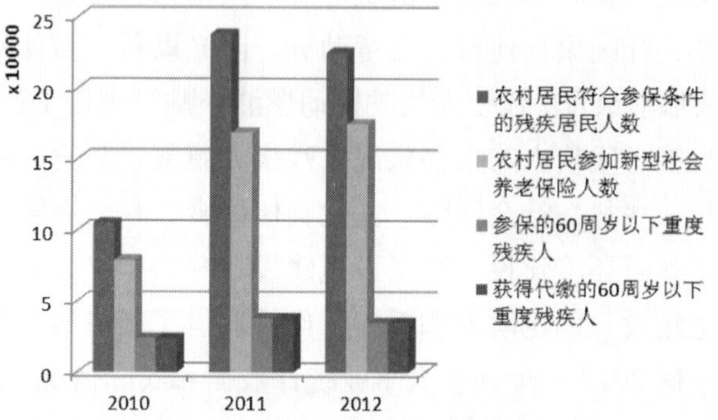

图 5 农村居民参加新型社会养老保险情况（万人）

城乡 19.2 万名残疾人纳入最低生活保障范围，其中城镇已纳入最低生活保障 5.5 万人，农村已纳入最低生活保障 13.7 万人；城镇集中供养和其他救助救济 1.5 万人；农村五保供养和其他救助救济 1.7 万人。

寄宿制托养机构 16 个，托养残疾人 1792 人；日间照料托养机构合计 46 个，托养残疾人 541 人；本年度享受居家托养服务残疾人 1.8 万人。

五、扶贫

本年度扶持贫困残疾人户 1.8 万户，扶持 2.7 万人，脱贫 8206 人，返贫 1666 人，接受实用技术培训的残疾人 2.1 万人次，投入培训经费 370.0 万元。

结对帮扶单位 1991 个，结对帮扶个人 5721 人；建立残疾人扶持基地 98 个，安置残疾人就业 1918 人，扶持带动残疾人 3570 户。

完成 1.5 万户农村贫困残疾人危房改造，投入危房资金 8,902.2 万元，受益残疾人 1.5 万人。

六、宣传文化

省级中央媒体采用稿件 50 件，主要新闻媒体刊播稿件数 260 件，报刊专版 3 个，残疾人专题广播节目 1 个，电视手语新闻栏目 1 个，省级残疾人事业新闻宣传促进会 1 个。

地市级主要新闻媒体刊播稿件数 1078 件，报刊专版 20 个，残疾人专题广播节目 24 个，电视手语新闻栏目 4 个，建立地市级新促会 3 个。

省级和地市级公共图书馆设立盲文及盲人有声读物阅览室已分别达到 3 个和 5 个，分别举办残疾人文化周 2 个和 59 个，举办残疾人文化艺术类比赛及展览分别是 3 个和 21 个，已成立残疾人艺术团队 1 个和 4 个。

七、体育

省级残疾人体育健身活动 6 次，参加人数 600 人，残疾人体育训练基地 4 个，聘任教练员 12 人。

地市级残疾人体育健身活动 31 次，参加人数 6365 人，残疾人体育示范点 4 个，残疾人体育健身指导员 14 人。

八、维权

制定或修改了关于残疾人的专门法规、规章地市级 1 件；县级以上人大执法检查或专题调研 14 次，政协视察和专题调研 14 次。

开展普法宣传教育活动 253 次，参加人数 6.5 万人；

开展法律培训班 39 次，参加人数 0.15 万人；

建立残疾人法律救助协调机构 46 个；

建立残疾人法律救助工作站 16 个，办理案件 98 件；

表 1　各级残联处理残疾人群众来信分类表（单位：件）

1. 涉法涉诉类	51
2. 康复类	510
3. 教育类	135
4. 就业类	393
5. 扶贫类	413
6. 社会保障类	292
7. 文化体育类	56
8. 机动轮椅车类	383
9. 意见建议类	109
10. 其他类	240

建立残疾人法律援助中心（工作站）86 个，办理案件 844 件；协助残联系统人大代表、政协委员提出议案、建议、提案 51 件，办理议案、建议、提案 39 件。

无障碍建设与管理法规、政府令 9 个；无障碍建设领导协调组织 43 个；系统开展无障碍建设市、县 2 个；贫困残疾人家庭无障碍改造 2070 户，无障碍检查 141 次，无障碍培训 848 人次，残疾人机动轮椅车燃油补贴 1.1 万人。

各级残联共处理残疾人群众来信 0.26 万件，接待残疾人群众来访 1.5 万人次，未发生集体来访。

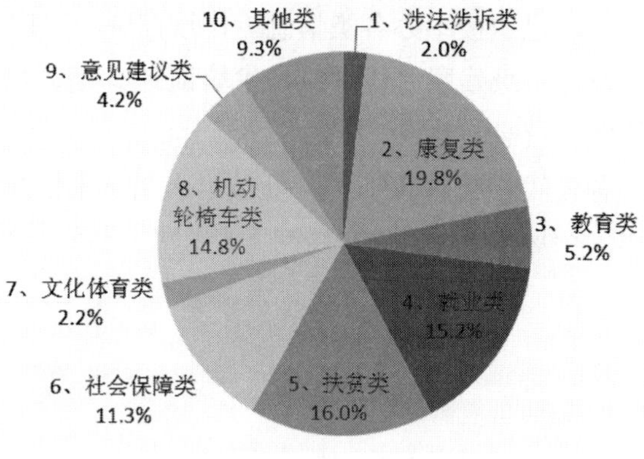

图 6　残疾人群众来信分类占比情况图

九、组织建设

2012 年，领导班子基本上都配备了残疾人理事长或副理事长，省级残联配备了 1 个驻会盲人理事，1 个驻会聋人理事。14 个地市级残联中，11 个地市残联的领导班子配备了残疾人理事长或副理事长。95 个县级残联中，57 个县级残联机关配备了残疾人干部。

在残疾人专职委员选聘方面，乡镇（街道）选聘残疾人专职委员 1326 名；社区（村）选聘残疾人专职委员 4320 名。

残联干部综合培训工作取得较好成绩。自治区各级残联实有人员已达 3071 人，干部培训工作取得新进展。

自治区共建立各类残疾人专门协会 546 个，其中盲人协会 110 个、聋人协会 110 个、肢残人协会 110 个、智力残疾人及亲友协会 106 个、精神残疾人及亲友协会 106 个、智力残疾人及亲友协会和精神残疾人及亲友协会二者合一的 4 个。

十、信息化

统计队伍建设进一步加强，各级残联共有96名专、兼职统计人员从事残疾人事业统计工作，统计人员业务素质培养普遍得到重视，省级残联举办培训班1期，参加培训的人员达到20人次；地市级举办培训班8期，参加培训的人员达到76人次。

地方残联全面推进网站建设，目前省级残联已开通了1个公众服务网站，有9个地市级残联网站和24个县级残联网站也已开通，网站总数比去年增加4个。这为今后残联系统网站集群服务奠定了基础，残联系统网上信息服务正在逐步覆盖全疆。地市级残联也积极举办各类信息工作培训班，2012年省级及地市级残联开设网站技术培训班5期，培训各级残联信息员达98人次。

各级残联共有132名专业技术人员从事信息化工作；省级残联共建立局域网1个，网上办公（OA）系统1个，邮件系统1个。

十一、基础设施

截止到2012年底，已竣工并投入使用的各级残疾人综合服务设施共计51个，在建项目共计18个，筹建项目共计7个。其中已竣工并投入使用的各级残疾人综合服务设施总占地面积11.1万平方米，总建筑面积12.0万平方米，总投资2.6亿元。

已竣工并投入使用的各级康复设施共计2个，已竣工并投入使用的各级康复设施总占地面积0.06万平方米，总建设规模0.2万平方米，总投资0.03亿元。

已竣工并投入使用的各级托养设施共计1个，在建项目共计1个，其中已竣工并投入使用的各级托养设施总占地面积0.3万平方米，总建设规模0.3万平方米，总投资0.09亿元。

2012年新疆生产建设兵团残疾人事业发展统计公报

2012年，兵团残疾人事业深入贯彻落实《中共中央、国务院关于促进残疾人事业发展的意见》，按照《兵团残疾人事业“十二五”发展纲要（2011-2015）》年度目标任务，紧紧围绕残疾人社会保障体系和服务体系建设，以改善残疾人基本生活为重点，扎实工作，各项工作有了新的起色，兵团残疾人事业发展呈现良好态势。

一、康复

通过实施一批重点康复工程，使各类别残疾人得到不同程度的康复。围绕“人人享有康复服务”的工作目标，充分发动和利用社会资源，积极推进社区康复示范团场创建活动。

14个师有11个师直单位和73个团场开展了社区康复工作，累计建立社区康复站99个，配备272名社区康复协调员。

全年完成白内障复明手术1671例；为452名贫困白内障患者免费施行复明手术；全年为1004名低视力患者配用助视器，培训低视力儿童家长17名。对212名盲人进行定向行走训练。

开展听力语言康复工作，新收训聋儿35人，其中机构训练14人，家庭训练21人，在训聋儿66人，培训聋儿家长62人；为成年听力语言残疾人提供康复技术服务68人次。

大力推广“社会化、综合性、开放式”精神病防治康复工作。在6个师开展精神病防治康复工作，覆盖总人口17.6万人，精神病人建档数9819人，有6882名精神病人得到有效监护，监护率达到70.08%，显好率达到44.89%，社会参与率达到35.58%，肇事率0.03%；对2912名重度精神病患者进行综合防治康复，对1876名贫困患者进行医疗救助，其中，通过“彩票公益金康复项目”资助800名贫困精神病患者免费服药，救助150名重症患者得到免费住院治疗，接受其他项目医疗救助926名贫困患者，各级投入经费227万多元。

对1036名肢体残疾人进行了康复训练，其中：实施救助项目资助25名脑瘫儿童进行机构康复训练,资助21名贫困肢体残疾儿童实施矫治手术。肢体残疾儿童社区、家庭康复训练训练94人，成人肢体残疾人社区、家庭康复训练917人。

对234名智力残疾儿童不同程度地开展了早期康复训练与服务，其中，实施救助项目资助35名智力残疾儿童进行机构康复训练；智力残疾儿童社区、家庭康复训练199人；成年智力残疾人社区、家庭康复训练159人。

开展辅助器具供应服务，全年供应各类残疾人辅助器具2261件，其中，为贫困残疾人免费发放1432件，为贫困残疾人矫形器装配43例，装配普及型假肢106例，验配助视器1006件。

二、教育

残疾人受教育权得到了更好保障，残疾儿童少年九年义务教育全面普及，学前教育阶段本年度接受残疾人事业专项彩票公益金助学项目资助30人次；认真做好残疾学生参加高考工作，有42名残疾学生被疆内外普通高等院校录取。

三、就业

城镇新安排774名残疾人就业。其中，集中就业残疾人216人，按比例安排残疾人就业372人，公益性岗位就业40人，个体及其它形式就业124人，辅助性就业94人，全兵团城镇实际在业人数15731人；职业培训基地2个,其中，残联兴办1个，依托社会机构兴办1个,1035人次接受了城镇职业培训。

培训盲人保健按摩38人，保健按摩机构共26个，医疗按摩机构7个；有9人和4人通过医疗按摩人员中级和初级职称评审。

四、社会保障

城镇残疾职工参加社会保险人数合计17511人，参加养老保险人数11179人，参加医疗保险人数12350人；城镇残疾居民参加社会保险达到24535人；城镇残疾居民参加城镇居民医疗保险人数为

21353 人，城镇残疾居民参加城镇居民社会养老保险符合条件的残疾居民有 11145 人，实际参保的残疾居民有 7580 人；在 60 周岁以下的参保残疾人中有 2282 名重度残疾人，1760 人和 164 人获得全额代缴和部分代缴优惠政策；城镇个体就业参加社会保险人数有 2515 人，个体就业参加养老保险人数 1900 人，个体就业参加医疗保险人数为 1271 人；城镇已纳入最低生活保障 20833 人，城镇集中供养和其他救助救济 8623 人。

残疾人托养服务工作稳步推进，寄宿制托养机构 18 个，托养残疾人 780 人；日间照料托养机构 2 个，托养残疾人 100 人；本年度享受居家托养服务残疾人 4820 人。

五、扶贫开发

扶贫开发成效显著，贫困残疾人生产生活状况得到进一步改善。扶持贫困残疾人户 8963 户，扶持 20169 人次，脱贫 2376 人次，返贫 610 人，接受实用技术培训的残疾人 11218 人次，投入培训经费 301.03 万元。

兵团财政预算投入扶贫资金 70 万元，使用中央财政专项贴息资金 76 万元，各级落实贴息资金 487.08 万元，为残疾人发放贷款 8323 万元，实际贴息贷款 7767.1 万元，扶持带动 2528 名贫困残疾人。1148 个单位和 2885 名个人对贫困残疾人开展结对帮扶；建立残疾人扶贫基地 8 个，安置残疾人就业 100 人，扶持带动残疾人 346 户。

将残疾人住房建设纳入兵团保障性住房建设年度计划，完成 3799 户贫困残疾人危房改造，投入危房资金 11298.5 万元，受益残疾人 3849 人。

六、维权

县级以上人大执法检查或专题调研 15 次；开展普法宣传教育活动 154 次，参加人数 50761 人；建立残疾人法律救助协调机构 2 个，建立残疾人法律救助工作站 1 个，办理案件 17 件；

建立残疾人法律援助中心（站、点）158 个，办理案件 139 件，有力地促进了法律援助和法律服务工作；残疾人参政议政工作得到加强，协助残联系统人大代表、政协委员提出议案、建议、提案 10 件，办理议案、建议、提案 3 件。

无障碍建设领导协调组织 5 个；开展无障碍检查 17 次；贫困残疾人家庭无障碍改造 348 户；为 1990 名残疾人发放机动轮椅车燃油补贴。

各级残联共处理残疾人群众来信 627 件，接待残疾人群众来访 2803 人次，其中集体访 1 批次，12 人次。

七、宣传文体

兵团残疾人事业宣传工作积极全面反映残疾人事业“两个体系”建设为残疾人生活带来的明显变化。圆满组织了以“加强残疾人文化服务保障残疾人文化权益”为主题的第二十二次全国助残日活动；积极宣传《无障碍环境建设条例》、《农村残疾人扶贫开发纲要》、《残疾人权利公约》履约等重大事件和重点工作。

省级主要新闻媒体刊播稿件数 290 件，电视手语新闻栏目 1 个，电视公益广告片 3 个，公益广告 15 个；地市级主要新闻媒体刊播稿件数 564 件，报刊专版 5 个，兵团“两刊”宣传工作荣获中国残联银牌奖。

残疾人文体工作趋于活跃，开展“残疾人文化周”、“全国特奥日”、“残疾人健身周”、“残疾人文化进社区”活动，省级和地市级举办残疾人文化周 1 和 17 个，举办残疾人文化艺术类比赛及展览分别是 1 和 3 个；2 名兵团残疾人运动员参加了第 14 届伦敦残奥会和残奥世界杯邀请赛并获得名次；省级残疾人体育健身活动 1 次，参加人数 50 人，残疾人体育健身指导员 2 人，聘任教练员 2 人；地市级残疾人体育健身活动 7 次，参加人数 1135 人，残疾残疾人体育健身指导员 12 人。

八、组织建设

兵团残联系统实有工作人员 300 人，其中省级实有工作人员 13 人，14 个地市级残联实有工作人员 49 人，省、地级残联下属事业单位 10 个，实有人员 39 人，县级残联 152 个，实有人员 190 人（兼职）；残疾人专职委员 68 人，志愿者登记在册总人数 1116 人。

省级以下共建立各类残疾人专门协会 53 个，其中盲人协会 10 个、聋人协会 9 个、肢残人协会 13 个、智力残疾人及亲友协会 10 个、精神残疾人及亲友协会10个、智力残疾人及亲友协会和精神残疾人及亲友协会二者合一的1个。

九、信息化建设

统计队伍建设进一步加强，各级残联共有177名兼职统计人员从事残疾人事业统计工作，统计人员业务素质培养普遍得到重视，省级残联举办培训班1期，参加培训的人员57人次；地市级举办培训班8期，参加培训的人员145人次。

推进网站建设，目前有1个省级1个地市级残联开通了公众服务网站。省级网站发稿量500篇，较上年多350篇。各级残联共有181名兼职人员从事信息化工作。

截至2012年底，兵团残疾人人口基础信息数据库累计采集、收录持证残疾人实名信息60983条。结合全国农村贫困残疾人扶贫调查，采集农牧团场贫困残疾人扶贫需求信息21623条。

十、服务设施建设

截至2012年底，已竣工并投入使用的各级残疾人综合服务设施共计11个，在建项目共计1个。其中已竣工并投入使用的各级残疾人综合服务设施总占地面积19393万平方米，总建设规模8102.19万平方米，总投资1307万元。

2012年黑龙江垦区残疾人事业发展统计公报

2012年是执行《中国残疾人事业“十二五”计划发展纲要》的攻坚年，在农垦总局党委的高度重视下，在中国残联的正确领导下，在全垦区残疾人工作者和广大残疾人的共同努力下，农垦总局残联全面完成了年初制定的工作目标，团结和带领全垦区残疾人在康复、教育、就业、扶贫、文化等各个方面取得了巨大的进步。现将2012年各项业务工作指标完成情况统计分析报告如下:

一、康复工作

紧紧围绕“人人享有康复服务”的目标，充分利用、整合资源，积极推进残疾人社区康复工作，使更多的残疾人享有康复服务并受益。

截止2012年底，全垦区共有21个农牧场开展社区康复服务，已开展康复服务的社区达37个，社区康复协调员累计达161人。已建社区康复服务档案人数37430人，占辖区内残疾人总数的41.44%，接受社区康复的人数累计达1372人，其中，本年度新增接受社区康复的人数为504人。

2012年，通过实施一批重点康复工程，使各类别残疾人得到不同程度的康复。全年完成白内障复明手术444例，为60名贫困白内障患者免费施行复明手术。低视力者配用助视器280人，培训低视力儿童家长120人，盲人定向行走训练280人。

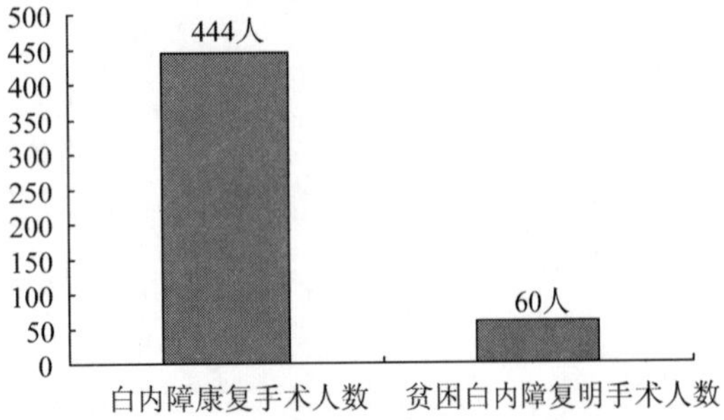

图1 2012年白内障康复手术人员统计图

大力推进精神病防治康复工作，按照“低水平覆盖”的要求，在全垦区范围内开展精神病防治康复工作，覆盖总人口163万余人，精神病总人数14440人，监护精神病人数6535人，显好精神病人数2363人。接受治疗的精神病患者2563人，精神病康复机构3家，在其中康复的精神病人数为627人。年度累计投入83万余元，其中，农场级年度经费投入74万元，管理局级年度经费投入9.4万元。

积极开展智力残疾人康复救助工作，为50名智力残疾儿童提供机构康复训练，为236名轻度智力残疾儿童提供社区、家庭康复训练。

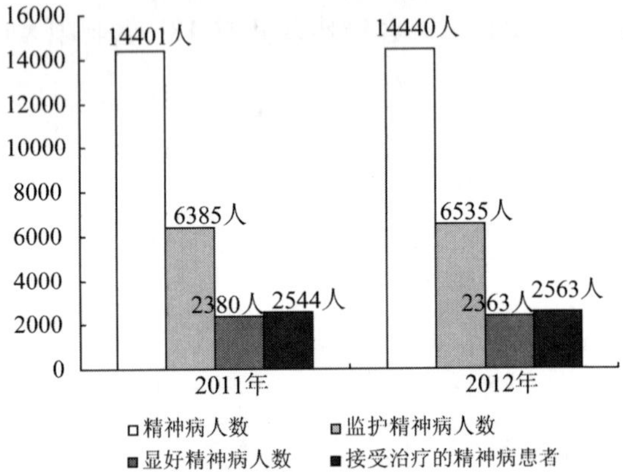

图2 2011-2012年度垦区精神残疾人康复工作一览

加强肢体康复训练工作，共为613名肢体残疾人提供训练，其中肢体残疾儿童机构训练13人，肢体残疾人社区、家庭训练600人。

加强对听力残疾儿童的康复训练，2012年，为32名听力残疾儿童提供家庭康复训练，新培训听力残疾儿童家长64名。

为了使残疾人出行方便，2012年共为35名残疾人装配了大腿假肢.为33名残疾人装配了小腿假肢，为各类残疾人免费配发辅助器具2020件，其中为重度残疾人配发辅具60件，使更多的残疾人得以恢复和改善肢体功能。

加大对残疾儿童的筛查和救助力度，目前有103个农场开展残疾儿童筛查工作。

为了更好的服务残疾人，2012年开展康复人才培训活动，培训康复管理人员59人，康复业务人员59人，培训社区康复协调员154人，极大程度的改善了康复人才不足的情况。

二、教育工作

在有关部门的共同努力下，残疾人教育事业取得了良好的成绩，尤其是义务阶段教育，在送教服务活动开展后，义务教育阶段辍学的残疾人儿童少年明显减少。目前，未入学的学龄残疾儿童少年共158人，其中视力残疾人3人，听力残疾人5人，言语残疾12人，肢体残疾人51人，智力残疾人71人，精神残疾人5人，多重11人，比去年减少13.3%。20名学龄前儿童接受彩票公益金助学资助。

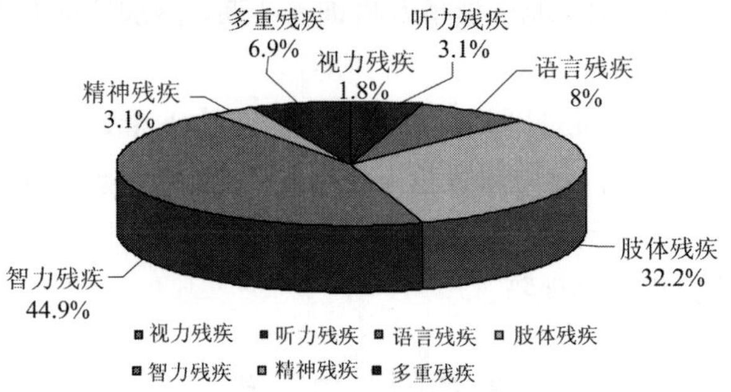

图3　2012年黑龙江农垦总局未入学学龄残疾少年儿童统计

三、残疾人劳动就业和社会保障

大力推进按比例安置残疾人就业工作，采取集中和分散相结合的方法，安置残疾人就业。鼓励有能力的残疾人自主创业。截至目前，残疾人就业人数15709人，其中集中就业51人，按比例就业5434人，个体及其他形式就业9929人，公益岗位就业295人。

为了更好的解决残疾人的实际困难，动员全社会的力量，开展"帮包带扶"工作。垦区目前有特困残疾人3774人，低收入残疾人17633人。本年度扶持贫困残疾人2582户，共5288人，脱贫1526人。为469名残疾人提供实用技术培训。为744户贫困残疾人进行危房改造，累计投入资金98万余元。全年参与扶贫的结对帮扶单位109个，帮扶个人695人，物资和资金投入24.1万元。

四、盲人按摩

卫生部、人力资源和社会保障部、国家中医药管理局和中国残疾人联合会联合制定了《盲人医疗按摩管理办法》出台后，垦区的盲人按摩有了更迅速的发展。目前，盲人医疗按摩机构1个，保健按摩机构2个，盲人医疗按摩人员中级的4人，初级的5人，盲人保健按摩人员5人。

五、社会保障

残疾人社会保障工作是当前残疾人工作的重点，这项工作残疾人受益面广，解决残疾人的实际困难比较彻底、稳定。2012年城镇残疾职工参加社会保险人数为8079人，残疾居民参加城镇医疗保险人数55881人，城镇个体就业参加保险人数5738人，其中，个体就业参加城镇居民养老保险人数3442人，参加医疗保险人数3752人。全年纳入最低生活保障范围的30534人，集中供养111人，其他救济4132人。机构托养残疾人321人，其中智力残疾16人，精神残疾290人，其他类别残疾人15人，享受居家托养服务残疾人1161人。

六、宣传文化

2012年残疾人事业的社会宣传力度得到进一步加强，社会舆论环境得到进一步改善。在主要新闻媒体刊播稿件数115件，在残疾人文化周举办残疾人艺术作品展，共收到刺绣、书法、绘画、摄影等艺术作品300余件，极大程度的丰富残疾人的文化生活。完善北大荒新月网站的各项工作，开设网上办公、法律援助、新月论坛、残疾人热线、整合残疾人数据库，建立覆盖垦区的电子数据传输平台，建立黑龙江垦区精神病人社会化服务管理系统，为精神病救助工作提供网络支持，也为垦区残疾人事业的发展和残疾人工作者之间的交流提供了良好的平台。

七、维权

继续完善残疾人事业法律法规，加大执法检查和监督力度，开展法律服务、法律援助和法制宣传，维护残疾人权益，为残疾人创造文明进步的无障碍环境。全年共开展普法宣传教育活动62次，参加人数2925人，印制普法宣传册13480册，为残疾人提供法律援助的案件60件。为推进垦区的无障碍建设，垦区共成立无障碍建设领导协调组织9个，共印发无障碍宣传材料300份。为1536名残疾人发放机动轮椅车燃油补贴。

信访工作的开展，有力的维护了残疾人的合法权益。全年共处理各类信访案件91件，其中康复类20件，教育类11件，就业类28件，扶贫类7件，社会保障类 23 件，机动轮椅车类 1 件，意见建议类 0 件，其他类 1 件。全年接待来访 1286 人次，无一起集体上访案件发生。整体上看，问题主要集中在就业、优惠政策方面，这说明残疾人的就业、生活问题仍然是我们迫切要解决的重大问题。

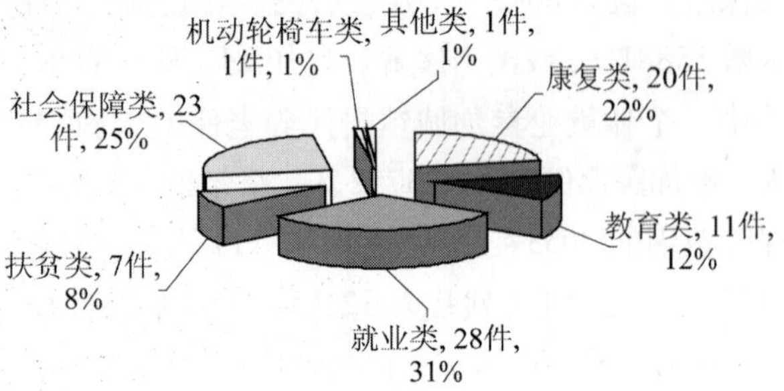

图 4　2012 年处理各类信访案件图

八、组织建设

残疾人组织是政府联系残疾人的纽带和桥梁，是做好残疾人工作的重要保证。全垦区共有各类残疾人 90715 人，持证残疾人有 28663 人，占残疾人总数的 31.6%。全垦区有专兼职残疾人工作者 204 人，其中行政编制 70 人，事业编制 134 人。配备残疾人专职委员 109 人。举办省级综合培训班 2 次，参加人数 80 人；地市级干部培训班 1 次，参加人数 13 人。

九、综合服务设施

截止到 2012 年底，已竣工并投入使用的各级残疾人综合服务设施共计 6 个，筹建项目共计 3 个，综合服务设施的投入使用将会给残疾人带来更大的方便。

十、信息化建设

统计队伍建设进一步加强，共有 113 名专、兼职统计人员从事残疾人事业统计工作，其中省级 1 人，地市级 9 人，县级 103 人。统计人员业务素质培养普遍得到重视，省级、管理局级统计人员均持证上岗。省级残联举办培训班 1 期，参加培训的人员 40 人次；地市级举办培训班 2 期，参加培训的人员达到 40 人次。

全面推进网站建设，有门户网站 1 个，发稿量 900 篇。信息化建设投入资金 37 万余元，系统维护费 3.3 万元，信息化专业人才 127 人，为垦区信息化建设提供保障。

十一、存在的问题和不足

2012 年，黑龙江农垦总局的残疾人工作较好地完成了各项计划任务，但由于经济和体制等原因，从工作整体来看，黑龙江农垦的残疾人事业发展与中国残联的要求还有一定的差距：一是贫困残疾人的医疗、康复、教育、就业、社会保障等方面还存在着一定的困难,不能满足残疾人的需求；二是改善残疾人参加社会生活的长效机制还不健全；三是残疾人无障碍建设环境还存在很大的不足，尤其是信息无障碍建设还处在起步阶段，残疾人工作者为残疾人服务的能力还有待进一步提高。因此，2013 年垦区各级残联将紧紧围绕中央 7 号文件和国办 19 号文件精神，全面推进“两个体系”建设，提高服务能力和保障能力，在保障民生等方面加大扶持力度，完善工作机制，保障残疾人的基本需求。

6

附录

Appendix

关于使用 2010 年末全国残疾人总数及各类、不同残疾等级人数的通知

残联〔2012〕25 号

各省、自治区、直辖市及计划单列市残联，新疆生产建设兵团残联，黑龙江农垦总局残联：

根据第六次全国人口普查我国总人口数，及第二次全国残疾人抽样调查我国残疾人占全国总人口的比例和各类残疾人占残疾人总人数的比例，推算了 2010 年末我国残疾人总人数及各类、不同等级的残疾人数，现通知如下：

全国残疾人总数为 8502 万人。

各类残疾人的人数分别为：视力残疾 1263 万人；听力残疾 2054 万人；言语残疾 130 万人；肢体残疾 2472 万人；智力残疾 568 万人；精神残疾 629 万人；多重残疾 1386 万人。

各残疾等级人数分别为：重度残疾 2518 万人；中度和轻度残疾人 5984 万人。

以上数据可在工作中使用并对外公开。

中国残疾人联合会

二〇一二年三月五日

第二次全国残疾人抽样调查残疾标准

（国务院2005年11月4日批准）

视力残疾标准

一、视力残疾的定义

视力残疾，是指由于各种原因导致双眼视力低下并且不能矫正或视野缩小，以致影响其日常生活和社会参与。

视力残疾包括盲及低视力。

二、视力残疾的分级

类别	级别	最佳矫正视力
盲	一级	无光感-＜0.02；或视野半径＜5度
	二级	0.02-＜0.05；或视野半径＜10度
低视力	三级	0.05-＜0.1
	四级	0.1-＜0.3

〔注〕

1. 盲或低视力均指双眼而言，若双眼视力不同，则以视力较好的一眼为准。如仅有单眼为盲或低视力，而另一眼的视力达到或优于0.3，则不属于视力残疾范畴。

2. 最佳矫正视力是指以适当镜片矫正所能达到的最好视力或针孔视力。

3. 以注视点为中心，视野半径＜10度者，不论其视力如何均属于盲。

听力残疾标准

一、听力残疾的定义

听力残疾，是指人由于各种原因导致双耳不同程度的永久性听力障碍，听不到或听不清周围环境声及言语声，以致影响日常生活和社会参与。

二、听力残疾的分级

听力残疾一级：

听觉系统的结构和功能方面极重度损伤，较好耳平均听力损失≥91 dB HL，在无助听设备帮助下，不能依靠听觉进行言语交流，在理解和交流等活动上极度受限，在参与社会生活方面存在极严重障碍。

听力残疾二级：

听觉系统的结构和功能重度损伤，较好耳平均听力损失在81-90 dB HL之间，在无助听设备帮助下，在理解和交流等活动上重度受限，在参与社会生活方面存在严重障碍。

听力残疾三级：

听觉系统的结构和功能中重度损伤，较好耳平均听力损失在61-80 dB HL之间，在无助听设备帮助下，在理解和交流等活动上中度受限，在参与社会生活方面存在中度障碍。

听力残疾四级：

听觉系统的结构和功能中度损伤，较好耳平均听力损失在41-60dB HL之间，在无助听设备帮助下，在理解和交流等活动上轻度受限，在参与社会生活方面存在轻度障碍。

言语残疾标准

一、言语残疾的定义

言语残疾，是指由于各种原因导致的不同程度的言语障碍，经治疗一年以上不愈或病程超过两年者,而不能或难以进行正常的言语交往活动，以致影响日常生活和社会参与（3岁以下不定残）。

言语残疾包括：

1. 失语：是指由于大脑言语区域以及相关部位损伤所导致的获得性言语功能丧失或受损。

2. 运动性构音障碍：是指由于神经肌肉病变导致构音器官的运动障碍，主要表现为不会说话、说话费力、发声和发音不清等。

3. 器官结构异常所致的构音障碍：是指构音器官形态结构异常所致的构音障碍。其代表为腭裂以及舌或颌面部术后造成的构音障碍。主要表现为不能说话、鼻音过重、发音不清等。

4. 发声障碍（嗓音障碍）：是指由于呼吸及喉存在器质性病变导致的失声、发声困难、声音嘶哑等。

5. 儿童言语发育迟滞：指儿童在生长发育过程中其言语发育落后于实际年龄的状态。主要表现不会说话、说话晚、发音不清等。

6. 听力障碍所致的语言障碍：是指由于听觉障碍所致的言语障碍。主要表现为不会说话或者发音不清。

7. 口吃：是指言语的流畅性障碍。常表现为在说话的过程中拖长音、重复、语塞并伴有面部及其他行为变化等。

二、言语残疾的分级

言语残疾一级：

无任何言语功能或语音清晰度≤10%，言语表达能力等级测试未达到一级测试水平，不能进行任何言语交流。

言语残疾二级：

具有一定的发声及言语能力。语音清晰度在11%-25%之间，言语表达能力等级测试未达到二级测试水平。

言语残疾三级：

可以进行部分言语交流。语音清晰度在26%-45%之间，言语表达能力等级测试未达到三级测试水平。

言语残疾四级：

能进行简单会话，但用较长句或长篇表达困难。语音清晰度在46%-65%之间，言语表达能力等级测试未达到四级测试水平。

肢体残疾标准

一、肢体残疾的定义

肢体残疾，是指人体运动系统的结构、功能损伤造成四肢残缺或四肢、躯干麻痹（瘫痪）、畸形等而致人体运动功能不同程度丧失以及活动受限或参与的局限。

肢体残疾包括：

1. 上肢或下肢因伤、病或发育异常所致的缺失、畸形或功能障碍；

2. 脊柱因伤、病或发育异常所致的畸形或功能障碍；

3. 中枢、周围神经因伤、病或发育异常造成躯干或四肢的功能障碍。

二、肢体残疾的分级

肢体残疾一级：不能独立实现日常生活活动。

1. 四肢瘫：四肢运动功能重度丧失；
2. 截瘫：双下肢运动功能完全丧失；
3. 偏瘫：一侧肢体运动功能完全丧失；
4. 单全上肢和双小腿缺失；
5. 单全下肢和双前臂缺失；
6. 双上臂和单大腿（或单小腿）缺失；
7. 双全上肢或双全下肢缺失；
8. 四肢在不同部位缺失；
9. 双上肢功能极重度障碍或三肢功能重度障碍。

肢体残疾二级：基本上不能独立实现日常生活活动。

1. 偏瘫或截瘫，残肢保留少许功能（不能独立行走）；
2. 双上臂或双前臂缺失；
3. 双大腿缺失；
4. 单全上肢和单大腿缺失；
5. 单全下肢和单上臂缺失；
6. 三肢在不同部位缺失（除外一级中的情况）；
7. 二肢功能重度障碍或三肢功能中度障碍。

肢体残疾三级：能部分独立实现日常生活活动。

1. 双小腿缺失；
2. 单前臂及其以上缺失；
3. 单大腿及其以上缺失；
4. 双手拇指或双手拇指以外其他手指全缺失；
5. 二肢在不同部位缺失（除外二级中的情况）；
6. 一肢功能重度障碍或二肢功能中度障碍。

肢体残疾四级：基本上能独立实现日常生活活动。

1. 单小腿缺失；
2. 双下肢不等长，差距在5厘米以上（含5厘

米);

3. 脊柱强(僵)直;

4. 脊柱畸形，驼背畸形大于 70 度或侧凸大于 45 度;

5. 单手拇指以外其他四指全缺失;

6. 单侧拇指全缺失;

7. 单足跗跖关节以上缺失;

8. 双足趾完全缺失或失去功能;

9. 侏儒症(身高不超过 130 厘米的成年人);

10. 一肢功能中度障碍或两肢功能轻度障碍;

11. 类似上述的其他肢体功能障碍。

智力残疾标准

一、智力残疾的定义

智力残疾，是指智力显著低于一般人水平，并伴有适应行为的障碍。此类残疾是由于神经系统结构、功能障碍，使个体活动和参与受到限制，需要环境提供全面、广泛、有限和间歇的支持。

智力残疾包括：在智力发育期间(18 岁之前)，由于各种有害因素导致的精神发育不全或智力迟滞；或者智力发育成熟以后，由于各种有害因素导致智力损害或智力明显衰退。

二、智力残疾的分级

级别	分级标准			
	发展商(DQ)0-6 岁	智商(IQ)7 岁及以上	适应性行为(AB)	WHO-DAS Ⅱ分值 18 岁以上
一级	≤25	<20	极重度	≥116 分
二级	26-39	20-34	重度	106-115 分
三级	40-54	35-49	中度	96-105 分
四级	55-75	50-69	轻度	52-95 分

精神残疾标准

一、精神残疾的定义

精神残疾，是指各类精神障碍持续一年以上未痊愈，由于存在认知、情感和行为障碍，以致影响其日常生活和社会参与。

二、精神残疾的分级

18 岁以上(含)的精神障碍患者根据《世界卫生组织残疾评定量表Ⅱ》(WHO-DAS Ⅱ)分数和下述的适应行为表现，18 岁以下者依据下述的适应行为的表现，把精神残疾划分为四级：

精神残疾一级：

WHO-DAS Ⅱ值≥116 分，适应行为严重障碍；生活完全不能自理，忽视自己的生理、心理的基本要求。不与人交往，无法从事工作，不能学习新事物。需要环境提供全面、广泛的支持，生活长期、全部需他人监护。

精神残疾二级：

WHO-DAS Ⅱ值在 106-115 分之间，适应行为重度障碍；生活大部分不能自理，基本不与人交往，只与照顾者简单交往，能理解照顾者的简单指令，有一定学习能力。监护下能从事简单劳动。能表达自己的基本需求，偶尔被动参与社交活动；需要环境提供广泛的支持，大部分生活仍需他人照料。

精神残疾三级：

WHO-DAS Ⅱ值在 96-105 分之间，适应行为中度障碍；生活上不能完全自理，可以与人进行简单交流，能表达自己的情感。能独立从事简单劳动，能学习新事物，但学习能力明显比一般人差。被动参与社交活动，偶尔能主动参与社交活动；需要环境提供部分的支持，即所需要的支持服务是经常性的、短时间的需求，部分生活需由他人照料。

精神残疾四级：

WHO-DAS Ⅱ值在 52-95 分之间，适应行为轻度障碍；生活上基本自理，但自理能力比一般人差，有时忽略个人卫生。能与人交往，能表达自己的情感，体会他人情感的能力较差，能从事一般的工作，学习新事物的能力比一般人稍差；偶尔需要环境提供支持，一般情况下生活不需要由他人照料。

多重残疾

存在两种或两种以上残疾为多重残疾。多重残疾应指出其残疾的类别。多重残疾分级按所属残疾中最重类别残疾分级标准进行分级。

中国残联统计调查项目目录

审批项目一览表

统计调查项目名称	批准文号	有效期截止时间
长江普及型假肢服务项目调查制度	国统制[2012]73 号	2014-08-06
盲人保健按摩师培训项目调查制度	国统制[2012]73 号	2014-08-06
中国残疾人事业统计年报报表制度	国统制[2012]81 号	2014-08-23
中国残疾人事业统计年报快报制度	国统制[2012]81 号	2014-08-23
中国残疾人事业统计台账制度	国统制[2012]81 号	2014-08-23
全国残疾人状况监测问卷	国统制[2011]91 号	2013-09-19

中国残疾人联合会文件

残联发[2006]1号

关于印发《中国残联系统统计工作管理办法》的通知

各省、自治区、直辖市及计划单列市残联，新疆生产建设兵团残联、黑龙江农垦总局残联:

为了加强统计工作的管理,规范统计调查行为，提高统计调查的整体效益，充分发挥统计工作的服务和监督作用，中国残联依据《中华人民共和国统计法》、《中华人民共和国统计法实施细则》、《部门统计调查管理暂行办法》，结合工作实际，对原有的《中国残联系统统计工作暂行规定》、《中国残联系统专项业务统计调查项目管理暂行办法》、《中国残联机关统计资料管理暂行办法》等进行了修订和整合，制定了《全国残联系统统计工作管理办法》，现予以印发，请遵照执行。

中国残疾人联合会

二〇〇六年一月三日

中国残联系统统计工作管理办法

一、总　则

第一条　为了科学、有效地组织全国残联系统统计工作，规范统计调查行为，提高统计调查的整体效益，充分发挥统计工作的服务和监督作用，依据《中华人民共和国统计法》(以下简称《统计法》)、《中华人民共和国统计法实施细则》(以下简称《实施细则》)、《部门统计调查管理暂行办法》，结合工作实际，制定本办法。

第二条　全国残联系统统计工作的基本任务是：对全国残疾人事业的发展状况和残联系统的业务工作进行统计调查、统计分析、统计预测和统计监督，为国家和各级人民政府制定与残疾人事业相关的政策、法规提供依据，为领导运筹决策和残联系统工作的发展提供有效的服务。

第三条　全国残联系统统计工作由：中国残疾人事业统计年报制度、中国残疾人事业统计快报制度、中国残疾人事业基础统计台账制度、专项业务统计调查工作组成。

第四条　各级残联应加强统计现代化建设，积极利用信息技术手段，使残疾人事业统计数据更加科学、准确、及时，逐步实现残疾人事业统计数据的电子化和统计数据的社会共享与服务。

二、统计机构、职责和统计人员

第五条　全国残联系统统计工作实行统一领导、分级负责。中国残联负责全国残疾人事业统计工作的组织、协调与管理，并对地方残联统计工作进行指导，具体由中国残联设置的统计机构负责组织实施。地方各级残联的统计工作由地方各级残联设置的统计机构或统计主管部门负责管理和组织实施，并接受上级残联统计机构和同级人民政府统计部门的指导、监督与管理。

第六条　中国残联的统计机构设在中国残联信息中心，负责组织、协调和管理全国残联系统的统计工作。其主要职责是：制定残疾人事业统计调查计划和项目，制定统计标准；组织协调各级残联搜集、整理、提供统计资料，管理统计资料的发布，开展统计分析、统计预测和统计监督工作；指导、检查全国残联系统统计工作，组织统计业务经验交流，开展全国残联系统统计科学研究；做好统计人员培训工作；制订全国残联系统统计工作现代化规划。

各省级残联应设置统计机构或明确统计主管部门并设专职统计人员，负责指导本行政区域内各级残联统计工作，组织管理本级残联的统计工作。其主要职责是：在完成好中国残联和上级残联下达的各项统计调查工作的同时，为本级残疾人事业提供各项统计数据，并开展统计调查活动。

各地级市残联应明确统计主管部门并设专(兼)职统计人员，其主要职责是：在完成好中国残联和上级残联下达的各项统计调查工作的同时，为本级残疾人事业提供各项统计数据，并开展统计调查活动。

各县级残联应明确统计工作主管部门或主管负责人，确定兼职统计人员。其主要职责是：做好基础数据工作，建立统计台账，完成好中国残联和上级残联下达的统计调查任务，为本级残疾人事业提供各项统计数据，并开展统计调查活动。

第七条　各级残联统计人员应保持相对稳定。统计人员的调动，应当征得本级统计主管部门或统计工作负责人的同意；省级专职统计人员的调动，应当征得中国残联统计机构的同意。统计人员调动工作或离职，应当由经过统计业务培训、能够胜任统计业务工作的人员接替，并办理交接手续。各级残联的统计人员应取得同级人民政府统计机构颁发的统计上岗证，具有残联系统业务知识和计算机操作能力。

三、统计报表制度的编制、修改与审批

第八条　中国残疾人事业统计年报、快报制度和统计台账制度中的指标、指标涵义、调查范围、

分类目录、计算方法和统计报表表式、统计编码以及报送时间，由中国残联统一规定，按照国家统计局的要求报送国家统计局进行审批备案。按规定程序经国家统计局批准或备案的统计报表，在报表的右上角标明制表机关名称、表号、批准或备案机关名称及其批准文号。被调查的部门、人员应当准确、及时地按报表规定填报。

不符合前款规定的统计报表（包括以搜集数字为主的调查提纲）是非法报表，被调查的部门可以拒绝填报。

第九条 中国残疾人事业统计年报、快报和统计台账应根据中国残疾人事业发展的需要及时进行调整和补充。中国残联各业务部门因工作需要，调整和补充有关指标时，应进行充分论证并与中国残联统计管理部门联系与协商，经中国残联理事会批准后，报国家统计局批准或备案。

四、统计台账管理

第十条 为了规范中国残联系统统计工作，做到依法统计，发挥统计服务和监督作用，根据《中华人民共和国统计法》和国家相关统计工作的规定，中国残联将制定中国残疾人事业统计台账制度，加强统计台账的管理与数据的报送。

第十一条 中国残疾人事业统计台账（卡）充分利用电子网络化的方式、将科学合理、准确实用的动态管理，与中国残疾人事业统计报表制度相衔接。台账填写内容要符合法律法规政策的要求，填写对象真实、准确；先填卡，后建帐，做到由台账中提取统计数字。

第十二条 各级残联必须依据中国残疾人事业统计台账（卡）中的数据，报送中国残疾人事业统计快报、年报和各项专项业务统计调查的统计报表，做到填报统计报表的数据全面、准确、及时、数出一门。

第十三条 中国残疾人事业统计台账在统一格式、统一软件下实施，由各级地方残联统计人员协调业务部门和人员用计算机或纸质台账、台卡方式进行专门管理。统计人员发生变动时，要严格履行交接手续。

第十四条 省级、地（市）级残联都应建立电子化台账。有条件的县级残联也要实行电子化台账，各级残联应积极推动电子化台账建设，加强统计台账的管理工作。在没有实行全面电子化台账之前，将实行电子化台账和纸质台账、台卡的同时保存。

第十五条 中国残疾人事业统计台账、台卡按中国残疾人事业统计报表逐级汇总上报。

五、专项业务统计调查管理

第十六条 中国残联和地方各级残联开展的专项业务统计调查，以及残联各业务部门与其他部门或单位联合组织实施的统计调查，其调查的统计指标与中国残联年报、快报指标交叉重复或需要对外公布统计数据的统计调查，均属于专项业务统计调查管理范畴。

第十七条 中国残联系统各级统计机构统一管理和协调本级业务部门专项业务统计调查。

第十八条 专项业务统计调查项目必须符合国家统计局《部门统计调查项目管理暂行办法》的基本原则与要求。专项业务统计调查项目的立项必须有充分的理由。调查要有明确的目的和资料使用范围。调查项目应当与中国残联职能范围和各项业务工作相对应。

第十九条 中国残联系统各级统计机构通过建立审批备案制度、调查项目公布制度、跟踪检查制度、举报制度，对会内专项业务统计调查进行管理。

第二十条 专项业务统计调查项目中的统计标准和分类必须与政府综合统计机构规定使用的标准和分类相一致。涉及政府综合统计机构规定以外的专业标准和分类，要与国家有关标准或行业标准相一致。尚无国家标准和行业标准的，必须严格按照标准化及分类科学的原则进行归纳和设计，并在使用前征求政府综合统计机构的意见。

第二十一条 中国残联新增设的统计调查项目在制定好统计调查方案后，须提交中国残联统计机构审核，报国家统计局批准后统一组织实施。

地方残联新增设的统计调查项目，由本级残联统计机构统一管理，报上级残联统计机构和同级人民政府统计局批准后组织实施。地方残联制发的统计调查表内容、指标涵义、计算方法、完成期限等，均不得与中国残联制发的有关统计调查表相抵触。

六、统计资料的管理与发布

第二十二条 残联系统统计资料实行归口管理。全国性残联系统 统计资料，由中国残联统计机构统一管理；地方性残联系统统计资料，由地方残联统计机构或统计人员统一管理。统计机构和统计人员必须建立统计工作责任制和统计资料整理、审查、管理制度，不断提高工作质量和工作效率，保证残联系统统计资料的准确、及时。

各级残联的文件、报告、简报、情况反映、信息等引用综合性的统计数字，必须经本级统计机构或统计人员复核。对外提供和公布的统计资料，必须经本级统计机构或统计人员统一复核和办理并由主管理事长批准。任何部门和个人不得擅自公开和使用未经正式公布的残联系统统计资料。

第二十三条 各级残联统计机构、统计人员必须建立健全统计资料档案，对原始记录、统计台账和综合分析等统计资料，按有关规定保管，不得损坏。对于属于国家秘密的残联系统统计资料，要按照《中华人民共和国保守国家秘密法》、国家统计局《统计资料保密管理办法》等有关规定，妥善保管。

七、奖励和惩罚

第二十四条 各级残联对有下列表现之一的残联统计机构或者人员，给予表扬或奖励：

一、在改革和完善残联系统统计制度、统计方法等方面，有重要贡献的；

二、在完成规定的残联系统统计调查任务，保障残联系统统计资料的准确性、及时性方面，做出显著成绩的；

三、在进行残联系统统计分析、统计预测和统计监督方面取得重要成绩的；

四、在运用和推广现代化信息技术方面，有显著效果的；

五、在残联系统统计科学研究方面有所创新的；

六、坚持实事求是，依法办事，同违反统计法规和本办法的行为作斗争，表现突出的。

第二十五条 各级残联对有下列行为之一的机构或者人员，给予批评或处分：

一、虚报、瞒报、拒报残联系统统计资料的；

二、伪造、篡改残联系统统计资料的；

三、无故迟报残联系统统计资料的；

四、侵犯统计机构、统计人员行使统计法规及本办法所规定的职权或打击报复统计人员的；

五、违反统计法规及本办法，未经批准，自行编制发布残联系统统计报表的；

六、违反统计法规及本办法，未经核定批准，擅自对外提供或公布残联系统统计资料的。

八、附 则

第二十六条 本办法由中国残联负责解释。

第二十七条 本办法自发布之日起试行。

中华人民共和国统计法

（1983 年 12 月 8 日第六届全国人民代表大会常务委员会第三次会议通过 根据 1996 年 5 月 15 日第八届全国人民代表大会常务委员会第十九次会议《关于修改〈中华人民共和国统计法〉的决定》修正 2009 年 6 月 27 日第十一届全国人民代表大会常务委员会第九次会议修订）

第一章　总　则

第一条　为了科学、有效地组织统计工作，保障统计资料的真实性、准确性、完整性和及时性，发挥统计在了解国情国力、服务经济社会发展中的重要作用，促进社会主义现代化建设事业发展，制定本法。

第二条 本法适用于各级人民政府、县级以上人民政府统计机构和有关部门组织实施的统计活动。

统计的基本任务是对经济社会发展情况进行统计调查、统计分析，提供统计资料和统计咨询意见，实行统计监督。

第三条 国家建立集中统一的统计系统，实行统一领导、分级负责的统计管理体制。

第四条 国务院和地方各级人民政府、各有关部门应当加强对统计工作的组织领导，为统计工作提供必要的保障。

第五条 国家加强统计科学研究，健全科学的统计指标体系，不断改进统计调查方法，提高统计的科学性。

国家有计划地加强统计信息化建设，推进统计信息搜集、处理、传输、共享、存储技术和统计数据库体系的现代化。

第六条 统计机构和统计人员依照本法规定独立行使统计调查、统计报告、统计监督的职权，不受侵犯。

地方各级人民政府、政府统计机构和有关部门以及各单位的负责人，不得自行修改统计机构和统计人员依法搜集、整理的统计资料，不得以任何方式要求统计机构、统计人员及其他机构、人员伪造、篡改统计资料，不得对依法履行职责或者拒绝、抵制统计违法行为的统计人员打击报复。

第七条 国家机关、企业事业单位和其他组织以及个体工商户和个人等统计调查对象，必须依照本法和国家有关规定，真实、准确、完整、及时地提供统计调查所需的资料，不得提供不真实或者不完整的统计资料，不得迟报、拒报统计资料。

第八条 统计工作应当接受社会公众的监督。任何单位和个人有权检举统计中弄虚作假等违法行为。对检举有功的单位和个人应当给予表彰和奖励。

第九条 统计机构和统计人员对在统计工作中知悉的国家秘密、商业秘密和个人信息，应当予以保密。

第十条 任何单位和个人不得利用虚假统计资料骗取荣誉称号、物质利益或者职务晋升。

第二章　统计调查管理

第十一条　统计调查项目包括国家统计调查项目、部门统计调查项目和地方统计调查项目。

国家统计调查项目是指全国性基本情况的统计调查项目。部门统计调查项目是指国务院有关部门的专业性统计调查项目。地方统计调查项目是指县级以上地方人民政府及其部门的地方性统计调查项目。

国家统计调查项目、部门统计调查项目、地方统计调查项目应当明确分工，互相衔接，不得重复。

第十二条　国家统计调查项目由国家统计局制定，或者由国家统计局和国务院有关部门共同制定，报国务院备案；重大的国家统计调查项目报国务院审批。

部门统计调查项目由国务院有关部门制定。统计调查对象属于本部门管辖系统的，报国家统计局备案；统计调查对象超出本部门管辖系统的，报国家统计局审批。

地方统计调查项目由县级以上地方人民政府统计机构和有关部门分别制定或者共同制定。其中，由省级人民政府统计机构单独制定或者和有关部门共同制定的，报国家统计局审批；由省级以下人民政府统计机构单独制定或者和有关部门共同制定的，报省级人民政府统计机构审批；由县级以上地方人民政府有关部门制定的，报本级人民政府统计机构审批。

第十三条　统计调查项目的审批机关应当对调查项目的必要性、可行性、科学性进行审查，对符合法定条件的，作出予以批准的书面决定，并公布；对不符合法定条件的，作出不予批准的书面决定，并说明理由。

第十四条　制定统计调查项目，应当同时制定该项目的统计调查制度，并依照本法第十二条的规定一并报经审批或者备案。

统计调查制度应当对调查目的、调查内容、调查方法、调查对象、调查组织方式、调查表式、统计资料的报送和公布等作出规定。

统计调查应当按照统计调查制度组织实施。变更统计调查制度的内容，应当报经原审批机关批准或者原备案机关备案。

第十五条　统计调查表应当标明表号、制定机关、批准或者备案文号、有效期限等标志。

对未标明前款规定的标志或者超过有效期限的统计调查表，统计调查对象有权拒绝填报；县级以上人民政府统计机构应当依法责令停止有关统计调查活动。

第十六条　搜集、整理统计资料，应当以周期性普查为基础，以经常性抽样调查为主体，综合运用全面调查、重点调查等方法，并充分利用行政记录等资料。

重大国情国力普查由国务院统一领导，国务院和地方人民政府组织统计机构和有关部门共同实施。

第十七条　国家制定统一的统计标准，保障统计调查采用的指标涵义、计算方法、分类目录、调查表式和统计编码等的标准化。

国家统计标准由国家统计局制定，或者由国家统计局和国务院标准化主管部门共同制定。

国务院有关部门可以制定补充性的部门统计标准，报国家统计局审批。部门统计标准不得与国家统计标准相抵触。

第十八条　县级以上人民政府统计机构根据统计任务的需要，可以在统计调查对象中推广使用计算机网络报送统计资料。

第十九条　县级以上人民政府应当将统计工作所需经费列入财政预算。

重大国情国力普查所需经费，由国务院和地方人民政府共同负担，列入相应年度的财政预算，按时拨付，确保到位。

第三章　统计资料的管理和公布

第二十条　县级以上人民政府统计机构和有关部门以及乡、镇人民政府，应当按照国家有关规定建立统计资料的保存、管理制度，建立健全统计信息共享机制。

第二十一条　国家机关、企业事业单位和其他组织等统计调查对象，应当按照国家有关规定设置原始记录、统计台账，建立健全统计资料的审核、签署、交接、归档等管理制度。

统计资料的审核、签署人员应当对其审核、签署的统计资料的真实性、准确性和完整性负责。

第二十二条　县级以上人民政府有关部门应当及时向本级人民政府统计机构提供统计所需的行政记录资料和国民经济核算所需的财务资料、财政资料及其他资料，并按照统计调查制度的规定及时向本级人民政府统计机构报送其组织实施统计调查取得的有关资料。

县级以上人民政府统计机构应当及时向本级人民政府有关部门提供有关统计资料。

第二十三条　县级以上人民政府统计机构按照国家有关规定，定期公布统计资料。

国家统计数据以国家统计局公布的数据为准。

第二十四条　县级以上人民政府有关部门统计调查取得的统计资料，由本部门按照国家有关规定公布。

第二十五条　统计调查中获得的能够识别或者推断单个统计调查对象身份的资料，任何单位和个人不得对外提供、泄露，不得用于统计以外的目的。

第二十六条　县级以上人民政府统计机构和有关部门统计调查取得的统计资料，除依法应当保密的外，应当及时公开，供社会公众查询。

第四章　统计机构和统计人员

第二十七条　国务院设立国家统计局，依法组织领导和协调全国的统计工作。

国家统计局根据工作需要设立的派出调查机构，承担国家统计局布置的统计调查等任务。

县级以上地方人民政府设立独立的统计机构，乡、镇人民政府设置统计工作岗位，配备专职或者兼职统计人员，依法管理、开展统计工作，实施统计调查。

第二十八条　县级以上人民政府有关部门根据统计任务的需要设立统计机构，或者在有关机构中设置统计人员，并指定统计负责人，依法组织、管理本部门职责范围内的统计工作，实施统计调查，在统计业务上受本级人民政府统计机构的指导。

第二十九条　统计机构、统计人员应当依法履行职责，如实搜集、报送统计资料，不得伪造、篡改统计资料，不得以任何方式要求任何单位和个人提供不真实的统计资料，不得有其他违反本法规定的行为。

统计人员应当坚持实事求是，恪守职业道德，对其负责搜集、审核、录入的统计资料与统计调查对象报送的统计资料的一致性负责。

第三十条　统计人员进行统计调查时，有权就与统计有关的问题询问有关人员，要求其如实提供有关情况、资料并改正不真实、不准确的资料。

统计人员进行统计调查时，应当出示县级以上人民政府统计机构或者有关部门颁发的工作证件；未出示的，统计调查对象有权拒绝调查。

第三十一条　国家实行统计专业技术职务资格考试、评聘制度，提高统计人员的专业素质，保障统计队伍的稳定性。

统计人员应当具备与其从事的统计工作相适应的专业知识和业务能力。

县级以上人民政府统计机构和有关部门应当加强对统计人员的专业培训和职业道德教育。

第五章　监督检查

第三十二条　县级以上人民政府及其监察机关对下级人民政府、本级人民政府统计机构和有关部门执行本法的情况，实施监督。

第三十三条　国家统计局组织管理全国统计工作的监督检查，查处重大统计违法行为。

县级以上地方人民政府统计机构依法查处本行政区域内发生的统计违法行为。但是，国家统计局派出的调查机构组织实施的统计调查活动中发生的统计违法行为，由组织实施该项统计调查的调查机构负责查处。

法律、行政法规对有关部门查处统计违法行为另有规定的，从其规定。

第三十四条　县级以上人民政府有关部门应当积极协助本级人民政府统计机构查处统计违法行为，及时向本级人民政府统计机构移送有关统计违法案件材料。

第三十五条　县级以上人民政府统计机构在调查统计违法行为或者核查统计数据时，有权采取下列措施：

（一）发出统计检查查询书，向检查对象查询有关事项；

（二）要求检查对象提供有关原始记录和凭证、统计台账、统计调查表、会计资料及其他相关证明和资料；

（三）就与检查有关的事项询问有关人员；

（四）进入检查对象的业务场所和统计数据处理信息系统进行检查、核对；

（五）经本机构负责人批准，登记保存检查对象的有关原始记录和凭证、统计台账、统计调查表、会计资料及其他相关证明和资料；

（六）对与检查事项有关的情况和资料进行记录、录音、录像、照相和复制。

县级以上人民政府统计机构进行监督检查时，监督检查人员不得少于二人，并应当出示执法证件；未出示的，有关单位和个人有权拒绝检查。

第三十六条　县级以上人民政府统计机构履行监督检查职责时，有关单位和个人应当如实反映情况，提供相关证明和资料，不得拒绝、阻碍检查，不得转移、隐匿、篡改、毁弃原始记录和凭证、统计台账、统计调查表、会计资料及其他相关证明和资料。

第六章　法律责任

第三十七条　地方人民政府、政府统计机构或者有关部门、单位的负责人有下列行为之一的，由任免机关或者监察机关依法给予处分，并由县级以上人民政府统计机构予以通报：

（一）自行修改统计资料、编造虚假统计数据的；

（二）要求统计机构、统计人员或者其他机构、人员伪造、篡改统计资料的；

（三）对依法履行职责或者拒绝、抵制统计违法行为的统计人员打击报复的；

（四）对本地方、本部门、本单位发生的严重统计违法行为失察的。

第三十八条 县级以上人民政府统计机构或者有关部门在组织实施统计调查活动中有下列行为之一的，由本级人民政府、上级人民政府统计机构或者本级人民政府统计机构责令改正，予以通报；对直接负责的主管人员和其他直接责任人员，由任免机关或者监察机关依法给予处分：

（一）未经批准擅自组织实施统计调查的；

（二）未经批准擅自变更统计调查制度的内容的；

（三）伪造、篡改统计资料的；

（四）要求统计调查对象或者其他机构、人员提供不真实的统计资料的；

（五）未按照统计调查制度的规定报送有关资料的。

统计人员有前款第三项至第五项所列行为之一的，责令改正，依法给予处分。

第三十九条 县级以上人民政府统计机构或者有关部门有下列行为之一的，对直接负责的主管人员和其他直接责任人员由任免机关或者监察机关依法给予处分：

（一）违法公布统计资料的；

（二）泄露统计调查对象的商业秘密、个人信息或者提供、泄露在统计调查中获得的能够识别或者推断单个统计调查对象身份的资料的；

（三）违反国家有关规定，造成统计资料毁损、灭失的。

统计人员有前款所列行为之一的，依法给予处分。

第四十条 统计机构、统计人员泄露国家秘密的，依法追究法律责任。

第四十一条 作为统计调查对象的国家机关、企业事业单位或者其他组织有下列行为之一的，由县级以上人民政府统计机构责令改正，给予警告，可以予以通报；其直接负责的主管人员和其他直接责任人员属于国家工作人员的，由任免机关或者监察机关依法给予处分：

（一）拒绝提供统计资料或者经催报后仍未按时提供统计资料的；

（二）提供不真实或者不完整的统计资料的；

（三）拒绝答复或者不如实答复统计检查查询书的；

（四）拒绝、阻碍统计调查、统计检查的；

（五）转移、隐匿、篡改、毁弃或者拒绝提供原始记录和凭证、统计台账、统计调查表及其他相关证明和资料的。

企业事业单位或者其他组织有前款所列行为之一的，可以并处五万元以下的罚款；情节严重的，并处五万元以上二十万元以下的罚款。

个体工商户有本条第一款所列行为之一的，由县级以上人民政府统计机构责令改正，给予警告，可以并处一万元以下的罚款。

第四十二条 作为统计调查对象的国家机关、企业事业单位或者其他组织迟报统计资料，或者未按照国家有关规定设置原始记录、统计台账的，由县级以上人民政府统计机构责令改正，给予警告。

企业事业单位或者其他组织有前款所列行为之一的，可以并处一万元以下的罚款。

个体工商户迟报统计资料的，由县级以上人民政府统计机构责令改正，给予警告，可以并处一千元以下的罚款。

第四十三条 县级以上人民政府统计机构查处统计违法行为时，认为对有关国家工作人员依法应当给予处分的，应当提出给予处分的建议；该国家工作人员的任免机关或者监察机关应当依法及时作出决定，并将结果书面通知县级以上人民政府统计机构。

第四十四条 作为统计调查对象的个人在重大国情国力普查活动中拒绝、阻碍统计调查，或者提供不真实或者不完整的普查资料的，由县级以上人民政府统计机构责令改正，予以批评教育。

第四十五条 违反本法规定，利用虚假统计资料骗取荣誉称号、物质利益或者职务晋升的，除对其编造虚假统计资料或者要求他人编造虚假统计资料的行为依法追究法律责任外，由作出有关决定的单位或者其上级单位、监察机关取消其荣誉称号，追缴获得的物质利益，撤销晋升的职务。

第四十六条 当事人对县级以上人民政府统计机构作出的行政处罚决定不服的，可以依法申请行政复议或者提起行政诉讼。其中，对国家统计局在省、自治区、直辖市派出的调查机构作出的行政处罚决定不服的，向国家统计局申请行政复议；对国家统计局派出的其他调查机构作出的行政处罚决定不服的，向国家统计局在该派出机构所在的省、自治区、直辖市派出的调查机构申请行政复议。

第四十七条 违反本法规定，构成犯罪的，依法追究刑事责任。

第七章 附 则

第四十八条 本法所称县级以上人民政府统计机构，是指国家统计局及其派出的调查机构、县级以上地方人民政府统计机构。

第四十九条 民间统计调查活动的管理办法，由国务院制定。

中华人民共和国境外的组织、个人需要在中华人民共和国境内进行统计调查活动的，应当按照国务院的规定报请审批。

利用统计调查危害国家安全、损害社会公共利益或者进行欺诈活动的，依法追究法律责任。

第五十条 本法自 2010 年 1 月 1 日起施行。

部门统计调查项目管理暂行办法

（1999 年 10 月 27 日国家统计局令第 4 号公布）

第一章 总 则

第一条 为加强对部门统计调查的管理和监督，规范部门统计调查行为，提高统计调查的整体效率，减轻被调查者负担，保障统计资料的准确性，提高共享性，根据《中华人民共和国统计法》及其实施细则，制定本办法。

第二条 本办法适用于国家机关、具有行政管理职能的事业单位、经授权代主管部门行使统计职能的国家级集团公司和工商领域联合会或协会、经国务院授权具有一定行政职能的人民团体开展的统计调查，以及上述部门和单位与其他部门联合组织实施的统计调查。法院、检察院组织实施的统计调查，参照本办法执行。

第三条 本办法所称的统计调查，是指部门搜集国民经济、社会和科技发展情况，用于政府管理目的的各类统计调查。包括以数字形式、文字形式或混合形式；以表格、问卷、电讯（电报、电话、传真等）、磁盘磁带、网络通讯（网络表格、电子邮件等）等为介质的普查、经常性调查、一次性调查、试点调查等。

第二章 部门统计调查项目的管理

第四条 政府综合统计机构统一管理和协调部门统计调查。国家统计局管理和协调国家一级部门制定的统计调查；县及县以上地方各级政府统计局管理和协调同级部门的统计调查。

第五条 部门的综合统计机构统一组织、管理和协调本部门各职能机构的统计调查活动，制定本部门的统计调查总体方案。部门内其它职能机构无权单独制定统计调查项目。

第六条 政府综合统计机构通过建立审批备案制度、有效期制度、调查项目公布制度、跟踪检查制度、举报制度，对部门统计调查进行管理。

第三章 制定统计调查项目的基本原则与要求

第七条 国家机关、具有行政管理职能的事业单位、经授权代主管部门行使统计职能的国家级集团公司和工商领域联合会或协会、经国务院授权具有一定行政职能的人民团体，可以制定与职能范围相对应的统计调查项目。

国务院临时机构，一般不得直接制定统计调查项目。工作需要的统计资料，应当向有关部门搜集、加工。确有需要调查的，须事先取得国家统计局的同意，方可制定统计调查。法院、检察院可制定业务情况统计调查项目。

第八条 统计调查项目的立项必须有充分的理由。调查要有明确的目的和资料使用范围。

第九条 统计调查的内容和调查范围必须与部门的职能相一致，必须符合既定的政府综合统计与部门统计的分工原则。

第十条 统计调查项目必须兼顾需要与可能，充分考虑基层调查人员和被调查对象的承受能力。必须符合精简、效能的原则。凡一次性调查能满足需要的，不搞定期调查；凡非全面调查能满足需要的，不搞全面调查。最大限度地减少调查频率，缩小调查规模，降低调查成本。

第十一条 调查项目中的报表表式和文字说明必须规范；指标解释和计算方法必须科学；调查内容要简明扼要，不能与其他调查重复、交叉、矛盾。

第十二条 调查项目中的统计标准和分类必须与政府综合统计部门规定使用的标准和分类相一致。涉及政府综合统计部门规定以外的专业标准和分类，要与有关国家标准或行业标准相一致。尚无国家标准和行业标准的，必须严格按照标准化科学及分类科学的原理进行归纳和设计，并在使用前征求政府综合统计部门的意见。

第十三条 所使用的调查方法要科学合理。要结合调查目的和要求选择最适当的调查方法，以获得最大的调查效益。避免由于调查方法使用不当给基层造成过重负担和产生数据质量问题。

第十四条 重大调查项目必须经过研究论证和试点，必须有完备的论证材料和试点材料。

第十五条 调查者必须依法使用调查资料，对属于国家秘密的统计资料，必须保密；对属于私人、家庭的单项调查资料和在统计调查中知悉的调查对象的商业秘密，负有保密义务。

第四章 审批及备案程序

第十六条 部门建立以系统内单位为对象的调查项目，须报同级政府综合统计机构备案；部门建立调查范围涉及到系统外单位的统计调查项目，必须报同级政府综合统计机构审批，在取得政府综合统计机构的同意或批准后方可组织实施。

系统内是指：与部门有直接隶属关系的单位及部门的派出机构；省及省以下与部门对口设立的管理机构；国家级集团公司所属企业。除此之外均属系统外。

第十七条 审批及备案程序的有关时间规定：

（一）政府综合统计机构在收到部门正式申请函及完整的相关资料后，在 20 个工作日内完成审批；在 5 个工作日内完成备案。完成时间以复函日期为准。

（二）部门收到复函后，在 20 个工作日内将布置调查的正式文件、调查方案和调查表式送达政府综合统计机构，以便及时在“部门统计调查项目库”中建立或更新记录，以及履行公文存档手续。

（三）对有关自然灾害、突发事件等不可预知、有特殊时效性要求的调查，政府综合统计机构将根据特事特办的原则，在最短的时间内完成审批工作，备案项目可事后补办。

第十八条 部门统计调查项目送审及备案时，须备齐以下文件：

（一）以部门名义发出的申请审批或备案的函。

（二）调查方案和表式。包括：总说明、报表目录、基层表式、综合表式、统计标准和分类目录、指标解释、逻辑关系及抽样方案（针对抽样调查）等。应明确表述调查目的、调查对象、统计范围、调查方法、调查频率、填报要求、报送渠道、时间要求等。

（三）相关文件。包括新建立该调查项目的背景材料、重大调查项目的研究论证材料及试点报告等。

第十九条 制定统计调查的部门，在将调查方案送审的同时，要认真填写《部门统计调查项目审批/备案登记表》。

第二十条 政府综合统计机构对送审的部门统计调查进行初审，提出修改意见和建议，部门应积极配合，及时作出说明和解释，并按照修改意见认真进行修改；如有不同意见，双方应进一步研究磋商达成一致。否则由国家统计局进行最终裁决，部门应按最终裁决意见进行修改。

政府综合统计机构对送备案的部门统计调查提出修改意见和完善建议。

第二十一条 政府综合统计机构对部门统计调查的具体审核工作完成之后，以统计局名义发函批复。批复分为：同意实施；不同意实施；建议暂缓实施三种。部门收到批复后，应严格按照批复执行。

第二十二条 部门收到同意实施的复文后，要及时印制调查方案和调查表式，起草布置实施的部门文件，部署调查工作。如遇特殊情况不能实施调查、延期实施调查或需调整变更调查方案的，须及时向政府综合统计机构报告说明。

第二十三条 调查范围涉及到省及省以下单位的部门调查，在将调查任务逐级布置时，应及时通知同级政府综合统计机构。

第二十四条 对部门内职能机构为监控生产经营活动的具体环节而建立的内容专一、分类至细、频率固定的业务统计项目，在其内容不与其它统计调查项目重复的前提下，可向政府综合统计机构提出申请，由政府综合统计机构研究同意后，授权部门的综合统计机构进行定期审批管理。部门的综合统计机构审批后，须将调查方案送政府综合统计机构，以便纳入“部门统计调查项目库”。

第五章 调查的法定标识和有效期

第二十五条 部门统计调查经政府综合统计机构批准或备案后，必须在报表的右上角标明法定标识。法定标识包括：（一）表号；（二）制表机关；

（三）批准机关/备案机关；（四）批准文号/备案文号；（五）有效期截止时间。

第二十六条 政府综合统计机构对部门统计调查实行有效期管理制度。批准的年度调查及其调查周期小于一年的定期调查的有效期为两年；普查、一次性调查、调查周期大于一年的定期调查，其有效期到该次调查的资料上报结束时止。备案的定期调查的有效期为三年；一次性调查的有效期到该次调查的资料上报结束时止。有效期皆以复函的日期为起点计算。

超过有效期的调查项目，一律自动废止。如需要继续执行，应当重新办理审批或备案手续。在有效期内发生变化的调查项目，应随时办理重新审批或备案手续。

第六章 监督与处罚

第二十七条 政府综合统计机构为了保护合法的部门统计调查项目顺利实施，采取以下监督措施:

（一）定期通过公共媒体向社会公布“部门统计调查项目目录”，以便建立全社会监督机制。“部门统计调查项目目录”的内容包括:

1、经过批准或备案的部门统计调查项目名称；

2、制定及组织实施该项调查的单位名称；

3、批准文号或备案文号及其日期；

4、调查项目的有效期。

同时公布经查实的违规调查项目和因超过有效期而被废止的调查项目。

（二）建立对违规调查的举报核实制度。在政府综合统计机构设立举报接待部门，根据举报线索，对违规调查的情况进行调查核实后予以公布。

第二十八条 为保护国家利益和被调查者的权益，减轻被调查者和各级数据加工部门的负担，政府综合统计机构对部门调查的资料使用情况、实施方案与批准方案的一致性进行监督，监督内容包括:

（一）检查调查取得的资料是否被正当使用。资料使用与调查目的是否一致；资料使用是否超出原定的范围；资料是否被私自用于营利目的；是否违反有关保密的规定；是否有其他损害国家利益和被调查者权益的行为。

（二）检查调查资料的有用性。对大部分内容使用频率不高、针对性不强的调查，建议修改、合并或停止实施。

（三）检查调查实施过程中是否严格按政府统计机构批准的方案执行，是否有擅自变更调查内容、调查范围、计算方法和报送频率等行为。

第二十九条 对违反本办法第十六条、第二十二条、第二十六条的规定，未履行法定的审批或者备案程序和擅自变更调查方案的部门统计调查，县级以上政府综合统计机构可以依法予以废止，并按照《统计法》及其实施细则的有关规定处理。

第七章 管理部门提供的服务

第三十条 为主动作好部门统计调查的管理工作，避免可能出现的问题，政府综合统计机构为制定统计调查的部门提供有关业务性咨询、调查方案设计指导。帮助部门掌握设计统计调查项目的基本方法，提高设计工作的效率和质量。

第三十一条 为了避免调查项目之间的重复、矛盾，政府综合统计机构建立并向部门开放“部门统计调查项目库”。部门在制定调查项目前可先进行查询，以达到避免重复调查，充分利用已有信息的目的。

第三十二条 对于部门利用已有资料，精简调查项目和调查内容的，政府综合统计机构给予充分支持和协助。对部门之间在利用对方资料中遇到障碍的，政府综合统计机构可出面协调。

第八章 附 则

第三十三条 对于政府综合统计机构与部门联合制定的统计调查项目，以政府综合统计机构为主制定的（使用政府统计机构的文号），参照政府综合统计机构调查审批程序办理；以部门为主制定的（使用部门的文号），参照部门调查审批程序办理，最后以会签文件作为实施依据。

第三十四条 本办法由国家统计局负责解释。

第三十五条 本办法自公布之日起施行。